Educating Ourselves
The College Woman's Handbook

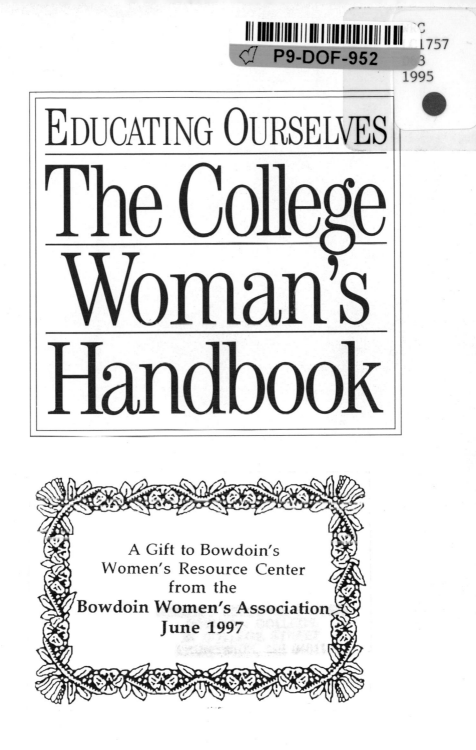

EDUCATING OURSELVES
The College Woman's Handbook

RACHEL DOBKIN & SHANA SIPPY

Illustrations by Virginia Halstead

WORKMAN PUBLISHING • NEW YORK

Library of Congress Cataloging-in-Publication Data

Dobkin, Rachel.
The college woman's handbook / by Rachel Dobkin and Shana Sippy.
p. cm.
Includes bibliographical references (p.) and index
ISBN 1-56305-559-7
1. Women--Education (Higher)--United States-- Handbooks, manuals, etc.
2. Women college students-- United States--Life skills guides.
3. College student orientation--United States--Handbooks, manuals, etc.
I. Sippy, Shana. II. Title.
LC1757.D63 1995
378.1'98'22--dc20
95-106 CIP

Cover design by Lisa Hollander
Interior design by Lisa Hollander with Lori S. Malkin
Book illustrations by Virginia Halstead
Back cover photo by Ken Karp
Typesetting by BPE

"How to Help Your Friend With a Drinking Problem," page 321, adapted by
permission of the Bacchus and Gamma Peer Education Network.

Workman books are available at special discount when purchased in bulk for
special premiums and sales promotions as well as for fund-raising or educational
use. Special editions or book excerpts also can be created to specification. For
details, contact the Special Sales Director at
the address below.

Workman Publishing Company, Inc.
708 Broadway
New York, NY 10003

Manufactured in the United States of America

First Printing, July 1995
10 9 8 7 6 5 4 3 2 1

**To our parents
Barbara and Eric Dobkin
and Roni Sippy and
Lachman Sippy**

ACKNOWLEDGMENTS

In many ways, this book was a collective project—it would not have been possible without the ideas, criticism, knowledge, and support of numerous individuals and organizations.

First, we thank the thousands of women at colleges across the country who spoke with us, sent in questionnaires, answered our probing questions about the most personal of topics, and continually reminded us why we are so excited about this project.

We would like to acknowledge the members of the Barnard/Columbia Handbook Collective whose work on the *Barnard/Columbia Women's Handbook* inspired and supported the creation of this book: Vicky Borgia, Colette Brown, Brinley Bruton, Hadar Dubowsky, Kim Egan, Inès Escandon, Soya Jung, Ilomai Kurrik, Stacy Marple, Jen Kelly Paradise, Laura Pérez, Becky Roiphe, Claire Shanley, Beth Stryker, Margaret Taylor, and Millicent Wilner. We would also like to thank those members of the collective who were actively involved in the creation of this book: Jill Colton, Cara DuBroff, Carolyn Farhie, Lorna Gottesman, and Lisa Olstein. And special thanks to Laura Norton for her permission to adapt her condom cartoon, and to Hilary Rubenstein and Carla Richmond, without whom neither the B/C book nor this one would exist. We also wish to thank the Duke Women's Handbook Collective for their initiative in writing their handbook, and for their continual inspiration.

The Women's Resource Center of New York served not only as our home base and the repository for truckloads of papers, pamphlets, and megabytes of resources in our first year of work, but also as a place where we met and worked with some remarkable women. Our heartfelt thanks to Gretchen Anthony, Andrea Baumgartner, Belinda Blum, Debbie Carlow, Martha Davis, C. Denise Gayle, Joslyn Levy, Christine Merser, Karen Mirko, Jenna Rayer, Manisha Thakor, Kathe Trilling, and the many other volunteers and staff who provided help and assistance.

We also want to thank the faculty and staff at the Barnard Center for Research on Women, the Institute for Research on Women and Gender at Columbia University, the Barnard Women's Studies Department, the Wellesley Center for Research on Women, the MIT Women's Studies Department, and the women's studies departments at the some 400 schools that handed out questionnaires to students.

The following individuals provided invaluable expertise, criticism, and editorial wisdom: Gillian Aldrid; Jim Bauer, Director of Financial Aid, Marietta College; Martin Bonilla, Associate Director of Minority Recruitment, University of Pennsylvania; Al Bingham; Tamara Cohen; Kelli Conlin; Dawn Davis; Eric Dobkin, MBA; Barbara Dobkin, MSSS; Dr. Ernest Drucker, PhD; Dr. Katherine Falk, MD; Dr. Harvey U. Fracht (El Gato), MD; Dr. John N. Gardner, PhD, Director, University 101; David Goldberg;

Suzanne Guard, Director of Financial Aid, Barnard College; Lynn Harris; Nick Jehlen; Kathy Jewell, RN, Barnard College Health Services; Sam Kreuger, COOL; Sharon Levin, CSW; Deborah Levine, Healthwise, Columbia University; Joanne Magdoff, MSW, PhD; Dr. Todd Mangum, MD; Diane Paylor; Julie Salzman; Robin Beth Schaer; Susan Weidman Schneider; Barbara Seaman; Jane Selwyn, Director, Barnard College Career Services; Dr. Barney Silverman, MD; E. Roni Sippy, MSCC; T.J. Sullivan, Director of Communications, BACCUS and GAMMA; Dr. Martin Tesher, MD; Carlene Tockman, ACSW; Marjorie Stamper, Assistant Director, Anti-Defamation League of Massachusetts; Patima Tanapat; Marsha Wagner, Ombudsperson, Columbia University; Dr. Polly Wheat, MD, Director, Barnard College Health Services; Mira Wasserman; Carol Wirtshafter, PhD; David Wirtshafter; Amber Weintraub; Judy Yu; and the amazing, indefatigable Sarajane Baysinger. Also thanks to Amy Batkin, Elizabeth Chen, Tina Chen, Jesse Drucker, Rabbi Lisa Greene, Ian Landau, Eve Landau, Marie Mockett, Tanya Nieri, Tanya Pearlman, Janice Rous, Ruth Silverman, and Lachman, Anjali, and Pravina ("the next generation") Sippy.

We are grateful to our agents, Gay Young and Charlotte Sheedy, who helped us through every step of the process. We thank them for their confidence in the book and in us, as well as for their always insightful advice.

And then there are the folks at Workman Publishing. We were truly lucky to have had the opportunity to work with such a talented, supportive, and (occasionally) zany bunch of people. Over the course of the writing and editing of THE COLLEGE WOMAN'S HANDBOOK, the entire staff at Workman became somewhat of a second family to us. (But unlike our other families, their advice and criticism were nearly always well taken.) We are extremely grateful to Suzanne Rafer, Beth Pearson, and Anne Magruder for their editorial input; Lisa Hollander and Lori S. Malkin for the book's great design; Lisa Mincey for publicizing it with panache; and to Virginia Halstead for her witty and wonderful illustrations. We wish to particularly thank Kristen Carr and Gail Greiner for their editorial prowess and ability to shape the most muddled of thoughts into clear, punchy sentences. And a *very* special thanks to our persistent, persnickety, and passionate editor Margot Herrera. Evidence of her boundless patience (tested with regularity), her sense of humor, her vast knowledge of all things college related, her willingness to listen, and her expertly wielded red pencil can be found on every page.

Finally, a thanks to all of those, too numerous to name, who provided moral (and immoral) support, brought us ice cream and fresh-baked stollen in the wee hours of the night, gave us room and board when we were visiting campuses, tech support when our computers crashed, and who didn't disclose the stuff we'd say when we were sleep-deprived and completely wired on caffeine. You know who you are and you know how grateful we are.

Contents

Part One: All Things Academic

Part Two: Money and Home

Part Three: Of Sound Mind and Body

Problem? • Getting Help • Helping a Friend With a Drug or Alcohol
Problem • Activist Ideas • Resources

Part Four: Sexual and Reproductive Matters

Part Five: Fighting Back

Part Six: Defining Yourself

Part Seven: Odds and Ends

How It All Began...

In the spring of 1992, after almost two years of planning, writing, editing, designing, and meeting on lumpy dorm couches, a collective of 35 Barnard and Columbia women students completed the aptly titled *Barnard/Columbia Women's Handbook*. The book was a friendly, straightforward compendium of information and resources for undergraduate women. Operating under the premise that information—and access to it—is power, we gleaned its contents from a sea of pamphlets, the college catalog, the university library, dorm meetings, and interviews with students, faculty, staff, and administrators. The objective was simple: to provide basic information about health, rights, opportunities, and the services available to women students on- and off-campus so that they could make informed decisions for themselves.

Although we were extremely proud of our little handbook, we were surprised by the overwhelming response it got—the 4,000 copies printed were all snatched up within four days. The book was praised in the school papers, it was honored with a student government award, and all over campus groups of students could be seen flipping through its pages and discussing the contents. After a week or so of basking in the glow of our accomplishment, we returned to our pre-handbook lives. We had extensions to beg for, jobs to find, finals to take, and last-minute gym credits to fulfill.

Some weeks later, an article about the book appeared in *The New York Times*, and the power of the press was revealed to us in no uncertain terms. We were flooded with calls from offices of student life at other colleges, individual women, and women's organizations from Indiana to India requesting copies of the book. And publishers called to inquire about creating a national version.

A national version? Suddenly visions of everything we'd wanted to include in the original but didn't have the time or space for began to dance in our heads. We imagined an in-depth guide that would address the issues that college women across the country face on a daily basis—something that would do for all college women what the Barnard/Columbia book did for that community. After discussing our ideas with several publishers, we signed on with Workman, and it was time to turn our imaginings into reality.

In June of 1993, the two of us started researching and writing the book in earnest. Our goal was the same as that which prompted the creation of the original: to provide readers with basic information and resources to enable them to navigate the sometimes tricky waters of the college experience, milk the undergrad years for all they're worth, and take care of themselves—and have a good time in the process. However, with some seven-and-a-half million college women at schools ranging from tiny to huge, rural to urban, single sex to coed, sectarian and non-, it was clear that we couldn't just rely on our own experiences to determine which issues should be included or how they should be addressed. We needed to get the input of women students from across the country.

To this end, we sent letters and questionnaires to women's studies departments; posted information on-line; networked with students through a multitude of organizations; attended myriad formal and informal programs on campuses; set up booths at conferences; made random campus visits; and talked with as many "experts" (students, faculty, administrators, activists, and professionals) as possible about everything from health to harassment.

The input we got as a result of this outreach was instrumental in shaping the book. The amazing quotes we collected about all aspects of college life enabled us to both get in touch with the salient issues on campus and to include the voices of real women. And although we were able to use only a small portion of these quotes in the book, all of them informed its topics, content, and tone.

One thing that we quickly learned was that there is no such thing as a "typical college woman," and that it would be impossible to adequately deal with

every concern of every female undergrad. But what we could do (and what we tried our best to do) was to address those issues that were common to the majority of college women. The way we see it, no matter where you're from or where you go to school, what you study or what you believe, by virtue of being a woman living in these times trying to get a higher education, there are certain things that you're likely to face. We all need a place to live, access to health care, and a way to finance our education. And it can't hurt to have information about our body and sexuality, to know our rights and what to do if they are violated, and how to find communities of people with interests similar to ours. And although they aren't course requirements, learning about how to cope with stress or how to help a friend through a serious problem are as much a part of a college education as term papers and chemistry labs.

Still, even though these experiences may be common among college women doesn't mean that we should all confront and handle them in the same way. Thus, this book strives not to prescribe solutions or dictate what's "right" and what's "wrong" (although our opinions do occasionally slip out), but rather to present basic information in a nonjudgmental way, along with some things to think about when making your own choices.

In case the information we present on each topic is not detailed enough for your purposes, we concluded just about every chapter with a resource section (cleverly titled "Resources") listing organizations and publications that can provide further information, advice, and/or support. We opted to include only those tried and true, big ol' rock-solid organizations that should be around for at least as long as this book sits on your shelf. This means that we had to leave out many excellent local groups, but we hope that by asking the organizations listed for referrals, you will find those local gems as well.

A few other omissions in the book: We left out very specific information that is constantly changing (such as experimental treatments for HIV and various state laws regarding abortion rights). In addition, we covered only cursorily such important topics as prenatal care and the politics of affirmative action—an adequate discussion of these would require far more ink than we could allot in a book like this. Again, we're counting on you, the reader, to use the resources to find the additional information you need.

Other issues emerged in trying to create a comprehensive book for a diverse population. For one, as women who strongly believe in using correct, up-to-date terminology, we found accommodating an entire country's worth of slang and usage no easy task. In most cases it didn't seem like a big deal. If we called a resident advisor an "RA" and in your dorm they're called "proctors" or "dorm moms," we imagined you'd figure it out, no problem. But when it comes to naming communities of people, especially communities that we are not members of, it gets trickier. Language is a very powerful thing—it shapes opinions, ideas, and identity—and we tried to choose those terms and expressions that are the most commonly used, most easily understood, and most empowering.

We also sought to be inclusive in our use of pronouns. We operated under the assumption that our readers are women (though most of the information contained in the book would be relevant to men's lives as well), and the "yous" and "wes" can be read accordingly. Usually, when talking about others—doctors, profs, friends, lovers, real-estate agents, bankers, and bigots—we tried to use gender-neutral expressions ("s/he" and "his or her"). Sometimes when this got too awkward, we simply choose a gender.

Our hope is that this book will help women help themselves, whether they need a crash course in financial aid or the phone number for the National Black Women's Health Project. We want it to inform, inspire, and empower women students, and if in the process it helps to expand the dialogue between college women nationwide, then so much the better. Ultimately, we hope the book compels you to discuss, share information, argue, organize, and most of all educate yourself now and long after commencement.

Rachel and Shana
June 1995

Part One

All Things

Academic

The Class System

Courses, Grades & Profs

"Education for a woman is the first step toward achieving equality and liberation. This includes social education as well as academic education. She must learn about herself, her sexuality, her body, her abilities, and her potential to contribute to society as an active, productive human being in order to achieve her goals."

—MARY WASHINGTON COLLEGE, '96

College's raison d'être is education, and a significant portion of our learning comes from our involvement with things academic: classes, discussions, reading, writing, presentations, labwork, research, and the critical and creative thinking that all this requires. However, probably the most valuable and useful stuff we learn would never appear on a multiple choice quiz.

We glean considerably more from the learning process than the countless facts, figures, fictions, and formulas forgotten ten minutes after the exam: We learn how to think analytically, how seemingly esoteric information is relevant to our lives, and how to ask questions about ourselves and the world (which often make us more confused and bring up more questions). We learn that there is rarely one right answer, opinion, or perspective. (But don't use this rationale when trying to contest a poor grade on a true/false quiz—it won't work.) We also gain some very important "real world" skills, such as how to deal with pres-

THE GENDER DISPARITY

In the academic world, men still hold most of the powerful positions, write most of what's studied, and fill most of the slots on boards of trustees. Academia idealizes a "tradition" that for the most part is not enthusiastically inclusive of women. Even the tallest and hippest ivory tower still has foundations in a society that holds rather unflattering beliefs and expectations about women's intellectual abilities. And for women who are not white, Christian, middle class, and/or heterosexual, the exclusion and discrimination can be all the more intense and prevalent. Knowing our rights, opportunities, and a few tricks to boot is especially important when we're made to feel like outsiders in the ol' boys' club. Being aware of the way in which discrimination may manifest itself in the college classroom, the curriculum, and the institution will better prepare us to overcome it.

sure, deadlines, and time management, as well as how to discuss, debate, collaborate, negotiate, and listen. Plus, we invariably get an exhaustive lesson on how the formal and informal political structure of an institution affects the working environment thrown in for good measure.

Considering all these opportunities for intellectual overstimulation, we may not give the process of picking classes, studying efficiently, relating with professors, and troubleshooting sexism in the classroom a second thought. But, developing the skills that enable us to succeed in our academic adventures may be some of the most important learning we do. Not only do these skills enable us to concentrate on the juicy stuff, but decision-making, getting the job done, negotiating the bureaucracy, and sticking up for your rights will be much more valuable to you after college than remembering the year *The Rime of the Ancient Mariner* was published.

CHOOSING CLASSES

Classes are the backbone of your academic career, so it's worth taking the time to pick them with care. Few things are as exhilarating as taking a great class with a stimulating prof. Conversely, there are few things as deadening as sitting through a whole semester of an uninspiring class taught by a total bore. Below are some tips to help you ensure that you have more of the former and fewer of the latter.

■ Pick courses first by professor, second by content. The best professor can make even the most boring topic fascinating, relevant, and enlightening, and the worst professor can make the most interesting topic a drag.

■ Don't enroll in a course solely on the basis of a riveting catalog description.

Ask other students (especially those majoring in the department), your advisor, or professors you like about good and, well, not-so-good profs and courses. But don't make any final decisions until you've gone to the first day, tried the professor, time, and syllabus on for size, and gotten a feel for the workload and whether or not you can handle it. Most schools give students a week or two to check out classes before final registration. Take advantage of this "shopping period."

■ Explore a little. Try a course that falls outside of your requirements. Three little credits could change the course of your college career.

■ Take courses that are at your level. Students often do poorly in courses that are too easy or too difficult. If the class is boring, there is a tendency to blow off studying and class, and to not put enough time and energy into assignments (not exactly the best way to maintain the health of your GPA). Take courses for which you have the prerequisite skills so that you will be able to fully participate in discussions and understand the material. If you are unsure whether you can handle the class, talk to the professor during pre-

registration. Come prepared with a list of college classes, AP classes, and test scores that may help determine whether you have the necessary background. However, even if you have taken the prerequisite courses (or their equivalents), you may find that a class is beyond you, most often because certain things weren't included in your high school curriculum.

Some schools require or recommend that you take a placement test before registering for classes in subjects such as foreign language or math. They are usually offered at the start of each semester or around the time of preregistration for the next term. Ask about them in the appropriate department. Even if you feel as though you want to take the most introductory class, it's a good idea to take the placement test. You may find that you know more than you thought and it would be better to take the next level up. You also may be eligible for exemption from requirements, course credit, or prerequisites in other areas.

■ Know the prof's history with women students. Every school has at least one professor that leers at the women in class, refuses to find work by and about women relevant, calls on men more often, or makes sexist comments. Do your best to avoid them.

The reality, however, is that no matter how vigilant you are, you're bound to come across teachers you're not crazy about. When you do end up with a not-so-hot prof or a mumbling TA, make the extra effort to engage with the material. Choose a paper topic that interests you so much it makes the class exciting. Come fully prepared so you'll want to participate.

If your prof is really offensive or engages in behavior that you find

"I took an advanced seminar my sophomore year. I learned a lot but I would have learned more and done better had I taken a more introductory course before jumping in. In retrospect I would tell everyone to think carefully before taking those advanced seminars."

—HARVARD UNIVERSITY, '94

from 42.6% in 1972. ※ 54% of grad students are women. ※

harassing or discriminatory, you may want to file a formal complaint. (See "Taking Formal Action," page 481.)

Don't Bite Off More Than You Can Chew

It is important to have a balanced and reasonable courseload. Don't take so many credits that you can't do the work for all of your classes, but don't take so few that if you have to drop a course you will run into credit prob-lems. Consider the kind of time com-mitment each class requires. The amount of work required by seminars, lectures, and lab classes is different. If there are just plain too many courses that are too exciting to pass up, con-sider easing some of the pressure by taking a class Pass/Fail or auditing. If you discover that you were a bit ambi-tious in your course selection, you can drop a course or, if it's too late to do that without penalty, take an incom-plete and finish the work later. (For information about these alternative grading options, see page 16.)

SO MANY CLASSES . . . SO LITTLE TIME

Overwhelmed by the tome that is your course catalog? Doubtful that there's enough time in the world to check out all the classes you're interested in during the shopping period at the beginning of the term? Below are things to consider when choosing classes to help you to pare down your list into a fairly reasonable semester's schedule.

▲ Subject matter that interests you

▲ Recommendations from peers, pro-fessors, advisors, and alums

▲ General and major requirements/credits

▲ When the class meets (Know thy-self: Not being a "morning person" is certainly not the best reason to can a 9:00 A.M. course, but it may be a consideration.)

▲ Professor (Check out the teaching assistant as well. You're likely to spend more time with her than the prof, anyway.)

▲ Workload

▲ Good prep for later life, or current life

▲ How a particular class will fill out/balance your transcript

▲ The classroom environment (is it a discussion or lecture class? Do the students give presentations or only the prof? Does everyone sit in a circle or face front?)

▲ Grading options

▲ Costs (Factor in lab fees, materials fees for visual arts classes, books you'll have to buy, transportation if it's off campus.)

▲ Level of other students in the class (Will the discussions be boring, insipid, inspiring, or completely over your head?)

▲ Provides a challenge

REQUIREMENTS: PRESCRIBED WISDOM

"I took math not because it particularly interested me, but because I needed to fulfill a quantitative reasoning requirement. I didn't want to take 'Physics for Poets.' I was like, 'Hey I'm an intelligent woman—sign me up for calculus! I'm not going to let you guys intimidate me!' I ended up loving it, and majoring in it."

—UNIVERSITY OF PENNSYLVANIA, '94

The goal of colleges and universities is to graduate well-educated, well-rounded students, armed with all the information and skills necessary to handle whatever's thrown their way. However, there is no cross-college consensus on exactly what this essential info is. What one school considers to be a topic with which every adult should be familiar, another may find less important. The content and structure of requirements vary accordingly from school to school. Some schools give students a lot of leeway in fulfilling requirements, mandating that students take at least one course in a variety of disciplines. Other schools designate exactly which courses students must take, which languages they must learn, and which concepts they must master before they are allowed to don the tasseled mortarboard. Then there are those colleges that have few requirements and ask the students to design their own curriculums.

Know Thy Requirements

In most cases you'll have two sets of requirements: general requirements (also called core or basic requirements) that everyone must fulfill, and requirements for your major (and minor, if you declare one). These requirements are not always academic. Some schools require that students take phys-ed, do volunteer work, or participate in campus activities. Depending on your major, you may also be asked to write a thesis, pass a standardized exam, give a performance, or curate an art show.

Familiarize yourself with your requirements. You can find out what they are by looking in the course catalog. Also consult with your advisor, who ought to know what you'll need to do to graduate, but don't rely solely on her. Keep a running list of those requirements you've already completed and those you have yet to complete. And to make extra-sure to avoid last-minute scrambling and tangling, pay the registrar a visit well before graduation to go over your transcript and make sure you have an accurate assessment of your requirement status.

"I thought all was dandy with my requirements. Then as I was choosing classes second semester senior year I found out that at my first school history was considered a humanities class, while at my new school it was a social science. If my history classes didn't count for humanities credit, I was one class short."

—BARNARD COLLEGE, '92

When Should I Take Requirements?

〜〜〜

Some people like to get all their requirements taken care of early and explore the eclectic later. Others prefer to take a lot of electives at first in order to get a taste of a variety of subjects before settling down to a major. Most choose to intersperse required courses with electives. And when it comes down to it, scheduling woes and class availability will often be the biggest factors in determining when you take your requirements.

Required courses that teach important skills (like English comp) and/or provide the groundwork for subjects you wish to study (like survey and 101 courses in your prospective major) should be taken as early as possible to reap their full benefits. Further, because these courses are planned with the needs of first-year students in mind, they will also be helpful in getting you acclimated to college academic life. And it may be unwise to save all of the heftiest and least appealing requirements for the last semester. The combination of a schedule full of difficult and dreary courses, absences for interviews and job hunting, and senior slump (the uncanny inability to concentrate that afflicts nearly every second-semester senior), can be deadly.

There is a chance that your school may institute new requirements while you're there. Students who have already matriculated are often not affected—check with your advisor, the course catalog, and the registrar. With so many schools doing requirement review, your requirements may differ from those of members of classes before and after yours. You should also check the requirement policy if you plan to graduate with a different class than the one with which you entered. Some schools base requirements on those of the class you enrolled with; others, the class with which you graduate.

In Case You Screw Up . . .

〜〜〜

If you did wait until the week before graduation to check the status of your requirements, and you've come up short, be prepared to run to the dean or to your academic advisor. You may need to ask them to make an exception, in which case you should be prepared to justify why a course or a combination of courses you took should count as filling the requirements. If petitioning doesn't work, you'll need to face the fact that your undergraduate days will last a bit longer. (However, even so, the school may allow you to participate in the graduation ceremony but you won't receive your diploma until you've completed that last requirement.) In most cases, schools will allow you to complete the course in summer school or at a (preapproved) school that may cost less to attend or is close to where you'll be living.

REGISTRATION

Despite the fact that nearly every college student has met at least one good friend while standing in line during registration, the process is almost always frustrating and stressful. Even the ultra-organized early birds among us are not immune to those last minute catalog corrections that change a perfect schedule into a list of five classes that meet Monday, Wednesday, and Friday at 8:00 A.M. Some schools are attempting to make registration less chaotic by allowing you to register by phone or on-line, but unfortunately the phone lines are often just as busy and frustrating as those corporeal.

One way to smooth the process is preregistration. Your best bet, (and sometimes only hope) in securing a spot in popular classes, especially at larger schools, may be to sign up months in advance. This is particularly true for lab courses that are in high demand, seminar courses, and other courses where the number of spaces is limited. Some schools go so far as to hold lotteries for the perennial

> ## QUEUING FOR CLASSES
> ※
>
> There are a few universal truths that you can't avoid when it comes to registration:
>
> ▲ No matter the size of your school, the registrar's office is always a mob scene.
> ▲ Your advisor will mysteriously disappear at the 11th hour and you will spend umpteen hours in quest of her "Jane Hancock."
> ▲ There is no mercy. Do it wrong, hand it in late, sign on the wrong line—pay a price.
> ▲ You will have absolutely no interest in taking at least one of the courses you preregistered for.
> ▲ At least once, you will spend the first two weeks of the semester begging and pleading with a prof to let you into his class and then spend the rest of the semester regretting it.

favorites. These can take place up to a year before you need to take the course, so think ahead. To find out about course deadlines, lotteries, and scheduling changes, ask at the department offering the class in question or call the registrar. If you go to a techno-savvy college, the information might be posted on-line as well.

It's not a bad idea to check up on all the courses that spark your interest a week before preregistration. Because college course catalogs must be completed long before registration, you can bet that there'll be changes in meeting times, professors, and course offerings.

WOMEN IN THE CLASSROOM

"If you ask one of the guys in my classes who has seen my work, he'd tell you I was a really good programmer. The other guys who don't know me or my work think that I'm just OK because I have a hard time joining in the chats after class and knowing what the jokes mean. I have to work twice as hard to show that I am a good programmer, even though what the guys talk about has nothing to do with what's important nowadays."

—*MASSACHUSETTS INSTITUTE OF TECHNOLOGY, '98*

"I was in an engineering school in which there were so few women that I always felt alone—it was difficult at times to make conversation with men in classes, to get lab partners."

—*COLUMBIA UNIVERSITY SCHOOL OF ENGINEERING AND APPLIED SCIENCE, '92*

By the time we begin college, we've already spent quite a bit of time in the classroom, and learned—often the hard way—that even though by law men and women have equal access to education, the education we actually receive is not necessarily equal to men's. There have been a number of studies proving and giving validity to what many of us have felt and noticed for some time: In coed classrooms, men participate in class nearly two times more often than women, and men are called on almost twelve times as much, even if they consistently have

nothing too remarkable to say. We've got a ways to go before coeducation means equal education, equal participation, equal encouragement and praise, and equal numbers of female professors, advisors, mentors, and role models. Though there has been considerable improvement in hiring women faculty, incorporating information by and about women in classes, and supporting women who enter "nontraditional" disciplines, women still feel invisible, ignored, and often discriminated against in classrooms and curriculums. This is especially true for women of color, lesbian women, and other "minority" group members who find fewer role models and representations of themselves in syllabi and are forced to fight against prejudices about their ability and aptitude.

Studies of classroom dynamics show that the way women have been taught they're "supposed" to act may be hindering their education. We're supposed to be modest, be polite, and let everyone else have a say. This has translated into a speaking style and classroom behavior that often gives the impression that we're less capable and less comfortable with the material than the men are. Becoming conscious of the deeper lessons we have been taught about being "feminine" and how they affect our educational experience is the first step in fighting sexism in the classroom. Once you are aware of them, you'll see their reflections everywhere—perhaps even in yourself.

Even when they make up less than ¼ of a seminar, men do ⅓ to ½ the

STUDIES HAVE SHOWN THAT . . .

▲ Women tend to think before speaking, while men tend to think out loud.

▲ Women are interrupted more often.

▲ Women often will begin statements or questions with phrases like, "this sounds stupid, but . . .," or apologize at inappropriate times. Women also speak softly or look down rather than directly at the prof or the student to whom she's responding. All of these give an impression of lack of authority.

▲ Women are likely to withhold comments in fear of saying something "stupid" or "wrong." Instead, women often save questions and comments for an after-class one-on-one with the prof. As a result, men dominate classroom discussions.

▲ Women are less likely to fight to get their voices heard, argue a point in class, and make a point to clarify a misunderstood or misattributed comment or opinion. Profs will pay more attention to those who demand it. Studies show that profs more often make eye contact with men, comment on their comments, and direct questions to them than they do women.

The problems are magnified for women who choose male-dominated disciplines. Traditionally men have been thought to have a natural affinity for and more interest in subjects such as math and the sciences than women. But as more women debunk the myths and rise to prominence in these fields, we will be accepted as full and equal participants.

For more information on discrimination in the classroom and how to deal with it, see page 468.

If You Don't Get Into a Class

〰〰〰

If you really want to take a course, be assertive. In most cases, even if a class is closed you can get in with persistence and by proving that you will be an asset to the class. Put your name on the waiting list as early as possible, ask professors directly if you can join their classes (and be prepared with good reasons why they should let you in)—even ask the professor if you can sit in on the class in case anyone drops it, and then come to class prepared and ready to participate in discussions. How can a prof refuse to accept such a bright and enthusiastic student? If she just can't let you in, chances are good that you'll be one of the first admitted the next time it's offered.

THE BIG DECISION: CHOOSING A MAJOR

It's no wonder that choosing a major is often a source of anxiety, soul-searching, and stress. We're taught to believe that the major designated on our transcript is the be-all and end-all. Do yourself a favor: Choose a major out of love, not out of obligation. Think about the subjects you enjoy and in which you have excelled. You might find, upon examining your program, that a major has pretty much chosen itself.

Just as when you pick classes, when you choose a major consider not just the subject but the department's professors, facilities, and academic and extracurricular opportunities.

"As the end of my sophomore year approached, I became a wreck. I had no clue what I wanted to do. I came to school sure that I wanted to be a doctor, but didn't love my science classes. I talked with the pre-med advisor and she said I could major in whatever I wanted as long as I took certain classes— not exactly helpful. My parents wanted me to go to medical school, law school, or business school. I really liked my anthropology courses. I ended up majoring in anthro and minoring in economics, but I didn't want to rule out med school, so I took summer school so I could get all my science prerequisites in."

—*UCLA, '94*

Though the reputation and popularity of the major are often good indicators of its quality, make sure they are still justified. Sometimes a reputation outlives the reality.

Also, resist the urge to jump on the major of the moment bandwagon. What's trendy now may seem like an academic footnote in a few years. And beware of choosing a major only because it ties into a hot new career. What industry reports say about the "best" fields have a tendency to shift after four years.

If you have a certain professional program or career ambition in mind, consider the prerequisites for the program before you select a major. But for the most part it is more important that candidates have the necessary background and knowledge than have chosen a specific major. With the proper prerequisites, medical schools accept English majors, art schools take math majors—and publishers will finance and promote a book for college women written by religion and women's studies majors.

Major requirements vary from school to school. You may just have to take a certain number of classes in the subject area or department, specific classes, or at least one course in each of a few areas, and/or a few courses in one area of the discipline. You may need to complete a thesis or an honors project, an internship, an independent study, or assistant-teach a class. You can find out about major requirements in the course catalog or by asking at departments.

The majority of students choose just one major, especially those at schools with very hefty core requirements. But the one-student one-major option isn't the only one. You can opt to do a double major in which you complete the major requirements in two distinct disciplines. Or you can do an interdisciplinary major (sometimes called an adjunct major). While traditional majors use one main analytic

perspective to examine a variety of topics, interdisciplinary majors (such as American studies or Middle-Eastern studies) use a variety of perspectives to examine one big topic.

No matter what major you choose, at some schools you may elect to declare a concentration, focusing your study on one aspect or period of the discipline, such as East Asian art if you're an art history major. Concentrations are meant to make a huge and unruly discipline more personal and manageable, and may also allow a student to delve into a subject that doesn't have enough course offerings or is considered too narrow to stand as a major on its own. Many interdisciplinary majors, including women's studies and African-American studies, grew from concentration status into full-fledged majors and disciplines in their own right.

If you don't find a major that suits your fancy, many schools allow you to

design one yourself. (For more on creating your own major, see page 35.) At some schools you can declare a minor in addition. Minors are like mini-majors and require a subset of the courses required for the major. Often students will complete a minor's worth of classes in a subject area, but not bother to declare it—having it listed officially doesn't seem worth wading

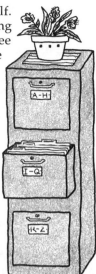

deep in the bureaucratic mire. But it might be simple and painless. Ask at the registrar.

At most schools, picking a major is in some sense like picking a family. You will be spending a good part of your academic career with a relatively small group of professors and students. Like a family member, your academic department is supposed to be accountable to you. It is a place to ask about jobs, get academic counseling, make complaints about problems with classes, ask questions about the discipline, or find out information related to the field.

Most students declare a major at the end of their sophomore or beginning of their junior year. But even though you'll have to fill out a card and choose a major advisor (and probably attend a "Thanks for Choosing Us" departmental fiesta), the decision is not cast in stone. People add majors, drop minors, pick up a new concentration and switch, almost up to the time the commencement program has been printed.

> "At the same time we had to select majors it became obvious to me that my boyfriend and I would probably be married right after graduation. He put a lot of pressure on me to drop my business major. I realize now that he just didn't want a wife that knew more about the business world than he did, but I was stupid enough to listen, and took psychology instead. Don't let anyone try to sway you from doing what you want, especially a guy."
>
> —UNIVERSITY OF ALABAMA, '93

CAMPUS HIGHLIGHT

Six Boston schools (Boston College, Brandeis University, Harvard University, Massachusetts Institute of Technology, Northeastern University, and Tufts University) joined together to create the Graduate Consortium in Women's Studies, housed at Radcliffe College. Its mission is "to advance women's studies scholarship through a series of team-taught seminars." Taught by profs from the various schools, the classes are offered free to a set number of graduate students who apply.

ADVISORS AND MENTORS AND PROFS (OH MY!)

Your advisor is supposed to offer suggestions and help you plan your schedule from the standpoint of being more familiar with the world of academia and school policies than you are. However, as in all aspects of life, there are some people whose every word should be followed and others who have a tendency to give terrible advice in an unfriendly way. When you and your advisor have very little in common, her suggestions, while well intentioned, may not be your best bet. If you and your advisor don't click, you can either ask for another or get additional advice from other profs, students, and administrators. And remember—you have ab-solutely no obligation to take your advisor's advice, you just need her signature on your registration form.

"While she may not know it, the director of the women and minority students committee has been quite a role model for me. She was a dynamic, down to earth, and simply brilliant professor. She has been a motivator, a teacher, and a friend. If I could offer entering women some advice—find someone to look up to, a woman willing to give you advice, to help you in your education and maturity."

—SIENA COLLEGE, '92

Forming Relationships With Our Professors

One of the most rewarding aspects of being in college is building relationships with professors. More than simply giving lectures, leading seminars, and advising lab work, professors are there to talk with you about the subject matter, help you with any problems that come up as you are studying, spark your intellectual, creative, and critical side, and learn from you while you're learning from them. They are your advisors, giving you help with course selection, future plans, and even personal issues. They are also your evaluators, and for the most part want to help you do well and enjoy the work. And they will, in the best of circumstances, match the amount of effort you put into the class. In addition, professors will be your recommendation-writers, and getting to know them can be a politically savvy move. They can also be your friends, employers, co-researchers, co-writers, and co-organizers.

If you have questions about subject material covered in class, problems with an assignment, or general thoughts about the course material, go talk with your professor during office hours or make an appointment for another time. Remember, you don't need to have a complicated question or a brilliant revelation to speak with a professor; just wanting him to know you enjoyed a particular lecture is a

A QUICK GLANCE AT WOMEN'S STUDIES

"Is the eventual goal of women's studies to work its way out of existence by spreading its methods and ideas throughout traditional fields? Maybe, and maybe we can't even imagine the kinds of things such departments will be freed to do when everyone takes for granted the importance of gender analysis. But until then, take an intro class. It'll change the way you understand yourself and the world. Plus you'll meet so many cooool women!"
—BARNARD COLLEGE, '93

One of the primary ways women scholars and scholars of work by and about women have addressed the basic inequality in the academy is through the creation of women's studies departments. Women's studies asserts that women are a serious category for academic inquiry and that research into any field can be enhanced and made complete through an examination of women's contributions and attention to questions of gender.

Women's studies also reevaluates academic language and methodology and reworks the traditional classroom environment. What goes on in the classroom—who has power, how works and theories are discussed, what subjects or materials are considered relevant to class discussions—is often as important as what's being studied in the classroom. Furthermore, women's studies makes the connection between the oppression, of women and other forms of oppression, and considers factors such as race, class, and sexual orientation in its scholarship. (See "Activist Ideas," page 19, for ways to incorporate a women's studies outlook into every class you take.)

Women's studies looks at experiences, contributions, actions, theories, perceptions, and words by and about women missing from (or barely covered in) traditional core curriculums. Because women's studies is interdisciplinary, women's studies departments may only offer a few courses; the majority of women's studies will be offered by other departments, including comparative lit, law, classics, history, and dance, to name just a few.

good enough reason to go to office hours. Most professors enjoy talking with their students, but because they have quite a few, it is usually your responsibility to start the conversation.

Not sure how to approach your prof? Here are some handy tips:

■ Don't call professors at home unless they say it's OK.

■ Attend class regularly, come prepared and ready to participate with your work and readings completed. It shows respect for what they do—and it won't hurt your education either.

■ Going to talk to a prof for the first time can be kind of scary. Many of us feel afraid of sounding dumb or of looking like we're trying to kiss up, when we're really in search of a mentor or a role model or simply need help understanding a certain principle or calculation. If you're nervous, think of what you want to ask or say in advance, take a deep breath, and go to those office hours.

> *"I think students are intimidated by the professors, especially at a big school like Michigan. Getting to know professors makes the class better, makes you feel like you're not anonymously floating in a sea of 200 people, and makes you want to do better and work harder, because you have a personal relationship with the teacher. I make it a point to meet at least once with all my professors."*
>
> —UNIVERSITY OF MICHIGAN, '93

FEMALE PROFS
※

The fact that the percentage of women faculty on university campuses is lower than the percentage of men translates into our having fewer available female role models. That is not to say that all women professors are good, nor that men can't be role models, but simply that the lower representation of women on the faculty is an injustice. Hopefully, you'll find at least one woman prof or administrator you can bond with.

Teaching Assistants
ဃဃဃ

Those of us who go to larger universities undoubtedly have some firsthand experience with teaching assistants (TAs), and have learned that

assignments
1. Work too hard.
2. No excuses.
3. Limit partying.
4. Make me proud that I am a professor.
5. Don't sleep in class.

despite the name listed in the course catalog, Nobel laureates rarely teach introductory seminars. In most cases, professors will lecture to a huge group a couple of times a week, and then smaller groups led by a TA will convene to discuss the topics in more depth. The good news about TAs is that they're often less intimidating and more accessible than the grand ol' profs. Because they're in the process of getting their degrees, they may be closer to the cutting edge of scholarship and to topics more relevant to the lives of undergrads than are the profs. They're often also closer in age to the undergrads and so more like peers than profs. As a result, the negative elements of the power differential are lessened, and it's easier to feel more comfortable with them. However, because they're professors-in-training, they may not be as powerful in the university (i.e., they may not be able to pull strings for you if you need it or be as good recommendation writers for

competitive programs or jobs) nor may they be as authoritative information sources. And some simply may not be very good teachers.

Remember that even if you spend most of your classtime with the TA, the prof is still the prof. If you feel the TA didn't grade your paper fairly or you just want to have a few words with the big cheese, request a meeting.

GRADES

Whether we think they're ridiculous, a necessary evil, or the most wonderful thing around, grades are given a lot of importance, and it's hard to ignore the pressure to get high marks. It's good to try hard, and a little cum laude never hurt anyone. But as long as your GPA is high enough to allow you to remain on the soccer team, or continue to receive

MAKE YOUR VOICE HEARD

Even though we're "just students," we have the power to influence classes, requirements, departments, and faculty. Most schools have some procedure for evaluating professors and courses—usually a questionnaire handed out the last day of class. Take the time to fill these out. You can also send either a signed or anonymous letter to the prof, the department, the dean of academics, or the dean of faculty if you have ideas about how a course could be made better, or want to give kudos to a faculty member or a class. Profs and deans take these evaluations quite seriously, and will turn to them when making syllabus and scheduling changes. The appraisals also will be used when deciding whether to grant or deny tenure. So make your voice heard. In addition to the evaluations, you may be able to join departmental committees and/or student/faculty review boards. Or you can nominate great teachers for awards.

receive only 35-40% of the PSAT-based National Merit Scholarships.

your scholarship, and to get you where you want to go, a low grade is *not* going to leave an indelible stain on you for the rest of your life. (You'll be surprised how quickly it doesn't matter.) In fact, some might argue that working hard, learning well, and enjoying the process should be given at least as much importance as getting good grades.

> *"As an RA, and someone who was in the real world for four years before going to college, I always tell my residents to chill out about grades. People think that one bad quiz or one C on their transcript will make it impossible for them to get a job. . . . All employers really care about is that you graduated. As long as you've got the degree, they'll hire you."*
>
> —SMITH COLLEGE, '95

Grading Issues

෧෧෧

At the beginning of the term, find out what your grades will be based on—beyond the obvious papers and exams. Sometimes attendance, quizzes, participation, homework, labs, evaluations from classmates, internship advisors, or fieldwork advisors will factor into determining your grade. Also ask what criteria each of your professors will use to grade papers, labs, presentations, and other "subjective" types of assignments. Find out how to compute your grade

point average by looking in the catalog. In general, GPA is calculated based on the grade received in a course and the number of credits a course was worth—classes worth more credits count more in your GPA. Some schools use a "weighted" system, where the difficulty of the class is also factored in.

So Many Ways to Make the Grade . . .

෧෧෧

In addition to taking courses for a letter or number grade, many colleges offer the option of taking classes Pass/Fail. Some schools prefer Pass/Fail's closest relative, Pass/D/Fail, where a D average will get you a D on your report card instead of a "Pass." There is usually a limit to the number of courses you can take Pass/Fail, and you are probably not allowed to take any courses that will count toward your major as Pass/Fail.

Another option is auditing a class. When you audit, you're basically an observer, sitting in on the class for the sheer thrill of learning. You don't have to write the papers or take the exam, but you don't get a grade or any credit for your time, either. But some schools will list audited classes on your tran-

script. Because you aren't getting credit, at schools that charge tuition by credits taken, an audited class may be less expensive, or even free. Some schools allow alums and locals to audit classes for free or for a small fee. The word around campuses is that it's considered impolite to dominate class discussions if you're auditing a class.

Here are a few other "non-grades" that may appear on your transcript:

■ **Withdraw:** If you wait until after a given time to drop a course, a W for withdrawal will appear on your transcript. This is most often used as a last resort when you would definitely fail a class and you were not able or did not want to get an incomplete.

■ **Incomplete:** If you ever find yourself in the truly abominable position of realizing that a crisis has left you unable to get your Feminist Theology term paper in before the end of the semester, think "incomplete." An incomplete is basically a placeholder for when a prof is not able to get a grade in by the deadline because a student has more work to hand in. Once the paper is submitted and graded the professor will change the incomplete to the final grade, most often without penalty. Unfortunately, not every professor will allow you to take an incomplete, especially if the reason you couldn't complete all the work was your own lack of organization (and not, for example, a medical emergency, a disability, or a family crisis).

While an occasional incomplete can be a lifesaver, don't acquire too many. You will still be responsible for the work and looming incompletes will make you feel as overwhelmed as you did when you decided to take them in the first place.

Also, be sure to assess your sched-ule to make sure that you can complete the outstanding work in the time alot-ted. You can't take an incomplete on an incomplete.

"A lot of my good friends took incompletes in college and I wish that I had taken a few. My friends who took them, took them responsibly because they knew their limits and it allowed them to do really well on their work instead of doing badly when there was no reason for them to."

—UNIVERSITY OF WISCONSIN - MADISON, '96

CHANGING OR CONTESTING A GRADE

For the most part, if a not-so-good grade makes its way onto your report card, you know deep down that the prof wasn't completely off base. But occasionally, students receive grades that seem completely illogical. Anytime you think that you have received an unfair grade, whether it is on a paper, an exam, or a report card, your first step should be to talk with the professor. Three things can happen. 1) Due to an administrative error, a computational error, or even simple carelessness, you did not in fact get the grade you deserved. The professor apologizes profusely and sends off a form to the registrar. 2) Your professor insists that the grade you received was correct, and as much as it hurts, you do understand her explanation. 3) You are not convinced by your prof's explanation. Your next recourse is to contest the grade by filing some sort of petition or complaint with the registrar, the dean's office, or the department. The school policy should be listed in the course catalog.

Depending on the situation, your grievance may be more with your professor than with the grade itself, in which case the procedure you follow may be different. If you believe that a professor evaluated your work unfairly or treated you in a manner that made you feel uncomfortable, embarrassed, threatened, or afraid (which, for obvious reasons, would have an effect on your performance), and you suspect it was because of your race, gender, or sexual orientation, you can file a discrimination complaint. (For information on dealing with discrimination, see "Breaking Down Bias" page 463.) The complaint will most likely have to be filed in addition to the request for a grade change.

Below are a few other points to bear in mind when you're considering contesting a grade:

■ Unfortunately, sometimes even when a professor who gave the grade asks for it to be changed, the registrar will refuse. In that case, ask if you (and perhaps also the prof) can submit a letter explaining the grade to be included in your transcript. There may also be a way to petition the registrar's decision—

check your catalog or talk with the dean's office.

■ When you contest a grade, whether formally or informally, you should be prepared with supporting evidence. Have copies of all or as much of your work as is possible. If your professor has some of your work and records of your grades, you are entitled to obtain copies for yourself.

> *"There are a lot of professors out there who think that any opinion that differs from theirs is wrong. I had a teacher who gave me a D on a paper because he said my argument wasn't based on fact. It was, only not the facts he gave us in class. I thought, 'I'm paying all this money to go to a school that punishes me when I want to think for myself?'"*
>
> —SPELMAN COLLEGE, '92

■ Remember, formally contesting a grade is serious business. Not that it shouldn't be done, but it's important to be aware of the possible ramifications. A professor may interpret your action as questioning her fairness, judgment, or ability to do a rather important part of her job. Your complaint could set off an antagonism that lasts throughout the semester— or semesters.

ACTIVIST IDEAS

■ Publish a student organized/student compiled booklet that evaluates classes. Start with first year seminars and comparisons of different sections of intro courses and other introductory seminars to help incoming students. Send out questionnaires that allow students to rate professor, class content, course structure, workload, and difficulty (for non-majors or majors) on a 1–10 scale with space for comments. See if you can gain access to the anonymous course evaluation sheets that many schools require students to fill out on the last day of class. If there are a large number of responses, the evaluations can become more than just a handy guide for students, but a message to faculty and administration about courses to expand and courses to drop. To fund the printing and distribution of the booklet, talk to the student government, student life office, dean of the faculty, and any other offices that deal with academic issues. Put copies on reserve in the library, on dorm and common area bulletin boards, or see if the student newspaper will include the list in editions that fall around the time of preregistration and registration. (This may be a good independent study project for students doing work in statistics or social science research.)

■ Support woman scholars by acknowledging other women's comments in class, using names (if you don't know, ask). Direct clarifications, comments, and questions to the student, not the professor.

■ Incorporate a women's studies outlook into every class you take. Check out the syllabus. Are there any women authors assigned? Research done by or about women? If not, it's perfectly acceptable to ask the professor why. If s/he responds by saying that there is no notable material, check it out by visiting the library or speaking with a professor who does work in women's studies. (Chances are it's not true.) Do your class project, paper, presentation, or research on a subject that addresses gender issues. Raise questions about the perception of women in the texts and how a study would have differed if women were included. Mention a woman writer/scholar/researcher in class. Be prepared to provide a brief bio.

■ Ask a librarian to offer a library tour of research materials by, for, and about women, and a class on how to find additional sources through on-line and CD-ROM database searches.

Note: For resources pertinent to academia, see the end of "Making the Leap," page 65.

Burning the Midnight Oil
Getting the Work Done

In college, classwork is a bit more serious, a bit more intense, and a bit more time consuming than it was in high school. Despite the fact that a seminar may meet only three hours a week, the volume of assigned readings, papers, and presentations far exceeds what was considered a semester's worth of work for a five-class-a-week high school course. Cultivating and honing the necessary study techniques and organizational skills —not to mention dabbling in the fine arts of speed writing, skimming, and cramming— is an essential part of being a college student. Following are some time-tested tips on all of the above.

MAKE A GAME PLAN THAT YOU CAN STICK TO

Once you've finalized your course schedule, but before you hand in your registration form, sit down with all your syllabi and your calendar. Looking over the whole semester, first mark all the events, holidays, and responsibilities that might be time consuming enough to throw your work schedule out of kilter if you don't plan ahead. (For example, factor in away games, religious holidays, conferences, due dates for financial aid forms, and projects at work.) Then, mark down test dates and when all significant papers and presentations are due inasmuch as you know these in advance. Some people like to help themselves plan ahead and mark down dates when they should begin papers and exam prep, not just the test and due dates. You may find that one of your classes will present so many conflicts that it might be better to wait and take it the next time it's offered. If you discover that you still want to (or have to) keep the class, but there is no way that you could ever get a certain paper in or pass a test without an extension, talk to the prof as soon as you spot the conflict.

Due Dates

At the beginning of the semester, your professors will probably give you the lowdown on their policies on late papers and missed exams. You may be marked down half a grade for each day a paper is late, for example, and you may not be able to make up a missed exam without a doctor's note or an equally valid and documented excuse. Some rules are school- or department-wide; others are professor-specific. (If the rule is administered by the school, the professor generally will have less leeway in granting extensions and exceptions.)

Professors know what it's like to be a student—they've spent a good portion of their lives not only working with them but being them. They know that college is a time when you're trying to get a lot more together than just your class assignments, and that you have a life beyond your academic responsibilities that can suddenly burst into chaos. Sure it's best to get everything in on time, and there are

some professors who wouldn't even dream of cutting you any slack. But most professors want you to do well, and often would rather you turn in a decent paper late, than a rotten paper in on time.

> "I hate studying in the library. I always run into people I know and it's easy to get sidetracked. I get tense the minute I walk in there. . . . Seeing everyone cramming makes me get pretty competitive. I study either in my room or in an empty classroom."
> —WASHINGTON UNIVERSITY, '96

But they can't be kind if you don't give them the opportunity to be. If you're going to be late—even if you haven't anything that resembles a legitimate excuse—call the professor as far before the due date as possible. Even talking to the prof after the class when you were supposed to hand in the paper is better than trying to convince yourself he won't notice. He *will* notice.

When you talk to your professor about why you're late, be specific. Show him what you've done so far, and try to explain what the problem is. Is your topic too big? Have you been unable to find all the information you need? Are you having a tough time formulating an argument? Even if you have to admit that you thought the paper would take less time and thus you planned your time poorly, describe what you've done so far. His guidance and ideas will probably be as valuable as the extension. You should also be able to say when he can expect to receive the paper. Be realistic in your assessment. Profs are usually not so gracious about giving second extensions. (Keep in mind that you'll have the added stress of knowing that your paper's late, and that you're expected to hand in something that makes good of the extension.)

Time Management and Study Tips

Wouldn't it be nice if there was one foolproof study technique that would work in all situations, with all subjects, no matter what our mood? Alas, it just plain doesn't exist, and developing and perfecting our study skills can be as difficult as the subject matter for which we employ them. Different techniques work for different people, and for different subjects, and at college, you'll probably have more than ample opportunity to give several techniques a whirl. Some of us do best in the daytime, others late at night. Some study best "an hour here, two hours there," others go for all-night marathons.

Where to study is also a matter of personal preference. You may need to shop around for a space, and some places may be better for studying certain subjects than others. You may like to take over a booth in an off-campus coffee shop, venture deep into the

"stacks," stay in your room, or settle into an empty classroom. You may need to be totally organized, or you might discover that if you waited until you were completely organized, you would never open a book. There are no hard and fast rules about how to study effectively; however, there are a few tips and tricks that many a student swears by.

■ At the beginning of each week, schedule time to sit down and block out your time. Take out your trusty calendar, syllabi, and random scraps of paper with homework assignments scribbled on them, and plan your days. Make a list of what's due for the week and what tasks you'll need to accomplish. Some people like to schedule specific tasks for specific time slots on specific days; others prefer to make a large "to do" list and not decide in advance what will be done when. (For big papers and exams, you should give yourself two weeks.)

■ Apply the concepts you learn in class to other areas in your life. Make connections to other subjects you're learning. Ask questions. Make comments. Draw diagrams. Discuss the material with friends. Get involved in related activities. Go see a French film. Visit a museum and see the work discussed in class. Try one of those psych experiments on your friends. You get the picture.

■ As important as knowing what to study is knowing what *not* to study. Figuring out which readings you can blow off (but do try to read the preface/introduction), which you can skim, and which should be pored over is a skill that should be learned early and used often.

MATTERS OF FAITH
—🌀—

It is illegal for your school to discriminate against you because of your religion. This means that you cannot be penalized for missing a class, an exam, or a lab due to a religious holiday. The fact that you cannot be penalized, however, does not mean that you are off the hook for the work—you are still responsible for getting the notes and doing the assignments that you missed.

■ Go to class. Pay attention. Take notes.

■ Reviewing your class notes and those you take on the readings right after you take them and (if you have time) right before the next session can help to reinforce what you learn. The more you engage with the material, the more you retain. Remember, too, that people learn differently: Some do better hearing and talking about information, others reading and writing it. Once you determine which methods are best for you, employ them!

■ Get to know your professors. The better a relationship you have with them, the more likely you are to be motivated and interested in the material and thus to do well in the class. Ask questions, go to office hours, etc.

■ You'll get more out of your study hours if you spend some of your free time doing something completely different. So even during crunch periods, allow yourself at least a little time off. If you're one of those people who lives in the library, make extra sure to schedule in time for fun—more than just the occasional study break.

■ Separate work time from play time. When it's time to work, make yourself sit down, ignore all the distractions, and work. When it's not time for work, don't even think about it.

■ If you find yourself having an impossible time concentrating, take a break instead of spinning your wheels. A study break can serve as motivation and give your mind the rest it needs to function at its peak. You will learn better, feel better, and work more efficiently if you allow yourself a short break every hour or two—walk around, grab a snack, listen to some music, complain about the amount of work you have, etc.

■ To avoid mixing up the material, don't study similar subjects back to

"In high school I was a cheerleader, tutored, worked in my church, hung out, and still got all my work done. I never had to actively balance schoolwork and fun. When I got to college I had fewer classes, spent fewer hours in class, but did a lot more work, and I did pretty poorly until I figured out that I had to schedule time for myself. If I didn't make time for hanging out with friends and doing fun stuff, I would end up slacking off, hating college, and feeling sorry for myself."
—UCLA, '97

hour, 60% goes within 24 hours, and 70% after 30 days. 🌀

back. After a meaningful session with Italian verbs, crack open your chemistry book (or better yet, take a break) before cramming for French. (If you need to review an entire semester's worth of macroeconomics formulas and don't have the luxury of maximizing brain efficiency in this manner, see "Hope You Like Cramming, Too," page 26.)

■ Studies show that for maximum retention, you should not spend more than two hours on a subject at a time, especially if you're trying to memorize material.

■ Get into study mode. Clear the desk of any extraneous materials. Assemble everything you'll need for studying. (Make sure you have a sufficient number of pencils or pens, the proper notebook, scrap paper, your textbook/reading, a calculator, graph paper, etc. Time and energy are wasted and concentration is broken when you have to find items as you need them.) If you're in your room, unplug your phone or

> "I am 35 and have been attending college for 17 years! Twelve of those years were spent in the community college system for my associate arts degree, four at the state university for the BA and MA, and now I am working on my PhD, which I will have in another two or three years. I have learned that I can do anything and that it doesn't matter how long it takes me to reach my goals."
>
> —UNIVERSITY OF SOUTHERN CALIFORNIA, PhD CANDIDATE

put the answering machine on with the volume down and close your door.

■ Avoid eye strain and fatigue, muscle soreness, general lethargy, and for goodness sake, repetitive stress injury. Look away from the book or computer monitor and focus your eyes on a distant object every 15 to 20 minutes. Stretch your arms, shoulders, back, and legs, wiggle your fingers and toes, do a neck roll or two, and shake out your wrists. Get up from the chair every once in a while and walk around for a few minutes. (In other words, the hokey-pokey is the ideal study-break activity.)

■ Some people like to study to music. If you do, keep it soft and stick to music without words. Also, steer clear of very familiar pieces like Beethoven's Fifth or tunes that are loaded with nostalgia and will make you want to hum along.

■ Actively resist the urge to drift away. Keep in mind that new, difficult, or boring material which requires the most focused thought is the most likely to send you off dreaming. If possible, study such material when you're most alert and capable of brushing away distractions.

The Procrastination Plague

❦❦❦

Many of us live by the old adage "Don't do today what you can put off until tomorrow." We've all experienced a sudden interest in cleaning our room, rearranging our closet, or calling a long-lost friend as a 40-page paper deadline looms in the not-so-distant future. Out of fear, frustration,

research sources; 2) go to periodical room for journals; 3) go to stacks for books; rather than chunks like, "do research." This can make the project less intimidating. But because procrastination can be connected with other issues, some may find that they need help to overcome it. Most schools offer study skills workshops and rap groups about procrastination. Meetings with your professor, advisor, or academic dean and/or therapy may also be helpful.

STUDY GROUPS

I f you're having trouble studying on your own, you might want to form a study group. A good study group can help you gain insight into the subject, give you a reality check on how well you know the material, provoke thoughtful, relevant, and appropriate discussions, and provide instant feedback. A bad study group, however, can leave you feeling overanxious, confused about the subject matter, and angry at the other members of the group for wasting your time. In a worst case scenario, you can end up studying material that isn't on the test, ignoring material that is, and/or memorizing incorrect dates, formulas, and definitions.

Here are a few tips on making sessions with your study group as productive as possible.

■ A key to study group success is to keep it very structured. Ask everyone to make up a possible exam question or two before meeting, then discuss the answers together. Or go over specific questions and problems from

anger, laziness, or some latent desire to self-sabotage, we put off work until the last minute, and put ourselves through hell when we finally are forced to get down to it. Of course, putting off an uninspiring or difficult task until the last minute makes the task even more unpleasant because of the stress of having to rush. It is disheartening to realize in the middle of an anguished push to finish a project that it could have been enjoyable (or at least well done) if you had allotted the appropriate amount of time for it.

To battle procrastination problems, try to break a project down into a series of doable tasks. Divide the project of, say, writing a paper into such pieces as: 1) make a list of possible

HOPE YOU LIKE CRAMMING, TOO

Just as important as good time management and study skills are cramming tricks, because even the most obsessively well-organized, computerized-calendar-toting student is not exempt from the dreadful "I've got two exams and a paper due tomorrow and I'm totally unprepared" scenario.

Cramming involves learning as much material as possible in the shortest amount of time. Shoveling information in at high speed is not a dainty process, but when done well, there is a certain art to it.

Some people cram by shifting their regular study techniques into high gear. However, there are a number of tricks to cramming that don't apply to regular, "maintenance" studying:

▲ Be realistic. You simply won't be able to learn an entire semester's information in one night. You'll have to make some decisions about what to study. Skim over the syllabus and your class notes. Then concentrate on learning the material that you know reasonably well. Work on the material that you have no idea about last— it's always better to have a really good grasp on some of the material than to barely know all of it, especially for essay tests. You may not ace the test this way, but hopefully it will allow you to pass.

▲ You have to be choosy about what to tackle when you are swamped with books and articles to read before sunrise. A popular tactic is reading the introduction and first and last paragraph of each chapter, the first and last sentence of every paragraph, and the summary or synopsis, if one exists. Of course, if you try this and feel like you're reading gibberish, try something else, like reading selective chapters that seem important.

▲ For most students, cramming just wouldn't be cramming without caffeine. However, too much can spell disaster. You don't want to drink so much coffee that you'll be too busy bouncing off the walls to open a book. The same goes for sugar. Eating a lot of sweets might give you a little energy boost at first, but chances are you'll experience a sugar crash within the hour.

▲ There are mixed opinions about the benefit of the all-nighter. Some claim that eight hours of sleep are essential before a big exam—and will get you further than if you spent those hours cranking the books. Others, while admitting that an all-nighter may take a bit of the edge off your cognitive acuity, believe that the extra study time, combined with the adrenaline rush that comes with exam-taking (which is often boosted by a couple of cups of java), more than makes up for it.

GET UP!
SNOOZE   GO TO
STUDY   School and go To work
STUDY
STUDY   Then Study
EAT

class, previous tests, homework, or the book by subject (rather than just throwing out random questions).

■ Unless everybody agrees that it would be helpful, spend as little time as possible going over questions that can be answered by simply looking at the text.

■ Study groups work best if they meet after all the members have finished, or have done a significant amount of studying on their own.

■ Don't study with people whom you can't be serious with, who will come completely unprepared, or who will give you more stress than help. And if you really need to get a lot of work done, think twice before studying with a potential romantic interest.

TIPS ON TACKLING TESTS

In order to do well on tests, you don't have to just know the material, you must be able to retrieve it quickly. Here are some suggestions on how to maximize your study hours.

■ Studying in an environment similar to the one in which you'll be taking the exam will make the retrieval of information easier. If you'll be taking the test at a desk in a dead-silent, well-lit lecture hall, try studying in an empty classroom rather than on your bed, listening to soft music.

■ The more sensory stimuli provided, the more ways your brain can take hold of the information and later regurgitate it. Instead of using those plain white rectangular note cards for flashcards, use colored paper cut into shapes.

"I believe that the way you feel about yourself has a lot to do with how you perform. I always take a shower, dress nicely, and take the time to have something to eat before an exam."
—UNIVERSITY OF NORTHERN IOWA, '97

■ Tape-record yourself reading the flashcards, waiting a few seconds before giving the translation, definition, etc. Make the tape be the first thing you hear in the morning and the last thing you hear before bed. (It sounds dorky, but it works.)

■ Write down those Swedish vocabulary words, chemical formulas, or psych terms over and over. Better yet, repeat the words out loud as you're writing. Use different colored pens— and save the really bright ones for the most important terms or those that you just can't seem to remember.

■ Mnemonic, or memory-assisting, devices like King Phillip Came Over From Germany Stoned to remember the classification of life (kingdom, phylum, class, order, family, genus, species), can be invaluable. Generally, silly mnemonics or ones about taboo topics (sex is always good) work best. Or change the words of your favorite song.

■ Group the information, and study related topics together. If you're taking a class in modern American history, instead of trying to cover every historically important event of the post-war era, break things down into smaller chunks. Take an umbrella topic, say, the civil rights movement, and get to know the main points of events like the Malcolm X assassination or *Brown v. the Board of Education* together. When grouping, try not to overwhelm yourself with more than seven or eight distinct pieces of information at once.

■ Analyze your profs. What is of interest to them? What do they ask in class? Do they like short or long responses? Are they detail-oriented? Do they go for the obvious or the obscure?

■ Write out (or at least outline) practice answers to a few probable essay questions.

■ In most humanities and social science classes, the bigger the test, the less minutiae will appear on it. Understand the overriding principles of the topics to be tested before getting bogged down in details.

AT THE EXAM

■ Confidence, baby, confidence. Though at times it may be difficult to summon, sometimes a positive attitude can mean the difference between passing and failing. When you think you get a question right, give yourself a mental pat on the back. Praise yourself for your essay-writing skills. Think about your success on similar exams. Convince yourself that staying up all night (or getting x number hours of sleep) was the absolute best method for getting yourself mentally and physically prepared. Leave the criticism of your study techniques and your abilities until after the test.

■ Beware the myth that you need not prepare for open-book exams. Being allowed to use your book and notes during an exam often causes more problems than benefits. Even though you have the material on hand, if it's not immediately accessible, you'll end up losing precious time. You should study just as you would for a closed-book test, and only use your notes or text for quick reference or to verify a fact. Make a sheet of information about important subjects (including page numbers if you want to refer to the book). Bringing along outlines of answers to possible questions never hurts either.

■ Don't forget about partial credit. If you know something—anything—about the question, get it down. Got only two minutes left? Get every last bit of relevant information down before time is called. Don't worry about complete sentences, articles, even verbs. Use an outline or a bulleted list of key points, and dashes if proper punctuation eludes you.

■ Studies have shown that students who stop studying at least 20 minutes (some say an hour) before the test do consistently better than those who thumb through flashcards up until the moment the blue book is opened. The time gives your brain a chance to rest, organize the material, and relax.

■ For an essay test, invest a buck and a half for a pen that writes smoothly and glides across the low-grade blue book-

OH, THE UBIQUITOUS ALL-NIGHTER

On many campuses there is a certain glamour in sacrificing one's rest for the pursuit of knowledge, and the telling (and retelling) of all-nighter "fish stories" is something of an unofficial varsity sport. Indeed, many students spend more time discussing sleep than getting it.

Hardly anybody makes it through her college career without spending at least one night in a stressed-filled battle against sleep, fighting to eke out a term paper or memorize a semester's worth of physics equations. The jury is still out on whether the benefits of the all-nighter outweigh the drawbacks. Critics contend that the staying up all night severely impedes performance. Proponents retort that without the knowledge gleaned in the wee hours of the morning, there would be no performance.

Still, there's no doubt that all-nighters are not a particularly efficient or enjoyable way to learn—and try remembering anything two days after the test. (For information on the physical effects of lack of sleep, see "The Anatomy of an All-Nighter," page 206.)

paper. As minor as it sounds, it really does make a difference. And it's never a bad idea to have a spare or two on hand as well.

PAPER PLEASURE

You can always identify a student in paper panic by her keyboard-flattened fingers, her monitor-zapped eyes, and the index-card-sized paper cuts between her fingers. Even the most computer- and math-minded among us won't be able to squeak through college without writing at least one 7–10 pager. Though you may despise paper writing while you're knee-deep in the process, the feeling of satisfaction upon completing 20 pages on a subject you never heard of before the start of the semester should be bottled and sold as an anti-depressant.

And there is no better way to really get to know material than to write a paper about it. In fact, one of the most common euphemisms for "expert on a subject" is "she wrote her term paper on that topic." Below are tips for making the means as satisfying as the end. Well, almost.

■ Trying to write a comprehensive paper on the dramatis personae in all of Shakespeare's major works will take you more than a night and more than five pages. Pick a topic that is manageable within the given time frame. Do everything possible to avoid the most common student paper problem: discovering at the 11th hour that your topic is too broad or too narrow. Even if it's not required, it's never a bad idea to talk with your professor or TA about your idea (or to seek their advice on coming up with one that is appropriate, interesting, and doable).

■ Do research before you do research.

Check the card catalog, computer, and reference sources and/or talk to a librarian about the availability of *accessible* sources on your topic. (It's not enough that they exist—you have to be able to get to them.)

■ Use appropriate sources. Encyclopedias and other reference material that provide a pseudo-objective overview may be helpful when doing preliminary research, but should not be used to back up points in papers.

■ For the sake of time, accuracy, a less painful bibliography and footnote/endnote experience, and plagiarism-avoidance, take excruciatingly well-organized notes while you're researching. (See "Cheating: Just Don't Do It," on the facing page.)

GETTING HELP

College is not easy. Along with chem labs that last near into dusk, 10-page research papers assigned for "a week from today," and the inevitable scheduling horrors that leave us with 3 final exams within 15 minutes of each other, we're trying to earn money, hang out with friends, get involved with our communities, and ingest some of that fine cafeteria food. Keep

in mind that time management is a skill that takes time to learn, and even longer to perfect.

Nearly all students will find themselves overwhelmed with work to the point that they don't know where to begin. Being overwhelmed itself is not a problem nor a bad thing. Not seeking help when you need it is. Learning what to do when you are in the midst of academic hell and can't get out alone is an important life skill, every bit as valuable as learning to manage your time and choose your classes.

Following are some words to the wise:

■ Don't let things get too far out of hand. As soon as you see the first sign of trouble, seek help.

■ Talk to your professor, even if your problem is not directly related to academics. (You do not have to, and perhaps in some cases should not, go into great detail.) For the most part, professors want to help students succeed in the class. They can give you help, recommend additional materials, even allow you to do an extra credit assignment or rewrite your paper to improve your grade. Visit during office hours, or else schedule an appointment.

■ Find a tutor. She might help only once or you might meet with her after

SCHOOL SUPPORT FOR DISABLED STUDENTS

❀

In compliance with the laws that require education to be accessible to all, your school is required to provide students with disabilities, (including learning disabilities) with the resources, accommodations, and services that will enable them to do their work, such as allowing them extra time on exams, or to give oral presentations in lieu of written papers.

Many schools have created offices or centers that offer support, services, and facilities to students with disabilities. These places can provide counseling (academic and therapeutic) and tutors, arrange for rides, and help you navigate the system to get what you need from the administration, health services, professors, library, campus housing, dining services, and the telephone/computing centers.

If a permanent or temporary disability prevents you from taking a full courseload, you should still be eligible for aid or awards designated for full-time students.

(For more on attending college as a disabled student, see "Community and Identity," page 533.)

---

every class to go over material. Departmental offices often have the names of tutors with reasonable rates.

■ Talk with fellow students. You don't have to wait until the night before a test to study with friends. Get together with classmates to go over problem sets or the class discussion or to chat in Mandarin.

■ Take advantage of school offerings. Academic offices, counseling centers, and other campus groups may offer workshops that teach study skills and/or address procrastination problems, as well as recommend books and pamphlets on time management.

■ If things get way out of hand and you do not pass a certain number of credits or you don't maintain the minimum required GPA, your school may ask you to take a semester or year off. (For more information, see "Leaves of Absence," page 41.)

CHEATING: JUST DON'T DO IT

"I see more cheating in "guts" [classes intended for non-majors, taken to fulfill a requirement], because people don't care about what they're studying. They think, 'So what? It's a stupid class anyway, what does it matter to me?'. . . Even though people tend to stress out in upper-level classes—especially when they want to go on to grad school or work in the subject—they don't seem to cheat as much."

—COLGATE COLLEGE, '93

The first nonsexist edition of Roget's Thesaurus was published in 1982. ❀

Whether or not you sign an explicit honor code at the beginning of each year or before each test, every school expects its students to follow basic social and academic guidelines. Cheating, including plagiarism, can result in failure, suspension, or even expulsion. Every college student knows what cheating is, and every college student has a rough idea of what could happen if she were caught. If you want to know about the specifics of your school's cheating policy, talk to someone in the office that deals with academic affairs, check out the course catalog, and/or tune in to the rumor mill.

Plagiarism

෨෨෨

Plagiarism—using others' words and/or ideas without proper acknowledgment—is one of the severest of intellectual crimes. Many schools will penalize for plagiarism even if the student is not aware that it occurred. It is a paper writer's responsibility to scrupulously check all sources and citations, so technically even accidental plagiarism—citing the wrong pages, forgetting quotation marks, failing to include endnotes—is punishable. (And because it's often professors like the one grading your paper who produce the work that is plagiarized, you can bet that they will be extra-sensitive to any theft of ideas, be it intentional or accidental.)

To avoid plagiarism:

■ Always cite your source, whether you quote directly or paraphrase. Some professors prefer you to avoid using quotes unless the manner in which the original author writes

significantly adds to its meaning or importance. A paper generally sounds better and works better when ideas are expressed in the student's words and style. However, paraphrasing can be a tricky business. Even if you properly cite your source but your paraphrase too closely resembles the original, you may be considered guilty of plagiarism. Similarly, even if you properly cite works, using them too extensively can be considered plagiarism.

■ In some cases, even quoting yourself without proper attribution could be considered plagiarism, as in the case of using the same paper for two or more classes without permission.

■ If you are unsure whether to cite an idea or include the source in your bibliography, ask the professor. It is better

"Even though it would be fairly easy to cheat here because the school's big and the professors don't know us as well as our high school teachers did, I think that people realize that their education's up to them now, and cheating would only hurt them. . . . We're paying a lot of money to be here, and we might as well take advantage of it."

—DARTMOUTH COLLEGE, '94

☼ 57% of females and 61% of males ages 13-17 say they've cheated on a test.

to err on the side of overdoing it than failing to do it.

■ Ask all your professors to delineate their preferred footnote/endnote/bibliographic format at the start of the semester. Depending on their schooling, discipline, and own personal preferences, professors will have different standards and rules for citations.

■ Most colleges publish pamphlets or booklets that spell out guidelines for paper writing and proper citation. Ask if one is available from the office of academic affairs, the writing center, places that offer study skills workshops, or the library. If the school doesn't publish anything of the kind, get your hands on a copy of one of the books listed in the Resources at the end of "Making the Leap," page 65.

CAMPUS HIGHLIGHT

Bowdoin College in Brunswick, Maine, requires students to sign an academic honor code upon matriculation—and everyone takes it very seriously. Bowdoin's Hawthorne-Longfellow library, the largest in Maine, has no electronic security devices. Exams are unproctored, and buildings are open late into the night. If a student is accused of cheating, plagiarism, or another honor code violation, the case goes not to the dean, but rather to a student judiciary board, which has full authority to decide the consequences.

ACTIVIST IDEAS

■ Arrange for someone from the academic support center and/or counseling services to give a workshop or hold a support group on study skills and procrastination issues.

■ If you're a whiz in a subject, offer tutoring on a sliding scale (where students pay what they can afford).

■ During high-stress times on campus, organize a workshop on stress management and relaxation techniques. Counselors in mental health services and RAs may know people who could lead the program.

Note: for resources pertinent to study skills see the end of "Making the Leap," page 65.

Off the Beaten Track

Less Traditional Educational Opportunities

What is considered the traditional college experience —spending four consecutive years at a school, majoring in a traditional discipline, getting all your credits by taking classes taught by professors and TAs (for most of which you need to write a term paper and take an exam or two)—is not the reality for a large number of college students.

There is a wide variety of academic options that give students a chance to complete their degrees at their own pace, do their learning in a number of different environments, gain experience working in the "real world," get academic credit for out-of-classroom work, and custom-tailor their academic work to fit interests that fall beyond the established curriculum and standard disciplines. Even if you're at the most traditional of the traditional colleges, a simple scan through the course catalog or a discussion with your advisor or the head of your department will likely reveal myriad ways you can get credit for learning outside the confines of the lecture / seminar / lab format, the classroom, or even the school gates.

CHECK OUT WHAT YOUR SCHOOL OFFERS

You may be surprised at what's under your very nose. In addition to the standard curriculum, your school probably offers unusual courses, ranging from the extremely practical (law writing, lobbying, and political action courses) the semipractical (architectural history and walking tours), and the wholly delightful and esoteric (the influence of the sonata on 18th-century literature). If you pore over the catalog and sleuth around the departments, chances are you'll discover visiting professors, last-minute course offerings, and ways to create independent-study projects. In addition, many schools offer student-taught courses, both for credit and not for credit, ranging from batik to vegetarian cooking.

GETTING CREDIT FOR WORK

For most of us, working is an established if unwritten part of the college curriculum—whether it be in a work-study situation, a career-related internship, or a job we're doing for the money only. However, there are a number of programs available at colleges that enable work experience to fulfill more than just your financial requirements. Many colleges include internships and work experience in their requirements for graduation for those in majors such as teaching or physical education, and some require them for all students. This enables students to get real-world experience, make contacts for future employment, and apply class work to out-of-classroom work. Even if your school doesn't require that you supplement your studies with an internship, you can often get some sort of credit for work through a formal program like The College Level Examination Program (CLEP) or on a case-by-case basis. CLEP administers standardized exams that, if you pass, enable your work to be accepted as course credit. The exams may be either general overviews or detailed subject tests. Students often take them to get credit for work or for self-taught, on-line, video, and other "correspondence" courses. Schools vary in how they award credit—they may give course credit, requirement exemption, placement in upper-level classes, or all three.

Even if a formal work-for-credit program does not exist at your school, you may be able to substitute an internship for a class project, or get credit for work through an independent study, by writing a paper on your work experience, by teaching the skills learned, or by incorporating the experience into a self-designed major. (See "All About Internships," page 160, for more information about how to find an internship.)

CREATING YOUR OWN MAJOR

If your school doesn't offer a major in what you want to study, you may be able to make one yourself. To create a self-designed major, you'll probably need to find a faculty sponsor, get support from professors in all the areas

A SPECIAL KIND OF EDUCATION—
WOMEN'S COLLEGES

"I've had all-women classes and classes with men ... some at Wellesley, some at the coed schools around here, and I notice a really big difference in the way women talk and their confidence level in the non-Wellesley classes ... I even notice a change in myself."
—*WELLESLEY COLLEGE, '95*

Women's colleges originated because there was simply no other way that women could get a higher education. Though diminished in number, they have continued to exist (and thrive) because of the equality and quality of educational experience they offer women. There are currently 83 women's colleges in the United States and Canada. They foster an environment in which women's work is valued and cultivated. Women at women's colleges study the same broad range of disciplines that they do at coed schools.

Students at women's colleges avoid much of the sexism that can occur in coed classrooms and universities. Though a large percentage of women's schools do allow men to enroll in classes, the classes generally maintain a woman-friendly environment. In the past few years, women's schools have enjoyed a popularity resurgence, testimony to the fact that women are making their education a priority and feel that the environment and opportunities that a women's college offers may be the best choice for them, academically and personally.

"Most of the women who broke ground and opened up places and opportunities for women today went to women's colleges. Most of the women I call my heroines, the women who wrote the books and did the experiments that I study, did too. And much of the scholarship that is adding a rich new voice to the 'classics' is coming out of women's colleges."
—*UNIVERSITY OF TEXAS AT AUSTIN, '92*

"Being at a black women's college has been the most powerful experience for me. There is no other place where I, as a black woman, would have been supported, encouraged, and engaged by my professors to succeed. Spelman exists to educate black women so that we can take our place of power in this society with pride, and have the knowledge of our people's history always with us."
—*SPELMAN COLLEGE, '94*

included in your major, and present a proposal to an academic committee. The proposal should include information such as the purpose of your major, why it's important to you, how the existing curriculum doesn't offer you what you need, and a list of all courses, independent-study projects, work, internships, and extracurricular experiences that will count toward the major. If you wish to design a major in an established interdisciplinary field, such as African-American studies, Near Eastern studies, urban studies, environmental studies, etc., that your school doesn't offer, obtain information about requirements and course syllabi from schools that do for guidance and to help with the approval process.

STUDY ABROAD

There are study-abroad programs to satisfy the wanderlust in nearly every student. Whether you're looking for a "traditional" academic program (with workloads ranging from the extremely rigorous to the "I'm getting a semester's credit for this?!"), intensive study on one topic, an exploration of a different language and culture, or a break from the college environment, you can probably find it (or create it). Colleges and universities, the government and governmental organizations, and companies (private and public, not-for-profit and for-profit) offer programs specifically designed for American students to study at a foreign school or research facility, for a semester or a year.

The benefit of entering a program sponsored by your school is that you should have no trouble getting credit for your work and not too difficult a time getting in. But bear in mind that a program sponsored by your school might be filled with your classmates and may not be the best choice if you're looking to "get away."

If your school doesn't offer programs abroad, or if none of the available programs interest you, do what the majority of students who go abroad do: Check out the foreign exchange programs at other schools or apply directly to a foreign university.

If you don't have a designated office that handles study abroad, the office of academic affairs, the dean's office, or the library should have information about programs around the world, usually organized by area of study and/or country. If you are interested in concentrating on a certain discipline or subject, the appropriate department at your school (or a notably strong department at another school) should have some suggestions. You can also get in touch with programs that are similar to what you're looking for. Faculty members from or familiar with the country or city in which you want to study may also be of help, even if your school doesn't have a formal program. You'll most likely be able to apply credits received at another institution toward graduation.

Before Going Abroad

ම⑨ම

■ Get the scoop on your options. Talk with the dean or faculty member in charge of study abroad. You can find out whom to speak with by asking in the dean's office or checking the catalog. They will probably have books you can browse through and will be able to make some recommendations. If you want academic credit, find out your school's criteria for getting credit and what specific programs fit them before you apply.

■ Settle the leave issues. Make sure you have filed whatever papers are required to take a leave of absence. (If you are in a university-sponsored or affiliated program your semester or year abroad may not be considered a leave.) For more on taking time away from school, see page 41.

■ Get your coursework approved ahead of time if possible. This ensures that when you return your credits will transfer. Often this means that you must take a program and course description to professors (frequently the chair of the appropriate department) and get signatures of approval. Have this put in your file. If for some reason you cannot get your courses approved in advance, be sure to keep any information about the courses, syllabi, samples of your work, and letters from your instructors abroad—this will make it easier to get credit when you return.

> *"I think everyone who has the chance should try to take at least one semester away. It's probably the last time that you can see the world and have someone else help you pay for it."*
>
> **—DUKE UNIVERSITY, '95**

■ If for any reason your school will not recognize a program you want to go on (as is often the case), you can sometimes get credit by doing an indepen-

dent study with a professor. This may require that you write a paper or give a presentation about your work when you return. There are lots of ways to get credit for even the most nontraditional programs.

■ The process by which to find out about, evaluate, and apply to schools or programs is very similar to that of applying to transfer or grad school. (See "Making the Leap," page 44, for tips on applying to schools.)

Bonnes Questions Before Bon Voyage

☙☙☙

While you're weighing your options, here are a few points to consider.

■ **Purpose:** What are you looking for? Something familiar, like taking courses in your major at an American enclave in a foreign country, or something wholly unfamiliar, like a homestay/cultural immersion program?

■ **Language:** Do you want classes to be taught in English, a second language you're proficient in and wish to master, or one that you'll have to learn from scratch (as quickly as possible) upon your arrival?

■ **Academics:** How hard do you plan to work? You may want to opt for a slightly lighter academic load if you're hoping to really get to know the place (and other places nearby).

"Until I went away, I took my free-dom being an American woman for granted. . . . After a year study-ing and traveling in four Muslim Arab nations—where I couldn't go out alone, I had to cover my body, and basically had very few rights—I returned a feminist."
—UNIVERSITY OF VERMONT, '94

■ **Credit:** How much academic credit do you need? If you can't get a full semester's credit for a program you're crazy about, can you fit an extra class in before you go or when you return to make up the difference?

■ **Living and social situation:** Do you want to live in a dorm with American students, with a family, in an indepen-dently rented apartment, or to be in-termingled with local students? Do you want to go on a meal plan (if one is available)?

■ **Goals:** Are you looking to gain spe-cial skills, knowledge, or experience? Consider more than just the academic portion of the program. Will you have an opportunity to travel, meet people, work/volunteer/intern, or participate in activities, rituals, and events specific to the area/time of year?

■ **Funding:** If you're enrolled in ROTC or on an athletic scholarship, you may not be allowed to take a leave. Also, certain grants and loans may be avail-able only as long as you attend your school or an affiliated school. Talk to the financial aid office about how going away might affect your present aid package, as well as strategies for funding your semester/year away. Remember to find out the cost of living in the new area.

■ **Personal needs:** Can the program accommodate a disability, a medical/psychological condition, your reli-gious and/or dietary needs? If the pro-gram has no provisions in place to fulfill your needs, find out if special arrangements can be made.

■ **Health insurance:** Will you be cov-ered by your school's health insurance if you are away? If not, does the pro-gram offer health insurance? Will your parents' plan cover you?

■ **Others' needs:** Are there other peo-ple involved in your decision whose needs must too be met? What about funding, accommodations, and/or work for a significant other or child? Are you going to have to give your parents the hard sell?

See page 526 for tips on staying safe while you're abroad.

CAMPUS HIGHLIGHT

Antioch College sponsors the Comparative Women's Studies Program, an intensive in-field research experience, every fall semester. Students from all over the country travel to Poland, Germany, the Netherlands, and England to study with scholars, activists, policymakers, and writ-ers in classroom and non-class-room settings. For the last month, students live in a homestay in Lon-don and finalize their research. For more information contact Idella Burmester, assistant direc-tor of Antioch Education Abroad at 1-800-874-7986.

At some schools, as many as 10% of incoming first-year students defer.

BEFORE YOU GO . . .
GET ALL THE NECESSARY DOCUMENTS

▲ VISA: Many countries require that you have a visa, which is a document issued by the foreign consulate or embassy of the country granting you permission to stay for a specified length of time to work, live, and/or study. There are different types of visas: student, travel, business, etc.

To get a student visa you may need to have proof of acceptance from or enrollment in the institution abroad. Foreign schools or programs can assist you in the process of getting your visa. You can also apply for one through the mail, but be sure to allow enough time—this can be a bureaucratic nightmare and a time-management hassle. If your visa runs out it is usually possible to get an extension if you want to stay longer.

You can find the address of the foreign embassy or consulate by looking in the congressional directory at your campus or public library.

▲ PASSPORT: A passport is required for entry into most foreign countries and re-entry into the U.S. Even if it is not required for the country you are traveling to, it's worth your while to get one. It's one of the best forms of identification around and will be your ticket to assistance from the American embassy or consulate in that country if you run into trouble. You can get a new passport, or have your old one renewed (in most cases they are good for 10 years), at U.S. government passport offices. Check the phone book. When you travel keep your passport with you at all times, or at least make sure it is in a very safe place. If it gets lost or stolen, report it to the embassy ASAP.

▲ IMMUNIZATIONS: Find out if you need any immunizations to travel to a specific country by contacting the local health department, your physician, or the Centers for Disease Control and Prevention (404-332-4559).

▲ THE INTERNATIONAL STUDENT IDENTIFICATION CARD: This identification card can give you discounts on travel, lodging (in hostels and the like), and museums and other tourist attractions; access to a 24-hour toll-free hotline for medical, legal, or financial emergencies; and illness and accident insurance. It is well worth the cost (under $20) and can be obtained through most student travel agencies, the Council on International Educational Exchange (CIEE), or the Institute of International Education (IIE). See the Resources at the end of "Making the Leap," page 65, for the phone numbers and addresses of these organizations.

"*I loved being at a small, rural, academically demanding school but I was intrigued by my older sister's stories of UC—San Diego, so I did an exchange semester. Because the school is part of the Twelve-College Exchange, it was a completely painless process. I recommend to students who aren't sure they want to go to a foreign country to do an exchange at a U.S. school. . . . After Dartmouth, UCSD was like going to a foreign country.*"

—DARTMOUTH COLLEGE, '90

ABROAD IN THE U.S.A.

You don't need to go out of the country in order to get a very different academic experience (let alone culture shock). Many schools are formally and informally affiliated with others at which you can do an exchange. (But affiliation is not required—you can just apply directly to the other school.) Taking a semester or a year at a school with a more (or less) diverse student body, that offers you the chance to study with the professor of your dreams, that is in a location that has the climate (both social and meteorological), surroundings, activities, and/or proximity to loved ones that you crave, can provide the perfect routine-breaker, without the effort, expense, credit dilemmas, and hassles of going abroad.

LEAVES OF ABSENCE

If the trend continues, students who finish their college requirements in four consecutive years before the age of 22 will be few and far between. Students defer starting school or take time off from their studies for a number of reasons: to pursue nonacademic interests, to save money, to give themselves time to deal with and recover from physical and/or emotional illnesses, to care for children, to get a clearer idea about where and how to focus their academic ambitions, to recharge after an unfulfilling or unpleasant experience, and to devote more time to other social, familial, religious, personal, or career responsibilities. By necessity, schools these days are generally very accommodating to students who choose to take time off.

Filling out all the required forms and notifying all the necessary people is the easiest way to make the process of post-leave readmission and reinstatement of aid as painless as possible. Before taking a leave, talk to folks in the registrar or dean's office to deal with the administrative issues and get the scoop on the institution's leave policy (including the requirements for return). Talk to the financial aid office about how taking a leave of absence will affect your aid package, as well as what (if any) steps you should take to ensure that you will get aid when you return. This is especially important if you are leaving mid-term. Some funding sources require that you complete a certain number of credits per semester—failure to do so can make you ineligible for future aid, make it more difficult to get aid, or mean you have

"I spent 13 years of my life in school, then applied to college like everyone else did without giving it any thought. But once I got there I felt like 'Why am I spending all this money and putting myself through this?' I finished the semester, and planned to take a semester off and get a job and think about what I really wanted. The semester turned into three years. When I went back to school, I felt like I was much more focused and sure of myself."

—WILLIAMS COLLEGE, '96

to repay the money, even if it has already been spent. (However, schools and funding sources are often sympathetic to students who must take a leave of absence due to a medical problem or another situation beyond their control. The dean's office, the financial aid office, and/or health services will often give advice, try to piece together additional financial aid for you, and may even notify appropriate professors. Nonetheless, you'll still have to do a bit of legwork and make a mess of phone calls.)

You should also discuss your leave with your academic advisor and a professor in your department. It's a good idea to have an accurate picture of where you stand academically, how your leave will affect your major, and if your absence from school will preclude you from taking specific classes or studying with certain professors. Avoid the unpleasantness of discovering upon your return that you don't

have the credit that you were certain you had at the time of your departure.

Taking a Medical Leave

To qualify for a medical leave, you might need to provide the school with verifying information (such as a doctor's note) and you may have to get the OK from health services before you can return. Schools may have different policies for readmission depending on the reasons for leaving. It's possible that you'll find yourself tangled in a bit more red tape when returning after a leave due to emotional or mental illness (such as depression, an eating disorder, or substance dependency) than physical illnesses, especially if the problem had a serious enough impact on your performance that the school required that you take a leave. Because schools are such high-pressure environments and offer little supervision, the powers that be want to be sure that your emotional health is stable before you return.

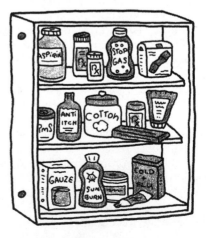

ACTIVIST IDEAS

■ Organize a study-abroad fair, where students who participated in programs can show slides and pictures, and a dean can explain the school policies on taking a semester or year at a foreign school.

■ If you have a skill or knowledge in a subject area, why not teach a class? Student-taught courses in topics such as basic word processing and other essential computing skills, women's health, guitar, and star-gazing (as well as many, many others) are very popular at colleges that have organized student-taught programs in their curriculums. If your school doesn't have a formal student-taught program, offer your course through a campus group or on your own.

■ Incorporate your volunteer and/or paid work into your academic work. Do an independent study that focuses on practical applications of the theoretical work you do in the classroom.

Explore the ideas about organizing, making social change, and building communities that you learn about in women's studies, African-American studies, sociology, and/or history by working with an activist organization. See how in-class discussions about law, public opinion, the political process, and public versus private power inform your work for a candidate, in a legislator's office, or reporting on current events for the campus newspaper, and vice versa. Do volunteer work in a hospital, clinic, or community for elderly adults to supplement your work in science, psychology, health care, or social work. Even if you can't get a course's worth of credit for this work, you can certainly make it a paper or in-class presentation topic.

Note: For resources pertinent to pursuing nontraditional educational opportunities, see the end of "Making the Leap," page 65.

Making the Leap

Transferring & Graduate School

Oh, doesn't it seem like just yesterday that you sent off those college applications, swearing that you'd never willingly put yourself through any such process again? There are few things more stressful than pulling together a multipart application, especially one that requires one or more essays and is seemingly so important to your future. But thankfully, as painful as the process is, it's almost always well worth the effort. Keep this in mind if you are about to break your promise never to write another personal statement by applying to grad school or transferring to another college. And perhaps it won't be as bad the second time around—especially if you use the tips and tricks provided below.

LOOK BEFORE YOU LEAP

Before you begin calling schools, formulating essays in your head, and announcing your transfer or grad school plans to the 37 relatives sitting around the Thanksgiving table, do some good, hard thinking. Take the time to discuss your plans with a friend, advisor, and/or family members (one or two at a time). Go over pros and cons; what the choice will mean socially, financially, academically, and emotionally; and be honest about the fears, ambitions, and pressures behind the decision. Though this won't guarantee that you end up making a choice you'll be forever grateful for, you'll at least go into it confident that you made the best decision you could.

Almost all students find themselves wondering if they made the right choice at least once during their college careers. Before transferring, take the time to consider whether it's really your school that's getting you down, or something else. (If you're applying to a more prestigious school or to one you wanted to go to but didn't get into when you first applied before, that's a different story, but still consider whether making the change is worth it.) You should give the same amount of serious thought before applying to grad school. When the reality of graduation looms near, and the notion of being hurled into the "real world" of careers, loan repayments, and unsubsidized housing sends shivers down your spine, grad school can seem like a rather pleasant alternative. That is, until you get there and realize that you never had and never will have any interest in the study of leech communities. Sometimes it takes a little distance from the academic setting to get an accurate picture of where your talents and interests lie. Don't be afraid to take it if you need it. The real world is not that scary.

FIGURING OUT WHERE TO APPLY

Having already spent quite a bit of time in school gives you insight into what to look for, but it doesn't mean that the process will be easy. Here are some things to consider when checking out schools:

■ **Students:** In grad school, there will be a relatively small group with whom you'll be taking most of your classes, collaborating on research projects, and spending untold hours in the library, lab, and studio. So, when checking out programs it's not a bad practice to check out your potential peers as well. Do they have academic and extracurricular interests and political leanings compatible to yours? Are they friendly? Do they like to have a good time? Are they at a similar level of seriousness and ambition as you?

■ **Professors:** Are they accessible? Do they do work in your desired area of concentration? Are there a fair number of women profs? Will any of the professors you want to study with be on sabbatical or otherwise inaccessible?

■ **Location and size:** Where is the school? How large is the student body? Is it culturally, ethnically, and/or economically diverse? Even a place with an excellent reputation and engaging profs can feel like a virtual hell if the city gal in you feels claustrophobic at a small rural school or the country girl in you feels uncomfortable walking to the library after dark.

■ **Costs:** How sky-high is the tuition? What's the funding situation like? Are there jobs available? How much will housing cost? What about food and entertainment? Will you be able to afford to travel home?

■ **Social life:** Is it easy to meet people? Are there organizations, and activities that interest you?

■ **Facilities:** What are the libraries like? Is the campus computerized? What services are offered to students by way of academic assistance, clergy, career planning, day care, counseling, and disability and health services?

■ **Job placement:** What percentage of graduates find jobs? How well-connected is the career services center? Does it sponsor programs like mock interviews, résumé writing, and job counseling? Is there on-campus recruitment? Is there an alumni network

COSTS TO CONSIDER

As if the process of applying to school weren't arduous enough, it can cost a pretty penny, especially if you're applying to more than three schools or plan to visit schools that are far away. Make sure you budget for the following:

▲ Standardized test prep materials and/or classes.

▲ First-class postage for recommendation letters and the applications. (You know if you're someone who'd best budget in the cost of overnight mail.)

▲ Photocopies of all the applications and the packet for professors writing your recommendations.

▲ Application fees. (Some schools will waive fees if the applicant would otherwise be unable to apply.)

▲ Standardized test registration fees.

▲ Fee to have test scores sent out (ETS will send your scores free to three schools if designated on the day of the test).

▲ Fee to have transcript sent out (don't forget to check it over for errors before it goes out).

▲ Cost to make campus visits (transportation, lodging, food).

▲ Long-distance phone calls to the admissions office and professors at prospective schools.

that helps students get jobs and internships? Do they help with job placement while you're still in school?

■ **Academic options:** Find out about your access to other classes, departments, and/or programs within your school, in the entire university (if you are at one), and other affiliated schools. For example, can you cross-register with other schools? Also, find out the policy on deferment and leave.

■ **Intellectual level and academic requirements:** Sit in on a class or two. Do you like the format? Are the profs engaging? Are the students' comments stimulating or vapid, very basic or

totally over your head? Is the atmosphere competitive or laid-back? How heavy is the workload? Will you be required to do a lot of work in areas that don't interest you?

■ **Prestige/reputation:** Every school has stronger and weaker departments. A school's prestige is not always an indication of the quality of the education you'll get or how well the school will suit you. Schools gain prestige because of research, famous alums, professors who may or may not be in your discipline, and selectivity, among other factors. You might be surprised to learn that a highly regarded school has a terrible department or program in your field of interest, has few women grad students and professors, and has poorly ventilated, decrepit laboratories.

GETTING THE SCOOP ON SCHOOLS

The best way to find out about a department or a school is by talking to folks who are already familiar with it, such as:

■ **Students in your department of interest:** Students are usually very candid about their likes and dislikes, and their friendliness, enthusiasm, and intensity can say a lot about the atmosphere of a school. The department you're interested in or the admissions office can probably help you find students to talk to and stay with.

Questions to ask: Why did they choose this school over others? Are they happy with that choice? What would they change? What are their professional aspirations? Does the school prepare them to meet their goals, and if so, how? What is the work (and workload) like? What are the departmental politics like? What are the professors who work in your fields of interest like? What are the big issues on campus? How are they funding their way through?

■ **Professors at your current school:** Academia is a small world so it's more than likely that your current profs will be able to give you some insight into other schools' professors, programs, procedures, and politics. They may even be able to hook you up with professors and former students at other schools. It also never hurts to show a potential recommendation writer that you think highly enough about her opinions to ask her advice about what you should do with your future.

Questions to ask: What professors at what schools are doing work in my area of interest? What schools could I realistically get into? What schools are known to be supportive of women students? Have other students of yours recently applied to similar programs? What were their experiences like?

■ **Professors at the prospective school:** You'll want to speak with them for a number of reasons: They'll play a large role in your educational experience, and they'll know the most about the program or department you'll be entering. At grad schools, admission into a program is greatly influenced, if not decided by the professors in the department. Before you speak with a professor, find out about his or her area of specialization. You can find out by reading the school's catalog or checking the library for any of their publications.

Questions to ask: What classes would you recommend to someone with my

field of interest? Do you like working here? What are the students like? What do students have the most problems with? What's the state of the department? Are any professors going on sabbatical? What kind of jobs/residencies do students find after graduation? What kind of funding is available? How secure is it?

Campus Visit

୭୭୭

It always helps to visit a school if you possibly can, although distance and finances often preclude it. Only a few schools will pay a prospective student's travel expenses, but almost every one will provide you with meal tickets and housing with a student, and will schedule appointments/, interviews with faculty members and admissions officers. If you are unable to convince the school to pass you up, there are a few options:

■ If there's a chapter of your sorority or coed fraternity on campus, a quick phone call will almost guarantee you a place to stay.

■ Try contacting students with similar interests by calling your prospective department or an organization you're interested in—the admissions office or the student life office can provide you with phone numbers.

■ Ask your friends at your school. Little did you know, but your physics study partner's best friend's sister is in the program that you're applying to, and has an extra bed.

■ If you do end up having to stay in a motel, the admissions office can undoubtedly recommend one.

APPLICATION CHECKLIST

Get the info. Request information and applications from the admissions office. Be clear about what program you'll be applying to. Some universities have separate applications and requirements for different programs. And while you're on the phone, it is always a good idea to ask about deadlines and financial aid forms. Sometimes you will have to call more than one office to gather all the information you need, especially if you are calling a large university. Make one big schedule of when the materials are due for each application and post it in a prominent location.

Take the requisite tests. Find out from the admissions office which standardized exams are required. If you need to take a test, get an information packet from the Educational Testing Service (ETS) and register for the exam. If possible, give yourself ample time to practice—statistics indicate that taking practice exams almost always improves scores. Arrange for your scores to be sent to the appropriate institutions or programs. (For more on standardized tests, see page 53.)

Line up recommendations. Determine who you want to write your recommendations—professors, employers, friends, your clergyperson, dean, or guidance counselor—and ask if they are willing to write them. If they agree, give them your recommendation forms with pre-stamped and pre-addressed envelopes and a packet of information about you. (For more on recommendations, see page 51.)

☼ In 1991, women received 180,686 masters degrees and

TO SUPPLEMENT OR NOT?

Grad schools and professional schools are not interested in your many talents and accomplishments that are not connected to the subject you'll be studying, so unless you're applying to a related program, do not send slides of your sculpture, the literary magazine in which your poetry was featured, or your exposé on corruption in the administration that appeared in the school newspaper. (However, if your art, poetry, or journalism won you any awards or acclaim, do mention it in your application.) The story's different if you're transferring. One or two quality items that demonstrate your prowess in the arts and extracurricular interests can really boost your application. But only send material that's sure to wow them. And always call before sending videotapes they are rarely viewed.

Have your transcript sent out. Official transcripts must be sent directly from the registrar. (Most programs require official transcripts, meaning that they must be stamped with an official school seal. If you don't need to send an official transcript, sending a Xerox of your own copy will save money and perhaps a lot of stress.) In most cases you'll have to fill out a form and pay a fee for any transcripts you have sent. Do this as early in the application process as possible, for as application deadlines approach, registrars become completely swamped with requests. Make sure you take a look at a copy of the transcript before it's sent to check for any misinformation or mistakes that need your correction.

If you're transferring and you've spent only a year or less at your current college, you will likely also have to provide prospective schools with your high school transcript.

Provide information about yourself. Fill out the application form perfectly and write a stellar essay. The latter is especially important, as it can help distinguish you from all the other applicants. If appropriate, send samples of your work.

Pull strings. If any relative, no matter how distant, went to the school, mention it. If you know of anyone who went to the school, especially if s/he still has contact with key professors in your department or big-wig administrators, or s/he has donated a building or two, have her or him write a letter of recommendation for you.

Go face to face. Even if the school doesn't require an interview, it is a good idea to have one, if possible. Making a connection with someone involved in the decision-making process can help make you stand out. So, set up an appointment with an admissions officer. It's also appropriate and in fact advisable for you to speak with professors with whom you might be interested in studying. (You can set up appointments with professors either by writing to them directly in care of their department or by calling the school or department).

14,538 PhDs to men's 156,482 masters and 24,756 PhDs.

THE EARLY BIRD . . .

A few compelling reasons to get your application in as early as possible:

▲ It shows you're on the ball, a self-starter, a go-getter, and all the other goofy sounding expressions that mean you're focused, directed, and will succeed in all you do.

▲ You'll face less competition. They'll look at your application before they're bogged down with thousands of applications that resemble yours. Theirs will seem old, boring, dry, and repetitive. Yours won't.

▲ It indicates that you're really interested in the school, and there's nothing better for alumni endowment, word-of mouth reputation, and the creation of an active, involved, and happy student body than accepting people who love the school.

▲ If last year's entering class was smaller than planned, they'll want to compensate by filling more slots early so they won't be under-enrolled for two years running.

▲ You'll save on overnight mail charges.

Figure out funding. If you are applying for any fellowships, financial aid, grants, or scholarships, you may need to fill out additional forms and get additional recommendations. (See "The Financial Aid Maze," page 75, for more information.)

For forms and general information, contact the admissions office at your prospective school(s) and the financial aid office at your school and prospective school(s).

For information on grants, loans, and fellowships, get in touch with your department at your school and prospective school(s), the career services, and the library.

MAKING IT ALL LOOK GOOD

P resentation is important. Because your application consists of only a few pieces of paper (and possibly an interview) every detail counts.

■ Most admissions offices say they don't care whether you type or neatly write your application. However, unless your handwriting is ultra legible, it's best to type.

■ Be sure to make copies of your application forms as soon as you receive them, and wait until you have successfully filled out a copy before you go near the real thing.

■ Get started early enough that if your application falls in a greasy, muddy puddle on the way to the mailbox, you have enough time to redo it.

- Have someone else read your application for spelling errors and typos before you send it.

- Dot your *i*'s and cross your *t*'s.

- If you discover a significant mistake after you mailed the application, send in a corrected copy with a cover letter.

Go the Extra Mile

- Be ruthless about making an impression (and a good one at that). The admissions game demands that you find a way to differentiate yourself from the thousands of other applicants clamoring to get in.

- Show the school how committed you are and how much you want to join the program. If it's your first choice, say so. Make yourself known (but don't make them feel like you're stalking them).

- Follow up on your conversations. After you speak with people who were helpful, write a note thanking them for taking the time to speak with you.

- Get as many people as possible at the school to want you there. How can the admissions committee turn you down when they've got notes from the person who interviewed you, the professor you met, the tour guide, and the student with whom you stayed, all saying what a smart, "joy to be around" kind of gal you are?

RECOMMENDATIONS

"I went to Oklahoma State University—over 15,000 undergraduates—and only once did I have a class with less than a hundred people, so when the time came around for me to apply to graduate school I had no professors that knew me well enough to write a recommendation that meant anything substantive. Suddenly I had to introduce myself to professors whom I had studied with and tell them about myself, in hopes that they could actually write a recommendation after the fact. I was at a complete disadvantage from students who went to smaller schools."

—OKLAHOMA STATE UNIVERSITY, '90

Although you may firmly believe that the receipt of your diploma will signal the end of your academic career and that you will never need recommendations from professors, it is always a good idea to keep your options open. It never fails that after graduating you change your mind and find that you need a recommendation from a professor you had five years ago who is on sabbatical in Nepal. Even if you are able to reach her, there's a good chance you could be a bit vague in her memory. (After all, hundreds of students have passed through her classes since the days you wowed her with your Pulitzer-quality essays.) Ask professors who are very familiar with you and your talents and abilities to write recommendations for you while they still remember you and while you know where and how to reach them. If you sign a waiver giving up your rights to see the recommendation, you can ask the professor to hand it directly to the registrar for inclusion in your file.

Asking for a Recommendation

ꙮꙮꙮ

When approaching a professor for a recommendation for a job, school, scholarship, or fellowship, be prepared to go into detail about what the recommendation is for. For example, if you are applying to a graduate program, you might tell your professor about why you are going, what you hope to do in the long run, and what makes you a good candidate for the schools you are applying to. Also be prepared to explain why you think he is a good person to write your recommendation.

Always give a potential recommendation writer adequate room to deny your request. A professor may feel that he will not be able to write you a recommendation that would be an asset to your application, especially if many of his other students are applying to the same program or he doesn't have the time. In some cases, a lukewarm recommendation or one from someone who seems unfamiliar with your work will make admissions officers, personnel departments, and funders wary. They assume that you would, as is the usual practice, get recommendations only from those who

are crazy about you, and the lack of such a glowing report will make them wonder why you weren't able to duly impress any faculty members. If recommendations aren't required, many admissions committees feel that no recommendation is better than a less than enthusiastic one. However, when you're applying to a competitive program, a not-so-personal recommendation from the highly esteemed Nobel Prize-winning head of the department may be an asset to your application. Talk to professors, administrators, or career services about how to best approach the recommendation tango.

Don't forget to thank your professors for writing recommendations, (a short thank-you note is always appreciated), and be sure to tell them the outcome of your application.

Creating a Packet

ꙮꙮꙮ

Especially in large schools, professors writing your recommendations may not have a chance to get to know you as well as they'd like. And even professors who do know you may have trouble remembering all the details about the classes you took, the grades you received, and the items that should be noted in their letters. To make recommendation writing easier for the writers and to ensure that everything that you want said is said, provide your professors with a packet of information about your academic and extracurricular interests and accomplishments. The more information you can give them about why they should recommend you, the better your recommendations will be.

Though creating a packet is no small task, it is time well spent. Not only will it prove itself invaluable as far as your recommendations are concerned, but once it is complete, you'll have everything you need for filling out the informational part of the application, getting together a CV/résumé, writing a cover letter, and preparing for an interview right at your fingertips. It'll also give you a big head start in writing your personal essay(s).

Include the following:

■ A cover letter that briefly describes what the recommendation is for and your short- and long-term goals.

■ CV/résumé. Tailor it to the program for which you are applying. For example, if you are applying for a PhD in biology and your grade point average for your science course is higher than your overall GPA, make a note of it. Put related academic and extracurricular work first. Remember, this is no time to be modest or to downplay your successes. (For more on résumé writing, see "Working Women," page 169.)

■ A list of all the classes that you took in areas related to your planned field of study. Include course title, professor, material covered, grade, and a description of papers/reports/presentations (or other significant classwork) you completed.

■ A sample of your writing, lab reports, etc.

The packet is an integral part of the application process—don't even consider handing it to anyone before it's spell-checked, formatted nicely, and paper-clipped or stapled.

Waivers

Many schools ask that you waive your right to see your recommendation. They do this because it's assumed that the person writing about you will be more candid if s/he knows you won't read what s/he writes. It is your right to choose whether or not you sign the waiver, but know that some schools do not even consider recommendations if the waivers have not been signed, and some take such recommendations less seriously than those that come with signed waivers. And the recommendation writer may prefer it as well. If you plan to sign the waiver, and it's not obvious on the recommendation forms you give to professors, be sure to tell them. Signing a waiver does not prohibit professors from giving you an (unsolicited) copy of their recommendation letters.

FILLING IN THE DOTS: STANDARDIZED EXAMINATIONS

The question is on everyone's mind: If these tests are supposed to provide an accurate and objective indication of the test taker's aptitude, why then has the ETS taken to completely revamping them every several years (some more frequently than others)? Regardless of one's opinion of standardized tests, they still figure prominently in the admission process at many graduate schools.

The Educational Testing Service (ETS) writes, administers, and grades the following tests:

The GRE (Graduate Record Examination), which is actually not one, but a number of tests used for graduate school admission. The general test, a three-and-a-half hour exam that tests vocabulary, math, and reading comprehension in six sections—two verbal, two math, and two "logical reasoning"—is similar to the SAT. In addition, there are 17 subject tests that applicants to grad school programs in languages, science, the humanities, and social sciences might be required to take as well. The GRE general test is scored by the ETS on a scale of 200 to 800; the subject tests are scored from 200 to 980 (and these are the folks who are assessing our logical reasoning skills?).

The LSAT (Law School Admissions Test) is required for admission to many law schools. It's made up of two logical reasoning sections, one analytical reasoning section, one reading comprehension section (approximately 100 questions total), plus a 30-minute writing sample. The LSAT is scored on a scale of 120 to 180.

The GMAT (Graduate Management Admissions Test) is the entrance exam for business school. It contains three verbal sections (reading comp, sentence correction, and critical reason-

A BIT ABOUT THE WRITING SAMPLE

Though the multiple choice questions on the grad school standardized tests are a pain, somehow they're not as scary as the essay. But, even though high-speed scribbling is never fun, the experience doesn't have to be an ordeal.

The ETS folks don't give a hoot about your opinion or your knowledge. What they do care about is that you can create a well-structured, clear, concise, and logical essay with squeaky-clean grammar. Though the essay will probably be copied and sent with your scores, don't waste time trying to impress them with your response—they've heard them all. Spend your time making sure it sufficiently proves your point, even if it's a bit boring to read. Save your wit, creativity, and quirky-cool writing style for the personal essay on your application. For the ETS essays think: straightforward. Avoid using fancy language unless it's absolutely necessary (it's not Scrabble—you don't get points for big words containing Q and X), and diligently stick to the topic. Many suggest taking the first five minutes to plan and make an outline, then spending the remaining time fighting the impulse to stray from it. (Don't forget to proofread, too.) A final note: The stress of writing a timed essay can do terrible things to hand-rendered letterforms. But remind yourself to keep it neat. Though you will not be graded on penmanship, the ETS folks won't be happy if they need a handwriting expert to decipher your chicken scratchings. No matter how brilliant it may be, if they can't read it, you'll get a zero.

> "Unlike the SAT, the GRE and the GMAT, LSAT, and MCAT scores are based only on the number of questions you answer correctly. You don't get penalized for wrong answers, so don't leave anything blank."
>
> —WASHINGTON UNIVERSITY, '94, UNIVERSITY OF MINNESOTA PHD CANDIDATE

BITE THE BULLET

✸

If you think you might go on to grad school someday, even if there's only a remote chance, take your tests now. In a study by the Graduate Management Admissions Council, the longer students are out of school, the lower their GMAT scores. In the study, those out of school for one year scored an average of 19 points below the college seniors; after two years it dropped to 27 points; after three years, 34 points, and after four years, 44 points.

ing), two writing sections, and three math sections. (The ornery data sufficiency math section, found only on the GMAT, is a source of anguish for many a test taker.) The objective portion of the test is scored on a scale of 200 to 800; the essays are scored from 0 to 6.

The MCAT (Medical College Admissions Test) is a six-hour doozy of an exam that includes four sections: physical science, biological science, reading comprehension, and two 30-minute essays. Each of the objective sections is scored on a 15-point scale, and the essays are graded from J to T.

In addition to the scored sections, many of these exams will include one unscored section, called the experimental section, which will help the ETS evaluate questions to include on future tests. You will probably not be able to identify the experimental section by its content, although the fact that you had to sit through an extra section of one type may be a tip-off. Since there is no way to be absolutely sure that a section is experimental while you're taking the test, give every section your all.

Depending on the program you're applying to, you may be required to take other tests. ETS also offers the PCAT (Pharmacy College Admissions Test) and the VCAT (Veterinary College Admissions Test), and psych students generally have to wrestle with the Miller Analogies test. Again, ask the admissions office about which tests you need and how and when to register for them.

Do I Need to Take a Standardized Exam?

〽〰〽

Schools vary in what standardized tests they require (if any) and how much importance they place on them. Some schools look only at scores from a few sections of the test. For example, they may not even bother with an application from a student who didn't score in the top tenth percentile on an analytical reasoning section, but not care a bit if a student only scored a 200 for signing her name on the math section. The best place to get the most current information on school policy is from the school itself, namely the admissions office or a visiting recruiter. Get the information in the earliest stages of planning your life after college so you can prepare accordingly, but don't forget to check again as application time draws near. Just as the ETS is in the process of changing many of their exams, schools are changing their minds about how helpful they are in determining an applicant's aptitude and predicting her future success.

However, even if none of the schools you are applying to requires that you take standardized tests, you may want to take them anyway. A number of merit scholarships are based on board scores, and schools may use scores to determine placement, exemption, or credit.

Preregistration

෨෨෨

As you may recall from your glorious SAT/ACT–taking days, you must preregister, usually six weeks in advance, in order to take these exams. Send in your preregistration form as early as possible. Not only do late registration penalty fees run maddeningly high, but because test sites are filled on a first come, first served basis, the later you preregister the less likely you are to get your test site of choice. If you're taking your test in a city such as Boston, which is filled to the gills with students, desks at convenient test sites fill quickly, and a late registration may mean you'll have to travel an hour and a half to color in the dots.

If you cannot afford the registra-

tion fee, you can always request a fee waiver by writing to the ETS. In some cases, they may require your school or the school you're applying to (if you're requesting a fee waiver for sending score reports) to do the requesting for you.

Alternatives to the Standard Saturday Test

෨෨෨

Depending on where you live and the test you're taking, you may be able to take your exam on a computer. The benefits of computer testing are that you can schedule the exam with more flexibility, you don't need to preregister as far in advance, and you receive your scores immediately. The drawbacks are that the computerized exam costs more money than the pencil and paper exam and you cannot, as of yet, practice the exam as it will be when you take it on computer.

For students who are unable to

> *"On my SATs I inadvertently skipped a question, and didn't realize it until 20 questions later. I had to redo all the problems because I couldn't remember the answers, and totally blew that section. From that point on I always marked my answer in the booklet or on a piece of scrap paper as well as on the score sheet, so if I screwed up again, it wouldn't get me into the same trouble."*
> —*UNIVERSITY OF MICHIGAN LAW, '94*

take the exam on a Saturday for religious reasons and who cannot (or don't wish to) take it on the computer, the test is offered at a small number of sites on the Monday following the Saturday date. To get a spot, you must register even earlier than if you were taking it on the regular testing day and include a note, preferably from a leader in your religious community, stating why you are unable to take the test on Saturday.

If you have a physical or learning disability, ETS will accommodate your needs. In order to have special testing conditions, you must include with your preregistration and fee a letter from you stating the nature of your disability and one from a physician or certified specialist confirming it. The letters should specify your special needs and the accommodations that need to be made, such as giving you extra time, letting you take an oral exam, etc. You will also have to provide documentation stating a similar situation in which you had like accommodations. If you cannot include such documentation, explain why not in your letter. They should make accommodations for other medical conditions as well. For example, if you take

"Wear comfortable clothing and dress in layers so it's easy to adjust to the temperature. It's always really cold when you first get there and really hot later on. Also bring something to drink and a good healthy snack like a piece of fruit or a granola bar for the break."
—CONNECTICUT COLLEGE, '95

medication and/or have a physical condition that gives you a dry mouth, proctors should permit you to have water with you during the test.

Preparation for the Tests

ⓦⓔ

While there are still some folks who believe that studying for the SAT won't necessarily up your score, studying for the standardized tests for grad school admission will almost definitely improve your results. For some tests, such as the MCAT, there is specific material—an enormous amount of facts, formulas, functions, and flow charts—you'll want to know. For others, like the general test of the GRE, brushing up on your vocabulary, reviewing SAT-level math, and getting familiar with the format will be enough to bring success.

There are myriad books and review courses devoted to teaching the ins and outs of the exams. If you're motivated, studying on your own using books and doing practice tests should be sufficient. If not, you may want to consider taking a class, although some can be on the pricey side. Many of the test-prep courses do award scholarships, and sometimes a group of students will chip in to send one person to the classes, who will then share the materials and lecture notes with the group. On-line services like America Online have ETS, Princeton Review, and Stanley Kaplan folks available to answer questions and give out tips, and there are materials to download. Libraries and career services offices usually have books available, and if you put up a sign right after a test, you'll probably be able to buy a book from a student for cheap. There is no one surefire method of study, but the increased confidence level of someone who has a clue about

> *"The questions get harder as you go through each section. So if there is an answer that seems really obvious at the end of a section, it's probably not the right one. . . . If you can't figure out the right answer, see if you can't eliminate at least one or two you are sure are wrong, and then guess."*
>
> —WORCESTER POLYTECHNIC
> INSTITUTE, '96

what's on the test is good for a number of points.

If you do choose to study, make sure your materials are up-to-date. Since ETS has taken to overhauling the tests every few years or so, test prep materials have a tendency to become outdated quickly. Sneak a peek at the date on your test prep materials, especially if you are preparing by doing practice tests. Then call ETS to make sure they haven't rewritten the test from ground zero since your material came out.

In addition, don't neglect to prepare physically as well as mentally. Sitting so long in a cramped tension-filled room can take a lot out of you. You'll need more than just a little adrenaline to make it through. Get your eight hours of sleep each night for three days before the test. Some students train for the test almost as if they were training for a marathon—eating lots of pasta and other high-energy foods, taking vitamins, drinking an abundance of fluids, steering clear of alcohol and other drugs, and getting enough exercise to clear their head and relieve stress.

Scoring

For most standardized tests, you (and the admissions committee) will receive three scores: a raw score, which indicates how many questions you got right; an adjusted score, which is a conversion of your raw score into the 800/980/180/15-point scale; and a percentile score, which tells how well you did in comparison with everyone else who took the test. If you are in the 66th percentile, you scored better than 66 percent of all other grad-school hopefuls who took the same standardized test on the same day. (The MCAT score reports give a few more stats than the rest.)

You probably won't receive your scores until a good six weeks after the exam, so make sure your application is not due before your scores arrive. If you didn't plan ahead you can, for a fee, have ETS rush your scores. Or call the admissions office to let them know the scores are on their way and the rest of your application will be on time. ETS will send a set number directly to schools for free if you designate them at test time. Otherwise, you have to pay to have score reports sent.

How Important Are Standardized Tests?

Some schools don't require them; other schools base almost everything on them. Most schools use them to some degree. Obviously a high board score can do nothing but help an applicant, and a very low score with no legitimate explanation will probably hurt. But doing poorly on the exam does not mean you won't get in to grad school. A strong GPA, impressive experience, a good interview, and stellar recommendations can do well to counter the damaging effects of low board scores. This said, some schools will automatically dump your application if your grades and/or scores are too low, and will not venture even a peek at the well-rounded you. Law schools are known to be especially fond of this technique, due in part to the work of the Law School Data Assembly Service (LSDAS). The LSDAS is responsible for taking your weighted grade point average, your LSAT score, and a few other pieces of information, slapping them on a piece of paper, and sending them off to the law schools of your choice to become the determining factor in the fate of your professional future. If a school uses this system, board scores will be more important, as you'll have less opportunity to balance low numbers with a remarkable personality and a glowing recommendation or two.

The application process is expensive, time-consuming, and exhausting, so it's worth your while to make sure that you have at least some chance of being accepted to every school you apply to. Don't be afraid to ask direct questions about the importance of board scores or if your grade point average will mean automatic rejection. With a little investigation you're apt to find a school that has what you want and seems to go for applicants with your credentials.

EYE ON TRANSFERRING

Unfortunately, there's no magical method for determining if a school is your perfect match—you may have to go through a less-than-completely-gratifying semester or two to realize that it just isn't for you.

It's not surprising then that every year a large number of students enter what they think is their perfect school and find that the college doesn't offer everything they need. They find their classes too challenging or not challenging enough, or that the school doesn't offer classes in their area of interest. They feel claustrophobic among a thousand students at a rural

academic performance of "older" students, particularly women.

school or completely lost at an urban campus teeming with tens of thousands of students. Or, as is occurring more and more often, they discover that their aid package doesn't cover the skyrocketing cost of tuition and expenses. Or they may transfer to a four-year college to get their bachelor's, after getting an associate degree at a two-year school.

"I transferred medical school programs because my boyfriend was going to school across the country and I wanted to be closer to him. It was a total disaster because my boyfriend and I broke up, I lost credits, and I was depressed for an entire semester because I missed my friends from my old school."

—YALE UNIVERSITY
MEDICAL SCHOOL, '95

There are no universal "good" and "bad" reasons to transfer (though it's important to think carefully before switching schools to be with the one you love). Many people who expected to spend the best four years of their life at their college have mixed emotions about transferring. It can feel relieving and upsetting at the same time. It can make you feel good that you refuse to let a less than ideal social, academic, or financial situation get in the way of your pursuing your education. Even if the decision is obvious, fear about "starting again," sorrow at leaving friends, wondering "What did I do wrong . . ." and the never-appetizing prospect of going through the application process again can cause some apprehension.

Tips on Transferring

℞℞℞

Before you transfer:

■ Give yourself time at school before you make the final decision. It takes a while to get adjusted to a new situation, especially one like college, which is heavily laden with mystique and expectations. First semester is not always a breeze, even for those who eventually find that they couldn't have made a better choice.

■ Avoid finalizing your transfer plans during exam period or other high-stress times. Every student of sound mind entertains thoughts of transferring when the going gets rough. Wait until you've gotten through the crunch and you have a chance to reflect upon the reality of your school experience before making a final decision.

■ In the long run, finding solutions to the problems with your school is easier, less stressful, less time-consuming, and less costly than transferring. Take the time to investigate other aid sources, talk to your advisor about taking a class or two at a nearby school, experiment with different courses and professors, go abroad, or check out other social scenes on campus.

■ Your grades, extracurricular activities, and professor/dean recommendations from your college will make up the bulk of your transfer application. If you have been wholly miserable at school, it has probably affected your academic performance, your relationships with professors, and your involvement in activities that would make an admissions officer drool. You may need to take an extra

"You always think you'll find the perfect school and then you'll find they are all the same. I went to a conservative all-women's school and then transferred to the very liberal Bennington, and then to another extreme in New York, and now all I want to do is graduate."
— MARYMOUNT MANHATTAN COLLEGE, '94

semester at your school (or another school) to get your grade point average up and develop relationships with professors who could write recommendations for you before you apply to the school of your dreams.

■ If you aren't sure you want to transfer, but you do want to take time away from your school, consider taking a semester at a potential transfer school. You'll definitely get a better idea of what the school has to offer than you would at one of those "prospective student weekends."

■ Get recommendations from professors at your old school while they still remember you. Have these recommendations placed on file at your transfer school as well.

■ It may be easier to get in if you apply for midyear/January admission (because there are fewer applicants at that time). The flip side is that starting midyear will be the most difficult socially.

After you transfer:

■ If you have the option, consider living on campus for at least your first semester (especially if you are transferring second semester). Being in the middle of the action, having easy access to school facilities, classrooms, and libraries, and being constantly surrounded by potential friends will help you get acclimated to the new environment more quickly and easily than if you were living off campus.

■ Working out credits and requirements is arguably the most frustrating part of transferring. Even if every one of your classes meets the criteria for credit approval (only possible with a touch of divine intervention), don't be surprised if you don't get credit for them all. Schools generally limit the number of credits from another school that you can apply to your degree. Most schools require you take a minimum number of "in-house credits" (a set amount of coursework, usually half the amount needed to graduate, that must be done at your new school in order for you to qualify for a degree from the institution). For this reason, transferring schools may mean that you'll either have to forgo your opportunity to study abroad or do an extra year.

"In this weird way, when I trans-ferred, I felt like I was failing. I felt that I was the one that couldn't make it at school, not that the school failed me—which was really the case. For some reason we get these ideas that the first school that we pick should be the school—but what is the big deal, anyway?"

—LOYOLA UNIVERSITY, '94

■ Even if you do not receive credit for some classes because you have more than the limit, because they don't suf-ficiently satisfy a requirement, or because similar courses are not taught at the new institution, the courses and grades will still appear on your official transcript.

■ Always keep course catalogs and syllabi from classes you took at your old school. In many cases, you'll need to give detailed descriptions of the content of classes you took in order to get credit or exemption from prerequi-sites or requirements. You may also need to get a note from a professor or department to verify that the course covered all the material necessary to satisfy a requirement.

■ Unfortunately, schools usually can't or won't evaluate how many of your credits will transfer and how many requirements your classes will fulfill until *after* you've transferred. How-ever, you can get some indication by meeting with faculty members in your major department and those that teach the required classes at your prospec-tive school. Be sure to bring catalog descriptions, syllabi, and even lab write-ups, problem sets, sample exams, papers, and other course mate-rials (the same things that you will submit to the registrar when they com-pute your credits).

■ Be prepared to take more require-ments. Schools can be quite strict about the classes that will satisfy their requirements, especially when they've been teaching the same core curricu-lum for a long time. At some schools, students may have up to five semes-ters' worth of required classes to take. Depending on your exemptions, you may need to take an extra year in order to fulfill all the general and major requirements.

■ Have the registrar delineate exactly how they decide if a course fulfills a requirement (ideally they should give you a list of all the subjects that a course should address, how often homework should be assigned, how many hours it meets per week, etc.). If the registrar does not grant you credit for a class, be sure to ask why. If you believe that a course does in fact meet the criteria for credit, ask the professor who taught the original course to write a letter saying it does. If one course doesn't quite meet the criteria, you may be able to show how another course you took filled in the gaps.

■ Along with losing credits, you may lose the opportunity to receive honors. This is more likely to be the case if your old school had a different grad-ing system or credit system, or if your transfer school applied credit for courses you did poorly in, but not those you did well in. Talk to the regis-trar about ways to address this.

■ If you played a sport or took physi-cal education at your first school, a letter from your coach, intramural advisor, the director of the athletic department, or your physical education teacher will often satisfy some or all of a phys-ed requirement at your transfer school.

GRAD SCHOOL SPECIFICS

The graduate application process is more intense and time-consuming than the undergraduate. In grad school you will be working closely with profs and other students, exploring subject areas in depth, and doing original research. Graduate departments are looking for someone who will add to class discussions, inspire new scholarship, and become renowned enough to raise the school's prestige meter an increment or two (and rich enough to donate a new sports complex).

Not only is getting in harder, but it might not even guarantee that you'll have the opportunity to get a degree. Some schools enroll more students than is "ideal" for the program, and after a year will invite only certain students, those who score above a certain GPA or who receive recommendations from key professors, to return. The atmosphere at schools that have students vying for a few coveted posi-

tions can be rather cutthroat; it is not uncommon for students with the intellectual capacity to do the work to bow under the pressure. Advocates for such a system contend that it makes students work harder and produce better work, and that the more competitive the program, the more highly regarded it will be. Others believe that the atmosphere hinders learning, because students are so concerned with competing against each other that they're afraid to share knowledge, and because the politics— knowing the right profs, publishing *anything*—takes time and energy away from study.

Unlike college, with grad school the acceptance process isn't always over once the letters arrive. It's common knowledge that grants and scholarships are not set in stone. If the aid package is not sufficient, or if another school is offering you a better deal, call the program or department and go to bat for yourself. Once they've accepted you, they want you, and they'll often find a way to beat out their competition's bid for you. Some feel that schools almost expect you to call and haggle. (See "Funding Graduate School," page 97.)

TRYING AGAIN

As hard as they try to make rejection letters sound nice, getting a thin, insignificant envelope from the school of your dreams—or any school, for that matter—is no picnic. Allow yourself to feel blue. Something that you were really vying for didn't work out. It's understandable that you feel let down. However, at the same time, keep the rejection in perspective and think realistically about your options. The admissions process is far from perfect, and because of limited space and funds, schools aren't able to take all qualified students who apply. A rejection doesn't mean that you aren't capable of doing the work, or that "you haven't got what it takes."

If you feel the rejection was truly unjustified, you can call the admissions office and ask for an explanation or, better yet, have one of the professors who wrote you a recommendation do it.

When you call the school, ask why you were not accepted, and what steps you could take to strengthen your candidacy should you wish to reapply. A school may recommend that you take another course or two, learn another language, improve your standardized test scores or your science GPA, get a recommendation from a higher-ranking professor, have another interview, or take a job or internship in an area related to the program.

As harsh as it sounds, and as hard as it is to hear, it is important for you to know if people think that you might not be cut out for a certain field. You shouldn't compromise and give up your dreams, but you may want to reevaluate them and try different approaches. For example, if it becomes really apparent that med school is out of your reach, pursue another area in health care. And if, after working with patients in the health care system, you still believe that being a doctor is

exactly what you want, you'll have experience that will both boost your application and help you with the academic and clinical work that med school requires.

If you are rejected but you really want to go (and you truly think you are academically and intellectually suited for the work that it would entail), think about these options:

■ Sign up for a summer school/noncredit class with an influential professor in your field, ideally at your desired school, and show her what you're made of. Once you've sufficiently impressed her, ask if she'll write you a recommendation.

■ Reapply. Applications from people going directly from college to graduate programs can look pretty similar on paper, especially if they went straight to college from high school and/or held a "just to pay the bills" kind of job, rather than one directly related to the prospective area of study. Supplementing your college academic record, recommendations, and extracurricular activities, experience with recommendations from employers, work (paid or unpaid) in your field of interest, additional courses to raise your GPA, and an indication that you've matured and focused yourself could be the ticket to entrance.

(If you feel that your being denied acceptance is related to your gender, race, or religion, see "Breaking Down Bias," page 463.)

ACTIVIST IDEAS

■ Organize a graduate/professional school fair. Fill the gym or the student union with alumni back from their MA, MD, LLB, MBA, or MFA programs. Have an informal program where everyone wears name tags and mingles, or something more formal where each guest sets up a table of information about her program.

■ Organize a workshop on how to write a killer personal statement. Ask an admissions officer or someone from the office of career services to lead it.

■ Find students who aced the standardized tests, and have them give a workshop on their best tips and tricks for soon-to-be test takers.

RESOURCES

Women's Educational Associations and Organizations

There are too many organizations that address the issues and concerns of women in specific fields of study and professional life to list them all here. The ones included below should serve as a good starting point. They should be able to provide referrals if they can't help you themselves.

ASSOCIATION OF AMERICAN COLLEGES AND
  UNIVERSITIES
PROGRAM ON THE STATUS AND EDUCATION
  OF WOMEN
1818 R STREET NW
WASHINGTON, DC 20009
(202) 387-3760
Monitors the status of women and provides information about women students, faculty, and staff at colleges and universities throughout the country. Maintains information about issues of specific importance to women in academia.

CENTER FOR WOMEN POLICY STUDIES
2000 P STREET NW, SUITE 508
WASHINGTON, DC 20036
(202) 872-1770
Conducts research on and provides information about women in education. Promotes equal educational access for women of all races, ethnicities, economic classes, abilities, sexual identities, and ages. Organizes political action/advocacy work and lobbies on behalf of legislation favorable to women in education. Publishes numerous materials on education, including *Women of Color in Mathematics, Science, Engineering: A Review of the Literature; The SAT Gender Gap: Identifying the Causes;* and *Looking for More Than a Few Good Women in Traditionally Male Fields,* among others.

AMERICAN ASSOCIATION OF UNIVERSITY
  WOMEN (AAUW)
1111 16TH STREET NW
WASHINGTON, DC 20036-4873
(202) 785-7700
FAX: (202) 872–1425

8 to 1. ❀ By 1992, 28% of American PhDs were women. ❀

Works to ensure the advancement of women through advocacy and emphasis on equity in education for women and girls. Fosters the aspirations of women, from teenage girls to doctoral candidates, through financial support, advocacy, and encouragement. Conducts research about educational opportunities and equity issues, especially those relating to discrimination in education. Offers numerous scholarships and grants to promote the advancement of women in education. Publishes numerous materials, including *AAUW Outlook,* which covers such issues as equity for women, education, community affairs, cultural interests, and funding opportunities, and *Action Alert,* which covers legislation related to education of women and girls. Maintains a library of information related to the study of women.

NATIONAL COUNCIL FOR RESEARCH ON WOMEN
530 BROADWAY
NEW YORK, NY 10012
(212) 274-0730
FAX: (212) 274-0821
Maintains a clearinghouse of information and resources to further and assist feminist research. Works to increase the visibility

and funding of research by and about women. Publishes numerous materials, including *A Women's Thesaurus: An Index of Language Used to Describe and Locate Information by and About Women; Opportunities for Research and Study; Sexual Harassment Research and Resources;* and *Women of Color and the Multicultural Curriculum.* Provides referrals to national organizations and to local libraries and centers for research on women in the U.S. and abroad.

AMERICAN ASSOCIATION OF HIGHER EDUCATION
WOMEN'S CAUCUS
ONE DUPONT CIRCLE, SUITE 360
WASHINGTON, DC 20036
(202) 293-6440
Works to improve the quality of higher education for women. Publishes numerous materials.

AMERICAN COUNCIL ON EDUCATION; OFFICE OF WOMEN IN HIGHER EDUCATION
ONE DUPONT CIRCLE, SUITE 800
WASHINGTON , DC 20036
(202) 939-9390
Works to advance Black, Latina, Asian Pacific, American Indian, and Caucasian women in the field of academic administration. Provides general information on programs, policies, and ideas about how to advance women students, faculty, staff, and administrators in higher education. Publishes *Sexual Harassment on Campus* and *The Fact Book on Women and Higher Education,* among other books.

NATIONAL ASSOCIATION FOR COLLEGE WOMEN
1325 18TH STREET NW, SUITE 210
WASHINGTON, DC 20036-6511
(202) 659-9330
FAX: (202) 457-0946
Works to promote and advance educational opportunities for women. Sponsors programs and grants to support research

by and about women. Publishes numerous materials, including *About Women on Campus* and *Initiatives*, which address topics such as funding sources for women students, educational equality, women's athletics, sexual harassment on campus, women's studies, and womens colleges. Runs an annual leadership conference for undergrad women to help them cultivate leaderships skills on campus and in their communities.

WOMEN'S COLLEGE COALITION (WCC)
125 MICHIGAN AVENUE NE
WASHINGTON, DC 20017
(202) 234-0443
Raises public awareness of women's colleges and the educational needs of women. Provides information, including statistics, about women's colleges.

Women's Studies

The women's studies department at your school is the best place to begin any search for women's studies resources. Some schools have centers for research on women, others may have library collections, women's centers, and the like. If your school does not have a women's studies department, find out if there is a women's studies advisor or talk with a professor who does work on or related to women. If that fails, you may try contacting one of the national organizations listed above to find out if there are women's studies departments at a school nearby or if they can refer you to an organization that will be of assistance.

NATIONAL WOMEN'S STUDIES ASSOCIATION
7100 BALTIMORE AVENUE, SUITE 301
COLLEGE PARK, MD 20740
(301) 403-0525
FAX: (301) 403-4137
Provides information about educational

opportunities and conferences on women's studies. Publishes a directory of undergraduate and graduate women's studies programs, as well as a journal. Makes referrals to other organizations and programs involved with women's studies.

Women's Academic and Professional Associations

Women's academic and professional associations, societies, organizations, and caucuses exist in all areas of study—everything from the Society of Women Engineers to the committee on the status of women of the American Philological Association. There are groups for women and about women in mathematics, history, literature, physics, biology, religion, folklore, and just about every other field. If you are interested in finding out about the women's groups in a specific discipline or field of study, it is best to start by asking a faculty member and/or administrator (preferably but not necessarily someone who is involved with women's issues) in the related department at your school. Find out if there are any specific women's organizations in the field. If not, ask about the professional/academic association in the field, as many will have women's divisions/caucuses. For example, the American Psychological Association has a division on the psychology of women, and the American Sociological Association has a committee on the status of women.

ASSOCIATION OF AMERICAN MEDICAL
    COLLEGES; WOMEN IN MEDICINE
    PROGRAM
2450 N STREET NW
WASHINGTON , DC 20037
(202) 828-0575
Works to support and coordinate efforts

designed to improve the environment for women faculty and students at the nation's medical schools. Provides information about the status of women in medicine.

ASSOCIATION FOR WOMEN IN SCIENCE
1522 K STREET NW SUITE 820
WASHINGTON, DC 20005
(202) 408-0742
Promotes greater communication between and advancement of women in science. Conducts research on the status of women in science. Provides networking and support services to women in the sciences. Publishes related materials, available upon request.

AMERICAN ASSOCIATION FOR THE ADVANCEMENT OF SCIENCE
NATIONAL NETWORK OF MINORITY WOMEN IN SCIENCE
1333 H STREET NW
WASHINGTON, DC 20005
(202) 326-6670
Promotes the advancement of minority women in science. Works to support and coordinate communication between minority women in science.

General Education Resources

EDUCATIONAL RESOURCES INFORMATION CENTER (ERIC)
ACCESS ERIC
ASPEN SYSTEMS CORPORATION
1600 RESEARCH BOULEVARD
ROCKVILLE, MD 20850
(301) 258-5500
ERIC consists of over 16 clearinghouses, 8 adjunct clearinghouses, and 4 support contractors on educational topics such as: teacher education; disabled and gifted students; languages and linguistics; adult, career, and vocational learning; higher education; junior colleges; science, math, and the environment; information resources, and others. Each of the subject-specialized clearinghouses conduct research and provide information. They maintain a collection of numerous publications, documents, policies, curricula, research, and statistics on their particular subject area. ACCESS ERIC can help you find your way through all the various ERIC databases.

NATIONAL EDUCATION ASSOCIATION
1201 16TH STREET NY
WASHINGTON, DC 20036
(202) 833-4000
Works to promote quality education for all. Has numerous divisions and caucuses, including the women's caucus and the higher education caucus, which monitor, conduct research on, and work to improve different areas of education.

STATE DEPARTMENTS OF EDUCATION
Collect and provide information about students, faculty, staff, finances, locations, and offerings of schools in their state. Look in your phone book under "State Government Agencies" to locate your state department of education. ·

Standardized Testing

EDUCATIONAL TESTING SERVICE (ETS) OF
  THE COLLEGE BOARD
PRINCETON, NJ 08541–6000
(609) 921-9000
ETS PUBLICATIONS: (800) 537–3160

Provides general information about all exams administered by ETS, such as the SAT, GRE, MCAT, and LSAT. Provides and sends information about registration, exam admission procedures, and score reporting. Makes referrals to the division of ETS appropriate for your needs.

Study, Research, or Travel Abroad

COUNCIL ON INTERNATIONAL EDUCATIONAL
  EXCHANGE (CIEE)
205 EAST 42ND STREET
NEW YORK, NY 10017
(212) 661-1414

Publishes numerous materials, including directories and handbooks on study abroad and funding sources. Provides information about funding study, travel, and research abroad, as well as study-abroad programs and opportunities. Administers some scholarships, such as the Education Abroad Scholarship Fund for Minority Students. Also offers scholarships for international education. Offers the International Student Identification Card, as well as information on international youth hostels.

INSTITUTE OF INTERNATIONAL EDUCATION
  (IIE)
U.S. STUDENT PROGRAMS DIVISION
809 UNITED NATIONS PLAZA
NEW YORK, NY 10017
(212)883-8200

Administers Fulbright Grants for graduate study and research. Ask for *Fulbright and Other Grants for Graduate Study Abroad,* which is published annually. Provides information and answers questions about international exchange programs for stu-

dents, funding, study, travel, and research abroad, as well as other opportunities for travel abroad. Publishes numerous materials, including directories and handbooks on study abroad and funding sources. Offers the International Student Identification Card, as well as information on international youth hostels.

ROTARY INTERNATIONAL FOUNDATION
ONE ROTARY CENTER
1560 SHERMAN AVENUE
EVANSTON, IL 60201
(708) 866-3000

Maintains the largest private international scholarship program in the U.S. Provides funding for foreign study and travel for undergraduate, graduate, and vocational students, journalists, teachers of disabled students, and recent graduates.

FOREIGN LANGUAGE AND AREA STUDIES
  (FLAS)

The federal government offers Foreign Language and Area Studies (FLAS) fellowships to study foreign language and culture, at schools either in the U.S. or abroad. They are administered by individual schools. Inquire in specific departments(s) and/or the financial aid office of your school.

Low Airfares

The following travel agencies often have very low rates for students. Before you call these numbers, you may wish to see if they have a local office by checking in your phone book (many do). Remember to check the restrictions on any ticket before you purchase it.

International Student exchange Flights
5010 East Shea Boulevard, Suite A104
Scottsdale, AZ 85254
(602) 951-1177

Student Travel Agency
17 East 45th Street
New York, NY 10163
(212) 986-9470

Health Information

The International Association for Medical Assistance for Travelers (IAMAT)
417 Center Street
Lewiston, NY 14092
(716) 754-4883
A nonprofit organization that provides medical health information for travelers, including a directory of affordable, qualified, English-speaking doctors, publications  on immunizations, climate, and the health and safety of food and water.

Passports and Visas

Passport Services
U.S. Department of State
1111 19th Street NW, Room 5813
Washington, DC 20520
(202) 647-0518
Provides information about how to obtain or replace a passport, including how to acquire the necessary documents if you have not already done so, and it allows you to report the loss or theft of your passport (which you can also do through a U.S. embassy abroad). Makes referrals to other agencies dealing with naturalization, travel

advisories, customs regulations, and immunizations required by specific countries.

United States Government State Department for U.S. Citizens Overseas
2201 C Street NW, Room 4800
Washington, DC 20520
(202) 647-5225
Provides information about visa requirements of specific countries for U.S. citizens and makes referrals to foreign embassies. Also provides travel advisories to the public about the advisability of traveling in certain areas or countries and assistance to U.S. citizens abroad in emergency situations. Also handles inquiries about the welfare or whereabouts of U.S. citizens abroad as well as makes notifications of deaths of U.S. citizens abroad.

Foreign Embassies

Before you travel to any country, it may be useful or necessary to contact the foreign embassy. All countries have foreign embassies located in Washington, D.C.; many have them in other U.S. cities as well. Call directory assistance in Washington, D.C., at (202) 555-1212 to locate the number of a specific embassy.

Home Exchange

Better Homes and Travel
Box 268
185 Park Row, Suite 14D
New York, NY 10038
(212) 349-5340
For a fee, provides a listing of opportunities for exchange programs abroad.

Intervac or U.S./International Home Exchange Service
Box 190070
San Francisco, CA 94119
(415) 435-3497

☀ In 1960 there were 4 million students (both undergrad-

Publishes directories of home exchange programs, available for a fee.

Funding Study and Travel Abroad

Published by Reference Service Press:
Financial Aid for Research and Creative Activities Abroad
Financial Aid for Study and Training Abroad
Published by Career Press:
The International Scholarship Directory: The Complete Guide to Financial Aid for Study Anywhere in the World.

Further Reading

Study Guides and College/University Guides

New study guides and college guides are published every year. There are books for gay/lesbian students, women students, black students, etc. available as well. You can find the most updated information by checking in your local bookstore; most have sections devoted entirely to educational reference books. Some of the largest publishers of educational guides and aids include Princeton Review, Barron's, The College Board/ETS, Peterson's, Arco, and Ten Speed Press.

Writing and Research Manuals

The Chicago Manual of Style, 14th Edition,. David Grossman, ed. (University of Chicago Press, 1993).
Elements of Style, William Strunk, Jr., & E. B. White (Macmillan, 1970).
MLA Handbook for Writers of Research Papers, Third Edition, Joseph Gibaldi & Walter S.

Achtert (MLA Association of America, 1988).
MLA Style Manual, Joseph Gibaldi & Walter Achert (MLA Association of America, 1985).
The Borzoi Handbook for Writers, 2nd Edition. Frederick Crews & Sandra Schor (Alfred A. Knopf, 1989).
The Handbook of Nonsexist Writing for Writers, Editors and Speakers, Casey Miller and Kate Swift (The Women's Press Handbook Series, 1989).
Fields' Reference Book of Nonsexist Words and Phrases (Fields Enterprises, 1987).
The Thesis Writer's Handbook: A Complete One-Source Guide for Writers of Research Papers, Joan I. Miller and B ruce J. Taylor (Alcove Publishing Company, 1987).

Traveling

Time Out: Taking a Break from School to Travel, Work and Study in the U.S. and Abroad, Robert Gilpin and Caroline Fitzgibbons, (Fireside, 1992).

For travel and guidebooks for specific countries and many specifically for women travelers; check the travel section of your local bookstore. The *Let's Go* and *Lonely Planet* series are both good ones for budget conscious travelers.

Feminist Publications

The University of Wisconsin publishes the quarterly journal *Feminist Periodicals: A current Listing of Contents; New Books on Women and Feminism,* a biannual publication listing books in English; and *Feminist Collections,* a quarterly listing faculty, students, and librarians doing work about women. Contact the Women's Studies Librarian, 430 Memorial Library, 729 State Street, Madison WI 53706; (608) 263-5754.

uate and graduate); today there are more than 14 million .

Part Two
Money &
Home

The Financial Aid Maze
Paying for Your Education

Getting financial aid for your college or grad school education means filling out a seemingly endless stream of forms, revealing everything about your and your family's financial situation, and, for some, writing essays on "why education is important" and running around campus getting recommendations. It also involves becoming exactly what the funders want you to be—assertive and focused, but needy; exceptional and strong, but still capable of pulling a heartstring or two; and unquestionably worthy of your dollars.

The majority of students who embark on this journey are successful in getting a workable financial aid package and a share of the billions disbursed annually in grants, loans, and scholarships. But for many students, what the school sees as "workable" just plain isn't, and other students miss out on getting the funding they need because they don't know where to seek it, because they are dissuaded by the process, or because they don't even bother to apply, assuming themselves to be ineligible. Understanding how aid works, what is out there, where it comes from, and how it is distributed can give you some say in the daunting process of financing your education.

> "The best recommendation that I can make about aid is that you should be known by the people in the financial aid office. Go and talk to them; avoid being a number. If they know your name and your face and you are friendly to them, they are more likely to help you out when you need it, and they have more invested in your coming to or staying at school."
>
> —HAMPSHIRE COLLEGE, '95

WHAT IS FINANCIAL AID, ANYHOW?

Financial aid is money that subsidizes, in part or full, the cost of your education. In most cases, aid is granted based on your financial need, academic merit, or both. However, you may also qualify for "targeted aid" by meeting specific criteria as a result of your background; community, political, and/or religious involvement; field of interest; or personal accomplishments or other attributes. Aid money comes from a variety of places, but the two primary sources are the federal government and schools themselves. Other sources include state governments, banks, and an enormous number of foundations, companies, and organizations. Aid is available in the form of outright grants, work-study programs, fellowships, scholarships, assistantships, and loans.

Most students agree that applying for financial aid is a drag. Not only is the process complicated, but it also requires a lot of time-consuming research and busywork. Still, it doesn't have to be torturous, especially with your financial aid office helping you navigate the ever-twisting financial aid maze.

For most undergrads, the student aid office is the primary (if not exclusive) source of all things aid related—advice, information, and the aid itself. But not all college funding is administered by the financial aid office. Most schools offer a variety of types of aid. Deans and professors may have access to departmental money reserved to finance the education of promising scholars who otherwise wouldn't be able to attend. In addition, schools also administer scholarships donated by alums on what may seem to be the most obscure criteria. Who knows, your Danish-Thai heritage and xylophone talent may be your ticket to an affordable education.

Although the aid folks require at least as much information as the IRS, their sole purpose is to give you money, not take it away; they wouldn't exist if they didn't want to find loans, grants, scholarships, and work-study positions that will make school afford-able for you. But in order to help you, they need your help, and your job is to make it as easy as possible for them to give you all the aid you need.

Are You Needy?

௸௸௸

The federal government provides the largest percentage of aid, and by law the vast majority of it is need-based. So in order to apply for govern-ment aid, you'll have to fill out the Free Application for Federal Student Aid (FAFSA), a form that has ques-tions about income, interest, taxes, assets, and expenses (this last can include such things as whether you or your parents are footing the bill for another knowledge seeker to attend school as well).

You can get the FAFSA from the financial aid office of the school(s) you're applying to, your high school college guidance office, or from the U.S. Department of Education.

In addition, the school(s) you apply to may require you to fill out a form called the Financial Aid Profile, which is administered by the College Scholarship Service (CSS), a division of the College Board. The information on this form will be used by colleges for awarding institutional financial aid (aid from a school's endowment, gifts, tuition, etc.). It has questions similar to the FAFSA, but more of them. Plus, it may contain a section tailored to the college(s) you're applying to. For ex-ample, say you're applying to two schools that require the Profile. The first part of the form will be the same for both schools, but at the end there may be a section of additional ques-tions specific to each school.

You can obtain a Profile Request Form from your high school college guidance office or the financial aid office at participating colleges.

When filling out aid forms (or any kind of application form), neatness, completeness, and deadlines count. Be organized. Double-check that you've filled out the forms completely in exactly the manner requested. (It's bet-ter to make approximations on the need-analysis form and notify the processor of changes later than to leave an item blank.) Omissions, writ-ing in the margins, or forgetting to sign can delay or even prevent your being considered for aid. If the direc-tions are confusing (as they usually are), call the organization or visit your school's financial aid office. And keep on top of due dates. Deadlines set by your school are often different from the federal deadlines and are, in most cases, "rolling"—first come, first served. Make copies of all forms before you send them off, and keep track of when you sent which form and any follow-up work required or com-pleted. Following are a few additional tidbits that may help when it comes to filling out these ubiquitous forms:

■ Even if you're pretty sure you won't qualify for aid, submit need-analysis forms anyway. Often schools need these forms to consider you for merit-based and other types of grants or scholarships.

■ To fill out the forms, you will proba-bly have to collect information from the following documents: your bank records; your and your parents' prior year's federal income tax records; medical expense records; W-2 and 1099 tax forms from the prior year; records of any money collected from interest income, Social Security, disability, veterans benefits, or public assistance; records of any investments and/or mortgages you may have; and a list of your current financial assets (all that you own that is worth money, or money itself, such as savings in the bank, and stocks).

■ If, because of a disability, you are unable to fill out an application as specified, call the financial aid office or the provider/underwriter.

■ If you feel there are extenuating circumstances that affect your ability to pay but are not adequately reflected on the financial aid form, write a letter to the director of aid at your school outlining the situation. For example, if you expect a change of income in your family during the next year, note the projected annual income instead of base income (in your letter).

■ You do not have to be admitted to a school to ask about financial aid procedures, and if you wait to ask, you risk being too late.

About four weeks after you submit your FAFSA, you will receive a Student Aid Report (SAR) indicating your Expected Family Contribution (EFC), which is how much the government has determined you and/or your family can afford to contribute toward your education. (All the schools you list on your FAFSA will also receive a copy.)

To determine how much you and your family can afford to pay, your school's financial aid office will consider either the assessment provided on your SAR, the Profile's analysis, or its own analysis, in combination with criteria specific to the school's aid policy. Your EFC is calculated by government-approved formulas (and there are a few governmental grants based on only these numbers), but it's ultimately up to each school to determine how much aid you qualify for, if any. So, even if your SAR says that you are filthy rich and aren't eligible for need-based aid (and it just ain't true), it doesn't mean your school or outside funding sources will necessarily agree. In addition, your actual financial "need" may be only one aspect, albeit an important one, of what the financial aid office considers when determining your aid package. If you qualify, a portion (or all) of your package may come from targeted and/or merit-based sources.

Your Financial Aid Package

୭୭୭

The money in your financial aid package will probably come from your school, the federal or state government, or all three, and will come in the form of loans, grants, scholarships, and/or work-study. The package is

---

IF THERE'S A PROBLEM

If you believe that your EFC is not consistent with your family's circumstances (as is often the case), ask your financial aid office to review your application and, if possible, make an adjustment. If the financial aid office won't reduce your EFC, you can always inquire about applying for other types of aid. (See "Getting It Yourself," page 89.)

basically your school aid office's plan to help you cover the cost of your education. So, even if the aid office determines that you have little or no need, it will still help you plan the financing your education and should assist you in finding (or at least directing you to) alternative sources of aid. Financial aid offices review financial need annually and make adjustments where necessary to reflect changes in the financial need of students, the costs of attending school, and the amount of aid they have to give away.

In a lot of cases, you won't need to do much more than fill out the forms. The school will take care of assessing and dispensing the aid, and will explain to you, step by step, what you will need to do. School-administered grant and loan funds may be automatically credited to your student account or given to you directly, or both. If you are given the monies directly—the funds may be received in increments or in one lump sum—you will be expected to take care of payment yourself. In such a case, budgeting is extremely important. (See "Budgeting Your Bucks," page 105.)

Keeping Your Aid

ෙ෧෧

Don't assume that just because you've gotten the aid you need the first year, you're on easy street until graduation. Unless you are instructed otherwise, you will have to reapply for funding each school year—which usually requires filling out forms about your and/or your parents' current financial situation. This way, if you or your family have a change in income—for example, you incur new medical costs, begin supporting grand-

parents, or your parents divorce—your new financial situation will be taken into account.

"I'm not an organized person, but when it comes to money for college, I have to be. So I have a system—when I hear about a grant or scholarship that sounds good, I write down the info on a special calendar. I prioritize them by prestige, amount, how much work it would require (can I use an essay I already wrote or do I need to write a 40-page paper from scratch?), how much bother, and how much the application fee is. This way even if I decide not to go for it, I can try for it the next year."
—VANDERBILT UNIVERSITY, '95

In addition, if financial aid is your key to getting an education, you should take very good care of it. Know how, when, and where to reapply for it; what your responsibilities for maintaining it are; and what factors, if any, could jeopardize your aid. In most cases, in order to continue to receive aid, students must remain in "good academic standing," based on grade point average, credits per semester, and disciplinary record in a degree program. To keep the aid flowing, take heed of the following:

■ Don't assume last year's deadlines, qualifications, requirements, and application forms are the same. In fact, it's best to request a new application even if the person on the phone tells you that the application form hasn't changed.

■ If you're considering taking a leave of absence (for any reason), taking more or fewer than the average number of credits, changing your course-load, dropping classes, or reducing to part-time, check with the financial aid office before you make your final plans or take action.

■ Before returning to school after a leave of absence or study abroad, give the financial aid office ample time to prepare. Try to get your forms in early and make sure they know how to reach you, if need be.

■ In general, aid that your school gives you will not be transferable to programs that are not affiliated with your school (such as study abroad). However, the aid office will be a good place to get assistance in seeking alternate sources of support.

■ If you get credit for AP classes, an exemption from a requirement based on a test score or outside experience, or transfer credits from a study-abroad program or another school, the finan-

cial aid office may deduct from your aid package an amount relative to the cost of those credits at your school.

■ Dropping an activity or leaving a program/department that gives you aid will usually result in the loss of that aid. For example, if you are at school on an athletic scholarship and decide to quit the sport, your aid from that program will usually be revoked.

■ You usually won't get aid if you have defaulted on a grant or loan received for attendance at any institution. For example, say you haven't kept up with an outstanding federal loan from a previous school. Federal laws prohibit schools from allocating funds until you have cleared your default status. (Specifics vary from school to school.)

UNTYING THE PACKAGE

Free Money

ଡ଼୭ଡ଼

Grants, scholarships, and fellowships are like "free money"—gifts you don't have to pay back as long as you meet your end of the bargain (which can be as simple as enrolling in school or as complex as writing a book). The distinctions between grants, fellowships, and scholarships are not universally defined, and funding sources, such as schools and foundations, may employ their own definitions of the terms. A large portion of the funds come from schools themselves, but individuals (often alumni); federal, state, and local governments; public and private foundations; corporations; and religious or secular organizations who have a vested interest in a partic-

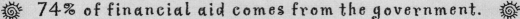

ular field of study or in students with specific attributes (such as academic, artistic, or athletic ability) also sponsor scholarships. They are awarded based on need and/or merit, and may cover expenses such as tuition, living, and/ or research. They may be part of your school's financial aid package, or you might seek them out on your own to fund research for your thesis, a project during winter break, or your living expenses while you are doing a specific, perhaps unconventional, educational project.

Though some grants/scholarships/fellowships come free and clear, others require the recipient to participate in certain activities (such as athletics) or to do academic work (such as lecturing, assistant teaching, or research).

Some grants, scholarships, and fellowships require that you apply; you have to be nominated for others. You may wish to ask professors, deans, or departmental advisors about the possibility of nominating you, as well as whether they have any recommendations about where you should apply for funding. (See "Applying for Grants," page 89.)

Two of the most common types of federal-government-sponsored need-based educational grants are:

Federal Pell Grant: Anyone who completes the FAFSA form automatically applies. Eligibility is determined by the EFC.

Federal SEOG (Supplemental Educational Opportunity Grants): A federal grant program that allocates funds to participating colleges for them to dispense to undergraduates with very low EFCs (with priority to recipients of Federal Pell Grants). Anyone who completes the FAFSA or the need-

analysis form required by her school automatically applies for this grant.

"After $10,000 in loan debt from undergrad, I am now racking up about $7,000 more for grad school. The only good part is that my school aid office has been really helpful and has taken into account the fact that I'm coming in with loans already. I am researching grants and loans outside of school, and I think that by combining what I get from school with my other sources of aid, I'll be able to manage."

— *EMORY UNIVERSITY, '97*

Loans

ଡ଼ଡ଼ଡ଼

The majority of financial aid at public colleges or universities is distributed in the form of loans (meaning we usually end up paying for our education, albeit over time rather than in one lump sum). A wide variety of loans are available to students and their parents. Some are earmarked for those who meet need-eligibility requirements, while others are available to all students and/or their parents or guardians, providing that they have a good credit history. Students can also take out personal loans that, although not specifically designated for educational purposes, can be used to help cover the cost of education.

The one thing that all loans have in common is that they must be repaid.

Everything else (minimum and maximum loan amounts, requirements, interest, fees, term, repayment policy, deferment options, and penalties for late payments) varies based on the type of loan. The major lenders include the federal government, state governments, banks, credit unions, and savings and loan (S&L) companies, as well as some schools, life insurance companies, and professional associations. In addition, numerous companies, organizations, and foundations offer special loans to students who meet specific criteria. Many such loans often have very low interest rates, and some are even interest-free.

In most cases, it won't be a big hassle applying for loans, because the processes have all been streamlined in recent years. However, if you do need to take out a loan yourself, the best deals are usually on loans specifically earmarked to cover school costs. This is because no matter whether you or the school does the legwork, most student loans are guaranteed by the federal government (i.e., should you not be able to pay the money back, the government is legally bound to cover you). Just because the government can "bail you out" does not change your responsibility to repay the loan or to suffer the consequences if you do not

> *"The most affordable school isn't always the one with the lowest tuition. Even though Bowdoin tuition costs are sky high, because they have such good financial aid programs it turned out that it was much more affordable than schools that cost a lot less on paper."*
> —BOWDOIN COLLEGE, '90

(to wit, your credit rating will be zapped and the IRS will put a lien on all future tax refunds). One additional benefit of government loans: In addition to providing money to pay for your education at a reasonable interest rate, they also give you a chance to establish credit in your own name.

The loans most commonly offered as part of school financial aid packages are:

Federal Perkins Loans (previously called National Direct Student Loans): Need-based federal loans available to undergraduate, graduate, and professional school students. Though these are federally funded, eligibility is determined by the school's financial aid office. These loans remain interest-free while you are a student. Repayment usually begins nine months after you leave school.

Federal Stafford Loans (previously called Guaranteed Student Loans): Federal loans available to qualifying undergraduate, graduate, professional, and vocational school students. Though eligibility for this loan is determined by your school's financial aid office, you may need to work out the logistics at the bank or another lending institution. But you won't have to do it all alone. The aid office takes some of the responsibility for securing the Stafford Loans and will direct you in fulfilling your responsibilities. There are two types of Stafford Loans: subsidized and unsubsidized. Subsidized loans are need-based and the federal government covers the interest payment for the period that you are in school or have other grounds for deferment. Unsubsidized loans are not need-based, and you are responsible for interest payments while you are in school, although most lenders will permit you to defer paying until you're out of school. But keep in mind that even though you aren't paying the interest, it is *accumulating*. Repayment of the principal usually begins six months after you leave school for both subsidized and unsubsidized Stafford Loans. (You may have both subsidized and unsubsidized loans as long as the total does not exceed annual limits.) If you take out a direct Stafford loan, which unlike other Staffords comes directly from the federal government, it will be administered by the financial aid office instead of a bank.

Specialized/targeted loans: Depending on your field of study, you may be eligible for federal or state targeted loans, such as those offered by the U.S. Department of Health and Human Services for future health professionals, or those administered through the Law School Admissions Council for law students.

PLUS Loans (Parental Loan for Undergraduate Students) are available to the parents of a dependent student regardless of income (as long as they have a good credit history). They usually have higher interest rates but allow for longer repayment periods than other federally guaranteed loans. These loans are available directly from commercial banks and other lenders, and have no deferment period—meaning you are responsible for making interest and principal payments during the time you are in school (except in very special cases). Though it is your responsibility to find the lender for these loans, you need approval from the financial aid office in order to get one, and it can be quite helpful in this process. You cannot borrow more than the cost of your education minus the financial aid you were awarded. Despite the name, PLUS loans are available to the parents of graduate and professional school students, as well as to parents of undergraduate students.

Personal loans: Of course, you and/or your family also have the option of taking out loans independently (such

> *"My first year of college, I took out a slew of loans to go to an oh-so-prestigious private school. But it turned out that the education wasn't any better than at my state school, so I transferred. Before you borrow yourself into centuries of debt, I would suggest that you consider the quality of education and how much you think you're going to make when you get out. In some cases, loans may be worth it, but I'm really glad that I transferred. It saved me from living a life of debt."*
>
> **—UNIVERSITY OF MICHIGAN, '94**

In 1992, more than 4 million students received Pell grants.

LOAN JARGON

CAPITALIZED INTEREST: Accrued interest (interest that you haven't yet paid but is being added to your principal anyway). In other words, you have to pay interest on your interest (as well as on your principal).

COLLATERAL: Something (such as personal property or another asset) used to guarantee a loan. Secured loans are those based on collateral; unsecured loans are those based on credit. With the former, if you default on your loan (that is, don't pay up), the lender is entitled to your collateral.

DEFERMENT: A delay in loan repayments granted to a borrower for a certain time period.

DEFERRED INTEREST: A delay in interest payments on the loan granted to a borrower for a defined time period.

FEES: Additional money you will have to pay to cover the costs associated with administering a loan—for example, origination, guarantee, and late payment fees. Often referred to as service fees, the fees may be paid up front, spread out over the life of the loan, or subtracted from the principal, depending on the loan.

INTEREST RATE: The percentage of the principal that is charged on borrowed money. It determines how much beyond the amount borrowed you will have to pay back. For example, if you took out a $100 loan with a daily interest rate of 10%, you would owe the lender $110 after the first day. Interest rates may be either fixed, in which case it stays the same throughout the life of the loan, or *variable*, in which case it fluctuates during the life of the loan according to changes in economic indices, such as the *prime rate* (the interest rate banks use when they borrow from each other) or the *90-day Treasury bill rate* (the interest rate the federal government uses when it sells its 90-day treasury bills). Banks usually set limits on how high (*caps*) and low (*floors*) the interest rates go on accounts and loans.

GUARANTEED LOAN: A loan in which another party (for example, your parents or the federal government) is legally responsible for the loan payments if the borrower defaults. This system, also called cosigning, allows borrowers with poor or no credit history to take out a loan.

LIFE OF THE LOAN/TERM: The time between when money is borrowed and when it's paid back in full.

PRINCIPAL: The original amount of money borrowed.

More than 2,100 groups give targeted aid to women and "minor-

PROMISSORY NOTE: The legal document you sign that states the terms of the loan. A promissory note must state the amount of your loan, the interest rate, and the date repayment begins; a list of all fees attached to the loans; a current description of the loans you owe to your school or lender, an estimate of your total debt, and your monthly payments; an explanation of default and its consequences; an explanation of consolidation options; and information about your prepayment options. You should ask for a copy of this agreement upon signing, and you should receive the original when the loan is completely paid off.

"Loans are excellent. I say take out as many as you can while you can. You'll never get such good rates again."
—CARLETON COLLEGE, '93

REPAYMENT PLAN: A plan for paying back your loans. It spells out the duration of the repayment period, the size of the installments, and how often payments will be due. For many loans, repayment responsibilities change once you graduate, and the repayment plan will make it clear whether you have a grace period after graduation before repayment begins or before interest begins to accrue. When discussing the repayment plan, ask if you can make payments through the mail or by an ATM, modem, or telephone, or if the bank can automatically deduct the amount from a savings or checking account.

as home-equity loans) to fund your education.

Unlike loans acquired through your financial aid package, money from loans like PLUS, the unsubsidized Stafford, and personal loans can help you to meet your Expected Family Contribution (EFC). (In general, loans secured through your financial aid office are intended to help you pay for your education but not to cover your EFC.)

Look Before You Leap

Whether you secure your loans with the guidance of school financial aid offices or get them totally independently, it's important to have a basic working knowledge of loan jargon (see the facing box), how repayment plans work, and what your rights and responsibilities are before you sign on any dotted lines. The specifications of a loan can be very confusing, so take the time (and demand it from the banker or financial aid officer) to ask a lot of questions and go over all the details before you commit yourself. For example, knowing the interest rate on a loan means nothing unless you know how long the repayment period is. A loan with a relatively high interest rate but a short repayment period could end up costing you less than one with a relatively low interest rate and a long repayment period. Calculate how much the loan will cost you in interest, principal, and various additional fees, and consider how long you'll be in debt (also find out whether there's a penalty or a reward for accelerated repayment). Try to keep convenience, flexibility, and your future plans in mind when assessing how good a deal a particular loan is.

Repaying and Deferring Loans

In order to approximate how much debt you can handle, you need to think about the long term. Consider how much you will be able to afford when your repayment starts, if there are foreseeable expenses that may make it difficult for you to repay the loan, if inflation rates will affect your loan, and if you anticipate changes in the incomes of anyone who is helping you with your loan repayments.

In most cases, banks defer principal payments (or even all payments) on a need-based student loan while the student is in school for at least half-time (even if you transfer or go right on to grad school) or serving in the Commissioned Corps of the U.S. Health Service, the armed forces, or the Peace Corps, Vista, or a similar volunteer service program. Deferment requests also may be granted during a time of temporary total disability, parental or medical leave, or economic hardship. Your debt may be canceled in part or full if you enter into specific professions that are considered to be important for the betterment of the country, such as professions in health care, or social service with low-income populations.

Repaying loans can be really frustrating and complicated, but you don't have to handle it on your own. Financial aid advisors recognize that upon graduation many students have yet to line up jobs or incomes that are sufficient enough to take care of college loan expenses. In an effort to help graduating students manage the looming responsibility of loan repayment, the financial aid office conducts entrance and exit interviews, during which they give advice, tips, and strategies for devising a loan repayment plan.

Consolidation

If you've taken loans out from a number of sources, repayment of all of them at the same time can be an impossible task. One solution is consolidation—that is, combining all your loans into one big loan. The consolidated loan has a new payment schedule and an interest rate based on those of the individual loans, plus a few percentage points. If all your loans are not from the same institution, you may need to use a loan consolidation service. Though consolidating loans makes it easier to meet payments, it ends up costing you a lot more money because the interest rate is higher and the payment period is usually longer. And unlike federal student loans, consolidated loans do not allow you to defer payment while attending school.

Although consolidation is one of the most frequently used methods of debt management, there are other options. Explore them with your aid office.

Work-Study, Research, and Teaching Assistantships

෨෨෨

Another way in which schools grant financial aid is by securing students jobs, and thus incomes, through work-study. Work-study jobs are funded in a large part by the federal government (through the Federal College Work-Study Program) and administered by individual schools. Usually, work-study jobs are just like any other job, except that students are paid through their school and eligibility is determined by the aid office or by your graduate department.

Work-study jobs run the gamut—students work as administrative assistants in academic departments, campus tour guides, food servers in dining halls, research assistants for specific professors, and so on. Though each school offers different opportunities, you will probably be able to select the type of work-study job you want and in some cases even create your own work-study job or find a job of your choice off campus (providing it meets specific criteria).

> *"In my sophomore year of college I was in a special internship/ work-study program. I worked for a nonprofit of my choice and they paid half of my salary and a grant from the school paid the other half. I ended up getting a job offer after graduation and I'm working there now."*
>
> *—VIRGINIA COMMONWEALTH UNIVERSITY, '94*

Once you have a work-study job, your aid office pays you with money from financial aid funds allocated specifically for this purpose. Salaries are usually paid directly to you by check. It is then your responsibility to ensure that college costs are met. Some schools allow you to do work-study over the summer, in any part of the country—ask about these opportunities in the aid office.

Graduate students often fund their education through teaching assistantships (TAships), research assistantships (RAships), or teaching jobs. The advantage of all of these is that they allow you to work in your field, earn needed money, beef up your résumé, and build relationships with professors. Research assistantships are usually funded by a professor's independent grant money. If you are lucky you might find a position in which you can conduct your own research while you work. RAships may also give you the opportunity to copublish with your professors—great for the personal satisfaction, the ego, and the résumé. At universities with large undergraduate populations, funding for graduate students normally involves some teaching and/or research. Ask explicitly about the availability of such positions and what is expected of graduate students when you are applying to and selecting your school. (See "Funding Graduate School," page 97.) In some cases undergraduates will also be eligible for research and teaching assistantships—ask professors in departmental offices about these job opportunities.

Although it is not a part of financial aid work-study programs, you always have the option of raising funds by getting a job on your own. In some cases this option may pay a higher wage and/or give you better experience than your work-study alternatives. (See "Working Women," page 158.)

"My professor asked me to be her research assistant and I really wanted to do it—I needed the money and wanted the experience. The only glitch was that she asked if I was eligible for work-study. Because I hadn't submitted the forms before, I had to wait a while to find out if I was eligible, and by then she had found someone else. The moral of the story: Submit all those financial aid forms, even if you don't think you'll need them, because you never know what's going to come up."

— WASHINGTON UNIVERSITY, '98

National Service

The National Service Program was established so that students would have the option to defray the costs of their education by working in their communities before attending school. Prospective students perform salaried community service work for one or two years and, upon completion of the program, receive additional money to fund their education—approximately $5,000 for each year of service. The program is intended to supplement, not replace, other forms of federal aid. If it is successful, the program will increase in size, participation, and presumably funding. The National Service Program is federally funded and administered by the individual states.

Reserve Officers Training Corps

The Reserve Officers Training Corps (ROTC) allows students to go to school while receiving payment for military training. In return for money for tuition, fees, and books and a tax-free stipend of approximately $1,000, students enrolled in ROTC are required to participate in a military training program and take courses in military science while at school, and after graduation they must serve from six months to four years on active or reserve duty in a branch of the armed forces. If you are interested but ROTC is not an available option at your school, you may be able to participate in the ROTC program at a school nearby. As there are many ways to meet the ROTC requirements, students can often tailor the program to their individual needs, interests, and schedules. However, ROTC is by no means a free ride. The time commitment that the extra coursework and weekend and summer training sessions require, as well as the physical and emotional demands of the program, can be intense. Plus, it is no secret that the military is not exactly a bastion of liberation, and many women have found being in ROTC difficult. Furthermore, because of the current military regulations, open lesbians (as well as openly gay men) are not eligible for ROTC. In addition to ROTC, the GI Bill provides funds and avenues for higher education to those serving in, or who have served in, the military. (For more information, call the Federal Financial Aid Information Hotline; see the Resources at the end of this chapter.)

GETTING IT YOURSELF

Despite the fact that there is a lot of financial aid to be had, there is relatively less these days than in years gone by—especially if you're applying for aid through the regular channels. This is partially because college endowments haven't grown at the same rate that tuition has. As a result, despite student demonstrations, lobbying, budget juggling, and fund-raising efforts, more schools are raising tuition and abandoning their need-blind admission policies (those that don't consider your financial need in the decision to offer you admission). If, for whatever reason, you find that you're unable to make ends meet, it's time to break your reliance on the aid

office and begin your own quest for private grants and scholarships.

Applying for Grants

ⓥⓐⓥ

Applying for grants (and scholarships and fellowships) to pay for anything from your tuition to the development of a performance art piece can be arduous, but, hey, money doesn't come cheap. And more than just helping you get funding, the application process can help you organize and clearly focus your educational interests or projects.

First, you should do some research to find the places that have an interest in the kind of work you are pursuing or project you are planning. Is it educational, religious, environmental, or scientific? Try to determine all the areas of interest that relate to your topic. For example, if you're interested in studying indigenous flora in the Brazilian rain forest, check places that fund projects in botany, environmental issues, general science, Brazil, world development, ecology, and women's research. Many foundations, corporations, government agencies, individuals, and nonprofits invest in specific areas such as health, education, minority issues, the environment, or women's studies, and you will probably need to fit into a number of categories in order to convince them to fund you.

Once you have found a funding source that matches your interests, you need to write a proposal. Find out about the funder and cater your proposal to its interests. This means that you will probably have to emphasize different elements of your project, experience, and life to different

KEEPING UP WITH THE DONKEYS AND ELEPHANTS

As elected officials come and go and new legislation is passed, policies about funding for education change. Everything from interest rate changes, budget cuts or increases, and new tax legislation to all types of economic and social reform can affect both your current financial aid package and your future funding options. Keep an eye on what's going on in Washington, DC, and the state and local governments where your school (and, if different, your legal residence) is located so that you can take advantage of any new programs or plan appropriately if it looks as if there will be a reduction in the type of aid you receive. In any case, you should ask the financial aid office and/or the federal aid information hotline (see the Resources) about any new programs and policies.

funders. Most foundations and corporations require the same information, while individuals may want more or, if you're lucky, less information. Government agencies tend to require *a lot* of information.

A basic proposal contains the following elements:

Cover letter: Should be short and concise. Its purpose is to inform the potential funder that you are enclosing a proposal for consideration and what kind of award you are applying for (i.e., is it for a specific award or a certain amount of money?). Try to get the name (with correct spelling) and title of the appropriate person to address. If you can't find out, you should address your letter to the executive director or president of the funding source.

Introduction: Should provide some background information about you and the project. Who are you? Why are you qualified to do the project? How will your findings contribute to the field? Here you should also establish the link between your work and the interests of the funder.

Summary: Should include all essential elements of the proposal. What are you planning to do? Why? How? In what time frame? How much funding do you need to do it?

Statement of purpose/intent: Should identify the focus of your project, highlighting the issues and/or population you will serve and problems and questions you will address. It should help the funder identify his or her interests in your proposal, thus building a case for support.

Methods: Should explain the technical aspect. How do you plan to carry out your objectives (i.e., how will you actually do your project)?

Timetable: Should lay out a clear schedule of things you need to do and when they will be done: Will the project take 1 year, 2 years, 18 months? (This may also help you in planning out your work/research.) If you are applying for a general grant to fund your education, then you should talk about how long you expect it to take to complete your requirements (if it is not obvious) and what you plan to pursue while in school and afterward.

Budget: Should show the funder your projected expenses. Try to estimate as closely as possible, but don't worry if you're a little off. Include items such as salary, travel, supplies, telephone, postage, and research fees.

Personal statement: Should detail who you are, what you want to do and why, why you are the person who should do it, and why you deserve the funds. Some grants will require you to discuss your goals for study in a specific field. In such cases it helps to be as specific as possible—the more focused you sound, the more likely you are to get money. In some cases, creativity will be acceptable (and even encouraged). Talk with deans and/or professors to see what is appropriate.

Evaluation plan: Should outline when and how you will determine if the project was successful and the objectives met. Evaluation processes vary depending on the project.

Tips for Getting Grants

■ Start your funding search early. It usually takes six to nine months from the time money is awarded to the time you actually get it. And the application deadline is likely to be three months before that.

■ Beat the deadline. The majority of financial aid sources do not consider late applications, and some give out aid on a rolling (first come, first served) basis.

■ Don't ignore the small grants. In addition to often being less competitive and requiring less work than bigger grants (not to mention that every cent helps), they do wonders for your résumé. A little grant money holds a lot of prestige and may attract a lot more grant money. Funders consider a woman with a number of academic awards a good investment. You may also be able to piece together a few small grants and make up a full financial aid package.

■ Keep letters of recommendation on file to send off at a moment's notice. (See "Recommendations," page 51.)

■ If a grant application requires you to do a large project or write a long essay, try to use the same piece of work for more than one application. In addition, many professors are understanding and supportive of students who compete for grants that require a lot of work, and may allow you to turn it in for academic credit.

foundations were either misdirected or filled out improperly. ❀

TARGETING TARGETED AID

When starting your search for funding, think about everything you've ever done, everywhere you've ever lived, everyone you're related to, and everything you want to study or have studied—those things that make you different and special (and the more unique you are the better). You'll be surprised how much money is available to women based on their various attributes. Below are some of the most popular criteria on which money is awarded.

ACADEMIC PERFORMANCE/EXPERIENCE: Your class rank, GPA, standardized test scores, previous academic experience, awards and degrees received, and what and where you're studying can all be your ticket to grant money. There are also grants earmarked for students in nontraditional programs, or for "returning" students, "older" students, part-time students, and full-time students.

GEOGRAPHY AND CITIZENSHIP: Some funders will give money based on the city, county, state, and country you're from, where you currently live, and where you're going.

PROFESSIONAL GOALS OR CONNECTIONS: A lot of funding is available to help future workers hone their skills, and to entice them into nontraditional or underrepresented fields. There are also grants available to students who pledge to work with a specific company or religious institution, the government, the military, and/or in a rural area or a developing country after graduation. Further, many companies and professional societies offer scholarships to their employees/members.

CLUB OR ORGANIZATIONAL AFFILIATION: A number of clubs and organizations, including fraternal organizations (such as the Elks, Masons, and Knights of Columbus), sororities and coed fraternities, academic societies, community groups, synagogues, and churches offer grants to their members, relatives of members, and sometimes to people with no affiliation whatsoever.

PERSONAL ATTRIBUTES: Personal attributes, including heritage, family, and special skills, talents, and/or interests are a basis for a huge number of scholarships. Your race, gender, ethnicity, ancestry/ies, religious affiliation, disability, age, sexual orientation, first or second language, athletic or musical ability, hobbies, and extracurricular interests will figure prominently in these types of grants.

- Remember, neatness counts.

- If you are applying for one grant, it is usually not so hard to apply for more. You have already formatted a proposal, written an essay, and requested recommendations. The more grants you apply for, the better chance you have of getting one of them.

- Follow up with funders after you have submitted a proposal. This should be done within two to three weeks by phone. They should tell you when you should expect to hear from them or call them again.

- Don't get discouraged if you are turned down—there are thousands of people just like you trying to get their projects funded. Keep trying!

Keep the Financial Aid Office Apprised

ඥඥඥ

If after you've filed your financial aid forms or your school has made an offer for aid, you receive funding from any other source, it is generally your obligation to notify the aid office. An adjustment will then be made in the financial aid award so that it will not exceed what they have determined to be your need.

Most schools have policies for figuring out how such outside aid affects your package. In most cases, you'll be allowed to receive a small amount of money from outside sources, such as from private grants, without it affecting your aid. If you do receive additional money, ask your aid office about any restrictions placed on outside funds before you raise your specific case.

IF YOUR NEED CHANGES

If your financial situation changes and you find you need more money to pay for school, there are a few possibilities for obtaining more aid. But remember, money might be hard to come by, because most institutions assume that a student's financial situation will remain pretty much the same throughout the entire time she's attending school (and certainly the same during the academic year), and they create aid packages based on this assumption. If you need a significant amount of money mid-semester (more than a few hundred dollars), you'll have little choice but to apply for one of the federal student loans or a personal loan from a bank. (See "Emergency Money," page 106.)

Your first step should be to speak with the financial aid office. Following are some hints on making your meeting go well.

- Before you make an appointment, find out and heed the school's policy for appealing or revising a financial aid package.

- Prepare a written statement, with all the necessary forms attached.

- Go to the meeting with a list of other potential sources of funding. This will show that you are willing to put time and energy into finding the aid you need—you won't sit back and expect the school to do all the work. Look through some of the financial aid books at the library, search an on-line database, and/or visit a community center that has information and resources about financial aid. Ask

GRANT SEEKING SERVICES

Because it is time-consuming to find out where to apply for funds such as grants, services exist to help you find funding sources. It may be worth your while to pay an agency to do your footwork—especially if time is short. But be warned: In most cases the information the services provide is readily available to anyone who has the time and energy to scour libraries, foundation centers, departmental bulletin boards, academic and professional association newsletters, and local, state, and federal agencies. If you are thinking about using a grant/scholarship/fellowship-seeking service, ask your financial aid office and previous users for names of reputable firms, especially those that refund your search fee if they don't come up with a designated minimum of sources.

at your department, dean's office, local and national sorority chapters, temple or church, job, or any other place that might provide financial assistance. Even if there's nothing too promising on your list, it might spark an idea of new places to look. Aid offices will be more energetic in helping find aid for a responsible student who values her education.

■ Come to the meeting organized, awake, alert, and neatly dressed. Show the financial aid officer how important this is to you.

■ Remind the school that you are a sound investment, definitely worth their time and money. Be prepared to talk about your educational and career goals, the ways you contribute to the school community, and how and why you and the school are so well suited to each other.

■ Recognize that because the bulk of student aid is dispensed at the beginning of the school year, if you apply mid-semester, the school will have less aid available. In the best-case scenario, financial aid officers may be able to scratch together enough of an aid plan to carry you over until the next financial aid review period when you can apply and be considered for federal aid. (The aid office should help you make the appropriate revisions to your financial statement.)

■ Be specific about the amount of money you need and what expenses it would cover, as well as why it is impossible for you to meet your costs without the additional aid. This approach is much more persuasive than just saying, "I need more money."

■ If you are applying for aid or an increase in aid because your family's financial situation has changed, you will need to provide information about (and perhaps documentation of) the reasons for the change (e.g., death in the family, loss of a job, new baby).

■ Try to stay as calm as possible. That way you can be sure the facts are straight and your ideas are heard, and most important, you won't irritate, anger, annoy, or upset the person who is your ticket to getting the aid you need.

■ Consider your options if you don't get all the aid you need. Perhaps a professor will let you put off handing in the final term paper and take an incomplete, so you can use the extra time now to put in more hours at work. Or you might request a deferred payment on loans or take a semester or a year at a less expensive school closer to home. Because funding school can be so difficult, many students find creative solutions. Be flexible.

■ If, after your conversation with the aid office, you still believe that your package is insufficient and was evaluated incorrectly, you may wish to ask about the procedure for appealing their decision and, in the meantime, start pursuing other options.

PARENTS AND FINANCIAL AID

Schools generally expect that the cost of your education will be borne, at least in part, by your parents if you are in any way dependent on them financially. There are, however, very specific guidelines that govern how your parents' financial information can affect the way your aid award is determined. It is important to know your rights and to ask the aid office any questions you have that pertain to your case.

"If your school is making you give parental information when it is very unreasonable, protest—not to the extent that the aid office hates you, but make them understand with formal letters, phone calls, and/or in person why their requests or stipulations are inappropriate. I led a protest at my school and got together petitions of a number of other students. The only way that the system is going to change is if you change it."
—UNIVERSITY OF MICHIGAN, '97

Separation and Divorce
☾☉☽

When determining aid, some schools consider the income and assets of both parents (as well as stepparents, if remarried). Such schools may require you to submit a "custodial parent form" or "divorced parents statement" detailing the finances of all your parents and stepparents. Neither federal nor state forms ask for this information. They base your EFC solely on the financial profile of the parent who is your legal guardian (and, if remarried, his or her spouse). (They do, however, request information about all contributions to your education, so if your noncustodial parent is helping pay for school, you have to say so.) If your school requests noncustodial financial information and it is either inappropriate to your situation or you cannot provide it, speak with the director of aid. The aid office will usually be flexible about this requirement.

Independent Status vs. Dependent Status

〰〰〰

The government has its own definition of who qualifies to claim independent status. You are eligible to receive federal financial aid as an independent if at least one of the following applies to you:

▲ You will be at least 24 by the last day of the year.
▲ You are a U.S. Armed Forces veteran.
▲ You're enrolled in a graduate or professional program.
▲ You're married.
▲ You have legal dependents (other than a spouse) for whom you provide at least half of the support.
▲ You're an orphan or ward of the court, or were when you turned 18.

There are other circumstances in which you might be considered independent (for example, if you were abused by your parents). Ask your aid administrator if you think you should qualify but don't meet the criteria. And know that even if you fit these criteria, if your parents give you a considerable amount of financial support, you may still be regarded as a dependent by some institutions.

Even if your school requires you to give parental information, if you are an independent, your parents' financial information *will not* be factored into the equation that determines your eligibility for federal aid. Therefore, although you may have to provide your parents' information on forms to be considered for school-based aid, the information you provide will not affect how much federal aid you receive.

TAXES AND AID

Some forms of aid may be taxable. Talk to the financial aid office or the administrator of your graduate department for specific information about your aid plan, your state tax code, and the federal tax code. The issue of taxes may be particularly pertinent when you are an independent.

In addition, federal and state legislation regarding federal tax breaks for educational expenditures can drastically affect the amount you or your parents have to pay in taxes, as well as how your need is determined. You can find out about the tax provisions by calling the federal aid information hotline or by speaking with a school financial aid officer.

Most schools have some leeway in making an assessment of someone's independence. If there is no possibility that your parents will contribute to or help you secure funds for your education, you should notify the aid office in writing, and send them letters from both your parents and yourself stating the situation. If you entered or enrolled in school with dependent status, be aware that some schools may

not recognize a change to independent status when they award school-based aid in the future.

FUNDING GRADUATE SCHOOL

The process of funding graduate school education is quite different from the process of getting aid for an undergraduate education. Because most of the government aid, which is primarily need-based, is reserved for undergrads, grad students have to depend more on loans and school aid (often in the form of assistantships and private grants, scholarships, and fellowships). Therefore, you should take the time to search through financial aid directories and write applications for any and all grants, scholarships, and fellowships for which you qualify. There are also special federal aid programs for students pursuing degrees in needed fields, such as education for disabled students or rural medicine, in which the government will cover, or at least partially cancel, your loan debt upon graduation.

Funding Professional School

Students in professional grad programs, such as law, business, or medicine, are less likely to receive grants, scholarships, and fellowships than are students in "nonprofessional" graduate programs, such as literature or science—the assumption being that once you graduate from programs in law or medicine you will be more likely to find a job with a high enough income to pay back any debts you incurred while in school. Hence, the most popular method of funding professional school is through loans. However, summer jobs can help relieve some portion of the financial burden, and there are still many scholarships available for people who fit the right criteria. For example, women and/or members of minority groups may qualify for special funding available to students entering fields such as business, medicine, or law. Also, tuition reimbursements, loan reductions and waivers, stipends (money intended to help cover the costs of basic needs or to supplement your income), salaried jobs, and/or scholarships exist for those students who intend to do certain types of public service work upon graduation. For example, the U.S.

"I have taken out more loans to go to school than I will probably make in my first three years of working. . . . I sort of understand the rationale of not giving out grants for students in some kinds of professional programs, but my friends and I are not in school because the professions are lucrative, we are going into them because we think we can do some good in the world—and yet in order to pay back the loans, a lot of my friends are "selling out" on their ideals and going into jobs where the money is."

—BRANDEIS UNIVERSITY
SCHOOL OF SOCIAL WORK, '97

for employees working toward MBAs or other advanced degrees. ☀

Department of Health and Human Services offers specific funding opportunities for students entering the health professions. Talk with your aid office about your options; they are usually well aware of the opportunities that exist for students in your field and can help you work out a strategy to pay for your education.

Funding Nonprofessional Graduate School

ᕙᕤᕙ

Graduate schools vary in how and when they offer aid. Some schools don't give you aid for your first year, while others don't guarantee that you will have aid *beyond* your first year. For the most part, individual departments, rather than a central school-wide office, dispense aid. Getting to know the professors during the application process (and after) may greatly influence how much aid you receive. If afaculty member feels that you would

> "The way that you get grad school money is all a bit clandestine—nobody really tells you what is going on. If a grad school offers you a stipend, make sure that they are going to help you fund your whole program and not leave you hanging. A lot of schools will guarantee you jobs teaching or doing research [for the first few years] ... and forget that you have to eat while you write your dissertation."
>
> —UNIVERSITY OF CHICAGO, PHD CANDIDATE, '95

be a great asset to the department, you have a pretty good chance of getting department/university-dispensed aid. Also, if you need to negotiate for more aid, having a contact in the department can be a real help.

When applying for grad school aid, you've got to be headstrong, creative, persistent, and crafty. It is no time to be modest—it's up to you to toot your own horn. Let the department know what makes you special and what you've done that makes you a stellar candidate.

If one school offers you a better aid package than the school you want to attend, call the latter school and use it as a negotiating point. It isn't easy, but aggressive networking, "personal PR," and making friends in high places (and occasionally groveling) have helped many a student get the help needed. The point is, it is not only acceptable for you to ask about getting more money when you are accepted to a school, it is expected. So don't be shy.

OTHER FUNDING ISSUES

Funding for Part-time/Returning Students

Although most aid is given to full-time students, the federal aid programs, as well as a large number of state and local aid programs, are available to part-time and returning students. In addition, if you are a returning student, you should explore special grants, scholarships, and fellowships targeted at your group. (See the Resources at the end of this chapter for names of student and grant directories.) If a permanent or temporary disability prevents you from taking a full courseload, you should still be eligible for aid designated for awards for full-time students.

Funding for International Students

In general, it is very hard for international students to receive aid in their first year of study in the U.S., because one of the requirements for federal and state aid is that you be either a U.S. citizen or an eligible non-citizen. If you are a foreign student, you'll probably find the most success if you contact agencies and funding sources in your country of origin that offer scholarships to students studying abroad. The office that handles the concerns and needs of international students on your campus may be able to give you pointers. If they are not helpful, try getting in touch with the office for international students at a university with a large foreign student population.

Funding Nontraditional Educational Projects

Although the bulk of aid offered by the government and schools is funding for traditional academic programs within a school setting, there are ways to get funding for nontraditional educational programs such as studying dance in Egypt, making a movie about pigeons, or building a school in

"I was really excited when I got a paper accepted to a big conference being held across the country. But I couldn't afford the price of a plane ticket, hotel for three days, food, etc. So I went up the school hierarchy. I went to my advisor, then the department, then the deans, asking about discretionary funds and special grants. I talked with the financial aid office to see if I could use some of my fellowship money. I called women's organizations and the professional organizations in my discipline and gathered together a couple hundred dollars."
—UNIVERSITY OF MINNESOTA, '98

Nicaragua. The bulk of this funding comes in the forms of grants and loans, and is offered by federal and state governments, schools, corporations, and foundations. Finding the money to fund your creative ideas may require some creativity itself. The first place to begin is in the dean's office—

inquire there about any school- or nationally sponsored grants to fund your projects. Many schools offer some type of grants for projects done over vacation periods. In addition, ask in the appropriate departments about any departmental or national scholarships for which you might qualify. (See the Resources at the end of this chapter, as well as "Targeting Targeted Aid," page 92.)

DISCRIMINATION

If you feel that any part of the aid process has been discriminatory (including the forms you are filling out, the interview questions, the selection process, and/or the requirements), talk with your director of aid. The U.S. Department of Education's regional offices can help in this situation as well. If you feel that you were discriminated against in getting a grant, send a letter to the funder, requesting an explanation of why you were rejected.

It is illegal to deny someone a loan on the basis of gender, race, national origin, religion, marital status, age, or disability, or because she receives federal assistance. If you were turned down for a loan, you are legally entitled to find out why in writing.

Most schools have their own policies about discrimination, which may be more inclusive than federal or state laws, and they cannot violate their own policies when awarding aid. For example, if you feel you were denied aid because of your sexual orientation, even though you are not protected by federal law, you may still have grounds for recourse based on the school's own policy.

ACTIVIST IDEAS

■ Have a grant-writing workshop with members of the college development office, financial aid office, and/or career services.

■ A big project but a worthy one: Make a list of foundations and companies that provide scholarships to under-graduate women. Make it available at the financial aid office, women's center, library, career services and post it on-line.

■ After you graduate, try to give money to your school's scholarship fund so aid will be available for future scholars.

Women's colleges make up only 2% of all 4-year institutions,

RESOURCES

Information About Federal Aid

THE U.S. DEPARTMENT OF EDUCATION
THE FEDERAL FINANCIAL AID INFORMATION
HOTLINE
(800) 433-3243 [(800) 4-FED-AID]
Provides information and answers questions about all areas of federal financial aid. Provides assistance with filling out federal forms, and gives information about funding options and alternatives. Provides need assessment and application forms for federal aid programs. Makes referrals to organizations that can best answer your questions or address your needs with regard to all federal funding for education. Publishes numerous materials; catalogs are available upon request.

THE DIRECT LOAN SERVICES CENTER
BORROWER SERVICES DEPARTMENT
(800) 848-0979
Gives information about all federally administered loans. Will check on the status of your loans and help you understand the ins and outs of payment plans. The Direct Loan Consolidation Center, also at this number, can help you with all matters consolidation-related.

State Financial Aid

Most states provide some funding for higher education. To find out about funds offered by your state, contact the State Office/Department of Higher Education or State Office/Department of Education, listed in the blue pages of your phone book under "State Government Agencies."

Foundation Centers

The Foundation Center is an organization whose purpose is to help individuals and nonprofit organizations find grant sources. It has affiliated libraries throughout the country that maintain large collections of funding directories as well as sell publications such as *Foundation Grants to Individuals*, *Foundation Directory*, and *National Directory of Corporate Giving*. You can find out the locations of affiliated libraries in your area, and/or request a catalog of publications by calling (800) 424-9836.

Major Grant/Scholarship/ Fellowship Funding Organizations

Following are some of the major funding organizations. The sources of financial aid for students, especially those entering into fields of study, such as health, law, business, art, and the humanities, are too numerous to list here. Your best bet is to talk with someone in the financial aid office and to search through the applicable financial aid directories listed below. In

addition, you can request listings of all federal grants, scholarships, and funds (of which there are many) by contacting the federal aid information hotline listed above.

Most funders require you to apply a full year before you will need the money. Applications for most educational grants, scholarships, and fellowships are due in the early fall for the following year.

NATIONAL SCIENCE FOUNDATION
PROCESSING CENTER
702 SOUTH ILLINOIS AVENUE
OAKRIDGE, TN 37820
(615) 483-3344

NATIONAL ENDOWMENT FOR THE HUMANITIES
PUBLIC INFORMATION OFFICE
1100 PENNSYLVANIA AVENUE NW
ROOM 402
WASHINGTON, DC 20506
(202) 606-8438

NATIONAL ENDOWMENT FOR THE ARTS
PUBLIC INFORMATION OFFICE
1100 PENNSYLVANIA AVENUE NW
ROOM 803
WASHINGTON, DC 20506
(202) 682-5400

Graduate Support

AMERICAN ASSOCIATION OF UNIVERSITY WOMEN EDUCATIONAL FOUNDATION
P.O. BOX 4030
IOWA CITY, IOWA 52243
(319) 337-1716
(202) 728-7603

NATIONAL RESEARCH COUNCIL (THE FELLOWSHIP OFFICE)
2101 CONSTITUTION AVENUE
WASHINGTON, DC 20418
(202) 334-2872
Administers numerous grants of private foundations for graduate support in many areas of study.

Further Reading

The Student Guide: Financial Aid from the U.S. Department of Education, is published annually and is an excellent guide to federal funding. For a free copy, call the Federal Student Aid Information Center at (800) 433-3243.

Directories

There are numerous directories of funding sources that list grants, scholarships, fellowships, and loans available to students. In addition, these directories and others list funding opportunities for projects ranging from making films to creating organizations. The directories can be found in deans' offices, offices of career services, financial aid offices, and, of course, in libraries. If your school or local library doesn't have the directory you are looking for, ask them to order it for you. (Remember, because directories tend to be expensive it makes sense for libraries to buy them, rather than you—but, because most libraries are poorly funded, realize that it may not be possible for them to fill your requests. If you don't find them in one location, look in another.) Some directories of particular interest to women students are:

Published by Reference Service Press:
Directory of Financial Aid for Women
Directory of Financial Aid for Minorities
Financial Aid for the Disabled and Their Families
Financial Aid for Veterans, Military Personnel, and Their Dependents
How to Find Out About Financial Aid

Published by Gale Publications:
Women's Information Directory
Scholarships, Fellowships, and Loans
Awards, Honors, and Prizes: An International Directory of Awards and Their Donors
The A.B.C.'s: Your Guide to Academic Scholarships

Published by Macmillan:
College Blue Book (volume 5 has information about scholarships, loans, fellowships, and grants)
The Complete Grants Sourcebook for Higher Education

Published by Garrett Park Press:
Financial Aid for Minorities—Awards Open to Students with Any Major

Financial Aid for Minorities in Business and Law
Financial Aid for Minorities in Education
Financial Aid for Minorities in Engineering and Science
Financial Aid for Health Fields
Financial Aid for Minorities in Journalism and Mass Communications
Directory of Research Grants

Published by the Foundation Center:
National Guide to Funding for Women and Girls
Foundation Grants to Individuals
The Foundation Directory
The National Guide to Funding in Higher Education

Also see:
The National Directory of Grants and Aid to Individuals in the Arts, (Washington International Arts Letter).
Financial Aids for Higher Education, (William C. Brown).
ARIS Funding Messenger: Creative Arts and Humanities Report, (Academic Research Information System).
The International Scholarship Directory, (Career Press).

Note: Since most of these directories are updated every few years, publication dates are not included here. Make sure that you are working with the most updated version.

Money Matters

Managing Your Personal Finances

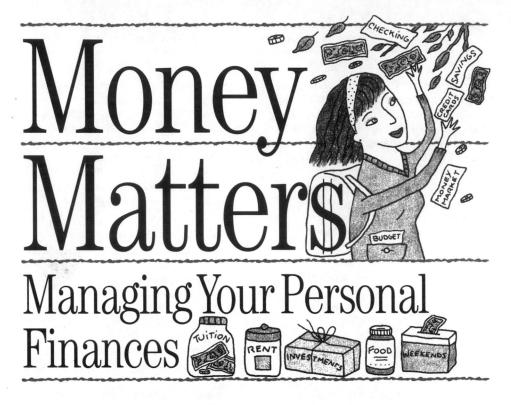

Although women have been responsible for money management throughout history (most notably in budgeting and overseeing family financial matters), it is only recently that people have acknowledged that financial prowess is not a trait found only on the Y chromosome. Because it was assumed that women would have difficulty grasping anything beyond "home economics," a woman's financial education rarely went further than balancing a checkbook. Even those women who worked outside of the home (and there were many) did not have opportunities to gain financial knowledge or financial independence equal to men's.

Though obstacles still exist, a very different reality is reflected in the lives of contemporary women. Access to information about how to establish credit, open and manage a bank account, deal with debt, file taxes, secure loans, and invest money has played an essential role in the forging of women's independence. Assuming responsibility for managing our finances not only makes a difference in our own lives, but increases the opportunities, access, and power afforded all women.

No matter whether we're financially dependent or independent or have a lot of money to manage or a little , an important part of college education is learning how to be financially responsible. For many women, college is a transitional period between having most financial matters taken care of for us and being "out on our own." Most of us get some help from our families and/or the aid office with paying the bills but are responsible for our day-to-day money management. Sticking to a budget, managing a checking account, and paying the bills on time—not to mention holding a job and applying for aid so there'll be money to use in the first place—can be hard work, even without all the other academic and personal responsibilities we have. But a bit of basic information (including how and where to find the not-so-basic information) will get you well on your way.

BUDGETING YOUR BUCKS

There's more to financing an education than digging up enough money to pay for tuition. Once we've earned, borrowed, and graciously accepted all the money we can, we have to make it cover all of life's expenses—aka making a budget.

The budgeting process requires a ruthless inventory and analysis of your financial situation and practices. If you take the time to do it well, you'll end up with an accurate picture of what you have, and what you can afford.

The first step in creating a budget is determining how much money you have to work with. Almost all of us have a certain amount of money with which to support ourselves each month. It may fluctuate a little—there may be semesters in which you'll work fewer hours, and there are always those birthday checks—but for the most part, your income is probably relatively stable. In addition to obvious sources of income, such as salary, aid, and perhaps an allowance, include outside grants or loans, gifts, and interest on savings and/or investments.

The next step is determining your expenses. Take time to figure out all of the things you spend money on. (Using past receipts and bank statements may help when determining seasonal expenses.) Then organize them into categories. You might use "essential expenses," e.g., those that you really can't avoid (this may include tuition, rent, utilities, food, transportation) "essentially essential" expenses, such as those that are pretty crucial but a little less predictable and offer you some flexibility (toiletries, clothes, school supplies, pesky fees); and "discretionary expenses" (entertainment, meals out, gifts).

Because college usually brings new expenses, new jobs, new means of support, and possibly, if you go away to school, new costs of living, it may take a few months to get an accurate picture of your money situation. Similarly, with every change in income—a promotion (or a lay-off), a revised aid package, a lottery win, or a change in expenses (a move, a new baby, a new boyfriend who lives across the country)—you'll have to revise your budget.

Where It All Goes

〰〰〰

■ The biggies: tuition, rent, food

■ Other potential academic costs: books and notebooks; fetal pig for bio lab; materials, studio, and lab fees (often charged in visual arts courses); paints; leotards and dance shoes; copy card; computer hardware, software, disks, and paper; grant and scholarship application fees; loan fees

■ Bills: utilities; student loan payments; health, dental, and other insurance; credit card payments

■ Look good/feel good expenses: clothing, toiletries, laundry, haircuts

■ Fun: tickets to school sporting events, movies, and plays; parties; other entertainment

■ Organization costs: club, church, synagogue, temple, and/or sorority/coed fraternity dues

■ Transportation costs: gas; subway or bus fare

■ Keeping-in-touch costs: E-mail accounts; stamps; telephone bills; travel expenses

■ Those loathsome, unanticipated expenses: parking tickets, medical expenses, overdue library book fines, bank fees, costs to drop or add courses, late registration fees

And don't forget to budget in money to be saved. Although this can be difficult to do (as many of us are up to our ears in debt), try to put a little money aside, as you never know when an out-of-the-ordinary expense will arise.

Living on the Cheap

ೲೲೲ

When it comes to budgets, the less money you have, the less flexibility you have in deciding where it goes; and the more strictly you need to stick to your budget, the more creative you have to be about pinching pennies. Below are a few time-honored scrimping tips.

Food and Shelter

The most common method of saving money on food and housing is living with a roommate or two, or renting a

EMERGENCY MONEY
🌀

Most school financial aid offices, and occasionally, deans, have some funds at their disposal earmarked for small, short-term emergency loans. These loans are usually interest-free and run between $500 and $800. They are generally not intended to cover tuition costs, but rather to help a student through a crisis, such as paying for food, medical care, or rent. Some schools require that you disclose what the loan is for. (This may present a problem if you need the money for a private matter.) Because it can take up to a week between approval and receipt of the money, try not to wait until the last minute to apply for an emergency loan.

room in a private home. Or consider becoming an RA (which usually offers room and board), working for your school's food service (free board), or living in co-op housing where you prepare your meals as a group. (See "Special Interest Housing," page 134.) Or get together with a bunch of friends and buy food in bulk, which can really cut costs. Working in a restaurant or volunteering in a soup kitchen often gets you free meals during the time you're there.

If you have access to a kitchen, cooking your own food (and buying it with coupons) is much less expensive than dining out—and a bag lunch that you prepare at home will be undoubtedly cheaper, healthier, and tastier than the average cafeteria fare.

Academic Expenses

You can save yourself some money by getting academic credit for off-campus work (including any classes, jobs, or internships related to your fields of study) or for a research position, or by taking summer classes at a less expensive university near you (make sure the credits will transfer). You can also offset school expenses by applying for grants or scholarships to fund special educational projects. (See "Applying for Grants," page 89.) Plus, if you or a family member is an employee of your college/university, you can usually get a tuition break. To save on books, buy them used and sell those you no longer need. Or, when possible, don't buy books at all—borrow them from the library (try a local library if what you need's on reserve at the college library). Another option is getting a job in the student bookstore—often employees get a hefty discount.

Keeping in Touch

Airlines, bus companies, local public transportation authorities, and many travel agencies offer discounts to student travelers. Many schools also have ride boards, where students who have room in their cars and students who need rides can find each other. Make all but local phone calls in the evening or on weekends, or sign up for a discounted calling plan (there are many options available from the various long-distance carriers). If you and your correspondent have computers and modems, take advantage of the free or cheap E-mail accounts that many schools offer. (And there's nothing cooler than surfin' the net.)

Shopping and Leisure

Many stores, organizations, and schools themselves offer student discounts on computers, tickets to events, and other products and services. Garage sales, thrift shops, flea markets, and community swap meets are generally plentiful in places where there are a lot of students. If you're looking for furniture, posters, or clothing, you can find a lot of great stuff free if you wander through the dorms at the end of the year, after everyone has moved his or her stuff out. (The best pickings are usually found in and around senior housing.) And don't forget about good ol' coupons. Just beware of the temptation to buy something you don't really need just because you have a coupon.

There are coupons available from some entertainment venues. Two-for-one coupons are a great way to save money doing something you do all the time or to inspire you to do something you wouldn't ordinarily do. They are found in newspapers and are given out at many establishments, but the best place to find them is in "entertainment" or "value" books, which are usually sold by churches, synagogues, or community groups to raise funds. Flip through the book before you buy to make sure you'll actually take advantage of the offerings. Although there is a fee for the books themselves, your savings may be well over the initial cost.

Seek out free cultural events on and off campus and patronize museums, amusement parks, movie theaters, bowling alleys, and restaurants that offer group or student discounts, and stores that discount sports equipment for school athletes. And finally, volunteer work provides a no-cost way to both have fun and give a little help to your community or favorite cause.

Many colleges have state of the art athletic facilities, the like of which are hard to find in the real world. Use those squash and tennis courts, that pool, and that weight room. Sign up for intramural, club, or varsity sports.

Health Care

It's probably hard to beat the cost of health care at your campus health services. You can usually get free over-the-counter pain relievers, throat lozenges, and cold remedies, substantial discounts on prescriptions

(including those for contraceptive devices), free therapy, and inexpensive gynecological care (including Pap smears and sexually transmitted disease testing). Local clinics and hospitals may also provide health care inexpensively (or on a sliding scale). And you can usually get free condoms, lubricants, and dental dams from health services or safer-sex education programs. (Many religiously affiliated colleges do not provide this service, but there are probably local groups, hospitals, and clinics nearby that do.) Remember, if you have a serious medical emergency, hospital emergency rooms will treat you regardless of your ability to pay. Do not let the fear of looming doctors' bills deter you from seeking medical help if you need it.

GETTING THE MOST FROM YOUR BANK

Keeping your money in a piggy bank on your dresser is certainly simple and convenient, but it's neither the most secure nor the most efficient way to stash your cash. A bank account with checking and/or savings options keeps your money safe but accessible and allows you to write and deposit checks, earn money through interest, and keep track of how much (or little) you've got. And once you have an account, you can call on the bank to obtain financial information or advice, get a credit card, purchase money orders (though they're usually cheaper at the post office), pick up some traveler's checks, rent a safe-deposit box for your valuables, get a certified check, or secure a loan.

TAKE YOUR ACCOUNT WITH YOU

Even if you have a checking account at home, if you are moving to a new place to attend school, it's not a bad idea to open a new account—not only for the convenience of having your bank nearby, but also because many stores will not take out-of-state/city checks. If your current bank has a branch near your school, it might be the best choice. You'll probably be able to transfer funds easily from one account to the other. Alternatively, if you receive a stipend or an allowance at set times during the semester, consider opening an account at a branch of the same bank the provider uses. This would allow funds to be transferred directly into your account, giving you immediate access to your money—you won't have to wait for checks to clear or worry about sending them through the mail.

Shopping for a Bank

Ask around at school for bank recommendations—fellow students are probably your best resource. Visiting banks in your area can be helpful, if you have the time. Pick up brochures and/or speak with customer service representatives. You can also call banks. Ask to speak with a manager—she'll probably tell you more than you'd ever want to know about the benefits of banking with her branch.

Your bank should be convenient—with a branch and/or a 24-hour ATM on or near campus (and/or close to home) and low-cost or free checking accounts. You'll probably find that most banks offer comparable services but that options, requirements, and fees vary. Ask specific questions about the types of accounts and services a bank offers. Take the time to probe enough to uncover any unpublicized fees or restrictions lurking beneath seemingly excellent deals.

All About Accounts

There are two main types of bank accounts: **Checking accounts** offer the convenience of paying "in cash" without having to carry around wads of bills or send cash through the mail. They also provide protection—a canceled check is an indisputable record of payment.

There are two main types of checking accounts. Regular checking accounts generally do not pay interest (and if they do, not only is it a very low rate, but you are required to keep a higher minimum balance). NOW accounts are "limited" checking accounts that pay interest. This means that you will only be allowed to write a certain number of checks a month and must maintain a minimum balance, but in return you'll earn interest. If you don't foresee having to write a large number of checks, and you have enough cash to maintain the minimum balance, this may be a good option. The restrictions are different at each bank, so check yours for details.

The main benefit of **savings accounts** is that they pay interest—athough the rates of interest vary by bank and type of account, all savings accounts offer a return on your money. You can withdraw money, but in most cases you can't write a check on a savings account. Many people keep both checking and savings accounts, and transfer money from the savings to the checking when they need it. The simplest types of savings accounts are passbook and statement. With a passbook account, all transactions and interest payments are recorded in a little book, which serves as your record.

> *"After working all summer to earn money for school, I didn't just put it in a checking or savings account. I bought 60- and 90-day Treasury bills [short-term bonds], which yielded a higher interest rate. It also helped me figure out and stick to a budget because the money wasn't available until the bills came due."*
>
> —UNIVERSITY OF NEBRASKA, '96

In a statement account, you receive an itemized statement every month or quarter in the mail, and you can usually use an ATM to withdraw and deposit money. Another savings option is a money market account, which pays a higher interest rate but usually requires a higher minimum balance. You may be allowed to write a few checks a month against money market accounts. (For more savings options, see page 116.)

Making Sense of Saving Cents

◎◎◎

When assessing banks, ask about special deals and limited-time promotions. Many banks offer student accounts "tailored" to meet your needs that sometimes include reduced fees and/or special benefits. Also ask about the following:

Insurance: Be sure that your bank is a member of the FDIC, which means that your money will be insured up to $100,000.

General fees: Find out what fees you'll encounter (accounting fees, monthly fees, etc.) and the cost of certified checks, money orders, etc.

Charges for transactions: Every written or deposited check and ATM withdrawal is considered a transaction. Some banks don't charge fees for transactions but may charge a monthly fee for the account. Some banks charge you for each transaction. Others charge for every transaction you make over a specified number per month. And some charge only if your balance falls below the required minimum. (*Note*: Even if the account is called "free," the bank may charge per check.) Some banks will charge you if you *don't* write a check or make a withdrawal every so often.

Minimum balance: Some banks require that you maintain a minimum balance in your checking and/or savings account, and will charge you a fee and/or stop interest payments if your balance drops below that amount. Many banks offer free checking privileges if you maintain a (usually pretty high) minimum balance.

☀ How many minutes will you wait in line at the bank? Divide the number

INTERNATIONAL STUDENTS

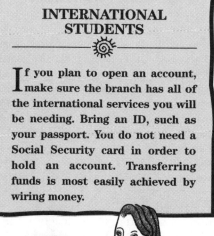

If you plan to open an account, make sure the branch has all of the international services you will be needing. Bring an ID, such as your passport. You do not need a Social Security card in order to hold an account. Transferring funds is most easily achieved by wiring money.

Automatic rollover: Some banks offer "automatic rollover" to their customers who have both savings and checking accounts. This means that if you don't have enough money in your checking account to cover a check, the bank will automatically cover the difference with funds from your savings account. Such accounts often have a fee attached, and the bank will most likely additionally charge you if they roll over funds, but you don't have to worry about the fines, hassles, and risks to your credit rating associated with bouncing checks.

Linked bank accounts (also called "relationship banking"): If you have more than one account at a bank, instead of being required to maintain a minimum balance in each account, the sum total of all accounts may satisfy the minimum balance. This can work to your advantage. If you have both a checking and a savings account, you can keep most of your money in an interest-earning savings account, and transfer funds to your checking account only when necessary.

> "The problem with ATMs is that they make you feel like it's free money. I never realize how much I take out. And no matter how organized I try to be, I usually end up just stuffing my pockets with receipts, never to be found again."
> —KALAMAZOO COLLEGE, '92

ATM (automatic teller machine) cards: Nearly every bank issues ATM cards. You should be able to use the card to get cash or to check your balance at machines of other banks and facilities; most banks require that you make deposits at your own branch, and may charge you a fee for making ATM transactions at other banks. An ATM card is very useful, not only because it's convenient, but also because you can use it to quickly access account information, such as whether that all-important check you deposited has cleared. If your ATM card is lost or stolen, report it to the

of people ahead of you by the number of tellers, then multiply by 2.5.

CAMPUS HIGHLIGHT

—☼—

The women at Scripps College in Pomona, CA, started an investment fund, giving students an opportunity to invest first hand. An alumna of the college gave the school money to help women to learn experientially about investing. The students make decisions about where to invest the money—in which income stocks, bonds, mutual funds, and growth stocks—and then give the profits to fund student groups on campus.

bank immediately. Some banks require that you pick up a new card in person; others will send one out to you in the mail within a few days.

Picking Your PIN

When you get an ATM card, you'll need to select and memorize a Personal Identification Number (PIN). You then use your PIN to access your account. Because the PIN is used to protect you against unauthorized withdrawals from your account, do not use an obvious number, like your birthday, address, phone number, or another number that someone who looks through your wallet could figure out. *Do not* write your PIN on your ATM card or even on a piece of paper in your wallet or datebook. Using a catchy word as your PIN can help you to remember it more easily. However, it is important to be careful here as well. As with obvious numbers, words can be decoded. Don't use your name or that of your pet or school.

Opening an Account

಄಄಄

You will generally have to open an account in person. Call the bank before you go in to be sure you have everything required. In general, you'll need money to deposit (in cash, money order, certified check, or traveler's checks—if your bank accepts a personal check, you will have to wait until the check clears before you can withdraw money); your Social Security number (if you don't have one, you need to call the Social Security office—the number is listed in the phone book); and picture identification (driver's license, passport, or student ID). The bank will have you fill out a signature card, which they'll keep on file to verify that the signature on your checks is, in fact, your own.

Introduce yourself to your new customer service representative, the tellers, and even the branch manager. Being known as a person rather than an account number has its advantages—a manager who knows your face is more likely to cut you some slack when you are in a jam.

Managing a Checking Account

಄಄಄

Each month, your bank will send you a statement listing all the deposits, withdrawals, and checks drawn on your account for the time period, along with any canceled checks. You should read through the statement, marking the checks that have cleared in your checkbook, and making sure that the numbers in your checkbook match those on the statement.

☼   Common bank fees, such as those charged for checking and

(Remember, if you wrote or deposited checks that haven't cleared by the time the statement was sent, you should take that into account when calculating the amount of money you have at your disposal.)

It's vital to save your statements, cleared checks, and deposit slips for tax purposes and for your protection. Some day you may find that you have a need to prove that you paid a bill or deposited money in your account. If you detect an error on your bank statement, contact your bank immediately (though you will usually be able to correct the error well after it is detected if you have evidence).

"I keep all of my receipts and ATM statements until after I've received my bank statement—then I check everything off. The hassle of keeping them far outweighs the misery I would face by throwing them away before it's time."

—SCRIPPS COLLEGE, '94

Stand up for yourself if an error occurs with any of your accounts. You can get erroneous bank fees repealed by speaking with a teller or customer service representative.

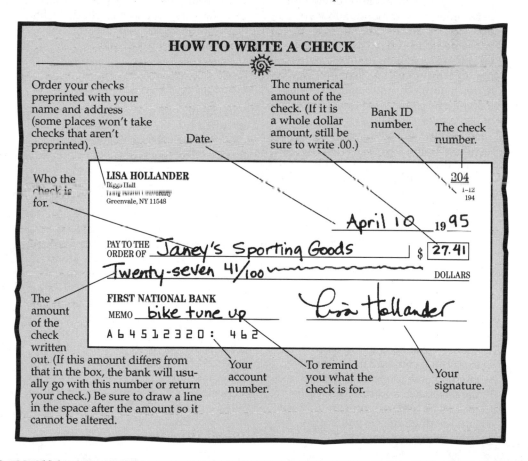

HOW TO WRITE A CHECK

Order your checks preprinted with your name and address (some places won't take checks that aren't preprinted).

The numerical amount of the check. (If it is a whole dollar amount, still be sure to write .00.)

Bank ID number.

The check number.

Date.

Who the check is for.

LISA HOLLANDER
Riggs Hall
Long Island University
Greenvale, NY 11548

204
1–12
194

April 10 19 95

PAY TO THE ORDER OF Janey's Sporting Goods $ 27.41

Twenty-seven 41/100 DOLLARS

FIRST NATIONAL BANK
MEMO bike tune up

Lisa Hollander

A 6 4 5 1 2 3 2 0 : 4 6 2

The amount of the check written out. (If this amount differs from that in the box, the bank will usually go with this number or return your check.) Be sure to draw a line in the space after the amount so it cannot be altered.

Your account number.

To remind you what the check is for.

Your signature.

ATM transactions, can vary up to 100% from bank to bank.

Writing Checks

By writing a check, you are stating that you have sufficient funds in your account to cover the amount of your purchase. And although it might take a few days for your account to reflect the debit, you no longer have access to that money. If you don't have enough money in your account, your checks will bounce.

Many places will ask for identification when you write a check. You'll probably need to show a picture ID with your signature (like a driver's license, passport, or school ID), a credit card, and/or an ATM card, and provide your address and phone number. Some places may not allow you to use a check unless you show a check guarantee card, which you can get at your bank when you open your checking account—they are usually free, so it never hurts to have one. An establishment may also wish to keep names of customers with check-writing privileges on file, and require that you fill out a form and receive a special card before they'll accept your checks. If you realize that you don't have enough money in your account to cover a check, you can ask the person or place to whom you wrote the check to wait until you have deposited money in your account to cash it, or, if agreed upon, you can postdate the check. In addition:

▲ Write all checks in pen.
▲ Write the amount clearly.
▲ If you make a correction on a check, initialize it so the bank knows it's you, and not someone changing the amount. If there is an illegal change and the bank cashes the check, the bank must reimburse you the difference if you notify them within a year.

▲ A signature that resembles chicken scratchings is much easier to forge than one that has well-defined letters. Take the extra second to pen something legible.
▲ Keep your checkbook up to date.

Cashing Checks

If you want to cash a check, you must either go to your bank or the bank where the check writer has his or her account, or pay a fee at a place that offers check-cashing services. If you don't have a bank account and you don't mind waiting for your money, you can sign the check over to a friend, then he can deposit the check in his account, and pay you the amount in cash after the check clears.

Depositing Checks

You can deposit checks by mail, at one of your bank's ATMs, or in person. You must fill out a deposit slip, available at banks, ATM machines, or in the back of your checkbook. Use a pen, and make sure that any carbon copies are legible. When making a deposit in person or at an ATM machine, be sure to get a receipt. (In most cases, if you deposit your checks by mail, a receipt will be mailed to you.) It's smart to write "For Deposit Only" on the check (so even if you misplace it, there's no chance someone pretending to be you could cash it) and you must endorse it by signing your name on the reverse side. Remember, depending on your bank and that of the check writer, it may take up to a week after you deposit a check in your account before you have access to the money. Out-of-state checks usually take longer to clear than in-state ones.

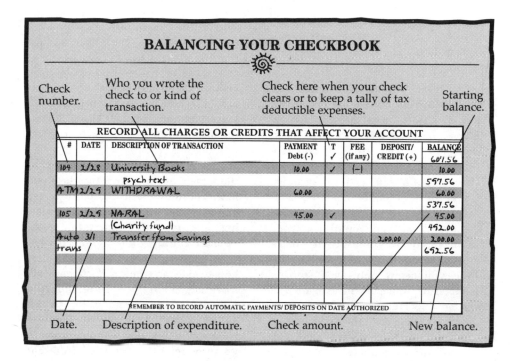

BALANCING YOUR CHECKBOOK

Check number.

Who you wrote the check to or kind of transaction.

Check here when your check clears or to keep a tally of tax deductible expenses.

Starting balance.

#	DATE	DESCRIPTION OF TRANSACTION	PAYMENT Debt (-)	T ✓	FEE (if any)	DEPOSIT/ CREDIT (+)	BALANCE
		RECORD ALL CHARGES OR CREDITS THAT AFFECT YOUR ACCOUNT					607.56
104	2/28	University Books	10.00	✓	(−)		10.00
		psych text					597.56
ATM	2/29	WITHDRAWAL	60.00				60.00
							537.56
105	2/29	NARAL	45.00	✓			45.00
		(Charity fund)					492.00
Auto trans	3/1	Transfer from Savings				200.00	200.00
							692.56

REMEMBER TO RECORD AUTOMATIC PAYMENTS/ DEPOSITS ON DATE AUTHORIZED

Date.   Description of expenditure.   Check amount.   New balance.

Bouncing Checks

Bouncing checks costs more than a bit of embarrassment: The bank may levy fees against both you and the party to whom you wrote the check, regardless of the check's size. If you do it too often, the bank may place limits on your account and cause credit problems for you. (See "The Value of Good Credit," page 124.) In addition to being slapped with a fee, the person or place to whom you wrote the check does not receive payment and usually faces a fee from their bank. Thus many stores will charge a penalty fee and/or revoke your check-writing privileges if you bounce a check. But if you handle the problem quickly and responsibly, you may redeem yourself.

> *"One thing you should never, ever do is bounce a check in your school bookstore. I did it as a first-year student and they didn't let me write a check again for an entire year.*
>
> *—AURORA UNIVERSITY, '93*

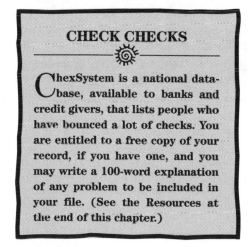

CHECK CHECKS

ChexSystem is a national database, available to banks and credit givers, that lists people who have bounced a lot of checks. You are entitled to a free copy of your record, if you have one, and you may write a 100-word explanation of any problem to be included in your file. (See the Resources at the end of this chapter.)

1,492 times and write 15,224 checks, 152 of which will bounce. ✸

INVESTING YOUR MONEY

Contrary to popular opinion, you don't need to be an economics major with a large pile of cash to invest. If you happen to have some extra money, there are many opportunities that can give you a higher return than a plain old savings account. Unlike bank accounts, however, most investments are not guaranteed, meaning that you could lose your savings. For this reason, if you're interested in investing, use the information below only as a starting point from which to investigate the myriad opportunities available. Read up on investing (see the Resources at this end of the chapter) and seek advice from a reputable, trusted advisor. As a general rule, the greater the potential return on your money, the more risky the investment.

Some investment options include:

CERTIFICATES OF DEPOSIT (CDS): CDs pay a fixed interest rate for a set amount of time. The rate is higher than those paid out by savings accounts, but you must deposit a larger amount than is required for most savings accounts, and the bank will stick you with a penalty fee if you withdraw any money before the end of the fixed term. In general, the higher the balance and the longer the term of the CD, the higher the interest rate.

MUTUAL FUNDS: Mutual funds pool the money of many investors into one large account, which is used to invest in a variety of stocks and bonds, creating a "diversified portfolio." The account is run by a professional manager who, presumably, knows the markets inside and out and chooses his investments wisely. By investing in a mutual fund you may not make as much as if you invested in the stock of one company, but you also don't have as great a potential for loss. Different funds hold different risks, and you'll need to choose the risk group you want your account to be in. Most banks sell mutual fund shares, but they may also be obtained through firms registered with the Securities Exchange Commission (SEC).

STOCKS/BONDS (INCLUDING SAVINGS BONDS): If you have quite a bit of money (around $5,000 or so) that you'd like to earn higher interest on, most commercial banks offer services

Lost or Stolen Checks

If your checkbook is stolen, you will not be held responsible for any checks written against your account as long as you alert your bank immediately. It is the bank's obligation to verify your signature against the one it keeps on file before cashing any check. If you notify your bank (usually within one year) of a forged check you found on your statement, your bank must take the loss. If you lose a check that someone wrote to you, notify the person immediately and ask her to stop payment on it and write you a new one. (It

to help you get involved in stocks and/or bonds. When you purchase a stock, you are buying shares of ownership in a company. Your shares then either increase or decrease in value depending upon the performance of the company—and you then benefit or suffer accordingly. For some stocks, if the company continually prospers, you will be paid money, or dividends, while maintaining your shares in the company. If the company does poorly, the stock does, too, and you stand to lose your investment.

With a bond, you are essentially loaning money to a company (or the government). In turn, either you are paid specified amounts of money (called coupons) at specified times of the year, or you receive the entire principal amount plus interest at the end of the term of the loan. The value of bonds changes with economic indices.

If your bank does not offer these services, you need to hook up with a broker affiliated with the (SEC), New York Stock Exchange (NYSE), and/or National Association of Securities Dealers (NASD). You can usually get a free consultation. However, be aware that you usually have to pay a broker whether or not you make money.

may be embarrassing, but it's important for your sake and hers.)

Stopping Checks

If a check you wrote is lost, you accidentally wrote a check for the same goods or service twice (i.e., you paid a bill twice because you were sent a second notice and you weren't keeping track), or you wrote a check to a party who did not perform the service you both agreed upon, *and* the check hasn't yet been cashed, you can prevent it from being cashed by asking the bank to stop payment. Most banks charge for this service. You'll need to know the check number, how much it was for, who it was made out to, and the date (another good reason to keep your checkbook in order). Be sure to warn the payee, in writing, that you are canceling the check, to avoid confusion and hassles when your check doesn't clear.

THE LOWDOWN ON CREDIT CARDS

Unlike checks, where you're using money that you have in an account, when you use credit and charge cards, you are essentially taking out a loan. The credit issuer "lends" you money for your purchases, which you must pay back either at once in full, or over a period of time, with interest (and usually very high interest at that).

Credit cards serve multiple purposes. They allow you to buy on credit, build a credit rating, purchase items by mail, and rent a car, and they may serve as a form of identification. It's a smart idea to begin building credit while you are still in school, and not too difficult, as credit card companies are vying for student membership. You will probably be offered a credit card application or two at the beginning of every term. Solicitors frequently station themselves outside of campus bookstores, registration offices, and dining halls, hoping to enlist us while we're young and gain our lifetime loyalty. You may also receive myriad offers in the mail. Typically, they say that you have been "preapproved" for the card, with a line of credit already set aside for your use. They often push you to accept quickly, "before it's too late."

Generally speaking, students with a valid ID from a four-year college or graduate school and a savings or checking account don't need a job, a minimum income, or a credit history to get a credit card, but requirements among banks and credit card companies vary.

If you can't or don't want to get a card on your own, you may be able to apply for a joint card with someone who has a good credit history (often a parent). The account will list both your and the other person's name—thus, if you are delinquent in your payments, the cosigner is responsible. The bills will still be sent to them, and the account will remain in their name; however, your card will have your name on it. (This is probably not a good idea if you'll be in perpetual struggle with the cosigner over how much money you spend or who is responsible for which payments. It also won't help you establish credit in your own name.)

Although many of the offers may seem attractive, remember that no credit card issuer would be foolish enough to create a deal for its customers that wasn't of benefit to itself. Issuers receive up to 5 percent of the cost of your purchase from the merchant for any transaction. (Some people avoid charging small purchases at places they care about, because writing a check or using cash saves the store money.) Although credit card companies derive an ample portion of their assets in this manner, late-payment fees and interest charges bring in a pretty penny, too. Avoid lining their pockets with your hard-earned cash by paying off balances on time and in full each month. (See "Avoiding the Credit Card Blues," page 124.)

Types of Cards

ᥫᩚᥫᩚᥫᩚ

Though they are all commonly called credit cards, there are slight differences between credit cards (Visa, MasterCard, Discover, and Optima), travel and entertainment (T&E) cards (American Express, Diners Club, or Carte Blanche), and charge cards. **Credit cards** are issued by either a bank or a credit card corporation. Even if you get your card through a bank, it is not necessary to have an account there. With credit cards, you are required to pay only a small percentage of your total bill each month, but you will be charged an extremely high interest rate (up to 20 percent a year) on the unpaid balance. **T&E cards** require payment in full each month. (If you don't pay your bill for a couple of months, the card company will freeze your credit, though if you call and inform them that "the check is in the mail," they'll usually free it up.)

Charge cards, issued by a specific store or gas station, can only be used to purchase the issuing company's products. Even if you don't regularly shop in one of the department stores or gas stations that have their own card, consider getting one, as you may get special bonuses or discounts (like 10 percent off on the first purchase) and improve your credit rating at the same

☀ 82% of college students carry at least one credit card. ☀

time. Just make sure that the card doesn't carry a minimum purchase requirement or a monthly or annual fee.

Though they look like credit cards, **debit cards** are more like plastic checks (without the time lag checks have). When you pay for something with a debit card, the amount is immediately deducted from your bank account. If you've used an ATM card to make a purchase, you've essentially used a debit card.

Shopping for a Credit Card

ᘉᘉᘉ

Before selecting a card, take the time to read carefully the fine print to learn what terms and conditions apply, as each one affects the ultimate cost of the credit you are issued. Also consider how you plan to use the card. If you intend to pay bills in full each month, it may be smarter to go with a card with a low or no annual fee rather than a low interest rate. On the other hand, if you expect to use credit cards to pay for purchases over time, the annual percentage rate should play more significantly in your decision.

Annual fees: Many credit card issuers charge annual fees, ranging from $15 to $75, or even higher for Gold or Platinum cards. Cards that offer free miles, or other special benefits can cost extra, too. Try to find a card with no annual fee. As a come-on, many card companies waive the fee for the first year; ask what it'll be the next year (unless you plan to cancel the card after a year).

Other fees: The card company may also stick you with transaction fees if you take cash advances on your card, late-payment fees if your payment's even just a day past due, and fees for exceeding your credit limit. You also might be required to pay a fee or a minimum amount each month whether or not you use the card. Ask about these.

Annual Percentage Rate (APR): The APR is the amount of interest you have to pay on any outstanding balance per year. The card issuer charges you a percentage of your unpaid balance in return for extending you credit. Some APRs are fixed, meaning they stay the same despite the economy; others are variable, meaning they change in accordance with certain economic indices. Rates vary drastically between cards, usually falling somewhere between 13 and 24 percent.

Convenience: Find a card that has an excellent reputation and is widely accepted. Even if a card has low fees, high limits, and great benefits, it won't be of much use if no one accepts it.

Customer service: Make sure the company provides a 24-hour toll-free number for questions, cancellations, and speedy replacement of lost or stolen cards.

Credit limit: Credit card companies limit the amount you can charge on the card, and many impose a fee if you exceed the limit. This credit limit (usually between $250 and $500 for first-

CHARGING THOSE SKY-HIGH EXPENSES

⟡

The one (and perhaps only) good thing about the high cost of college is that if you charge your tuition on one of those credit cards that gives you frequent-flier miles for every dollar you spend, you may very well get a free round-trip ticket each year. And if you charge your loan payments, books, and room and board, you'll be able to pop in on your grandma in Sydney, Taiwan, or Bali. But be sure to pay off your balance in full as soon as you get the bill—otherwise, high interest rates will make the cost of school even more astronomical. In some cases you can pay by credit card and then use loan money to pay the bill immediately. Talk to the school bursar's office for more information.

time cardholders) protects both you and the credit card company from having to face the repercussions of a boundless spending frenzy. If you charge as close to the credit limit as possible without going over each month and pay the bill on time in full, your credit limit will increase, which will improve your credit rating. It's a good idea to keep track of how much you charge each month, as you would with a checking account, in order to avoid going over your limit, as well as to check your monthly bill for errors.

Grace period: The time between when you make a purchase and when your payment is due is called the grace period. It's also called the "free period," as you aren't charged interest on the amount (although if you have any outstanding balance at all, many cards *will* charge interest on new purchases. Thus the "free period" may really only be free to those who start the billing cycle with a zero balance). If there is no grace period, the card issuer will begin calculating your APR from the date you use your credit card or from the date each credit card transaction is charged to your account.

Special services: Many card companies provide special services to card members, such as increased warranty on purchases; replacement of lost, stolen, or damaged purchases; additional flight or rental car insurance; price protection (if you find an item you bought being sold for less within 60 days of purchase, and you can produce an ad or price quote to prove it, the card company will reimburse you the price difference); and replacement of a lost or stolen card in a day or two. Other programs offer benefits like frequent-flier miles or long-distance telephone credits, special deals on hotel rooms and car rentals, cash advances, discounts on computers, or donation of a percentage of your total bill to charitable organizations. These programs often charge an annual fee. Make sure that your benefits substantially surpass any fees, because if you rarely make long-distance calls, don't drive, or are acrophobic (and therefore refuse to fly), these deals may not be so great.

⟡ In 1989, 71.3% of students said their number 1 reason for go-

Plastic Protection

☙☙☙

Credit card fraud is pretty common. The following should help you keep track of your credit card expenditures and avoid financing another person's shopping binge.

Basic Tips

■ Save your credit card receipts until your bill/statement arrives so that you can check your purchases against the statement.

■ Report lost or stolen cards right away. (See "If Your Card Is Lost or Stolen," on the next page.)

■ Never give out your credit card number to unknown telephone solicitors.

■ Correct billing errors immediately. (In general, you need to alert the company of the mistake, in writing, within 60 days.)

■ If you cancel your card within 40 days of your receipt of the statement that contains the charge for the annual fee, you do not have to pay the fee. (You *do* have to pay the charges made on the card, of course.)

■ For added protection, you can now obtain a card with your picture on it. But, as they say, if you look anything like your credit card picture, you're probably too sick to shop.

■ Sign a new card the moment you receive it.

When Making Purchases in Person

■ If a store uses a "manual slide" machine to record credit card sales, make sure that either you or the salesperson rips up the carbons so the numbers are no longer legible and throws them away after the sale is completed. The same goes for any receipts with your card numbers on them.

■ When making a purchase, double check that the clerk charges you the right amount.

■ By law, you do not need to provide your address or phone number when charging in person. You may need to show a form of identification, but the salesperson should only need to note what form of ID you presented, not the information contained on the ID.

■ After you make a purchase, be sure that the salesperson hands you your card back. In other words, "don't leave the store without it."

READ THE MOUSE TYPE

The fine print on the back of your monthly credit card statements lays out your rights as a cardholder. You'll find information about how to report a missing card; refuse payment to places that did not provide you with the goods and/or services for which you've been charged; obtain a refund for merchandise you purchased with the card and then returned; take advantage of the extended warranty and protection against lost, stolen, or defective merchandise that many card companies offer; and report and rectify a possible billing error. You are entitled to have the payments you make credited to your account promptly.

■ Draw a line through any blank spaces above the total when you sign receipts.

■ Unless it is mandatory (as when you rent a car), never sign a blank receipt.

When Making Purchases by Mail

If you use your credit card to pay for mail order or phone purchases, it's especially important to keep an eye on your monthly statements to ensure that all the charges are valid. Orders can get mixed up, and though problems are rare when dealing with reputable companies, there is always a risk that your number will fall into the wrong hands when you give out your credit card information.

If You Detect a Billing Error

ගගග

If you detect either unauthorized purchases or billing errors, call your card issuer immediately. (The number to call will be printed on the back of your statement). After calling, send a backup letter stating the problem, the dates of both the bill and the call you made, the name of the person you spoke with, and what was resolved. This will give you recourse in case something goes wrong.

If Your Card Is Lost or Stolen

ගගග

It is important to keep a record of all your credit card numbers and expiration dates in one safe place (obviously not in the wallet or purse you carry the cards in), as well as the numbers to call to cancel the cards. This way, you'll have everything you need if your card is lost or stolen. Report a missing card to the company immediately. The vast majority of card companies have 24-hour toll-free numbers for this purpose. If someone takes your card for a spending spree before you cancel the card, the company can legally hold you responsible for the first $50 charged, but in most cases it won't. To be extra safe, you may also want to send a letter to the card company confirming the cancellation.

Once you cancel your credit card, the card is no longer usable. If you find the card, cut it up so the numbers are illegible, and throw it out. Once you receive a new card, be sure to notify any places that automatically bill to your card of your new number.

Drowning in a Sea of Plastic

ගගග

"I thought I was in good shape—I paid the minimum on my credit card each month, and didn't really worry about the interest—it was less than 2 percent each month. But that added up to a lot over the course of a year. If I had gotten a T&E card, rather than a credit card, I would have been required to pay the entire bill each month, and would have avoided this big mess."

—SARAH LAWRENCE COLLEGE, '91

One of the most common financial woes of college students is discovering the hidden trap of credit cards. Many a woman has thought all was well in financeville, diligently keeping up with her minimum credit card payments only to discover that the account balance on the card was slowly but surely growing out of control. In an effort to regain financial stability, she focuses attention on paying off the balance, to the neglect of other bills, and late-payment fees begin to pile up. Then the angry letters from the phone company arrive, and she finds herself totally frazzled and overwhelmed.

If you find that your credit card balance becomes unmanageable (or if you are unable to make loan and/or bill payments), there are things you can do to reduce the potential damage to your credit rating and your stress level while still maintaining some level of financial independence.

■ Whatever your situation, contact your creditors as soon as you realize there is a problem. Try to work out an adjusted payment plan that will reduce your payments to a more manageable level.

■ Do not wait until your account is turned over to a debt collector. If you thought the creditor was hounding you, just wait and see what debt collectors do.

■ Cut up your charge card.

■ Put in ghost payments (see "Avoiding the Credit Card Blues," on the next page).

■ The old trick of paying off a credit card debt with another credit card can be the kiss of death. Don't be tempted.

"I made the mistake of living off my charge card for a year, paying for everything with 18 percent interest tacked on.... I tried paying the minimum on the bill but it never seemed to end. After the bank started calling, I had them turn my case over to a collection agency. They set me up on a payment schedule and interest on the overdue bill stopped accruing. I was so ashamed of my financial problems, but I didn't need to feel that way."

—UNIVERSITY OF ROCHESTER, '92

Help Is on the Way!

෨෨෨

Consumer Credit Counseling Services (CCCS), as well as other nonprofit programs at universities and credit unions, offer assistance to those who are having difficulty dealing with debt, at little or no cost. They provide help by dealing with creditors, working out payment plans that suit all the parties involved, and advising you on setting up a budget and regaining control of your finances. It's a good idea to shop around for the best service in your community—the quality of assistance provided varies greatly from agency to agency. Before signing on at one of the "credit repair" services, check them out by calling the CCCS, the Better Business Bureau, or another consumer protection organization. (For more information, see the Resources at the end of this chapter.)

list of their concerns; 67% said money was the top issue.

AVOIDING THE
CREDIT CARD BLUES

If used responsibly, credit cards can offer convenience, consumer protection, and an opportunity to build your credit rating. However, between the fees, the deceptively low interest rates, and "benefits" with strings attached, they can send you into debt faster than you can say "compounded interest." Below are some tips and tricks for escaping being crushed under a plastic avalanche.

▲ Beware of deals and options that seem too good to be true—they usually are. For example, many card companies "allow" you to defer payments for a month or two (most often right after the winter holidays). What they don't tell you is that they won't stop charging you interest during that time.

▲ Don't be fooled by what appear to be low monthly interest rates. You pay compounded interest on credit cards. Every month interest will be computed and added to your monthly balance. The next month interest will

be computed on the principal plus the interest already accrued, and so on. In effect, you'll be paying interest on your interest.

▲ Beware of the minimum-payment option. Aim to pay the entire bill each month, or at least as much as you possibly can.

▲ You don't necessarily have to wait until you get a statement to pay. Make ghost payments (money given between the specified due dates) to save on interest if your card has no grace period or if you have an outstanding balance on your card. In other words, because interest rates are so high, making payments to reduce your debt, no matter how small, can go a long way toward saving you money.

▲ Read the fine print. Seemingly insignificant differences in grace periods, interest rates, and fees can add up to a pretty penny over the course of a year or so.

▲ If you can't manage your debt, get help ASAP.

THE VALUE OF GOOD CREDIT

Your credit rating is an evaluation of how responsible you have been with money matters. It is a determination of how credit worthy you are, based on information about your present financial situation (bank

accounts, loans, credit limits on cards) and how responsibly you've upheld financial obligations in the past (loan, bill, and credit card payments, bounced checks). You'll need a good credit rating to rent an apartment, borrow money, or lease a car.

It's important to establish credit in your name. Traditionally, all of a family's money matters and credit information would be recorded under the male head of the household's name. This made it very difficult for women to assume financial independence. Single women often had to fight to get credit and married women found themselves in financial limbo upon separation, divorce, or widowhood. If you share financial responsibilities, or have a joint bank or credit card account with a husband, a partner, or another family member, under the Equal Credit Opportunity Act you can insist that all credit information be listed under both your names. There are a number of things that you can do to both establish and maintain a good credit rating: Get and use a credit card or store charge card; make sure that you don't drop below the minimum balance required on your bank accounts; do not bounce checks; and make your loan and bill payments on time.

> **"If you need to take out loans, see if you can do it in your name because if you pay your loan back, your credit rating will improve."**
> —UNIVERSITY OF THE PACIFIC, '92

There are three national credit bureaus (TRW, Equifax, and Trans Union) and over 1,000 local bureaus that keep credit records and provide the information upon request. Your credit report keeps track of your payments on credit cards, installment loans, and other credit accounts. Credit reports include your credit card information for up to three years back and show any late payments you made on a loan (30 days, 60 days, and 90 days past due) even if you eventually paid, and any outstanding loans and/or bills and sometimes any checks you bounced. Credit report

updates happen very slowly. Profoundly negative episodes in your financial past, such as bankruptcy, that you'd rather soon forget can remain on your record for as long as ten years. If unfavorable information about your credit history is correct but you have a reasonable explanation for it, you have the right to send a very brief letter of clarification to the credit bureau to be included in your report.

You are allowed one free credit search a year from TRW (the cost of additional searches depends on the state you live in), and the two other credit bureaus charge less than $10. If you've been denied credit, employment, or insurance within the last 60 days (and have a letter to prove it), they are always free.

For a copy of your report, send a request to a local bureau; it should include your Social Security number, present and past addresses, birthdate, a copy of a utility bill or driver's license to verify your address, and all the names you've ever used. You should also ask them to send a correction form with your report, in case you find an error in the information.

The credit bureau is required to investigate disputable items on your credit report as long as they're not frivolous. Be aware, though, that they take their time when correcting inaccurate information. Thus, problems that were resolved may not yet appear as such on your report. Warn anyone receiving your report of the potential discrepancy.

Creditors consider your credit report with other

factors such as your salary, collateral, and the credit rating of your cosigner, if you have one. If a bank or another company turns down your application (for a loan, credit card, apartment, etc.) because of bad credit, you are entitled to a written statement explaining why, including a list of the credit bureaus or any other places from which they obtained information that affected their decision.

TAXES—APRIL *IS* THE CRUELEST MONTH

Once a year in April, every tax-worthy American must pay his or her dues to the Internal Revenue Service (IRS). It is not a time we relish—and no wonder, since federal and state taxes may claim a nice chunk of our incomes. Plus, because each state has its own tax forms and regulations, the federal ones aren't exactly simple to understand, and tax laws are in perpetual flux, finding out whether we need to file, what we need to report, and what we may deduct can be as painful as writing the check to the IRS. (To find how to get the most current information regarding taxes, see the Resources at the end of this chapter.)

Tax Tips

§§§

■ You may need to file even if you don't hold a steady job. Baby-sitting revenue, investment returns, and interest on money in your name all count as earnings.

■ To facilitate filing, you'll need to save your receipts of expenses (such as medical bills and charitable donations) and earnings (including investment returns and interest payments).

■ If someone else is filling out your forms and you suspect he is doing so incorrectly, don't sign. Seek a second opinion. You are responsible for the validity of the information given on the forms, even if you do not prepare your own return. Therefore, go over your returns carefully and completely.

■ Tax forms must be postmarked by April 15, or an extension must be filed.

■ If you meet certain criteria and can provide the appropriate verification, you may be able to take a tax deduction for charitable donations, job-related moving expenses, or tuition.

■ Some forms of financial aid may be taxable, while some portion of tuition costs and/or loan repayments may be tax-deductible. The financial aid office should have all the details.

ACTIVIST IDEAS

■ Take an economics class—learn about the bigger picture so that you can make informed decisions about savings and investments.

■ Put your money where your mouth is. Patronize places with pleasing politics. Find out if a company's political action committee supports candidates, legislation, and movements that you like/don't like through the *Boycott News* newsletter, Standard & Poor's listings, and political action committee reports.

■ Use the memo section of your check to express your political views. Write "Pro-Choice" or "Vote for So-and-so." Your check will pass through a few hands. Why not have it do some campaigning?

■ Buy food and household products in bulk with your friends to save money and, because you're avoiding unnecessary packaging, the environment.

RESOURCES

Consumer Protection

You can find your local Consumer Protection Office by looking in your phone book under one or more of the following: "State/City Government," "Attorney General," "Consumer Protection Agency," "County Attorney's Office," "Department of Consumer Affairs," "Consumer Protection Division," "Consumer Fraud Division," or "Consumer Affairs Unit."

To find out the scoop on businesses and companies or to file complaints, contact one of the following two organizations:

FEDERAL TRADE COMMISSION
BUREAU OF CONSUMER PROTECTION
OFFICE OF CONSUMER AND BUSINESS
   EDUCATION
WASHINGTON, DC 20580
(202) 326-3650
Makes referrals to local consumer protection agencies. You can also find the federal trade commission of your state, county, and city government by looking under state/city/government agencies in your phone book. These offices provide assistance in dealing with complaints against businesses. Many offices investigate and work to resolve problems with local businesses.

COUNCIL OF BETTER BUSINESS BUREAUS, INC.
NATIONAL HEADQUARTERS
4200 WILSON BOULEVARD
ARLINGTON, VA 22203
(703) 276-0100
Makes referrals to local Better Business Bureaus. Accepts complaints against businesses.

To find the local office, look in your phone book under "Better Business Bureau." These offices provide general information on products, services, reliability, and previous complaints filed against local businesses. They also work to mediate and resolve complaints filed by consumers.

CONSUMER INFORMATION CENTER
CATALOG
PUEBLO, CO 81009
(719) 948-4000
Provides information about all areas of consumer protection. Send a postcard with your name and address on it to obtain a

free copy of their Consumer Information Catalog.

THE FEDERAL INFORMATION CENTER (FIC)

P.O. BOX 600
CUMBERLAND, MD 21502
(301) 722-9000
TTY/TDD: (800) 326-2996

Provides information about all federal government services, programs, and regulations, including those dealing with money and housing. Makes referrals to the federal agency which can best assist you and to state FIC offices. Publishes numerous materials, available upon request.

To find your state FIC, look in the phone book under "State Government" or "Federal Government" Agencies—they are usually toll-free numbers.

Banking

OFFICE OF CONSUMER AFFAIRS
FEDERAL DEPOSIT INSURANCE CORPORATION (FDIC)

550 17TH STREET NW
ROOM F-130
WASHINGTON, DC 20429
(202) 898-6777
(800) 424-5488

Provides information, answers questions about banking, and addresses complaints about FDIC-insured banks. Provides information about FDIC-insured and state-chartered banks and their compliance with consumer laws and the Truth-in-Lending Act. You can also acquire this information by contacting a local FDIC-insured bank, regional office. Publishes numerous materials about ways to protect yourself and make wise investments.

State Banking Authorities

You can find your local banking authority by looking in your phone book under one or more of the following: "State Government Agencies," "State Bank Commissioner," "State Comptroller," "Department of Banking and Finance," "Commissioner of Banks."

Low-Cost Checks

If you don't get free checks with your checking account, consider purchasing them from a private company which generally sells checks for less than banks do. Two of these companies are:

CURRENTS, INC.

(800) 533-3973

CHECKS IN THE MAIL

(800) 733-4443

Credit Cards

BANKCARD HOLDERS OF AMERICA

560 HERDON PARKWAY, SUITE 120
HERNDON, VA 22070
(800) 553-8025

Provides educational information, including listings of the lowest rate and nonfee credit card companies, and listings of banks that have no annual fees. Offers a computerized credit card payment plan to help deal with debt in the most efficient way possible.

VISA USA

(800) 847-2511 800 [VISA-511]

Provides free information on credit card fraud and credit management.

CREDIT CARD AND COMPUTER FRAUD
OFFICE OF INVESTIGATION
U.S. SECRET SERVICE

U.S. DEPARTMENT OF THE TREASURY
1800 G STREET NW
WASHINGTON, DC 20223
(202) 435-6100

Accepts complaints and conducts investigations about the fraudulent use of credit cards, ATM cards, telephone cards, as well as other types of computer access fraud.

Consumer Reporting Agencies

There are numerous consumer reporting agencies, which conduct credit checks for individuals and companies. If someone has conducted a credit check on you, find out what agency conducted the check to get their specific report and/or to file any complaints. The three main national agencies are listed below.

TRW
P.O. Box 2350
Chatsworth, CA 91313-2350
(800) 682-7654

Trans Union
P.O. Box 390
Springfield, MA 19064-0390
(800) 851-2674

Equifax
P.O. Box 105873
Atlanta, GA 30348
(800) 685-1111

Dealing with Debt

National Foundation for Consumer Credit
8701 Georgia Avenue, Suite 507
Silver Spring, MD 20901
(301) 589-5600
(800) 388-2227
Makes referrals to local Consumer Credit Counseling Services. Local offices provide low-cost assistance and counseling to help individuals manage debt and develop repayment plans.

You can also locate such services by looking in the white/yellow pages of your phone book under "Credit" or "Credit Reporting Agencies."

Federal Trade Commission
Debt Collection Practices
Federal Trade Commission
Washington, DC 20580
Enforces the Fair Debt Collection Practices Act. Write a letter to this agency to report any problems or complaints with debt collectors.

In addition, most states have their own laws about fair debt collection; contact the state attorney's office to find out the local laws and to report any problems.

Tax Assistance

Local post offices serve as the central distributor for federal and state income tax forms and information packets and brochures. For a more thorough understanding of tax law, consult your local library.

Internal Revenue Service (IRS)
(800) 829-1040
TTY/TDD: (800) 829-4059
If you call the 800 numbers above, a representative should be able to provide information and answer any questions regarding tax forms, requirements, filing, and all tax-related issues. Or contact your local IRS office listed in the front of your phone book in the blue pages under the section "U.S. Government Agencies," "Internal Revenue Service." Your state will also have an Internal Revenue Service, listed in the phone book under the section "State Government Agencies." However, telephone inquiry lines are often more trouble than they're worth. It is not uncommon to be put on hold for half an hour, only to be frustrated by their incapacity to answer your questions. Make sure to write down the date and full name of the person who helps you, in case you have any problems or further questions.

greater than getting a royal straight flush in an opening poker deal.

IRS PUBLICATIONS
(800) 329-3676
Publishes numerous free materials and information about taxes, including *Publication 4: The Student's Guide to Federal Income Tax*. All information is available free upon request.

IRS DIRECTOR OF PRACTICE
1111 CONSTITUTION AVENUE NW
WASHINGTON, DC 20224
Provides a copy of your tax return (if you have not received it automatically).

Professional Tax Assistance

AMERICAN INSTITUTE OF CERTIFIED PUBLIC ACCOUNTANTS
(800) 862-4722
Provides a list of CPAs in your area.

NATIONAL ASSOCIATION OF ENROLLED AGENTS
(800) 424-4339
Provides a list of enrolled agents in your area.

Information on Investing Bonds

U.S. SAVINGS BONDS DIVISION
TREASURY DEPARTMENT
WASHINGTON, DC 20226
(800) 487-2663
Publishes information and answers questions about bonds. Provides information about current savings bonds interest rates, in addition to other information.

Mutual Funds

INVESTMENT COMPANY INSTITUTE
NATIONAL TRADE ORGANIZATION FOR MUTUAL FUNDS
P.O. BOX 27850
WASHINGTON, DC 20038-7850
Publishes numerous materials on mutual funds. Write to the above address to request a catalog of public publications.

Stocks, Securities, or Commodities

NATIONAL ASSOCIATION OF SECURITY DEALERS (NASD)
OPERATIONS CENTER
9513 KEY WEST AVENUE
ROCKVILLE, MD 20850-3389
PUBLIC DISCLOSURE PHONE CENTER: (800) 289–9999
Provides information on NASD Firms, any complaints filed against organizations. Publishes numerous materials about investing, including *Investing Wisely*; available upon request.

NEW YORK STOCK EXCHANGE (NYSE)
11 WALL STREET
NEW YORK, NY 10005
(212) 656-3000
Publishes numerous materials about stocks and investments, including *The Investors Information Kit*, available upon request.

Further Reading

Making the Most of Your Money, Quinn, Jane Bryant (Simon & Schuster, 1991).
The Wall Street Journal Guide to Understanding Money & Investing, Morris, Kenneth M. and Alan M. Siegel (Fireside, 1993).
The Wall Street Journal Guide to Understanding Personal Finance, Morris, Kenneth M. (Fireside, 1993).

Financial Magazines
Forbes, Money, Kiplinger's Personal Finance, Fortune, Card Trak, and *Smart Money* magazines among others can serve as good resources to learn more about credit cards, banking, and investing.

47% of men and 26% of women prefer sex to money; 16% like both equally.

A Room of Your Own

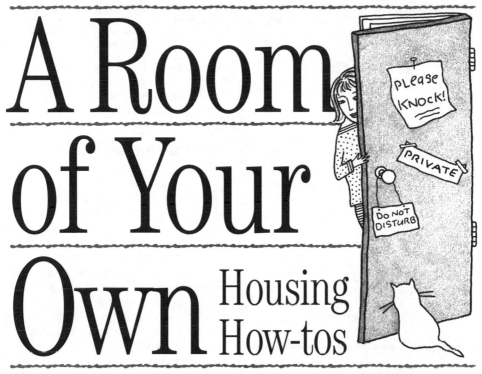

Housing How-tos

Where you choose to live has an all-important influence on your college experience. Like picking a major or even a school, it's one of those fundamental choices that affects everything from your social life to your studies. Whether you decide to live on or off campus, with a total stranger from a faraway town or your nearest and dearest high school pal, you'll want to be as comfortable and happy in your surroundings as possible.

Every college has its own housing policies and options. Depending upon your needs and resources and those of your school, your choices may include dorms, sorority (or coed fraternity) houses, co-ops or other special interest housing (like the Spanish Club, Hillel, or a women's center), and university apartments. Or you might choose to live off campus, renting a place yourself or with friends or living at home with your family. Your options will depend on several factors—for instance, whether there's a housing crunch driving students off campus, whether you're attending a residential or a commuter college (one that doesn't provide housing for most students), or whether your school's housing lottery gives first year students last picks on prime real estate.

> *"Think about yourself. If you covet your privacy, need quiet, and hate when people touch your stuff, sharing a room with four other women might not be the best idea. However, if you feel lonely when fewer than 10 people are around, a remote single miles from campus probably won't make you too happy."*
>
> —*BARNARD COLLEGE '92*

73% of women say they look forward to going home at the end of the day.

LIVING ON CAMPUS

~~~~~~~~~

Convenience is the operative word when it comes to living on campus. Nearly everything you need —the dining halls, academic buildings, laundry room, health clinic, and library—is usually just a short walk or bike ride away from your room. If you're very involved on campus, dorms are the ideal place to be. Late-night meetings and early-morning practices are much easier to bear if your bed is a Frisbee's throw from the student government office or the gym.

GIMME SHELTER
❋

Create a little corner (at least) of your own—a place where you can relax, sleep, study, work, get romantic, hang out with friends, dance, and hide away.

Living on campus is also an almost guaranteed way to kickstart your social life. In fact, only the determinedly reclusive will be able to avoid the heavy-duty socializing that occurs when 60-odd undergrads are thrown together on one floor. There's nearly always someone around to procrastinate with, play backgammon with, discuss the meaning of life within a late-night philosophizing session, get advice from, and have a crush on. On a more practical note, on-campus housing usually has relatively good safety and security. Plus the school will often supply you with furniture,

lightbulbs, garbage bags, (scratchy) toilet paper, free repairs (if the damage isn't your fault)—the works.

Dorm, Sweet Dorm
☙❧☙

University housing can also provide an almost mindboggling array of services. Many dorms are equipped to fulfill the combined functions of apartment buildings, health clubs, cafeterias, and counseling, computer, and entertainment centers. Dorm dwellers can keep themselves amused with aerobics classes, movie screenings, pizza orgies, *Jeopardy* marathons, and myriad other activities.

Perhaps the most important thing a dorm can offer its residents is a healthy support network. Resident advisors (RAs) are a principal part of the network. RAs are students who have been singled out by dorm higher-ups as having (a) highly developed people skills and (b) boundless supplies of patience and Kleenex. They can help you deal with everything from an unwieldy class schedule to an uncooperative roommate, and are typically required to be on hand on an almost round-the-clock basis. They may serve as advisors to the mini-governments some floors form to keep things running smoothly. They also plan events, organize programs, and serve as liaisons to the housing administration, which generally oversees things like room switches, punishment for severe breaches of floor etiquette (such as nine-keg room parties), and the minutiae of dorm management. Not surprisingly, RAs frequently wind up as floor disciplinarians, a role some inhabitants find hard to swallow and others grudgingly appreciate, especially when there's someone fighting with a roommate or throwing up in the hallway at 4:00 A.M. Another aspect of the network might include support sessions for people coping with drug habits or eating disorders or seminars on topics ranging from good study habits to bike maintenance. Finally, some dorms may even offer peer tutoring or "buddy" programs for residents with physical disabilities.

People may not always live up to their reputations, but dorms often do. It's true that a given dorm may not be 100 percent filled with high school stereotypes like the Jock, the Brain, or the Artsy Type, but a proximity to the fieldhouse, round-the-clock quiet hours, or a funkier decor might make some dorms apt to attract birds of a certain feather. Also, some dorms work harder at enforcing policies on alcohol use or opposite-sex overnight guests. All-women's dorms are likely to be cleaner and quieter, and you'll avoid early-morning hallway or bathroom encounters with groggy unshaven men, though you may have your fair share with groggy unshaven guests. And then there's that near-universal campus feature, the party dorm, known far and wide for its bacchanalian excesses and beer-slimed elevators.

"I transferred and lived off campus. It was hard because it made it difficult to meet people. I finally moved on campus second semester, and it made all the difference in the world."
—RUTGERS UNIVERSITY, '94

While they may be fun places to be on the weekend—or on weeknights, for that matter—they can seriously impede your quest for quality study time. That may sound like your parents talking, but it's no fun having a high-decibel heavy-metal broadcast force you out of your snug little room into a library carrel.

The downside of dorm life involves the size of the rooms (and the number of people simultaneously trying to get ready for class in them), the post-party Sunday morning mess, the lack of privacy, the mildew in the bathroom, the noise level. All that can get a little grating after a month, a semester, or, for the very tolerant, a year or two.

The specific policies on choosing and applying for campus housing vary from school to school. Many places operate on a seniority system, in which the seniors get first dibs and the sophomores are left with the closet-size triples on the outskirts of campus. Curry favor with the housing gods by turning in your request or application as far ahead of the deadline as you can manage—it may not help, but it certainly can't hurt. Special interest housing is often allocated separately from the general housing lottery, and usually requires that you apply to the group that's running it, even if the building is owned and maintained by the school.

White Hall, is the tallest occupied building in the whole state.

Special Interest Housing

ᘐᘖᘙ

Members of a special interest house (or dorm or floor) share a religious, linguistic, political, ethnic, and/or social commonality. Food co-ops, Newman Centers (a Catholic student organization), women's centers, and African heritage houses can be found on campuses nationwide. Many colleges also have cooperative housing, or co-ops, which are a form of special interest housing that doesn't adhere to any specific belief or practice—instead, they're composed of basically like-minded individuals who're looking for an alternative to dorms.

Living in special interest or co-op housing can be great. As in dorms, you've got a built-in social life. But while dorms are often random assortments of people with whom you may have nothing in common, in special interest or co-op housing you're sure to have at least one thing in common with those who live around you, whether it's your religion, ethnic/racial identity, diet/abstention from eating certain foods, politics, gender, language, sport, or hobby. In addition, special interest housing can be less expensive than dorms. It's usually governed by consensus—the group determines such issues as guest policies and how to handle housekeeping and expenses. Sometimes there are committees that deal with meals, clean-up, repairs, entertainment, and the budget.

Like dorms, special interest and co-op houses may lack flexibility, privacy, and quiet. In some cases, you must take on house responsibilities that range from party planning to cooking meals to scrubbing bathrooms

> "The ultimate irony about room draw is that by the time I was a senior and had a low enough lottery number to get a decent room, I no longer had any desire to live on campus."
> —NORTHWESTERN UNIVERSITY, '90

to attending weekly meetings. If the house has food service, you may be required to take all meals there. You also might have to pay dues above and beyond rent. If your special interest housing or co-op is university-sponsored, the university's policies on alcohol, coed night visitors, and the like will still apply.

Sororities and Coed Fraternities

ᘐᘖᘙ

Perhaps your mother, your grandmother, and your great-aunt Mimi were all do-or-die members of Pi Beta Phi. Or maybe you just like the idea of an organization strong on charity fund-raising, female bonding, and great sweatshirts. In any case, depending on your college, sororities can offer some of the best housing around. The lovely Victorian mansion shown in movies may not be a reality, but many sororities *are* known for their comfy digs.

The thing about sororities is, you don't just fill out an application and get in. Sororities and fraternities recruit, or rush, new members during a week- to two-week-long period just before or during fall semester. On some campuses, rush is postponed until second semester to give incoming first-years the chance to get their bearings before making a commitment. Some schools send you a rush preregistration form in their housing materials; others have you sign up soon after you hit campus. Most schools do charge a rush fee ranging anywhere from $30 to $70. (For more information on rush, see "Sororities— Sisterhood Is Powerful," page 592, or call the Panhellenic office on your campus.)

Once you're in a sorority, you may or may not be able to move in right away, depending on the space available and campus rules. If there's a seniority-ranked waiting list, it may take a while, but you'll probably get your chance. Many sororities *require* you to "live in" for a year or two, typically as a sophomore or junior.

Joining a sorority involves making a considerable financial investment. Fees for room and board vary greatly from house to house and campus to campus, but they should be comparable to living in a dorm. Then there are dues, which you have to pay in addition to room and board and range anywhere from $500 to $1,500 a semester. Plus, there are incidental expenses that can strain your budget if you're not careful. Sorority life offers boundless opportunities to run up a major tab on Greek-themed T-shirts, hats, boxer shorts, key chains—you get the idea. Parties can get expensive, too, and so can the little gifts that members often swap. Some houses build in a per-semester party fee, but you can also expect fairly regular bills for dresses, flowers, and alcohol.

One of the great things about joining a sorority is that you've got an instant gang of friends and social life. But they come with a price, in that, when you are living in the house, there are few ways to escape the endless committee meetings, meals, out-of-town formals, and parties and gatherings of every hue. At times you may feel like you're eating, sleeping, and breathing your sorority, and you'll have to work harder at finding time for your other interests, not to mention your independent friends.

For those who like Greek life but would prefer a male presence, joining a coed fraternity may be a good alternative if your campus has them. Coed fraternities are often looser and less traditional than single-sex Greek organizations.

THERE'S NO PLACE LIKE HOME

For those of us who live close to campus, staying at home may be a good choice—if not the only choice. Besides the fact that you usually can't beat the rent, some of us may have to stay home if there are siblings or parents who need to be taken care of or other responsibilities that need our attention.

But even if there's no pressing issue keeping you at home, there may still be good reasons to stick around. If

---

SPEAK UP

Let the housing office know well in advance if you have specific housing needs, such as a room that is wheelchair-accessible or on a low floor.

rating? 60% of tag sale customers arrive before 10 A.M.; 90% by noon.

STUCK ON CAMPUS

Some financial aid packages require that you live on campus, or will cover only on-campus housing costs. Be sure to talk with the aid office before you make any housing decisions. Also, many schools require first-year students and first-year transfers to live on campus. If this is economically (and/or socially) undesirable, talk with the housing office as quickly as possible. You may need to file an application for permission to live off campus.

your only alternative is to live alone in a pricey matchbox-sized studio or your school's housing offerings are truly grim, it might be tempting to keep your home fires burning. And there's something to be said for open-fridge privileges and laundry service that doesn't require a fistful of quarters. Home can also be a source of emotional security if you're looking to ease into a college existence.

Still, awkward and even combustible situations can result when your newfound sense of independence bumps up against parental authority. (See "Negotiating Relationships," page 559, for information on handling your changing relationship with your family.)

Some ways to aid your day-to-day transition from home to school:

■ Find a place on campus that can act as a sort of base when you're between classes or activities—be it a corner of the student center, a booth in a coffee shop, or a carrel in the library.

■ Check into getting a locker—that way you won't have to carry your things everywhere.

■ Find out if a place exists on campus where you can stay the night for a small fee if you're ever in a jam.

■ You may want to get your own phone line at home (and an answering machine that lets you call in for messages). Or see if you can get a voice mailbox. This way you avoid relying on your folks to tell you who called and can pick up messages as often as you want.

GETTING YOUR OWN PLACE

For all the conveniences that campus life offers, when you tire of hauling your toothbrush down to the communal bathroom, when you find out that going off board will save you money, or when you want to experience some of the freedom of apartment life, it might be time to move out of the dorm.

You may not have to leave the bosom of the university to do this. Many schools rent apartments to students, and these can be some of the best deals around. With your school's housing office as your "landlord," you usually won't have to worry about handing over a check every month (as you'll most likely pay at the beginning of the semester or on a quarterly basis), repairs will usually be made in a timely fashion, and the buildings will generally be safe and secure. However, there are probably more rules and supervision when you're in a school apartment than when you're renting a place on your own. You may even have a resident advisor living in the apartment complex—which, depending on your point of view, may or may not be a good thing. The one big advantage to campus housing is that your lease is generally up at the end of the academic year. If you want to leave for the summer, you won't have to bother with subletting.

Moving Off Campus

ⓥⓐⓥ

If your college doesn't offer apartments or houses as a living option or if the whole point is to get *away* from school, you'll have to move off campus. The freedom and independence of renting go hand in hand with the occasional aggravations—namely, the extra travel time to and from campus, the leaky toilet that was supposed to be fixed a week and a half ago, those pesky utility bills. . . . However, there's a comparatively vast spectrum of living situations to choose from—many involving your own bedroom!!!—and unlike campus housing, you won't automatically be kicked out at the end of your academic year (unless your lease is up then). The legwork, brainwork, legal work, and avoid-the-scam work are all left to you, but then, so is the satisfaction of knowing you found the perfect—well, almost perfect—place to live.

Finding a Place

ⓥⓐⓥ

Before you start looking, you should form a pretty clear idea of what you're after. Decide on the neighborhood, your price range, the size of the apartment, and the number of bathrooms required to avoid the daily spectacle of you and your roommates leg-wrestling for the shower. Make a list of which items you're willing to negotiate on and which you aren't. If you are looking with one or more people, it's a good idea to get together before the great search begins and discuss your expectations. Sketch out some advance compromises when they don't match up—if one roommate simply must have a southern exposure, maybe she'll be willing to forget about the Jacuzzi requirement that doesn't fit another roommate's budget. This way, you'll avoid most tension-producing surprises when you're out pounding the pavement, and you'll be ahead of the game in finding that rare apartment that makes everybody happy. Incidentally, you should start hunting for housing approximately one semester or, in some cases, a year before you need to have your new place. It probably won't take that long to arrive at the lease-signing stage, but a housing search is not something you want to put off until the last minute.

Finding an apartment or house is equal parts excitement (when you're first starting out), exhaustion (when you can't bear to darken the doorstep of one more "great find!"), and elation (when that last appointment finally pays off). Your search may demand saintly measures of patience and fortitude, particularly when you're looking in a city that you

TO GO OR NOT TO GO

L iving off campus has its upsides and downsides:

PROS

▲ More space to yourself (usually)
▲ Flexibility on choosing a roommate (like a dog, a boyfriend, or an iguana)
▲ Your own kitchen and bathroom
▲ A break from meals of delicacies like tater-tot casserole
▲ Can be cheaper than a dorm, especially if you share a place with a bevy of roommates
▲ You can keep the place as long as you want (usually)

CONS

▲ Spending time and energy on things you didn't have to do in the dorm, like shopping, cooking, and cleaning a bathroom and kitchen
▲ Waking up earlier to get to class
▲ The extra money you might have to spend on transportation to and from school
▲ The extra work you may have to put into meeting people and keeping abreast of late-breaking news, gossip, and social activities
▲ Apartment hunting can be a drag

---

don't know well. However, many resources exist in every community to make the apartment-finding process as painless as possible.

■ Tell everybody—your friends, profs, advisor, etc.—that you're looking. They may know of the ideal place for you.

■ Classified ads in local and school papers not only may help you find a place, but are invaluable tools in figuring out what's available and what rents are like.

■ School housing offices sometimes keep rental listings on file or may have a bulletin board covered with housing opportunities. (Find out if your school has an off-campus-housing or affiliated-housing office.) Religious, community, athletic, and women's centers often post housing notices, and you might also try bulletin boards in restaurants, libraries, and supermar-

kets. If the desperation factor is running high—you're under serious time constraints, or the market you're looking in is especially tight and the competition's cutthroat—you might post flyers promising a small reward to anyone who provides the lead that results in your renting a place.

■ Academic departments are also good places to look. Check departmental bulletin boards and ask around—professors going on sabbatical often rent their homes to responsible students, and they are often furnished nicely and filled with good books.

■ Brokers and/or realtors are other sources to consider, albeit potentially expensive ones. A landlord who has space for rent will list his or her apartment with a broker, who in turn advertises and shows it to would-be tenants. Brokers' fees can run as high as a whopping 15 percent of the first year's rent. The savings-conscious would do better to contact landlords directly, if possible. When reading the real estate section, keep an eye out for listings that say "No fee" or "By owner." And bear in mind that many brokers' fees are negotiable.

■ Take a walk around the neighborhood where you'd like to live, stop in buildings that suit your fancy, and ask any friendly-looking tenants you see whether there are any apartments available. Even if there aren't, try to find out the landlord's name and phone number—s/he may know of a late-breaking development in the building. Also be on the lookout for "open houses"—available apartments or houses open for home hunters to pop in and look around.

■ If you are in the market for a summer rental, many colleges rent empty dorm rooms. Often fraternities or sororities will sublet their rooms (to members and nonmembers alike), as will students living in off-campus housing.

■ Starting your search before everyone else does can help give you a jump on the competition. When you hear about or read an appealing listing, call to make an appointment to see the place ASAP.

Checking It Out

◎◎◎

Don't sign anything before you know exactly what you're getting into. Your "dream" apartment or house could be a nightmare waiting to happen. To help ensure it's not, carefully examine every inch of the place. If the electricity is off, ask if it can be turned

on. If not, ask to see the place in the daytime and bring a flashlight (and even a friend) to help you inspect the nooks and crannies. You'll also want to eyeball the neighborhood you'll be living in. Is the apartment near all the necessary conveniences, like a grocery store, dry cleaner, and public transportation? Find out.

Don't be afraid to go over things with a fine-tooth comb. So what if it looks like you're being fussy or nosy? It may prevent heartache down the road. Keep your eyes and ears open for the following:

Security: Obviously, the security issues will vary based on where you live. If you are moving to a big city, you have to be pickier about the sturdiness of the door, the locks, and the gates on the windows than you do in a small, friendly town. In addition, ask who has keys to the house or apartment, if it's possible to have the locks changed, and what type of security the building offers—for instance, a burglar alarm, a buzzer/intercom/video system, or a security desk or doorman (if it's an apartment). Do the windows lock or have bars (especially important if the apartment is on the first floor)? Do the doors have deadbolts? If not, have them installed (you'll probably have to pay for this, so make sure

CLASSIFIEDS DECODED
————❀————

Here's what some of that gibberish means:

AC = air conditioner
CAC = central air-conditioning
EIK = eat-in kitchen
No fee = no broker's fee
1BR, 2BR, 3BR = one bedroom, etc.
W/D (or wshr/dryr) = washer/dryer
DW = dishwasher
Stu = studio
Vu = view
WIC = walk-in closet
S expos = southern exposure
WBFP = woodburning fireplace
B'stone = brownstone
Full reno = fully renovated
N/S = no shares allowed
G/H inc = gas and heat included
24 hr D/M = 24-hour doorman
Hdwd fls = hardwood floors

they're the kind that can be removed and reinstalled in your next place). How safe is the building and neighborhood? (Ask a neighbor, preferably a woman, if she feels comfortable walking alone at night.)

Water: Check hot water and shower pressure—flush the toilet and turn on a couple of faucets. (Do this at the same time, to see if you'll have to wait until your roomie finishes washing the dishes before you'll be able to take a good hot shower.) Find out if water's included in the rent or is a separate utility. If the lead content in your water is a concern, contact the EPA's safe drinking water hotline at (800) 426-4791 for more information on testing lead levels in your water.

Kitchen: Check the shelf and counter space, lighting, and ventilation. Make sure all the appliances work. If they don't, indicate needed repairs on your lease.

Space: Is there enough room for you, your roommates, and your stuff? What kind of closet space is available? Do you have to pass through two bedrooms to get to the bathroom?

Energy: Ask about the state of the building's electrical wiring (especially if you will be using a computer). Can the wiring handle large appliances like air-conditioners, microwave ovens, and dishwashers? Look for loose wires. Check how many outlets are in the dwelling and if they are conveniently located. Find out whether you have control over your own climate and access to the fuse box. Is heat included? Is electricity included? (If not, find out the amount of the average monthly heat/electric bills.)

Bugs: Try to determine if the apartment has problems with whatever pests are indigenous to your area (cockroaches, rodents, lizards, or any combination thereof). If the floor is scattered with mousetraps, roach bait, flypaper, and gecko poop, get the hint. Ask the landlord when the exterminator comes, and who pays for it.

Structural damage: Check for stains on the ceiling, peeling paint, or a warped floor—they're usually good indications of previous water damage due to pipe or roof leakage and/or flooding.

Landlord/superintendent (or whomever you are supposed to contact if a problem arises): Ask a neighbor or two about the superintendent and/or landlord. Does s/he respond to calls

❀ 1 in every 5 families moves each year—that's 43 million people.

promptly, have reasonable ideas about what heat and hot water are, and make repairs in a timely fashion? Does s/he live on the premises? If so, the building will probably be both safer and better cared for.

Other tenants: The population makeup will determine both the noise levels and the social opportunities that exist in your building. Who are your neighbors? Are they mostly students? Families with small children? Singles? Couples? Older folks? Are people generally friendly, or do they keep to themselves?

Mail: Ask if there is someone available to sign for your packages when you're not home.

Pets: If you are planning to have a pet in your apartment, make sure you know the rules concerning animals in the building.

Fire alarms/escapes: Are both plainly in evidence and in good condition? Check out possible escape routes: Will you need to sprout wings in order to make a safe exit?

Insulation: Check windows for proper insulation. If there are portable heaters around, it's usually a sign of insufficient heat.

Noise level: How noisy is the street facing the building, or the courtyard behind it? Ask the super or another tenant about the noise level within the building. Do your potential neighbors play heavy-metal music until 3:00 A.M. every night? Does everyone go to sleep at 9:00 P.M. and complain if someone tiptoes too loudly?

Accessibility: Is there an elevator or stairs? If only the latter, are you going to mind walking up five flights with your laundry, groceries, and book bag? Is the building and the apartment wheelchair-accessible? Are the appliances and shelves at a height you can manage?

Affordability: How much will it *really* cost to live there (in addition to rent, consider utilities, and transportation to and from school)? How expensive is the neighborhood? (Check out the prices at grocery stores, gas stations, laundromats, and restaurants in the area.) Before deciding to spend even just a little more than your limit, make sure you truly will be able to afford it—or whether you're willing to cut costs in other areas to finance those parquet floors.

> *"There is a fine line between being annoying and persistent, but if you really want a place, call the landlord and tell her or him that you think it's beautiful and that you'd be such a good tenant. Essentially, kiss up."*
>
> —**HAYWARD STATE UNIVERSITY, '92**

HOUSING AND THE ADA

I t is illegal to deny a person housing (or to evict one) solely on the basis of gender, race, national origin, religion, marital status, and/or disability (e.g., your landlord and/or realtor is not allowed to ask whether you're married or what your religion is). The revised Americans with Disabilities Act further protects people with disabilities from discrimination and sets specific standards for the accessibility of public and private buildings. The new regulations include the following:

▲ Schools are required to make only "readily achievable" modifications (those that do not require much expense or difficulty) to existing buildings. However, most schools have (or will) go beyond this and put in the effort and money to make necessary changes in dorm, social, and academic buildings to accommodate the needs of individual students.

▲ If you are renting a private dwelling, you are allowed to make reasonable modifications to your dwelling and common-use areas at your expense (though the landlord may assume some or all of the expense), if you restore them to their original condition upon leaving. These changes (such as the installation or removal of carpeting, placing braille labels in elevators, or constructing ramps) should be agreed upon in writing, and attached to your lease.

▲ In all new public buildings, commercial facilities, and large private buildings, public common areas must be accessible to persons with disabilities, doors and hallways must be wide enough for wheelchairs, and all units must have an accessible route into and through the unit. Light switches, electrical outlets, thermostats, and other environmental controls must be placed within easy reach, and bathroom walls must be reinforced to allow later installation of grab bars.

▲ Guide dogs are allowed in "no pet" buildings.

▲ If you request a reserved parking space near your apartment, your municipality should make every effort to accommodate you.

(For more information on the Americans with Disabilities Act, and attending college with a disability, see pages 486, and 548.)

You Love It!

ᏁᏁᏁ

I f you've done all your homework and you're still convinced this is the place for you, grab it. Make sure the landlord knows you love it and find out exactly what you'll need to do to ensure that you'll get it. If there are others who need to see the place before you can make a final decision, ask the landlord when you could arrange to do so. Ask how soon you will find out if it's yours.

Be prepared to put a deposit down to hold the apartment. If you end up not getting the place, you should get your money back. However, if you back out, you'll probably lose your deposit.

How Does the Landlord Choose?

ೋೋೋ

Most landlords are at least somewhat human, and will tend to pick those who seem nice, responsible, eager (without being pushy), and excited about the apartment. And it's common knowledge that the fastest way to a lease is through a mutual friend (the closer, the better). However, some landlords are "strictly business" and will rent to the first applicant who checks out OK, using some or all of the following criteria:

Recommendations: The landlord may call past landlords, employers, or other listed references to find out if you're a generally responsible person, the type who'll get the rent in on time.

Guarantor: Understandably, the landlord wants to feel confident that you'll be able to afford to pay your rent. Full-time students, especially those without much (or any) credit history, aren't exactly a landlord's dream tenants. (Even if you're holding down a full-time job, you still have enormous expenses that eat up a large portion of your paycheck.) You may be required to have someone with a good credit history and income (often a parent) cosign the lease with you and thus agree to be responsible if you default on your rent.

Credit check: The landlord may want to do a credit check on you and/or your guarantor. In most cases, you'll have to pay for it—TRW, a widely used national credit service, charges around $30 for a credit check. However, if you are paying all the rent up front (as occasionally happens in the case of a summer sublet) the credit check shouldn't be necessary.

THE NITTY GRITTY

"Make sure all the roommates sign the lease. Even if you all have an understanding that everyone's equally responsible, it's really just not the same if only one or two people are on the lease. If you can't all sign a lease, make up a contract between all the roommates. It may seem silly at the time, but it's really important to have in writing what happens if someone leaves, how much rent each person pays, how long each person will be there, and that you are all responsible for paying bills on time."

—UNIVERSITY OF MICHIGAN
LAW SCHOOL, '94

The Lease

ೋೋೋ

The lease, meant to protect both you and your landlord, outlines the rights and responsibilities of both parties. Leases should include the date you take possession, the amount of rent you pay, which (if any) utilities are included in the rent, the term of the lease, repairs to be done, rules about pets, the conditions under which you can be evicted, and the maximum number of tenants allowed in your rental. The lease should also include details on subletting, as well as renewal rights. (Call a tenants' rights association to find out if your locality has a ceiling on yearly rent increases.) The lease should also state that neither the landlord, the super, nor any workers or inspectors may enter the apartment without your notification and approval. No matter how boring or indecipherable it seems, *read* your lease. If you're at all unsure about any of your lease's clauses, have a lawyer or someone familiar with tenants' rights look it over.

■ Remember that the terms of the lease may be negotiable. If an apartment is exactly what you want but the rent is too high, the deposit is too much for you to manage, there isn't a specified option for renewal, etc., negotiate these terms with your landlord. All

TYPES OF RENTAL AGREEMENTS

Not all leases specify how long you're allowed to stay or are signed directly with the landlord. You many sign a month-to-month (also known as a "tenant-at-will") agreement. This is a lease that may be terminated with 30 days' notice by either tenant or landlord.

Or you may choose to sublet. When you enter into a sublease, rather than renting from the landlord, you are renting from the person whose name is on the lease. As your name will not appear on that lease, regardless of how long you plan on subletting, you will need to make your own lease with the original tenant. It is important to work out a formal, written agreement each and every time you sublet, even if it's just for a month or two.

▲ Even though you are living there, the original renter is still responsible for paying rent to the landlord and covering the cost of damages. Because of this, many subleasers ask for the full rent up front.

▲ Utilities are frequently paid for by the person from whom you are renting the space. Make sure you know what the policy is before signing the lease.

▲ Not all subleases are legal. Legal means that the landlord knows and approves of what you and the original tenant are up to, and perhaps even has a sublease agreement of his or her own for all the interested parties to sign. Unfortunately, many subleases are enacted without the landlord's approval and thus can be deemed illegal. Enter into a illegal sublease at your own risk. Illegal subleasing is a widespread practice, and admittedly, many landlords remain blissfully or purposefully ignorant of the new neighbors in their building. But keep in mind that illegal subleasing could leave both you and the original tenant out in the cold.

Because cold air falls and hot air rises, aiming the air conditioner

changes made by you or your landlord to your rental agreement should be initialed and attached to the lease.

■ Before signing the lease, tour the place with the landlord, and make a list of any damage you find so you won't be charged for it when you move out. Also note any repairs that need to be made before you move in. Both you and the landlord should sign and retain a copy of the list (or better yet, attach it to the lease). If everything isn't in working order (as agreed on) when you move in, you are entitled to a rent reduction or, in some cases, to terminate the lease.

■ Many landlords will paint the walls white (or another color, if you spring for the paint) and clean the floors before a new tenant moves in.

■ You should retain a signed copy of the lease and keep it in a safe place. (It's a good idea to keep a file of all your housing information.)

■ At the lease signing you will probably need to fork over a hefty sum, covering the first month's rent, and the security deposit and sometimes even the last month's rent, too. If you need to deposit money in your account to cover the check, make sure you do so a week in advance if there are checks that will need time to clear. Many landlords ask for a certified check.

Security Deposits

〰〰〰

A security deposit is the money (usually equivalent to one month's rent) that a renter must give to the landlord up front, to cover possible damage to the apartment during the rental period (above and beyond normal wear and tear). Get a receipt for the security deposit, and ask your landlord whether you will receive interest on the deposit (after all, it *is* your money, and any interest it generates in a bank account should be yours, too—as long as you pay your rent on time).

Your lease should state clearly when you will get back your security deposit and on what grounds it might not be returned to you. If this is left completely up to the landlord, the reason you don't get your security deposit back may be totally arbitrary. When you move out, you and the landlord should walk through the apartment together and assess the extent of the damage (if any) and how much it will cost to fix. (If you feel your landlord's assessment is off the mark, call your local tenants' association.) Any money left over should be returned to you.

"One of the nifty things I learned at college is that you can "erase" little holes made from tacking stuff on white walls by rubbing in a little white toothpaste."
—WILLIAMS COLLEGE, '90

Utilities

〰〰〰

Once you've found the place and signed the lease, you'll need to start an account with the local utility and phone companies (and close the accounts at your old residence, if applicable). It is best to give them a call one to two weeks before the move so everything will be ready when you arrive. Ask your landlord or a neighbor-to-be for the names and numbers of the utility companies that service your apartment, or check a phone book. Be prepared to pay a one-time connection fee for some utilities. Many companies give you the option of paying the fee in one lump sum or over the course of a year.

Power

■ Most gas and electric companies will arrange a hookup over the phone, but you may be required to bring a copy of your lease to their office, especially if it's the first time you'll be setting up an account in your name.

Phone

■ Read the front pages of the phone book—it's guaranteed that you'll learn something useful about everything from rates to special services to area codes to payment options to your rights and responsibilities.

■ If you want to get an easy-to-remember number, tell the phone company representative that you have a small child living with you.

■ If you'll be moving into a previously occupied place, you'll need the landlord or the old tenants to terminate their phone service. You might be able to leave the phone connected and simply change the names on the bill (a cheaper option than disconnecting the phone and getting a new number), provided the old tenants are willing to do it this way and you're willing to

give out their new number if anyone calls for them. If there are already phone jacks in your new home, the phone setup should be fairly painless. A call to the phone company will get you hooked up.

■ Ask about what's included in basic service. Also ask about the costs of special options, such as call waiting and call forwarding. Some companies offer special deals on these.

■ Many long-distance companies have special deals for college/university students—ask at the housing office (or the place that handles on-campus phone service), or call the companies directly. Sometimes students sharing a suite or apartment elect to use their own calling cards instead of signing up for long distance service to avoid the hassle of splitting the bill.

■ Bear in mind that direct calls are almost always less expensive than calling-card calls, which are almost always less expensive than collect or person-to-person calls.

■ If your name is on the bill, your name is in the directory, unless you pay extra to keep it out. For a fee, your other roommate(s) can be listed, too. (Many women prefer to use a first initial instead of their first name to avoid possible harassment.)

■ If you or someone you are in touch with needs to use a TDD (Telecommunications Device for the Deaf) or a TTY (Telecommunications Teletype), contact the phone company. You may choose intead to use a computer-modem combination on a regular phone line.

So you've found a place, the phone's hooked up, the electricity's cranked and it's time to move. . . .

To turn off call-waiting for the duration of a phone call, dial *7O.

MOVING

Be prepared to shell out a bit of money to cover your moving and "start-up" costs—everything from stocking the fridge to buying hangers and hooks to telephone installation fees—especially if you are from out of town and you don't have a nice friend with a pickup. Raid your local convenience or grocery store for freebie boxes and start packin'.

If the job's going to be too big for you, your friends, and that 1978 wood-paneled maroon station wagon, you can either rent a truck, call some folks with a van, or hire a full-fledged moving company.

Renting a Truck

Your first stop: the yellow pages. Jot down a few listings and call around. Some places will charge a flat fee; some will charge by the day, hour, or mile. When comparison shopping, be sure to ask about discounts for students, reduced night or weekday rates, additional charges for one-way trips, and special deals for credit card users (some companies offer free insurance or reduced rates if you use plastic to pay your bill).

A small local company may cost less for a one-day job. However, if you're moving farther away you might find that you'll get the best deal from a larger company. If you don't want to drive round-trip to return the truck, rent from a bigger chain that will allow you to drop off the vehicle at a different place from where you picked it up (providing they have a rental location near your new home). They also usually supply directions, maps, and emergency road service if the truck breaks down.

Before you hit Phil's Haul-It-Yerself, find out what you'll need to bring (e.g., your credit card and driver's license).

In most states, you'll need to be at least 25 years old to rent a truck. Most companies also require a hefty cash or credit card deposit.

Meeting the Movers

༄༅༅

By far, the best way to find a mover is through recommendations. You can also get names from local papers, community bulletin boards, the yellow pages, and the chamber of commerce.

When you do your comparison shopping, you'll need to have a rough idea of how many boxes you'll be hauling. Ask the movers how they determine charges (per box, flat hourly rate, or per person per hour) and for an estimate of what your job will cost. Also ask about any special charges you might incur (including overtime charges); liability, delivery, and pick-

---

MOVING CHECKLIST

☼

KEEPING IN TOUCH

Notify the following of your new address:

▲ Post office (Before you move, fill out a mail-forwarding card at the post office. You can also pick up change of address cards there to send to everyone.)
▲ School
▲ Colleagues, friends, and family
▲ Workplace personnel office
▲ Subscription services (papers and magazines, book or disk of the month club, on-line services)
▲ Organizations you belong to
▲ Bank
▲ Credit card company
▲ Any place giving you a grant, scholarship, or loan
▲ Insurance company
▲ Doctors and dentist
▲ Anyone who regularly sends you money, mail, products, etc.

HEALTH ISSUES

▲ If you're moving far, make sure to get addresses of your current doctors, dentist, etc., so your new practition-ers can have your old medical records sent.
▲ Ask your current practitioners for recommendations of practitioners in your new area, especially if you take prescription medication. Pharmacies cannot fill out-of-state prescriptions, so you'll need to find an in-state prac-titioner to write up a new prescrip-tion for you.
▲ Contact your health insurance provider to give them your new address and phone number, as well as to find out if the move will affect your coverage in any way.

CLOSE DOWN THE OLD

▲ If appropriate, discontinue utility services at your old residence (cable, phone, electricity).
▲ Discontinue delivery service—newspapers, milk (if you're lucky enough to live in a place where there's still a milkman).
▲ Call your soon-to-be-ex-landlord to set up a time when you can meet, walk through the apartment, and get your security deposit back.

☼ A claim for movers' loss or damage must be filed within 9 months. The

up policies; and insurance coverage. Beware of any hidden costs you may incur—for example, some movers charge extra for each flight of stairs. A few other moving pointers:

■ The muscle-bound guy with a van will almost definitely be less expensive than a moving company, but he will most probably not be insured.

■ Before you hire a moving company, call the Better Business Bureau to find out if it has left behind a trail of unhappy customers.

■ As soon as the movers arrive—before they pick up the first box—you should confirm the details you discussed in your original phone call. Remind the movers of any special instructions you may have.

■ Don't forget to read the small print on the contract.

■ Though moving companies will help you pack, having everything packed (as much as possible) before they come will save you time (read: money) and confusion (you'll know exactly what's in each box) and provide security (you won't be afraid something's been overlooked). However, you might want to take advantage of their expertise and have the movers help you pack fragile or special items. Another reason to let them pack breakable items: Many companies insure only boxes packed by them.

■ Keep an inventory of all the boxes (and a summary of what they contain), and whether you packed your things or the mover did, and keep it in a safe, accessible place. It is the only proof you have that the company has your things, and the document you'll need should you have to file a claim for compensation of any lost or damaged possessions.

■ Pack a bag with your valuables (e.g., passport, jewelry, important documents) and essentials (toiletries, some clothing, address book, wallet, bank cards, medications) and keep it with you during the move, for convenience, security, and peace of mind.

■ Make sure you have a bit of cash to tip the movers after the job is done. Count on 10 to 15 percent of the bill.

Handy Tips on Moving

ᥢᥢᥢ

■ Reconfirm your move date and time with your new landlord, the existing tenants, and the moving company.

■ If you are moving locally, garbage bags are a good alternative to boxes for lighter things.

■ Don't put too many heavy things (e.g., books, dishes, computer equipment) in one box, especially if you will have to carry it yourself.

■ Use your move as an opportunity to get organized, and rid yourself of some of the clutter in your life. Be ruthless. Do you really need to keep that single orange-and-brown-striped sock? Recycle all your unnecessary papers, magazines, and newspapers, and give your clothes the one-year test: If you haven't worn it in a year, it goes to charity.

■ Label all of your boxes and/or bags so that you will know where everything is. And pack room by room so that things that belong together will stay together.

company must make a settlement offer within 120 days of receipt. ☀

■ Use clothing, sheets, and towels as packing material.

■ If you are planning to paint the new place, try to have it finished a day before the move.

■ Treat anyone who's helping you move to some cold drinks, some tasty munchies, and endless thanks.

■ Give yourself a break. Moving is one of the most exhausting and frustrating ways to spend your time. Plus, it will take a while before you'll feel totally at ease in your new home. Allow yourself time to relax and get everything in order.

ONCE YOU'RE IN

▲ **Give your new place a good cleaning.**
▲ **Cruise the neighborhood. Check out all your options regarding grocery stores, dry cleaners, banks, veterinarians, and shopping areas.**
▲ **Locate the nearest hospital and police and fire stations. Post their numbers in a highly visible place near the phone.**
▲ **Ask your landlord, the super, or a neighbor about trash collection and recycling.**

THE RENT

After you've unpacked the boxes (and hidden the scratchy pink-and-blue-plaid guest towels your mother sent you as an apartment-warming gift), you should be set for smooth sailing. There's just one minor detail left . . . the rent.

The best way to make your landlord happy is to get your rent in on time (and it's never a bad idea to keep the landlord happy). This means that if you'll be mailing your rent, send it far enough ahead of time so that the landlord will receive it on or before the due date. If you're late with your rent (and we know it won't become a habit), most landlords will give you a grace period of a week or so to pay up before they add a late fee.

■ If you're paying in cash, ask for a receipt with your name, the amount you paid, what it was for (e.g., "July rent"), the date of payment, and the signature of the person who took it. Remember never to mail cash. Canceled checks can also serve as receipts. Save *all* of your receipts (more fodder for your housing file).

■ If your landlord wants to raise your rent, s/he must give you 30 days' notice before doing so, at which time you may decide to move. Typically, rent can't be raised unless it's lease-renewal time or your landlord has made major capital improvements, so call your tenants' association if your landlord tries to up the rent mid-lease or the renewal rate seems high.

When the Landlord Does Not Hold Up His End of the Deal . . .

☙☙☙

In theory, you and your landlord are linked in a mutually beneficial relationship: You pay the rent, and your landlord upholds the terms of the lease (which are dictated in part by state and local laws as well as ordinances regarding livability standards for residential premises). But if a problem arises—you don't have heat or hot water, the doorknobs keep falling off, or the noise level is too high—call the person who is in charge of maintenance (usually the super). If s/he doesn't fix the problem in a timely fashion, you may have to take further steps.

1. Write down when the problem began. If there is damage, take pictures. Send a copy of your list of complaints to your landlord.

2. Unless the damage is truly your fault, the landlord should pay for repairs. If the problem is serious (for example, a possible gas leak or a flood) and your landlord or super is unavailable or won't deal with it even after being alerted to it, call a plumber or the gas company (the number is located on your bills or in the front of the phone book) yourself. Get the repairperson to bill your landlord or, if you have to pay, send the receipt to your landlord and deduct the amount from your next month's rent.

3. If your landlord refuses to respond in a reasonable way, and the problem makes your dwelling unsafe and/or unlivable (you are without heat in the middle of winter, you have no hot water, the roof is leaking, there is a problem with the electrical wiring

EVICTION
✺

A landlord may evict a tenant for only three reasons: non-payment of rent, failure to comply with requirements of a lease, and expiration of the term of that lease. A tenant has to be given at least five days' notice before s/he must move. If you are being evicted for reasons other than the three listed above or you were not given advance notice, talk to a tenants' rights group and file a complaint against your landlord with your local department of housing.

and your toaster blew up), send him a letter (by certified mail so he can't pretend he never got it) that clearly reports the problems and your attempts to get him to fix them. In it state that if he does not make the repairs within a certain amount of time, say, a week, you will file a complaint with the housing department. Keep a copy of the letter for your files. If he still doesn't address the problem, call the tenants' association and notify your landlord that you are filing an official complaint. The tenants' association will be able to guide you through the procedure.

The housing department may send an inspector over to check out your place. Have all your documentation and pictures ready. When the inspector comes, walk her through the dwelling and point out the violations. If the inspector finds the landlord in violation of housing codes, she will file a complaint against the landlord, specifying the violations and the time

 On average, women clean for 59 minutes a day; men, for 26 minutes.

frame allowed for repairs (usually 30 days). If your landlord fails to act upon this complaint, a second one will be filed with the municipal court and the landlord will be taken to court and fined. If after all of this, your landlord still fails to make repairs, talk with your city's health department to see if there is an emergency repair program that will come to your rescue. If the city considers your house or apartment unsafe or a health hazard, the repairs will be made and billed to your landlord. If there is no such program, you can continue to withhold rent until the repairs are made, make the repairs yourself and bill your landlord, or break your lease.

4. If your ceiling is not falling down in large chunks, but the problem is aggravating and was supposed to be fixed months ago, call a tenants' rights group, the local housing department, and/or the Better Business Bureau. Find out if your legal rights are being violated, and if so, register a complaint. Even if it's not an official violation, they will often give you advice on steps to take.

SHARING A LIVING SPACE

"Don't sweat the small stuff, and it's all small stuff."

—LEWIS AND CLARK COLLEGE, '95

You don't have to be cosmic twins to be great roommates. You should, however, be compatible on the nitty-gritty, pragmatic level and agree on some basic ground rules. Even if you don't particularly like each other, you and your roommate(s) have at least one thing in common: You want to feel comfortable in your living space. You may not need to discuss your relationship, but you will need to deal with the basics. Don't wait for a fight to break out to do it.

Finding a Compatible Roommate

The first rule of finding a good roommate is to know thyself. With that in mind, ask yourself:

■ Will you be able to tolerate living with a smoker or a righteous non-smoker?

■ What hours do you keep? Are you a morning or night person? When will you want to study, play music, etc.?

■ How often will your girlfriend/boyfriend/friends be staying over? Do you expect a lot of visitors?

■ Are you generally neat? Messy?

"At school, I live with three of my closest friends. At first, it was pretty difficult. I think we all expected to get along just as well as roommates as we did living apart. But after the initial problems were resolved, things got better quickly. . . . I can't say that there haven't been any problems, but I wouldn't change things. Having a close community of women to live in is really amazing."

—COLBY COLLEGE, '94

■ Are you allergic to anything, such as incense, plants, smoke, animals, etc.?

■ Are you into sharing clothing and CDs—with permission, of course—or do you prefer to keep your stuff to yourself? How about splitting the cost of staples like milk, toilet paper, garbage bags, toothpaste, etc.?

■ Do you like to spend a lot of your time at home?

■ What are your pet peeves? What are your worst habits?

■ Do you follow a special diet, for instance, kosher or vegetarian?

■ How much are you willing (or able) to spend on rent?

■ What are you looking for in a roommate? Someone you'll spend time with? A situation where you'll take

"My freshman-year roommate and I didn't get along at all. It's not so much that we fought, it's just that we had absolutely nothing in common. And what's worse, I just stayed in that position because I didn't know what else to do."
—NORTHWEST SCHOOL OF ART, '96

care of and watch out for each other or where you'll share rent and space and little else?

■ What are your tastes when it comes to furnishing your place? If you're a Martha Stewart groupie, will you be able to deal with a living room that looks like a Greg Brady original ("I just want a place to hang my beads . . .")?

ROOMING WITH YOUR BEST FRIEND

Not only do you not have to be best friends with your roommate, but it's often better if you aren't. Although you may get along great in social situations or make terrific study partners, living together can be another matter entirely. For example, where you might be fairly easygoing, your friend could be precise and particular. While this wouldn't necessarily affect the friendship if you didn't live together, it can be difficult to deal with as roommates. You also may discover that you don't have as much in common as you thought you did. These unexpected conflicts can often be resolved with some hard work, effort, and good intentions, but fair warning. Some very wonderful relationships have suffered as the result of living together.

On the other hand, there are some definite benefits to living with friends. When you live with people with whom you can hang out, who know how to deal with all your quirks, who (usually) don't bring up touchy subjects at the wrong time, and with whom you feel completely comfortable and at ease, your home becomes more than just a place to sleep, eat, and shower—it becomes a nurturing, supportive, and just plain fun place to be.

Exactly what questions to ask a prospective roommate will depend upon your living situation. If you'll be sharing a bedroom, smoking, neatness, and overnight guests will be important issues. If you'll each have your own room, it's more important that your roommate pays bills on time and respects your space.

House Rules

୭ର୭

The sooner you get the standard operating procedures for your apartment settled and agreed upon, the likelier it is that you and your roommates will never fight over anything more serious than k. d. lang vs. Aretha Franklin. There's no such thing as getting these issues out in the open too quickly—why even wait for the ink to dry on the lease?

Rent: How will the rent be paid? (Who will write the check, how will the rent be divided?)

Community items: How will household needs be paid for? (Everyone could contribute about $20 or so to a "pot" that would cover specific items like toilet paper, paper towels, lightbulbs, cleaning supplies, milk, etc.; when the pot is depleted, everyone contributes more. Or you could have a receipt jar and figure out expenses at the end of each week or month. Then again, you might all decide to fend for yourselves—good luck!)

Food: Will everyone be responsible for buying her own food? (You might want to have labeled shelves so that your items will stay your items. Or keep track of who bought what when.) Will you have collective meals?

Early departure: What happens if someone wants or has to leave before the lease is up? In what circumstances is she still responsible for the rent? How will you all go about finding a replacement? If a roommate will be away for the summer, can she sublet her room?

Phone: What will be the system for taking phone messages? How will you deal with the bill? (Getting separate phone lines is a common method of dealing with phone and phone bill problems.)

Bills in general: When and how will they be divided and paid? Whose name will they be in? Where will they be kept?

Quiet time: Is there a time when there's to be no loud music, no tap dancing, no meetings of the Primal Scream Society?

Chores: How will the chores be divided? (To avoid resentment building up, it's good to agree on some kind of a system, even if it's loose. You can make up a schedule or "work wheel" and hang it on the fridge, or agree to do what needs to be done when it needs to be done.)

Guests: What's the policy on throwing parties, or having guests stay on the

living room couch, use the phone, eat community-purchased food?

Special rules: Are there religious holidays that other roommates should be aware of? Any things that should not be mentioned when parents or partners are around?

Getting Through the Rough Spots

ⓥⓥⓥ

House rules or not, there has probably never been a college student who has not found herself, at least once, burning in roommate hell. But when tensions are running high, and you would rather avoid or scream at your roommate than deal with the situation in a constructive manner, it's the most crucial time to take a deep breath and explain as calmly as possible why it bothers you when her boyfriend brings a case of beer and his swigging buddies over the night before your physics final. Uncomfortable situations will inevitably occur. Knowing when you're upset is easy—knowing how to deal with it is the hard part.

Problem Solving With Roommates

■ Nip problems in the bud. Don't wait until they grow and fester to the point that they can't be dealt with calmly and quickly.

■ Do not leave notes to address problems—speak with one another. A note on the fridge asking a roommate to "PLEASE deal with your disgusting cat" has never been an effective means of alleviating tension and solving problems. (It usually exacerbates the situation.)

"I was placed with a transfer student my first year. I was all excited about living away from home, and she didn't want to be in school at all. All she wanted was to live with her boyfriend. Plus, as a junior, she expected to live in a single—I was not in her plans. When I realized all of this, I asked to be moved. My room change was granted, only she was the one that had to go."

—POMONA COLLEGE, '96

■ Never use the silent treatment when dealing with others. It's not fair, and more important, it doesn't accomplish anything. (For more on conflict resolution, see "Taking the Beast by the Horns," page 572.)

Changing Roommates

ⓥⓥⓥ

You've tried everything short of couples therapy, but nothing seems to work. The two of you are driving each other crazy and there's gonna be a showdown in No. 2F if one of you doesn't get out soon.

Well, now, just simmer down, cowgirls. If you're on campus, talk to your RA or the residential life office to learn what procedures are necessary for a room change. Keep in mind that school-sanctioned room changes usually take an exceedingly long time (which seems even longer). At most schools, the process will take less time if you can find a person to swap rooms with on your own.

If you're not in campus housing, and one of you moves out, you'll need to deal with the following issues:

■ Will you/she be able to get your/her portion of the security deposit back?

■ Who is responsible for finding a replacement?

■ How will items bought together be divided?

■ How will mail and phone messages be handled? (Even if a mail-forwarding card is filled out at the post office, a few stray letters will usually slip through the cracks, and second- and third-class mail will generally not be forwarded at all. As for the phone, leaving the departing roommate's new number on the answering machine message for a month or so and posting her new number near the phone for easy reference works well.)

■ If the name of the person moving out is on the lease, you may want to talk to the landlord about resigning the lease with the new tenant. Be aware that the landlord may feel you are breaking the lease and refuse to make the changes. If this is the case, you may be able to sublease her place to someone else. As always, get everything in writing: You and your remaining roommates should draft and sign a contract with the departing party that transfers all legal obligations and responsibilities to the new tenant.

ACTIVIST IDEAS

■ Start a neighborhood/dorm/university recycling program. Talk with your local sanitation department and/or recycling center for information about what to collect, how it should be bagged or tied, how pick-up can be arranged, and other details.

■ Start a housing board and/or a ride board on campus, a place where both those looking for and those offering housing or rides can post information and messages.

■ At the end of the school year, when everyone is packing to go home, collect unwanted posters, clothing in good shape, dishes and silverware, rugs in decent condition, curtains, and lamps to donate to battered women's shelters, homeless shelters, and/or other charitable organizations, or organize a huge swap day on campus, where folks can trade their no-longer-wanted stuff for other people's clutter.

RESOURCES

OFFICE OF FAIR HOUSING AND EQUAL OPPORTUNITY
DEPARTMENT OF HOUSING AND URBAN DEVELOPMENT
451 SEVENTH STREET SW, ROOM 5116
WASHINGTON, DC 20410-2000
(202) 708-2878
Provides copies of housing laws and regulations.

MAIL PREFERENCE SERVICE
DIRECT MARKETING ASSOCIATION
P.O. BOX 9008
FARMINGDALE, NY 11735-9008
A nonprofit national removal service that, if you write them, will help you avoid getting unsolicited (junk) mail.

TELEPHONE PREFERENCE SERVICE
DIRECT MARKETING ASSOCIATION
P.O. BOX 9014
FARMINGDALE, NY 11735-9014
The same as above, except that it helps curtail the number of unsolicited phone calls you receive.

ENVIRONMENTAL DEFENSE FUND
(800) 225-5333
Provides information about local recycling programs and the environment, available upon request.

You can also find out about local recycling programs by looking in your phone book under "Recycling" or "Sanitation Department."

NATIONAL CONSUMERS LEAGUE
815 15TH STREET NW, SUITE 928
WASHINGTON, DC 20005
(202) 639-8140
Provides informational pamphlets about consumer issues such as housing rights and environmental health.

AMERICAN MOVERS CONFERENCE
2200 MILL ROAD
ALEXANDRIA, VA 22314
Provides information and brochures with tips for moving. Write to request free information.

TELE-CONSUMER HOTLINE
1910 K STREET NW, SUITE 610
WASHINGTON, DC 20006
(202) 223-4371 (VOICE/TDD/SPANISH AVAILABLE)
Provides information about special telephone products and services for persons with disabilities, selecting a long-distance company, money-saving tips, reducing unsolicited phone calls, and telemarketing fraud.

TELECOMMUNICATIONS FOR THE DEAF, INC. (TDI)
814 THAYER AVENUE
SILVER SPRING, MD 20910
(301) 589-3006
Provides a listing of TDD manufacturers. TDI is a national organization that oversees matters relating to TDDs. It has authorized agents, whose roles are to recondition donated surplus teletype machines for practical TDD use, and to sell various types of portable TDDs.

State Utility Commissions:
State utility commissions provide information about utilities and customer rights, as well as regulate consumer services and rates for gas, electricity, and a variety of other services within your state. Many also handle consumer complaints.

You can find your local utility commission by looking in your phone book under "State Government," "Public Utilities Commission," or "Department of Public Utilities."

13 incandescent bulbs and uses only ¼ the electricity.

Working Women

Jobs, Internships & Careers

Just about all of us will have to hunt for a job at some point in our college career. We may need to find something to fulfill a work-study grant. Or we may need to make money to help pay for tuition or living expenses. We may want to beef up our résumé so that when it comes time for the "real job" search during senior year, we'll have relevant experience. We may want to learn more about an industry, company, or issue for an independent project or to help decide what to do with the rest of our lives. Or perhaps, owing to a light load, we have some time to get involved with a local activist group that does work we believe in.

FIRST THINGS FIRST

Once you've determined how a job fits into your short- or long-term plans, your next step should be to pinpoint what kind of job you want. If you're working while still in school, you'll need to find something that will fit your schedule, and, hopefully, something that won't leave you so stressed and exhausted you'll have no time for schoolwork. You'll need something that's nearby and won't require you to waste too much time and money on commuting. This doesn't mean that you're limited to slinging hash at the local greasy spoon. (Not that this is necessarily a bad prospect, considering you'd probably get a free meal or two. . . .) You can choose something school related, such as working in the reserve room at the library, working in

ANGLING FOR WORK

Think of the job hunt as if it were a fishing trip. First you have to decide what you're fishing for (determine your goals), then find the right spot (research possible fields), then get your equipment together (write a cover letter and résumé). Once you're all set, cast your net as widely as you can (consider small companies and large ones). And then if it's necessary, you'll have to cast it again. Finding the right job at the right time takes not only organization but patience.

the school day-care center, or getting a position with a prof doing breast cancer research. Or you can do something totally unrelated, such as working in an office off campus or baby-sitting in the local community, and have some time away from school.

If you're looking for a job for after graduation, you'll probably have to think a bit more broadly. Consider the required skills, what's to be learned, any contacts you might make, as well as the pay. For example, if you're interested in advertising, do you want to work for a glamorous Madison Avenue agency, where you might get a fancy title and work on high-profile national accounts but where you'll do only clerical tasks? Or do you want to work in a small company, where you participate fully in the creation and execution of a local campaign? Or do you want to work at a nonprofit, where you get paid almost nothing but may have complete control over the

look and feel of an advertisement and where it's placed?

Your options are almost unlimited, as there are any number of ways to gain work experience, including:

Volunteer positions/internships: Both provide excellent opportunities to boost your skills, meet new people, strengthen your résumé, get the scoop on an organization, and learn the ins and outs of your field of choice. Though the terms are often used interchangeably, internships are generally regarded as more structured and prestigious than volunteer positions, and some internships are paid. Some places use the title "intern" for all regularly scheduled volunteers, and some use it only for the hand-picked few who made it through a grueling selection process.

Part-time jobs: The vast majority of students work at some type of part-time job, whether it's to fulfill work-study requirements, earn extra money, or explore career options.

Summer jobs/internships: Use summer jobs to gain experience, to make money (a summer's savings should buy at least a few classes' worth of books), get more deeply involved in your present job, and/or to explore different fields.

Full-time jobs/careers: When it's time to take the inevitable plunge into the working world, ideally you'll have used your summer and part-time jobs, classes and extracurricular activities to help you pinpoint the type of full-time job that will bring you joy. You're not alone, however, if after going through 15 jobs and 3 majors and reading every career guide in the local bookstore, you still haven't a clue as to what you want to do.

 Women start new businesses at twice the rate of men.

ALL ABOUT INTERNSHIPS

Internships come in many shapes and sizes. They may be paid, unpaid, structured, loose, short-term, or long-term. In the best circumstances, you're treated like a member of the team, given challenging projects, and exposed to the way an organization—be it a performing arts company, a publishing house, or a research lab—functions. But often, the duties aren't very glamorous. As low woman on the totem pole, you may be asked to perform tasks you find somewhat tedious: hang up costumes, photocopy manuscripts, or clean lab equipment. Still, it's a great opportunity to see whether you like the industry and/or the specifics of the job. And because there are at least three summers before graduation, you can sample several industries you find interesting. For example, if you've always been curious about arts management, but you're not exactly sure what type of arts you'd most like to manage, first you can try interning at a museum; then with a major metropolitan symphony; and then at a tiny theater company in the country. On the other hand, if you discover you don't like the way arts companies operate, and you're considering veterinary school, you can use the following winter break or semester with a light course load to intern at a vet's office.

Experience isn't the only benefit of an internship. It can be an ideal way to get in good with a company you eventually want to work for full-time.

Along the same lines, it's a great way to make contacts that will stand you in good stead when you're looking for another job and need recommendations. If you can find an internship related to your field of study, it might be possible for you to arrange for school credit. An internship can also help you shape your academic plans—if you fall in love with a field, you can take related coursework.

And nowadays, quite a few internships pay. If you find one that has no salary to speak of but is irresistible, try moonlighting. See if you can handle an evening job like waiting tables. Or maybe you can intern three days a week and work for pay the other two. At a bare minimum, try to get your employers to provide a small cost-of-living stipend, at least enough to cover transportation to and from work and lunch.

FINDING INTERNSHIPS

Use the career services office or one of the many internship directories in the library; some of these are organized by region, others by field, and others seem to have no organization whatsoever but can still be quite helpful. If your search doesn't yield the perfect internship, consider creating one of your own. If there's a company you'd really like to work for and it doesn't have a formal internship program, ask about the possibility of coming in to work on office tasks they simply don't have time to start or finish.

75 to 80% of women interns subsequently found a job as a result

STARTING THE HUNT

To help find the job that best suits your needs, interests, and ambitions, you should make a priority list. Even if you have a pretty solid picture of what you're seeking, putting it down on paper can help you sharpen your focus.

You may find that you'll have to compromise, but that's to be expected. It's a rare job that will fulfill all of your needs, especially when you're in school or just starting out.

If you're in school, flexibility—e.g., the ability to take the day off before final exams or to shift your work schedule every term to fit your class schedule—may take precedence over high wages. Or you may vacillate between working for peace, equality, freedom, justice, and the general betterment of society and making a decent salary that'll enable you to pay back your loans. A priority list that includes the following should help with some of these difficult decisions.

■ What are your "must haves"—your absolute requirements? (A salary sufficient to support you, an office that is wheelchair-accessible or close to campus, health insurance?)

■ What are your "really wants"—requirements, things that you'd prefer not to sacrifice but might consider giving up for an exceptional job? (A job with a health club in the building, a company that has a good track record for promoting women, access to a word processor so that you can type your papers?)

■ What are your "would likes"—things that you know you could work without but are still important? (An informal atmosphere where you can wear jeans or study during the slow periods, a smoke-free environment, a job in New York, a fancy title?)

■ What are your "it would be great but it won't be a deciding factor" wishes? (Your own secretary, flexible hours, a corporate credit card?)

■ What are your "hope nots"—things you'd like to avoid but might be persuaded to accept if everything else were fabulous? (A long commute, weekly meetings every Monday at 7:30 A.M.?)

■ What are your "definitely nots"—things about the job that would call for an immediate veto? (A job that puts you on the road three weeks out of four, a job that doesn't offer health insurance?)

In making your list, it may help to consider whether the following things matter to you and rank them in order of importance:

▲ High salary
▲ Company's commitment to social values
▲ Training programs
▲ Fulfilling work
▲ Time and energy commitment
▲ Company's "good track record" in terms of women and minority employees
▲ Prestigious job title
▲ Prestigious company name
▲ Friendly coworkers
▲ Nice boss
▲ Decision-making opportunities
▲ Promotion opportunities
▲ Fast-track company
▲ Good benefits
▲ Flexible hours
▲ Subsidized or on-site child care

▲ Travel opportunities
▲ Big/small company
▲ Working conditions/atmosphere
▲ Own office
▲ Convenient location
▲ Tuition reimbursement
▲ Opportunity to meet interesting people
▲ Potential for promotion
▲ Vacation time

RESEARCHING JOB OPPORTUNITIES

There are a number of places you can turn to for help in your search for the ideal job. Some may be more useful than others, depending on what you're looking for and the time and energy you're willing to commit. ,

Student employment office: If you need a little pocket money and you're looking for a part-time job while you're in school, you might try here for both on-campus work and jobs available in the community. They usually require you to fill out an application and/or submit a résumé, which they will then send out to companies looking for skills comparable to yours. They also may call you if an appropriate opening comes in, or they may require you to drop by and check out the listings. If you're looking for a career-related internship or a job after graduation, you might head toward the career services center.

Campus career office: Many schools have baby-sitting, catering, and bartending services that you can sign up with. (At some schools the college career office functions as the employment office.) Your school wants to help you find a job that you'll like and be well compensated for. Their motivation is not purely economic (though no school would be angry at an alum who sends in a thank-you check). Statistics on the percentage of graduating students landing full-time jobs have a grand effect on the school's ranking, which in turn affects the school's ability to attract "highly competitive" applicants, alumni support, research grants, and prestigious professors.

Thus, it's in the school's best interest to have an active, viable career services office where job and internship opportunities are posted. In addition, these offices usually have information on recruiters (organizations/employers that come to campus) as well as a list of alums who may be willing to help you land a job. Many schools have mentoring programs specifically for women, and women's colleges are notably good at setting up alumnae with students and recent grads. Take advantage of whatever services your campus's career services offer. Most also provide career counseling, information and assistance on

RECRUITMENT ON CAMPUS

M any organizations (usually large for-profit companies like banks, insurance companies, advertising agencies, consulting firms, etc.) come to campus to recruit young talent. Find out from your career services office or the school's newspaper which companies are coming and when. Recruitment is usually a two-step process. First, recruiters come to campus to host an informational session, where they boast about their company, answer students' questions, and pass out information, usually annual reports or promotional brochures. They also encourage interested students to send in their résumés by a certain date.

Use the session to find out as much information about the company as you'll need to send in the most competitive cover letter and résumé possible. Ask intelligent questions about the types of positions they have available, the company's record on promoting women, the number of spots they're trying to fill, and anything else that interests you.

The second step involves on-campus interviews. Once the recruiters have screened the résumés, they send letters or call students to invite them to interview for jobs. Then, they return to the campus to interview a select number of students. Bear in mind that recruitment is very, very competitive. If you don't get called, write to the recruiters. Without groveling, let them know how disappointed you were not to get an interview, and suggest that if they can schedule one more, you're sure they won't regret it. Remember, too, that recruitment is only one way of reaching these companies. You can always contact the human resources department of a company you like directly.

Recruitment is generally reserved for seniors and graduate students, but there are exceptions. If you have a while before you graduate but you're interested in a summer position, attend the session anyway. If you'd like to work for a company while you go to school, ask about projects you could work on part-time.

writing a résumé and cover letter, and tips on helping you interview more impressively. Many jobs listed in career offices are specifically targeted toward students or recent graduates, so you may find it a little less discouraging than looking through the help-wanted ads.

While campus career offices are usually indispensable, they're not miracle workers. Once you find a job that looks good to you, you'll still have to work at making yourself stand out from the dozens to hundreds of other qualified students applying for the same position.

Libraries and newsstands: Libraries and newsstands are key places to look for newspapers, newsletters, and magazines that list new openings. Check local, campus, alternative, community, and free papers as well as trade (industry-specific) papers/journals and community newsletters for listings of jobs in specialized fields like not-for-profit, arts and entertainment, environmental, service, and women's organizations.

Also take a look at the library's job guides, directories, and magazine indexes, especially publications like the *Encyclopedia of Associations* or the *Directory of Organizations*. Many associations will send you regional and/or corporate lists free of charge. *The Job Bank Series* (a city-by-city guide to major employers) is also very useful. You can also consult specialized directories that list internships by industry—the arts, publishing, and so forth—or by region. If your library does not have these publications and other reference books, take the names and publishers of the books you want to the librarian and ask if s/he can order them. They may take a few weeks to arrive, so plan in advance.

Job boards: Many community, cultural, religious, ethnic, women's, and political organizations have job board listings. Consult them regularly.

Your network of friends, family, and professors: Often, just telling everyone you know that you're looking for a  job will lead to interviews and opportunities. While your personal dignity might not allow it, friends and family members are likely to go out of their way to ask around and toot your horn shamelessly. Be as clear as possible about what you want, so they can associate you with a specific job or opportunity. Professors are often privy to job information in their specific fields, so be sure to consult your deparment head or advisor if you're looking for work connected to your research or academic interests.

Departmental bulletin boards: Many academic departments have job listings in related fields. Also, if you are interested in working abroad you might ask a professor about positions in foreign countries. If, for example, you wanted to improve your Italian, ask a professor in the foreign languages department who teaches Italian if she can put you in contact with a company or university abroad where you might investigate work or research opportunities.

Field experience/cooperative education offices: Many schools require, urge, or allow students to count work experience toward graduation requirements, and have an office that specializes in helping students find and arrange it.

Former employers, supervisors, coworkers: Folks who know you and the quality of your work from past jobs or internships are the perfect people to call on when you're looking for a job. Even if they can't offer you employment, they will probably be able to recommend places and people to contact.

Placement offices/employment agencies: These organizations are often hired by companies to screen applicants and provide them with a pool of qualified candidates appropriate for a given job. When the agency places a candidate, it receives a commission from the hiring organization. So it's in the agency's best interests to see you land a plum job. But beware: Though headhunters can be very helpful, they can also be very pushy when they want you to take a job—even if it's not the job you want.

Temp agencies: If you need money while you are looking for a permanent job, or if you want a job with very flexible hours so you can work when your schedule permits, temping may be the answer. Though there are some drawbacks, temp jobs do pay relatively well and require very little commitment—assignments can last anywhere from one day to one month, and beyond. It's not unheard of for a temp job to turn into a permanent full-time job. By working in-house, you're usually the first to know about new openings. And if you've made a good impression on a coworker or two, you probably have a contact who will go to bat for you to get the job (or at least an interview with the head honchess). For more on temping, see page 178.

Other organizations: Contact the chamber of commerce in the area you'd like to live to find out about a specific organization or request a list of companies in your field(s) of interest.

Classifieds: The help-wanted section of the local and major daily newspapers in your metropolitan area lists new job openings at least every Sunday, and usually two or three other days per week. Look for ads that include the words "entry-level" or "college graduate" if you're worried about not having enough experience. If you see an interesting ad, act immediately. Openings are often filled right away. Also check the help-wanted sections of alternative papers.

Electronic/on-line job services: The job bulletin board has gone cyberhip. On-line bulletin boards are proliferating, and most schools provide students with free Internet access through the library or computing center. Some on-line services like America Online and CompuServe list openings in a variety of fields; others are field-specific. Remember, though, that on-line listings are usually for technological jobs and probably won't be helpful if you're looking for a job in, say, publishing or fashion. If you already know the field you're interested in, contact your industry's trade association, if it has one, to find out whether it posts jobs on-line.

GETTING YOUR FOOT IN THE DOOR

Once you're more or less sure about what you're looking for and you've found a few organizations that interest you, all you have to do is get them to hire you. Though it's easier said than done, the following steps should help you land a job.

Learn about the organization. Before you write your cover letter, have an interview, or apply for a job, learn as much as possible about the organization you're applying to. Potential employers respond favorably when you are familiar with what they do. If the company produces literature about itself, read it. If your interviewer knows you had a chance to read about the company (through published annual reports, recruitment brochures at the career services office, or recent newspaper articles), he will probably

36% to 51%, lawyers, 13% to 21%, and architects, 7% to 18%. ✺

expect that you have done so. The more you know about a prospective employer, the better equipped you'll be to tailor your comments and questions and emphasize the skills you have that could be useful.

When you schedule the interview, ask to have an annual report, quarterlies, a press release, or any other literature about the company sent to you. Or go to the library and check newspapers and magazines for relevant articles. If you're applying for a job with a store or other service provider, walk in as a customer and see what it is like.

If you find yourself with an interview at a company that you don't know (and can't find out) much about, call ahead and ask for information. You may wish to say, "I would really like to know more about what your company does" or "Can you tell me exactly what the company does?" If you are unable to get the scoop before the interview, ask there.

Write letters. Write to the company to express your interest in employment. Be sure to address your letter to the attention of the person who does the hiring. If you don't know who that is, call and ask. If you have a contact in the company or have a mutual acquaintance with or went to the same school as the person you'd like to impress, mention her/him/it, without

overdoing it. (Alternatively, you can ask your contact to write a letter of introduction on your behalf.) Mention that you will call "early next week" to see if it's possible to set up an interview or an informational meeting. Informational interviews are courtesy meetings at which you can ask questions about the field, what you should do to get your foot in the door, and when and where positions might be opening up.

Volunteer. Volunteering where you want to work could very well lead to a job. And while you are at it, you'll presumably be doing something you believe in and enjoy—all the while gaining experience. Even if you don't get a job at the organization, you'll show prospective employers that you aren't afraid of hard work, and if you've been a dedicated volunteer, your supervisor will probably be glad to provide you with references or contacts at related organizations.

Organize events on campus. Plan special events or seminars that center on your prospective field. For example, invite a VIP from the office of a politician you'd like to work for to speak on campus. With the assistance of career services or a department, plan a conference where speakers from a number of companies discuss trends in the economy, the state of women's health care, or different perspectives on the future of America. By organizing an event, you've (1) shown initiative, (2) made connections—ones you can call on when you are looking for a job, (3) become more familiar with the field, and (4) done a good deed for your fellow students.

Use your research. Do a class project, or write a paper or an article for a campus publication. Write to an influential person at a company whose work you admire, asking if she'd consider meeting with you to discuss her business or research ideas. You'll not only get an opportunity to meet her, but in all likelihood, you'll also flatter her by showing an interest in what she does. Most important, you'll have made a connection, someone you can later turn to for advice on finding a job.

The Nine Commandments of Job Hunting

ꙮꙮꙮ

Jobs are not just sitting around waiting for any takers. As the demand for graduates right out of college with little or no experience shrinks to new lows, it takes more skill, assertiveness, and confidence than ever to get the job you want. (Of course, a little luck never hurt anyone.)

1. Be assertive. When you hear of an appealing opportunity, find out more about it. In interviews, convey your confidence that you can contribute to the organization.

2. Be speedy. Respond quickly to news of job openings. Read the classifieds the moment they come out and have your résumé and cover letter ready to send out at a moment's notice.

3. Be attentive. Keep an eye on trade publications—look for news that signals new opportunities: start-up departments, new clients, promotions, mass defections (but first find out why people are leaving), new businesses/ stores (particularly good for part-time/summer work), or new organizations that may be hiring.

4. Be informed. Know the current news about your chosen industry and company. In your cover letter or during the interview, if you have researched an organization or read a recent article about it, find a way to make that clear. Also indicate how you got your information or found out about the job, especially if you were particularly creative. This will show that you have initiative (a desirable skill).

5. Be resourceful. Use every last one of your personal contacts. This point cannot be stressed enough. Using connections won't get you the job—only you (and your accomplishments) can do that—but your friends and family may put you in contact with someone who would likely otherwise have been inaccessible.

Everyone has connections—even when you think you don't, you do. For example, if you are interested in public health and you think you know no one in the field, think again. At worst, you know your doctor or health practitioner—call her up and ask if she knows anyone in public health whom you could speak with. Ask your profs, your roommate, your parents, your parents' friends, and your friends' parents—you never know who knows whom. Have no shame. It never hurts to slip the fact that you're looking for a job into a conversation. A little chutzpah (just a little, mind you) can go a long way.

6. Be prepared. Always bring your résumé to an interview or informational session—even if you sent it in previously. In fact, if you are on a job hunt, don't go anywhere without a résumé or at least an address book. You never know when you'll run into someone who can help you land a job.

If it appears that you've met some such person, say something like, "I'm looking for a job. Can I give you a copy of my résumé to give you a sense of my background, so if you hear of anything that might be right for me, you could let me know?"

7. Be creative. Present your résumé, cover letter, and yourself creatively. How imaginative you should be will depend on the field you're targeting. For example, while a résumé printed in an unusual font might be acceptable to a design firm, it probably won't go

---

ACTION WORDS FOR RÉSUMÉS AND COVER LETTERS

Accurately	Contacted	Improved	Purchased
Achieved	Contributed	Independently	Quickly
Actively	Coordinated	Increased	Raised
Acquired	Counseled	Influenced	Ran
Adapted	Created	Initiated	Received
Administered	Cut costs	Instituted	Recommended
Allocated	Dealt with	Instructed	Recruited
Analyzed	Decided	Instrumental	Reduced
Appointed	Demonstrated	Insured	Regularly
Arranged	Designed	Interpreted	Reorganized
Assigned	Developed	Investigated	Replaced
Authored	Devised	Involved	Reported
Awarded	Directed	Issued	Researched
Began	Distributed	Knowledge of	Revised
Built	Doubled	Launched	Scheduled
Calculated	Earned	Lectured	Secured
Changed	Edited	Managed	Selected
Chosen	Efficiently	Marketed	Set up
Collaborated	Elected	Oversaw	Simplified
Combined	Eliminated	Planned	Skillfully
Commended	Enhanced	Prepared	Sold
Compiled	Established	Presented	Specialized
Completed	Estimated	Priced	Spoke
Composed	Evaluated	Processed	Studied
Computed	Exceeded	Procured	Substantially
Conceived	Executed	Produced	Succeeded
Concluded	Expanded	Proficient	Summarized
Condensed	Expedited	Profitability	Supervised
Conducted	Expressed	Projected	Tackled
Consistently	Facilitated	Promoted	Taught
Consulted	Familiar with	Published	Tested

21% of women-owned businesses offer tuition reimburse-

over well on Wall Street. Do things that will make prospective employers notice you, but not so they'll remember you as someone to bar from the building.

8. Be conscientious. Always follow up. Thank anyone who interviewed you, spoke with you (even for just five minutes), gave you suggestions about places to look for a job, etc. Follow through on promises you made. If you say, "I'll call on Tuesday," call on Tuesday. Always write follow-up letters. Say you were excited by their work (the more specific you can be about how and why, the better) and thank them for their time and guidance. In your notes, aim for a tone that's honest and sincere, not overly ingratiating.

9. Keep good records. A job search is an ongoing process, and it can be very helpful to know with whom you talked, when, and what was said. Write it all down.

THE RÉSUMÉ

A résumé is a summary of your educational, work, and volunteer experiences. Most jobs require you to submit a résumé or fill out an application that includes the same or similar information. If an application is requested, you may wish to give them your résumé in addition to filling out the form.

Your résumé should be succinct yet comprehensive, highlighting your skills, talents, honors, and awards. To the extent possible, these should be tailored to match the requirements of the particular position you are applying for. Although résumés must be short (one page is standard), putting them together can be one of the most time-consuming tasks around.

When you are writing a résumé for the first time or adapting one for a specific position, it's useful to create a list for yourself of anything and everything you have ever done that's worth mentioning. It's also a good idea, even if you aren't looking for a job, to keep your résumé updated or to have a basic résumé that you can work from when you suddenly find yourself in need of one.

■ There are a number of acceptable résumé styles. Some people like to create a column for the date and a column for descriptions, others like to list them together. You can use bold and/or italic fonts, bullets, line spaces, and/or indentations to establish sections and organize the material. Pay a visit to the career section of the bookstore or to career services for a cornucopia of sample résumés.

■ It is standard to list items in reverse chronological order (most recent first).

■ If applying for a job during college or right after you graduate, you'll probably want to list your academic experience first; after a few years, employment experience comes first.

■ Be simple, terse, and clear. Rather than full sentences, use concise phrases beginning with active words, forgoing personal pronouns and articles. For example, "I coordinated the tutoring program" becomes "Coordinated tutoring program."

■ Resist the urge to skew type, add drop shadows, or use the computing center's entire font library. This is especially true if your résumé will be scanned into one of the automated systems popular in large or otherwise techno-savvy companies, since fancy type and layouts may be garbled by the computer. And don't forget to leave some white space for easy readability.

■ Don't put past salaries or wages on your résumé. You are being hired for a different job and presumably have more experience and maturity than in your last job. Thus the pay should be different.

■ Emphasize your trainability, specific skills, knowledge, responsibilities, and unique contributions you made to past jobs. Make yourself sound interesting, capable, and indispensable.

■ When you are being considered for a job, it is common for employers to request references. These recommendations can come from past employers and supervisors (at previous internships or summer, part-time, or full-time jobs), professors, advisors, and in some cases clergy or friends. Pick people who believe in your work and keep a list of their up-to-date addresses and phone numbers easily accessible during your job hunt, so when prospective employers call to request them, they are indeed available. Before you give out people's names, it is customary (and courteous) for you to ask if it's OK for you to use them as references. When you approach them, update them on your life and explain why you want the job you're seeking so that they can give you the best possible references.

■ Keep copies of your résumé (both print-outs and on disk) for your files. You never know when you'll need one.

■ Tailor your résumé to different job requirements. You may want to high-

CURRICULUM VITAE (CV)

A curriculum vitae, or CV, is a highly detailed academic résumé. It lists speaking engagements, more extensive job descriptions, publications, and the like. Used mostly for applications for grants or scholarships or to graduate or professional programs, academic postings, and so on, it is not appropriate for most job applications.

light or deemphasize certain things, depending on the job description. Information that is important for one job may not be for another. For example, if you are applying for a job at a homeless advocacy organization and you have done five years of volunteer work with the homeless, you should highlight this work, even if on other résumés it's the least prominent of your experiences.

■ Proofread like you've never proofread before. Read your résumé over before you send it out, then read it again. (A run through the spell checker is not enough.) And then, when you think it's letter perfect, give it to a meticulous friend to proofread yet again.

RÉSUMÉ COMPONENTS

YOUR NAME
HOME AND/OR SCHOOL ADDRESS
PHONE NUMBER

KEY WORDS Be sure to include the following (either in their own section or sprinkled throughout) if you're applying for a position in a large company that scans résumés into the personnel computer system: the name of your school, your major, your degree(s), your career goals, leadership roles, and languages and computer programs you are fluent or proficient in.

OBJECTIVE An optional line that says what you're looking for. It can range from the general "sales" to the specific "A public high school biology teaching position." Many recommend against putting objectives on résumés (especially when you're applying for a specific position), as it may end up closing you off to positions that don't exactly match your stated objective.

EDUCATIONAL EXPERIENCE List degree(s) received, major and/or field of interest, minor, year (or expected year) of graduation, and thesis or honors project title, if applicable. Some recommend removing high school from your résumé after sophomore year, but others say it can remain until graduation. Include special schools and programs (study abroad, performing or visual arts schools, etc.). Your GPA is needed only if you are applying to the most competitive positions or if your school recruitment program recommends it. In most cases, your GPA is not necessary.

AWARDS Include this section only if you have two or more honors to list.

WORK EXPERIENCE (or EXPERIENCE or EMPLOYMENT) Mention full-time, part-time, summer, paid, and unpaid jobs, internships, and leadership positions in campus and community organizations.

If you have held a series of short-term jobs not related to your intended career, you can write something along the lines of "Additional work experience includes baby-sitting, tutoring, and temporary office work" instead of listing them all individually with dates.

ACTIVITIES Activities that emphasize teamwork, leadership, finding innovative solutions to tricky problems, and/or creativity, and that demonstrate that you had the respect of your classmates (e.g., elected positions) are all good résumé fodder.

SKILLS Languages, computer knowledge (good words: fluency, proficiency, working knowledge of . . .) and other skills that might make you shine among the thousands of other job seekers.

And the optional last line: "References available upon request."

U.S. labor force; in 1992, 69% were earning paychecks.

THE COVER LETTER

Many people tend to spend so much time on their résumé that they have no time to write a memorable cover letter. Shame, shame. The cover letter is more than a formality—it's an opportunity to elaborate on your skills, impart a bit more of your dazzling personality, and show how good you are at writing a business letter. When employers are judging you based on two pieces of paper (especially when you're up against a sea of students and recent grads with nearly identical résumés), the cover letter is your first opportunity to stand out.

As with your résumé, remember to proofread and spell-check your cover letters (and anything else you write for a prospective employer). Triple-check the proper nouns—there's no more effective way to send shivers up the spine of a potential employer than to misspell her name or the name of the company. For most job openings, employers usually receive

---

COVER LETTER COMPONENTS

SALUTATION (OPENING)

▲ Call the company to verify the address and person to whom you should send your résumé. If you can't get a name, "Dear Sir or Madam" (or Madam or Sir) or "To Whom It May Concern" should do just fine.

BODY

▲ Where you heard about the job and what the job is.
▲ Who you are and why and how you are qualified (or better yet, perfect) for the position. Be specific about how your attributes complement the job and the company. You may wish to highlight past experience. Include both those things that obviously relate (e.g., a work-study position in a lab for a research job) as well as those things that might not be as obvious (e.g., being the head of the a cappella singing group required you to manage both the creative and business ends—perfect for working in a talent agency or PR firm). If you are sending a general letter of introduction and inquiry rather than applying for a specific position, you'll probably want to expand on your résumé and make yourself seem like the perfect candidate for any and every job they have available.

CLOSING

▲ Depending on the circumstances, you may ask for an interview, and tell them that you look forward to meeting them or hearing from them. Be sure to thank them for their consideration.

General Notes: Keep it simple, natural and friendly. Sound eager, enthusiastic, and confident, but not desperate or pompous. You want to show that you're qualified without sounding as if you think you have nothing left to learn.

---

so many qualified applications that they look for reasons to reject candidates. Sending in a cover letter or résumé with a typo is like handing them an ax with which to chop you from the forest of applicants.

Keep the following tips in mind as you compose a cover letter that, with minor adjustments, can be used to apply for almost any job:

■ Cover letters usually follow a semi-standard format. You will need headings that include your address and the date as well as the name, title, company, and address of the person to whom you are writing.

■ Say who you are, how you became aware of the opening, and why you are interested in it.

■ Briefly express why you are appropriate for the job. Mention coursework, experience, activities—anything that connects you with the job.

■ Type your cover letters on good-quality paper (the same kind you used for your résumé) and use matching envelopes.

■ Keep letters short and to the point.

■ Try to be warm and enthusiastic, but don't overdo it. Nobody likes an unctuous cover letter.

■ State that you have enclosed your résumé and thank the reader for his or her consideration.

■ Be focused. If you are interested in a certain position, say so. Don't just say you're great, say why you're great for the job.

■ Don't include information unrelated to the job, and for goodness sake don't include anything negative. Resist the urge to employ the oft-used line

"Although I don't have any experience in . . ." Positive, positive!

THE INTERVIEW

Interviews, as superficial as they may seem, are about making impressions. They offer you the opportunity to let the employer know more about you, to expand on your experience and interests, and to learn more about your prospective employer. People seem to either like interviews or hate them—it's a personality thing. Whether you excel at interviews or shake in your boots at even the thought of sitting across the desk from an interviewer, before your next interview try the following:

Anticipate questions. Ask your friends, your parents, career services, and any former supervisors about the types of questions you can expect. Some common questions: "Where do you hope to be in 5 to 10 years?" "What skills, interests, and experience do you have that we need?" "Why should we hire you?" "What are your biggest strengths and weaknesses?" "Why do you want to work for us?" "What was your most enjoyable experience in college?" "Why did you choose to go into this field?" "What do you hope to accomplish?" "What are your long-term goals?" Some interviewers may simply ask you to describe yourself and explain why you majored in a particular area. Even if they don't ask about it directly, they all expect to hear about your qualifications for the job, and the types of jobs you are applying for and why.

You should also be prepared for

"I found mock interviews to be really helpful—you can see how you are coming across, your body language, how many "ums" you say in a five-minute stretch, how often you flip your hair, and stuff like that."

—Columbia University, '92

what's known as the behavioral interview: A prospective employer poses a problem and asks you to describe something you've done in the past that illustrates your ability to solve it. Think about what kinds of scenarios could come up in the job you're applying for, and be ready to refer back to stellar problem-solving moments of your past.

Also be prepared to ask questions about the job and the company or organization. Interviews usually end with the interviewer asking you if you have any questions, and even if s/he has been crystal clear in describing the job and the company, you are expected to have them. Think of some ahead of time, just in case no questions spring to mind during the interview.

If the interviewer doesn't tell you when you'll hear about the job, it is appropriate to ask when you can call to learn of the decision or when you can expect to hear from her.

Practice. It is a good idea to outline what you want to convey about yourself before walking into the interview. Stress the areas you've excelled at in college or projects that have earned you positive reactions. To hear how you come across, you might practice saying what you'd like to express about yourself out loud.

Many career services offer mock interviews to help you practice your technique. Mock interviews are intended to strengthen the areas you are weak in, prepare you for possible questions that might come up, and boost your confidence. Most career counselors will provide feedback and evaluate your performance—some even videotape the interview and let you see yourself in action. If your school doesn't offer mock interviews, you may wish to have friends, family, or professors interview you as if you were in the real setting.

Consider your appearance. It is important to dress "appropriately" for the interview, meaning you should consider the type of job you are applying for, the dress code in the office, and the impression you hope to make. In most cases, it is better to dress more conservatively than less. It is also better to be overdressed than underdressed. For example, even if you know that employees are allowed to wear jeans, wait until you're hired

to don your Levis. People understand that you are trying to make an impression, and even expect it, so you should look professional.

Plan ahead. Before you leave for the interview, double-check the address and get clear directions. Give yourself plenty of time to get there. Even if you have already sent in your résumé or application, bring a copy to the interview. Then, when the interviewer is fumbling for your résumé, you can offer him one. Also bring a pad and pen and keep everything in a portfolio, so that you look neat and organized.

> "When I was on the train on the way to my interview, some idiot spilled a huge cup of coffee all over me. I didn't have time to go home and change before the interview. I had no choice but to walk in and tell the executive director of the only organization I ever wanted to work for what had happened. He understood and I got the job anyway. My advice: Be honest about your situation and it won't hurt you too much."
> —MOUNT HOLYOKE COLLEGE, '90

Accentuate the positive. Think of an interview as an opportunity to focus almost exclusively on your skills and those things about yourself that most qualify you for the job. This may be difficult, as studies indicate that women aren't trained to talk about themselves or to convey their strong points in the same way most men are. Remember, many employers realize that much of your experience will come from non-job-related arenas, so don't forget about drawing on your volunteer work or activist experience to highlight your leadership and organizational skills.

Be impressive throughout. If the measure of a successful interview is whether or not you made a good impression, the "interview" actually begins before you walk in the door. It begins when you send in your résumé and cover letter, or when you speak with the interviewer and request an informational interview. Once you're at the interview site, remember that you are not only making an impression on your interviewer, but also on everyone else in the office. In many cases, in fact, employers ask their coworkers (including the receptionist) about the impression a prospective applicant made on them. So be nice to everyone.

Show up on time. Never show up for an interview late. And if you arrive more than a few minutes early, take a walk around the block or find a quiet place to hang out before being announced. Most professionals find it very annoying to plan out their day fairly rigidly, only to have someone throw off their schedule by coming too soon.

Be yourself. It's not just a cliché: In any interview, the most important thing is to be yourself. Don't try to be something you're not, or say you have skills you don't. The point of the interview is to convince the interviewer that you are the right person for the position. If you are thrown hard questions—like "You have no computer experience, and the job requires it, so how could you handle it?"—confidently respond that while you're not yet a computer expert, you plan to enroll in a course, you just bought a book on the subject, or are a quick learner, and are sure you could pick up the basics in a short time. Such answers demonstrate motivation and initiative. Also, try to draw on examples of situations in which you have been forced to learn quickly and how you rose to the occasion. In essence, think about how to turn difficult questions into opportunities to give reasons for hiring you.

Pay attention to the interviewer's style. Is she casual, friendly, serious? Try to follow her lead. If it seems as if she is a very detail-minded person, you may want to be especially detailed in your answers. Don't make jokes with someone who is very serious. Always try to make eye contact—it is considered one of the most important parts of interviewing.

Listen. Match the skills you emphasize to the skills the interviewer is looking for. When the employer gives cues about the type of person wanted for the job, present yourself accordingly. For example, if a job requires contact with customers, respond by mentioning any experiences or courses that have prepared you to deal with people.

Turn potential pitfalls into assets. Listen carefully to the questions you are asked by your interviewer and try to hear the message *behind* each question. For example, if an interviewer asks you about the diverse interests listed on your résumé, she may be concerned about your lack of focus and your decision-making abilities. Or she may be excited by your interest in a large number of fields, and see you as a multifaceted person. Try to figure out which. You might want to respond by turning the question around: "I have explored a number of fields, and my exploration kept leading me back to this." And remember, it's usually a good idea to bolster your answers with concrete examples from your past. If you don't hear a question clearly or are unsure of its meaning, politely ask your interviewer to repeat the question.

If it seems as if the interview isn't

HANDY TIPS ON BALANCING SCHOOL AND WORK

▲ Make sure your employer knows and respects the fact that you're a student.

▲ Figure out when you're most efficient, and try to leave at least some of those hours free for studying.

▲ Let your employer know ahead of time about exams, and schedule time off to study.

▲ Consider trying to find a job that will enable you to study while you work (e.g., a receptionist position in a slow office).

▲ Learn to be more efficient with your study time.

▲ Know your limits. Accept that you're not Superwoman.

working out, you probably can still salvage it by remaining confident and conscientious. Don't get upset or start to worry. Believe it or not, interviewers realize you are only human. When you make a mistake, admit it and correct yourself. Also, if as things are coming to a close, you realize you have left out important points about yourself, when the interviewer asks if you have anything more to add or any questions, you might say, "Although I didn't get a chance to express this earlier, I think it might be helpful for you to know about my experience with . . ." or "Would you be interested in hearing about . . . ?"

Evaluate how you did. Although it's small consolation if you don't get the job, interviews are always good learning experiences. At the end of every interview, ask yourself what you could have done to make it go better and which questions you would have answered differently and why. This will only stand you in good stead for the next one.

Follow up. Send a typed follow-up note within 24 hours. In it you should reiterate how right you are for the job, stress how much you enjoyed meeting the interviewer, and thank him for his time. You should also indicate that if you haven't heard from him by a certain date, you'll follow up with a phone call. Such a letter is a sign that you're interested, it puts your name in his mind again, and it gives you another opportunity to show him who you are. If the interview was informational, thank him for his advice. Depending on how formal or informal the situation is, you might call the person you met with as well, especially if something you learned in the interview led you to a new direction or a job.

YOU GOT IT— SHOULD YOU TAKE IT?

Congratulations! You were offered the job. As heady as it can feel to be wanted, however, don't fall into the trap of accepting your first offer. Before you do, find out everything you can about the job. Ideally, you'll find someone within the company to talk to. Ask whether people enjoy working there. What's your potential boss really like? Will you be expected to put in overtime without compensation? Are you going to be working under a lot of deadlines? Will there be a lot of travel? (And if so, is it to places you want to go?) Don't let the prestige (or lack thereof) of a job title fool you. Find out what your real responsibilities and growth potential are.

Tips on Negotiating Terms

Assume your terms are negotiable. Even if you're truly desperate for a job, don't accept the salary and benefits right off the bat if you're not entirely satisfied. They are probably not carved in stone. Once you have an offer in hand but *before you accept the job,* you may take steps to negotiate. Don't be afraid to do so; it's perfectly acceptable to ask for more money, a bonus linked to performance, more vacation time, better benefits, etc.

Be bold and confident. While maintaining the favorable impression you've made, assert your worth.

Talk to people familiar with the field. If you want to know if your salary is competitive, talk to someone in the industry or at career services and/or check the library for Department of

TEMP TIME

Temp work has supported many a student through times when having a regular job wouldn't be feasible or desirable. Granted, being a temp doesn't offer you the perks of full-time employment, such as job security, benefits, coworkers who call you by your given name, or freedom from being a permanent fixture at the bottom of the office totem pole, but the pay-to-flexibility ratio is hard to beat. And it's no secret that many companies hire their temps to fill permanent jobs. Why should they go through a whole long job search, then spend time training someone when they know, after seeing you work, that you'd be perfect? Below are a few tried and true temping tips:

▲ You may be able to find temporary jobs through campus and community bulletin boards, career services, the student employment office or the campus or local paper, or by asking around. But, if you're looking to work at least a couple days a week for an extended period, you might want to hook up with an agency. Temp agencies match workers (you) with companies that need short-term help. They usually have a stable of temps they farm out to jobs, and they'll negotiate your pay (and pay you even if the company stiffs them), and work out difficulties between you and them should they arise. Companies turn to agencies for prescreened temporary workers.

▲ Shop around before you settle with a temp agency. Ask each agency about its connections, pay, how and when it will contact you (the night before, the morning of, you call them, they call you, you go into the office), and what kinds of jobs are common. Give a call to the local Better Business Bureau, the career services office, or friends who work in large companies who use temps and ask if they know anything about the agency's reputation.

▲ When you call to set up an interview with the agency, ask about what you should bring and what you should expect. In most cases, you should bring a résumé and be prepared to talk about your background, training, and experience. You'll probably be given a typing test, and if you say you're competent on the computer, a word processing test. Specialized temp agencies have been cropping up in cities big and small. If you are a Macintosh guru, know a few languages fluently, have experience as a medical or dental receptionist or day-care worker, or have other special skills, see if there's an agency that deals only in your area of specialization. It's more likely that you'll get work you're interested in, and you'll probably be paid pretty well for your expertise, too.

▲ In order to get the good jobs, you'll probably need to rack up a few hours in temp-job hell. You'll eventually get first pick at the plum positions and a good salary if you are available when you say you will be, are willing to take a few of those jobs that no one else wants, and do such a good job that you improve the agency's reputation (and your own). So don't be picky—and certainly not just

72% of temps are female and 48% are between ages 16 and 34.

for the sake of looking good in the agency's eyes. It's well documented that even the oddest jobs can be the beginning of an exciting, worthwhile, and lucrative career, a source of new friends, good material for your novel, or a way to learn some marketable skills and chalk up some experience. If nothing else, you will have a chance to confirm that you never want to have anything to do with a specific company, task, or industry again—very useful info to know.

▲ Temps aren't always treated with love and respect. Dealing with people who throw you a "why should I bother to be friendly, she'll be gone in a day" attitude goes with the territory. Don't take it personally.

▲ Act professional. Dress appropriately, ask questions, get there on time (or even a bit early). Don't make personal calls or take a long lunch. Before you pick up the first phone call, type the first letter, or file the first file, ask how your supervisor would like it done. Assume every place does everything differently.

▲ Sometimes you'll find that companies want you to do different tasks than those you were told to expect. Try to be flexible and rise to the occasion. However, if you are asked to do something that makes you uncomfortable, or you are asked to do something you're not qualified to do, call the temp agency.

▲ If you really like a company (and they like you), ask your supervisor to tell the agency so you will get first crack at any future assignments there.

Labor statistics (and private statistics). Remember not only to compare salary-by-position but also to consider experience, educational level, special skills, and the financial state of the company.

Consider questions you might be asked and how you'll respond. If you're asked what you made in the past, hedge the question by explaining that this job is different and you expect that your salary will be different as well.

If they ask what your salary requirement is, likewise try to avoid answering. Ask what they had in mind. However, if you are pressed to give a figure, give one that's a little higher than what you want so there's room to negotiate. Many employers understand that most students right out of college have never negotiated a salary, and they often will offer you a salary without asking what you want first.

Can I Live on It?

ᘉᘇᘉ

■ First, figure out how much money you'll need to get by. (See "Budgeting Your Bucks," page 109.)

■ Figure in taxes. What your salary is on paper is not what you'll be taking home. Because deductions vary by state, company, and occupation, it is important to find out how much you'll have to pay for the following before you make a final salary estimate: local, state, and federal taxes, Social Security payments, union dues, insurance premiums, professional organization membership dues, and licensing fees.

■ Also, find out if you will be working by the hour, on commission, for a flat wage, what benefits the company will provide that you won't need to pay for (meals, clothing, child care, car, rent, commuting, and so forth), and the cost of living in the area.

■ If, once you've factored in all of the above, you discover that there's no way you'll be able to make ends meet on the proposed salary, explain your situation. Your future boss may be able to cough up a little more dough. If she tells you she can't go any higher and you still want to take the job, see if you can get her to agree to a performance review in, say, four to six months. A positive review should be tied to a raise. If she or the powers that be won't even agree to that, then—well, are you sure you really want to be working for this outfit?

PROTECTING YOURSELF ON THE JOB

Though school is competitive, the stakes seem much higher in the workplace. One of your coworkers may see you as a threat, especially if there's only one person targeted for promotion from assistant to associate this year. Pressure to be profitable, make deadlines, and produce perfect documents for the big boss also contributes to the stress. If your work environment is like a pressure cooker, things are bound to explode. When they do, you'll want to make sure you've covered your tail.

■ Keep copies of all of your work. Although it may seem silly or unnecessary, if anything gets lost or anyone questions what you have done, you will have backup and proof.

■ Verify your work. Proofread and spell-check everything. If you're working with numbers, get in the habit of spot-checking every now and again.

■ Report mistakes to your supervisor right away. Unlike in college, if you screw up, you can't make it up on the midterm or final. In the corporate world, mistakes cost money, and thus it's best to correct the mistake as soon as possible.

■ Keep others informed. Every once in a while, if it is not obvious, let others know what you are doing. You can do this casually, in a conversation at the water cooler, say, or more formally by sending around a memo or bringing it up at a staff meeting.

■ Keep a general log of what you do and how you use your time.

■ In case of conflict, keep a record. If you are experiencing any problems with people at work (coworkers, supervisors, etc.), keep a written record of what is going on. After meetings (or confrontations), write down what was said (or, if appropriate, take notes during the meetings).

■ Have periodic progress meetings with your employer. It is always a good idea to have your work evaluated by your supervisor. In this way, if you are making mistakes, you'll be able to smooth things out sooner rather than later.

■ Find a mentor. Someone who knows the ins and outs of the company or field can be your best asset. It's always

BENEFITS

Not all benefits are equally beneficial. They range from the good (a comprehensive health insurance plan, with a very low deductible or none at all) to the bad (catastrophic coverage with a $5,000 deductible) to the marginal (season tickets to curling matches). An advantage of working for a big, established company is that they usually offer more attractive benefits packages than small companies, independents, start-ups, or nonprofits. When you review your benefits package, keep the following in mind:

HEALTH INSURANCE: For many people this is the most important benefit to get, as health insurance is expensive to buy individually. Many employers do provide some level of health insurance. However, since there are a variety of different kinds of plans, it is not enough just to verify that an employer is offering you a health insurance plan. Find out exactly what your coverage includes—catastrophic only, eye care, mental health, etc. Also, consider what your deductible (the amount that you have to pay out of pocket before the coverage kicks in) will be. Is it $50 or $1,000? Do you have to contribute to the premiums? Can you go to any doctor, or must you go only to doctors who participate in the plan?

DENTAL INSURANCE: Some health insurance packages include dental coverage, and the deductible varies from plan to plan. Find out if your plan covers only preventive—regular cleanings and checkups—or if it also includes major dental—e.g., the dreaded (and expensive) root canal.

EDUCATION REIMBURSEMENTS: Many jobs provide partial or full funding for employees to take courses or work toward a degree.

401(k): This is a savings plan to which you can make pretax contributions, meaning that if you want to contribute $50 a week, that's $50 less of your salary that's taxed. Some companies will make contributions to your account as well, matching all or a portion of your contribution—for every $50 you contribute, they can contribute up to $50.

OVERTIME: You should find out the type of compensation, if any, you will receive for overtime.

DISCOUNTS ON CERTAIN ACTIVITIES OR PRODUCTS: Depending on your interests, this may be a greater or lesser perk. For example, if as a part of your job you receive free tickets to dance performances you would attend even if you were footing the bill, you may be saving yourself a lot of money.

VACATION/TIME OFF: Find out the number of paid days given for vacation and the number of sick and personal days allowed. Once you take the job, you should find out about procedure. For example, how far in advance do you need to request vacation time?

75% will lose their job at least once during the course of their career.

useful to have someone in your corner who can both vouch for your work and make sure you get your share of good assignments.

■ Leave on good terms. It is particularly important when leaving a job to try to do so amicably. If at all possible, keep in touch with past employers and internship advisors, as they can be great contacts when you are looking for a job in the future. It's also good to leave things in order. Write memos detailing where everything is, walk someone else through your intricate filing system, and teach him or her what your abbreviations mean. It is helpful to leave a number where you can be contacted if questions arise.

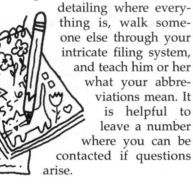

Discrimination and Harassment in the Workplace

இஇஇ

It is illegal for anyone to deny you a position or fire you solely because of your sex, race, ethnicity, religion, national origin, age, physical or mental disability, or union activity, and/or because you have filed complaints or assisted in procedures related to enforcing antidiscrimination legislation. Individual companies may also have their own antidiscrimination policies, many of which include provisions protecting against bias based on sexual orientation. There is also legislation protecting you from sexual harassment in the workplace. (See "Breaking Down Bias," page 463, for more information on defining bias, making formal complaints, and protecting yourself.)

ACTIVIST IDEAS

■ With the help of career services and campus community service groups, form a local internship matchmaking service if your school doesn't have one already. Fill a notebook with the names and phone numbers of community groups and a listing of what they do and what their needs are. Organize the information by topic/subject: environmental concerns, assistance to the elderly, women's issues, homelessness issues, etc. Students can page through and make their own contacts.

■ Organize panel discussions with alumnae about their careers. Have one

on business, medicine, law, art—depending on which majors are most popular, as well as on suggestions from fellow students. You can get in touch with alumni through the campus alumni office.

■ During on-campus information sessions, make a point to ask about in-house child care, parental leave, and the number of women employees in different departments of the company. It's good for companies to be reminded that potential employees care about such issues.

RESOURCES

Information About Women in the Workplace, Job Training, and Career Counseling

U.S. DEPARTMENT OF LABOR
200 CONSTITUTION AVENUE NW
WASHINGTON, DC 20210
(202) 219-6660

Provides information about all laws concerning employment, wages, and discrimination, as well as general statistical information about the workforce. Publishes materials about résumé writing, cover letters, and job search strategies.

Also houses the **Women's Bureau** of the U.S. Department of Labor ([800] 827-5335), which provides information about women in the workforce, including educational and statistical data, and publishes materials about women in the workforce. Also housed there is the Glass Ceiling Commission, which studies obstacles for minorities and women in career advancement, and works to promote diversity in the workplace.

Also houses the **Bureau of Labor Statistics**, which conducts research on all aspects of the labor force in the U.S. Publishes materials, including *Occupational Outlook Quarterly*, a magazine that provides information about current job trends, as well as advice about finding jobs, internships, and new job opportunities. They also publish *The Occupational Outlook Handbook*, available at most public libraries, which provides listings of careers—what they are like, what type of educational training is required, and projections for the prospects for each job type.

Also houses the **Office of Job Corps**, which provides information about job corps opportunities and applications. Publishes materials about job corps, including a directory listing the 105 job corps centers and their offerings, available upon request.

State Employment Service offices are listed in your phone book under "State Government Agencies." They will provide career counseling and assistance in finding jobs.

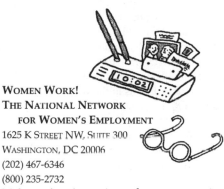

WOMEN WORK!
THE NATIONAL NETWORK FOR WOMEN'S EMPLOYMENT
1625 K STREET NW, SUITE 300
WASHINGTON, DC 20006
(202) 467-6346
(800) 235-2732

Makes referrals to places that can provide women with job training, counseling, networking, job placement, and other types of assistance.

EQUAL EMPLOYMENT OPPORTUNITY COMMISSION
1801 L STREET NW
WASHINGTON, DC 20507
(202) 663-4264
(800) 669-4000
TTY/TDD: (800) 800-3302

Local EEOCs exist in every state and can provide you with more specific information and assistance. Makes referrals to local EEOC offices. Provides information and answers questions about all areas of employees' rights, including information about policies on hiring, firing, unemployment, discrimination, and sexual harassment. Accepts and processes complaints against employers.

**9 TO 5: NATIONAL ASSOCIATION OF
WORKING WOMEN**
235 WEST WISCONSIN AVENUE, SUITE 700
MILWAUKEE, WI 53203-2308
(414) 272-2870
(800) 522-0925
Has local branches across the country. Provides information about women in the workforce. Provides crisis counseling and detailed advice for dealing with sexual harassment and other forms of discrimination in the workplace. Works to promote the improved status of women in the workplace and to introduce legislation to reduce occupational health hazards as well as sexual and racial discrimination.

Makes referrals to local organizations that can provide assistance to women dealing with problems in the workplace. Maintains a national speakers bureau of women in all fields of work. Conducts research on issues of importance to women in the workplace such as affirmative action, medical/family leave, and health issues.

Publishes numerous materials, including the *9 to 5 Newsletter*; *9 to 5 Working Women's Guide to Office Survival*; *Hidden Victims: Clerical Workers, Automatons, and the Changing Economy*.

**NATIONAL SOCIETY FOR INTERNSHIPS AND
EXPERIMENTAL EDUCATION**
122 SAINT MARY'S STREET
RALEIGH, NC 27605
Publishes numerous materials on getting, making the most out of, and keeping internships, including *The National Directory of Internships*, and *The Experienced Hand*.

**NATIONAL ASSOCIATION OF FEMALE
EXECUTIVES**
30 IRVING PLACE, 5TH FLOOR
NEW YORK, NY 10003
(212) 477-2200
FAX: (212) 633-6489
Promotes women's success in the work-

place. Provides information and advice about résumés, writing, interviewing, and networking techniques. Sells career books at a discounted rate. Makes referrals to women's professional and networking organizations. Publishes numerous materials, including *Networking; Stress Management; How to Get a Raise; Guide to a Winning Résumé; Market Yourself for Success;* and *Achieve Your Goals*.

NATIONAL COMMITTEE ON PAY EQUITY
1126 16TH STREET NW, ROOM 411
WASHINGTON, DC 20036
(202) 331-7343
Provides information and answers questions about equal and fair pay issues. Publishes numerous materials, including *Pay Equity: An Issue of Race, Ethnicity and Sex; Briefing Paper: The Wage Gap;* and *Bargaining for Pay Equity: A Strategy Manual*.

FAMILIES AND WORK INSTITUTE
330 SEVENTH AVENUE
NEW YORK, NY 10001
(212) 465-2044
FAX: (212) 465-8637
Provides information about and assistance for women trying to both work and raise a family. Publishes materials about women, work, and family.

NONTRADITIONAL EMPLOYMENT FOR
WOMEN
243 WEST 20TH STREET
NEW YORK, NY 10011
(212) 627-6252
Provides information about and assistance to women pursuing nontraditional careers. Publishes materials and makes referrals to local networking and professional organizations.

CATALYST
250 PARK AVENUE SOUTH
NEW YORK, NY 10003
(212) 777-8900
Works to promote advancement of women in the workforce. Conducts research and provides information and statistics. Maintains a speakers bureau. Publishes numerous materials, including career books and brochures on job hunting and development. Makes referrals to women's networking and professional organizations.

Networking/Professional Organizations for Women

Numerous networking organizations exist for women in all fields. The national working women's organizations listed above should be able to provide you with referrals to the professional organizations in your area of interest. For example, if you are interested in construction, you may want to contact the Association of Professional Women in Construction, if you are interested in being a firefighter, you might want to contact Women in the Fire Service, and so on. Such organizations often

■ Offer mentoring programs.

■ Facilitate or arrange internships.

■ Gather and provide information about the status of women in the field.

■ Work to promote greater equity for women in the field and to address discrimination problems.

■ Make referrals and recommendations for employment opportunities.

■ Serve as networking and support organizations for women already in the field.

Further Reading

ꙮꙮꙮ

Breaking With Tradition: Women and Work, The New Facts of Life, Felice N. Schwartz (Warner Books, 1992).

The Minority Career Guide, Michael F. Kastre, Nydia Rodriguez Kastre, and Alfred G. Edwards (Peterson's, 1993).

The Smart Woman's Guide to Career Success, Janet Hartner (Career Press, 1993).

The Smart Woman's Guide to Interviewing and Salary Negotiations, Julie Adair King (Career Press, 1993).

The Smart Woman's Guide to Résumés and Job Hunting, Julie Adair King, and Besty Sheldon (Career Press, 1993).

Work of Her Own: How Women Create Success and Fulfillment Off the Traditional Career Track, Susan Wittig Albert (G.P. Putnam's, 1992).

Work Sister, Work: How Black Women Can Get Ahead in Today's Business Environment, Cydney Shields and Leslie C. Shields (Fireside, 1994).

Offbeat Careers: The Directory of Unusual Work (Ten Speed Press, 1988).

What Color Is Your Parachute? Richard Nelson Bolles (Ten Speed Press, 1995).

The Wall Street Journal: Résumés, Taunee Besson (Wiley, 1994).

The Wall Street Journal: Interviewing, Arlene S. Hirsch (Wiley, 1994).

The Wall Street Journal: Networking, Douglas B. Richardson (Wiley, 1994).

97% of the senior managers are white, and nearly all of them are men. ☼

Part Three
Of Sound Mind & Body

The Big Three
Nutrition, Exercise & Sleep

In order to be a healthy and productive human being, you have to eat nourishing food, get some rest, and move around a bit. Combined, good nutrition, exercise, and sleep give you the strength to ward off disease, the stamina and acuity to take a three-hour essay test, and the chemical balance to keep your mood on a relatively even keel. On the simplest level, food is the fuel that gives the body energy, and exercise and sleep keep the body in good shape so it will use the energy efficiently and run for a long time. The better the fuel and the healthier your machine, the better your output will be.

The good news is that eating, working up a sweat, and getting REM sleep are some of the more enjoyable ways to pass time. The bad news is that at college, there often seems to be a serious shortage of places to eat healthy, quick, inexpensive food and little time to sleep and work out between classes, meetings, and all your other responsibilities. But it is possible to find the grub and the time to make your body happy without sacrificing all that you came to college to experience.

NUTRITION

If the old adage "You are what you eat" were entirely true, there wouldn't be so many attractive college students. It's not that we aim to eat poorly, but with the average cafeteria fare being what it is—vending machines and snack bars abounding, and at least four pizza places that deliver into the wee hours of the night—it just happens. And the fact that junk food just tastes so darn good

doesn't help the cause much, either. So how's a gal to eat right?

It's not as hard as you'd think. Eating right doesn't have to mean a steady diet of tofu-and-sprout sandwiches with a side of brown rice. It might mean skipping the extra cheese on a late-night pizza—or forgoing the pizza altogether. It might mean hitting the cafeteria's salad bar several times a week, or calling your mother for some of her quick-and-easy recipes you took for granted all those years (she'll be so flattered). But mostly, it's eating the foods that both taste good and are good for you. That's not to say that candy, chocolate chip cookie dough, or french fries can't be included in a healthy diet—you just might want to consider helping yourself only occasionally to such treats. A healthy diet must be realistic, affordable, and palatable, as well as supply the body with the essential nutrients. Because for most of us, even if it's healthy on paper, if we can't afford it, don't have time to do it, and/or it's not the least

bit fulfilling, it's not going to make us feel good.

Things can get even trickier if you're on a meal plan and your college's food isn't the most nutritious or delicious. While food service directors increasingly have been taking nutrition and fat content into consideration, dining hall fare usually still leaves a lot to be desired. It can be barely edible or full of fat or salt or all three.

Going away to school may also mark the first time you've ever had complete carte blanche in selecting not only what to eat, but how much you can have. Seconds, thirds, and even fourths are not a problem when it comes to cafeteria dining, though they might become one if you have to charge up a wardrobe that's a size or two bigger. But if you know the basics of nutrition, there are usually ways of finding something reasonably tasty to eat that will provide the essential vitamins and minerals and keep you clear of the dreaded "first-year fifteen."

EAT YOUR WORDS

One of the biggest assets of living and eating on campus is the communal aspect. Take advantage of the thrilling conversation just waiting to happen while you're noshin' in the dining hall. The pleasure of sitting back and discussing the latest movies, politics, an assignment, or the novel you have yet to put on paper can almost make you forget how utterly inedible the food is.

A VITAMIN AND MINERAL PRIMER

Vitamins and minerals are necessary for almost all body functions—from energy production to growth and repair to maintaining the body's various systems. They help keep our eyes seeing, our hearts beating, our bones strong, and our skin soft as a baby's bottom. Because the body is incapable of producing any of the essential minerals and most of the vitamins, they must be obtained from outside sources.

The best source of vitamins and minerals is food. The body can absorb and use the nutrients in food much more easily than it can those in most supplements. And unlike supplements, fruits, vegetables, and grains contain large amounts of fiber, which aids in the absorption of nutrients. That said, if you're like the vast majority of students and do not get 100 percent of the recommended daily allowance (RDA) of vitamins and minerals, it may pay to take a multivitamin.

Although you don't need a prescription to buy vitamins, it doesn't mean that they are all safe in large doses. Some vitamins (such as vitamin C and the B complexes) are water-soluble, meaning that if they are not used relatively soon after ingestion, they are excreted in urine or perspiration. You'll need to replenish these every day or so. Other vitamins (such as A, D, E, and K) are fat-soluble—if the body can't use them right away, they're stored in body fat or in the liver. (It's especially important to avoid massive overingestion of these. Because they can be stored, it's possible for them to build up to toxic levels.) Your body also needs small amounts of minerals—including calcium, potassium, magnesium, sodium chloride, phosphorus, sulfur, iron, iodine, zinc, and fluoride.

Keep in mind that volumes are written on the subject of nutrition, and new (often contradictory) information appears regularly. To learn the latest findings on what vitamins do, or what's generally thought to be good or bad for you, call upon a nutritionist, pay a visit to the ever-expanding nutrition section of your local bookstore, or contact an organization listed in the Resources at the end of this chapter.

Vitamins

ᗯᗯᗯ

VITAMIN A (Retinol)
Function: Helps maintain bones, hair, and skin; keeps eyes and organ tissue healthy; maintains organ linings. Functions as an antioxidant.
Best sources: Liver, eggs, yellow orange and dark green fruits and vegetables, fortified dairy products, and fatty fish, such as cod, salmon, halibut, and tuna. Beta-carotene, the vitamin A precursor, is found in such vegetables as parsley, carrots, squash, broccoli, cantaloupe, peaches, and apricots.
Other: A vitamin A deficiency can hinder night vision and cause other eye and skin problems.

VITAMIN B₁ (Thiamine)
Function: Maintains nervous system and muscles; facilitates energy production by aiding in the metabolism of carbohydrates. Functions as an antioxidant.
Best sources: Pork, fish, dairy products, eggs, whole grains, bran, brown rice, fortified cereals and bread, soybeans, peas, and potatoes.
Other: Your need for thiamine goes up when you're sick or working out a lot, or any other time you might need to burn extra carbohydrates. Thiamine may aid in the treatment of mental health problems. Part of the B-complex vitamin family.

ANTIOXIDANTS

Antioxidants, which include vitamins A, C, and E, are one of the newest health fads. Their merits have been lauded on magazine covers, in scientific and medical journals, and on health food store flyers. They've been touted as actually preventing disease and have begun to play a role in treatments for heart disease, cancer, and immune system disorders. Some scientists even believe they slow the aging process. They do their magic by helping to eliminate tissue-damaging free radicals, which are unstable oxygen molecules that are toxic by-products of basic cell metabolism and ordinary immune response. A healthy immune system is equipped to take care of free radicals before they cause trouble, but some health practitioners believe that consuming foods that are rich in vitamins A, C, or E, such as broccoli or carrots, is beneficial anyway. If your immune system is functioning less effectively because of stress or illness, it might be in your best interest to take an antioxidant supplement.

VITAMIN B₂ (Riboflavin)

Function: Keeps eyes and skin healthy; aids in lipid and protein metabolism.

Best sources: Liver, red meat, milk and other dairy products, eggs, whole grains, green leafy vegetables, and beans.

Other: Deficiencies cause eye fatigue, flaky skin or dermatitis, and irritability. Part of the B-complex vitamin family.

VITAMIN B₃ (Niacin)

Functions: Keeps skin healthy; aids in carbohydrate and protein metabolism.

Best sources: High-protein foods such as liver, red meat, poultry, fish (especially tuna), dairy products, eggs, whole grains, peas, beans, and peanuts.

Other: Can lower blood cholesterol and may help take the bite out of menstrual cramps. Oral contraceptives may inhibit absorption. Part of the B-complex vitamin family.

VITAMIN B₆ (Pyridoxine)

Function: Helps regulate the nervous system; aids in the production of hemoglobin (which allows red blood cells to transport oxygen from the lungs to all the body's organs and tissues); keeps skin healthy.

Best sources: Liver, herring, salmon, eggs, whole-grain products, wheat germ, brown rice, nuts, and most fruits and vegetables.

Other: Oral contraceptives may inhibit absorption. May help ease pain caused by carpal tunnel syndrome. Part of the B-complex vitamin family.

FOLIC ACID

Function: Aids cell growth and repair and formation of red and white blood cells.

Best sources: Liver, poultry, green leafy vegetables, whole-wheat bread, beans, nuts, orange and grapefruit juice.

Other: Required in high doses by pregnant women. One piece of fresh fruit or one serving of an uncooked veggie per day is all you need for a folic acid fix. Part of the B-complex vitamin family.

VITAMIN B₁₂ (Cobalamin)

Function: Aids in the formation of red and white blood cells; essential for a healthy nervous system.

Best sources: Liver, red meat, lamb, poultry, fish, milk, and eggs.

Other: As B₁₂ is found in animal products only—cows and sheep manufacture it in their digestive tracts— vegetarians and vegans should pay extra attention to the inclusion of sufficient B₁₂ in their diets. A deficiency of B₁₂ can lead to anemia. Oddly enough, not part of the B-complex family.

VITAMIN C (Ascorbic Acid)

Function: Stimulates immune system and bolsters resistance to disease; aids in mending wounds by helping blood clot and tissues heal; helps in the body's absorption of iron; is needed for the formation of collagen, which builds teeth and connective tissue; functions as an antioxidant.

Best sources: Fruit (especially oranges, strawberries, and cantaloupes), broccoli, potatoes, brussels sprouts, collard and mustard greens, kale, cabbage, turnips, and green peppers.

Other: May help decrease the severity and duration of the common cold.

VITAMIN D (Cholecalciferol and Ergocalciferol)

Function: Keeps teeth and bones healthy; helps heart and nervous system function properly; increases body's uptake and use of calcium.

Best sources: Sunlight, liver, fortified dairy products, eggs, whole grains, and fatty fish, such as tuna, sea bass, halibut, herring, and cod.

Other: May help prevent kidney disease, hypertension (high blood pressure) and osteoporosis. Antibiotics and sleeping medications may inhibit absorption.

VITAMIN E (Tocopherol)

Function: Aids in the growth and maintenance of cells; can help heal wounds and reduce scar formation; functions as an antioxidant and anti-carcinogen by protecting the body against environmental toxins, such as lead, mercury, and cigarette smoke. Some scientists feel that vitamin E prevents cells from wearing out, thus slowing down the aging process.

Best sources: Liver, fish, whole grains, green leafy vegetables, and vegetable oils, such as corn, saffron, and cottonseed.

Other: Too much vitamin E may inhibit absorption of vitamins A, D, and K. If applied in liquid form to the skin can help soothe and heal minor burns.

VITAMIN K

Function: Essential for blood clotting.

Best sources: Liver, tomatoes, egg yolks, whole grains, fruits, cabbage, spinach, and mustard greens.

Other: Since the friendly intestinal bacteria manufacture vitamin K, there is little danger of deficiency. However, if you are taking antibiotics which kill these bacteria, you should be sure to get your K from outside sources.

Minerals

಄಄಄

CALCIUM
Function: Helps build teeth and bones; aids blood clotting; helps muscles contract (especially the heart); activates enzymes.

Best sources: Milk, yogurt, hard cheeses, tofu, spinach, collard and dandelion greens, and salmon and canned sardines eaten with bones.

Other: Getting sufficient calcium is especially important from early childhood to early adulthood, when bones are growing. But even after they are fully grown, women need to make sure they get adequate calcium to help ward off osteoporosis, a condition in which bones become weak and susceptible to fracture. Women get osteoporosis more often than men in part because the lack of estrogen in the body following menopause can adversely affect bone density. Caffeine, antacids containing aluminum, and certain antibiotics can inhibit the absorption of calcium. Remember, though, that bones need much more than calcium to stay strong and healthy. Exercise and good nutrition are equally essential.

FLUORIDE (or Fluorine)
Function: Helps maintain strong bones and teeth.

Best sources: Fish, tea, fluoridated drinking water, and soybeans.

Other: Toothpaste with added fluoride helps maintain healthy teeth, as does the fluoridated water found in most areas of the country.

IODINE
Function: Essential to the health of the thyroid gland; facilitates hormone production.

Best sources: Seafood (particularly shellfish), dairy products, iodized salt, seaweed and sea vegetables.

IRON
Function: Aids in the production of hemoglobin (which transports oxygen to cells throughout the body); helps maintain circulatory and respiratory systems; increases resistance to stress and disease.

Best sources: Beef, liver, shellfish, poultry, milk, whole grains, breads, cereals, fruits, potatoes, spinach, broccoli, and nuts.

Other: Because menstruating women lose a significant amount of iron every 28 days or so, we are prone to iron deficiency. This is why it's important for pre-menopausal vegetarian women to be extra careful to include generous amounts of whole grains, enriched breads, and (if necessary) supplements in their diets. Iron deficiency can lead to anemia, causing tiredness, headache, breathlessness, and sores inside of or in the corners of the mouth. Caffeine may inhibit absorption.

MAGNESIUM
Function: Helps keep teeth and bones healthy; maintains healthy nervous and muscular systems; regulates body temperature.

Best sources: Seafood (especially tuna and clams), tea, milk, nuts, rice, oats, and green vegetables.
Other: If you eat normally, you can get all the magnesium you need without even trying. Deficiencies are extremely rare.

PHOSPHORUS

Function: Pairs with calcium to help keep those teeth and bones healthy; aids in the release of energy from carbohydrates.
Best sources: Red meat, poultry, fish, dairy products, whole grains, peas, beans, and nuts.
Other: Deficiencies are uncommon, as phosphorous is found in a wide variety of foods.

POTASSIUM

Function: Maintains healthy nervous and muscular systems; particularly useful in regulating heartbeat; may help alleviate muscle cramping.
Best sources: Red meat, dried fruits, bananas, orange juice, peanut butter, dried beans, and potatoes.
Other: Insulin and diuretics may lead to deficiency, but for the most part, potassium deficiencies are rare in people who eat normally. If, however, you have a severe bout of diarrhea or vomiting, you may be at risk for a deficiency.

SELENIUM

Function: Essential for immune system functioning. Prevents the breakdown of fats into toxic by-products. Functions as an antioxidant.
Best sources: Red meat, shellfish, chicken, egg yolks, whole grains, mushrooms, and garlic.
Other: Little is known about this mysterious mineral. Some studies indicate that selenium prevents cancers of the digestive system.

SODIUM (Salt)

Function: Helps muscle contraction; regulates the body's fluid balance.
Best sources: You won't have trouble finding sources—salt is a major ingredient of the average college student's diet. Think of all your favorite fast foods and snacks.
Other: Generally, there is no need to supplement your diet with sodium; if anything, you should watch your consumption, particularly if you are prone to high blood pressure.

ZINC

Function: Aids in the body's growth and in healing wounds; helps in the digestion and metabolizing of food.
Best sources: Red meat, seafood (especially canned tuna and oysters), eggs, poultry, whole grains, and milk.
Other: A zinc deficiency may affect appetite. The best way to get enough zinc is to eat a varied diet containing animal protein.

COPPER

Function: Helps in the formation of red blood cells.
Best sources: Liver, nuts, shellfish, various legumes, cocoa powder, and bran flakes.
Other: You should get a sufficient amount of copper without even trying—most diets supply more than enough.

CHROMIUM

Function: Helps metabolize carbohydrates and regulate blood sugar levels.
Best sources: Red meat, cheese, whole-grain cereals and breads, dried beans, peanuts, and brewer's yeast.
Other: May help prevent diabetes.

Food Building Blocks

〰◉◉◉〰

Carbohydrates, proteins, fats, and cholesterol are the building-block elements of food. They are the raw materials the body needs to fulfill its functions, be they refueling, growth and repair, or fighting disease.

CARBOHYDRATES
Function: The body's primary source of energy; whole grains provide the body with fiber, which facilitates good digestion and helps satisfy appetite.

Sources: Found in starches such as potatoes, rice, corn, breads, pastas, grains, dried beans, and cereals, and in the complex sugars in fruits and vegetables. "Empty" carbohydrates are the refined sugars found in cakes, cookies, ice cream, soft drinks, and other snacks.

Other: There are a host of good reasons to make whole grain complex carbohydrates the featured players in your diet: They are the best source of digestion-enhancing fiber, and they fill you up far better than sweets and fats do, and they can be rich sources of nutrients. Whole grains and beans in particular are nutritional bargains, and some types of beans have a protein content that puts them on a par with beef (at a fraction of the price).

PROTEINS
Function: Help build and maintain muscles, skin, hair, teeth, bones, organ tissue, and hormones. Not surprisingly, protein accounts for 50 percent of the body's dry weight.

Sources: Complete proteins (the animal proteins found in red meat, poultry, fish, dairy products, or eggs) contain all or nearly all of the nine amino

---

SWEET TALK
◦〰◦

The average American consumes 128 pounds of sugar a year. Whether it's the white stuff in the bowl on the kitchen table or those *-ose* ingredients listed on the back of the cereal box, we all eat far more sugar than we realize or need. All sugar, whether it's brown, white, raw, or honey, has the same nutritional value—which is, of course, zero, zippo, zilcho.

Lots of people rely on sugary foods for a quick energy boost, but it's a short-lived fix. As soon as the sugar hits your bloodstream, your pancreas secretes insulin to bring the level back to normal, or below normal, and you can be left even more hungry or tired than you were before. The next time the sugar urge hits, fight it off with a snack that won't cause you to crash. A piece of fruit, a bagel, or other complex carbohydrates take the body longer to break down, providing a steady supply of energy that curbs the appetite and keeps you going.

---

acids the body needs to manufacture its own special proteins. Vegetable proteins (which are found in whole grains, beans, yams, pasta, and nuts) may be deficient in one or more amino acids; to compensate it's best to pair complementary vegetable protein sources. (See "Vegetarian and Vegan Diets," page 199.)

Other: Chances are you eat more protein than you need, especially if you're

---

 Aspartame (Nutrasweet™) is just as caloric as sugar, but

not a vegetarian. All a 125-pound woman needs to satisfy her recommended daily allowance is 48–52 grams of protein, which is the equivalent of about six ounces of chicken. Consuming too much protein is thought to contribute to cancer and heart and kidney disease. But eat too little and you'll lose muscle.

FATS
Function: The body's most concentrated source of energy; supply fatty acids for many of the body's chemical reactions; aid in the the absorption of fat-soluble vitamins; provide cushioning for organs; and help regulate body temperature.

Sources: There are three kinds of fat in food: *saturated* fats which are solid at room temperature (these include beef or chicken fat, butter, coconut oil, and palm oil); *monounsaturated* fats, which are liquid at room temperature (these include olive, peanut, and canola oils); and *polyunsaturated* fats, which are liquid at room temperature and when refrigerated (these include corn, safflower, soybean, and sunflower oils).

Then there are the partially hydrogenated vegetable fats, like margarine and the shortening contained in so many of the foods on the supermarket shelf that are "bad for you." These are synthetically created saturated fats and they affect cholesterol levels like their animal-fat-saturated cousins. But because they are unnatural, the body isn't as efficient at breaking them down.

All fats, whether polyunsaturated, monounsaturated, or saturated, have the same number of calories per gram. If you're interested in cutting down on your fat intake, saturated fats are the ones to avoid because they are the ones connected to high cholesterol levels and heart disease, while monoun-

saturated fats are widely considered to be the healthiest choice.

Other: As little as one tablespoon of dietary fat a day can be all you require to produce the necessary fatty acids, but you may need more than this to maintain a body fat level that's necessary to the other functions listed above. However, nutrition experts suggest that no more than 30 percent of your total calorie intake per day should be derived from fats.

CHOLESTEROL
Function: Cholesterol is an essential component of cell structure, and it helps in the formation of hormones.

Sources: Cholesterol can be produced in the body by the liver and in the small intestines. It is found only in animal products, although certain highly saturated vegetable fats, such as coconut and palm oils will raise blood cholesterol levels. Roughly 85 percent of your cholesterol requirement is filled by your body; 15 percent comes from food sources.

Other: Cholesterol is possibly the most highly debated issue in nutrition today

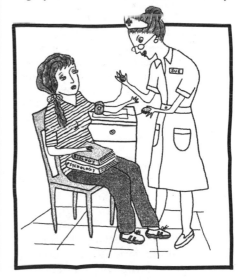

and is infamous for its role in causing atherosclerosis, or hardening of the arteries. The two types of cholesterol are low-density lipoproteins (LDL), or "bad" cholesterol, which cause heart disease, and high-density lipoproteins (HDL), or "good" cholesterol, which may actually prevent it. Your genetic background, your intake of fats, and the amount of exercise you get (HDLs increase with exercise) all affect cholesterol levels. Have your blood tested to determine if your cholesterol level is within the normal range (below 200) so that if necessary, you can take special steps to reduce your consumption of it.

Balancing the Basics

〇〇〇

A surefire method for covering all your nutritional bases is by following the recommendations set forth by the USDA in their ubiquitous Food Pyramid, which divides food into six categories. It suggests that on a daily basis you consume 6–11 servings from the bread, cereal, rice, and pasta group; 3–5 servings from the vegetable group; 2–4 servings from the fruit group; 2–3 servings from the milk, yogurt, and cheese group; 2–3 servings from the meat, poultry, dry beans, eggs, and nuts group; and that you use fats, oils, and sweets "sparingly." Lest this sound like enough food for an army, bear in mind that the serving sizes are not large. For example, a slice of bread is one serving, as are 2½–3 ounces of cooked lean meat, and ½ cup of cooked vegetables. When it comes to following the USDA suggestions, remember the cliché, "Variety is the spice of life." If you eat a wide range of foods from the various groups, you'll have a good nutritional foundation.

VEGETARIAN AND VEGAN DIETS

For ethical, religious, health, medical, or financial reasons, or simply because of taste, many women have cut meat and/or dairy products from their diets. But a healthy vegetarian diet involves more than substituting a soyburger for a steak. When you place restrictions on your diet, you need to pay extra attention to getting all the nutrients you need. Fortunately, with a bit of planning and knowledge, it's not too hard to lose the meat and/or dairy and keep the vitamins and minerals. And as suggested earlier, the wider the variety in your diet, the better the chances that you are getting the nutrients you need.

The most common problem for vegetarian and vegan (those who do not eat any animal products at all, including eggs and dairy products) women is iron deficiency, for not only is the form of iron that our bodies use most easily available in animal products, but iron-rich meat is often replaced by soy products and fiber, both of which inhibit iron absorption. Vegans also have a harder time getting enough of the essential vitamin B_{12} (though it is found in fortified cereals and soy milk), and zinc.

Another common problem is a tendency toward protein deficiency. When a food has all nine of the amino acids the body needs, it is considered to be a "complete" protein. Almost all animal products (even milk and egg whites) are complete proteins, but plant products often don't contain sufficient amounts of all the necessary amino acids. Vegetarians and vegans have to eat foods that contain "complementary" proteins in order to fulfill their protein requirement. It is not necessary for every meal to have complete proteins, but for maximum benefit, it's best to eat the complementary proteins within three to four hours of each other. To get complete protein, combine legumes (peas, lentils, and dried beans) and rice, legumes with wheat, and/or nuts with rice.

In addition, vegetarians and vegans (and meat eaters, too, for that matter) would be wise to combine foods in

---

LACTOSE INTOLERANCE

Consuming dairy products can be a little tricky if you're lactose-intolerant. People who are lactose-intolerant don't have enough lactase, the enzyme that the body uses to break down lactose, a sugar that's in milk and other dairy products. An inability to break down lactose can cause gas, bloating, intestinal discomfort, cramps, and/or diarrhea. If you're experiencing these indigestion-like symptoms regularly, ask your doctor if you should be tested for lactose-intolerance—it can spring up at any age. If you are moderately lactose-intolerant, but don't want to give dairy products up, don't despair. With the number of low-lactose dairy products and over-the-counter lactase supplements available at supermarkets and drugstores, you should be able to have your vanilla fudge ripple ice cream and digest it, too.

---

ways that will optimize their vitamin intake. For example, eating iron-rich food with food that contains vitamin C helps the body absorb the iron.

Vegans have to pay especially close attention to getting all their nutrients. In particular, they must ensure that they get enough vitamin D and calcium. Normally, these are found in fortified dairy products, but D can be obtained through sunlight, and calcium is present in tofu, green leafy veggies, and legumes.

And remember, just because you are cutting meat and/or dairy out of your diet, don't assume that you will automatically be healthy—a healthy diet is dependent on what you *do* eat, not only on what you *don't*.

NEVER SAY DIET

A decision to lose weight most often comes from a desire to look good, feel good, and be healthy. To diet in the traditional "deprive yourself until you can't stand it anymore" mode is counterproductive on all three counts. If you drastically cut your calorie intake, your metabolism compensates by slowing down (making it even more of a struggle to lose weight). And you'll lose muscle, which is essential to burn fat. Plus, haphazardly cutting calories usually means cutting back on nutrition, making you more susceptible to illness. And we all know that being hungry makes us grumpy and spaced out (and able to concentrate on only one thing—food).

However, the fact remains: The only way to lose weight is to burn more calories than you take in. Just be sure to choose a safe, sane, and relatively pain-free way to do it. Instead of going on a crash diet, learn the basics about nutrition, and you'll have the tools to figure out a diet that makes sense for you. It may take more thought and effort than blindly following a regimen printed in a beauty magazine, but knowing what you're doing and why will give you more incentive to stick with the program. And there is no need to "go off" a reasonable program that you've tailored to fit your schedule and lifestyle. The goal here is to do something to make your mind and body as healthy as possible—it's *not* to feel bad about what you aren't doing.

The majority of college women who think they need to lose weight don't. Before you embark on major changes in your eating patterns, check with your doctor. If you find out that you are indeed carrying more weight than you should be, cutting fat is more important than cutting calories, and eating healthfully and exercising are safer, more practical, and more effective alternatives to dieting. As a general rule, aim to lose one to two pounds a week at most. The more gradual your weight loss, the more likely you are to keep the pounds off.

For more on dieting, body image, and eating disorders, see "Real vs. Ideal," page 274.

Diet Pills

◑◑◑

The number of diet products lining drugstore, health food store, and supermarket shelves is overwhelming. They range from appetite suppressants and meal plans to powdered food substitutes and reduced-calorie

"So many girls at my school diet by taking Dexatrim. It's not like we don't know how bad it is for us and that we'll gain the weight back, but we do it anyway, like it's some magic cure. And when our face breaks out or our hair loses its shine or we feel really tired, we don't think that the pills could be part of the problem."

—UNIVERSITY OF NORTH CAROLINA AT CHAPEL HILL, '94

foods. In 1982 the FDA established safety and marketing guidelines for over-the-counter diet aids, and approved the use of a number of drugs, the most common of which is phenylpropanolamine hydrochloride (PPA).

PPA, which was originally used as a decongestant and is still present in many over-the-counter cold remedies, is contained in many appetite suppressants, including Dexatrim, In Control, and Acutrim. It has a similar chemical structure to amphetamines and, like them, binds with receptors in the area in the brain that is responsible for hunger.

Though the average diet pill has a PPA level that is considered safe by FDA standards, it is not uncommon for women to experience side effects such as dizziness, headaches, high blood pressure, anxiety, and insomnia. In addition, PPA can pose serious health risks for women with high blood pressure, diabetes, or heart, kidney, or thyroid problems, or who are taking antidepressant medication. Unfortunately, thyroid problems, high blood pressure, and diabetes are prevalent in overweight women—the same women who may turn to diet pills in response to social and medical pressure to lose weight.

How Do I Eat More Healthfully?

ᥫᥬᥬ

Although there are more diet tips out there than there are stars in the sky, here are a few of the best and the brightest.

■ Few of us get our eight glasses of water a day. Try doing it for a week, and see if you don't feel healthier and less tired and have better skin and more energy.

■ Choose low- or nonfat fortified dairy products. If you don't eat dairy products, make sure you are getting

"I am one of those people who started a diet every few months, and broke it a week later. All the diets seemed reasonable at first, but then I'd have a schedule that didn't give me time to go home and broil three ounces of chicken for lunch . . . [so] I'd end up grabbing a burger instead. . . . As soon as I'd break it once, it was over. I met a nutritionist at a party and I was joking about my dieting, and she said that my inability to stick to the diets showed that there was a problem with the diet, not a problem with me."

—BOSTON UNIVERSITY, '94

enough calcium and vitamins A and D from other sources.

■ Eat breakfast. The urge to blow off the first meal of the day when you're trying to make it out the door is a strong one. But after eight hours with nary a crumb, you need a little bit of nourishment to get you going; even if it's just cereal and OJ, your mood and motivation level will be higher than if you hadn't eaten. Eating a big, nutritious breakfast, a medium lunch, and a smallish dinner can help you lose weight, too, by making you less snack-prone during the crucial mid-morning and mid-afternoon stretches. If you're on the run, grab a couple of pieces of fruit, some toast, a bagel, or even a sandwich you cleverly packed the night before.

■ Snacking has a bad reputation, not because it's an unhealthy practice, but because what we usually choose to snack on isn't exactly the most nutritious chow. Instead of chips, ice cream, candy, or cheese fries, you might want to satisfy the bulk of your between-meal stomach rumblings with some unbuttered popcorn, veggies, fruit, rice cakes, low-fat cheese with crackers, Popsicles (there are even sugar-free types available), fruit, cereal, bagels, nonfat yogurt, or no-oil corn chips.

Tips When Shopping for Food

■ Don't shop for food while you are hungry.

■ Go shopping with a list. Think twice before buying anything that is not on your list.

■ Buy fresh, healthy foods. Fresh foods are not only better for you than processed foods, they are also faster and easier to prepare. Frozen vege-tables are also easy to steam or microwave, and because they are packaged at their peak of ripeness (or so say their ads), they are also very nutritious.

EXERCISE: WORKING IN WORKOUTS

Your high school phys ed teacher was right: Exercising actually leaves you with *more* psychological, physical, and mental energy, not less. Exercise also relieves stress, helps you sleep better, and elevates your mood. It can also boost your concentration and your metabolic levels, and strengthen your immune system, your bones, and your muscles (including the most important one, your heart). It is generally believed that consistent, moderate exercise will reduce your susceptibility to cardiovascular diseases, osteoporosis, cancer, and PMS, among other things. Best of all, it doesn't require an enormous effort, a huge time commitment, or a triathlete's training intensity to reap the rewards.

"People think that working out requires that you do aerobics or go running. I've been doing yoga for three years now, and I feel much better than I ever did when I did aerobics three times a week. I not only feel physically fit, but I am centered."

—ADELPHI UNIVERSITY, '91

Integrating Exercise Into Your Schedule

෧෧෧

Exercising is like flossing. For best results, you've got to do it on a consistent basis. (Exercising 3 times a week for 30 minutes each time is recommended.) But doing it occasionally is better than not doing it at all.

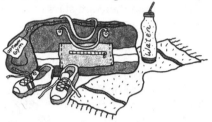

For those who don't like to exercise or don't have time to exercise, there are ways to work it in without it being painful, tedious, and/or schedule-wrecking. Here's how to incorporate exercise into your life without even noticing.

■ Walk, bike, Rollerblade, or cross-country ski to class.

■ Take a study break; turn on the radio and boogie with your roommate for 15 minutes.

■ Get a map of your area, round up a few of your fellow exercise-phobes, and explore the nooks and out-of-the-way places on foot or by bike.

■ When you're going a few flights, take the stairs instead of the elevator.

■ Do a 20-minute hokey-pokey.

■ Run errands on foot.

■ Volunteer your time to an organization that involves physical activity—do a little housework or run errands for the elderly, or help out at an after-school program for little kids.

HOW TO FIND YOUR TARGET HEART RATE

For aerobic exercise to be beneficial and safe, you need to monitor the intensity of your workout, which you can do by measuring your heart rate. To determine your heart rate: During the most intense period of your exercise, stop and use your fingertips (not your thumb, which has a beat of its own) to take your pulse either on your opposite wrist or on your neck an inch or so below your ear. Count the number of beats in 15 seconds, and multiply by 4. To determine your target heart rate range: Subtract your age from 220. For your minimum level, multiply this number by 60 percent (that's .6); for your maximum level, multiply by 85 percent. During the most intense period of your workout, your heart rate should fall somewhere between those two numbers. If it is too high, slow down.

Monitor your heart rate periodically during exercise to gauge the intensity. While a high-intensity workout might seem like the fastest route to fitness, continuously exceeding your target heart rate can be counterproductive and dangerous.

■ Play on a dorm, intramural, or varsity team. (It's a great way to meet people as well.)

Exercise increases endurance and stimulates the bones and muscles to renew themselves and become stronger. Beyond this, specific benefits depend on the type of exercise you engage in. Twenty to 30 minutes of aerobic exercise (which increase your heart and breathing rates) such as walking, jogging, running, circuit training, cross-country skiing, Rollerblading, and swimming does great things for your heart, arteries, and lungs. Even after you've finished your workout, your metabolism will stay revved up so you'll continue to burn calories at a faster pace. Depending on the specific exercise, you can also build and tone muscle. Plan your workout to include warm-up and cool-down periods. Stretching your arms, torso, and legs before and after the main event helps get your blood moving and reduces your chance of soreness and injury.

Exercise doesn't need to be very rigorous or high-intensity to be beneficial. In fact, it's more important that it be repetitive, rhythmic, and continuous, enough to increase your heart rate and breathing rate and make you sweat a bit for at least 20 minutes. To really reap the rewards, you will need to put a little oomph into your workout. However, if you're breathing so hard you can't speak, let alone groan, or your face reddens like a big ol' tomato, relax your pace. A good workout should rev you up, not make you keel over.

Aerobic exercise is highly touted, and for good reason, but if you can't or don't want to do it, there are a number of other options. Exercise such as yoga, stretching, and weightlifting won't give the same cardiovascular workout or burn calories to the same extent as aerobic exercise will, but it can increase balance and flexibility, strengthen joints and muscles, and release tension like nobody's business. Weight training and yoga also help strengthen your bones as well as your muscles. Along with a calcium-rich diet, exericising to increase bone strength is helpful in preventing osteoporosis.

In the Beginning—Getting Over the Hump

ⓢⓢⓢ

When you first start your new exercise regimen, you may find that you have to dig deep down for the willpower to stick with it. It hurts. It's frustrating. It's exhausting. You're sore. You don't see any changes. Everyone else in the gym seems more coordinated, faster, stronger, and healthier. It's just plain no fun.

When you begin to exercise, especially after leading a sedentary existence, you need to prepare yourself for the fact that the first few weeks may be rough, and plan accordingly. Make your program easy enough, fun enough, invigorating enough, and realistic enough to get you through this period. Don't set yourself up for failure by trying to start jogging outside in the dead of winter when streets are paved with ice, or to begin weight training the week that you have three papers due. Don't make such a strict regimen that you find yourself dreading the thought of working out.

Vary your exercise so you don't get in a rut. Start slowly—if you overdo it, chances are you'll be in so much pain that you'll be unable to exercise (or even walk) for a week. Remember, it can be as simple as walking the long way to class, taking an African dance workshop, or going ice-skating with friends.

It can help to find an exercise buddy—someone who is willing to work out with you on a regular basis. Fitness experts say that having a partner gives you the best odds for sticking with a program. If you are the type who works better with a set regimen, get help in creating one. Sign up for a fitness planning class, or get in touch with a personal trainer if you can afford it. Call or post a flyer in the athletics department—chances are there are plenty of physical education majors who'd help you come up with a routine for little or no money.

It may be difficult, but try to keep in mind that once you get into a routine and start seeing some progress, you'll find it easier and easier to stay

EXCUSES, EXCUSES

Believing that you have to be in great shape to exercise is by far the strangest of the various exercise excuses. This slightly skewed line of thinking is the most common among former high school athletes, whose once strenuous exercise regimen petered out when replaced by new interests and responsibilities once they got to college. If your frustration over "I used to be in so much better shape" is interfering with your enjoyment and frequency of exercise, remind yourself how utterly illogical it is. So enough with the excuses already!

motivated. You'll look healthier. You'll feel *much* healthier. You'll even start to miss it if you have to skip a day.

Working Out Smart

ᨠᨠᨠ

While being in shape is not a prerequisite for exercise, being in fairly good health is. It's always a good idea to talk to a doctor before you start a new exercise program, and to listen to your body while you're doing it. Don't let yourself get overheated or dehydrated. Be careful on hot days (or in warm gyms) and drink water before, during, and especially after you exercise, even if you don't think you sweat that much. (During exercise, fitness experts recommend taking only small sips of water—just enough to wet your mouth. Taking big gulps of liquids in the midst of a high-intensity workout can cause cramping.) Because exercise has a tendency to decrease appetite and can inspire us to eat less, there is often a temptation to cut too much out of one's diet when starting an exercise program, and protein sources are often the first to go. Don't fall into that trap. This is precisely the time to maintain or even increase your protein intake, because your body will need it to build those muscles.

Having the proper equipment and knowing how to use it correctly is another requirement for a sound exercise program. If your plan includes pumping iron, ask someone to show you how to use the free weights or machines and to watch you for your first few reps (you probably won't have trouble finding help—serious weight trainers usually enjoy showing off their technique). Also make sure your workout garb is up to snuff. Wearing a good pair of shoes, the right amount of high-quality protective gear, a supportive bra, and a comfy, stretchable, "breathable" outfit can make an enormous difference in the enjoyment and overall safety of your workout.

If you get hurt, allow yourself time to fully heal before working the injured muscle or limb. Don't mess around. If left untreated, small injuries can easily become serious injuries. But if it's just plain soreness, exercise that's taken down a notch or two in intensity can help rather than harm. When muscles are worked harder and longer than they're used to, lactic acid builds up and causes tiredness, tightness, and soreness the next day. Getting your aching body warmed up and moving will help flush out the lactic acid and relieve some of the pain and stiffness. And remember, once you get into a regular exercise routine, you won't get as sore.

SLEEP, PRECIOUS SLEEP

Students are notorious for never getting enough sleep. If we're inundated with work, the first thing we're willing to sacrifice is rest. Instead of catching some z's, we could be finishing up those papers or studying for an exam. But sleep is essential for good health. It allows the body to use energy more efficiently, and a well-rested body is better at fighting illness than a sleep-deprived one. It's no secret that lack of sleep makes us spacey, unable to concentrate, cranky, achy, and generally not much fun to be around. Sleep also gives relief from stress both by relaxing the body and

THE ANATOMY OF AN ALL-NIGHTER

Pulling an all-nighter means you miss out on delta sleep, which is when the body does its most intensive repair work, releasing a growth hormone that renews worn-out tissues. Tellingly, when you're totally exhausted and finally do go to sleep, your body chooses to refill its non-REM sleep requirement first.

It's not just your body that feels the ill effects of lack of sleep. Stay up for 24 hours straight, and your attention will wander, you'll have trouble performing routine tasks, and your mood may fluctuate. You may also experience headaches and burning eyes.

Fortunately, there's an easy cure for the ill effects of an all-nighter: Eight hours or so of solid snooze the next few nights will leave you bright-eyed and bushy-tailed. (For more on all-nighters, and study techniques to help you avoid them, see "Burning the Midnight Oil," page 29.)

by forcing us to take a break from bosses, profs, roommates, parents, boyfriends, and girlfriends (and ourselves) for a few hours. But even though you won't be able to deal with the actual stresses in your life while you're snoring away, there's no promising you won't be dreaming about them. Your more stressful day-to-day encounters are the ones most likely to appear in your dreams, albeit in some scrambled or twisted form.

Does It Matter When We Sleep?

Not only is the amount of time you sleep important, but also when you do it. There's an assumption among many busy students that as long as they can slip in their requisite number

"During finals, the campus transforms into the night of the living dead. Everyone has dark circles under their eyes, coffee breath, and lives in sweats. The guys don't shave. Everyone meets in the library and complains about how much work they have to do. Anyone who looks peppy or has a manageable amount of work is considered an enemy of the people."

—STANFORD UNIVERSITY, '91

of Z's within a 24-hour period, they're adequately rested. Not so. Snoozing for an hour facedown on a desk in the library then dozing for a while in a lounge between classes won't give you nearly the same benefits as sleeping a consecutive number of hours will. Most people need about 7½ hours a night, but anything between 6 and 9 hours is considered normal. Some scientists feel that there's no reason to worry about going above or below that range as long as you're running on all cylinders after that 4—or 14—hours.

Continuous sleep allows your body to cycle through all the sleep stages, a requirement for feeling well rested. Also, staying up all night and dozing during the day can throw your mood, metabolism, hormones, and natural chemical balance off-kilter.

What Happens When We Sleep?

ⓥⓖⓥ

As you sleep, your body shifts through clycles of two sleep "speeds": REM and non-REM. The first phase is non-REM or slow-wave sleep, named for brain waves that are regularly and widely spaced. As non-REM sleep progresses, your body movements become less and less frequent, your senses shut down, and you become next to impossible to wake up. The last and most restorative stage of non-REM sleep is called delta sleep.

Next comes REM sleep, which begins about 70 to 90 minutes after you first zonk out. REM, (pronounced *rhem*) stands for rapid eye movement —aptly named, as during this time your eyes move rapidly in their sockets. Additionally, your breathing gets faster, your fingers and toes twitch, and your brain waves speed up and become irregular. REM sleep is also when you do your heavy-duty dreaming. The first REM cycle may last only a few minutes, but REM sleep can grow to 30–45 minutes on its third or fourth cycle. All told, you're in this phase for about 1½ to 2 hours per night.

Although there are countless theories about the psychological and cultural significance of dreams, scientists still aren't certain about their exact purpose. However, they do know that dreaming is a crucial part of our sleep cycle, thanks to studies showing that sleepers deprived of REM sleep make up almost the exact amount they missed the following night. Dreams may serve as a safety valve for the release of emotional tensions, and they may help us work out tricky dilemmas or complex issues. Research has shown that dreams may also help us reorganize information into patterns that make it easier to learn and remember. One study revealed that students who got a good night's rest before an exam fared better than those who did not.

Insomnia

ⓥⓖⓥ

An all-too-common scenario: You are so zonked that you have to sit near an open window to keep from dozing off in class. Eyes at half-mast, you go through the day consumed with thoughts of your cozy bed. But when you climb into said bed, all geared up for some quality rest, you're more awake and alert than ever. Visions of

 Two-thirds of insomniacs who seek treatment are women.

the fight with your mom, your upcoming comp lit presentation, and your skyrocketing debts are tap-dancing in your head, making such a racket that they could very well wake your roommate. And so you lie there, frustrated, knowing your lack of sleep will make you even more of a zombie tomorrow.

Insomnia, or a prolonged inability to sleep, may be the result of a number of factors. Stress and anxiety are quite common ones. Too much coffee, too much exercise too close to bedtime, illness, excitement, depression, and napping during the day can also make it difficult to sleep at night. Some helpful hints to put insomnia to sleep:

■ Exercise, do your most brain-intensive homework, and deal with traumatic issues during the day or early evening, but not immediately before you lay down to sleep. Strenuous physical, mental, or emotional activity right before bed can make it hard to relax.

■ Give yourself some wind-down time before bed. Read a book (how about something that's not on your syllabi?), take a bath, or drink a cup of herbal tea. Don't do anything that is going to make you feel stressed or anxious.

■ Avoid taking naps. It's better to go to sleep a bit earlier

"I never had any problem sleeping until I got to college. It wasn't easy getting accustomed to sharing a bedroom with two other girls and the noise at all hours of the night. I guess I am a lot more stressed-out now than I was before, too, and I'm eating a lot more junk. . . . Everyone is always drinking coffee to stay up, and I only wish I could fall asleep."
—UNIVERSITY OF OKLAHOMA, '97

earlier than you normally do than to sleep during the day. Otherwise, when it finally comes time to sleep, you may not really be tired.

■ Don't forget the old favorites: a glass of warm milk or a warm bath (not a shower, which is better for a morning wake-up).

■ Try a relaxation exercise. (See "Learning to Relax," page 250.)

■ If you are tossing and turning, get out of bed and read, take a walk, or write a letter. Wait until you're ready to sleep before climbing back into bed.

■ Avoid caffeine for at least five or six hours before you plan to go to bed. This includes not only tea and coffee, but soft drinks, chocolate, and some over-the-counter medicines as well.

■ If the insomnia is persistent, you might want to talk with a doctor and/or therapist.

Though you may be tempted, don't resort to alcohol, sleeping pills, or other sedatives to help you drift off. They make you feel drowsy, but they can actually interfere with your getting a good night's sleep. The drugs disturb the natural sleep cycle, which results in sleep that is rarely sound or deep enough to make you feel refreshed and alive in the morning. This is why you'll often wake up feeling groggy and unrested in the morning after a keg party or a big dose of Nyquil.

ACTIVIST IDEAS

■ Support the women's sports teams at your school. Not only will a sea of smiling fans improve the players' game and make a better team (and bring even more fans), but cheering bodies in the stands will guarantee that the team continues to receive funding—the more popular a team, the less likely they'll cut it. In this era marked by hefty school budget cuts, a show of support can mean the difference between a team's life and death.

■ Don't wait until you're ready to keel over and die before you take care of your health. It *is* true that even just one week of eating right, exercising, and getting adequate sleep will improve your looks, your energy level, your health, and your academic ability. Why not try it?

■ Get together with a group of "we want to exercise but don't know where to start" buddies who shudder in the presence of a stair-climber. Reserve a room on campus, lug over a stereo and some extremely danceable CDs, and boogie in the name of exercise.

RESOURCES

Nutrition and Food Information, Education, and Referrals

INTERNATIONAL ACADEMY OF NUTRITION
AND PREVENTIVE MEDICINE
P.O. BOX 18433
ASHVILLE, NC 28814
(704) 258-3243
Promotes and conducts research on the relation of nutrition to health and prevention of disease. Provides information and answers questions about health, disease prevention, nutrition, and preventive medicine. Makes referrals to local health care providers who are involved in nutrition and preventive medicine. Publishes numerous materials on all aspects of nutrition, available upon request.

THE AMERICAN DIETETIC ASSOCIATION
216 WEST JACKSON BOULEVARD, SUITE 800
CHICAGO, IL 60606-6995
(312) 899-0040: GENERAL INFORMATION
(800) 366-1655: NUTRITION HOTLINE
Provides information and answers questions about nutrition. Callers may speak with a registered dietitian directly or may listen to regularly updated recorded nutri-

within 5 minutes of your head hitting the pillow; sleeping late on weekends.

tion messages. Maintains a resource library and database. Publishes numerous materials on nutrition, available upon request.

CENTER FOR SCIENCE IN THE PUBLIC INTEREST
1875 CONNECTICUT AVENUE NW, SUITE 300
WASHINGTON, DC 20009-5728
(202) 332-9110
FAX: (202) 265-4954
Conducts research on the relationship between technology and food safety and nutrition. Organizes political action/advocacy work on behalf of improved health and nutrition policies. Provides information and education about the impact of technology on food safety and nutrition. Engaged in public policy issues, including testing, labeling, and advertising of foods. Publishes numerous materials, including *Nutrition Action Healthletter* and bibliographies on nutrition.

FOOD AND DRUG ADMINISTRATION (FDA)
U.S. DEPARTMENT OF HEALTH AND HUMAN SERVICES
5600 FISHERS LANE
ROCKVILLE, MD 20857
(301) 443-3170
(301) 599-1012: CENTER FOR DRUGS EVALUATION AND RESEARCH
(202) 205-5251: CENTER FOR FOOD SAFETY AND APPLIED NUTRITION
Provides information and answers questions about foods, drugs, products, regulations, recalls, and labeling. You will have to leave a message and a specialist will return your call. Accepts complaints about specific foods, drugs, and medical devices. Provides referrals to local FDA offices. Makes referrals to the division of the FDA that can best address your questions. Publishes numerous materials, including many on nutrition, available upon request.

To find your local Food and Drug Administration office, look in your telephone book's blue pages under "United States Government Offices, Health and Human Services Department, Food and Drug Administration."

THE CENTER FOR NUTRITION POLICY AND PROMOTION
1120 20TH STREET NW, SUITE 200
WASHINGTON, DC 20036
(202) 418-2312
FAX: (202) 208-2322
A branch of the United States Department of Agriculture. Provides information and answers questions about nutrition. Publishes numerous materials on nutrition, available upon request.

NATIONAL DAIRY COUNCIL
(800) 426-8271
Provides information and answers questions about nutrition. Publishes numerous materials on nutrition, available upon request.

VEGETARIAN PRESS
P.O. BOX 61273
DENVER, CO 80206
Publishes books on all aspects of vegetarian life. Write to request their free catalog.

Exercise, Sports, and Physical Fitness

WOMEN'S SPORTS FOUNDATION
EISENHOWER PARK
EAST MEADOW, NY 11554
(800) 227-3988
Provides information about women's nutrition and fitness as well as sports and sports medicine. Publishes materials with specific focus on college women, including *Nutrition/Weight Control.*

AMERICAN ALLIANCE FOR HEALTH, PHYSICAL EDUCATION, RECREATION, AND DANCE
1900 ASSOCIATION DRIVE
RESTON, VA 22091
(800) 321-0789
(703) 476-3400
Provides information about different types of physical activity and dance.

THE AMATEUR ATHLETIC UNION
AAU HOUSE
P.O. BOX 68207
3400 WEST 86TH STREET
INDIANAPOLIS, IN 46268
(317) 872-2900
Provides information about all areas of fitness, wellness, and exercise.

Further Reading

ೞೞೞ

Everywoman's Guide to Nutrition, Judith E. Brown (University of Minnesota Press, 1991).

The Nutrition Desk Reference, revised edition, Robert Garrison, Jr., and Elizabeth Somer (Keats Publishing, 1990).

The Columbia Encyclopedia of Women's Nutrition, Carlton Fredericks (G.P. Putnam's, 1989).

Prescription for Nutritional Healing: A Practical A–Z Reference to Drug-Free Remedies, Phyllis and James Balch (Avery, 1990).

The Bodywise Woman: Reliable Information About Physical Activity and Health, Melpomene Institute for Women's Health Research (Prentice-Hall, 1990).

The Mount Sinai School of Medicine Complete Book of Nutrition, Victor Herbert and Genell Subak-Sharpre, eds (St. Martin's Press, 1990).

Jane Brody's Nutrition Book, Jane Brody (Bantam, 1987).

The Complete Sports Medicine Book for Women, Mona Shangold and Gabe Mirikin (Fireside, 1985).

Sports and Recreation Periodicals

WOMEN'S SPORTS AND FITNESS
2025 PEARL STREET
BOULDER, CO 80302
(303) 440-5111
Includes information and inspiration to help women improve their lives through sports and fitness.

YOGA JOURNAL
2054 UNIVERSITY AVENUE
BERKELEY, CA 94704
(510) 841-9200
A magazine devoted to the practice of yoga.

Staying Healthy
Prevention & Remedies

Staying healthy means being attuned to our bodies so that we can recognize when something is wrong and we need to seek outside help. It means getting the information we need about our health and staying well from books, counselors, health care practitioners, and friends. And it means making the necessary trips to the doctors, dentists, acupuncturists, or therapists, learning how to do a breast self-examination (and doing it!), and choosing the right medications.

Should you fall ill or become injured, you'll want to find a treatment that not only makes you feel better as quickly as possible, but that fits into your personal philosophy of well-being—for example, one woman may hit the corner drugstore for a cold remedy, another might head for her local herbologist, and still another might tough it out without any medication. Choosing a doctor or other practitioner is another decision in which personal and practical factors carry near equal weight.

PREVENTIVE ACTION

A key to prevention is simply doing everything possible to keep your body balanced and strong enough to resist illness. It requires that you focus your attention on health care, not disease care, and not wait until you feel run down to start eating well, getting enough rest, exercising, and reducing stress. There is no better way to keep troublesome bugs from gaining a foothold in your body than to keep it healthy. Because no matter how careful you are, where you go, or whom you hang out with, it is literally impossible to avoid exposure to a wide

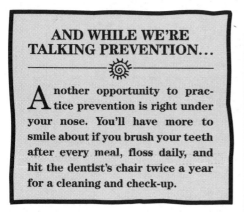

AND WHILE WE'RE TALKING PREVENTION...

Another opportunity to practice prevention is right under your nose. You'll have more to smile about if you brush your teeth after every meal, floss daily, and hit the dentist's chair twice a year for a cleaning and check-up.

assortment of viruses, bacteria, and other creatures.

To keep germs outside the body, wash your hands frequently with soap and warm water, especially right before meals or before putting on makeup (or any other time you're touching your mouth, nose, or eyes). And take care of your skin. It is your number one defense against germs, so keep it healthy. This may require special attention during cold months, as the combination of the cold with indoor heating can rob your skin of moisture, leaving it more prone to cracking and cuts. Invest in a humidifier or place a pan of water on the radiator to keep the air moist, drink at least eight glasses of H_2O a day, and use a moisturizer.

Still, those pesky protists *will* find a way in. Your overall best bet for staying healthy is to keep your immune system strong and primed to flush germs out before they have a chance to wreak havoc. One way to do so is to eat a well-balanced diet. Take a multivitamin if you suspect you're not getting all the essential nutrients. Also, get enough sleep, and make managing and relieving stress a priority. Though even the healthiest of bodies can't always obliterate a bug before it takes

hold, a strong, a well-cared-for immune system will decrease the frequency, duration, and severity of the illness.

WHEN THE BUG BITES

It's sometimes hard to figure out whether all we need is OJ, TLC, and R&R, or whether we should join the ranks of coughing, sneezing, aching students in the overcrowded waiting room of the student health center. Knowing what you've got can help you decide where to go to get rid of it. For example, viruses, which cause most colds and flu, generally need to be waited out. All you can do is treat the symptoms: the dry cough, the runny nose, the scratchy throat, the aches and pains, the headaches, and the fatigue. (See the chart on page 223 for some quick ways to treat these symptoms.) Unless you can't breathe without difficulty, haven't been able to shake your illness for over a week or two, or have one or more of the other danger signs listed on page 221, a doctor probably won't be able to offer you much more of a remedy than "Take two acetaminophen (Tylenol) gargle, drink plenty of fluids and pay this bill." (Vaccines can prevent the onset of some viral illnesses, like influenza or hepatitis, but they won't help once you have the bug.)

On the other hand, doctors should be seen for bacterial infections. Bacterial infections like pneumonia or strep throat can appear on their own or be triggered by a virus. It's not always easy to tell whether you have a virus or a bacterial infection, so if you suspect it might be the latter or find that

MONITORING YOURSELF: HEALTHY COMPUTING

Computers are wonderful things, whether you're using them to run miles of spreadsheets, write 40 pages of blood, sweat, and footnotes for a lit class, or chat with an E-mail buddy at another college across the country. Those long days at the keyboard, though, can result in some special health hazards, including back problems, eyestrain, and repetitive stress injuries, the most serious of which is carpal tunnel syndrome. Carpal tunnel syndrome—the tennis elbow of the technologically savvy—results when nerves in your wrists are damaged by the continual strain of typing. Your wrists swell, and the swelling pinches the nerves leading to your hands, causing pain, tingling, numbness, and/or weakness. Treatment for carpal tunnel includes rest, anti-inflammatory medication, corticosteroid injection, and in severe cases, surgery.

The following tips can help you prevent the neck pain, cramped fingers, and other assorted aches and pains (or worse) that could result from a prolonged encounter with your PC.

FIRST, LIMBER UP A BIT

1. Flex those digits! Clench your fists tightly and release, spreading and wiggling your fingers.
2. Hang on to the fingers of one hand and bend back your wrist. Hold for a five-second count, and repeat with the other hand.
3. Take the thumb of one hand and pull it back. Hold for five seconds—you should be able to feel the stretch. Repeat with the other hand.
4. Give yourself a hand massage. Or better yet, swap massages with someone else.

As you're working, take an occasional break—get up and walk away from your computer, stretch out a bit, and do neck and shoulder rolls. Another good tension releaser is to raise your arms in the air while clenching and unclenching your hands. Eyestrain can be alleviated by looking away from the monitor at least every 15 minutes and focusing on something far away.

If you're in front of the computer on a daily basis, look into buying an ergonomically correct chair, one that follows the contours of your back and distributes your weight comfortably. When typing, keep your wrists at the same level as your hands. You also should consider investing in a wrist rest, a padded bar that fits on the front of your computer keyboard to help you maintain the proper form. Make sure there's not much of a reach between you and your computer keyboard—adjustable keyboard stands and a desk that's the correct height can help in this department. Finally, position the papers or books you're working from so you don't have to twist sharply to one side to read them. Better yet, buy a copy stand that puts materials at the same height and on the same plane as your computer screen.

even with rest and fluids you just aren't getting better, see a doctor. If you do indeed have a bacterial infection, your doctor will prescribe an antibiotic. Failure to deal with an infection quickly and efficiently (and to take the medicine until it's gone, not just until you feel better) can lead to very serious problems.

COMMON MALADIES

It's winter, your psych lecture sounds like a tuberculosis ward, and your three closest friends have been coughing, hacking, sneezing, and heaving away for the past week. You're starting to feel like you may be coming down with something.

Listed below are some common illnesses, their symptoms, and a few proven remedies to help put you on the road to recovery.

ATHLETE'S FOOT
What it is: A fungus lurking in damp places like shower stalls or on sweaty feet that can't "breathe" in poorly ventilated socks or shoes.
Symptoms: Itchy, reddened, peeling skin on the feet, especially between the toes.
Relief/treatment: Keep your feet dry; use an over-the-counter antifungal cream or powder; dry your feet well after swimming and showers (get in between your toes) and sprinkle them with cornstarch; wear cotton socks; invest in a pair of thongs/flip-flops to wear in the locker room or other heavy-traffic showers.

BRONCHITIS
What it is: Inflammation/infection of breathing tubes.

Symptoms: Coughing (especially coughing up colored phlegm), difficult/painful breathing.
Relief/treatment: See a doctor; it could worsen and become pneumonia.

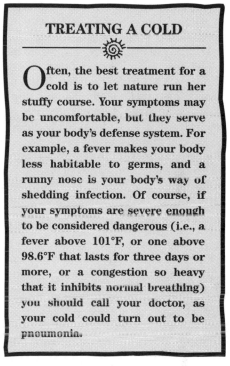

TREATING A COLD

Often, the best treatment for a cold is to let nature run her stuffy course. Your symptoms may be uncomfortable, but they serve as your body's defense system. For example, a fever makes your body less habitable to germs, and a runny nose is your body's way of shedding infection. Of course, if your symptoms are severe enough to be considered dangerous (i.e., a fever above 101°F, or one above 98.6°F that lasts for three days or more, or a congestion so heavy that it inhibits normal breathing) you should call your doctor, as your cold could turn out to be pneumonia.

COLD
What it is: A virus.
Symptoms: Sniffling, sneezing, sore throat . . . you know the rest.
Relief/treatment: There's no vaccine capable of zapping a cold virus, which mutates slightly every time it enters a new host. When faced with a virus, your body usually has to begin the immune response from scratch each time—unless it's one you've already had, in which case you'll use antibodies left over from the last time to help get rid of the current bug faster.

linked to B$_6$ deficiency, which is linked to Carpal Tunnel Syndrome.

MONONUCLEOSIS

What it is: Mono, or the "kissing disease," is caused by the Epstein-Barr virus. It is transmitted by saliva exchanged during kissing or sharing a toothbrush, drinking glass, or cigarettes, for example.

Symptoms: Tiredness accompanied by swollen glands, achy muscles, sore throat, and sometimes fever, and/or rash, and enlarged spleen. Detected by blood test. (Practitioners often take a throat culture to rule out strep throat, which has many of the same symptoms.) Can have different degrees of severity—it can last from a few weeks to several months.

Relief/treatment: There is no cure for mono, but you can relieve symptoms by taking acetaminophen, drinking tons of fluids, and resting. Avoid heavy exercise for two months (not that you'd have the energy) and stay clear of alcohol. Severely taxing your immune system or getting run down can bring on Chronic Fatigue Syndrome.

THE FLU

What it is: A virus.

Symptoms: High fever, sore throat, aches, congestion, watery eyes.

Relief/treatment: Once you've got it, you've got to wait it out. Get plenty of rest, drink tons of fluids (especially hot drinks), take acetaminophen for fever, and pseudoephedrine (found in Sudafed) for congestion.

CONJUNCTIVITIS (pinkeye)

What it is: Essentially, a cold that's taken up residence in your eyes. Conjunctivitis is highly contagious—you can get it through hand-to-eye contact or from shared towels or makeup.

Symptoms: Your eye (and the surrounding area) turns pink or red, discharges watery or puslike white fluid,

and itches. You may wake up with your eye stuck shut.

Relief/treatment: Avoid touching or rubbing your eyes—if you must, wash hands immediately after. If infection persists for more than a day or two, you'll need prescription-only antibiotic drops. Wipe pus away with warm water and a cotton ball.

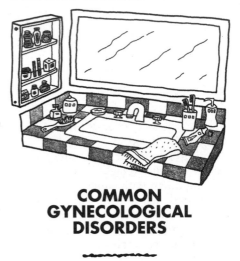

COMMON GYNECOLOGICAL DISORDERS

Almost as prevalent as colds on college campuses (although perhaps less discussed) are those pesky gynecological problems. Here's a look at some common disorders and how to treat them.

YEAST INFECTIONS (*Candidiasis*)

Cause: Yeast infections happen when there is an overgrowth of yeast organisms in the vagina. Though yeast infections can be sexually transmitted, they usually occur when factors such as stress, antibiotics, birth control pills, diabetes, and pregnancy upset the natural pH level in the vagina.

Symptoms: Itching and burning in the vulva; a red, sore vulva; small, red sore spots on the vaginal lips; and/or a thick, white discharge with a pastelike

HANDY TIPS ON AVOIDING VAGINAL INFECTIONS

Many healthy bacteria that grow inside the vagina help to curb the overgrowth of such harmful organisms as yeast and fungi. When the presence of these healthy bacteria is diminished, the other organisms will multiply and secrete wastes into the vagina, which causes infection. You can maintain and replenish the healthy vaginal bacteria in a number of ways:

▲ Take care of your general health. Strengthening your immune system through exercise, proper diet, and enough sleep and vitamins will work to increase your resistance to infections.

▲ Wash your vulva and anus with mild soap and water.

▲ Avoid deodorant tampons and pads, highly perfumed soaps and bubble baths, and feminine deodorant sprays or washes.

▲ Do not douche. Douching can wash away the healthy bacteria lining the vagina, as well as disrupt the vagina's natural pH level. (A healthy vagina maintains a slightly acidic environment, unsuitable for the growth of most problem-causing bacteria. When it's disrupted, the unhealthy bacteria can thrive.)

▲ Use only plain white, unscented toilet paper.

▲ Keep your sugar intake to a minimum—too much can affect the vagina's pH balance.

▲ Wear underpants, tights, and pantyhose with cotton crotches only and avoid skintight pants. Nylon underwear and tight-fitting pants retain heat and moisture, which create favorable conditions for the growth of unhealthy organisms.

▲ Always wipe from front to rear so that bacteria from the anus will not get into the vagina or urethra.

▲ Make sure that your sexual partners and your sex toys are clean. When having sexual intercourse with a man, use a condom for extra protection against infection. If you are having anal intercourse, make sure your partner washes his penis and changes condoms before you have vaginal intercourse. (The same goes for dildos and other sex toys.)

▲ Choose a sterile, water-soluble lubricant like K-Y Jelly, Wet, or Astroglide (and not Vaseline, baby oil, or other oil-based substances) for use during genital and anal sex.

▲ Take acidophilus supplements (lactobacillus) in the form of capsules, liquid, or yogurt that contains live, active cultures (look for the National Yogurt Association seal), especially when using antibiotic drugs. Acidophilus in its various forms is available in health food stores. For best results, they should be kept in a refrigerator. The tablets or yogurt may be taken orally or used vaginally.

▲ If you have an infection, make sure that both you and your partner get treated, even if s/he is asymptomatic, to avoid the "ping-pong effect" (you give it to your partner, your partner gives it back to you, and so on).

infections are the 2nd most common reason women visit the doctor.

or cottage cheese–like consistency. Yeast infections can also cause pain during sexual intercourse. Abdominal pain, strong- and unpleasant-smelling discharge, or fever could be a sign of a problem more serious than a yeast infection, such as an STD, an infection not cured by over-the-counter medication, or another illness that needs a doctor's attention. Do not treat these symptoms as a yeast infection, as over-the-counter creams could interfere with your practitioner's ability to diagnose the problem.

Relief/treatment: Most yeast infections are easily treated with an over-the-counter medicated cream or suppository, like Monistat 7 or Gyne-Lotromin. It is important to use the medicine as directed (usually once a day for three to seven days), even after symptoms subside. If you prefer to use alternative treatments, inserting acidophilus yogurt into the vagina or using garlic suppositories (wrap a peeled, uncut clove of garlic in gauze) at the first sign of a yeast infection may be helpful (once the infection's in full swing, garlic may not help much). Aloe vera gel or over-the-counter hydrocortisone cream can temporarily relieve external itching and burning. Persistent infections may require a prescribed antifungal medication.

Other:

■ Yeast infections are very common and are rarely more than a bother. Recurring, incurable, and persistent yeast infections may signal a serious problem like diabetes, a different type of vaginal infection, or HIV.

■ Thrush, caused by an overgrowth of yeast organisms in the mouth is characterized by a cottage cheese–like coating in the mouth and throat, bleeding and sores in the mouth, and a dry mouth. It is usually treated with prescribed Nystatin drops.

■ The creams and suppositories can be messy—you might want to wear a panty liner or pad during treatment.

■ Avoid sexually transmitted yeast infections by using condoms and dental dams during genital, oral, and anal sex. If you have sex while you have a yeast infection, remember that most of the over-the-counter treatments contain vegetable oil, which weakens the latex in condoms and diaphragms and can interfere with the effectiveness of spermicides. Do not rely on these methods to prevent pregnancy and STDs when treating a yeast infection.

■ The Western medical method of treating yeast infections with medicated cream or suppositories is based on the assumption that the yeast problem is one that is restricted to the vagina. But yeast infections are rarely confined to just the vagina—evidence of the infection may also appear in the rectum, colon, intestines, bladder, and urinary tract. This explains why so many women get recurring yeast

AVOIDING "HONEYMOON CYSTITIS"

Because the vagina, clitoris, and urethra are so close together, many women find that after the pleasure of sex subsides, the pain of a urinary tract infection (UTI) sets in. If you are susceptible to UTIs, there are a few things you can do to keep your urethra healthy while satisfying your libido:

▲ Make sure you are well lubricated (either naturally or with the help of water-soluble lubricants) before having intercourse.

▲ Urinate before and after sex. Doing so before alleviates pressure on the bladder; doing so after helps wash away those nasty germs that can cause UTIs. (And there are fringe benefits to emptying your bladder, as most women are not able to have an orgasm if they have to urinate . . .)

▲ Some sexual positions such as rear entry may aggravate UTIs in women who are susceptible.

▲ If you're having heterosexual intercourse and are bothered by UTIs, consider your birth control method. Since the diaphragm puts pressure on the bladder, it is generally not recommended for the UTI-prone, but if you really love your diaphragm, make sure your practitioner prescribes the smallest-sized diaphragm possible (that will still, of course, provide effective contraception). Ribbed/textured condoms may "rub the wrong way," and some spermicides may be irritating. (But you can squeeze a bit of spermicide in the *inside* tip of the condom to get the added contraception and STD prevention that spermicides provide.)

---

infections. Though our vaginas may be clear of the infection after treatment, we have not fully addressed the bacterial imbalance in our bodies, and thus, in a matter of time, the itching and discharge return.

BACTERIAL VAGINOSIS

(*Gardnerella; Nonspecific Vaginitis*)
Cause: Bacterial vaginosis is caused by an overgrowth of certain organisms in the vagina. It may arise spontaneously or be transmitted sexually.
Symptoms: White or gray discharge that may be either thick or watery and has an unpleasant odor. Pain during urination and intercourse is also common.

Relief/treatment: Oral antibiotics prescribed by your practitioner, such as metronidazole (Flagyl), ampicillin, or sulfa-based creams and suppositories. An over-the-counter pain reliever will help soothe the discomfort.
Other:
■ As the infection can be passed through genital-genital and genital-anal contact—sexual partner(s) should be treated simultaneously.

■ Metronidazole can cause very serious side effects if combined with alcohol, and may complicate pregnancy.

■ Avoid using a diaphragm, a cervical cap, spermicidal jelly, or a tampon during treatment.

URINARY TRACT/BLADDER IN-FECTIONS (*Urethritis; Cystitis*)

Cause: Urinary tract infections (UTIs) and bladder infections occur when bacteria travel into the urethra (the tube that connects the bladder to the urinary opening) and bladder, or when the urethra becomes irritated. They can result from transfer of fecal bacteria from the anus to the urethra, a sudden increase in the frequency of vigorous genital stimulation, particularly vaginal intercourse ("honeymoon cystitis"), or prolonged pressure on the urethra. They may also be caused by sexually transmitted diseases such as gonorrhea, chlamydia, or trichomoniasis.

Symptoms: Frequent urination; burning during urination; blood or pus in the urine; cloudy, strong-smelling urine. If these symptoms are accompanied by a high fever, vomiting, or lower-back pain, they may indicate a kidney infection, which requires immediate medical attention.

Relief/treatment: UTIs are diagnosed by a urine test performed by a health practitioner, and can be treated with antibiotics, such as sulfa. (A relatively new test, the Uri-Three, can give results as quickly as 18 hours.)

For treatment and prevention: Drink a lot of fluids (two or three glasses of water an hour when infection is present); urinate frequently and completely empty your bladder each time; after urinating, gently blot—don't wipe; to keep your urinary tract acidic drink unsweetened cranberry juice, take cranberry capsules (available in health food stores), or take vitamin C; avoid caffeine, spicy foods, and alcohol (all of which irritate the bladder), and citrus fruit and juice (which make the urine alkaline). For relief from pain and discomfort, take a warm bath (without oil or bubbles), hold a warm compress to your urethra, and take over-the-counter painkillers. Do not engage in activities that could irritate the urethra during the treatment period (such as genital intercourse and clitoral stimulation).

Other:

■ If you are prone to urinary tract infections, keep in mind that use of the diaphragm can irritate the urethra.

■ Pregnant women are especially susceptible to UTIs.

■ The same antibiotics that can cure your UTI can cause a vaginal infection, because they kill both the unwanted bacteria that cause UTIs as well as the healthy bacteria that prevent vaginal infections. Conversely, the over-the-counter creams and suppositories that treat yeast infections can irritate the urethra and trap unwanted organisms, causing UTIs. To avoid this rather unpleasant cycle, take acidophilus when taking antibiotics, and avoid activities that may irritate the urethra when treating a yeast infection. (See the tips above.)

■ Interstitial cystitis, a condition once thought to affect only postmenopausal women, is now appearing with greater frequency in younger women. Symptoms resemble those of UTIs, except that antibiotic treatment does not bring relief. There are a number of organizations that offer information and support to women with interstitial cystitis. (See the Resources at the end of this chapter.)

INFLAMMATION OF BARTHO-LIN'S GLANDS

Cause: The two Bartholin's glands (located on the back wall of the vagina, near the vaginal opening) secrete a fluid to keep the vaginal opening moist and supple. If the area becomes irritated (often from an STD), the opening of one or both glands may become blocked and they may swell up.

Symptoms: Feels like a bump just below the skin. If the inflamed gland becomes infected, it will be painful—especially during vaginal intercourse.

Relief/treatment: If the inflamed gland isn't painful or obtrusive, it is generally not necessary to seek treatment from a health care practitioner.

However, if it becomes infected, antibiotics, warm baths, anti-inflammatory medication, hydrocortisone cream, and/or interferon shots and, if need be, surgically lancing and draining the infected gland will usually remedy the problem. In cases when it becomes chronic and causes great pain, doctors may recommend that the glands be removed.

Other: Also called vestibular vaginitis, vestibulitis, or vestibular gland inflammation. May be misdiagnosed as anything from vaginismus to allergies to stress to "It's just your imagination, relax."

(For information about fibrocystic breast disease, fibroadenomas, uterine fibroids, endometriosis, ovarian cysts, or premenstrual syndrome, see "Know Your Body," page 343. For information about PID and sexually transmitted diseases, including HIV/AIDS, see "STDs, HIV, and AIDS," page 369.)

VISIT THE DOCTOR IF YOU HAVE . . .

▲ Cold or flu symptoms that don't abate for a week of fluids and rest.

▲ A fever that lasts three days, goes above 101°F, or is accompanied by swollen glands or severe diarrhea.

▲ A change in the color, size, or shape of a mole or freckle.

▲ Bleeding that won't stop after several minutes of pressure; a severe or persistent bloody nose; blood in urine or stool; blood or a substance resembling coffee grounds (digested blood) in vomit.

▲ Vomiting or diarrhea for more than two days.

▲ Dramatic, unexplained changes in appetite, weight, or bowel movements.

▲ Pus in your throat.

▲ Fatigue lasting over three weeks.

▲ Low back pain lasting a few weeks.

▲ A change in your menstrual cycle.

▲ An overdue period (more than two weeks late) and you've had sexual intercourse.

▲ Swollen glands for several weeks.

▲ Abdominal pain increasing in severity, especially on your right side.

▲ Changes in vaginal discharge accompanied by lower abdominal discomfort, if you are sexually active.

SYMPTOMS AND SOLUTIONS

PROBLEM	TRY THIS	WHEN TO SEE A DOCTOR
Diarrhea	Drink lots of clear liquids, such as flat ginger ale, to help flush out your digestive system and replace lost fluids. Avoid spicy foods, fruits with skins and seeds, and dairy products in favor of bananas, rice, and other bland foods. As a last resort, try an over-the-counter diarrhea medication.	If diarrhea lasts longer than three days or keeps you up all night, or you have blood in stool, coal-black stool, or if you are vomiting and/or have fever.
Stuffy nose/ congestion	Lean over a sink or basin filled with steaming hot water with a towel draped over your head. (Try adding a bit of peppermint or eucalyptus for an extra kick.) Do this for 10 minutes or so a few times a day. (You'll probably want to use a little moisturizer on your face after steaming.) Get plenty of rest, vitamin C, and fluids. If you decide to turn to a decongestant, use only one that does not contain antihistamines.	If it lasts longer than 10 days, or you have difficulty breathing, or you're producing green or yellow mucus.
Constipation	Drink plenty of fluids, and eat high-fiber foods like bran, fresh or dried fruits (prunes are always a favorite), and vegetables. Try some light exercise or relaxation techniques. As a last resort, try an over-the-counter laxative or a glycerin suppository.	If constipation is accompanied by dizziness, weight loss, or severe stomach pain, or lasts longer than five days.
Heartburn	Eat slowly and in smaller amounts; avoid wearing tight clothing; wait two to three hours after a meal before you lie down. Cut back on spicy or acidic foods, alcohol, chocolate, and caffeine. Don't smoke, especially right before or after a meal.	If the problem becomes chronic, lasts for three days, or causes extreme pain and/or bloating.

☼ 17.6% of women and 5.7% of men get migraines. ☼ Ameri-

SYMPTOMS AND SOLUTIONS

PROBLEM	TRY THIS	WHEN TO SEE A DOCTOR
Stomach pains/ cramps	Avoid spicy, acidic, and fried foods, and dairy products. Ingest only clear liquids and/or bland foods, until the pain goes away. If resting, try lying on your stomach. If pain is gas-related, reduce consumption of gas-producing foods (fiber rich food like bran, beans, broccoli, cabbage, brussels sprouts). Don't chew gum, smoke, or suck hard candies, which make you swallow more air. Also, eat slowly and stay away from carbonated drinks. Walking or light exercise may help relieve discomfort. If pain is menstruation-related, a warm compress or heating pad can relieve cramps. (See page 361, for more information.)	If you have a very intense, dull ache or very sharp pain that lasts more than 24 hours (especially if it's on the right side), accompanied by fever above 101°F, chills, cold, clammy skin, and/or trembling.
Sore throat	Gargle with a mixture of warm water, baking soda, and salt. Take ibuprofen or acetaminophen to relieve inflammation or pain. Sip weak tea with honey and lemon. Suck ice cubes, hard candy, or zinc lozenges, or take spoonfuls of honey.	If accompanied by other cold symptoms or low fever for more than three days, or if fever over 101°F. If you have diffi culty swallowing or breathing, a very swollen neck, pus on your throat, or if symptoms are accompanied by a rash.
Headache	Lie down and rest. Try a relaxation technique and/or take an analgesic. If it's a migraine (intense pain, usually on one side of the head, often accompanied by nausea and/or blurred vision), avoid foods that contain tyramine, such as red wine, hard cheese, hot dogs, nuts, and chocolate.	If headache lasts more than a day; if it appears after bumping your head; if you feel dizzy or disoriented. If you suffer from migraines, talk to your doctor about prescription remedies.

SYMPTOMS AND SOLUTIONS

PROBLEM	TRY THIS	WHEN TO SEE A DOCTOR
Fever	Rest; drink a lot of fluids; take acetaminophen. Do not take aspirin when you have a fever—there is a possibility you could have Reye's syndrome, a viral illness that can prove fatal combined with aspirin use.	If temperature is elevated for more than two days or rises above 101°F. Also call if fever is accompanied by dizziness or disorientation.
Nausea and vomiting	Drink as many clear fluids as possible to avoid dehydration. (Flat ginger ale is a favorite, along with clear broth, weak tea, Jell-O, or Gatorade.) If you can't keep anything down, try sucking on ice cubes or popsicles, or sipping small amounts of liquid as frequently as possible. If you have a virus, your whole body or head will ache. If you have food poisoning, usually your stomach will be affected. When nausea eases, try eating small amounts of bland foods like rice, pasta, crackers, or toast. Avoid spicy foods, veggies, fruit, and dairy products.	If vomiting lasts more than 24 hours or is accompanied by fever; if there's blood or a substance that resembles coffee grounds in vomit; or if appetite fails to return after three days.
Cough	Only take over-the-counter cough suppressants for nonproductive or "dry" coughs (which don't produce phlegm), and then only if the cough is keeping you up at night or is overly exhausting. Do not take cough expectorants for con-gested coughs—they may prolong symptoms. Instead try taking a hot, steamy shower or breathing steam over a basin with a towel draped over your head, sleeping with your head slightly elevated, or even eating some hot soup.	If cough lasts more than a week, you're bringing up green or yellow phlegm or blood; if cough is accompanied by painful or difficult breathing, or lasts for three or more days.

☼ Can't swallow a pill? It's easier if you place it at the

KNOW YOUR DRUGS

Your take on medicine—or rather, how, when, and why you take medicine—is a big part of a health philosophy. Some of us will bend over backward to avoid a Tylenol capsule, while others prefer to force an ailment into submission with a wide range of pharmaceuticals. In either case, when you do take medicine, it's smart to know what you're taking and when to stop taking it, whether it's an over-the-counter or prescription drug.

For most people, the search for a self-cure starts at the local drugstore. Most over-the-counter medicines have descriptions of their effects and instructions for their use on the side of the box or in an insert. If the information in or on the package is insufficient, ask your pharmacist for written and/or oral instructions on how it should be used.

Don't let a drug's over-the-counter status make you take it less seriously. It's important to follow the directions on the package to the letter (unless modified by your health practitioner).

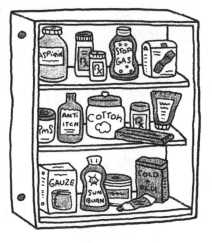

Also pay close attention to what other medications, foods, drinks, and activities should be avoided while you're on the drug. (If you're pregnant, avoid any and all medications, unless you have a doctor's OK.) Finally, if your symptoms haven't cleared up within a few days of using an over-the-counter drug, call your doctor.

Prescription Questions

It may become all too apparent that you can't make short work of an illness or injury without taking something. Below is a list of important questions to ask your health care provider about the medications she prescribes or recommends.

■ What is the name of the drug? (Get the brand name *and* the generic name.) Is there anything I should not be taking while I am using the drug? (*Never* leave the doctor's office without finding out the answer to this question. You should confirm the answer with your pharmacist.)

■ What symptom(s) or medical problem(s) is the drug being prescribed for? How does the drug work?

■ Is the drug expensive? Will insurance cover the cost? If it's a brand-name drug, is there a safe generic substitute that costs less? (You might also want to ask if your doctor could supply you with any of the many free samples he is likely to have received from pharmaceutical companies.)

■ What form does the drug come in (capsules, tablets, liquid, cream, suppositories)? How often and at what time should I take it? For how long—

back of your tongue, then drink from a bottle, not a glass. ☼

A BURNING ISSUE: SUN SAFETY

It's March, the bikini's packed, and you've got a plane ticket to some sandy haven in your hot little hand. Whoa there, missy—where's the 15 SPF sun lotion?

Spring break affords millions of lucky collegiate sun-worshippers a perfect opportunity to become sun-abusers, so skin protection is something you'll want to have on hand whether you're jogging, walking, swimming, Rollerblading, or shopping. Choose a sunscreen with at least a 15 SPF (sun protection factor), and try to get one that protects against UV-A rays as well as UV-B rays. (UV-A rays cause wrinkling and a severe form of sun cancer called malignant melanoma, while UV-B rays cause sunburn, cataracts, and other forms of skin cancer.) Other hints:

▲ Remember to wear sunscreen on overcast days, as harmful rays can penetrate clouds.
▲ Use a 15 SPF lip balm, as lips are particularly sensitive.
▲ Watch out for reflective surfaces, such as water or sand (and snow, if you're skiing). All can give you a wicked burn.
▲ Wear a hat—the bigger the brim, the better.
▲ If you do get burned, drink plenty of water and take an analgesic. See a doctor if your skin is blistered or raw.
▲ Try to stay out of the sun between 10:00 and 3:30, the sun's strongest hours.
▲ Be especially careful if you've had chicken pox in the past six months, as exposure to the sun can cause hyperpigmentation of the skin.

No matter what your complexion, watch out. Although the tanning temptation may be hard to resist, remember, there is no such thing as a healthy tan. If you must have the bronzed-goddess look, check out one of the many self-tanning products on the market.

---

until the entire prescription is gone, or until the problem goes away?

■ Should I take the drug on a full or empty stomach? Should I avoid certain foods or alcohol while on this medication? Can I drive or exercise while I'm taking it? Is there any problem with taking this drug and using contraception?

■ Are there any potential long- or short-term side effects? What should I do if I experience them?

■ How long will it take before I feel better?

■ What should I do if I miss a dose?

■ Why is it necessary to prescribe this drug? Is there a nonprescription or nonmedicated way that I can treat or alleviate the problem?

■ Are there any "alternative" or complementary ways to treat the problem? What are they? Can you recommend a holistic practitioner?

Americans fail to take medicine as ordered ½ the time, costing

COMMON MEDICINES

ACNE MEDICATIONS

Description: Benzoyl peroxide is the active ingredient in most over-the-counter acne medications. Three common prescription treatments are tretinoin, a vitamin A acid in liquid, cream, or gel form, sold under the brand name Retin-A; antibiotics such as tetracycline and Cleocin T; and Accutane (isotretinoin), a powerful vitamin A derivative taken in pill form, and used when standard treatments fail to treat cases of severely disfiguring cystic acne.

Effects: Benzoyl peroxide prevents and heals pimples by killing bacteria in the pores and mildly irritating the outermost layer of the skin, causing it to peel away. Antibiotics kill acne-forming bacteria. (For more on antibiotics, see below.) Tretinoin (Retin-A) is thought to help prevent pore blockage and stimulate the manufacture of new skin cells. It is particularly effective in the treatment of blackheads. Though it is not completely clear how Accutane works, studies show that it shrinks oil glands in the skin. The three-to-five-month treatment is highly effective—90 percent of patients' conditions clear up after two courses of Accutane, and improvement continues after treatment ends.

Keep in mind: When using Retin-A, several weeks will pass before you notice any improvement. Some people, especially those with sensitive skin, may experience raw, dry skin or breakouts before they get positive results. Retin-A causes increased sensitivity to the sun. No matter how dark your skin is, during the course of tretinoin treatment you should wear a sunscreen when outdoors. Though Retin-A has passed all of the stringent FDA safety requirements, it is a fairly new drug and its long-term effects are not known.

Many patients on Accutane experience dry and itchy skin, dry mouth, nosebleeds, and conjunctivitis outbreaks as side effects. It also impairs night vision and can cause headaches, nausea, vomiting, lethargy, insomnia, and mild depression. Patients should have their liver functions, triglycerides, and cholesterol checked before and during treatment. Accutane causes severe birth defects if used during pregnancy. If you are heterosexually active, you must use contraception for a month before, and take a pregnancy test two weeks before starting the drug. You'll also need to sign a form stating that you have been informed of the potential side effects. During treatment, you must use two forms of birth control and have a monthly pregnancy test.

For some women, soap and water and an over-the-counter medication will solve an acne problem. Others may require a washing regimen and prescribed medicine.

ANALGESICS

Description: Aspirin works to reduce fever and inflammation and relieve pain; it also has blood-thinning properties, and is commonly used to prevent blood clots in people who are at risk for heart attacks and strokes. Ibuprofen (found in Advil and Motrin, among others) is both a pain reliever and an anti-inflammatory and is slightly more effective than aspirin for the relief of muscle pain caused by sprains, strains, and menstrual cramps. Acetaminophen (the main ingredient in Tylenol) is equally as

effective in relieving pain and is gentler on the stomach, but it isn't as effective as aspirin or ibuprofen at reducing swelling or easing cramps.
Effects: See above.
Keep in mind: Taking aspirin or ibuprofen can cause stomach upset, and long-term use can cause ulcers (especially when taken on an empty stomach) which can, in turn, lead to anemia. Viral illnesses should not be treated with aspirin, because the combination can lead to Reye's syndrome, a potentially fatal disease. Acetaminophen is not recommended for women with kidney or liver problems, or those who are heavy drinkers.

ANTACIDS
Description: Antacids neutralize the stomach acid that's responsible for your heartburn or indigestion. The most popular over-the-counter varieties contain calcium, aluminum, magnesium, and/or sodium to help with the neutralizing process and to coat the stomach. Some also contain ingredients to help relieve gas pain.

Effects: Antacids containing sodium bicarbonate (the bubbly ones like Alka-Seltzer) provide potent and fast-acting relief of indigestion; magnesium-based antacids (which may contain large doses of calcium [Tums], or aluminum [Maalox or Mylanta]) coat and soothe the stomach; antiflatulent (gas-preventing) antacids break up troublesome gas bubbles.
Keep in mind: If you have high blood

pressure, stay away from bubbly antacids, as they contain high amounts of sodium. Most doctors feel that simethicone-based antiflatulents don't live up to their claims. Take antacids in liquid form, which is cheaper than tablets and more effective. Antacids should not be used for more than two weeks (unless your doctor OKs it). Avoid antacids if you're taking aspirin, as nausea, cramping and diarrhea can result. Also, don't use them if you have tarry, black stools or are vomiting blood or a substance resembling coffee grounds (digested blood), or have bone or kidney disease.

Antacids containing aluminum can deplete the body of calcium and fluoride, which over time can weaken bones. However, for those who do not have kidney problems, they are considered safe if used according to the directions in the package.

ANTIHISTAMINES
Description: Antihistamines are frequently used to relieve symptoms of the common seasonal allergy known as hay fever, which include an itchy, runny nose, sneezing, a tickle in the back of the throat, and watery, irritated eyes—all courtesy of the pollen and dust filling the air in spring, summer, and fall. Asthma, hives, and severe reactions to insect bites can also be treated with antihistamines.
Effects: Antihistamines counteract the symptoms produced by histamines, which are chemicals that are released after you've inhaled or ingested a substance your body perceives to be harmful.
Keep in mind: Drowsiness is a major side effect of most antihistamines; even the least-sedating one will slow your reactions. Other side effects include dizziness, nausea, and occasion-

THE LIQUID CURE

Fluids can practically be cures in themselves when you're sick—they can soothe a sore throat, replace what you've lost from fever, vomiting, or diarrhea, and flush the unfriendly invaders from your system. Try weak tea, water, or flat ginger ale if you're having stomach problems, or juice if you're not. If you've lost a lot of fluid, you may want to sip Gatorade or another "sports drink" that will help replace essential nutrients and minerals and restore your electrolyte balance.

Because caffeine can act as a diuretic, drink coffee, colas, and caffeinated teas in moderation, if at all. (Watch out for caffeine as an ingredient in over-the-counter drugs, too.)

and inhibiting the growth of bacteria. They are injected, taken orally in pill or liquid form, or applied to the skin.

Effects: The curative powers of antibiotics depend on how they are used. Take the entire prescription in order to get rid of the bacteria causing the illness, even if you feel "cured" before it's finished—otherwise, the bacteria can become immune to the antibiotic and cause a more serious illness requiring even stronger medicine. Doses should be spaced out as evenly as possible to ensure an effective level of the drug in the body.

> "Just because a drug is legal doesn't mean it's completely safe and won't give you problems. I know more people who have had a bad reaction to antibiotics than to smoking pot. I'm not saying that antibiotics are bad and marijuana is good, just that any drugs can have bad effects."
>
> —UNIVERSITY OF WISCONSIN–MADISON, '95

ally restlessness and insomnia.

The best treatment for allergies is figuring out what you're allergic to and then avoiding it (if possible). But if you suffer from hay fever, it's hard to escape those difficulties with pollen and dust unless you barricade yourself with an air filter. Antihistamines may be addictive and/or tolerance-forming. If your usual dose doesn't "do what it used to," tell your doctor.

Note: They are completely ineffective in treating cold symptoms.

ANTIBIOTICS

Description: Antibiotics such as penicillin, erythromycin, tetracycline, amoxicillin, and Cleocin T are used to treat and prevent infection by killing

Keep in mind: Birth control pills may not work as well if you're taking antibiotics; to be safe, it's best to use an additional form of contraception for the remainder of your cycle. They also increase your susceptibility to yeast infections, as antibiotics don't know the difference between the "unhealthy" bacteria that make us sick and the "healthy" bacteria that help regulate our bodies.

A few words of warning about using antibiotics: Alcohol, milk, citrus fruits, carbonated beverages, and antacids containing calcium, magnesium, or aluminum can weaken an antibiotic's effectiveness. Never use antibiotics past the expiration date, as outdated antibiotics can be toxic to the kidneys. Finally, if taking the antibiotic causes you to feel warm and flushed, or if you develop a rash or joint pains, contact your doctor immediately—you may be allergic to it.

COUGH MEDICINE

Description: Cough **suppressants** help to prevent coughing. **Expectorants** promote your body's efforts to rid your lungs of mucus.

Effects: Cough suppressants work by suppressing the cough reflex in the brain, and should only be used for nonproductive coughs. (A nonproductive cough is a dry cough that does not bring up mucus, as opposed to a productive cough, which helps you loosen and get rid of the goo.) Expectorants help you cough up mucus by breaking it up in the airways. Studies of expectorants done by the FDA have not yielded any proof that they actually work.

Keep in mind: The only cough suppressant you should consider taking is one containing the drug dextromethorphan (DM), which carries the fewest side effects. Cough expectorants should be generally avoided in favor of taking a steamy bath or shower, or even eating a bowl or two

> ### MEDICAL ALERT
> ※
>
> If you have a medical problem, such as a severe allergy to penicillin, painkillers, anesthesia, or other medications often used in emergency situations, or have a medical condition that emergency technicians should be aware of, wear a medical alert bracelet or necklace. You can find out about where to get one at a hospital, pharmacy, or campus health services. You should also carry a card in your wallet alerting any attendant of your special medical needs as well. List your name, age, blood type, special medical issues, address, phone number, phone number of someone to call in an emergency, and physician's phone number.

of hot soup. Both remedies will soothe the lungs, open the air passages, and loosen mucus.

DECONGESTANTS

Description: Decongestants relieve a runny nose and other symptoms of nasal congestion.

Effects: Decongestants shrink swollen nose and inner ear passages by restricting blood flow to the area.

Keep in mind: Take only decongestants without added antihistamines (such as Sudafed).

HYDROCORTISONE

Description: Hydrocortisone is commonly used in cream form to treat skin conditions, eye infections, arthritis, and other ailments that produce inflammation.

※ **Chewing ginger is one of the oldest remedies for motion sickness.**

Effects: Inflammation and rashes are actually signs of the immune system working to heal the body. Cortisone cream suppresses immune response and thus reduces swelling.

Keep in mind: Hydrocortisone cream, like all over-the-counter medications, is intended for short-term use. If the problem doesn't go away within the time frame indicated, see a doctor. Using cortisone creams for a long time (as in not per the package instructions) can increase your risk of getting viral, parasitic, and fungal infections. Weaker forms of hydrocortisone (.25 percent strength) may not be effective. For minor skin rashes, calamine lotion works just as well as hydrocortisone to relieve itching and inflammation, and is probably a safer choice. Other sources of relief: taking oatmeal baths, avoiding scratching, applying cool compresses to affected areas, and wearing soft, loose clothing.

LAXATIVES

Description: Available in pill, liquid, or suppository form, laxatives treat constipation by softening stool and/or stimulating the colon.

Effects: Bulk form laxatives contain indigestible fiber, which adds bulk to stool, which in turn holds water in the intestine and stimulates the colon. Saline laxatives contain non-absorbable salts, which draw water into the colon. Laxatives containing phenolphthalien chemically irritate the walls of the intestines, causing muscle contraction. Lubricant laxatives make the colon slippery, thereby easing evacuation. Stool softeners penetrate and loosen stool. Laxatives—other than bulk forms like Metamucil, which is safe to take regularly—should be used infrequently, if ever. Their prolonged use can seri-ously impair bowel function, making it difficult to evacuate without the help of an ever-increasing amount of the laxative. Overusing laxatives can cause dehydration, acute stomach pain, and diarrhea, as well as colitis (irritation of the colon).

Keep in mind: Occasional constipation is just a fact of life. When it strikes, reach for some fiber-rich foods like prunes and other dried fruits, prune juice, bran cereals, and the like, and stay clear of rice, bananas, crackers, and other starchy foods.

Do not take laxatives if you have severe stomach cramps, nausea, or vomiting. These symptoms can signal a more serious problem than constipation, and laxatives can only exacerbate these problems, not alleviate them.

NASAL SPRAYS AND DROPS

Description: Nasal sprays and drops containing saline solution alone or in combination with other ingredients help shrink the nasal passages. They are squirted into the nose as you inhale.

Effects: Nasal sprays and drops offer only temporary relief of your symptoms. They should only be used for three days, tops. Use of these over-the-counter remedies for longer than a few days can lead to bleeding, addiction, and an increase in stuffiness as the medication wears off. Also, don't use nasal sprays or drops if you think your near constant congestion is caused by an allergy. Long-term use can lead to permanent damage of the nasal membranes, and you may find that you won't be able to breathe through your nose without them.

Keep in mind: Again, it may be better to stock up on the Kleenex and allow your nose to run so your body can evacuate the infection.

Peppermint gum or candy may also be good for nausea relief.

THE ROAD TO RECOVERY
On-Campus Health Services

❧❧❧

The first place most students turn to when they're feeling ill is the student health center. Almost every four-year college and over half of all two-year community colleges have some type of health care available for students, though the extent and quality of that care varies dramatically from school to school. Services range from a vending machine where students can buy Band-Aids and aspirin to a federally funded health center offering everything from general health and counseling services to sports medicine and family planning. Student health centers typically spon-

"Before you graduate, milk student health services for all they're worth. Unless you move to Sweden, it's probably the last you'll see of free or low-cost health care. Get a physical and gynecological exam, and stock up on discount birth control. If you're facing the loss of your insurance when you graduate, see if your school offers some kind of short-term plan to tide you over until you get on-the-job insurance. . . . And don't forget to nab a copy of your medical records on your last visit to the health center."

—KANSAS UNIVERSITY, '95

sor programs, information sessions, and support groups related to a variety of topics, such as safer sex, stress management, birth control, nutrition, substance abuse, and exercise planning—to name just a few. Schools may offer insurance plans that cover some or all of the cost of prescriptions (including birth control), eyeglasses, and lab work for Pap smears, urine and blood tests, HIV screening, and throat cultures.

Evaluating Campus Health Services

❧❧❧

Apply the same standards when evaluating student services as you use in evaluating off-campus practitioners. Consider the following:

■ Are the practitioners board-certified or board-eligible?

■ Are the practitioners and staff sensitive to the needs of women?

■ Is there a system for specialist consultation and/or emergency referral?

■ Is after-hours care and/or advice available?

■ Are you offered a choice of providers? Can you continue with the same provider?

■ Do they take the time to listen to you? Do they take you seriously?

■ Are they responsive to suggestions or complaints?

■ Is prevention and health education a part of the care provided? Will practitioners help with student programs if asked?

■ Is your health center in compliance

HERBAL CURES

❋

The following are a few of the most common age-old "home remedies."

ACIDOPHILUS: A bacteria that prevents and clears up yeast infections. Available in capsules, liquid, or in unsweetened yogurt that contains live acidophilus cultures. Helpful in replacing "healthy" bacteria killed by antibiotic use.

ACTIVATED CHARCOAL: Available in pill form, can be used to soothe stomach problems brought on by flu or food poisoning.

ALOE: Great for healing burns and fading scars. Buy aloe gel or get an aloe plant. (Breaking the stalk releases the healing Vaseline-like substance inside the plant.)

CASTOR OIL: A warm castor oil compress will soothe bumps, aches, and pains.

GARLIC: Eaten raw or cooked or taken in tablets or capsules, works as a natural antibiotic.

GINGER: Use fresh, in capsules, or in powder form to treat digestive ailments. Boiled fresh, it also makes a nice tea that's handy for soothing sore throats and other cold-related symptoms.

HERBAL TEAS: Drinking chamomile tea soothes nerves, promotes sleep, and relieves indigestion. Fennel tea is good for coughs, and peppermint tea will help relieve nausea, headaches, and fevers.

WITCH HAZEL: Use on cuts to stanch bleeding quickly or reduce the sting of insect bites and skin inflammations. Witch-hazel-soaked cotton balls ease strained, red, and tired eyes.

APPLE CIDER VINEGAR: Put it in a bath to treat dry, flaky skin.

---

with the Recommended Standards for a College Health Program, developed in 1991 by the American College Health Association?

■ Is there a health-services advisory committee? Does it have student members?

Affordable Off-Campus Options

෧෧෧

If your school doesn't have free health services—or if you don't want to use them—there are other quality, low-cost options available. It is almost always possible to find something in your price range. Many community organizations, local or women's health clinics, mental health centers, and other cultural, religious, and special interest organizations provide medical or counseling services that charge on a sliding scale; i.e., what you pay depends on what you can afford. For leads on practitioners who charge student-friendly fees, call the medical or psychology departments at school, or check campus papers, job boards, and employment opportunity listings for other low-cost options.

If you have a practitioner you like who seems to be out of your price range, explain your financial constraints to her. She may be able to adjust fees, work out an alternate payment plan, or at least suggest another, more affordable practitioner.

OUR DOCTORS, OURSELVES

Knowing how to find and evaluate doctors and other health care providers is a crucial part of taking care of yourself. Your doctors do not have to be your best friends, but they do have to be people you trust. If you don't feel comfortable talking about health problems, voicing concerns, and asking questions, or your practitioner can't or won't take the time to explain things clearly, look for another practitioner. It's not easy to demand a doctor's time and attention. Most of us have been taught to regard doctors as infallible, so questioning them may feel a little intimidating. But, for the sake of your health, ask as many questions as you need to.

Also, it's important that your doctor be readily accessible. If phone calls aren't returned, you have to wait three months for an appointment, or you have to travel by boat or camel to get to the office, you should probably find another practitioner.

Ask or at least consider the following questions when you're deciding on a new doctor.

■ What type of practitioner are you? What is your training? Are you board-certified/licensed? Do you practice by yourself, in a group, or in an HMO?

■ Are you involved in teaching medicine? How do you keep up with the latest developments in your field?

■ What are your hours? What is your availability in case of emergencies? Do you make evening appointments? Can I call you with questions? Will you give advice about a minor complaint over the phone, or is an office visit required?

■ Can I get to your office via public transportation? Is it wheelchair-accessible?

■ At what hospital(s) do you have admitting privileges?

■ What are your fees? Do you charge on a sliding scale, or do you have a special rate for students? What methods of payment do you take? Do you accept my insurance plan? Will you bill me or bill my insurance company?

■ Do you wear gloves or take other preventive measures to ensure that HIV and other infections aren't passed along in your office?

■ Do you prescribe medications and treatments with a woman's physical issues in mind?

■ Is there someone who covers for you if you're ill or on vacation?

■ What if I need medical attention after-hours?

FIRST AID TO GO

Put together a little first-aid kit that includes Band-Aids, gauze pads, antibiotic ointment, a plastic bag for ice, acetaminophen, ibuprofen, an Ace bandage, hydrogen peroxide, rubbing alcohol, tweezers, cotton balls, a thermometer, calamine lotion, and petroleum jelly.

Male doctors interrupt their patients twice as often as female doctors.

Coming Prepared

ᛉᛉᛉ

You'll get the most out of your visit if you provide the doctor with all the necessary facts about you and your condition. In particular, you should:

■ Tell the practitioner/receptionist why you are making the appointment when you call, so you'll be scheduled for the amount of time you'll need for consulting with your doctor and having any necessary tests done. Also ask questions when making the appointment. Find out whether the doctor will perform any tests that require you to refrain from eating or urinating before the exam.

■ Come armed with the basic facts about your medical history, including dates and circumstances of major/chronic illnesses, operations, hospitalizations, allergies, past or current pregnancies, and physical and/or learning disabilities.

■ Be sure to inform your doctor of any prescription and/or over-the-counter drugs you are taking (including birth control pills, vitamin supplements, antacids, laxatives, diet aids, acne medicine, and pain relievers).

■ Be prepared to tell all about your menstrual history: When did you start your periods? Are your periods regular? How long do your periods usually last? What was the starting date of your last period? You may be asked about your sexual history as well.

■ Be ready to relate the medical background of your immediate family. Relate any incidences of cancer, heart disease, high blood pressure or cholesterol levels, diabetes, kidney problems, genetic disorders, mental illness, and

---

INFORMED CONSENT

⟐

The informed-consent policy was created to protect us from undergoing operations, tests, or treatments that could prove to be costly, risky, painful, or just plain unnecessary. By law, before you OK any medical procedure or operation, it must be clearly explained to you why the procedure is necessary, what it entails, its risks, its success rate, and any possible alternatives, including no treatment. You should also have information about the costs of the operation and of any care you'll need afterward. You have the right to say no, to seek another opinion, or to simply think it over before going ahead with it.

---

drug or alcohol abuse. If you're adopted, do not neglect to tell your doctor about your adoptive family history (as well as your birth parents' medical histories, if you know anything about them). The environment and culture in which you were raised has a great impact on factors like your mental health, your diet, and whether you smoke, drink, or use drugs.

■ When going in for your first visit or for a second opinion, bring your medical records (including test results and X rays, if necessary) with you or have them sent ahead of time.

■ Studies show that patients who come to a doctor's appointment with a written list of their symptoms receive better care. Be as specific as possible about the nature of your symptoms (Is

---

80% of women ages 18 to 35 use an ob/gyn as their primary physician. ⟐

the pain sharp or dull? Is the nausea constant or does it come and go?), when they appeared, and how they affect you (you can't sleep because of the headache, you have difficulty breathing because you're so congested). Also note how you've tried to treat your symptoms. What has helped, what hasn't?

■ Bring a pad and pen and write down what your doctor says. Not only will it help you remember what you need to know, but a doctor will be less likely to gloss over or forget details if he sees you taking notes. At the end of the appointment, read or show him what you have written and ask if there's anything else you should add.

■ If it's not your first appointment, don't forget to keep your practitioner updated on any changes in your health or lifestyle (if you've moved, given up smoking, or decided to take up vegetarianism, your doctor should know about it). Report back on any

treatments, medications, or other practitioners she may have recommended to you.

Questions to Ask About Tests

ⓈⓆⓈ

You're in your paper nightie and the doctor tells you she recommends testing. Before you say, "OK, tell me where to go" think about asking the following questions.

■ What does the test consist of and what will you be looking for?

■ How does the test work? How accurate, reliable, and conclusive are the results? Where will the test be done? By whom? Will I need to prepare for it ahead of time by not eating or drinking? How long will the procedure last?

■ What would a positive or negative result signify? How would it alter my

---

MEDICAL EMERGENCY

※

If a medical emergency arises:

▲ Call campus EMS, security, or 911 immediately.

▲ Do not attempt to move an injured person unless you absolutely must.

▲ Have one person go wait for help to arrive and someone sit with the hurt person to comfort and tell her that everything's going to be OK.

▲ Do not do CPR unless you're trained.

▲ If the person is bleeding uncontrollably, apply firm, even pressure to the wound with a towel, blanket, or sheet. Do not remove the towel to check if the bleeding has stopped. If the towel gets soaked, do not remove it, just place another on top.

(For dealing with drug or alcohol related emergencies, see "Use and Abuse," page 313. For dealing with emergencies after rape or other forms of sexual and/or physical assault, see "Ending the Silence," page 491.)

---

treatment? Will you interpret the results for me or will someone else?

■ Are there any risks involved? Are there less risky alternatives?

■ How much will the test cost? Will my insurance cover the cost of the procedure?

■ And of course: Will it hurt?

Questions to Ask About the Diagnosis

◎◎◎

■ What exactly is the diagnosis? Are there other names for this illness or condition? Is there anything else it might be?

■ Am I going to feel worse before I feel better? How long should I wait before I engage in a specific activity (such as going swimming, having sex, drinking alcohol, running a marathon, or giving blood)? How long will it take before I'm entirely recovered? Is there any chance of my relapsing or of the illness recurring? Does the illness/condition have any long-term effects?

■ What treatments/therapies/medications/operations will be necessary to help me feel better? Are there any alternatives to the course of treatment you're recommending?

■ Do I need a follow-up appointment?

Confidentiality

◎◎◎

Doctors are required to write down all important information on your medical records, for your protection and theirs. If you're over 18, this information and the subjects you discuss with your doctor are confidential, period. Your medical records cannot be released without your written permission. One instance in which you may have to give your consent, however, is in obtaining insurance. Insurance companies often require access to your records in order to determine what your coverage will be.

Note: Insurance companies are not bound by the same standards of confidentiality. When you file a claim for treatment or medication, that diagnosis or supporting information may no longer be confidential.

If You Have Not Been Treated With Respect

◎◎◎

If your practitioner says or does something that is patronizing or condescending, ideally you'll be able to resolve the matter simply by bringing it to his or her attention. Point out the problem immediately—if possible, don't leave the office until you've made it perfectly clear why you don't consider the comments or actions acceptable. Admittedly, this may take more presence of mind than you're capable of summoning on short notice. You might want to wait until after the exam is over and you're dressed to bring up the offensive comments or behavior—you'll feel less physically

"My boyfriend and I were very sexually active, and I would keep getting urinary tract infections. When I went to my doctor, who had always been friendly, warm, and courteous, he chastised me for having so much sex. I felt completely insulted, embarrassed, ashamed, and extremely angry, but unable to say anything.... He acted like I was doing something wrong.... Could you ever imagine that a doctor would tell a guy that he was having too much sex?... I left the office feeling like hell. About a year later, I confronted him on it. He didn't remember the episode, but he apologized and said that I must have misinterpreted his remarks. He told me that if anything happens like that again I should tell him right on the spot."

—BARNARD COLLEGE, '92

and emotionally vulnerable in your street clothes than in a flimsy paper gown.

If you don't feel comfortable bringing up the issue at the time of the appointment, your next best bet is to write a letter that explains your feelings about the incident in no uncertain terms, and mail it within a week of your appointment. You may want to follow up your written complaint with a phone call.

If your doctor is physically or emotionally abusive and is affiliated with campus health services, you'll want to report him or her to the director of health services or a health services advisory committee. Members of the faculty and/or administration, a women's/students' advocacy center, or a campus legal services office might also be willing to help you take the appropriate steps to resolve the problem. If you are on campus, you may even want to ask friends and acquaintances if they have had a similar experience; if you work together to get your complaints noticed, you might be able to find a cure for the poor treatment you received. If you saw an off-campus practitioner, write a letter to your state department of public health, county medical association, and/or state and national medical licensing board. (See the Resources at the end of this chapter for contact information.)

COMPLEMENTARY/ ALTERNATIVE MEDICINE

Unlike Western medicine, which has become increasingly specialized, holistic medicine starts with the whole body. Practitioners of holistic medicine and supporters of holistic health believe your health is connected to all aspects of your being— physical, emotional, nutritional, and environmental factors all interact to determine your overall health. Holistic practitioners "treat the individual, not the problem." In other words, instead of targeting symptoms, they try to bring the whole body into balance (or keep it there). For example, instead of treating a yeast infection with a vagi-

Women are prescribed drugs twice as often as men are, and

nal cream, a holistic practitioner will investigate what conditions in the body are permitting or provoking a yeast overgrowth in the vagina. She might then prescribe a diet, supplements and/or medication, and stress-reducing exercises to help rebalance the body's systems.

Holistic approaches can be used alone or paired with other therapies to treat a huge variety of physical and mental afflictions, even HIV/AIDS and substance abuse. Patients take a great deal of responsibility for their own well-being; if you choose a holistic method, expect to play a very active role in your own wellness and recovery.

In the United States, holistic practices are used by medical doctors, nurses, physician's assistants, and other licensed health professionals. The best ways to find out about different techniques and reliable practitioners are talking with health practitioners, doing library research, and contacting the groups listed in the Resources at the end of this chapter. Because many methods of complementary medicine are not regulated, meaning there are no established and enforced standards of practice, you should see only those practitioners recommended by people you trust. Once you've decided on a holistic method, it's a good idea to set up a consultation appointment with one or more practitioners. The therapies listed below represent just a few of your choices.

■ **Acupuncture** is a nearly 6,000-year-old Chinese technique that uses small needles inserted at specific places on the body to open energy channels. Acupuncture can be used to relieve chronic pain from arthritis, cramps, headaches, and carpal tunnel syndrome. It can also be used to help overcome addictions to smoking, alcohol, and drugs, or even as anesthesia.

■ **The Alexander Technique** teaches more effective, healthy ways of movement with a strong emphasis on self-improvement. Your teacher or practitioner will gently show you how to improve your body's alignment, bringing new qualities of flexibility and ease to the way you stand and carry yourself.

■ **Homeopathy** is based on the philosophy that you "cancel out" a set of symptoms with the same substance that causes them in a healthy person. Homeopathic medicines are derived from extracts of animal, vegetable, or mineral sources that have been diluted many times. Remedies should be taken only one at a time and in very small doses.

■ **Biofeedback** is a kind of "guided relaxation" that helps you learn how to alleviate physical signs of stress by becoming aware of your body's response to it. You are hooked up to a machine that monitors subtle changes in your muscle tension, breathing rate, heart rate, and temperature; the machine beeps if any of these rise above a certain level. Your goal: to learn to detect signs of stress yourself and to use relaxation techniques to relieve them.

■ **Chiropractic** is a widely available method that helps keep your body aligned through adjustments to the spinal cord. The chiropractor's adjustments fine-tune the connections between your muscles, nerves, and organs. Realignment releases tension and eases restrictions on movement, so that you can walk, sit, and stand with less strain. Chiropractors try to enact positive changes in your emotional well-being, too. Specifically, chiropractic can help you recover from strains, sprains, and breaks, can relieve tension, and can even be useful in treating allergies.

■ **Hydrotherapy** literally means "water healing"—using hot baths, showers, whirlpools, mineral baths, or hot or cold compresses to improve circulation and ease cramped, aching mus-

cles. Hydrotherapy has been used to relieve arthritis, as physical therapy for injured athletes, and to improve motor coordination in senior citizens. It is also useful as a relaxant or as a stimulant.

■ **Hypnotherapy** is when a patient is put into a trance by a therapist, who then gives the patient very specific suggestions on improving his or her health. Hypnotherapy is used to treat habit-related problems like smoking, overeating, and nail biting, or stress-induced problems like asthma, high blood pressure, and headaches.

■ **Massage therapy** is one of the oldest forms of body therapy. Practitioners concentrate on your muscles, rubbing, pummeling, and tapping those fibers into shape. Massaging your contracted or untoned muscle helps increase blood flow to the cells, nourishing them and carrying off wastes. Swedish massage can be one of the most relaxing and soothing therapies. *Shiatsu massage*, also known as *acupressure*, is a Japanese technique that uses massage of specific points to release tension and energize the body. It is used to prevent and relieve the symptoms of physical and emotional disorders.

ACTIVIST IDEAS

■ Sponsor a program on women and health. Bring speakers on such subjects as the latest research findings about women's health, eating healthily on campus, how to describe symptoms to your practitioner, alternative medicine, and special health issues for women based on their race, ethni-

city, sexual orientation, and sexual practices.

■ Make up pamphlets with the help of health services that describe the most common maladies on campus and the best treatments. (Use the information in this chapter as a guide.)

Before the NIH launched the Women's Heath Initiative in 1993,

■ Praise wonderful health services practitioners and help the not-so-wonderful ones change their ways. Set up a task force to evaluate health services, make the services they provide fit students' needs, hear student complaints and suggestions, and publicize policies, especially those about confidentiality and ethical conduct. You may even be able to do it as a class or independent-study project, or as part of your work-study job.

RESOURCES

General Heath Information and Referrals

NATIONAL HEALTH INFORMATION CENTER
P.O. BOX 1133
WASHINGTON, DC 20013-1133
(301) 565-4167 IN MARYLAND
(800) 336-4797
An office of the U.S. Department of Health and Human Services Department of Disease Prevention and Health Promotion. Conducts research. Provides information about health information resources and issues to health professionals, the media, and general public, including specific information about women's health issues. Maintains a library and computer database. Publishes numerous materials, including resources lists on major health topics, and special concerns for women about specific diseases. Provides listings of toll free information numbers that give out free health information, available upon request. Houses and runs the National Information Center for Orphan Drugs and Rare Diseases, sponsored by the Food and Drug Administration. This organization concentrates on diseases that affect fewer than 200,000 people and drugs that have not been researched extensively or made readily available.

NATIONAL INSTITUTE OF HEALTH
OFFICE OF COMMUNICATIONS
BUILDING 1, ROOM 344
BETHESDA, MD 20892
(301) 496-4461
Publishes numerous materials about all areas of health, available for free, upon request. Provides information about all areas of health. Conducts free database searches. Houses the Office on Research on Women's Health, which encourages and promotes research on diseases and disorders, among other health concerns that affect women; works to ensure that women are represented in and gender is considered in medical research, they are particularly concerned with research conducted by the NIH. Conducts research, in affiliation with the Women's Health Initiative, an in-depth study of women's health concerns and issues. Encourages development and advancement of opportunities and support the advancement, retention, and recruitment of women in medicine. Also home to the Office of Alternative Medicine,

which awards grants for research, runs a national database and information clearinghouse, investigates and assists alternative therapy research, education, and policy development.

PUBLIC CITIZENS HEALTH RESEARCH GROUP
2000 P STREET NW, SUITE 600
WASHINGTON, DC 20036
(202) 833-3000
Organizes political action/advocacy/lobbying. Publishes numerous materials, available upon request. Publications include: *Best Pills, Worst Pills, Women's Health Alert, Medical Records: Getting Yours,* and *Questionable Doctors* (an annual publication). Conducts research in order to protect consumers.

**AMERICAN ACADEMY OF ALLERGY AND
    IMMUNOLOGY**
611 EAST WELLS STREET
MILWAUKEE, WI 53202
(800) 822-2762 [ASMA]
Provides information about allergies and immunizations. Makes referrals to local doctors/practitioners who work with allergies. Publishes numerous materials about allergies and immunizations, available upon request.

AMERICAN COLLEGE HEALTH ASSOCIATION
P.O. BOX 28937
BALTIMORE, MD 21240-8937
(410) 859-1500
Conducts studies on issues relating to college/university health. Organizes college/university health care professionals. Provides information about health issues of primary concern to college/university students. Publishes numerous materials about common health issues for college/university students, available upon request. Although this organization primarily serves college/university health care professionals, you may be able to find out about general ethical and medical standards/guidelines for college/university students; file a complaint about a specific school health services, if the venue for doing so doesn't work at your school, and you may be able to obtain information about college/university health issues.

Patients' Rights

AMERICAN HOSPITAL ASSOCIATION
PATIENTS BILL OF RIGHTS
840 LAKESHORE DRIVE
CHICAGO, IL 60611
(312) 422-3000: GENERAL INFORMATION
(800) 242-2626: FOR PUBLICATIONS
Provides information about the rights of patients and ethical guidelines for doctors and other health professionals. Publishes numerous materials; call to request.

AMERICAN DENTAL ASSOCIATION (ADA)
211 EAST CHICAGO AVENUE
CHICAGO, IL 60611
(312) 440-2500
(800) 621-8099
Conducts and funds research, accredits dental schools. Publishes numerous materials. Provides referrals to local organizations and dental referral programs, as well as providing information about a dentist's background/training. They will provide details of where a dentist attended dental school, year of graduation, year of licensing, any complaints filed against her/him, as well as other information. Provides information about dental problems and health.

AMERICAN MEDICAL ASSOCIATION
DEPARTMENT OF PHYSICIAN SERVICE
515 NORTH STATE STREET
CHICAGO, IL 60610
(312) 464-5199
Provides information about a physician's background/training. Write a letter requesting information and include the name of the physician. They will send the details of where a physician attended medical school, year of graduation, her/his place and field of residency and year of licensing, any complaints filed against her/him, as well as other information.

BUREAU OF HEALTH PROFESSIONALS
HEALTH RESOURCES AND SERVICES
ADMINISTRATION
5600 FISHERS LANE, ROOM 8-05
ROCKVILLE, MD 20857
(800) 767-6732
Provides information about all disciplinary actions, malpractice claims, or other complaints against licensed health professionals. Makes referrals to the appropriate organization to file any complaints against medical practitioners.

Chronic Fatigue Syndrome

CFIDS ASSOCIATION
P.O. BOX 220398
CHARLOTTE, NC 28222
(704) 362-2243
(800) 442-3437
Publishes numerous materials about chronic fatigue syndrome, available upon request. Provides information about current research and symptoms. Makes referrals to local support groups and practitioners dealing with chronic fatigue syndrome.

Gynecological Disorders

THE VULVAR PAIN FOUNDATION
P.O. DRAWER 177
GRAHAM, NC 27253
(910) 226-0704

Offers support for women suffering from vulvar pain. Makes local referrals to organizations, groups, and practitioners who address vulvar pain. Provides information upon request.

INTERSTITIAL CYSTITIS ASSOCIATION
P.O. BOX 1553
MADISON SQUARE STATION
NEW YORK, NY 10159
(212) 979-6057
Makes referrals to local support groups and practitioners dealing with interstitial cystitis. Provides information for women who suffer from interstitial cystitis, the most common urinary tract infection.

Women's Health Organizations

The number of organizations that deal with women's health issues are too numerous to list completely. However, if the organizations listed below cannot address your needs, they should be able to provide you with a referral to an organization that can.

NATIONAL WOMEN'S HEALTH RESOURCE
CENTER
2440 M STREET NW, SUITE 325
WASHINGTON, DC 20037
(202) 293-6045
Provides information and education on all issues relating to women's health. Publishes numerous materials; available on request.

NATIONAL WOMEN'S HEALTH NETWORK
514 10TH STREET NW, SUITE 40
WASHINGTON, DC 20004
(202) 347-1140
FAX: (202) 347-1168
Organizes political action/advocacy to increase the participation and inclusion of women in the U.S. health care system. Maintains a clearinghouse of information to help women make well-informed health care decisions. Provides information on all

areas of women's health, available upon request. Monitors the health-related regulatory agencies and reviews proposed federal legislation. If they cannot meet your needs, they will make referrals to organizations that can.

FEDERATION OF FEMINIST WOMEN'S HEALTH CENTERS

633 EAST 11TH STREET
EUGENE, OR 97401
(503) 344-0966

Makes referrals to local women's clinics and practitioners who are members of the federation. Most organizations they refer to offer gynecological services. Publishes numerous materials about women's health, catalogs of publications, available upon request. Organizes political action/advocacy work to promote greater access to and options in women's health care.

WOMEN'S HEALTH CONNECTION

P.O. BOX 6338
MADISON, WI 53716
(800) 366-6632

Provides information, answers health questions, offers guidance and advice about topics such as how to talk with your doctor. Publishes numerous materials including listings of health resources and bibliographies on health topics of particular interest to women, available upon request.

NATIONAL BLACK WOMEN'S HEALTH PROJECT

1237 RALPH DAVID ABERNATHY BOULEVARD
ATLANTA, GA 30310
(800) 275-2947 [ASK-BWHP]
(404) 758-9590
FAX: (404) 758-9661

A self-help and advocacy organization on health issues facing black women and their families. Encourages mutual and self-help advocacy among women, urges women to seek out available health care resources and to communicate with health care providers, become aware of self-help methods and to communicate with other black women to allay feelings of isolation and powerlessness. Organizes political action/advocacy work to promote the betterment of black women's health care, and to encourage greater attention and consideration of black women in medical research. Involved in coalitions to improve the health care provided to women of color, and women in general. Provides information on issues related to black women and health care, available upon request. Publishes numerous materials, including *The Black Woman's Health Book: Speaking for Ourselves* and *Vital Signs,* a quarterly periodical advocating activism to reduce black women's common health problems, reports of research, and information and discussion of black women's health issues.

THE NATIONAL LATINA HEALTH ORGANIZATION

P.O. BOX 7567
OAKLAND, CA 94601
(510) 534-1362
FAX: (510) 534-1364

Organizes political action/advocacy work and promotes the inclusion of Latina issues in the national reproductive health care debate. Engages in health education, promoting self-help methods and bilingual access to health care. Provides information about health care issues of special concern to Latina women, available upon request.

NATIVE AMERICAN WOMEN'S HEALTH EDUCATION RESOURCE CENTER

P.O. BOX 572
LAKE ANDES, SD 57356
(605) 487-7072

Organizes political action/advocacy work and provides educational information on issues that effect Native women's health, including such issues as reproductive health care issues, the environment, AIDS, and fetal alcohol syndrome.

THE CAMPAIGN FOR WOMEN'S HEALTH
666 11TH STREET NW, SUITE 700
WASHINGTON, DC 20001
(202) 783-6686
Organizes political action/advocacy work to promote the improvement of women's health care in the U.S. and to increase public awareness about women's health issues. Also works to promote increased research into women's health issues. Publishes numerous materials, including statistics and information about women's health.

SOCIETY FOR THE ADVANCEMENT OF
  WOMEN'S HEALTH RESEARCH
1920 L STREET NW, SUITE 510
WASHINGTON, DC 20036
(202) 223-8224
FAX: (202) 833-3472
Organizes political action/advocacy work to promote medical and health research that considers gender as a factor and to raise awareness about issues of concern in women's health. They focus on the inclusion of women in medical research trials. Publish numerous materials, available upon request.

Alternative/Complementary Medicine

NATIONAL COMMISSION FOR THE
  CERTIFICATION OF ACUPUNCTURISTS
1424 16TH STREET NW, SUITE 501
WASHINGTON, DC 20036
(202) 232-1404
Provides free information about acupuncture treatments. Makes referrals to local practitioners.

NATIONAL CENTER FOR HOMEOPATHY
801 NORTH FAIRFAX STREET, SUITE 306
ALEXANDRIA, VA 22314
(703) 548-7790
Makes referrals to homeopathic centers and practitioners. Publishes materials and provides information about homeopathy.

AMERICAN MASSAGE THERAPY ASSOCIATION
820 DAVIS STREET, SUITE 100
EVANSTON, IL 60201-4444
(312) 761-2682
Publishes numerous materials about massage, cost varies. Maintains a listing of local practitioners who will take referrals.

AMERICAN HOLISTIC MEDICAL ASSOCIATION
4101 LAKE BOONE TRAIL, SUITE 201
RALEIGH, NC 27607
(919) 787-5146
Makes referrals to local holistic practitioners throughout the country. Publishes numerous materials about holistic medicine.

Further Reading
◈◈◈

General Health, Prescription, and Over-the-Counter Drugs

The College Student's Health Guide, Sandra Smith and Christopher Smith (Westchester, 1988).
Campus Health Guide: The College Student's Handbook for Healthy Living, Carol L. Otis and Robert Goldingay (College Board, 1989).

The Complete Drug Reference (Consumer Reports Books & United States Pharmacopeial Convention, 1991).

Physicians' Desk Reference for Nonprescrition Drugs (Medical Economics Data).

Physicians' Desk Reference (Medical Economics Data).

PDR Family Guide to Prescription Drugs (Medical Economics Data).

Handbook of Over-the-Counter Drugs and Pharmacy Products, Max R. Leber, Robert W. Jaeger, Anthony J. Scalzo (G.W. Manning, 1992).

Natural Alternatives to Over-the-Counter and Prescription Drugs, Michael T. Murray (William Morrow, 1994).

Herbes of Choice: The Therapeutic Use of Phytomedicinals, Tyler, V.E. (Pharmaceutical Products Press, 1994).

The Honest Herbal: A Sensible Guide to Herbs and Related Remedies, Tyler, V.E. (Pharmaceutical Products Press, 1994).

The Alternative Health and Medicine Encyclopedia, James Marti (Gale Research, Inc. 1994).

Holistic Medicine: A Meeting of East and West, Henry Edward Altenberg (Japan Publications, 1992).

Women's Health

The New Our Bodies Ourselves, The Boston Women's Health Collective (Simon & Schuster, 1992).

The Woman's Guide to Good Health, Consumer Reports Books Editors (Consumer Reports, 1991).

Everywoman's Health: The Complete Guide to Body and Mind, 4th edition, Douglas S. Thompson (Prentice-Hall, 1990).

The New A–Z of Women's Health: A Concise Encyclopedia, Christine Ammer (Hunter House, 1991).

Woman: Your Body, Your Health, Josleen Wilson (Harcourt, Brace, Jovanovich, 1990).

Women's Health Alert: What Most Doctor's Won't Tell You About Birth Control, C-sections, Weight Control Products. . . . , Sidney M. Wolfe and the Public Citizen Health Research Group, with Rhoda Donkin Jones (Addison-Wesley, 1991).

Women's Bodies, Women's Wisdom: Creating Physical and Emotional Health and Healing, Christine Northrup (Bantam, 1994).

A Women's Guide to Alternative Medicine, Liz Grist (Contemporary, 1988).

Alive and Well: A Lesbian Health Guide, Cuca Hepburn and Bonnie Gutierrz (Crossing Press, 1988).

For information about health insurance, see the Resources in "Safety First," page 528. For more information on gynecological disorders, see the Resources in "Know Your Body," page 366.

☼ 84% of those who try alternative medicine do so again. ☼

More Than Just the Blues

Mental Health & Therapy

College is a time filled with constant change and endless demands, so it's natural for us to run into rough patches now and again—that's simply part of life. But sometimes problems can escalate beyond manageable proportions: We're so stressed out we feel like we're going to explode, we're so incredibly low we can't even get out of bed, or we don't feel in control of our emotions or our actions.

You may not have thought about your mental health much before college, but now is the time to start taking it every bit as seriously as you do your physical health. You've got to learn to do what it takes to deal with difficulties you face: When you are hurting inside, find someone to talk with; when you are in need of support, ask for it. And, maybe hardest of all, try to recognize when what you're doing isn't enough and you need to seek further help.

SENDING OUT A STRESS-O-S

College life is inherently stressful. Even under the highly improbable circumstance that we've finished this week's reading and don't have a paper or a midterm looming, there's likely some combination of relationship issues, extracurricular commitments, job woes, family problems, phone bills, unanswered letters, and/or roommate hell to worry about. And unlike financial aid, stress-inducing events don't go away upon graduation. How we deal with stress now will in large part determine how we'll deal with it later in life. College, therefore, is a good time to learn how to anticipate stressful times, and to figure out healthy, constructive ways of getting through them.

15% of college students spend ½ their waking hours worrying.

> *"When you're a stress-muffin or upset, everyone seems smarter, more organized, more directed, and more talented than you. You have to remind yourself that stress can play tricks on your mind and that just because there are a lot of talented people at your school it doesn't mean that you're a stupid, clumsy clod."*
>
> —BROWN UNIVERSITY, '98

What Exactly Is Stress, Anyway?

ᕙᕗᕙ

Stress is our body's way of rising to meet a challenge. It can make us more alert in a new job, more clear-headed in an exam, more focused during a presentation, and quicker during a swim meet. It's a physiological reaction, the old fight or flight response, designed to help all us animals fend off or escape predators: Our heart and respiration rate go up, the blood supply to our brain and muscles increases, and the blood supply to our stomach, intestines, sex organs, and skin decreases. It's actually a great system, when used occasionally. The problems arise when it goes into overdrive in reaction to chronically stressful situations, like an impossible course-load or an intractable family problem, that cause the body to be in a constant state of agitation.

How Stress Affects Us

ᕙᕗᕙ

We can't underestimate the toll chronic stress can take on our bodies. It can be the culprit behind headaches, stomachaches, muscle tightness, neck pain, back pain, insomnia, nausea, eating disorders, menstrual irregularity, acne, hives, eczema, high blood pressure, ulcers, depression, and heart disease.

It is guaranteed that our bodies will tell us when they have crossed their stress threshold. Unfortunately, because we're under so much stress, we're probably not listening. And sometimes the signs are subtle or manifest themselves slowly. Pay attention to your body. If you are experiencing any of the above problems, see a health practitioner and make a commitment to deal with the stress in your life.

Managing Stress

ᕙᕗᕙ

We all have ways we cope with stress. The problem is that often our coping mechanisms only make our lives more stressful and difficult. Unwinding with a glass of wine, a hit of pot, or an entire pint of ice cream might give you temporary relief. But, if they become the primary means of coping they can actually make things worse. When we're under a lot of pressure, we tend not to take time out to think about what would be best for ourselves. By making the things that give us pleasure a part of our day even when we have lots to do, we can help to lighten the load. Simple things like taking a walk, listening to

COLLEGE WOMEN AND STRESS

"I have a 30-hour-a-week job, 16 credits, a Take Back the Night march to plan, a welding project to finish, a boyfriend who thinks that I don't spend enough time with him, and a roommate who has spent the last three days with a bucket next to her bed nursing what the Times calls 'the worst flu to ever hit New York,' and you ask me why I'm stressed????"

—COLUMBIA UNIVERSITY, '95

These may or may not be the best years of our lives, but one thing is for sure: They are some of the most difficult. We're in a new environment, navigating demanding classes, trying to get good grades, and probably working to finance at least part of the experience. And for many of us, college is the first time we've been away from the support and structure of home. This separation can be extremely difficult, especially for women, as we haven't been conditioned to break away.

And while we're doing all this separating, we're also forming new attachments—meeting people, making new friends, and working out new love relationships. We might have our first serious relationship, which can be stressful in and of itself, and our first serious breakup, which can be completely devastating. Pile on top of this roommate trouble, overextension, poor time management, and the pressure many of us feel to be perfect and we've got an ulcer in the making.

music, making a vegetable stir-fry or hanging out with friends all help to defuse the stress, leaving us more relaxed and prepared to face the next challenge. And it's no big secret that talking about feelings, problems, and fears—instead of keeping them pent up inside—is one of the best ways to feel better. Here are a few other good techniques:

■ Try to pinpoint what's stressing you out. Break it down into manageable components. If, for example, you have a terrifying chem final coming up, you have to learn your lines for a play, *and* you're fighting with your roommate, address each problem separately. Declare a time-out with the roomie, plan to spend the next two days in the library studying chemistry, and have breakfast, lunch, and dinner with the guy who's playing Romeo to your Juliet so you can practice your lines. More often than not, problems that seem huge and unwieldy are actually quite manageable and simple when looked at as a series of smaller tasks.

"Too much stress is a bad thing, but a little stress gives me a little kick and makes me more alert. . . . I do better on tests if I'm a little nervous than if I'm totally calm."

—NORTHWESTERN UNIVERSITY, '95

responded that student stress level was "high" or "very high."

■ Be realistic about your expectations and abilities. Not even Superwoman could take 25 credits, work two nights a week on the rape crisis hotline, support her best friend through her recovery from a substance abuse problem, maintain a loving long-distance relationship, work at the bookstore 20 hours a week, pledge a sorority, and pass environmental psychology with that famous wunderkind professor all at one time.

■ Try to keep your perspective—admittedly an arduous task when you're feeling like your entire world is about to cave in. But ask yourself: Will it matter in 10 years that I had to get an extension on my history methodology paper? For that matter, will it make a difference in two weeks? Stand back and take stock. Is there something that isn't really that important that you could let slide for a few days, at least until after basketball season, parents' weekend, or the GRE?

■ Hit the gym. Exercise is not only one of the best ways to release stress, it's also an important aid in its prevention. A fit body is more capable of handling the curve balls college life flings your

LEARNING TO RELAX

Learning to breathe properly is one of the most important elements of stress management. Deep breathing is extremely calming and when you're stressed and your body's working in overdrive, you need all the oxygen you can get. To make sure you are breathing deeply, place your hand on your stomach and inhale through the nose, so you can feel your stomach push out. Concentrate on filling your lungs with air without letting your shoulders or chest rise. When your lungs are filled to capacity, hold the air in, count to five, then slowly release the air through your mouth. Feel your stomach go down again as you empty your body of the breath. With each exhalation, try to visualize and feel your shoulders, neck, face, and chest muscles spreading out, loosening, and relaxing. Let your hands go limp and slack. Do this 10 times.

When you are feeling stressed or tense—say, before an exam or a class presentation, when you are crying, or when you are about to blow up with anger or frustration—deep breathing works wonders to relax the body and mind. Combine deep breathing with meditation, yoga muscle relaxation exercises, and other forms of stress and tension reduction techniques, or do it while standing in line at the cafeteria, before bed, in the shower, or when you see your ex strolling across campus with another woman.

❄ The scent of vanilla can reduce stress levels as much as 63%.

way. If you exercise regularly, chances are you'll sleep better, concentrate better (due to increased oxygen to the brain), feel better, and look better, all of which help reduce stress. Be sure to choose a workout method you enjoy, set reasonable goals, and don't get all crazy about it if you miss a session— just sweat until you can sweat no more.

■ Procrastinate not. We all know how thinking about the work we have to do and not doing it makes us ever so much more miserable than just doing the work. So instead of putting it off until tomorrow, do yourself a favor and get to it.

"Before I got to college I literally believed that I could do anything if I just worked hard enough at it, but that because I was stuck at my high school I wasn't able to realize my full potential. When I got to college I had very high expectations because I had no more excuses. As a result, if something didn't go perfectly, it sent me into a tailspin. I had to learn that even if I had all the time in the world I still wouldn't be guaranteed that my life would go exactly as I wanted it to, and that that was OK." **—REED COLLEGE, '97**

CHANGE

We are constantly facing change in our lives, and most of the time we just take it in stride without much thought. But the more dramatic the change (whether good or bad), the more of an effect it has on us, the more energy is required to adapt to the new situation, and the more anxiety and stress it's apt to produce.

If you're going through a lot of changes at once (such as in the beginning of a term or after a breakup) things are bound to get extra stressful. If possible, introduce changes into your life gradually. And when that's impossible, take especially good care of yourself. Give yourself time to relax, and remember to do the things that make you feel good. It doesn't matter what they are, as long as they give you pleasure and don't add to your stress.

them up, burn them, and/or flush them. Knowing that the paper will be destroyed and unreadable might make it easier to get the feelings out.

■ Keep a datebook. It frees your mind from having to remember everything. Make it a habit to write down assignments, appointments, reminders and important phone numbers in one handy place.

■ Learn about yourself. Take some time to think about what gets you stressed—the little things, the big things. Write them down, and try to find consistencies. That way you can

■ Keep a journal. Scribble down your thoughts, the things that you can't say to anyone. Or, simply put down your deepest darkest feelings and opinions, read them over once or twice, then rip

try to avoid (or at least prepare your-self for) those situations that are bound to stress you out.

DEPRESSION

"It's really hard to explain what depression feels like. It's scary to feel so bad for no good reason ... and feel like it's not ever going to go away. It feels like someone puts a dingy glass cage around me—I feel trapped and can't get a perspective on things."

—GEORGETOWN UNIVERSITY MEDICAL SCHOOL, '97

We all get the blues. We feel down after bombing a test, after fighting with a friend, or during midterms. The blues are a normal, though not a terribly fun, part of life. But when the blue feeling lingers for weeks or months, when it keeps you from getting to sleep at night or getting out of bed in the morning, you may be clinically depressed.

Depression, a painful, debilitating, but treatable problem, is an affective, or mood, disorder that is said to afflict over 10 million Americans. As college women, we are especially at risk. According to a 1990 report by the American Psychological Association on women and depression, a third of college students suffer from depression (compared to a fifth of the general population), and twice as many women as men of all ages get depressed. Nobody knows exactly why this is the case, but theories suggest that it's a combination of factors. One of these is that as women we're rarely encouraged to express anger, so our tendency is to turn our anger inward which can result in depression. Unhappy relationships and cultural traditions that diminish women's value may also contribute, as may the fact that many of us were raised to place our emotional needs second to the needs of others.

Mood disorders can display themselves in several ways. There's bipolar disorder (or manic-depression), in which your mood is unstable and may swing from dizzying highs to debilitating lows; dysthymia, or chronic, low-grade depression, in which a feeling of sadness may last for weeks and recur every few months, but you can still function; and major depression, in which you are unable to function in at least one daily activity, are plagued by feelings of loneliness, helplessness, and despair, may over- or under-eat, may oversleep or have insomnia and/or may have thoughts of suicide.

Depression is often unrecognized or goes untreated because of the stigma of mental health problems, the expectation that we should be able to control our moods, and the lack of understanding that depression is fre-

NO PANACEA

Be careful about using drugs, including alcohol to help temper the blues. Although it may seem like they will make you feel better, they will usually increase the feelings of depression, rather than lessen them.

🔆 1 in 4 women will be depressed during her lifetime; 1 in 8 men will. 🔆

IF YOU ARE FEELING SUICIDAL . . .

If you are feeling suicidal you should get professional help immediately. Call a suicide prevention hotline (the operator or information will be able to connect you or provide the number) or tell a friend how you are feeling and ask him/her to get you help. The following steps are not meant to replace professional help.

▲ Don't act on your suicidal feelings. Wait. You probably won't feel better overnight, but these feelings can and will pass. Even though you may feel as if you want to end your life, it is really your pain you want to end. And with help, it is possible to end your pain.

▲ Don't condemn yourself for feeling depressed or suicidal. It's not something you have control over. This may be an important transition period in your life. By talking with someone who understands you, you may find new and creative answers to the problems you are experiencing.

▲ Though it may not seem as if your friends and family care about you, remember that they can't necessarily know how you are feeling unless you communicate it to them. By letting them in, you give them the opportunity to show that they care.

▲ Despite the way it may feel, you do have options. Your life, health, and happiness are more important than any academic, professional, or even personal responsibilities. Ask for help. You can take a leave of absence from school, get incompletes and finish your work later, and/or take a break from a difficult relationship. Talk with deans, professors, or counselors about your options. Allow yourself to take the weight off your shoulders.

---

quently a problem of biochemistry and physiology. And just like any medical problem, if symptoms of depression cause you pain and disrupt your life, it's important to get a proper diagnosis and treatment from a competent mental health professional. Because as with many illnesses, the longer it remains untreated, the more serious depression becomes.

The 12 Signs of Depression

୭ଵ୭

If you are suffering from one or more of the symptoms listed below, you may be depressed and should consider getting help.

▲ Continual feelings of sadness, emptiness, and helplessness that seem to have no cause

▲ Loss of interest or pleasure in ordinary activities, including sex

In the U.S., 12-13 million people are depressed; 7-8 million are women.

IF YOUR FRIEND IS SUICIDAL . . .

"One question many people ask about suicide is, 'Is she just trying to get attention?' and if so, it's brushed off as an immature and pathetic move. Someone hurting herself for attention often means that she doesn't know a better way to ask for help, and the only way she can be taken seriously is to do something drastic, even if she doesn't realize that at the time. It's a sad state of affairs that so many people have to bleed before their pain is noticed or they feel like they justifiably can get help."

—HUNTER COLLEGE, '96

If you think your friend may be thinking of suicide, take the following steps.

▲ Talk to her about it. Ask her questions such as, "How are you feeling," "What are you thinking about," and "What's going on in your life?" Show her you care by listening without judging, urging her to talk, and demonstrating that you believe what she says to be true. Don't dismiss her thoughts and feelings, no matter how off the mark they may seem to you, by saying things such as, "Don't worry about that," "You're making a big deal out of nothing," or "You're interpreting this all wrong." Show her unconditional caring—that no matter what she feels, what she did, or what happened, you'll be there for her.

▲ Address the issue in a calm way. Don't be judgmental, but do be direct. Ask:

"Are you thinking of hurting yourself?" If she is not considering suicide, asking her will not "give her the idea" to do it. And if she has been thinking of suicide, she will probably be relieved that she is able to talk about it openly and honestly with you.

▲ If she is thinking about suicide, you should first encourage her to seek help. Say something like, "I feel like you need to talk to someone who can give you better help than I can. So, do you want to call counseling services/ talk to the RA or should I?" If she is willing to go see someone, walk her over. If she is willing to talk to someone on the phone, ask her if she wants you in the room with her. If she says no, wait outside the door so you can be there with her after she is through. If there are no campus resources available, call a suicide hotline. Even after talking to the hotline worker, it is still important that she gets further, more personal help, so she or you should contact health services, an RA, a priest, minister, or rabbi, or another trained counselor who you trust. (It's probably best if that someone is affiliated with the school.)

▲ If she is unwilling to call, make the call to health services or to security yourself. Tell them that your friend needs to see a therapist immediately, and ask about the correct procedure and your alternatives.

▲ After you have alerted the proper people, remain a source of support for your friend, but leave the counseling and professional decisions to the professionals. If you feel like she is not getting the care she needs or the counselor is missing the point, either address your concerns with the therapist directly, or get another opinion by talking with another counselor (don't use your friend's name).

▲ If you are unsure of what the best resources are, call campus security, health services, or the operator or 411 (if you're off campus) who will connect you to a suicide hotline. If you cannot get in touch with a suicide hotline, call another crisis hotline or a psychiatric emergency service connected to a hospital facility. Call 411 or 911 for the number. The people answering the calls should be equipped to handle suicide issues.

▲ If it is an emergency—she has the means to hurt herself on hand or she is not otherwise physically safe, call campus security or 911.

▲ You may want to get help for yourself. All the on- and off-campus support and counseling options listed in this chapter may be appropriate and/or useful.

▲ There is absolutely no such thing as overreacting to a potential suicide threat. If you're worried, trust your instincts and get help. Don't waste time by trying to guess why or when. Remember, breaking a promise not to tell that a friend is contemplating hurting herself is not betraying her. It's caring for her.

▲ Decreased energy, fatigue, feeling slowed-down
▲ Sleep problems (insomnia, waking at odd hours, oversleeping)
▲ Eating problems (loss of appetite, increased appetite, bingeing)
▲ Difficulty concentrating and making decisions
▲ Feelings of guilt, worthlessness, and helplessness
▲ Irritability
▲ Excessive crying
▲ Chronic physical aches and pains that don't respond to treatment
▲ Feelings of hope-lessness
▲ Thoughts of death or suicide, or suicide attempts

Helping a Depressed Friend

ගගග

How can you tell if a friend is just going through a difficult time or if s/he is experiencing a major depression? Check "The 12 Signs of Depression," above, and if your friend has had one or more of the symptoms for longer than two weeks, s/he may need help. Don't assume that someone else is taking care of the problem. Negative thinking and inappropriate behavior need to be addressed as quickly as possible. Not only does treatment lessen the severity of depression, it may also reduce the duration and prevent further bouts.

Encourage your friend to get help. If s/he doesn't, it's appropriate to and important that you speak with a counselor, RA, or advisor about the problem. (See "A Friend in Need," page 327, for more on helping others.)

often by a direct threat or statement of intent to hurt themselves.

SAD: SEASONAL AFFECTIVE DISORDER

I f come every fall when the temperature drops and the light fades, your mood drops and your energy level fades, you're unable to concentrate, have no energy, and tend to sleep too much, you may have seasonal affective disorder (SAD), and you are not alone. SAD, the aptly acronymed malady, causes 15 to 25 million Americans to feel blue in the winter months, and women are four times as likely as men to be affected by the disorder. It's not known exactly why people get SAD, but it's thought that it may be related to the hormone melatonin, whose secretion is affected by light.

Exercising (preferably outdoors), keeping warm, and maintaining a healthy diet have all proven helpful in relieving some of the symptoms of SAD. Studies have also shown that full-spectrum light therapy, or "phototherapy," has been successful in treating approximately 50 to 75 percent of SAD cases. In light therapy, sufferers sit (or better yet, exercise) in front of a full-spectrum light source for a period of time every day. The lamp mimics sunlight (but does not cause tanning or burning) and fools the body into thinking it's summer. Portable

CONSIDER THERAPY IF . . .

▲ You have issues that are plaguing you, and talking to friends and/or family doesn't help.

▲ You need to talk, but you don't know of anyone to talk to or can't talk to anyone you know.

▲ People you trust and who care about you suggest it.

▲ Your behavior, feelings, and mood make you nervous or scare you.

▲ You feel like you need some help getting control over your life.

▲ You recognize that you have a problem with food, drugs, and/or dealing with the pain of past experiences.

▲ Chronic anxiety or concern over issues in your life is preventing you from functioning.

▲ You are experiencing signs of depression and they are interfering with your life.

▲ You're having trouble dealing with a crisis.

▲ You want to get to know yourself better.

▲ You're afraid to talk about something that's consuming you.

▲ You want to work out your relationship with a lover or a member of your family.

▲ You need to get out of or change a present situation but are unsure of how to go about it or need some support to help you through it.

▲ You don't know what is bothering you but it won't go away; you can't seem to snap out of it.

▲ You would like someone else's perspective on your situation.

▲ You just feel like it might be a good idea.

Younger women tend to eat and sleep more when they are de-

light units for home use are available, but expensive. Some insurance plans will cover the cost if prescribed by a physician. If you think you might suffer from SAD, consult a doctor, who can make a diagnosis and tell you about treatment options.

OTHER MENTAL HEALTH DISORDERS

Depression, SAD, and the myriad difficulties brought on by stress are some of the most common mental health problems to befall college students. There are, however, other mental illnesses that tend to manifest themselves in late adolescence or early adulthood, which for many means the college years. These include: schizophrenia (a disorder of thinking characterized by delusions, hallucinations, incoherent speech, etc.), anxiety disorders, panic disorder, obsessive-compulsive disorder, multiple personality disorder and other personality disorders.

These are all very serious but treatable disorders. If you suspect that you or someone you know is suffering from one of the above, it's extremely important to get professional help as soon as possible.

THERAPY

When we have a virus we don't give a second thought to going to the doctor, nor do we feel guilty, ashamed, or embarrassed about

"In my family, if you had a problem, you dealt with it yourself. If it was a big problem, you might talk to the preacher about it. Then this little Alabama girl finds her way to a big, liberal New York City school, where 'everyone is in therapy, was in therapy, or should be in therapy.' I was afraid that if I wasn't in need of therapy, maybe I wasn't digging hard enough. . . . I finally feel like I don't have to be in therapy to understand myself, but if I did need help, I wouldn't feel bad or guilty for seeing someone."

—*THE NEW SCHOOL/PARSONS SCHOOL OF DESIGN, '97*

it. In a perfect world, we would look at seeing a therapist the same way, but in our society the importance placed on solving our own problems and being in control, the notion that therapy is an extravagance, and the afore-mentioned stigma associated with mental illness cause many people who would benefit from therapy to shy away from it.

Talking It Out

If you are going through a difficult period, talking with friends and relatives will often provide you with all the help and support you need. But in certain cases, even the most understanding friend can't pull you out of the doldrums. It sometimes takes the skill and experience of a trained professional or the support, focus, and structure of a group to help you to uncover conflicts and fully address problems.

Therapy can be a valuable tool in helping you to gain insight into both your feelings and behavior. A good therapist or group can help you find the strength within to confront pressing issues and to understand, question, cope with, and make changes in your life.

There are many reasons you might feel the need for therapy: to deal with present concerns like academic pressure, homesickness, or the stress of trying to balance school, job, and family. You may want to face and work through a crisis in your life or memories from your past. You may go with a partner or a family member to iron out sticky relationship issues. You may just want to talk with someone who can help you gain perspective on your, life, someone who can help you get to know yourself better. Or you may have already entered into therapy to deal with specific issues but discovered that the therapeutic process brought out new ones that also need to be addressed.

Starting therapy is essentially a commitment to take care of yourself and to help yourself feel better about your life. It isn't a magic cure, and there is no single perfect therapy method. Cultural and personal backgrounds profoundly impact the way people respond to and process the experiences in their lives; therefore, people will respond differently to each approach and practitioner. To find a therapist and therapy style that is best suited for you emotionally and financially you should consider what you need and want, and obtain information about the many options that are available to you.

TYPES OF THERAPY

There are almost as many types of therapy as there are clients and practitioners. All of the forms of therapy fill different needs and can work alone or in conjunction with one another. Pinpointing why you want or need therapy will help you determine what type will work best for you.

Individual therapy. There are many different styles of individual therapy. What they share is that you're talking with someone who is focused only on you—what you're saying, how you're acting. This enables you to address the specificities of your situation and receive very personal feedback and (sometimes) advice.

Psychopharmacotherapy. Psychopharmacotherapy looks at the psychobiological issues—the interaction of the brain and the mind—most often by combining talk therapy with medication to treat mental health problems.

"Crisis counseling" hotlines and crisis centers. This kind of counseling provides one-on-one anonymous support and/or referrals to places that provide the help you need. They are not intended to fill the same needs or perform the same functions as a counselor you see on a regular basis; instead, they provide immediate help when you are facing a crisis.

Support groups/group therapy. These can help you gain perspective on your life and find solutions to problems through talking with others. Depending on the makeup of the group you may get feedback from people who aren't familiar at all with what you're

Only 1 in 3 depressed people seeks help.   With treatment,

going through, those who have themselves had similar experiences, or something in between—all of which can be helpful. While group therapy is usually professionally led, support groups (sometimes known as self-help groups) are most often collectively, or peer-run, and may keep to a set structure based on a particular formula or process, such as the 12 Step (Anonymous) meetings. Groups most often cost less than individual therapy, and many are free.

"When I went looking for a support group I was overwhelmed by the specificity of them all. There were groups to deal with every issue under the sun: bereavement, living with HIV, eating disorders, and the list went on. I wanted a more general one to talk about what's going on in my life. I finally just went to a rap group at the women's center and I suggested that we make it a regular thing, and it turned into the kind of support group I needed."

—UNIVERSITY OF CHICAGO DIVINITY SCHOOL, '98

Couples and family therapy. Couples or family therapy allows you and your partner or family member(s) to look closely at your relationship and better understand the dynamics and hidden issues that affect how you treat each other and yourselves. The sessions provide you with a safe place to raise questions, cite problems, air feelings, and explore different solutions for working through your conflict.

"Therapy doesn't work out the problems for you, but it gives you the tools to work them out for yourself. For example, anytime a problem arose between me and my father, we couldn't talk to each other, and any conversation ended in screaming. Seeing a therapist together helped us to listen to each other and figure out a way to talk to one another."

—BENNINGTON COLLEGE, '95

Nonverbal and/or holistic forms of therapy. Therapy is not always just sitting in a room and talking. Many therapeutic approaches use other media to help you. Some of these forms include techniques that provide a nonverbal means of expressing and conveying emotions, such as art therapy (through drawing, painting, sculpting, ceramics, and other visual media) and dance therapy (through movement). Also common are techniques that aid in relaxation, stress management, and alleviating physical and emotional tension (such as massage therapy, biofeedback, rolfing, and Alexander Technique). Martial arts, keeping a journal, recording dreams, and meditation are also methods of exploring yourself and working out issues.

Hospitalization and inpatient care. Inpatient care can offer the security,

MEDICATION

Medication is one of many methods used to treat such mental health disorders as depression, eating disorders, bipolar disorder, obsessive/compulsive disorder, anxiety, and addiction/dependence, among others. For many, medication helps relieve pain, confusion, nervousness, and sadness, and is most effective when used in combination with talk therapy. Like all forms of medication, psychiatric medications can help things tremendously, a bit, or not at all, and may have adverse side effects.

If your therapist recommends medication, find out why, how it works, how it will help, and any potential side effects. If you have doubts about your therapist's diagnosis, or just want more information, get a second opinion.

Psychiatric medication must be prescribed by an M.D. (preferably a psychiatrist). If you choose to take medication, you should meet regularly with a psychiatrist to monitor its effects.

Different people will react differently to the same medication, and need to take different amounts for different lengths of time. Your doctor may have you try more than one drug to find the one that works best for you, and even once you do, there may be a period during which s/he varies the dosage to arrive at what's best for you.

Alert the doctor immediately to any side effects and discuss any of your doubts, questions, or concerns about your medication.

If you feel you need to cut down on the amount of medication or want to stop taking it altogether, do so only after consulting with a psychiatrist. Quitting cold-turkey can have disastrous consequences.

---

safety, intensity of treatment, and individual attention that outpatient treatment rarely can. When a problem becomes too intense or interferes with normal functioning; when other, less intense treatment methods aren't providing the help you need; or when you need a structured environment like an inpatient facility to assure your physical safety, a therapist may recommend hospitalization as an appropriate option. Before you take that step, however, be sure to investigate thoroughly whether a change in therapy methods (like starting, stopping, or changing medication, for example) could preclude hospitalization.

Types of Therapists

〽〽〽

The term "therapist" encompasses a wide range of professionals.

Before you go to see a therapist you may wish to find out what the certification, licencing, and/or training requirements for his or her type of practitioner are in your state. Although therapists may be affiliated with national associations, it is most often the individual state associations that determine certification requirements and regulate the standards for practice.

"For the first time in my life I felt like I was failing—I couldn't get up the energy to do my work and I didn't care about anything. Schoolwork became unimportant, I stopped practicing the cello, I stopped running, and I didn't return calls or make plans with friends—all I wanted to do was sleep. I started therapy and it has helped me to see why I was depressed, and slowly I'm beginning to put my life back together."

—YALE UNIVERSITY, ON LEAVE

The most common types of mental health practitioners are:

▲ Psychiatrists (who are medical doctors and have the authority to prescribe medication)
▲ Psychologists (who hold PhDs and so may be called "Doctor," but are not medical doctors)
▲ Certified psychoanalysts
▲ Social workers
▲ Marriage or couples, family, and child therapists
▲ Mental health counselors
▲ Psychiatric nurses
▲ Certified pastoral counselors
▲ Nonverbal/holistic practitioners (there are many different kinds)

Though it is useful to understand what a therapist's title means, bear in mind that training and degree do not always indicate his or her area(s) of expertise, approach, demeanor, attitudes, amount of clinical experience, or, most important, ability to help with your problems.

FINDING A THERAPIST OR GROUP

Finding a therapist with whom or a group with whose members you feel comfortable and can build trust is essential. In your search for a therapist, look for someone who is easy to talk with, who helps you understand your situation, focuses on your well-being, listens carefully to your thoughts and concerns, is receptive to trying a variety of treatments, and can work within your financial constraints. The same requirements apply if you are interested in a group (perhaps with the exception of "receptive to a variety of treatments"). And in either case, make sure your confidentiality will be respected.

On-Campus Therapy

"I wish I had known that as students we were entitled to a certain number of hours of free therapy as long as we were enrolled. . . . I might have dealt with my problems differently, more effectively. A friend of mine took advantage of her free sessions and said they helped her immensely."

—MARY WASHINGTON COLLEGE, '94

Many college health centers offer both individual and group therapy services for students, and costs are usually covered by student health

Within 2 years of FDA approval, 650,000 people were on Prozac.

insurance. The process of setting up an appointment varies: Some places require that you meet for an initial consultation in order to find the best therapist for your needs; some will schedule a session for you with the first available therapist; some set aside certain drop-in hours when you can talk to a counselor without an appointment. In order to accommodate as many students as possible, many schools limit the number of sessions allowed. But in most cases, if you and your therapist decide you should continue counseling after this time, your therapist will help you find someone who can meet your personal and financial needs and your schedule.

The good news about therapy offered by campus health services is that it's free (or very inexpensive) and convenient, and the practitioners and on-campus therapy groups are familiar with and cater to the specific issues and concerns of college students. The bad news is that the services usually offer only a limited choice of practitioners. This may pose a problem, because the background, style, and experience of the individual therapist (or group) play a significant role in how comfortable you are with him or her.

Tips on Dealing with Campus Health Services

■ Ask around about which therapists are good and which should be avoided at all costs.

■ When you call to make an appointment, tell the receptionist why you're seeking help, whether you need to see someone as soon as possible or can wait, and your special preferences (if you'd like to see a woman, for example). This will better enable him or her to choose a compatible person.

■ If you see someone you think isn't the perfect therapist for you, keep in mind that a counselor who does not fit your every ideal can still be very capable of helping you work through your issues.

"I liked working with a campus counselor because she had experience working with college students. She knew the school and the atmosphere and was tuned in to the pressures I faced being a student here. I didn't have to take the time to explain everything."
— BROWN UNIVERSITY, '95

If the wait for an appointment is long, the available therapists are notoriously awful, or your problem would be better served by an alternative to health services, explore other options. Maybe a support group run by a school organization would do the trick. You can probably find ethnic, religious, women's or gay/lesbian/bi groups that address issues of identity, as well as groups that focus on crisis and recovery issues for those coping with eating disorders, past rape or sexual assault, and substance dependency. If you can't find an appropriate group, look for a practitioner off campus.

Finding an Affordable Off-Campus Practitioner

༄༅༅

If you can't or don't want to take advantage of the services offered at your school's health center, there are quality, low-cost therapy options available in the community, and it is almost always possible to find something in your price range. One of the best ways to find a practitioner is to get a recommendation from a friend, doctor, or clergyperson. Asking people you know who have had positive experiences with their therapists is also a good idea.

In addition, many community organizations, local or women's health clinics, mental health centers, and other cultural/religious/special interest organizations provide therapy and charge on a sliding scale—that is, what you pay depends on what you can afford. Following are a few other ideas on where to find an affordable therapist:

■ Universities that offer graduate degrees in medicine, psychology, or social work; hospitals with a psychiatry residence program; or other facilities that train therapists may provide free or inexpensive counseling. Call the schools, ask psychology departments, and check campus papers and bulletin boards for information about low-cost options.

■ Many hospitals, health care advocacy organizations, and city health and human services departments have referral servies that list professionals based on location, specialty, cost, and other categories.

■ County or state medical societies, medical specialty boards, and national, state, and local chapters of professional associations (such as the American Medical Women's Association [AMWA], the American Medical Association [AMA], the National Association of Social Work [NASW], American Psychiatric Association [APA], or the American Psychological Association [APA]) may provide referrals or listings of practitioners in your area.

■ The Yellow Pages can also be of help. Look under "Social and Human Services"; "Counselors—Marriage, Family, Child, and Individual"; "Mental Health Services"; "Psychologists"; "Physicians and Surgeons–Medical (Psychiatry)."

Questions to Ask a Therapist or Group

༄༅༅

Following are some questions you should ask both a potential therapist and group leader.

Professional Background. What type of therapist are you? What is your training? Are you certified and licensed? Are you affiliated with a hospital/clinic?

Practice. Do you limit your practice to (or is the group limited to) the treatment of certain issues (e.g., eating disorders, sexual assault, substance abuse, disability/chronic disease) or certain people (e.g., families, couples, women, students)? Are you taking new patients/members?

Payment. What are your fees? What do you charge for an initial consultation? Do you charge on a sliding scale? Do you have a special rate for students? What methods of payment do you accept? Do you accept/have experience with my insurance plan? Do you need payment at the end of every session, or will you bill me? Will you bill my insurance company directly?

Sessions. Will sessions be held in a regular place at a regular time? How often and how long are sessions? Where and in what type of environment will sessions be held? How far in advance do I need to cancel in order to avoid being charged?

Convenience. Do you have evening appointments? Where is your office/the group located? Is it located near public transportation? Is it wheelchair-accessible?

Personal issues. Can you give me quality care within the confines of my religious/ethical/moral beliefs? What cultural, religious, philosophies or beliefs do you/does the group embrace?

Questions for a Therapist

What is your experience in working with individuals with my issues/problems? Is there someone who cov-

ers for you if you're unavailable? Do you have an answering service or beeper? Will you talk to me about issues over the phone, or is an office visit required? In what capacity will you be available outside of the regular sessions if a crisis arises? What is your experience with/opinion of medication? (If not a psychiatrist: Do you have a working relationship with a psychiatrist who can prescribe medication if the need arises?) How far in advance do I need to call to schedule/reschedule an appointment? Is there a way I can call to find out if you're running late?

Questions for a Group

What is the size of the group? What is the makeup of the group—gender, ages, sexual orientation, ethnic/cultural background? Are members of the group in individual therapy? Is this a group of people just beginning therapy? Is the group general or issue-specific? Are the same topics discussed each session? Is the group for a limited time or is it ongoing? Am I entering

> *"I'd thought that a lot of self-disclosure would make me uncomfortable, and at first I did not want anyone to know so much about me. That fear subsided after a session or two because I realized the more I told, the better I felt. I didn't feel better instantaneously, but I felt better eventually. I shared things I was embarrassed about, but I learned those things were important to get out, too."*
>
> —SMITH COLLEGE, '93

 Beginning in the year 1973, the American Psychiatric Associa-

the group at its formation or entering into an ongoing group? How is the group run? Does everyone speak during each session? What is the attendance policy of the group? When does the group meet? How is the confidentiality of the group maintained?

CHOOSING A THERAPIST

If you need to find a practitioner quickly, then you might choose to screen only a few therapists over the phone and/or go by the recommendation of someone whom you trust. However, if you can take the time, it can be a good idea to do a little shopping around.

Calling potential therapists on the

"I really wanted to see a woman therapist, but at the time, there were none available that fit my schedule. I reluctantly went to see a man—expecting to see him until a woman was available. I didn't think I would be able to talk about sex issues. To my surprise, it worked out—he helped me through my crisis." —COLORADO COLLEGE, '95

phone and doing initial screenings will help you decide if you want to go in for a face-to-face consultation. (If you call a therapist and get an answering machine, it is perfectly acceptable to ask that s/he be discreet when returning your call or leaving a message. (It's smart to specify the times that are good

---

SPECIAL CONSIDERATIONS FOR LESBIAN, BISEXUAL, AND QUESTIONING WOMEN

Until relatively recently, homosexuality was considered to be a mental health disorder, and although this is no longer "on the books," it remains in the minds of far too many mental health practitioners. When selecting your therapist, make sure to screen her by asking her questions about her attitudes toward sexuality and her experience (if any) working with gays and lesbians, and if she has any experience working with people with issues similar to yours (such as coming out, family problems, relationship problems, or being a lesbian on a homophobic campus). In order to find

a supportive, lesbian-friendly therapist, try asking at lesbian/gay community centers and lesbian/gay health collectives, and also asking lesbian and gay friends.

It is essential that your therapist be supportive and accepting of your sexuality and that she have experience with (or is open and aware enough to understand) issues that you may face as a lesbian, bi, or questioning woman. Although many women feel most comfortable seeing a therapist who is lesbian or gay, her ability to help you is more important than her sexual preference.

---

tion stopped classifying homosexuality as a mental health disorder.

for him or her to call you back.) Most therapists will talk with you on the phone for 5 to 10 minutes without charge. For the sake of time, select the most important questions, the ones that will help you determine if the two of you could be compatible on the most basic level. If you feel comfortable talking to her, and she has the credentials, experience, and philosophy suited to your needs, make an appointment for an initial consultation.

Remember, having a consultation or diagnosis, or even seeing a therapist five times, does not commit you to seeing him or her for long-term care. Most therapists know that clients shop around, and they will understand if you choose someone else.

What to Expect

◉◉◉

When you begin therapy, you'll probably find that even just the act of trying to articulate your thoughts and feelings is illuminating. This process is one of the central aspects of talk therapy, and it often helps you identify for yourself what is wrong and how to go about changing it. In "alternative therapy" methods, this process may be predominantly nonverbal—you may articulate your thoughts through art or dance—or it may combine both verbal and nonverbal components.

Therapists will differ in how much they share about themselves, what they prefer to be called ("Dr." or first name), and how active

or passive a role they take in discussions. Some therapists will let you decide what to talk about—they are listeners who talk very little. Other therapists may probe, confront, and offer insight and occasionally advice.

In your first few sessions you'll probably be talking to your therapist/group about your reasons for being in therapy, your present situation, your past, and your personal history. You'll likely discuss:

The basics: General information about yourself, the makeup of your family, your and your family's medical history (both physical and mental health).

> *"One of the most wonderful parts of therapy was discovering that all the embarrassing, disgusting, humiliating things that I could never talk about with anyone weren't really that bad."*
>
> —VIRGINIA COMMONWEALTH UNIVERSITY, '96

Your reasons for being there: Why are you in therapy? What do you hope/expect to get out of therapy?

The present: How are you feeling? How long have you been feeling this way? When did you begin to feel this way (or have you always felt this way)? What new experiences and/or changes have come about in your life recently? Who are the significant people in your life, and how do you relate to them?

☀ Depression is said to cost the country upwards of $276 billion

TELLING OTHERS YOU'RE IN THERAPY

"I have been in therapy for six months and I haven't told anyone—it's my private thing and I think it is good for me to keep it private. The problem is that now I have to tell my parents so I can get their financial support because it is draining me to pay for it alone. This is going to be so hard and I don't want to tell them, but because I am not totally independent I am not free to make the choice of not telling them about my life, at least not right now."

—*University of Georgia, '96*

Remember, your decision to be in therapy is a sign that you are taking care of yourself, and that is not something to be ashamed of. At the same time, however, you should not be pressured to disclose more than you want or need to (to an insurance company, for example) about why you are in therapy and the issues you discuss there. If you need to bring it up with someone, but are having a difficult time doing so, ask your therapist for help. Even if he doesn't have experience with similar situations, he can help you work out the best approach.

The past: What significant life experiences or events have had a major effect on you? Can you trace the beginning of your problems to a specific event or time? Is this your first time in therapy? If not, what was your previous experience like?

Though a therapist might be good at sensing how you're feeling and providing insight into your situation, s/he can't read your mind. It is your responsibility to tell your therapist what's bothering you and anything else that you think might influence your situation. Remember that therapists have heard it all and your stories won't surprise or shock them.

Keep in mind that opening yourself up and discussing your feelings and problems can be exhausting, difficult, and painful, even when you realize that it's an essential part of the process of feeling better. Sometimes sessions with your therapist or group will be intense. Those times when you feel you would rather do *anything* than go to therapy may well be the times when it's most important that you stick with it. Often the more uncomfortable you are in therapy, the closer you are to hitting on some important insights. It's only when you go to sessions and provide as much information as possible about yourself and your feelings that your therapist or group members can best be able to provide insight, help, and advice.

"Actually, at some points, therapy seemed to cause more confusion than before, because I had to actually deal with my problems and emotions constructively instead of suppressing them."

—*Rollins College, '95*

PROBLEMS IN THERAPY

*"Being pissed off with your thera-
pist for a couple of weeks doesn't
mean that you should find another
therapist. . . . Let me tell you, getting mad in therapy is probably
one of the best things that can
happen."* —NEW YORK UNIVERSITY
PHD CANDIDATE, '96

Not Liking Your Therapist

Therapy requires you to open up bottled emotions, share deep thoughts
and experiences, and confront fears
and problems with someone you may
not know very well, so it is natural that
you will not always feel comfortable.
Thus it can be difficult to assess
whether or not the reason you're feeling uneasy, angry, or upset is due to the
difficult process of therapy itself or
unhappiness with your therapist. If
you find that after three or four sessions you feel worse, not better, talk to
him or her about it. Try to be specific
about what's bothering you, and if possible, suggest changes that would
make your sessions more beneficial. If
it can't be worked out, don't let the sessions drag on; see another therapist.

Sometimes therapists and patients
don't click. The relationship between a
therapist and a patient is a very personal one, and even a therapist whom
you like as a person, or who has come
highly recommended, may not be
right for you. Though this can be frus-

trating and upsetting, it does not mean
that therapy in general won't work
for you.

Ethical Issues

If you are seeing a licensed therapist,
you are entitled to receive proper,
professional treatment. If you feel you
have been mistreated by your therapist or that s/he has breached ethical
codes, you have options for recourse.

CONFIDENTIALITY ISSUES FOR MINORS

If you are under 18, a therapist
may be required to get parental
consent to treat you. If you do not
want your parents to know you're
in therapy, discuss this with your
therapist. In certain instances,
such as cases of sexual assault or
abuse (by a parent or anyone
else), you probably will not need
to get your parents' permission.
However, the therapist may be
required by law to break confidentiality and report cases of
suspected abuse to the proper
authorities. This shouldn't deter
you from going to therapy, but if
you have any concerns or questions, call the state associations
and ask about policies pertinent to
your case. This is also something
you can discuss with your therapist in your initial consultation.
(See the Resources at the end of
this chapter to help find the appropriate state association.)

Violating confidentiality (except in cases when your therapist is legally required to do so) and engaging in romantic or sexual relationships with patients are unacceptable behaviors that may result in the loss of the therapist's license to practice. Yet for the most part, the lines between appropriate and inappropriate behavior are not clear-cut. If you feel your therapist is crossing acceptable boundaries, and talking with him or her about your uneasiness does not help, consult with another therapist, a person from a mental health advocacy group, or your state's licensing board. (See the Resources at the end of this chapter.) You do not have to use names when inquiring about the appropriateness of a therapist's conduct.

Though a therapist's approach may be considered legally, medically, and socially acceptable, it may still not be right for you. The bottom line is that if you do not feel able to talk openly and freely with your therapist, whether as a result of unethical behavior or not, there is little benefit to working with him or her and you should try to find someone else.

ACTIVIST IDEAS

■ If you go to a school that doesn't see too much sunlight during winter months, try to get health services to invest in a few lightboxes to set up in a centrally located room on campus. Students can sign out the room key from health services, an RA, or the student union.

■ Educate students about depression, and depression in women in particular. Have a panel discussion that includes both women who can talk about their experience with depression and counselors from mental health services who can talk about treatment options. End the program with a question and answer period that will help dispel the myths about depression and the stigma associated with it.

■ Post information about campus and community mental health resources, including hotlines, support groups, places to find on- and off-campus therapy as well as stress management tips. Put the info in highly visible places during high stress times on campus.

RESOURCES

L isted below are a number of national organizations and hotline services, many of which can make referrals or help you find local groups. In addition, almost all cities and states have local mental health organizations, support groups, and hotlines available. There are a number of excellent organizations that deal with specific mental health issues and illnesses not included here, but the organizations that are listed should be able to provide referrals.

National Mental Health Organizations

NATIONAL ALLIANCE FOR THE MENTALLY ILL
[NAMI]
2101 WILSON BOULEVARD, SUITE 302
ARLINGTON, VA 22201
(800) 950-6264
(703) 524-7600
A network of self-help groups and organizations. Makes referrals to local support groups, mental health professionals, and organizations through their chapters in every state. Provides information about mental health issues. Conducts research and advocates on behalf of mentally ill persons and their families.

NATIONAL FOUNDATION FOR DEPRESSIVE
ILLNESS
P.O. BOX 2257
NEW YORK, NY 10116
(800) 248-4344
Provides general information on affective illnesses. Makes referrals to national and local organizations that can provide additional information on specific conditions and makes referrals to the type of mental health practitioners and/or support groups that can address the issues at hand.

NATIONAL MENTAL HEALTH ASSOCIATION
1021 PRINCE STREET
ALEXANDRIA, VA 22314
(800) 969-6642
(703) 684-7722
Provides information on mental health and mental illnesses. Makes referrals to local support groups, mental health centers, self-help clearinghouses, and other organizations. Publishes materials and sends free information upon request.

THE NATIONAL MENTAL HEALTH CONSUMER
SELF-HELP CLEARINGHOUSE
1211 CHESTNUT STREET
PHILADELPHIA, PA 19107
(215) 753-2481
Provides individuals and groups with information, materials, assistance, and advice on all areas of running self-help groups. Makes referrals to local groups.

AMERICAN SELF-HELP CLEARINGHOUSE
25 POCONO ROAD
DENVILLE, NJ 07834-2995
Makes referrals to and provides information about local support groups that are free and/or low cost.

NATIONAL INSTITUTE OF MENTAL HEALTH
(NIMH)
5600 FISHERS LANE, ROOM 7602
ROCKVILLE, MD 20857
(301) 443-4513,
(301) 443-4514: PUBLICATIONS

An arm of the National Institute of Health concerned with mental health and illness. Conducts research on mental health disorders. Provides information and answers questions about mental health issues. Publishes numerous materials. Sends information upon request.

Suicide Prevention/Crisis Counseling

Most suicide prevention and crisis hotlines are local. Call the operator or directory assistance (411) for a local hotline number.

PRIMARY HEALTH
(800) 765-4320 (24 HOURS)
Offers confidential suicide and crisis counseling over the phone. Makes referrals to local groups, organizations, practitioners, hotlines, and crisis centers that can address the problems.

Professional Associations

The following professional associations may be able to:

■ Make referrals to mental health professionals in your area.

■ Provide information about requirements for certification in specific specialty fields and background information about specific practitioners—their history, any complaints against them, and the proper procedures for addressing ethical problems, filing complaints, or any other related questions that you may have about a practitioner.

Many of these associations/organizations have divisions that focus specifically on the concerns of women and mental health—ask them if they have a women's division and/or if they can give you a referral to an organization that works specifically on

women's issues. If the following associations can't answer your questions, ask them to refer you to a national or local organization that can.

AMERICAN ACADEMY OF CHILD AND ADOLESCENT PSYCHIATRY
3615 WISCONSIN AVENUE NW
WASHINGTON, DC 20017
(202) 966-7300

AMERICAN ASSOCIATION FOR MARRIAGE AND FAMILY THERAPY
1100 17TH STREET NW, 10TH FLOOR
WASHINGTON, DC 20036
(202) 452-0109

AMERICAN ASSOCIATION OF PROFESSIONAL HYPNOTHERAPISTS
P.O. BOX 29
BOONES MILL, VA 24065
(703) 334-3035

AMERICAN FAMILY THERAPY ACADEMY
2020 PENNSYLVANIA AVENUE NW, #273
WASHINGTON, DC 20006
(202) 994-2776

AMERICAN GROUP PSYCHOTHERAPY ASSOCIATION
25 EAST 21ST STREET, 6TH FLOOR
NEW YORK, NY 10010
(212) 477-2677

AMERICAN MENTAL HEALTH COUNSELORS
   ASSOCIATION
P.O. DRAWER 22370
ALEXANDRIA, VA 22304
(703) 823-9800
(800) 326-2642

AMERICAN PSYCHIATRIC ASSOCIATION
1400 K STREET NW
WASHINGTON, DC 20005
(202) 682-6000

AMERICAN PSYCHOLOGICAL ASSOCIATION
750 FIRST STREET NE
WASHINGTON, DC 20002
(202) 336-5500
(202) 336–6044: THE DIVISION OF THE PSYCHOLOGY
   OF WOMEN
Houses the Division of the Psychology of
Women, which works to promote the equal
treatment of women in psychology; supports increased research on women and
mental health; and publishes materials on
women and psychology.

NATIONAL ASSOCIATION OF SOCIAL
   WORKERS
750 FIRST STREET NE
WASHINGTON, DC 20002
(202) 408-8600
(800) 225-6880

AMERICAN WOMEN IN PSYCHOLOGY ROSTER
C/O KNOW
P.O. BOX 86301
PITTSBURGH, PA 15221
(412) 241-4844

Publishes a listing of feminist psychothera-
pists throughout the country; available
upon request.

Legal and Advocacy Groups

AMERICAN BAR ASSOCIATION COMMISSION
   ON MENTAL AND PHYSICAL DISABILITY
   LAW
1800 M STREET NW, SUITE 200
WASHINGTON, DC 20036
(202) 331-2240
Addresses legal issues relating to mental
and physical disability discrimination and
ethical violations by practitioners.

BAZELON CENTER
1101 15TH STREET NW, SUITE 1212
WASHINGTON, DC 20005
(202) 467-5730
Does advocacy work to increase the legal
rights of people with mental disabilities.

Stress Prevention and Management

Most colleges and universities, well
aware of the correlation between being
a student and being stressed, offer
stress management courses through
health/mental health services. In addition, yoga, biofeedback, meditation,
and other holistic healing approaches
have proven very useful in the prevention and management of stress.
Check your school health services and
physical education department for a
referral.

AMERICAN INSTITUTE OF STRESS
124 PARK AVENUE
YONKERS, NY 10703
(914) 963-1200
Provides information about the effects of
stress and strategies for stress management. Makes referrals to local groups and
professionals who teach stress management.

Further Reading

〇〇〇

Therapy and Mental Health

Getting Help: A Consumer's Guide to Therapy, Christine Ammer with Nathan T. Sidley (Paragon House, 1990).

A New Approach to Women and Therapy, Miriam Greenspan (McGraw-Hill, 1983).

Women, Power and Therapy, Marjorie Baud (Harrington Press, 1988).

In a Different Voice: Psychological Theory and Women's Development, Carol Gilligan (Harvard University Press, 1982).

Silencing the Self: Women and Depression, Dana Crowley Jack (Harvard University Press, 1991).

Trusting Ourselves: The Sourcebook on Psychology for Women, Karen Johnson and Tom Ferguson (The Atlantic Monthly Press, 1990).

Toward a New Psychology of Women, revised edition, Jean Baker Miller (Beacon Press, 1986).

The Other Side of the Couch: The Healing Bond in Psychiatry, Gail Abert, PhD (Faber and Faber, 1995).

The Lavender Couch: A Consumer's Guide to Psychotherapy for Lesbians and Gay Men, Marney Hall (Alyson Publications, 1985).

Winter Blues: Seasonal Affective Disorder, Dr. Norman Rosenthal (Guilford, 1993).

Stress

The Female Stress Syndrome: How to Recognize and Live with It, Georgia Witkin-Lanoil (Newmarket, 1984).

Gender and Stress, Rosalind C. Barnett, Lois Biener, and Grace Baruch, eds. (Free Press, 1987).

Lives in Stress: Women and Depression, D. Bella, ed. (Sage Publishing, 1982).

Women Under Stress, Donald Roy Morse and M. Lawerence Furst (Van Nostrand Reinhold, 1982).

Successfully Managing Stress, Lynn Brallier (National Nursing Review, 1982).

Coping with Stress in College: Everything Students Need to Know to Manage the Pressures of College Life, Mark Rowh (College Board, 1989).

Kicking Your Stress Habits: A Do-It-Yourself Guide for Coping with Stress, Donald A. Tubesing (Whole Person Press, 1988).

slow the pulse down and temporarily lower blood pressure. ☀

Real vs. Ideal

Body Image, Dieting & Eating Disorders

As women, we have learned that our appearance is considerably more significant than simply "what we look like"—it is seen as a symbol of our worth, desirability, and self-control. Despite all the changes in society in the past 20 or so years, a woman's "value" is still largely determined by the way she looks, especially in terms of how attractive she is to men. Even women who are full participants and extremely successful in what was once considered a "man's world" are still expected to conform to traditional standards of beauty and femininity. Society tells us that heavy women are unhealthy, lazy, and have no control over themselves and that disabled women are sexless. We are told implicitly and explicitly that if we just had smaller feet, bigger breasts, a narrower nose, larger eyes, a flatter stomach, or longer, slimmer legs, our lives would be grand. And though on a rational level we may know how ridiculous this is, we nevertheless put ourselves through physical and emotional torture (and cut our self-esteem to shreds) in an effort to be what we think we're supposed to be. We fret over our weight and try to diet away "excess" pounds. We squeeze ourselves into high heels and uncomfortable clothing. We shave, cut, bleach, wax, pluck, dissolve, and electrocute "undesirable" hair. We scrutinize the way we smile, laugh, walk, and talk.

However, spending a great deal of time assessing and obsessing does not guarantee that we have an accurate perception of what our bodies look like. In fact, for many (if not most) of us, there is a discrepancy between what our bodies actually look like and how we perceive them. We think we're too fat or have noticeably large feet or walk like an armadillo when it just isn't the case. And even if we are showered with compliments about how fit we are, how dainty our feet are, or how gazellelike our gait is, there's no convincing us of the truth. This disparity between how we think we look and how we really look is caused by a distorted body image.

> "About three years ago I saw a woman on the train wearing a shirt that said 'Women: TAKE UP SPACE.' It really had a powerful effect on me. So much of what women are supposed to be like is based on us not taking up space. We're supposed to be thin, speak softly, be meek, and be on the sidelines, supporting others, rather than in the spotlight."
> —New York University, '97

WHAT IS BODY IMAGE?

Body image is how we perceive our bodies: the way we think they look and how we feel about it. It is what we see when we look in the mirror, and what we think others see when they look at us. Body image is not just about body size; it includes our whole appearance: how we move; how our voices sound; the way we stand; our smiles. Even though our body image is related to our physical bodies, to a large degree it is shaped by our feelings *about* our bodies (and ourselves in general). Factors such as how stressed we are, how important we feel it is to have "the perfect body," how much we believe in one objective standard of beauty, how we feel about the state of our lives, and how our mood is can all contribute to how we feel about ourselves and can directly influence the creation and perpetuation of a distorted body image.

REAL AND IDEAL

Open any mainstream fashion magazine, turn on MTV, pay a visit to a department store cosmetics counter, watch a movie, and you can't miss idealized images of women. The media, the cosmetics/beauty, fitness, diet, and fashion industries, to say nothing of religious, cultural, and ethnic traditions and other social norms and trends, all create and perpetuate images of what a woman is supposed to look like, act like, and be like. These messages, both positive and negative, affirming and deprecating, have been instrumental in molding our thoughts and behavior. They provide us with looks to emulate and to strive for. And then, because we almost invariably pale in comparison to the ideals, we feel inad-

BODY IMAGE AND SELF ESTEEM

How we feel about our bodies both affects and is affected by our self-esteem. Self-esteem is about realizing and asserting that you are important, that you deserve to be treated with respect, and that you have worthwhile thoughts, feelings, and ideas.

Having good self-esteem has a broader importance than just creating an accurate body image. It is an essential component of enjoying life, coping with difficult times, and having healthy relationships in which you can give and receive love, support, and trust.

In a society that makes it quite clear how we're supposed to look, act, and be, developing and maintaining a positive self-image and good self-esteem is often hard work. Instead of spending time and energy focused on finding flaws, make a decision not only to accept yourself (warts and all) but to actually like yourself and your body. Make a concerted effort to stop negative and self-deprecating thoughts, engage in activities that make you feel capable and confident, spend time with people who make you feel appreciated and important, and prioritize your health, safety, and happiness. Too many of us, consciously or unconsciously, let unattainable social and personal expectations get in the way of noticing and celebrating our strength, talent, and power.

"I was in a rush, and accidentally grabbed my younger sister's pants instead of mine. When I couldn't get them on, I felt completely depressed. I went and looked in the mirror and "saw" the weight I gained on my face, and how chunky my legs looked. . . . I went to the bathroom and stepped on the scale and found I had lost half a pound. Then I realized what I'd done. It was a really profound example of how you can totally manipulate yourself."

—*SCRIPPS COLLEGE, '93*

equate—dissatisfied with ourselves, our bodies, and our ability to meet what are presented as realistic and attainable goals. (Even the models—the ideals personified—don't look much like their glossy photos without the aid of a generous amount of makeup, flattering lighting, camera tricks, and photo retouching.)

The fact that the ideals conflict, are unattainable, or are even undesirable doesn't dilute their potency. Even though we can be (and probably often are) critical of the messages about "the perfect woman," they are so ingrained in our culture that it may take work to analyze and recognize how they affect us. Simply educating ourselves about the issues often doesn't make us immune to all of the messages about

Too-narrow, high-heeled shoes account for $2 billion in health care

*"I read **The Beauty Myth.** I know about how women are exploited by media ideals and the damage that it does, and I really resent it. But I also have to get along in this world. So when I go to a job interview, do I put on heels and makeup and 'act the part'? You bet I do. I'd like to change the world, but I don't want to starve while doing it."*

—MOUNT HOLYOKE COLLEGE, '94

how our bodies are supposed to look, how our voices are supposed to sound, and how we are supposed to sit, walk, run, laugh, throw a ball, dress, and wear our hair. The ideals are so pervasive that they seem normal and have evolved into real standards by which we judge ourselves and evaluate our control over our lives, our worthiness, our success, our potential, and our womanhood. For example, we hardly think twice when we see a model who is 5'11" but only weighs 110 pounds. However, emulating images that are physically unattainable inevitably leaves us disappointed and frustrated with ourselves. And even if we don't believe in traditional body ideals, we're still affected by them by virtue of their pervasiveness and the fact that we live in a society that rewards those who fit its ideals.

COLLEGE WOMEN AND BODY IMAGE

Although women of all different ages and from all different environments and backgrounds are dissatisfied with their appearance, body image problems are most prevalent in women 25 and under—an age group including a large segment of the college population. In an oft-quoted study of college women, three-quarters of those surveyed felt they were overweight when, by medical definition, less than one-quarter of them actually were. Clearly, the reality of how college women look has little to do with how they believe they look. This may be related to a number of factors that are specific to both our age and situation:

■ During college we are taught to analyze and scrutinize everything we read and see, and we apply our newly honed skills to ourselves.

■ Looking inside ourselves and dealing with difficult issues is often rewarding and helpful but is also very hard work—sometimes it's easier to focus on how we look than what's within.

■ Not only are women in their late teens and twenties the target population for most fashion magazines, but the vast majority of models also fall into this age range. When the media messages and images are aimed directly at us, they can be pretty hard to ignore.

■ Because college is one of the first opportunities that we have to "reinvent" ourselves more or less independently of the baggage of our past, we look to ideals for guidance about who and what we should be.

■ For many of us, the college years serve as our transition into adulthood. It's up to us to "forge our destiny." It seems as if every decision we make

now will directly and permanently affect our future happiness and prosperity, and that we can control every aspect of our lives. This can make even the most mellow and confident person feel stressed and edgy.

■ Though most would agree that perfectionism is problematic, being a perfectionist is not only socially acceptable, it's socially desirable.

■ Body- and self-criticism are well-practiced rituals for a large number of college women. We bond over dieting together, comparing pinched inches of fat and putting ourselves and our appearance down. In this way, we reinforce each other's insecurities about our bodies.

SO MANY MESSAGES, SO LITTLE TIME

"My grandmother is always telling me that I should eat and be strong and healthy, but when I do, she tells me to watch what I eat or I'll never find a husband."
—DAVIDSON COLLEGE, '98

What we look like, what we think we look like, what we think we're supposed to look like, and what we want to look like are often four different things. There is no one universal ideal but many, and we are taught which one (or usually, which *ones*) we should aspire to, based on our heritage, class, race, and environment. Communities hold different standards of beauty and interpret symbols and behaviors differently. What is considered "just right" by

some standards is often thought too small/big/loud/flashy/messy/prim by others. Not to mention that these standards are ever-changing. The latest offering from the pop music industry, a newly elected first lady, and scientific discoveries about the harmful effects of too much sun all affect the look we're supposed to emulate. Trying to fit the latest mold set by all the communities to which we belong can be an impossible task.

"I feel trapped between two worlds because I believe that what is African is really beautiful, and I don't want to look like a white model . . . but I do still think that being thin looks good."
—SPELMAN COLLEGE, '96

Though both men and women are overweight in equal percent-

■ We continually find ourselves in situations in which appearance is particularly important: We're making first impressions, rushing sororities, interviewing for jobs and internships, trying to impress professors and mentors, and lookin' for love.

"IF I COULD LOSE 10 POUNDS, MY LIFE WOULD BE PERFECT"

"I got to college and I never saw so many beautiful girls in my life.... I never had much of a problem with my looks, but suddenly, there were all these tall, thin, blond girls with perfect figures everywhere I looked, and I totally felt short, fat, and ugly." —UCLA, '96

Considering the importance placed on appearance, the benefits that come with "beauty," and the prevalence of women with distorted body images, it's no surprise that so many of us spend so much time trying to change the way we look. We minimize and maximize, tuck and bind. Some of us even turn to surgical remedies for those "problems" that we can't get rid of ourselves. And we diet. *A lot.* In 1993, the diet industry took in $37 billion pushing its products, programs, and promises into the shopping carts and belief systems of American women (and occasionally men). The diet companies rarely tout a message of the health benefits of getting and staying fit. (Perhaps this is because many of the pills, formulas, and diet plans are unhealthy and sometimes dangerous, even when used as directed.) Instead, they entice us with promises of happier, more fulfilling lives, implying that being thin is the answer to all our problems.

Even though we know the facts (and we do know the facts), we all too often ignore them. We know that crash diets don't work—not only do they make us miserable, but the weight almost always comes back. This happens because when we suddenly reduce our food and calorie intake to a trickle, our bodies go into starvation mode, lowering metabolism (and thus causing calories to burn more slowly) and using energy stored in muscle, not fat. So even though we can finally fit into that itsy-bitsy teeny-weeny yellow polka-dot bikini at the end of a two-week-long monogamous relationship with lettuce, we still have all the fat we started with—and we're less able to lose it. Thus, when we eat normally again, we end up weighing more than when we started the diet.

"I think about how much time, energy, aggravation, and money we spend on ways to change the way we look. Instead of being pissed and disgusted that our thighs bulge, we should be pissed and disgusted that we get pissed and disgusted—our thighs are supposed to bulge!"
—AMERICAN UNIVERSITY, '97

If you go on diets that feel like "die with a t" and expect that you'll magically be transformed into the person you've always wanted to be, you're almost guaranteed to end up gaining even more weight than you lost and feeling lousy and disappointed with yourself to boot. On the other hand, eating well, enjoying food, and taking the time to exercise are excellent ways to make you and your body happy. Establishing healthy eating patterns is different from dieting—it's a basic part of taking care of yourself. Regardless of your weight, it's important to eat nutritionally balanced meals, a variety of foods, and foods that are both physically and emotionally satisfying. (See "The Big Three," page 189.)

"Somewhere along the way, so many women's priorities have become screwed up. Instead of doing what it takes to make us healthy, taking care of our bodies, and doing everything possible to make us feel good about ourselves, it's like we're doing everything in our power to make ourselves feel lousy about the way we look and guilty about missing one aerobics class." **—WELLESLEY COLLEGE, '92**

It is not bad to care about what you look like or to feel good about looking good, and trying to get your body in shape can be a positive thing. Being clinically overweight can put you at risk for a number of serious disorders (such as diabetes, heart attack, high blood pressure, and back pain), and becoming physically fit can do wonderful things for your health, energy, mood, and self-esteem. But feeling inadequate, unsexy, embarrassed, self-conscious, or uncomfortable because you fail to resemble an unattainable social ideal is time poorly spent. There is never a good reason to hate or feel ashamed of your body, and your weight is not a measure of your success or worthiness. Making a decision to lose weight should come out of caring for your body.

WHY FOOD?

Undisputed scientific fact: We must eat in order to live and in order for our bodies to function normally. But food does not function simply as an energy source. For those under personal or social pressure to be thin, food becomes transformed from a thing to enjoy, celebrate with, and nourish ourselves with into an adversary—an evil enemy that tempts us on dessert trays, on supermarket shelves, and in pizza parlor windows. Further, the preparation and eating of food, as well as the food itself, often has cultural, historical, religious, sentimental, and social meaning. Even just the mention of Thanksgiving turkey, tea, apple pie,

WHAT THEY DON'T WANT US TO KNOW

~❀~

You've heard this before, but listen this time: Not one of the hundreds of powders, formulas, pills, creams, herbs, tapes, books, seminars, or pieces of equipment available has yet been proven to be the miracle, magical solution for effortlessly taking and keeping weight off. Despite the claims of celebrities, those women-just-like-you-and-me, and the throngs of doctor/writers, fitness guru/writers, and dietitian/writers, more than 95 percent of those who diet gain back the weight they lose, and then some.

"Even though I knew rationally about the statistics about how many women had eating disorders and I could see obvious signs that many women on campus were also bulimic, I felt totally alone— like no one could possibly understand my problem."
—BATES COLLEGE, '91

HEALTHY AND UNHEALTHY EATING

━━━━━

The line dividing "normal" eating patterns and eating disorders is often blurry, because so many women in this country, although not suffering from clinically defined eating disorders, have unhealthy eating patterns. Occasionally drowning your sorrows in an ice cream sundae is absolutely normal and acceptable. But using food on a regular basis as a means to satisfy an emotional hunger rather than a physical one; to assert control over your life; to numb feelings; to punish, comfort, or calm yourself; or to cope with difficult feelings can have dangerous physical and emotional ramifications.

milk and cookies, barbecue, champagne, or Grandma's stollen, can be enough to conjure up feelings and memories. Our personal experiences— with our families, our friends, and our communities—influence the ways in which we understand food and use it in our lives.

Much of what we like about food and think about food has more to do with nostalgia, habit, social codes, and the roles it has played in our lives than with satisfying hunger and our bodies' needs. We use food to relieve anxiety, enhance celebrations, reward ourselves for a job well done, comfort or punish ourselves, and demonstrate love. Our relationship to food and the eating patterns we've developed is complex—it evolves from and reflects both conscious and unconscious emotions, attitudes, memories, and purposes.

Too many women feel guilty about eating, and some of us have a hard time knowing when to stop eating (or when to start) and/or are unable to tell when we are hungry or full. If you experience any of these problems, you may want to examine your eating patterns, perhaps with the help of a professional.

WHAT CAUSES EATING DISORDERS?

Eating disorders are often linked to our backgrounds, family and social experiences, perceptions about ourselves, the messages we receive about how our bodies should look and the way we react to these messages, and/or psychological conditions. They can develop as ways of coping with issues such as alcoholic family members, difficult transitions, racism, homophobia, depression, perfectionism, emerging sexuality, fear of success, a changing body, mood swings, and childhood abuse.

You cannot "get" an eating disorder from dieting per se, but for those susceptible, the physical and/or emotional effects of extensive dieting may trigger the development of an eating disorder. The frustration and stress of "yo-yo" dieting, acclimation to irregular eating patterns, and lack of sufficient calories and nutrients (especially in combination with all the caffeine in the diet pills, coffee, and diet soda that dieters tend to consume instead of food) may lead to mood swings, feelings of depression and inadequacy, and a distorted body image, all of which can deal a hefty blow to one's self-esteem.

EATING DISORDERS

The term "eating disorders" is used to define those eating patterns and behaviors that are clinically diagnosed and are physically or emotionally dangerous, such as anorexia nervosa (anorexia), bulimia nervosa (bulimia), and binge-eating disorder. In these conditions, food (or the denial of it) becomes the primary outlet or focus of one's energy—one's intake of food becomes a literal and symbolic way to assert control over one's life. Eating disorders are not just related to what we ingest or how our bodies look; they are one way in which we physically express the presence of often painful personal issues. Eating disorder behaviors affect, change, hide, and reveal our emotions. Although it may seem as if food is the central issue, because how it's eaten, whether it's eaten, what is eaten, when it's eaten, and what others are eating consume our thoughts, food actually serves as a distraction—a handy way to avoid dealing with charged issues that we may or may not be aware of. Once we begin the process of using food to "stuff feelings" and avoid dif-

> *"One of the biggest steps in my recovery was finding the strength to ask myself what the hell I was doing.... Why would I, a nice-looking, intelligent person with good friends and the potential for a good future, be literally starving myself to death?"*
>
> —SAN FRANCISCO STATE, YEAR WITHHELD

90% of people with anorexia or bulimia are women.

ficult issues, many of us find ourselves less and less capable of dealing with feelings without it. As with any addiction, the person in its grips becomes dependent on using food to get through the day while trying to convince herself and others that she "can stop anytime."

Eating Disorder Behaviors and Physical Effects

ගග

Anorexic, bulimic, and binge-eating behaviors are not mutually exclusive. In fact, so many women with eating disorders exhibit both anorexic and bulimic behaviors that a growing number of practitioners use the term "bulimarexia" in their diagnosis.

One does not have to display all of these behavioral symptoms to have an eating disorder. Nor does one have to have a clinical eating disorder to get help from any of the places that treat such disorders. If food, weight, or self-hating thoughts are intruding upon your life, if you are continually preoccupied with your last meal or your next meal, and/or if you are feeling sad, confused, lonely, or desperate, you might want to talk it over with a friend, a counselor, or your doctor. There are many places to find help and understanding. (See the Resources at the end of this chapter for organizations that can provide help and understanding.)

Anorexia Nervosa

ගග

Anorexia is a potentially life-threatening disease characterized by self-starvation, an intense preoccupation with food, and the physical and psychological issues and effects related to this behavior.

Anorexic Behaviors Often Include

▲ Not eating
▲ Preoccupation with food: fixation on how, when, and where it is eaten and prepared
▲ Obsession with weight: constantly weighing oneself, talking about weight
▲ Distorted body image: perception of body unrelated to actual weight or appearance
▲ Inability to recognize the signs of hunger and/or consciously ignoring signs of hunger
▲ Excessive exercise
▲ Wearing baggy clothing to hide one's body
▲ Moodiness
▲ Feelings and expressions of insecurity, loneliness, inadequacy, helplessness
▲ Depression
▲ Perfectionism
▲ Difficulty concentrating or focusing

Risks and Effects of Anorexia-Related Starvation

Anorexic behavior prevents the body from functioning normally because it deprives the body of essential nutrients and energy it would regularly get from food. This action of starvation depletes energy stores (specifically those found in muscle and fat), which results in the body lowering its metabolism in an effort to conserve energy. It also rations what energy it does have to maintain only the most basic functions. As a result, the following may occur:

▲ Changes in menstruation—irregular or light periods or none at all (amenorrhea)
▲ Stomach and digestion problems, including pain, bloating, and constipation
▲ Loss of 15 to 25 percent of body weight
▲ Increased sensitivity to cold
▲ Growth of fine hair on the arms, legs, and face

▲ Lowered pulse rate and blood pressure
▲ Chronic bad breath
▲ Dehydration
▲ Lowered body temperature
▲ Dull nails, hair, and skin
▲ Slowed reflexes
▲ Head hair loss
▲ Lowered sex drive
▲ Feeling weak and/or tired
▲ Feeling dizzy and/or fainting
▲ Insomnia
▲ Difficulty concentrating
▲ Increased susceptibility to illness (lowered resistance and weakened immune system)
▲ Irregular metabolism

RECOGNIZING EATING DISORDERS

"Because I'm tall and black, people didn't think it was odd that I was so thin, and they never suspected that I was anorexic."
—UNIVERSITY OF CONNECTICUT, '92

Eating disorders have traditionally been seen as a white, straight, middle-class women's issue. Although a large percentage of people with eating disorders are white and middle and upper-middle class, eating disorders are by no means exclusive diseases. Women from every racial, ethnic, and religious group, disabled women, and lesbian women (among others) struggle with eating disorders. Even women who do not aspire to the idealized images of women are not immune to them.

Because our concept of who suffers from eating disorders is not wholly accurate, we sometimes fail to identify eating disorders even when the obvious signs are present. Just as looking thin does not mean that someone is anorexic and being "overweight" does not make a binge-eater, having a body that looks "healthy" or "normal" doesn't mean that someone couldn't have an eating disorder. Behaviors and the feelings behind those behaviors indicate whether or not someone suffers from an eating disorder.

"I know so many women who fit the stereotypical eating disorder stat— middle class, overachiever, attractive—that when my Asian roommate was starving herself it took me a while to recognize it as anorexia because I thought her eating patterns were cultural."
—UNIVERSITY OF MICHIGAN, '96

86% of people with an eating disorder develop it before the age

Bulimia

ᘒᘒᘒ

Bulimia is a potentially life-threatening disease characterized by episodes of binge-eating (eating large amounts of food in one sitting) followed by one or more methods of purging (ridding the body of the food in order to avoid weight gain), and the physical and psychological issues and effects related to this behavior. The most common methods of purging are throwing up, taking laxatives or diuretics, and rigorous exercise. Some bulimic women will alternate periods of binge-eating with periods of intense dieting or fasting. Unlike women with anorexia, women with bulimia are generally at "average" or "normal" weight.

Bulimic Behaviors Often Include

▲ Eating high-calorie and/or large quantities of food followed by vomiting, fasting, taking laxatives, or compulsive exercise (called the "binge-purge cycle")
▲ Preoccupation with food, weight, and appearance
▲ Distorted body image
▲ Eating in secret
▲ Constantly trying to lose weight
▲ Feeling out of control while eating—fear of not being able to stop eating
▲ Self-criticism
▲ Being nervous or agitated when prevented from being alone after eating
▲ Low self-esteem
▲ Feelings and expressions of insecurity, loneliness, inadequacy, and/or helplessness
▲ Depression
▲ Perfectionism

"My bulimia had become so incorporated into my life that I couldn't imagine what life would be like without it. I felt like I would completely fall apart and lose control. . . . It was especially hard for me to get help because I wasn't thin, obsessed with my body, or pretty like all the people I knew who had eating disorders, so I wasn't sure I really had a problem, even though I was throwing up many times a day."
—University of Minnesota, '93

Risks and Effects of Repeated Purging by Induced Vomiting

The harmful effects of purging can appear after a short or long period of time, and may be temporary or permanent. As is the case of anorexia, many of the effects are not immediately obvious; by the time they appear they may already be serious.

▲ Tooth decay and gum disease
▲ Chronic bad breath
▲ Dehydration
▲ Stomach and digestion problems, including pain, bloating, constipation, and involuntary regurgitation
▲ Irritation and tearing of esophagus
▲ Headache
▲ Electrolyte imbalance (which can lead to kidney or heart problems)
▲ Fatigue and dizziness
▲ Scratched or scarred knuckles (from scraping against teeth)
▲ Broken blood vessels in the face and eyes
▲ Weight fluctuation (but note that

many women with bulimia do not lose weight)

▲ Bloated face (swollen glands, especially around chin and throat) and/or stomach
▲ Irregular metabolism
▲ Lack of sufficient nutrients and calories

Risks and Effects of Laxative and Diuretic Overuse

▲ Stomach and digestion problems, including pain, bloating, constipation, and uncontrollable diarrhea
▲ Developing tolerance and dependence (a greater amount of laxative is required to do the trick)
▲ Dehydration
▲ Dizziness
▲ Electrolyte imbalance (which can lead to kidney or heart problems)

Because laxatives and diuretics cause the release of excess water, which can give the illusion of weight loss, they are sometimes mistakenly thought to rid our bodies of excess calories. But that's a myth. In fact, the laxative effect doesn't kick in until after the body has taken the calories from the food.

Physical Effects of Bulimia-Related Starvation

As a result of induced vomiting or intense dieting and/or fasting, women with bulimia often do not get the necessary amounts of nutrients and calories. The risks and effects are the same as those discussed on page 283.

Warning Signs of Compulsive Exercise

Compulsive exercise can be difficult to define and recognize, because it's more about one's attitude than one's behavior. Regular exercise is an essential part of a healthy lifestyle. It relieves stress, boosts metabolism, and strengthens and tones muscles. However, when a person exercises obsessively, it can be physically and/or psychologically dangerous. Warning signs include:

▲ Shirking your responsibilities, obligations, and basic needs in order to exercise (e.g., cutting classes, missing appointments, skipping meals)
▲ Using exercise to punish yourself
▲ Becoming depressed and distraught if you don't perform up to your expectations
▲ Continuing your regimen even when you are sick or injured
▲ Friends expressing concern about the amount of time you spend exercising or thinking about exercising and/or your attitude toward exercise

"Eating disorders at my school were a huge problem, and the bathrooms started to get clogged, the plumbing ruined and everything. The administration responded by closing the women's bathrooms near the dining hall—then, they thought, women won't throw up after meals. This "solution" is so representative of the stupidity with which some people treat eating disorders—'Oh, we'll close down the bathrooms and that will solve the problem.'"

—WELLESLEY COLLEGE, '89

☼ If Barbie were a real woman her measurements would be 39-23-33,

"I would eat in the middle of the night. I'd be in a trance, eating everything in sight, and if there wasn't anything to eat I'd feel like I would explode, and get dressed and run to the store. I was gaining a lot of weight, and I would try to diet, but no matter how hard I tried, I would always get out of control at night. Finally, I couldn't take it anymore. I was so depressed about my looks, and felt nauseous all the time, and had no energy, and couldn't afford it anymore, so I made an appointment with one of the [school] psychologists." —CORNELL UNIVERSITY, '92

Binge-eating

ꮒꭹꮒ

Binge-eating disorder is characterized by eating large amounts of food (usually high-calorie) in one sitting. Binge-eating has only recently been recognized as an eating disorder in and of itself.

Binge-eating Behaviors Often Include

▲ Eating when not physically hungry
▲ Feeling out of control around food
▲ Eating in secret
▲ Eating "normally" or "dieting" in public, but eating large quantities of food in private
▲ Feeling guilty and/or depressed, especially after a binge
▲ Difficulty expressing feelings

▲ Wearing oversized clothing to hide one's body

Physical Effects of Binge-eating

▲ Weight gain
▲ Stomach and digestion problems, pain, constipation
▲ Bloating
▲ Irregular metabolism
▲ Increased risk of developing heart problems, diabetes, and high blood pressure (due to weight gain)

GETTING TREATMENT

The sooner an eating disorder is identified and treated, the easier and faster the recovery, and the smaller the potential for permanent physical and emotional damage. Effective treatment for an eating disorder involves treating the whole self. It should acknowledge and address behavioral issues (learning how to regain healthy eating habits and how to feel and respond to hunger again); physical issues (repairing the damage done to the body as a result of the disease); and psychological issues (understanding and coping with the reasons behind and problems related to the eating disorder).

The prevalence of eating disorders doesn't necessarily make it any easier for women to confront the problem, and self-identifying and seeking help for eating disorders may be very difficult. Deciding where to go and whom and how to tell about your secret can be painful, scary, and confusing. Remember, you deserve to have support, and support does exist. Consider turning to a friend, a dorm counselor

and she would have so little body fat that she wouldn't menstruate. ☼

or RA, or your family for assistance. You can also go to campus health/mental health services or find an off-campus therapist or doctor (see "Finding a Therapist or Group," page 261, and "The Road to Recovery," page 232, and/or call a local group or one of the Resources at the end of this chapter).

Treatment Options

ⓥⓥⓥ

There are numerous methods of recovering from an eating disorder. Whichever you choose, seek out those professionals who have knowledge about and experience working with people with eating disorders, or who are at least willing to put time and energy into learning about eating disorders and how to treat them. Because of the complex nature of eating disorders, treatments that involve the advice, expertise, and support of two or more of the following are usually the most successful:

■ **Medical and dental care:** To address the effects bingeing, purging, and/or starving have had on your body. Have complete dental and physical exams, with regular follow-ups to monitor your physiological state. Choose a practitioner whom you can tell you have an eating disorder.

■ **Individual therapy/psychiatry:** To help you discuss and analyze the many ways in which the eating disorder affects your life. Due to the high incidence of depression in women with eating disorders, as well as the increased evidence of the effectiveness of antidepressants and similar medications in the treatment of eating disorders, consider having a consultation

with a psychiatrist (who has the training and authority to prescribe medication if necessary) or a therapist affiliated with a psychiatrist. (For more on therapists, therapy options, and medication, see "More Than Just the Blues," page 247.)

"I can't tell you how incredible it is to finally not feel guilty and nervous about eating. And no more lying to the supermarket cashier, telling her I'm having a party to explain why I'd be buying so much junk food so late at night."
—UNIVERSITY OF MINNESOTA, '93

■ **Family therapy:** To gain insight into and deal with issues that lie behind and result from the eating disorder.

■ **Therapy/support groups:** To talk with and get support and advice from others who have (or had) similar experiences. Many campuses and communities have both formal and informal groups specifically for women dealing with eating disorders. Two such groups, Overeaters Anonymous (OA) and Food Addicts Anonymous (FAA), are open to anyone dealing with eating or food issues (not just overeating), are based on the 12 Step philosophy of the other Anonymous groups, and hold meetings throughout the country. (For more on 12 Step programs, see "Use and Abuse," page 318.)

■ **In-patient care:** In-patient care for eating disorders is important when the effects of an eating disorder have become physically or emotionally dangerous and/or when outpatient treatment has not been effective. There are a number of hospitals and treatment facilities that are able to provide the comprehensive and intensive care that many women need in order to recover. In-patient care usually involves working with a team of trained professionals, such as medical doctors, therapists (in individual and group therapy and support groups), nutritionists, and/or exercise therapists, in a structured environment. Unless it coincides with a vacation, undergoing in-patient treatment will likely require taking a leave of absence from school. (See "Leaves of Absence," page 41.)

■ **Nutritional counseling:** To evaluate your nutritional needs, help plan a healthy, realistic, nonthreatening diet plan, and address the damage done to the body from restricting, bingeing, and/or purging food.

■ **Exercise counseling:** To help create a safe and healthy exercise program and monitor progress.

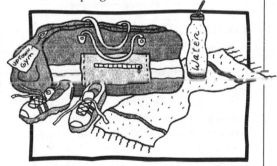

■ **Dance, music, or art therapy, martial arts:** To reveal, express, confront, and cope with issues and emotions in a nonverbal manner.

■ **Holistic care:** Hypnosis, biofeedback, massage, herbal therapy, aromatherapy, and body alignment work may be helpful in repairing physical and emotional damage, developing stress-management techniques, learn-

ing and adjusting to new behaviors, uncovering and coping with painful memories and emotions, improving body image, and restoring inner balance and peace.

Treatment Issues

ഗൈ

"I was hospitalized for anorexia and bulimia, and during our first session the psychiatrist asked me to think of all the things that made me feel good about myself. When I told her the only thing was when I felt skinny or lost weight, she said, with total sincerity, 'I am so glad that at least you have something that makes you feel good about yourself.' I will always remember the impact her gesture made on me. Instead of the accusing, punitive response I felt from others, she gave me permission to care for myself in the only way I knew how." —BARNARD COLLEGE, '92

Letting go of an eating disorder can be a terrifying prospect, even when you are aware of the damage it's causing. Though rationally you may know you need help and are ready to work toward recovery, you can still feel like you're losing your stabilizing and motivating force, and the one thing that is special or unique about you. Though you may feel ready to give up the disorder, you may not feel ready to feel the pain and other emotions you've used food to avoid. It does take a lot of hard work to transform self-destructive thoughts and behaviors into healthy, self-affirming ones, but considering the pain of living with the eating disorder as well as the potential long-term damage that can result, it's worth it.

HELPING A FRIEND WITH AN EATING DISORDER

E ating disorders do not affect just the women who have them. When someone has an eating disorder, it changes her relationship with her friends, family, acquaintances, and lovers. Watching her be obsessed with food—acting like she's blind to the problem when she's usually insightful and aware—and feeling pulled in but pushed away can be frustrating, frightening, and truly difficult to bear. If food becomes such a prominent issue in your friend's life that she can no longer be responsive to your needs and you can no longer hold a decent conversation or have fun with her, your friendship will invariably suffer. You can support her and try to "be there" for her, but you won't be able to solve the problem for her, no matter how badly you might want to. Learning how to be caring and helpful without becoming enmeshed in her issues can be a real challenge. (For advice on talking with or confronting your friend, supporting her through recovery, and knowing how, when, and where to seek out a professional, see "A Friend in Need," page 327. Anyone who helps people struggling with eating disorders is usually there for their friends and families, too.)

SUBSTANCE ABUSE AND EATING DISORDERS

I n eating disorders, food (or the denial of it) has a function similar to that of alcohol or other drugs for a person with a substance dependency problem. It's not uncommon for women to have a dual addiction, to use both food and the mood-altering substances more commonly associated with substance abuse as a means of numbing pain and/or avoiding difficult issues. Though the recovery process for a woman trying to overcome an alcohol or other drug problem will have some differences from that for a woman with an eating disorder, the basic elements—discovering, confronting, and working out issues; learning how to cope without the use of a substance; recognizing the role that the substance played in our life—are exactly the same. The largest difference is the new role that the previously abused substance will play in your life. The most popular drug recovery programs prescribe abstinence. However, that's not exactly a reasonable option when food has been your drug of choice. Those healing from an eating disorder are required to relearn how to feel hunger, eat sensibly, and use food to nourish the body, not to numb the feelings.

In 1940, the woman pictured on White Rock soda cans was 5'4"

ACTIVIST IDEAS

■ Make signs that say "This Insults Women" and stick them on posters and advertisements that portray women in demeaning or disrespectful ways. Write letters to companies that use offensive advertising. Promote and support the use of images that more accurately reflect what most women look like and show women as powerful, capable people.

■ Organize a peer-support training session for a group of women who have recovered from eating disorders, specifically for the purpose of supporting women students who need someone to talk to who understands. You can make a confidential referral list of the women's names and numbers available through campus mental health services, campus hotlines, peer support groups, and/or dorm counselors.

■ Plan a "no-diet day" at your school. Organize a display and place for women to ceremoniously deposit diet pills and milk-shake formulas, clothes that they'll never fit into, and all those diet foods that we eat instead of the foods that we really want. Bring speakers on issues such as images of women in the media; the diet industry; eating disorders and body image. Contact the International No Diet Coalition ([914] 679-1209) for more ideas.

■ Stop yourself from saying self-deprecating things and from thinking self-deprecating thoughts. Don't allow yourself to endure insults, harsh words, and criticism from yourself that you wouldn't take from others.

RESOURCES

Information and Referrals

AMERICAN ANOREXIA/BULIMIA ASSOCIATION
293 CENTRAL PARK WEST, SUITE 1R
NEW YORK, NY 10024
(212) 501-8351
Provides information and referrals and organizes self-help groups.

ANOREXIA NERVOSA AND RELATED EATING DISORDERS, INC.
P.O. BOX 5102
EUGENE, OR 97405
(503) 344-1144
Provides general information about eating disorders; offers support groups, and counseling; makes referrals; conducts workshops, seminars, conferences, and training programs.

NATIONAL ASSOCIATION OF ANOREXIA NERVOSA AND ASSOCIATED DISORDERS (ANAD)
P.O. BOX 7
HIGHLAND PARK, IL 60035
(708) 831-3438
Offers referrals to clinics, support groups, and therapists dealing with eating disorders; raises awareness about eating disorders and works to help professionals improve the treatment of eating disorders.

and weighed 140 pounds. Today she is 5'8" and weighs 118 pounds. ☼

OVEREATERS ANONYMOUS
117 WEST 26TH STREET, SUITE 2W
NEW YORK, NY 10001
(212) 206-8621
An international network of support
groups based on the 12 Step philosophy of
recovery for people dealing with food
issues. Provides referrals to local support
groups.

Advocacy

**NATIONAL ASSOCIATION TO ADVANCE FAT
    ACCEPTANCE**
P.O. BOX 188620
SACRAMENTO, CA 95818
(800) 442-1214
An organization that addresses and raises
consciousness about the rights, issues, and
public perceptions of fat people. Provides
support groups in local communities,
fights against size discrimination (especially in the areas of jobs and health care,
offensive advertising, and public accommodations), and promotes a self-affirming,
body-positive outlook for people of all
shapes and sizes. Publishes a newsletter
and other materials.

Further Reading

🌀🌀🌀

Bulimarexia: The Binge-Purge Cycle, Marlene
    Boskind-White and William C. White,
    Jr. (W. W. Norton, 1987).

*Beauty Secrets: Women and the Politics of
    Appearance,* Wendy Chapkis (South End
    Press, 1986).

The Hungry Self, Kim Chernin (Harper &
    Row, 1985).

The Obsession, Kim Chernin (Harper &
    Row, 1981).

*Transforming Body Image: Learning to Love
    the Body You Have,* Marcia Germaine
    Hutchinson (Crossing Press, 1985).

*Making Peace With Food: Freeing Yourself
    from the Diet-Weight Obsession,* Susan
    Kano (Harper & Row, 1985).

*Controlling Eating Disorders with Facts,
    Advice, and Resources,* Raymond Lem-
    berg, ed. (Oryx Press, 1992).

*SomeBody to Love: A Guide to Loving the Body
    You Have,* Lesléa Newman (Third Side
    Press, 1991).

Fat Is a Feminist Issue, Susie Orbach
    (Berkley, 1982).

*Hunger Strike: The Anorectic's Struggle As a
    Metaphor for Our Age,* Susie Orbach
    (Avon, 1988).

The Beauty Myth, Naomi Wolf (William
    Morrow, 1991).

*Feeding the Hungry Heart: The Experience
    of Compulsive Eating,* Geneen Roth
    (NAL/Dutton, 1982).

Breaking Free From Compulsive Eating,
    Geneen Roth (NAL/Dutton, 1984).

☀ Size of the times: Marilyn Monroe wore a size 12. ☀

Use & Abuse:

A Rational Look at Alcohol & Other Drugs

Drugs are a fact of life on college campuses. At almost every college or university, you don't have to look too hard to find everything from marijuana and beer to grain alcohol and heroin, not to mention an obscene amount of caffeine. This variety of drugs is used in a number of ways: socially, experimentally, habitually, medicinally, and sometimes quite dangerously. However, despite the prevalence of drugs and drug use, there generally isn't a corresponding amount of drug awareness and education.

When it comes to getting the lowdown on drugs, it's hard to know what to believe. We are constantly exposed to conflicting messages. What you hear about one drug might be based on one person's good or bad experience, and what you read about another may be exaggerated to suit the needs of a particular political agenda. We're discouraged from asking questions about those drugs that are considered "taboo" (illegal drugs), and we don't think to ask questions about those drugs that are considered "safe" (prescription or over the counter and/or legal drugs). And even if we had access to all the current information out there about drugs, most of it would still be inadequate as far as women are concerned, because the bulk of drug research has failed to consider the biological and sociological factors that make many drugs affect women differently than they do men.

To make informed decisions, it's useful to question both the information we receive and its source. And if you choose to use drugs, you should know how the drugs work, what their effects are, and how to get help if the need arises.

KNOW WHAT YOU INGEST: A DRUG LEXICON

The following "drug lexicon" should be used as a first step in learning about the effects and risks of alcohol and other drugs that you may encounter on campus. Because at this time there hasn't been sufficient research done on the effects of drugs on women, the bulk of the information included here describes generic cross-gender effects.

It goes without saying, but it's important enough to say anyway: Driving, operating heavy machinery, or doing anything else that requires agility, alertness, awareness, quick thinking and/or reflexes while under the influence of most of the below substances can be illegal, dangerous, or even fatal.

Alcohol

Description: Alcohol, a by-product of grain fermentation, is a depressant.

How it works: Alcohol affects the areas of the brain that regulate and control reason and judgment, balance, coordination, consciousness, and breathing.

Under the influence: Paradoxically, alcohol's sedative effect on the brain can, in small doses, make you feel "up." Because it sedates the reason and judgment center of the brain, you may feel fewer inhibitions, more confidence, giddy, buzzed, friendlier, and more relaxed in social situations. In larger amounts, alcohol can cause dizziness, loss of coordination, nausea, vomiting, depression, loss of memory, and violent aggression. Overdose can cause

PREGNANT AND NURSING WOMEN TAKE NOTE

Using any drugs when you are pregnant (or have cause to think you might be) or nursing may pose serious risks to yourself and your fetus or newborn. Consult your physician before taking any drugs—legal or illegal, over-the-counter or prescribed—during pregnancy. Be honest with your physician, even if you think she won't approve. There are programs designed specifically to help pregnant women and new mothers deal with drug use. (See the Resources at the end of this chapter for organizations that can provide referrals.)

unconsciousness, coma, and death.

Alcohol affects the body almost immediately (but effects will vary depending on how much you have eaten, how rested you are, etc.). The less you weigh (and the greater your percentage of body fat), the longer it will take for your body to process the alcohol and the longer the effects of the alcohol will last.

Long-term effects: Alcohol may be addictive, especially in those with a genetic or familial propensity toward alcoholism. Longtime or heavy users who try to quit may experience severe physical and psychological withdrawal symptoms. Long-term overuse can weaken the immune system and cause heart, kidney, brain, nerve, and liver problems. Other effects are depression, fatigue, and memory and learning problems. It can also render an individual unable to metabolize alcohol, increasing the likelihood of developing alcohol-related health problems. Alcohol affects the REM sleep phase, causing bad dreams as well as restless and interrupted sleep.

And bear in mind: It is extremely dangerous to combine alcohol with stimulants, sedatives, or narcotics. Avoid alcohol if you're taking antihistamines, cough medicine (especially those that contain codeine), tranquilizers, sleeping pills, and other prescription and nonprescription painkillers. This even goes for aspirin and/or ibuprofen: Alcohol can cause an upset stomach and promote gastric bleeding when taken in combination with these medicines.

Alcohol can also diminish the healing effects of antibiotics. And when taken with metronidazole

"Because we see all those ads that make drinking look so casual, because it is part of our culture, and because we associate it with romantic ideas, it's easy to overlook the fact that alcohol, like many other drugs, is not generally healthy for us, and it is an addictive drug. . . . It's also hard to escape the fact that it's easier to get someone who's been drinking into bed than someone who's stone cold sober."

—HARVARD UNIVERSITY, '93

(Flagyl), an antibiotic often prescribed to treat vaginal infections, it can cause severe stomach upset, stomach cramps, and headache.

Alcoholism is considered a hered-

TWO OR MORE . . .

When you take more than one drug at a time, the way the drugs interact with each other, combined with the way that they interact with your body, can greatly alter the the drugs' effect. Combining drugs can cause a loss or gain in their potency, bring on strange but benign side effects, or make for some pretty serious consequences. For example, aspirin taken with caffeine may increase the effects of the aspirin; alcohol and barbiturates taken together are such a potent combination that they can cause serious prob-

lems, including coma and even death. When taking a prescription medication, ask your doctor or pharmacist before using any other drug at the same time, including over-the-counter medications. Also, if you are planning to use illegal drugs, ask your doctor about how they interact with any medication you are already taking. If you feel uncomfortable asking face to face, you can also call a drug hotline or the drug company hotline—the number will be on the prescription insert. (See the Resources at the end of this chapter.)

3½ drinks per week; students with "D" or "F" averages consumed 11.

ALCOHOL: THE DRUG OF CHOICE

*"My drinking crept up on me fresh-
man year. There was the Wednesday
night frat party, the Thursday night
"study break," the Friday night beer
run, and the Saturday night
blowout. I didn't even consider
myself much of a drinker, but before
I knew it I was drinking four out of
seven nights in the week."*
— *SCRIPPS COLLEGE, '90*

Alcohol can lower our inhibitions
and thus help us speak more
freely, take more risks, be more out-
going, dance more outrageously, feel
more comfortable, and/or "make the
first move." But with lowered inhibitions often come increased vulnera-
bility, intensified emotions, and
impaired judgment. Of all the drugs
used on campus, alcohol is probably
the most prevalent. And because it's
so widely available, accepted, and not
generally viewed as a drug, alcohol is
probably the easiest substance to
abuse. Particularly during the first
year, when the newfound freedom can
cause people to go a little crazy, it's
not unusual for drinking to get out of
control.

Because of the prevalence of alcohol on campus, it is important to be
aware of its effects and be prepared
to confront situations of overuse.
This may mean dealing with someone who has gotten sick or violent or
who has passed out from drinking,
or it may mean being able to recognize when your own or someone
else's drinking has become a prob-

lem that requires help. (For more
information, see "Dealing with
Emergencies," page 313, "Signs of a
Drug Problem," page 315, and "Help-
ing a Friend with a Drug or Alcohol
Problem," page 321.)

*"I had a tough time at the beginning
of school because I don't drink, and
parties were where everyone was
meeting each other. Sure I had a
choice not to drink, but when parties with alcohol are the places you
meet people and people use alcohol as an excuse to fool around, it's
not so fun being sober."*
— *VANDERBILT UNIVERSITY, '95*

SHOTS VS. MINT JULEPS

There is a double standard for
women and men when it comes to
alcohol use. Drinking is very much a
man's ritual ("A sip of this'll put some
hair on your chest"), and the places
that people drink—frats, bars, and
sporting events—are often male dominated. When men get drunk, rowdy,
obnoxious, or even aggressive,
they're "just bein' boys," they're frequently defended as cool, fun, or
funny. And even when a guy drinks
alone, he may become not antisocial
or a closet drunk, but "a tragic hero
of our time" à la Humphrey Bogart in
Casablanca.

On the other hand, drunk, raucous
women are seen as sloppy, out of control, unsociable, or "just asking for
sex," and they are considered to be
"making a spectacle of themselves."

 35% of college women say they sometimes drink alcohol for the

itary disease: A child of an alcoholic is more prone to developing an alcohol problem than a person with no alcoholism in her family.

Using, selling, possessing alcohol if you're under the age of 21 is illegal unless it's used in a ritual or is served by a parent or guardian in a private home.

Special considerations for women: Due to a number of recent studies, there is now an influx of information that explains why and how alcohol affects women differently than it does men. In general, women's bodies are smaller than men's, and weight and body mass greatly influence alcohol tolerance. Further, because women have a higher percentage of body fat than men, and fat does not absorb alcohol, even a woman who weighs the same as a man will have more rapid, intense, and long lasting effects from alcohol. On top of this, the enzyme responsible for alcohol metabolism is more active in men than women, which means that even if men and women consume the same amount, more alcohol will enter into women's bloodstreams and will remain there longer. This is one reason why a higher percentage of female alcoholics suffer from alcohol-related physical problems than do their male counterparts.

Alcohol inhibits the absorption of vitamins and nutrients such as folic acid, which is used in the production of red blood cells. During menstruation, when iron levels are lowest, alcohol is more likely to cause fatigue. This is heightened in women who take oral contraceptives, which also inhibit absorption of nutrients.

Studies indicate that consuming more than four ounces of alcohol may set the libido aflame, but it can also decrease physical arousal and the intensity of, as well as the ability to reach orgasm. It also may inhibit the production of vaginal lubrication, making sexual intercourse painful.

Research is also being done to determine whether there are any connections between alcohol and the menstrual cycle, specifically whether alcohol affects us differently at different points during the cycle, whether estrogen increases the rate of alcohol absorption, and if alcohol use can heighten PMS symptoms and/or affect fertility.

Alcohol use during pregnancy can result in fetal alcohol syndrome and birth defects. Nursing mothers should also avoid drinking, as studies have suggested that the alcohol that passes into breast milk might retard motor development in babies.

Alcohol is also involved in more than 90 percent of incidents of campus sexual assault, as well as a large number of automobile accidents.

Amphetamines

Speed, uppers, pep pills, bennies, dexies (dextroamphetamine), meth (methamphetamine), black beauties (biphetamine)

Description: Amphetamines are usually swallowed in pill form, but may also be injected. Freebase methamphetamine (called *ice* or *crystal*) is smoked.

How they work: Amphetamines affect the areas of the brain associated with alertness, arousal, reward, and mood.

Under the influence: Amphetamines increase energy and alertness, suppress appetite, and bring on feelings of excitement and euphoria. They increase heart rate and blood pressure, and may cause tremors, nervousness, mood swings, irritability, sweating, and insomnia. Overdose can cause convulsions, heart attack, coma, and death.

Long-term effects: Overuse can cause brain damage, muscle dysfunction, loss of appetite, insomnia, anxiety, hallucinations, paranoia, and death. Amphetamines (particularly methamphetamine) are highly addictive and cause extremely severe withdrawal symptoms.

And bear in mind: "Ice" also refers to freebase methamphetamine mixed with heroin or cocaine; both are potentially deadly combinations. Using, possessing, or selling amphetamines without a prescription is illegal.

Special considerations for women: In the past, amphetamines were often prescribed as diet pills for women, without much consideration of their addictiveness.

Women should avoid amphetamines if they are pregnant or nursing.

Caffeine

Description: Caffeine, a stimulant, appears naturally in many plants, like coffee, tea, the kola tree, cacao, and ilex.

"Caffeine is definitely the college student's drug of choice. I couldn't imagine getting through finals without it." —BATES COLLEGE, '97

How it works: Caffeine stimulates the central nervous system, increasing heart and breathing rates.

Effects: In small doses (approximately one cup of brewed coffee or two cans of colas or three cups of tea), caffeine can make you feel awake and alert; in higher doses it can make you feel anxious and jittery. It also acts as a diuretic. Effects depend on the individual's sensitivity and tolerance.

And bear in mind: Caffeine has been shown to irritate the bladder, which can cause problems for those who suffer from chronic urinary tract and bladder infections. Because it may have inflammatory effects, caffeine can also aggravate arthritis, and other muscle and joint problems. It also increases calcium loss—a problem because the vast majority of college women don't get enough calcium, and they have a tendency to replace milk with caffeine-rich beverages.

Because caffeine is addictive—many "need" a cup of coffee to wake up in the morning—stopping abruptly can cause you to feel headachy, irritable, edgy, depressed, tired, and generally out of sorts and achy. If you want to cut down on your caffeine intake, it's best to do it gradually.

On the up side, caffeine may help relieve headaches.

Special considerations for women: PMS symptoms, such as cramps, headache, and moodiness, can increase with caffeine use, depending on how much and how often caffeine is

Because they cause increased urine production, drinking caf-

consumed. If PMS is a problem, it may help to avoid caffeine right before and during your period. But, despite the growing connections being made between PMS and caffeine, many over-the-counter pain relievers and PMS remedies contain caffeine (Aqua-Ban has the same amount as NoDoz, and maximum-strength Midol has more than a can of cola). Check the ingredient list on the package to be sure.

Caffeine intake during pregnancy has been related to birth defects in animals, and although at this time there is no definitive information about the effects of caffeine on human fetuses, it is best to be moderate in the consumption of caffeine during pregnancy.

Caffeine has been linked to fibrocystic breasts, so if you have cystic breasts, you may want to cut your intake.

> *"Coffee is a social drug—it's what we drink when we go to cafés to relax—and it's a productivity drug—it's what we drink when we are stressed out of our minds trying to get work done. In this town almost everyone I know is a coffee snob, so beyond just drinking a lot of it, we drink this blend or that blend . . .*
>
> —UNIVERSITY OF CALIFORNIA, BERKELEY, '96

Cocaine

Coke, snow, flake, blow, toot, White Lady, sugar, cane, crystal, nose candy

Description: Cocaine is a stimulant extracted from coca leaves and processed into a potent white powder. It is most often inhaled (snorted), injected, or, in the case of crack co-caine, can be smoked.

Crack or "rock," is cocaine that has been processed into a less expensive, more potent form, resembling translucent beige pebbles. Smoking is an extremely rapid method of delivering drugs to the brain. Therefore even small doses of crack can be very potent and very disorienting or overwhelming. It's like taking a fast shot of grain alcohol rather than sipping a beer.

How it works: Cocaine works very quickly, binding with brain receptors responsible for pleasure and alertness, and mimicking the effects of an excess of the naturally occurring neurotransmitters. This produces the "high." In an at-tempt to correct the imbalance, the brain then inhibits the production and reabsorption of these neurotransmitters. This results in a crash, which takes the form of depression, exhaustion, and a craving for more of the drug.

Under the influence: Cocaine can cause feelings of increased mental and physical ability, mastery, confidence, and euphoria. It can also cause sleeplessness, increase or decrease sexual desire, and decrease appetite. It raises body temperature, blood pressure, and heart rate, constricts blood vessels, and can induce muscle spasms, stroke, high fever, and convulsions. Some heavy or frequent users experience hallucinations and delusions, like "coke bugs" (the sensation of insects crawling all over their body). As the rush wears off, a user may feel paranoid, anxious, irritable, and depressed. Crack produces a short, intense high and an extremely intense crash.

Long-term effects: Cocaine use can cause acute medical problems, including heart and lung failure and blood clots, which are especially hazardous because the drug constricts blood vessels, making a blood clot more likely to cause blockage. Heavy use can also cause insomnia, anxiety, paranoia, depression, sexual dysfunction, and dangerously rapid weight loss, and can impair learning and concentration. It is extremely physically and psychologically addictive, especially when smoked or injected. Because users build tolerance and then need more of the drug to achieve the desired effect, risk of overdose increases with use.

And bear in mind: Cocaine is often cut, or diluted, with other substances, such as Ajax, talc, vitamin C, or bleach, which can cause effects other than those listed above.

Snorting cocaine can cause nosebleeds, runny noses, congestion, sinus infections, damage to the nasal septum, and lung problems.

Injecting cocaine can cause skin abscesses, inflamed veins, and infection. Sharing needles invites the spread of TB, hepatitis, and HIV (see "Cleaning Needles," page 304, as well as "STDs, HIV, and AIDS," page 369).

Occasionally, cocaine is used medically as an anesthetic. In all other cases, using, possessing or selling cocaine is illegal, punishable by fine, imprisonment, or both.

Special considerations for women: Avoid if pregnant or nursing.

Hallucinogens

Description: Hallucinogens, or psychedelics, alter perception of reality. LSD (*acid, cubes, blotter*), which is taken orally, is synthesized from lysergic acid, an odorless, colorless, and tasteless chemical. Mescaline (*mesc, cactus*) is extracted from the peyote cactus and can be smoked or taken orally. Psilocybin occurs naturally in certain mushrooms (*magic mushrooms, shrooms*) and is taken orally. Phencyclidine (*PCP, angel dust, killer hog, peacee pill*) is a synthetic hallucinogen and can be smoked, inhaled (snorted), injected, or taken orally. It is used as an animal tranquilizer.

How they work: Hallucinogens block and inhibit the function of certain neurotransmitter receptors, affecting the way the brain communicates and processes information.

Under the influence: The effects begin 30 to 90 minutes after ingestion (almost immediately if snorted or injected) and trips usually last 6 to 12 hours, but may last longer, depending on the dosage. Mushrooms, mescaline, and LSD (the most potent of the three) are taken orally and intensify colors, sounds, and emotions, cause hallucinations and delusions, and induce a dreamlike state. Some claim to experience religious and personal revelation while under the influence. Physical effects can include dilated pupils, increased heart rate and blood pressure, trembling, nausea, loss of appetite, and mood swings.

The effects of PCP are unpredictable. It can cause feelings of depression, slurred speech, blurred vision, confusion, loss of judgment and coordination, violent aggression, euphoria, drowsiness, and insensitivity to pain. Overdose can induce a psychotic state and cause heart and lung failure, coma, and death.

Hallucinogens can bring on a bad trip, characterized by feelings of panic,

SEXUAL ASSAULT AND DRUGS

※

It's no surprise that in the vast majority of incidents of sexual abuse (and sexual encounters regretted after the fact) on campus, some or all of the people involved were "under the influence." Drugs impair one's ability to reason, to accurately assess risk, and to make well-thought-out decisions, and they make us more likely to engage in activities we wouldn't ordinarily consent to. We might also be unable to voice a lack of consent or physically remove ourselves from a dangerous or undesirable situation while under the influence of drugs or alcohol. Additionally, if we are with someone who's drunk or high, s/he may not be able to read our discomfort or hear (let alone understand) a "no." (See "Ending the Silence," page 491.)

Although inebriated women don't technically lose their legal rights, they can lose many of their social rights. Despite the laws that clearly state that sexual activities with a person unable to consent is sexual assault, a woman who is assaulted when drunk or high simply doesn't receive the same sympathy and support as does a woman who was not inebriated. And in many cases these women are openly or tacitly blamed for the assault.

Even consensual sex in these circumstances can be dangerous. When drunk or high, one often forgets or ignores the possibility of becoming pregnant or getting a disease, and thus contraception and condoms may not find their way out of their containers or wrappers. (See "Contraception and Safer Sex," page 399.)

When you are under the influence or with people who are, it's especially important to be careful and conscious of who you are with, where you are, and any potential for the situation to become at all dangerous.

---

confusion, suspiciousness, anxiety, paranoia, helplessness, and loss of control.

Long-term effects: Users can experience flashbacks, which are sudden recurrences of the drug's effects without taking the drug again. Overuse of hallucinogens may result in impaired memory and attention span, confusion, depression, and difficulties with learning and abstract thinking. Though hallucinogens are not considered to be physically addictive, a user may develop a tolerance to them

requiring more of the drug to achieve the same effect. The risk of overdose increases with use.

And bear in mind: Some Southwestern Native American tribes include smoking or eating peyote in ceremonial rituals. This is the only legal use of hallucinogens. Possessing, using, selling, or synthesizing hallucinogens is illegal, punishable by seizure of the drug as well as fine or imprisonment, or both.

Special considerations for women: Avoid if pregnant or nursing.

---

become addicted.   ※   Alcohol is involved in 90% of campus rapes.   ※

Heroin (see Narcotics/Opiates, on the facing page)

Marijuana

Cannabis, pot, grass, weed, ganja, cheeba, herb, reefer, spliff, joint, smoke, toke

Description: Marijuana is the dried green leaves and flowering tops of the hemp plant. Hashish, (or hash), the concentrated dark brown resin of the hemp plant, is the more potent form. Marijuana is most often smoked, although it is sometimes added to brownies or other foods.

How it works: The active ingredient in marijuana is THC (one of the over 400 chemicals in the hemp plant), which binds with the receptors in the brain responsible for coordination and memory.

Under the influence: Effects begin within a few minutes and last for two to four hours. Marijuana can make you feel content, giddy, "stoned," mellow, hungry (commonly known as the munchies), anxious, paranoid, and/or tired, and it can alter perception of space and time. Common symptoms of use are bloodshot eyes, dry mouth, slow reflexes, and increased heart rate.

Long-term effects: Though marijuana is not considered physically addictive, it can be emotionally addictive. Long-term, regular use can "burn out" short-term memory, wear down the immune system (making you more susceptible to illness), cause weight fluctuations and mood swings, and affect motivation, concentration, and alertness. Marijuana contains many of the same cancer-causing substances as tobacco, but in greater concentration. Since marijuana smoke is held in the lungs before it is exhaled, its damaging effects are compounded.

And bear in mind: Marijuana can contain traces of pesticides or be laced with drugs (like PCP, in which case it may be called *supergrass*), LSD, or cocaine) that cause effects other than those listed above. There is increasing evidence that marijuana has medicinal benefits, and it is sometimes prescribed to treat eye diseases, such as glaucoma, and to relieve the pain and nausea associated with chemotherapy and AIDS. In many cultures, marijuana is used socially, religiously, and medicinally.

It can take as long as a month for THC to leave the body completely (which has particular implications for drug testing).

At present, possession and use of marijuana for nonmedical or nonreligious reasons is illegal in most states. There is a small but vocal minority working for the legalization/decriminalization of marijuana.

Special concerns for women: Marijuana may cause menstrual irregularity, a temporary loss of fertility, and a decreased sex drive. (It can have similar affects on male sex drive and may reduce sperm count.)

Some women use marijuana to help alleviate the pain of menstrual cramps.

Women should avoid marijuana if they are pregnant or nursing.

MDMA

Ecstasy, Adam, XTC, X

Description: MDMA, taken orally, has both mild hallucinogenic and stimulant effects. The drug gained popularity in the late 1970s and early 1980s as a "truth serum," and was thought to create strong emotional bonds between those who used the drug together. It became illegal in 1985.

How it works: MDMA is believed to affect the areas in the brain that regulate aggression, mood, sexual activity, sleep, and sensitivity to pain.

Under the influence: Effects start approximately a half an hour after consumption and last four to six hours. The drug can make you feel friendly, loving, insightful, open, energetic, uninhibited and sexually excited, but can also cause confusion, insomnia, and anxiety. Other effects include increased heart rate and blood pressure, muscle and jaw tension, teeth chattering, nausea, dizziness, blurred vision, sweating, and backache.

As the effects wear off, users can feel jittery, exhausted, depressed, and anxious. Although MDMA is generally short-acting, because it is frequently cut with amphetamines, LSD, or other types of drugs, the effects may last longer and differ from those described here.

When using MDMA it is impor-

tant to avoid dehydration and overheating (from which there have been several deaths at "raves"—see below). If you choose to use it, drink plenty of water while under the influence and periodically take breaks to cool down if dancing.

Long-term effects: In rare cases it can cause symptoms resembling those of Parkinson's disease or spinal injury. Other effects include depression, irritability, and loss of mental acuity.

And bear in mind: MDMA may be cut with a variety of substances, from rat poison to baby powder, that cause effects other than those listed above.

MDMA has become increasingly popular over the past few years, especially in connection with "raves": all-night dance parties which often include techno music and videos or special effects, and where the majority of the partygoers have "X-ed" (taken Ecstasy) beforehand. Synthesizing, using, possessing, or selling MDMA is illegal.

Special considerations for women: Avoid if pregnant or nursing.

Narcotics/Opiates

Opium, heroin, morphine, codeine, methadone, Demerol, Percodan

Description: Narcotics are natural or synthetic drugs that contain or resemble opium (a drug extracted from the poppy flower) and are taken orally, injected, smoked, or snorted. In the U.S., all the narcotics listed above except heroin (*horse, smack*) and opium are prescribed as painkillers. *Black tar* (also called *gumball* or *tootsie roll*) is a cheaper, highly potent form of freebase heroin.

CLEANING NEEDLES

※

If you use any drugs that are injected, to prevent transmission of HIV, you should only use new, clean needles (or those that only you have used). If you must share, it is imperative that you clean your works well before each use. You should never use a needle that you haven't opened yourself without cleaning it first. You can clean your works with bleach in the following manner:

▲ RINSE: Draw *cold* water into the syringe until it fills the setting and empty it (not into the clean water). Do this three or four times.

▲ CLEAN: Draw 100 percent bleach into the syringe until it fills the setting, let it sit for 30 seconds, then empty it (outside the container). Do this three or four times.

▲ RINSE: Draw cold, clean water into the syringe to flush it out. Do this four times.

▲ Do not reuse bleach or water.

▲ Under no circumstances should you share cookers or cotton.

How they work: Because of the large number of opiate receptors present in the brain, opiates can produce a variety of effects in addition to alleviating pain. Heroin activates receptors responsible for pleasure and physical dependence, which accounts for the highly addictive nature of the drug.

Under the influence: Opiates medically prescribed for pain usually cause drowsiness and "spaciness." Heroin's effects usually last one to three hours, depending on the dose and user tolerance. Soon after injection or inhalation, a user feels a brief euphoric rush (often accompanied for new users by nausea and vomiting), then enters into a serene state. Overdose can cause a user to stop breathing, and can lead to death.

Long-term effects: Narcotics are highly addictive if used regularly, and users who try to quit can experience severe withdrawal symptoms. Heavy use can negatively affect mental, phys-

ical, and psychological well-being. Long-term use can cause depression, low self-esteem, aggression, and edginess, and increase impulsiveness and the need for instant gratification. However, when administered and regulated by a competent health provider, narcotics can provide exceptional pain relief with little risk of addiction.

And bear in mind: Heroin is often injected, which carries its own set of risks, like skin abscesses, inflamed veins, and infection. Sharing needles invites the spread of TB, hepatitis, and STDs, including HIV / AIDS. (See "Cleaning Needles," above and "STDs, HIV, and AIDS," page 369.)

It is extremely dangerous to combine opiates with sedatives (like alcohol and tranquilizers) or stimulants (like cocaine). Using, possessing, or selling heroin or other opiates without a prescription is illegal.

Special considerations for women: Avoid if pregnant or nursing.

※ Clean needle exchange programs decrease needle sharing but do not

Nicotine

Description: The addictive drug contained in tobacco is nicotine. Tobacco is most often smoked (rolled into cigarettes and cigars, or put in pipes). In the form of chewing tobacco, nicotine is absorbed through the gums.

How it works: Nicotine is a highly addictive drug that stimulates the central nervous system. It may also calm the user down. The combination of nicotine and the hundreds of other chemicals in cigarette smoke are responsible for cigarettes' detrimental effects on the body.

Under the influence: When nicotine reaches the brain, blood pressure rises, breathing quickens, and heart rate may increase or decrease. A user may feel relaxed, alert, better able to concentrate, and more in control. In high doses, nicotine can cause tremors, vomiting, intestinal cramps and diarrhea. Although nicotine is the drug responsible for smoking addiction, it is the hundreds of other substances in tobacco that pose the most health risks to smokers. For example, carbon monoxide inhibits the absorption and distribution of oxygen in the body, and tar leaves a cancer-causing residue in the mouth, throat, trachea, and lungs.

Long-term effects: Cigarette smoke can cause cancer, heart and lung disease, ulcers, high blood pressure, difficulty breathing, yellow fingers and teeth, and premature wrinkling.

And bear in mind: Breathing second-hand smoke poses similar health risks to smoking cigarettes, although to a lesser extent.

Active antismoking organizations are lobbying for banning cigarette smoking in all public places, raising

WEIGHT GAIN AND STOPPING SMOKING— LUNG CANCER OR A SOFT BELLY?

The fear of weight gain is the most common reason that women put off quitting. Nicotine increases your metabolism and can act as an appetite suppressant, so in the first few weeks of quitting, the majority of smokers will gain some weight. Also, new ex-smokers often retain water, which can give the illusion of weight gain, but it is only temporary, like menstrual bloating. Another reason for gaining weight is that new ex-smokers may eat more to satisfy an oral craving. If you're used to smoking after meals, after quitting, that sense of closure disappears, and you may end up eating another dessert. Or having a cigarette with a friend may become having a snack.

However, not all quitters gain weight, and even if they do, it's usually only in the short term. To keep weight gain to a minimum, stock up on healthy, low-fat foods like carrots and other crunchy veggies, leave the table after meals, suck on a straw or chew sugar-free gum, and start an exercise program. (Not only does aerobic exercise quell hunger pangs, but it also boosts metabolism.)

cigarette taxes and stronger enforcement of the law prohibiting the sale of cigarettes to those under 18. They have also been publicizing the dangers of

HELPFUL HINTS FOR QUITTING SMOKING

"I'm really good at quitting smoking because I've done it so many times."

—OHIO WESLEYAN UNIVERSITY, '94

There are many different methods used to quit smoking: cold turkey, cutting down slowly (with or without the help of a commercial program, such as Cigarrest), hypnosis, acupuncture, therapy and support groups, nicotine replacements like "the patch" or nicotine gum, or chewing on a straw or "smoking" a fake cigarette. Whichever method you choose, here are some hints that might make quitting easier:

▲ Set a date for quitting. Be realistic about the date. If you smoke at work, try to quit while on vacation. Alert your family and friends. Prepare for that day: Make a dental appointment to get your teeth cleaned. Clean your house and do laundry to get rid of the smoke smell. Get rid of your ashtrays and every last cigarette. If you have a car, remove the cigarette lighter, and clean the ashtray and use it to hold change and toll tokens.

▲ Quit with a friend or a family member.

▲ To help alleviate withdrawal symptoms, drink a lot of fluids (but stay away from caffeine and alcohol, which can bring on cravings of the worst kind), snack on healthy food like carrot sticks, suck on hard candy or chew gum, soak in a hot tub or take a walk to relieve stress and tension, and be sure to get a good night's sleep.

▲ Write down a list of the reasons you want to quit. Include everything from cancer risk and bad breath to "My lover hates it" and "I want to work on an ash-free desk." Review your list at the beginning and end of each day, as well as anytime you feel the urge to smoke.

▲ Avoid situations that lead you to smoke. Spend time in no-smoking places—study in the library rather than in your room, go to a museum, eat in a no-smoking section.

▲ Find a support group, or put together your own.

Nicotine is considered to be one of the most highly addictive drugs around, so quitting smoking can be very difficult. Upon stopping, most people feel worse before feeling better. In the three or so days it takes your body to flush out the nicotine, you might feel irritable and tense, tired, or hungry, and might experience headaches, coughing, constipation, and temporary fluid retention. Remind yourself that these unpleasant initial withdrawal symptoms are temporary, and are signals that the body is beginning to recover from the effects of smoking. Within a week, your sense of smell and taste will improve, your breathing will become easier, your skin will clear up, your eyes will brighten, and your energy level will begin to increase.

Each day, 1,600 teen girls smoke for the 1st time.   Women

cigarettes using a variety of methods, and protesting the way in which the cigarette companies have targeted specific segments of the population (including women, children, and African-Americans) in their advertising. There are also a number of "smokers' rights" organizations that work to preserve individuals' rights to choose to smoke.

Special considerations for women: Smoking may speed up our bodies' estrogen metabolism, which can affect fertility, bring on earlier menopause, and increase breast cancer risk.

Smoking inhibits the absorption of calcium. Lack of sufficient calcium can contribute to osteoporosis.

Smoking while pregnant poses serious health risks for the baby, such as low birth weight and premature birth. Smokers on hormonal contraceptives (the Pill, Norplant, Depo-Provera) put themselves at triple the risk of heart attack and stroke.

Smoking-related cancer is the number one killer of women in the United States.

New studies indicate that nicotine affects women more strongly than men, making it more difficult for women to kick the habit.

The tobacco industry spends millions of dollars targeting young women. It seems to be working—women under 23 are now the fastest-growing group of new smokers, and since 1978 statistics have shown that more high school girls than boys smoke. The organization Women and Girls Against Tobacco Smoke is running a campaign against tobacco companies' manipulative advertising tactics.

Sedatives/Hypnotics

Barbiturates: barbs, downers, phenobarbitol, secobarbital (reds, red devils), pentobarbital (yellow jackets). Benzodiazepines: Valium, Librium, Dalmane, Tranxene. Methaqualone: Quaaludes, ludes

Description: Commonly called depressants and tranquilizers, sedatives/hypnotics fall into three categories: barbiturates, benzodiazepines, and methaqualone. These drugs are available by prescription (though they are also sold on the street), and are usually taken orally, though they may be injected.

How they work: Sedatives/hypnotics depress certain areas of the brain, causing the individual to feel calm and sleepy.

Under the influence: These drugs reduce anxiety and aid in sleep. In higher doses, they may act as painkillers or anticonvulsants. They cause drowsiness and calmness, though some may produce a brief period of excitement or euphoria before the sedating effect begins. Other effects can include nausea, confusion, impaired judgment, loss of coordination, slurred speech, and tremors. Overdose can cause stupor, coma, and death.

Long-term effects: Sedatives/hypnotics are highly addictive, and can

who smoke are twice as likely to get lung cancer as men who do.

produce severe withdrawal symptoms if use is abruptly discontinued. Symptoms of habituation can occur within a week or two with regular use. Long-term use can cause agitation, insomnia, depression, impaired memory, tremor, and loss of appetite, and often leads to taking more of the drugs to get rest.

And bear in mind: It is extremely dangerous to combine sedatives/hypnotics with alcohol.

Because they relax muscles, sedatives/hypnotics may be prescribed as antiseizure medication.

Intravenous Valium is often used as an anesthetic, especially for those allergic to narcotics.

Using, possessing, or selling sedatives that weren't prescribed to you is illegal.

Special considerations for women: Seventy-five percent of tranquilizer prescriptions are written for women. As a result, many more women than men are dependent on these drugs.

Women should avoid sedatives/hypnotics if they are pregnant or nursing.

LEARNING THE FACTS, WEIGHING THE RISKS

All of the drugs listed above have two things in common: They can be used to produce desirable effects, and they can pose serious risks. They may relieve pain, keep you awake, or help you lose weight or temporarily forget about problems, but they can also bring on depression, insomnia, addiction, or, in some cases, death. Responsible drug use, there-fore, means making an informed decision about whether the desirable effects of a drug outweigh the potential dangers.

Factors Determining How a Drug Affects You

෧෧෧

From published research, professional advice, word of mouth, old wives' tales, and personal experience, you may have a general idea about what is supposed to happen when you take specific drugs. However, a large number of factors determine which of the long list of "normal" reactions and side effects you will experience. The way a drug affects you (the positive, the negative, the dangerous, and the benign) varies not only among individuals, but with each use. A drug may "work" (do what it is intended and expected to do) for some people—such as provide pain relief or make them high—but not for others. And a drug may cause you no problems the first 10 times you use it, but then, without warning, send you staggering to the bathroom or the emergency room on the 11th try. Even the most common, extensively tested, FDA-approved drugs, though certainly more predictable than unregulated drugs, are still not completely consistent in their effects.

Each of the following factors will influence the way in which you react to a substance. For your safety, health, and well-being, consider these when making a decision whether or not to use a drug:

■ **Health:** Your general health—whether you're rested and strong or tired and run down—influences the

SOCIAL PRESSURE

"When keg parties are the biggest social event on campus and all your friends are drinking, it's kind of hard not to reach for a beer. It's almost a matter of holding something in your hand and taking sips. Although I suppose a glass of juice would work just as well, it's not the same as a beer, partially because the effects of the beer can make the conversation seem better than it is."

—*NORTHWESTERN UNIVERSITY, '97*

"I smoked pot and dropped acid a bunch of times in college. I didn't do it because I enjoyed it, but because it was just what you had to do to be a part of the social scene. It was horrible and I always felt like I was dying. . . . I've talked to a lot of my friends since then, and most of them weren't doing it because it was fun, but rather because it was what our group of friends were doing."

—*MACALESTER COLLEGE, '91*

Social pressure does affect our decision whether or not to use drugs, but it never happens as it does in the filmstrips the health teacher would show year after year: "C'mon, Sally, just one puff! We won't ever talk to you again if you don't! What are ya, scared?? Everyone's doin' it. Don't be a chicken!" *Beeeep.* The teacher advances to the next frame. Our heroine, with a strength and conviction never before evidenced, stands up straight, opens her mouth, and lets out a resounding "NO!" Music swells. The end.

Social pressure to use drugs *is* real, but most often it's more subtle than our friends threatening us. Just by being at a party where alcohol is the main focus, you may feel obliged to drink, even though no one is overtly forcing you; the pressure felt comes more from your own need to be included than it does from others trying to get you to participate. (This same pressure dynamic can exist around any drug or behavior—not just alcohol at college parties.) It's not too fun being the only sober person at a party; none of the jokes seem funny, and everyone else seems to be having a better time. There is a sort of bonding that goes on when people use drugs together. When playing drinking games and ordering rounds, you've got to drink in order to participate.

When you are in a communal setting it is often difficult to differentiate between what you want to do and what the group dynamic is suggesting you do. Try to pull back from the action a moment and decide what you really want. If you feel like going along, fine. But if you don't, that's OK, too. Realize that just because you choose not to do drugs doesn't mean you can't still go out, socialize, and have a good time. But next time you might want to choose an activity that doesn't "require" you to drink or do drugs.

sume 4 or more drinks in one sitting) than their peers not in college.

way a drug affects you. Further, certain drugs may cause problems if taken while you're sick with certain illnesses. For example, drinking while you have mono can be very dangerous.

■ **Family medical history:** Your family history may indicate that you may be predisposed to bad reactions to drugs or to problems that can be exacerbated by certain drugs.

■ **Emotional state/stress level:** How you are feeling can, depending on the drug, alter the way in which the drug affects you. In many cases drugs will intensify emotions you are already feeling. But they can also work as an emotional anesthetic.

■ **Weight:** In general, the less you weigh, the more a given quantity of a drug will affect you.

■ **How much you slept:** The less you sleep, the more your body is affected by everything, including any drugs you take.

■ **Food consumption:** Drugs affect us differently depending on how much or what we ate; for example, if you drink alcohol on an empty stomach, its effects will be quicker and stronger.

■ **Other medications you're taking:** Make sure that what you want to take is compatible to what's already in your bloodstream. (See "Two or More," page 295.)

Illegal drugs

☙☙☙

Not all the risks of drug use are physical. The choice to use illegal drugs brings with it additional risks.

■ Every state has different laws regulating drug use and possession. Break-

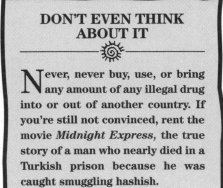

DON'T EVEN THINK ABOUT IT

Never, never buy, use, or bring any amount of any illegal drug into or out of another country. If you're still not convinced, rent the movie *Midnight Express*, the true story of a man who nearly died in a Turkish prison because he was caught smuggling hashish.

ing those laws can have serious consequences, from fines to jail.

■ The legal drinking age in the U.S. is 21. If you are underage, drinking, possessing, or trying to buy alcohol can result in everything from a slap on the wrist to a revoked driver's license, fines, and/or court-mandated community service.

■ Your school may also have its own set of rules regarding drug and underage alcohol use on campus. Breaking these may have serious consequences, such as suspension or expulsion.

■ Because illegal drugs aren't regulated, you can never be completely sure of what they contain and how they'll affect you. And the more you take of an unregulated drug, the more likely you are to be affected by any impurities in it.

SAFER DRUG USE

Although there are always some risks when taking any drug, whether it's aspirin or acid, there's no denying that some drugs carry higher risks than others. This said, here are some valuable tips to help keep you and your friends out of harm's way:

■ Watch out for your friends and ask them to watch out for you. If you're going to use drugs, it's best to do so around people you can trust.

■ If you are going out, make sure you have money on you and a safe means of transportation home. Even if you have a designated driver, you need to be responsible for yourself.

■ Know what you're taking. Even though it's impossible to ever really know what an illegal drug contains, you're better off avoiding drugs from sources you don't know and trust. (See "Learning the Facts, Weighing the Risks," page 308.)

■ Ask before you ingest. Don't take something without asking exactly what it contains just because everyone around you is doing it. You can't always tell what a drug's effects will be from its look, taste, and smell. (Grain alcohol, for example, has no particular taste but has a very high alcohol content. It can affect you quickly before you realize what has happened.)

■ Know what you can handle. Depending on your experience with the substance, you may know how it will affect you and in what ways. (If you've never used a drug before, unless it's prescribed, don't use as much as an experienced user would.) But remember, how a drug affects you can vary based on a number of factors, some of which you can control (e.g., how much you take) and others of which you can't (e.g., exactly what's in it).

■ Practice safer sex. If you're going to engage in sexual activities while under the influence (or anytime), protect yourself. Be prepared: Carry latex (condoms and/or dams). As a rule, it is better not to go home with someone when you are plastered out of your mind. But then, if you *are* plastered out of your mind, it can be difficult to make coherent decisions. You may want to ask a friend to watch out for you if you're planning a particularly wild night out.

■ Don't share needles. Drugs that are injected pose the risk of HIV transmission when unclean needles are used. If you are injecting drugs, make sure to use clean needles. (See "STDs, HIV, and AIDS," page 369, and "Cleaning Needles," page 304.)

■ Be smart. Don't do drugs when you are responsible for other people (e.g., baby-sitting or driving everyone home after the party).

■ Be moderate. Moderation is a key element of responsible drug use. Repeated use of certain drugs causes your body to build up tolerance to some or all of the drug's effects. This increased tolerance or resistance causes you to need greater amounts of a drug to get the same effect. As you take more of the drug you increase your chance of running into problems—everything from being affected by the impurities in the drug to using

SOME WAYS TO AVOID DRIVING
UNDER THE INFLUENCE

We all know that driving under the influence is a stupid thing to do. But what do we do when it seems like a driver who's been doing drugs is your only way home? And what if that driver is you? (Remember that although we usually think that driving under the influence refers to driving under the influence of alcohol, it refers to driving under the influence of any drug that impairs your sense of judgment, reflexes, and coordination, including a number of prescription drugs.) If you or someone else is going to be driving under the influence, it might not seem like an emergency at the time, but it's important to realize that it is.

▲ Call someone to drive you home. Always try to keep some money on you for emergencies, but otherwise scrounge up the appropriate change or call collect. It's OK to wake up friends or family when the alternative is driving under the influence.

▲ Walk home with buddies or take public transportation. If you came by car, leave it where it is. If it's not in a safe place, ask someone else to put it in a lot or another safe place and pick it up later.

▲ Call a taxi. If you don't have cash, ask the driver to stop at an ATM machine or to wait for you outside your destination while you get money.

▲ Always have one or two designated drivers (a person who agrees not to drink or do drugs) so that there is always someone sober to drive.

▲ If you don't have a designated driver, or know that everyone is going to be doing drugs, plan on taking a cab or public transportation together. Check schedules ahead of time to make sure that you don't get stuck.

▲ In many communities there are car services or "safe ride" organizations that give free rides home to anyone in need. Find out about one in your community and put the number in your wallet. You can get information through campus/community drug and alcohol awareness organizations; local BACCHUS, SADD, or MADD chapters (see page 322 and the Resources at the end of this chapter); the department of public safety; or campus security.

▲ Call your local police station. They should be able to make a referral or offer some help.

▲ It can be very difficult to tell someone, especially someone who is drunk, that you don't think that they should drive, or that you aren't going to go with them. Remember that it is not your responsibility or obligation to make them feel good or to be "nice." Tell them that you are getting home another way and that you think they should do the same. If the person is clearly incapacitated, try taking away their car keys or somehow preventing them from driving.

▲ These same guidelines apply if you are operating any machinery that might hurt you (or someone else) or driving any vehicle, including a bike.

too much of it, which may cause an overdose.

■ Pace yourself. If you are drinking, intersperse your drinks with something nonalcoholic to lessen the potency of the alcohol. Spread your drinking out over a period of time. And remember that mixing alcohol with other drugs can be fatal.

■ It is generally a good idea to eat foods high in carbohydrates and/or protein before you drink or do drugs.

■ If you don't want to participate and you expect that you may be pressured, think of something snappy to say in advance so you'll be prepared when you are offered drugs. By the same token, don't force drugs or drinks on people. Be sensitive to people who don't want to do drugs, and try to make them feel comfortable with their decision.

■ Whether drugs are in the picture or not, it's a good idea for you to let people know where you are going. If possible, tell someone the name(s) of who you are going out with and where you are headed.

■ Learn the consequences of being caught by your school and state using or possessing any drugs that you choose to do.

Dealing with Emergencies

Because drug use poses risks, it brings with it responsibilities. You should be prepared to deal with emergencies should they arise. Rule number one is to think fast (which, needless to say, can be difficult if you are under the influence).

Get Immediate Help if

■ The person can't be aroused by shaking or shouting.

■ The person's breathing is shallow and irregular (less than eight breaths per minute).

■ The person drank alcohol in combination with sedatives, tranquilizers, or antihistamines.

■ The person has sustained a blow to the head or an injury that is causing bleeding.

■ The person drank a large amount of alcohol in a short period of time and then collapsed.

If the Person Is Very Drunk or High or Passed Out

■ Check regularly for breathing and consciousness. Roommates and friends should arrange to stay near the person until he seems to be out of danger. It's best if two people can stay, in case one has to get help. Make sure the person is lying on his side, with knees bent. This position should prevent choking should the person vomit.

■ If the person vomits, stay with her to make certain that the vomit is not swallowed or breathed in.

■ Get help immediately if the person has difficulty expelling vomit or gags on it.

■ Don't give the person any food, drink, or medication. Doing so might induce vomiting.

■ Don't try to walk or otherwise exercise the person.

■ Don't give the person a cold shower; the shock may cause him to pass out.

If the Person Is Aggressive When Under the Influence of a Drug

■ Your biggest responsibility is to protect yourself and others from physical harm.

■ Approach the person cautiously and keep your distance.

■ Explain anything you intend to do before you do it. Speak in a reassuring but firm manner.

■ Don't laugh at, ridicule, provoke, threaten, or argue with the person.

■ Don't attempt to restrain the person.

■ If the person becomes uncontrollable, violent, or in need of medical attention, call campus security or your local police station.

If You Are Drunk or Have a Hangover

■ Drink lots of water, take a multivitamin (one that includes B vitamins, potassium, and vitamin C), take an analgesic, drink a glass of orange juice. A good rule of thumb is to have as many glasses of water as you had drinks.

■ Rest and sleep it off.

■ A little baking soda, an antacid, Pepto-Bismol, and/or dry toast or crackers can help soothe the day-after tummy hell.

■ Though a little caffeine can help ease

a hangover and pep you up a bit, too much can dehydrate you and make your hangover worse.

WHAT CONSTITUTES A DRUG PROBLEM?

I t is not always easy to tell when drug use becomes a drug problem. The signs are often not clear, and it can be a difficult thing to admit. The warning signs generally appear slowly and over a long period of time, and it may be easier to ignore them than to face the possibility that you need help. Therefore, if you are using drugs, it's important to be aware of some of the common signs and symptoms that will help you recognize and admit problems.

The terms "substance abuse" and "addiction" are often used interchangeably; however, you can abuse a drug without being addicted to it. Having a substance abuse problem can

"I was the last one to see my drinking problem. A bunch of my friends confronted me on it, and instead of thinking about what they were saying and that they were trying to help, I got really angry at them and told them to stop meddling in my life. It wasn't until I broke my leg while on a drinking binge that I was able to start to recognize my problem and get some help."

—EMORY UNIVERSITY, '93

☀ Hangovers are caused not only by alcohol but by "congeners," which

"There's a real difference between trying a drug or using a drug occasionally and actually abusing a drug. But the simplistic 'Just say no' mentality forgets that. How many of those Washington officials don't drink at dinner parties and cocktail parties and official brouhahas? Aren't they using drugs? It is possible to use some drugs and not ruin your life."

—CARLETON COLLEGE, '97

simply mean that you use a drug or drugs in unhealthy ways. Sometimes it is not even the substances themselves that are the problem, but rather how you are using them and how you are affected by that use.

Addiction refers to a physical and/or psychological dependency on drugs that disrupts aspects of your life. Dependence on both the emotional and physical effects of a drug can grow over time—you come to need it to function normally (meaning you can't face the day, wake up, and/or get to sleep without it). Both emotional and physical dependence on a drug make it difficult for one to "just stop," and some drugs can cause extreme withdrawal symptoms when you try to quit abruptly.

Naturally, there are varying levels of drug problems and dependency. Not all drug use is inherently a problem, but if you suspect that yours or someone else's is, trust your instincts and address it. In many cases changing or stopping habits you have developed around drug use will require the help of others. (See "Getting Help," on the next page.)

Signs of a Drug Problem

ഇஇஇ

When you can't control your drug use or when using drugs becomes the focus of your time and energy, you have developed a problem. "Needing" a drag of a cigarette, a line of coke, or a stiff drink can be the first warning sign. Below is a list of other red flags. If you (or someone you know) is exhibiting any or all of them, you (or s/he) may have a drug problem. (See "A Friend in Need," page 327, and the Resources at the end of this chapter.)

Seek Help When Drugs . . .

■ Adversely affect daily life and personal well-being (e.g., cause hangovers, memory loss, blackouts).

■ Cause problems with or deterioration of communication with family, friends, professors, and/or employers.

■ Are used alone, rather than or in addition to socially.

■ Are used increasingly frequently and/or the amount of the drug that's used increases.

■ Cause changes in mood or behavior, or in eating, personal hygiene, and/or sleeping habits.

An Individual May Have a Problem When She . . .

■ Seeks new sources for the drug because the person who supplied it (bartender, doctor, friend) refuses to continue providing it.

■ Exhibits defensive behavior when drug use is questioned or mentioned.

■ Is embarrassed by or afraid of her behavior when under the influence.

■ Uses drugs in response to pressure, anxiety, depression, stress, tension.

■ Takes drugs more often than recommended by her doctor.

■ Mixes different drugs, using one drug to replace an addiction to another or to alleviate the negative effects of another drug.

■ Uses drugs regularly to aid in sleep and/or to get going in the morning.

■ Finds herself in situations that would not be likely to occur if she were sober.

■ Feels bored, tense, or upset when not using the substance.

■ Is depressed, lethargic, and/or withdrawn.

■ Frequently borrows money for drugs or has spent significant amounts of money on drugs.

GETTING HELP

For some people, dealing with a drug problem may mean simply regulating their use of the drug(s). For others, though, it may mean swearing off the drug(s) forever. Regardless of what category you fall into, it could be very helpful, and possibly essential, to have one or more forms of support.

Seeking help is an important first step in addressing drug dependency. However, finding the right help can be a daunting task; it isn't always easy to ask questions about treatment strategies, and often each program touts itself as "the only way." In reality, women have a plethora of options for dealing with drug problems, and you should be aware of all the choices available to you. Remember that every program has proven useful to some people and none have proven useful to all people. Therefore, if one approach does not work for you, or you feel uncomfortable with a certain group's ideology or methods, try not too feel discouraged—push yourself to seek alternatives. Many people find that one program doesn't give them all they need, and find it beneficial to use it in conjunction with another method.

Getting Help on Campus

಄಄಄

You may want to take advantage of one or several of the following:

Health/mental health services: Campus health/mental health services may be a good place to start. If no adequate treatment is available, they should be able to provide you with a listing of local organizations and referrals. (*Note:* Some schools may be less helpful and supportive than others,

"I was in a co-op where smoking pot was a major activity, and I realized I had to move out of my house and stop hanging out with my best friends because I needed to cut down. When I finally got up the courage to tell my friends, they got really defensive at first, and saw it as a critique of them. One even said that I was getting all high and mighty on myself and who was I to judge what they were doing. After they realized it was about me and not about them, they totally understood and stopped smoking so much when I was around."

—OBERLIN COLLEGE, '92

and some may have policies that require them to inform other members of the school administration about your problem. Inquire about confidentiality before you make an appointment. There may also be a local community health or crisis center where you can talk to a counselor or doctor about yourself or a friend. Some schools have support groups (including 12 Step programs) on campus.

Friends: They can obtain information for you about where to get help, accompany you to your first meeting, doctor's appointment, or therapy session, offer support, help keep you afloat while you are trying to deal with your issues, talk with you, join you in drug-free activities, distract you, and help you enjoy life.

Dorm advisors/RAs: They may be able to offer help and suggestions of specific places to call. Conversations with an RA may not always be confidential, so if you're worried about confidentiality, ask about it before you start the conversation. (This can be as simple as saying, "Can I talk to you confidentially?")

Hotlines: Hotline counselors are available to talk with you anonymously and give advice and referrals.

Women's centers: They may be able to offer referrals and/or support groups.

The housing office/deans: The housing office may be able to help you find a living space that is designated as alcohol-free or is at least supportive of your situation and needs.

Treatment Options

ⓥⓐⓥ

"If our society could stop stigmatizing and blaming people who get treatment for their drug problems, it would be so much easier to get help.... People wouldn't wait until after they'd hit rock bottom."

—COLORADO COLLEGE, '95

There are numerous ways to treat drug problems. Some of the options listed below will suit certain women's needs better than others.

Individual therapy/psychiatry: Therapy can help you gain perspective on your life through speaking with a trained professional. It may be an essential part of dealing with a drug

make up less than ¼ of all the patients in public treatment programs. ☀

problem, because drug abuse is almost always related to other issues; the process of treating a drug problem will often reveal concerns that have been masked by drug use, and quitting a drug often raises new issues.

When choosing a therapist, look for one with experience in treating substance abuse problems. If the drug has serious physical withdrawal symptoms, it may be helpful to work with a doctor or someone else who can address the issues raised by your physical addiction. As always, you need to find someone with whom you feel comfortable and can speak with openly. If you are working with a professional off campus, confidentiality is guaranteed. (For more detailed information, see "More Than Just the Blues," page 247.)

"Therapy is really helping me deal with all the issues that drinking allowed me to avoid thinking about, but I also go to AA for advice, support, and meeting other sober people my age. Getting and staying drug-free is not easy—I try to find help and support in as many ways as I can."

—COLLEGE OF THE HOLY CROSS, '95

Support groups: Joining a support group is one of the most effective ways to deal with a drug problem. Support groups can help you realize that others have many of the same problems you have, and can help you to find solutions while being supported by others who understand your situation. Some campuses and almost all communities have support groups that deal with the issues and problems related to alcohol and other drug use.

Step programs: Step programs are support groups with clearly defined philosophies about the means to recovery. These programs have developed steps that each member uses as a guide throughout the recovery process. Most step programs are modeled, at least in part, after the 12 Step (Anonymous) programs.

12 Step programs: The 12 Step (Anonymous) programs are the most prevalent step programs in the country. They maintain that all forms of substance abuse follow a pattern, and that the 12 Steps are an effective means to recovery for all people, regardless of gender, race, age, class, sexual orientation, and religion. Essentially, 12 Step programs subordinate difference, in an attempt to focus on similarities and unity. Although this is extremely important in creating support and acceptance between group members it doesn't always address the ways in which personal issues affect substance abuse and recovery.

All 12 Step programs are free and open to the public, and their philosophy is nonpolitical and nonsectarian. They maintain anonymity by using only first names, and they require that the content of all meetings be kept confidential. Groups can generally be found throughout the country, and meetings are held frequently. Each member is paired with a sponsor (a group member who has been with the program for a longer time) upon whom s/he can call for support. Serving as a sponsor is considered to be an integral aspect of recovery.

The 12 Step philosophy was initially conceived of for men and is based on Christian concepts of God

※ 9 months of treatment for a drug-dependent woman costs about $5,000;

"The AA group in my hometown was really great. When I went off to school I had to deal with all the pressure and anxiety that everyone feels, plus I had to deal with not being able to go to my local AA for support. The AA near school was completely different from what I was accustomed to: It was almost all men my father's age, I was one of only two black people, and the new group emphasized the religious aspects of AA much more than I could deal with. Luckily, I found out about a women's group sponsored by health services. I'm still partial to my hometown AA, but the school group is really good, too."

—UNIVERSITY OF CALIFORNIA
AT BERKELEY, '96

and the individual, which can raise issues for women and those who have non-Christian religious beliefs and/or conceptions of the world. The Anonymous programs have started to recognize this problem, and some communities offer specialized meetings and materials for women, gays and lesbians, Jews, and people of color, among others. (See the Resources at the end of the chapter for 12 Step contact information.)

Women's groups: Studies indicate that many women (although certainly not all) who are dealing with drug problems have problems with low self-esteem. They feel inadequate, are

questioning their identity or sexuality, have body image issues or mental health disorders, are in abusive relationships, and/or feel like they have little control over their lives. Some critiques of 12 Step programs suggest that they do not address the complex issues of women's drug use and self-esteem adequately. Alternative programs and approaches exist, as do step programs based on different philosophies. One such program is Women for Sobriety, which was created by a woman for women. Using 13 "Statements of Acceptance," the program helps women recover from substance abuse by encouraging them to take responsibility for the abuse and gain control over their lives, which in turn increases their self-esteem. Their philosophy is in contrast to the 12 Step philosophy, in which members recognize their powerlessness over alcohol (or whatever) and look to a higher power to give them strength in changing their lives.

Medical treatment: Detoxification (aka detox)—ridding your system of the drug—is an essential stage in almost all medical treatment programs. The physical effects of withdrawal can require full-time care in a hospital or an inpatient detox facility. In some cases, the detox process is aided by treatment with another chemical, such as methadone in the case of heroin addiction. At the very least, withdrawal requires outpatient care by a doctor or an addiction specialist. Determining which treatment is most effective will depend on the type of addiction, any complications caused by past drug use, and your physical condition.

Even if you are still using drugs and therefore are not suffering from

20 days of medical care for a drug-exposed baby costs about $30,000.

withdrawal, it is important to get a complete physical examination to assess the effects the drugs have had on your body. Find a doctor with whom you can talk openly about your past and current drug use.

Most doctors view drug abuse as an illness that can be treated only with professional help. This is an appropriate outlook and can be useful when you are seeking support. Friends, family, and employers are often more understanding when they are able to see problems with drug use as a disease rather than a character flaw.

If your drug use has put your life or the lives of others in imminent danger, it is vital that you be admitted to an inpatient facility. This type of treatment center may also be recommended in cases where the effects of withdrawal pose serious medical risks. In addition to offering medical treatment, most inpatient facilities offer support groups and individual therapy. The strength of these programs is also their weakness: By taking you out of your environment, they are often very successful in ending the drug use, yet when the program is over it might be difficult for you to maintain your sobriety.

Holistic healing approaches: "Holistic" literally means "relating to the whole," and holistic healing approaches acknowledge the interrelationship between the emotional and the physical. By focusing on how the mind affects the body (e.g., stress can make our muscles tighten or cause a host of other physical effects), many people are able to uncover the reasons why they were using the drug in the first place. By doing exercises that address this mind-body connection, they are able to relieve the stresses and cope with the difficulties inherent in changing patterns of drug use. Holistic approaches are used alone or in conjunction with other forms of treatment to deal with drug problems. Some of these methods include martial arts, massage therapy, art therapy, yoga, acupuncture, and acupressure.

"When I stopped drinking I had these terrible pains in my stomach. At first I was afraid that I did something to my liver, but then I found out that the drinking hadn't caused the pains but it had stopped me from feeling them. They were probably why I was drinking so much to begin with. Through massage the physical feelings and pains started to go away and I didn't even feel the need for alcohol anymore."

—NORTHEASTERN UNIVERSITY,
MA CANDIDATE, 1998

"I began doing yoga and martial arts my junior year of college after I faced the fact that I was an addict. I started using coke when I was in high school to numb everything, and when I finally stopped using coke I had to figure out a way to deal with the pain and issues that came up then.... I find that doing yoga and t'ai chi really helps me to focus my energy and feel strong."

—DIABLO VALLEY COMMUNITY COLLEGE, '95

HELPING A FRIEND WITH A DRUG OR ALCOHOL PROBLEM

Having a friend with a drug or alcohol problem can make you feel powerless, but there are some things you can do to help. The following are adapted from the BACCHUS and GAMMA Peer Education Network guidelines for helping a friend with an alcohol problem. BACCHUS is an intercollegiate group that promotes responsible alcohol use. The guidelines can also apply if your friend has a problem with another drug.

1. Decide to do something. Doing nothing doesn't help your friend, and your worry and concern will grow.

2. Talk with your friend. Ask your friend "What's going on?" or other nonthreatening questions. Don't attack, but make sure your friend sees what you see and knows that you've been affected as well.

3. Be prepared for any number of responses. Stay calm and don't take anything personally.

4. If your friend responds negatively, try again after the next instance of abusive behavior.

5. If your friend responds positively, work with him or her to develop a plan to get help and support. Don't become a caretaker; just be a supportive friend.

6. If your friend's drinking habits do not change, set some limits for yourself. Don't spend time with your friend when s/he is drunk, and don't ever cover up for your friend.

7. Get the support you need. This is a tough thing to go through. You need to express your concerns and frustrations to someone else.

8. Know when to quit. If talking to your friend doesn't work, you may need to remove yourself from the situation. Remember that it was your friend's drinking or drug use that ended the relationship, not you. You shouldn't feel guilty. You have to take care of yourself.

If you are in a relationship with someone who has a drug problem (parent, friend, sibling, lover, etc.), there are support groups to help you confront the ways in which this drug use has affected your life and the issues it has raised. See the Resources at the end of this chapter for organizations that may be of help.

⊚⊚⊚

For information on over-the-counter drugs and prescription drugs not covered in this chapter, see "Common Medicines," page 227. For information on diet pills, see page 200.

Half of women in alcohol treatment programs are under 35. ☀

ACTIVIST IDEAS

■ Work to put the curb on drunk driving by encouraging designated driver programs, getting local restaurants and bars to serve free nonalcoholic drinks to designated drivers, establishing "safe ride" programs in your communities (safe rides are free rides that people can call anytime they are in need of a safe way home), disseminating information about alternative ride sources (campus shuttle, security, taxis, public transportation, etc.), posting information about the drunk driving laws in your state, making sure that nonalcoholic beverages/nondrug options are available and acceptable choices at all parties, helping people too inebriated to drive find a way home or a place to stay, and not letting friends drive drunk.

■ Work to increase the number of studies that explore issues around women's drug use. Hold letter writing campaigns that target not only the scientific and medical organizations doing the research but their funding sources as well.

■ Raise awareness about women's substance use and abuse on your campus by sponsoring panel discussions or information sessions with medical/psychiatric professionals (from campus health services or your local community), and making information about substance abuse support services for women accessible.

CAMPUS HIGHLIGHT

BACCHUS and GAMMA Peer Education Network is a student alcohol awareness and health education program with more than 15,000 members and chapters on over 550 college campuses across the country. Through programs and initiatives that range from the serious to the outrageous, BACCHUS chapters promote responsible and informed decision making about drinking and other campus health issues. Chapter size, focus, and makeup varies from campus to campus. If you would like to start a BACCHUS chapter on your campus, or hook your peer-education programs into the BACCHUS network, write to P.O. Box 100430, Denver, CO 80250-0430, or call (303) 871-3068.

RESOURCES

Information, Education, and Referrals

NATIONAL CLEARINGHOUSE FOR ALCOHOL AND DRUG INFORMATION
P.O. BOX 2343
ROCKVILLE, MD 20847-2345
(800) 729-6686
TTY/TDD: (800) 487-4889
Provides information and answers questions about drugs, the affects of drugs, and drug treatment. Publishes free materials and fact sheets, including specific information about women and drugs, available upon request.

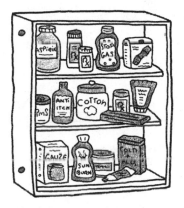

AMERICAN COUNCIL FOR DRUG EDUCATION
136 EAST 64TH STREET
NEW YORK, NY 10021
(212) 758-8060
Provides information about drugs and drug education. Publishes numerous materials.

INSTITUTE ON BLACK CHEMICAL ABUSE RESOURCE CENTER
2616 NICOLLET AVENUE SOUTH
MINNEAPOLIS, MN 55408
(612) 871-7878
Provides information for community-based organizations that treat chemical dependency, with attention to the particular needs and interests of African-Americans. Makes referrals to local organizations that address the specific needs of drug-dependent African-Americans.

COCAINE ABUSE HOTLINE
(800) 262-2463 [COCAINE]
Provides information about cocaine and the effects of its use. Makes referrals to local drug treatment organizations. Offers phone crisis counseling. Publishes numerous materials, available upon request.

INFORMATION CENTER ON SUBSTANCE ABUSE PREVENTION FOR PERSONS WITH DISABILITIES
1331 F STREET NW, SUITE 800
WASHINGTON, DC 20004
(202) 783-2900
Provides information and answers questions about substance abuse and disabilities. Provides educational materials to assist in substance abuse prevention. Makes referrals to local organizations that address the needs of disabled persons.

ALCOHOL AND DRUG HELPLINE
(800) 821-4357
Provides referrals to local treatment centers.

THE CENTER FOR SUBSTANCE ABUSE DRUG ABUSE INFORMATION AND TREATMENT REFERRAL HOTLINE
(800) 662-4357 [HELP]
SPANISH: (800) 662-9832 [66-AYUDA]
TTY/TDD: (800) 228-0427
Provides information and answers questions about drugs and their effects. Makes referrals to local treatment centers. Pub-

lishes numerous materials, available upon request.

AMERICAN COUNCIL ON ALCOHOLISM
2522 ST. PAUL STREET
BALTIMORE, MD 21218
(800) 527-5344
(410) 889-0100

Provides information on alcoholism prevention programs for adults and children. Offers phone counseling. Makes referrals to local treatment programs.

NATIONAL COUNCIL ON ALCOHOLISM AND DRUG DEPENDENCE, INC.
12 WEST 21ST STREET
NEW YORK, NY 10010
(800) 622-2255 [NCA-CALL]
(212) 206-6770
AND
1511 K STREET NW
WASHINGTON, DC 20005
(202) 737-8122

Organizes political action/advocacy work to raise awareness about the needs of alcoholics and other drug-dependent persons and their families. Works with national organizations to increase the attention given to alcohol and other drug issues in their agendas. Provides information about drugs and drug use, as well as developing prevention and education materials. Makes

referrals to local organizations providing treatment.

Organizations Offering Local Mutual-Support Groups

WOMEN FOR SOBRIETY
P.O. BOX 618
QUAKERTOWN, PA 18951
(215) 536-8026

Makes referrals to local Women for Sobriety mutual-support groups, for women dealing with all types of substance dependency. Publishes numerous materials for women who are drug-dependent, addressing such topics as depression and self-esteem; available upon request.

ALCOHOLICS ANONYMOUS (AA) WORLD SERVICES
475 RIVERSIDE DRIVE
NEW YORK, NY 10115
(212) 870-3400

Makes referrals to local groups. Ask specifically about women's groups within AA; there are many women's groups that have formed out of local chapters. Provides information about alcoholism.

COCAINE ANONYMOUS (CA)
6125 WASHINGTON BOULEVARD, SUITE 202
LOS ANGELES, CA 90230
(800) 347-8998

Makes referrals to local support groups for users of cocaine. Provides information about cocaine and related drugs and their effects. Publishes numerous materials. Sends information upon request.

SECULAR ORGANIZATIONS FOR SOBRIETY (SAVE OUR SELVES)
5521 GROSVENOR BOULEVARD
LOS ANGELES, CA 90034
(818) 964-5054

Makes referrals to local SOS mutual-support groups for people dealing with substance dependency.

☀ 20-40% of the hospital beds in the U.S. are occupied by people

RATIONAL RECOVERY
P.O. BOX 800
LOTUS, CA 95651
(916) 621-4374
Makes referrals to local Rational Recovery mutual-support groups for people dealing with substance dependency.

For Friends and Families of Those With Drug Problems

AL-ANON FAMILY GROUP HEADQUARTERS, INC.
P.O. BOX 862
MIDTOWN STATION
NEW YORK, NY 10018-0862
(800) 356-9996
FAX: (212) 869-3757
Makes referrals to local self-help groups for people who have family members and close friends who are drug-dependent. Provides information and answers questions about the effects of drug dependency on friends and family members.

CO-DEPENDENTS ANONYMOUS (CODA)
P.O. BOX 3577
PHOENIX, AZ 85067-3577
(602) 277-7991
Makes referrals to local support groups providing counseling.

NATIONAL ASSOCIATION FOR CHILDREN OF ALCOHOLICS (NACOA)
11426 ROCKVILLE PIKE, SUITE 100
ROCKVILLE, MD 20852
(301) 468-0985
Provides information, including facts and statistics about children of alcoholics. Organizes political action/advocacy work to increase public awareness about the issues and problems faced by children of alcoholics. Makes referrals to local organizations and support groups for children of alcoholics. Publishes numerous materials, including the *NACoA Network* newsletter.

Additional self-help groups exist for friends and family members of those who are dependent on drugs other than or in addition to alcohol. The groups listed above should be able to provide you with appropriate referrals.

Political Action, Advocacy, and Education

THE DRUG POLICY FOUNDATION
4455 CONNECTICUT AVENUE NW, SUITE B-500
WASHINGTON, DC 20008-2302
(202) 537-5005
FAX: (202) 537-3007
Conducts research about drugs and drug policies. Organizes political action/advocacy work to reform drug policies.

STUDENTS AGAINST DRIVING DRUNK (SADD)
255 MAIN STREET
MARLBOROUGH, MA 01752
(508) 481-3568
Organizes political action/advice and educational programs to raise awareness about drunk driving and to promote its prevention. Provides information and advice about how to organize prevention programs on campus.

MOTHERS AGAINST DRUNK DRIVING (MADD)
511 EAST JOHN CARPENTER FREEWAY, SUITE 700
IRVING, TX 75062
(800) 438-6233
Works to end drunk driving. Supports victims of drunk driving.

NATIONAL ORGANIZATION FOR THE REFORM OF MARIJUANA LAWS
1001 CONNECTICUT AVENUE NW, SUITE 1010
WASHINGTON, DC 20036
(202) 483-5500
Organizes political action/advocacy work to promote the reform of laws prohibiting sale and possession of marijuana. Publishes

who are suffering from complications related to alcohol abuse.

numerous materials about marijuana and its effects. Information available upon request.

UP FRONT DRUG INFORMATION CENTER
5701 BISCAYNE BOULEVARD
MIAMI, FL 33137
(305) 757-2566
Provides information about drugs, the effects of drugs, and the relationship between drugs and society. Conducts research about drugs and drug policy. Publishes numerous materials, available upon request.

Further Reading

෨෨෨

Practical Approaches in the Treatment of Women Who Abuse Alcohol and Other Drugs (U.S. Department of Health and Human Services, 1994).

Double Bind: Women Affected by Alcohol and Other Drugs, Dorothy Broom, ed. (Allen & Lewis, 1994).

Gender, Drink and Drugs, Maryon McDonald, ed. (Oxford University Press, 1994).

Changing the Research Story: Proceedings of the Women and Drugs Research Workshop, Jill Astbury, Lisa Frank, and Christine Burrows, eds. (The Institute, 1991).

Alcohol and Drugs Are Women's Issues, Paula Roth, ed. (Women's Action Alliance, 1991).

Women and Drugs: Getting Hooked, Getting Clean, Emanuel Peluso and Lucy Silvay Peluso (CompCare Publishers, 1988).

Women and Drugs: A New Era for Research, Barbara A. Ray and Monique C. Braude, eds. (U.S. Department of Health and Human Services, 1986).

Nice Girls Don't Drink: Stories of Recovery, Sarah Hafner (Bergin and Garvey, 1992).

The Recovery Book, Arlene Eisenberg, Howard Eisenberg, and Al J. Mooney (Workman, 1992).

The Recovery Resources Book, Barbara Yoder (Fireside, 1990).

A Friend in Need

Helping Others Through Rough Times

You break up with your boyfriend and you're absolutely sure you'll never fall in love again. You botch your intro psych exam and you know you won't ever find a job after graduation. You aren't accepted into the sorority of your choice and you're considering dropping out of school. It feels like the end of the world. We've all been in these or similar situations, so we know how to be supportive when our friends are floating in this boat. But when problems go beyond the small crises (which never feel small at the time), we may be at a loss as to how to help. Substance abuse and dependency, eating disorders, and depression are just a few of the problems that can rear their ugly heads in college. The components of helping someone navigate through the manageable and the more tricky waters are basically the same: Showing that you care and trying to find a way to give her what she needs. But when you're frustrated with, fearful for, and alienated from your friend because of her behavior, it can be harder to give support and easier to get hurt and overwhelmed in the process of trying.

WOMEN AS CAREGIVERS

Women, as a group, tend to spend a lot of time helping others. (And we do a darn good job, if we do say so ourselves.) Many of us have a knack for figuring out what to say and do on the fly, and how to console friends when they're blue, confused, and frustrated. Faster than you can say pop psychology, we can transform ourselves into Ann Landers/Dr. Joyce Brothers/Florence Nightingale/Lucy Van Pelt, ready to give a hug, proofread a thorny term

"If you look around, it's women who are doing the caretaking. And I'm not just talking about taking care of kids. If you want to talk to someone who will listen, who's less likely to judge you, who will try and figure out what you need, not give some pat solution, you go to a girlfriend. . . . These days being in a support position is much less valued than being in charge, but I don't think it's valid. Without someone there to give emotional support, nothing could ever get done."

—University of North Carolina at Chapel Hill, '96

paper, lend a shoulder and an ear, confirm that yes, the ex-boyfriend *is* a jerk, and help think through difficult dilemmas. Is it that we've been blessed with more than a double helix's worth of those prized "nurturing, always being there" genes? Possibly. But more likely we have, for the most part, grown up seeing women playing the role of listener, caregiver, and emotional problem solver, and have followed suit.

College is a time when we have a chance to hone our skills at helping others. After all, these years are often tumultuous. We leave a community in which we may have spent our whole life (or a significant portion thereof) for a new home with new people who don't know us from Eve. We have not only the opportunity but in some cases also the mandate to reinvent ourselves and make some major life decisions. In both our academic and social lives

we're likely to be confronting ideas that may challenge many of our assumptions. Combine this with living on top of hundreds or thousands of other people going through similar transitions, and it's likely that if you're not having a crisis, someone nearby is.

The reality is, it's impossible to hide problems behind closed doors when 3 people are sharing a bedroom and 30 people are sharing a bathroom. After a grueling day of fighting with her lab partner, getting a D on her midterm, and being cut from the varsity soccer team, your roommate has nowhere to go but to the space you share. Her bad mood resulting from those problems can be tough, but chances are she'll get over it pretty quickly. If she has a substance abuse problem, eating disorder, or is in a depression, however, there is almost no way to remain distanced from her misery, and it's unlikely that the problem will go away all by itself in a couple of days.

In a nutshell, college often requires us to help friends who are dealing with issues that can't be taken care of by a talk and a hug. We may realize we can't solve their problems ourselves (especially if a friend doesn't

think anything is wrong), but we don't know who or what else to turn to. What follows is a guide to how to be a good friend when the going gets tough. Remember, above all, that your goal isn't to become your friend's caretaker. Your mission is to help your friend help herself.

HELPING A FRIEND WHO WANTS HELP

If your friend recognizes she has a problem, you are both lucky, as that is the first step toward recovery. Maybe she has a drinking problem, a miserable family situation, or a case of chronic procrastination that has snowballed into an academic nightmare. She might be, as they say, on the verge of a nervous breakdown, an umbrella term that refers to anything from incapacitating depression to incapacitating crying jags (the key word being incapacitating). Or she might be the survivor of a violent crime or past or present abuse. Whatever the problem, she knows that it's interfering with her life and she needs help.

As obvious as it may sound, showing and telling her that you care is one of the most important things that you can do for her right now. She may be frightened that if others know that everything in her life isn't rosy, she won't be loved anymore. She may fear that you will be disgusted with, label, judge, or stop trusting and/or respecting her. Therefore, it is crucial to let her know that this isn't how you feel at all.

The next thing you may want to do is shine some light on the situation, literally and figuratively. Turn on a lamp, open the shades, go outside and talk in the sun. Get a pen and paper to write down a list of "where to go from here." Everything seems more manageable when written out in the light of day. If your friend is depressed, for instance, the best support you can give is to help her see the situation clearly and figure out a plan of action: "It seems like you're really blue; you might even be in a depression. Talking with a doctor or a counselor could help." The combination of your being outside of the situation yet knowing your friend and having some insight into how she thinks puts you in a unique position to help her. You can probably offer a perspective that is both more realistic than hers and still appropriate to her personally. You might intuit, for instance, that she would be more comfortable going to a

BE REALISTIC

When you're helping someone, you need to be realistic about what you can and can't accomplish. You *can* offer support, help her find information she needs, offer distractions when appropriate, and listen. You *can't* solve the problem, make it go away, force her to get help, or make others understand. You also can't take responsibility for the problem. You may be a powerful person, but you certainly don't have the ability to have single-handedly caused a depression, a drinking or drug problem, an eating disorder, or any other serious problem.

private doctor than through the campus counseling services. And because she trusts you, she's apt to listen.

"I remember when I was little being amazed at how my mother always knew exactly what to do to make me feel better. Now that I'm expecting my first child, I asked her, 'How am I going to know what my kid needs?' She reminded me how I helped my best friend in college when her drinking got out of hand. I became her confidante, her parole officer, her teacher, her referral service, her disciplinarian, and her support all at the same time. Thinking about it, if I could get through D.'s drinking problem, I should have no problem with parenthood...."

—YALE UNIVERSITY, '91

HOW TO LISTEN

Listening is one of the most helpful things you can do. In fact, just letting her know that she can talk about what's going on in her life may be enough to start her on the road toward getting better.

The more you get your friend to talk, the better. By asking open-ended questions instead of making statements, you will make it easier for her to express her feelings. When she is talking, support her with verbal and nonverbal expressions, like "uh-huhs" and nods, which indicate that you are listening. Eye contact is also often very reassuring. Reiterate important points and feelings that have been brought up in the conversation by saying such things as, "So you're saying you feel x when y happens." Summarize important feelings and points throughout, so that you can better identify what is going on and how best to help.

Don't be a blabbermouth. Give her the floor. Listen to what she has to say and accept it as her view of things. Below are some more strategies that may help:

■ **Educate yourself about the problem.** By knowing a little about your friend's issue, be it bulimia or depression or past abuse, you can be more supportive and offer useful suggestions for getting help. Call organizations and people who routinely deal with the problem. Resident advisors are often knowledgeable about these things, but remember to respect your friend's confidentiality. If appropriate, talk with mutual friends who might be able to offer support or advice. Try the related chapters in this book, or find journals, magazines, or other books that deal with the subject.

■ **Talk with her about the problem.** Use what you've learned to discuss with her how she might approach the difficulties in her life. (But remember, a little reading up doesn't make you an expert; try to avoid making assumptions about how she's feeling.) Your friend may just need a sounding board for her own ideas about what to do. Or she may need you to take the reins— more of an "OK, let's figure out what you've got to do to get through this" approach. Helping her come up with a pragmatic, step-by-step plan (or dic-

DON'T PLAY THERAPIST

In the midst of all this, it's important to remember your role: You are not your friend's therapist, you're her friend. While you may have a clear picture of the *symptoms* of her problem—not being able to get out of bed, bingeing and purging, abusing drugs—it is nearly impossible for you to know or unravel the underlying causes, and *that's not your job.*

tating one to her, as the case may be) might be necessary to prod her out of her rut.

"When my friends all confronted me about my bulimia, they met with someone to find out about the disease and read up on everything they could find, because they wanted to give me the best help they could. Unfortunately, by knowing so much they were sort of unable to really listen to what I was saying—they 'knew' what I was going through. Though I've got to admit, in hindsight, they did have a pretty good idea, I really resented them using terms and expressions that came from experts and books, rather than from me."

—SCHOOL AND YEAR WITHHELD

■ **Offer to help with practical, everyday things.** Do her laundry, clean her room, and offer to lend her the notes from the biology classes she missed.

■ **Give her referrals** to places and/or people who can give help, information, advice, and/or support. (See below.)

■ **Take care of yourself.** You will be better able to support your friend and to continue to manage your own life if you remember to make yourself a priority. Find your own sources of support, be they your friends, a partner, your family, or a therapist. It is important to allow yourself the time to deal with how the problem has affected your life as well as your friend's.

GIVING REFERRALS

Giving a friend a list of places and people she can call or visit for information, advice, or general help allows her to choose her own course of action. Should she not be interested in the list when you give it to her, let her know that if she changes her mind and wants the information, you will have it.

If possible, check out a resource's appropriateness before you make your recommendation. When you call or visit, ask if and how the organizations/practitioners will be able to evaluate or meet what you perceive to be her needs. If possible, try to refer your friend to a specific person, rather than to an office or organization. This makes things more personal and cuts down on the work your friend has to do. When you give the resource, it may be helpful if you also include informa-

GUIDING YOUR FRIEND TOWARD OUTSIDE HELP

Though it may sound like a platitude, recognizing that you don't have the expertise, time, energy, distance, or wherewithal to help your friend is an indication of maturity. Seeking additional support for your friend means you are aware of your limitations. Referring your friend to a counselor, the local chapter of AA, or a rape crisis center does not mean that you're too busy or uninterested—it shows that you care. (For information on places and people to contact, see the Resources at the end of "More Than Just the Blues," page 270, "Real vs. Ideal," page 291, "Use and Abuse," page 323, and "Ending the Silence, " page 510.) Below are some signs that may help you determine when to seek outside help:

▲ When a friend comes to you for help with a problem that is beyond your scope of knowledge.
▲ When you don't feel comfortable with the issues.
▲ When your history would get in the way of your giving help (perhaps someone in your family has a similar problem and it brings up negative associations for you).
▲ When you're too close to the person involved to be effective.
▲ When you've tried to help but it doesn't seem to be working.

When looking for outside help, it's important that you:

▲ Respect your friend's confidentiality. Do not use her name or identifying characteristics when resource hunting. You may even wish to get her permission before discussing the content of your conversations with anyone, unless it is an emergency, in which case you should use as much discretion as possible while still communicating the essentials.

When talking to others about your friend, especially those affiliated with her school, be discreet. Remember that therapists, educators, and other helping professionals may be required by law to break patient confidentiality if someone's life or well-being is in danger (including yours or hers). You can ask preliminary questions without revealing anyone's identity.

▲ Determine the consequences if the school administration finds out about what is happening. You can ask an administrator, such as a dean, to tell you the school's policy, and what if anything the school can do to help. You are in no way obliged to divulge the name of the student or any information about her. You are entitled, by law, to know the school's policy about such issues.

tion about when she can call or go in for an appointment and when meetings are held.

After you give the referral (especially if she asked for it, but even if she didn't), do not drop the subject. Follow up on it, ask if she made any contact, and whether it was helpful. If it wasn't, you can offer to help her find another source.

HELPING A FRIEND WHO WON'T RECOGNIZE HER PROBLEM

I f you're in the position of watching someone's life go down the drain because of something she is or is not doing, your first inclination might be to have a heart-to-heart talk and try to come up with solutions. But what if she's not aware that she has a problem? Even the most brilliant person can be oblivious to what is staring her in the face. If this is the case, you can't discuss the problem with your friend until you've confronted her with it. While the thought of having such a talk might make you uncomfortable, (you may worry that she'll be angry and/or that you'll jeopardize the friendship) remember that a confrontation isn't about fighting or judging, it's about making your friend realize that she needs help.

Confronting Your Friend

Y ou should think of the confrontation as an opportunity to help your friend acknowledge that there is a problem. Stay focused on the problem and how it's affecting her; don't bring up how it has affected you, or other issues that aren't directly related. The closer you keep to the point, the harder it will be for her to evade what's really going on. And don't expect your conversation to be a magic cure. Just hearing what you have to say can be important for her, even if she's not ready to act on it.

Ultimately you'll have to use your instincts to guide you through the confrontation, but there are some specifics to keep in mind:

■ **Be prepared for her reaction.** She may get angry, accusatory, spiteful, or upset; deny what you are saying; avoid acknowledging her problem; or say things that she doesn't mean. Remember, you are raising sensitive and charged issues.

■ **Expect denial.** If the problem is big enough for you to notice and be concerned about, you know that it's a problem that she must be aware of on some level. But denial is a very common and powerful defense, and you should be prepared for her to attempt to avoid the truth. If the denial persists, you may need to end the discussion and bring it up another time. Unfortunately, for many people it takes "hitting bottom" (or coming close) before they'll recognize that something's wrong.

take care of an inebriated friend at one point or another. ☼

Your Game Plan

〰〰〰

Where and when you confront your friend are both important. Pick a time that is low-stress—don't do it right before parents' weekend or her big track meet, or during finals. Also, it's useless to bring up your friend's drinking when she is drunk or her eating disorder during or right after a meal. You have to catch her between acts, so to speak. Make sure you have enough time for a long conversation. If you have to cut it short for some reason, say something along the lines of, "This is an important conversation, and we should talk more soon" and try to schedule a time to continue (the sooner the better). Pick a place where you can have privacy and be free from distractions and interruptions. Don't bring up a friend's problem in the student center, in the middle of the library, or anyplace else where confi-dentiality isn't guaranteed. You might want to suggest going on a walk, or to an out-of-the-way café.

Talkin' the Talk

〰〰〰

There is no perfect way to say what you have to say. What's important is that you stick to your intention of trying to get your friend to face that she has a problem. The tips below may be helpful in getting you started.

■ **Use your judgment.** Different approaches work for different people. Sometimes a straightforward confrontation works well, other times a gentler tack is warranted. Depending on your friend, humor might also be an effective way of broaching the subject and relieving tension.

■ **Be yourself.** Address your friend as a person, not a case study. Try not to

---

"ENABLING"

Sometimes even when you think you are helping your friend, you may in fact be hurting her by enabling her to perpetuate her problems. What may seem to be the kindest, most helpful gestures may be just the opposite. For example, writing a paper for your friend or lying to professors on her behalf may actually help perpetuate her problem. Regardless of how painful it is for you to see her fall apart in one way or another, it's important that you let her—to an extent—as she needs to see the consequences of her behavior.

By the same token, being a watchdog won't help. It is not your job to police her. You shouldn't follow your friend to the bathroom, call her therapist to make sure she went to her appointment, force food down her throat, or continually ask her how many drinks she's had. In most cases, these actions only lead to resentment on both of your parts, and they don't really address the problem.

Two thirds of the stress-inducing situations in women's

SENDING IN THE MARINES

"My friend confided in me about her drug problem. She made me promise not to tell anyone, but I had to. It was the hardest decision, but I'd rather have her hate me for betraying her trust than lose her altogether."
—*University of Cincinnati, '96*

Sometimes it's enough to give a friend a referral (see "Giving Referrals," page 331), but what if she won't get help on her own and her problem is escalating? In that case, it may be appropriate to have someone else intervene. Your best resource in a situation like this may be your RA or the school's counseling service.

Depending on your school's policy, you may want to discuss the problem hypothetically—"I have this friend . . ."—to find out how the situation should be handled.

If you learn that telling the administration about your friend would compromise her school status in some way, you may want to discuss other possible options with your RA, or a doctor or therapist. But remember that your ultimate goal is to get your friend the help she needs, that keeping her secret is probably not doing her any good, and that—as harsh as it may sound—it's not your job to protect her.

---

sound like you're reading from the pages of a recovery book.

■ **Watch what you say.** Language can be very powerful. Avoid throwing around words like "bulimia," "addict," or "alcoholic" without thinking. Although these may be easy words for you to say, they may not be easy words for her to hear. Instead, try an approach like, "I've noticed that you are missing all of your classes because you can't get up in the morning after drinking every night."

■ **Do not try to diagnose the underlying problems.** Deal with the problem itself. For example, even if you know that your friend has issues with her parents that might relate to her problem, it isn't a good idea for you to start playing therapist. Trying to help her recognize that her bingeing is out of

control is difficult enough without bringing up subjects that are apt to get her angry and defensive.

■ **Don't fill in all the silences.** They allow both you and your friend to think, and your silence will emphasize that you are listening. These conversations are very difficult—even the most talkative of us can find ourselves at a loss for words.

■ **Be honest about how you're feeling.** It's OK to admit that you are scared or that it is difficult for you to bring the problem up. You may want to say to her: "Try to listen more to what I'm saying than to how I'm saying this . . ." or "This is hard and I don't know how to do this . . ."

■ **Emphasize your concern.** Make it clear that you're only doing this because you care.

■ **Do not push your point or start an argument.** Recognize when it is time to back off. If she won't talk about it, there is little point in continuing.

WHAT TO DO IN A CRISIS

When a crisis hits, you don't have the luxury of being able to carefully choose your time, place, and words. If your friend is in immediate danger, or her behavior is endangering others, you have to act first and think later. If your friend has overdosed or has collapsed due to anorexia-induced weakness, if she is ranting uncontrollably or has been the victim of a violent crime, she needs immediate medical attention. Call the campus or another emergency medical service (EMS) and tell them what happened, when it happened, where you are, and how to get there. If they don't tell you first, ask them what you should do until they arrive. If you don't have an EMS number, call the campus or local police and give them the same information. They have a direct dispatch to the EMS. Never try to deal with an emergency of this nature alone. Seek help immediately.

Similarly, in the case of a suicide threat, there is no such thing as overreacting. You are in no position to judge whether or not she could or would do

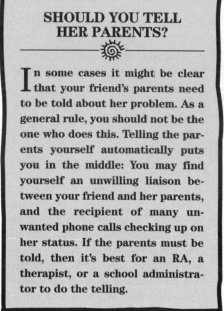

SHOULD YOU TELL HER PARENTS?

In some cases it might be clear that your friend's parents need to be told about her problem. As a general rule, you should not be the one who does this. Telling the parents yourself automatically puts you in the middle: You may find yourself an unwilling liaison between your friend and her parents, and the recipient of many unwanted phone calls checking up on her status. If the parents must be told, then it's best for an RA, a therapist, or a school administrator to do the telling.

it. If a friend confides in you that she's thinking about suicide, you need to react quickly and carefully. You are not betraying your friend if you get her help. (See "If Your Friend Is Suicidal," page 254, for information about identifying and helping someone who is suicidal.)

HELPING OTHERS WHILE TAKING CARE OF YOURSELF

Helping others is noble and important, to be sure, but somehow, in our schooling on "how to be there for everyone" an essential lesson was often left out: how to help others through their crises without having their problems become our own.

All the problems mentioned in

this chapter affect more than those struggling with them. When people you know—be they friends, roommates, or lovers—are having a hard time, you may find it physically, mentally, and/or emotionally draining to be constantly faced with the turmoil in their lives.

"My closest friend is completely obsessed with her weight and food—how fat she is and how bad she is if she eats anything. I know she needs my support, but when I try to talk to her about her problems she gets really defensive. Our relationship is so focused on her problems, I never feel as if I can talk to her about my life. I feel stuck because I care about her and she needs me, but the relationship is completely draining me."

—UNIVERSITY OF WISCONSIN–MADISON, MA CANDIDATE, '95

Making Sure You Don't Get Hurt

ଚ୨ଚ

"At a certain point in college, I realized that I couldn't handle having any more friends with serious issues, and when I met a woman whom I genuinely liked but I knew was anorexic, I decided not to become friends with her. . . . I couldn't be someone else's caretaker and it was clear to me that if I became friends with her I would have to help her. . . . I needed to do it for myself, but it's sad that I couldn't help her when I knew she needed it, and I also think I lost out on someone who would have been a friend."

—CORNELL UNIVERSITY, '93

Learn to acknowledge your friend's feelings and show support without becoming immersed in the situation. Watch what your body does when you're with her. Do you tense up? Are you starting to lose sleep or have difficulty concentrating? It's important, of course, to be empathic, but at the same time you need to remember that her problems are not your problems. It might be helpful to imagine putting up a clear barrier between the two of you as a reminder not to make her problems your own. There is no quantitative way to judge if you are spending too much time helping a friend by doing things for her, listening to her problems, and/or offering comments

WHEN TO BREAK AWAY

❀

You have tried everything for your friend and she still refuses to acknowledge that she needs help. Your friend is in a seemingly never-ending cycle of "getting better" and then relapsing. She is continually abusive to you, either emotionally or physically. You are not getting anything in return for your friendship and your efforts to help her. She seems to thrive on the constant drama that multiple crises supply. If any of these scenarios sound familiar, then it may be time to end, or at least limit, your friendship. True, the problem may very well not be her fault, but be that as it may, a true friendship is one that works both ways, and if your relationship has gotten to the point that the focus and energy is entirely on her, then it's not much of a friendship anyway.

and advice. If you are feeling overwhelmed, you might want to consider pulling back. But before you do, tell your friend how you feel. She may be so wrapped up in her problems that she has no perspective on the friendship. Hearing your side of it might be enough to change the dynamic. If not, at least you tried.

No matter how difficult a time your friend is having, regardless of the circumstances, she has no excuse to hurt you in any way. If someone is causing you pain, intentionally or unintentionally, you have the right to get angry and the responsibility to make sure that it doesn't continue. This may mean that you have to separate yourself from the person who is hurting you, or at least set up some rules about how she can or cannot treat you and when you can or can't be there for her. It also may mean finding help for yourself—talking to a friend or professional who can support you. (If your friend is hurting you physically, see page 491.)

While it's important to remember that your friend isn't a bad person but a person with a bad problem, it is perfectly OK to feel angry at her, and it's natural for the anger and hurt to color your general concern. Your feelings are valid, and there is no reason for you to feel guilty about them. These things—your anger, hurt, and possible feelings of guilt—are just some of the reasons you may want to seek support (either from a friend or a professional).

"A friend was struggling with depression and really leaned on me for support. But there'd be times when she acted like I was the problem. Once I went over when she was in an argument with someone else and she turned on me. Later she claimed that she'd had a 'nervous breakdown' because of what I'd done. It really hurt. I started to think maybe I did do something to flip her out."

—COLBY COLLEGE, '95

❀ Drinking contributes to approximately $2/3$ of all violent be-

ACTIVIST IDEAS

■ Start a "supporters" support group —a formal or informal forum where people who are supporting friends, lovers, or family members through a rough time can get a little help for themselves.

■ Run a workshop on how to confront a friend who has an eating disorder or a drug problem. Include on a panel students who are in recovery who can shed some light on what the friend may be experiencing and give tips and tricks on tactics to use. Also have counselors from health services on hand to address feelings and problems that may arise pre- and post-confrontation.

■ Simplify the art of referral. Create preprinted cards that list names, numbers, and descriptions of resources available on your campus and in your community that people can hand to a friend in need. They should be issue specific (one for eating disorders, one for alcohol and/or drug dependency, one for depression, etc.) and available from mental health services, RAs, the student union, security, or other easily accessible sources.

RESOURCES

See the Resources at the end of "Use and Abuse" page 323, "Real vs. Ideal" page 291, "More Than Just the Blues" page 270, and "Ending the Silence" page 510 for additional or ganizations and books that may be useful.

Further Reading

Many organizations, like the American College Health Association (see the "Staying Healthy" Resources, page 241), publish materials on how to help friends with specific problems; see also the Resources at the end of the chapters mentioned above.

Codependent No More: How to Stop Controlling Others and Start Caring for Yourself, Melody Beattie (HarperPerennial, 1987).

It Will Never Happen to Me, Claudia Black (Ballantine, 1987).

Codependence Misunderstood—Mistreated, Anne Wilson Schaef (HarperPerennial, 1986).

Too Good for Her Own Good: Breaking Free from the Burden of Female Responsibility, Claudia Bepko (HarperCollins, 1990).

When Helping You Is Hurting Me, Carmen Berry (HarperCollins, 1989).

Bulimia: A Guide for Family and Friends, Roberta Trattner Sherman and Ron A. Thompson (Lexington Books, 1990).

Surviving an Eating Disorder: New Perspectives and Strategies for Family and Friends, Michele Siegel, Judith Brisman, and Margot Weinshel (HarperPerennial, 1988).

How to Help Someone Who Doesn't Want Help, Vernon E. Johnson (Johnson Institute, 1986).

havior on campus and ¹/₃ of academic and emotional problems. ☼

Part Four

Sexual &
Reproductive
Matters

Know Your Body

A Few Gynecological Basics

![spiral icon] You might not be able to pinpoint when you went from thinking of your body as an abstract, sticklike figure to understanding it as a complicated network of tissues, organs, and muscles with a hormone or two thrown in for good measure. But chances are, it happened somewhere around the time commonly referred to as puberty, when perhaps without warning, strange and exciting changes started making their mark on your body.

Because traditionally women have not been encouraged to get to know their bodies inside out, many of us know far less about ourselves than our doctors or lovers do. But it's important to know the basics of your body, especially about the aspects unique to you as a woman. If you take the time to learn about your sexual and reproductive organs and how menstruation affects you both physically and mentally, it'll be easier to know what's nor-

mal and what's not and what feels right and what doesn't, and you'll be better able to keep your body healthy.

THE GYNECOLOGIST'S OFFICE

A good place to start learning about your sexual and reproductive system is in the gynecologist's office. (Some women prefer to see an internist, a general practitioner or family practice physician, a registered nurse, a physician's assistant, a nurse-practitioner, or a nurse-midwife for their routine gynecological care.) Watching and understanding what's going on during a gynecological exam will not only give you a chance to learn about your reproductive system, but may also make you feel more comfortable. If you ask, nearly every practitioner will give you a mirror to hold and will point out which organs are which, as well as explain how s/he can tell if everything is in good shape. Because most gynecologists are extremely busy (especially those who work at college health services), ask the receptionist who makes your appointment to schedule in a bit of extra time for you if you'd like a guided tour.

THE PELVIC EXAM

~~~~~~

Routine pelvic examinations are crucial to good gynecological health. It's recommended that

ESCAPE THE DRAPE

A gynecologist may choose to drape a sheet over your legs during the pelvic exam. Though the practice is intended to make you more comfortable by blocking your view and depersonalizing the exam (deemphasizing the fact that someone is feeling around in your "private parts"), it may do the opposite. The sheet can be a subtle way of reinforcing the idea that we should feel ashamed of our bodies and should not be interested in what they look like and how they work. But in fact, most women feel more at ease when they know what's going on. If you think you'd be more comfortable without the sheet, tell your gynecologist that you don't want it.

women begin gynecological care by the time they're 18 or as soon as they become sexually active. There are many female gynecologists and nurse-practitioners today, so if you want a woman to provide you with gynecological health care you shouldn't have a problem finding one. Whomever you choose, it is essential that you be comfortable and honest with him or her, and that you feel confident you will receive quality, attentive care. If you are unsatisfied with someone you've seen, you should find someone new. (For tips on finding a practitioner, see "Our Doctors, Ourselves," page 234.)

At your first visit to the gynecologist the practitioner will take a medical history and ask if you have any special health concerns. Then you'll be brought into an examining room and left alone to take off everything but your socks and to put on a paper or cloth hospital gown (it opens in the front). Next is a short, general physical exam that includes weight, height, and a check of your blood pressure, lungs, thyroid, and abdomen. Then comes a thorough look at your sexual and reproductive organs: a breast exam and an internal and external pelvic exam.

For the actual pelvic exam, you'll lie on an examining table or sit in a special chair with your feet resting in elevated stirrups, which support your legs in the proper position. Your legs will be spread apart, exposing your genitalia. Almost everyone feels uncomfortable and vulnerable the first few times they are in this position. Try to remind yourself that nearly all women go through this, and take a deep breath and relax.

As with any other medical procedure, if you tense up your muscles, the exam will be more difficult. Being

GYNECOLOGICAL HEALTH CARE FOR ALL WOMEN

✺

Many of the reasons women visit the gynecologist are for reproductive and heterosexual sex issues, such as contraception, painful intercourse, pregnancy, and sexually transmitted diseases. However, that doesn't mean that women who don't have sex or who engage in sex with women need not regularly see the gynecologist as well.

Studies show that lesbians have fewer gynecological procedures like Pap smears, mammograms, and tests for STDs and other disorders than do "straight" women. Perhaps this is because doctors make lesbians feel uncomfortable by assuming they're heterosexual. Or perhaps it's because

doctors are not traditionally aware of health issues and problems specific to women who are sexually involved with women. For example, if a woman says she's never had intercourse, a practitioner may assume she's not at risk for STDs, and not discuss them or check for them. Or a doctor may not know much about female to female transmission.

Whatever the case, since gynecological disorders are equal opportunity assailants, it's important for all women to get regular checkups. If you don't feel comfortable with your doctor, find a new one. Women's groups on campus can most likely provide referrals.

informed ahead of time about what the exam involves and feeling comfortable with your practitioner are probably the most effective strategies for quelling the jitters. The pelvic exam should not hurt. If at any point it does, let your practitioner know.

The External Exam

Your practitioner will visually examine your vulva for discoloration, irritation, swelling, and other abnormalities, and will gently feel your glands and other organs.

The Internal Exam

There are two parts to the internal exam. The first involves a speculum, which is a metal or plastic instrument that the practitioner inserts into the vagina. The metal one is more popular, as the plastic one has been known to pinch (albeit infrequently). However, for those who have ever experienced an ice-cold speculum, the plastic ones are a welcome sight. (Practitioners with their patients' needs in mind will usually warm the speculum before insertion.) The speculum is shaped almost like a duck's bill, and once it is inserted into the vaginal canal it can be gently expanded to open the interior vaginal walls. (The vagina is collapsed in its relaxed state, but it can widen easily to accommodate a tampon, finger, penis, or baby.) As the vaginal walls are spread, the practitioner is able to see clearly up the vaginal canal to the cervix, where s/he looks for discoloration, growths, abnormal discharge, lesions, and signs of infection.

The Pap Smear

In the process of the examination, the practitioner will take a Pap smear. The Pap smear is a screening test for cervical cancer. If cervical cancer is detected early, it is usually treatable and curable; if not, it can be fatal. For this reason, you should have a Pap smear once a year.

The Pap smear entails using a cotton-tipped swab (or other long stemmed-instrument) to collect a sample of the cells in the cervix. (Some women feel a slight cramping sensation when their cervix is touched.) The collected cells are smeared onto a slide and sent to a lab. At the lab your slide will be examined by a technician, who should be a certified cytotechnologist. Ideally, the lab itself will be directed by a qualified pathologist with expertise in cytopathology. The technician will examine the slide for abnormalities of the cells in the cervix, which may indicate infection or disease, including cervical cancer. For quality control,

PAP PREP

In order to make for the most accurate reading possible:

▲ Don't douche for three days before the test—it washes away the surface cervical cells that are collected in the Pap smear.

▲ Because spermicide and semen can obscure the sample, if you have intercourse the day before, do not use a cervical cap, diaphragm, sponge, or spermicidal foam or jelly, and be sure to use a condom without spermicide in the lubricant. (Instead, squirt a bit of spermicide *inside* the condom.)

▲ If you're using vaginal creams and medications, call your doctor and ask if they'll affect the Pap smear and whether you should stop using them for a few days or reschedule the test.

▲ Try to avoid scheduling your appointment to fall during your period (unless, of course, you are going to see your gynecologist for a reason that would require you to do so).

federal regulations require that 10 percent of a lab's negative (or "normal") Pap smears be read by an outside technician to determine the lab's "false negative" rate. Ask your doctor what percentage of samples are "rescreened"—that is, read by more than one person. If the number is higher than 10 percent, it is a sign that the lab is especially concerned with the accuracy of its readings.

Since the Pap test came into general use in the 1950s, the

The Pap smear does not test for pregnancy, sexually transmitted diseases, vaginal infections, or other types of gynecological problems. If you want comprehensive testing, you should ask before the Pap smear.

Note: You may find a trace of blood in your vaginal discharge after a Pap smear. If you bleed more than just a little, call your doctor.

After the Pap

The second part of the pelvic exam is called the manual (or bimanual) exam. After removing the speculum, the practitioner will insert one or two fingers into your vagina and press with his/her other hand on the outside of your lower abdomen. In this way s/he can feel the uterus, fallopian tubes, and ovaries, and check for any swelling or tenderness. S/he may also insert a well-lubricated finger into your rectum to further examine your ovaries and feel for signs of endometriosis or other gynecological disorders. (The rectal exam is possibly the most dreaded, and thankfully the shortest, part of the exam.)

What's Down There, Anyway?

⊚⊚⊚

Men in our culture are generally raised to be proud of their sexual organs, whereas women grow up feeling at best indifferent and at worst ashamed of their own genitals. Familiarizing yourself with your sexual organs is important from both a health perspective and one of personal empowerment. Following, then, is a quick look at what's down there.

Female Genitalia

Vulva: The external genitalia, consisting of the clitoris, the clitoral hood, and the labia majora and minora.

Mons veneris: The soft, fatty tissue covered with pubic hair that lies on top of the pubic bone.

Clitoris: The highly sensitive sexual organ made of erectile tissue and located near the top of the vulva within the labia majora. The external part of the clitoris, called the glans, is covered by a hood of skin. When aroused, the clitoris fills with blood, becoming harder and more sensitive, and the hood retracts. The sole purpose of the clitoris is sexual sensation, and if sufficiently stimulated it will produce orgasm.

Labia majora (outer lips): The soft folds of skin that form flaps on the outer part of the vulva.

Labia minora (inner lips): The folds within the labia majora, which surround and cover the openings of the urethra and vagina.

Perineum: The area between the inner lips and the anus.

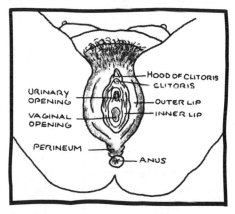

Female genitalia

GETTING A GOOD LOOK INSIDE: DOING A PELVIC SELF-EXAM

"When I finally got the guts to examine myself, I couldn't believe it—it was nothing like I thought, nothing like the pictures. Using a mirror put it all in perspective—put together the parts that I could see with the part I could feel. I was so excited I told my boyfriend about it. He hadn't really thought about the fact that I couldn't see myself and I didn't know what my vagina looked like, because it's no secret that guys spend a lot of time checking out their penises."

—*BRYN MAWR COLLEGE, '95*

The thought of closing the door and gazing into your vagina can elicit feelings ranging from excitement and curiosity to fear. There's definitely something taboo about spreading your legs wide, inserting a speculum into your vagina, and staring at your "private parts" for any length of time. (Not to mention that you'll need to use a mirror and a flashlight and get yourself into positions that you most probably wouldn't want the dean of students to see you in.) But it can be interesting and enlightening to see inside yourself—it'll help you know when something's wrong and also give you a better idea of how your body works.

For information about how to do a self-exam, see the Resources at the end of this chapter. In addition, many colleges, community health organizations, and women's collectives offer courses and sponsor workshops in women's health and human sexuality that teach how to give self-exams.

Female Reproductive System

Urethra: The tube leading from the bladder to the urinary opening.

Hymen: A thin membrane surrounding and partially covering the vaginal opening that may become stretched and/or broken when a finger, tampon, penis, or other object is inserted into the vagina, or during sexual intercourse. Sometimes other vigorous physical activity will cause the hymen to break, too. Because the hymen doesn't totally cover the opening of the vagina, you can use a tampon and have a pelvic exam and it can still remain intact.

Vagina: The muscular canal that leads from the vaginal opening to the uterus. The vagina has a natural discharge that changes in consistency and odor depending on where you are in your menstrual cycle. Menstrual blood also comes out of the vagina.

Cervix: The base of the uterus, which extends into the vaginal canal. In its center is a small opening into the uterus, called the cervical os.

Uterus (womb): The pear-shaped, organ, made up primarily of muscle tissue, that's situated in the pelvic cavity. The uterus receives and nourishes

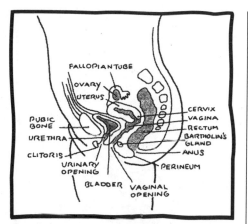

Female reproductive system (side view)

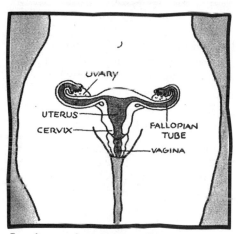

Female reproductive system (front view)

the fertilized ovum (egg), and contains and protects the fetus until birth.

Ovaries: The two small almond-shaped organs located on either side of the uterus, in which ova (eggs) are stored and grow to maturation.

Fallopian tubes (oviducts): The two slim tubes that are between 2¾ and 6 inches long and extend from the ovaries to the uterus, through which ova travel.

BREASTS

There is no such thing as a "normal" breast. Genes, age, pregnancy and nursing experience, "time of the month," birth control pills, diet, health, and lifestyle all factor into how your breasts look and feel. The size, shape, color, and texture of the breast, nipple, and areola (the pigmented area around the nipple), as well as sensitivity to touch, vary among women. Some women have hairs growing around the nipple, raised pimple-like bumps on the areola, or whitish, reddish, purplish, or brownish stretch marks, (which are generally caused by rapid growth or weight gain) on the sides of their breasts. Some women have inverted nipples, or nipples that look pushed in, which are more common among women with large breasts. And despite what we see in bra advertisements, on Barbie dolls, and in magazine centerfolds, it's very common to have one breast that is slightly larger than the other.

BREAST SELF-EXAMS

Along with having routine breast exams by your health practitioner, performing a breast self-exam once a month (right after you finish your period) is one of the most important steps in the early detection of breast cancer. Even if you're at extremely low risk for breast cancer—under the age of forty, healthy, and without a family history of the disease—it's still important to get into the habit of giving yourself a monthly breast exam. Taking the time to familiarize yourself with what your normal breast tissue feels like will better enable you to detect any potential problems in the future.

These self-examinations should serve as a complement to, not a substitute for, an expert's exam. If, in between your regularly scheduled visits to your health practitioner, you are concerned about a lump, by all means, get it checked by your health practitioner. But in general, if you are not at high risk of developing breast cancer, doctors often suggest that you monitor it for a month or two. A lump that comes and goes (or changes size) with your menstrual cycle or is affected by changes in your diet (try cutting down on fat, sugar, salt, and caffeine) is probably not malignant. If, however, you feel a lump that is hard, stationary, and not painful, see your practitioner immediately.

Examining Yourself

〰️〰️〰️

The relative firmness or softness of your breasts differs not only among breasts, but also within each breast. But generally, the arrangement of muscle, fat cells, fluid, and ducts that give breasts their shape can feel like lumps in the breast tissue.

Because the consistency and sensitivity of your breasts changes throughout the menstrual cycle, you should examine your breasts at approximately the same time in the cycle. The best time to do this is right after your period; it's easy to remember, and it's when your breasts are least tender and lumpy.

When you examine your breasts, look and feel for lumps, thickening,

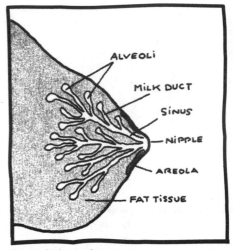

Breast (side view)

puckering, dimpling, discharge from nipple, and any changes in the shape, size, color, or texture of your breast or nipple and/or areola.

Stand and Look

Stand in front of a mirror. Examine yourself when you are in the following positions, as well as when you are switching from one position to the next.

1. Stand with hands at sides.

2. Clasp hands behind head and try to make your elbows touch in front of you.

3. Keeping hands clasped behind head, pull elbows back.

4. Place hands on hips and slouch shoulders and elbows in.

Stand and Feel

Keeping your hands flat, use the pads of your three middle fingers to press firmly on your breasts. Unless you do the exams right before your period, or when pregnant, it should not hurt. A bit of oil or lotion (or doing the exam in the shower) will make your hand glide smoothly.

   1. Raise your left arm.

   2. Starting on the outside edge of your left breast, near the armpit, spiral in slowly and thoroughly. Pay special attention to the area between the breast and underarm and the underarm itself.

   3. Be sure to check the areola area, too.

   4. Gently squeeze the nipple and look for discharge. (If discharge is present, see a doctor.)

   5. Repeat on your right breast.

Lie Down and Feel

Repeat the "Stand and Feel" while lying flat on your back. You can place

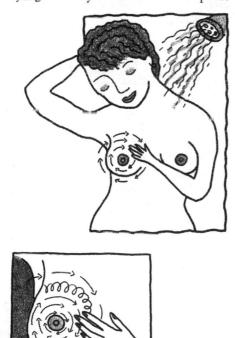

Breast self-examination

a pillow or folded towel under the left shoulder when examining the left breast (and the right for the right) to make the examination easier.

"My first breast self-exam scared the hell out of me. I had no idea that my boobs were supposed to be lumpy, so I was sure that I (at the age of 16) had cancer. At my next checkup (which came after a few months of serious fretting), I asked my doctor about it. She first gave me an exam, then she went over step-by-step the proper way to do a self-exam, and taught me about where and what the natural lumps in my breasts were."

—University of California, Berkeley, '92

Noncancerous (Benign) Lumps

ᓂᓂᓂ

Eighty percent of breast lumps are not cancerous (i.e., benign). They are either cysts, which change in size according to your menstrual cycle, or fibroadenomas which are independent of the menstrual cycle. Fibroadenomas are painless, hard, moveable lumps. Cysts feel like rubbery lumps and are largest and most painful right before the period. Heredity plays a key role in your likelihood of developing cysts, which are commonly referred to as fibrocystic breast disease, or FBD. Caffeine

SURGICAL ALTERATIONS

"I have really big breasts. Guys I don't know make obnoxious comments, and girls I barely know ask me if I ever thought about getting a breast reduction. There have been times that I wished my breasts were smaller, but two discoveries have made them totally OK. The first is wearing two jog bras when I work out. The second is that spending the money for a good-quality bra that really fits can make all the difference in the world."

—NEW YORK UNIVERSITY, '96

In the strictest sense breasts' function is to produce milk for babies, but they've certainly come to mean a lot more. Like body size, breast size has been translated into a symbol of femininity and beauty (although what is considered to be the ideal breast size changes on a regular basis and varies among different cultural communities).

All of us have probably wished our breasts looked different at some point or another, but some women are so dissatisfied with their breasts that they elect to alter them surgically. Women who want bigger breasts may opt to have implants inserted. Implants can be filled with either saline solution or silicone. Unless you've really had your head in the books, you probably know that there have been serious medical problems linked with silicone implants. As a result, there have been a number of class action lawsuits against implant manufacturers, as well as a movement toward having them banned. If you have implants, you should take the necessary precautions as prescribed by the United States Food and Drug Association (FDA). (See the Resources at the end of this chapter for more information).

Women who want smaller breasts may choose to have a breast reduction. Though most breast reductions are done for cosmetic purposes, they are also done to alleviate back, neck, and shoulder problems caused by the weight of the breasts.

If you are thinking of breast surgery, be sure to talk with a highly recommended and respected board-certified plastic surgeon and read up on the latest techniques and risks before making your final decision. (See "Our Doctors, Ourselves," page 234, for tips on finding a doctor, and the Resources at the end of this chapter to find more information on breast operations.)

has also been linked to FBD. It is recommended that women with the problem cut down on caffeine and take vitamin B complex and vitamin C to help decrease the size and pain of the cysts.

Though benign lumps are *not* malignant (cancerous), if their size or placement affects normal body functioning, or would make it difficult to detect cancer, they are often removed.

Am I at Risk for Breast Cancer?

෧෧෧

Breast cancer is a serious illness. If detected early, it can be treated successfully; if not, it is often fatal. The recent increased awareness and publicity about breast cancer has resulted in earlier detection, more accurate diagnoses, and more research into prevention, treatment, and cure.

"Both my mother and my aunt have breast cancer, so I know . . . that I am at greater risk of getting the disease. . . . As soon as my mom was diagnosed I did a lot of research about breast cancer—I called organizations, found out about treatments, and found a support group for her and for me. Having information helped me be less scared about what will happen to my mom, my aunt, and myself."
—COLUMBIA UNIVERSITY, '93

There is no one conclusive set of conditions and behaviors that can be used to accurately predict whether or not a woman will develop breast cancer. Statistically, women with a family history of breast cancer (especially those with a mother or sister diagnosed before age 50), are at a higher risk than those without. This genetic correlation has been confirmed by the recent discovery of a breast cancer gene. Still, the most significant factor is age: Studies show that breast cancer risk increases dramatically with age,

with women age 50 and older in the highest risk category. In addition to age and heredity, studies have shown that estrogen, a naturally occurring female hormone, may play a part in the development of breast cancer in some women. Researchers are now doing studies to determine if women who began to menstruate at an early age and/or reached menopause at a late age and/or were never pregnant or never breastfed—all of which would increase the body's exposure to estrogen—have a higher rate of incidence of breast cancer.

Proactive Steps

෧෧෧

■ There may be a connection between a high-fat diet and breast cancer, so it can't hurt to eat a veggie-rich, low-fat, high-fiber diet. And go easy on the booze: it's possible that regular alcohol consumption (as little as one or two drinks a day) may increase your risk of developing the disease—even for women under 30.

■ Have a health practitioner give you a breast exam and, if necessary, a mammogram as often as recommended (based on risk). Normally mammograms are not given to women under the age of 35.

■ Perform a breast self-exam monthly.

■ Because of the possible connection between estrogen and breast cancer, women at risk are sometimes advised against using birth control pills (which contains the hormone) and undergoing estrogen-replacement therapy at menopause.

The earliest known breast reduction surgery dates back to the 1600s. ☀

FEAR NOT

The information on breast cancer is overwhelming, and studies are constantly revealing new information about risk factors, how to prevent breast cancer, and so forth. Read the information and keep informed, but don't be defeated by it. The vast majority of women—even those who are in more than one high-risk category —do not develop breast cancer. As far as the experts know, individual biology is the primary determining factor of who gets breast cancer.

■ Find out about your family medical history with regard to breast (and other) cancer and discuss it with your practitioner.

■ If you are in a high-risk group, talk with your health practitioner about other steps you can take in terms of prevention.

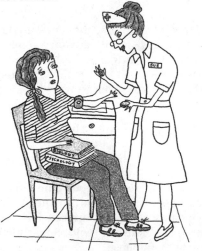

MENSTRUATION

Menarche (the onset of menstruation) signifies the beginning of one's reproductive years, and usually occurs during puberty (typically between the ages of 12 and 16, although it may come earlier or later). One of the main functions of menstruation is to enable our bodies to become pregnant, but the hormonal changes affect much more than just our reproductive organs and abilities. They can affect everything from our mood to how we feel physically to how tired or energized we are to our breasts' shape and tenderness.

Menstruation is full of cultural and social significance. It's been seen as both a sign of impurity and a sign of prosperity, at times called "the curse" and at other times "the blessing." Your choice in what you call menstruation and the way you feel about it are probably connected in some way to how menstruation is viewed by your family and your ethnic, religious, and/or cultural background.

"Who hasn't talked with other women about the trials and tribulations of her period? The best example that I can think of is when I went to study abroad in Turkey my junior year. The first way I bonded with the women there was by talking about our periods; it helped break the huge cultural barriers that I felt when I arrived."

—EARLHAM COLLEGE, '96

The Menstrual Cycle

ⓥⓥⓥ

*"One of my friends had a menstru-
ation ritual and ceremony created
for her by her mother and her
mother's friends. In retrospect, I
think the ceremony was a really
neat idea and I definitely like the
symbolism of coming into womanhood with older women surrounding you and having them celebrate
you, but when I was 12½ I didn't
want to celebrate the fact that I
was going to bleed every month, I
wanted to hide it."*

—BRANDEIS UNIVERSITY, '95

Though most of us only think of our menstrual cycle as the 5- to 7-day period, menstrual bleeding is only one part of the (on average) 28-day cycle of hormonal actions and reactions and body responses. Varying levels of the naturally produced hormones progesterone, estrogen, luteinizing hormone (LH), and follicle-stimulating hormone (FSH) regulate the menstrual cycle, which can be broken down into three phases.

The first phase of the cycle begins on the first day of bleeding. The menstrual fluid you shed is composed not only of blood but also of mucus and endometrial tissue (which lines the walls of the uterus). It generally takes four to six days for the uterus to completely expel this lining, though this process may vary in duration and flow from month to month and from woman to woman. On average, women only "bleed" about four to six tablespoons of fluid each period (about two fluid ounces), although it can sure seem like more.

During the second phase, a follicle in one of the ovaries matures into an egg. About 14 days before the beginning of your next period, an egg is released from the ovary into the fallopian tube, where it then travels toward the uterus. This is called ovulation. Within 24 hours after ovulation, while the egg is in the fallopian tube, a sperm can fertilize the egg and begin a pregnancy.

Some women feel a twinge or other sensation—ranging from a tickle to cramping pain—in their lower abdomen while ovulating; this is called *mittelschmerz*, which is German for "middle pain." Mittelschmerz can be soothed the same way you'd take care of cramps (see page 362). If you are unable to find relief, you may wish to see a doctor.

Also during this phase, the uterine lining begins to thicken with the blood and endometrial tissue that would be used to nourish a fetus.

In the third phase, (if you have a 28-day cycle, this phase will last about two weeks), one of two things can occur. If an egg is fertilized, it will travel down to the uterus, attach to the uterine wall, and begin to grow into a fetus. If no fertilization occurs, the egg dissolves and most of the uterine lining will be shed through the vagina (menstruation) as the cycle begins all over again.

When It's Not Every 28 Days to the Minute

ⓥⓐⓥ

"During our sorority initiation, all the pledges had to spend so much time together that our periods got in sync. We all had our periods during hell week."

—UNIVERSITY OF ROCHESTER, '92

Though the average cycle lasts 28 days, there is no universal timetable. It is as normal to have a menstrual cycle that lasts 23 or 34 days as it is to have one that lasts 28 days. Some women's menstrual cycles are regular (always about the same length), but many women have cycles that consistently vary in length.

Menstrual cycles can also be irregular in terms of flow (i.e., be unusually long, short, heavy, or light). And what's irregular for you may be completely normal for your roommate. A number of factors, both external and internal, can contribute to an irregular period—stress, travel, high-intensity exercise, excessive dieting, or too little body fat. Age can also be a factor: Irregularity is especially common for young women.

Because the cycle is hormonally regulated, hormonal imbalances (both naturally occurring or those that occur as a result of birth control pills, Depo-Provera, or Norplant) will inevitably affect menstruation. Irregular periods may also come as a result of extreme anemia, tumors, or other serious and not-so-serious gynecological disorders. And there's always pregnancy, breast-feeding, and menopause—times when the body naturally ceases to menstruate. However, some women are just "regularly irregular." Other than the relative inconvenience of not being able to predict when you will ovulate or get your period, there is nothing wrong with having an irregular cycle.

If you previously had a regular cycle and you suddenly become irregular or stop getting your period, see your doctor.

"FEMININE PROTECTION" PRODUCTS

As far as menstrual products go, our two main choices are pads and tampons, although recently more environmentally sound menstrual options have appeared on the market. (See page 360.)

Pads, or sanitary napkins, as they are called in polite company, come in a variety of shapes, sizes, and absorbencies. Most have an adhesive strip on the bottom that enables you to stick them to your underwear. Even when pads are securely fastened and hidden away in their proper place, they can

"I still only use pads. It isn't that I haven't tried to use tampons. I can't get them in or they are just totally uncomfortable. Some of my friends got really grossed out when they found out I still used pads, but I really don't mind; it's what I've done for a good 11 years now and it suits me just fine."

—UNIVERSITY OF NEW MEXICO, '96

Verbal skills are at their highest when estrogen levels are: You'll be

feel like they're slipping or showing through your clothes. (Oh joy!) But for women who are uncomfortable using tampons, are using vaginal medication that is contraindicated with tampon use, or want to play it safe in the toxic shock syndrome department, pads do the trick. Some women use a combination of pads and tampons.

Tampons are made of soft cotton and are inserted into the vaginal opening and rest in the vaginal canal to absorb menstrual fluid. They come in different sizes, absorbencies, with or without "deodorant," and with or without applicators. (If with, the applicators can be made of cardboard, or plastic, or be straight or curved for easier insertion.) Once you've decided to try tampons, you might want to test out different brands and styles to find the one that's best for you. Women can use tampons even if they haven't had sexual intercourse, and using tampons does not affect virginity.

How to Use Tampons . . .

To insert a tampon:

■ Unwrap the tampon. Be careful not to pull or push the applicator plunger (if it has one) or it will be difficult to insert. Tampons with applicators usually have two parts, one that surrounds the tampon and is inserted into the vagina, and a thinner tube that acts like a plunger to push the tampon out of the plastic or cardboard.

■ Relax. Either stand with one foot up on the toilet or sit with your knees apart. Make sure the tampon string is hanging out of the bottom of the applicator. Hold the tampon at the bottom of the larger tube (where it meets the smaller tube) between your thumb and third finger.

■ Gently insert the tampon into your vagina until your fingers touch your outer vaginal lips. Some women find it easier if they spread their lips with

VAGINAL DISCHARGE

Even when not menstruating, every woman has a vaginal discharge. This discharge is cervical mucus, which provides lubrication and acts to keep the vagina clean, the vaginal walls supple and elastic, and the pH level slightly acidic to help prevent infection.

Due to changing hormone levels, during ovulation the discharge is normally thicker, slipperier, and wetter than at other times of the month; after ovulation and menstruation, women usually have a lighter discharge. These changes help guide sperm cells to the fallopian tubes when an egg is present, and inhibit their movement when an egg isn't. (By paying attention to your discharge, you may learn to get a sense of where you are in your cycle.) Vaginal discharge should be clear or slightly whitish-yellow. If you notice that your discharge has a very strong smell and/or is discolored, or if you experience irritation and/or excessive dryness or wetness, it could be that you have an infection or another problem. (See "Common Gynecological Disorders," page 217.)

better at tongue-twisters during ovulation than right after your period.

CAN I HAVE SEX DURING MENSTRUATION?

It's fine to have sex during your period, as long as you take extra precautions. You have to be extremely careful when blood is present, because (in those infected) blood contains a higher concentration of HIV, the virus that causes AIDS, than any other body fluid. Thus, when you are engaging in sexual activities during your period, there is a higher likelihood of the transmission of the HIV virus than there would otherwise be. In addition, if you think you can't get pregnant during your period, you're wrong.

In protecting yourself, it's important to remember that not all contraception (such as the cervical cap and the contraceptive sponge) is safe and/or reliable to use when you have your period. (For more information, see "Contraception and Safer Sex," page 399.) Since diaphragms catch the blood and therefore reduce the chances of possible fluid exchange, you might consider using one, as this will enhance your partner's safety. Your partner should also use a condom, latex gloves, and/or dental dams.

their other hand or use a lubricant on the tip of the tampon (a water-soluble one like K-Y Jelly is your best bet). Another tip for first-time users is to squat over a mirror. You may feel some resistance from your vaginal muscles. If you do, relax, take a deep breath, and gently continue to insert the tampon. It may help if you jiggle the tampon gently. Don't be deceived by the initial resistance your vaginal canal gives; once you get past this tighter section, you will find that there is plenty of space for the tampon. You'll notice that rather than going straight up, your vagina tilts toward your back. You are in no danger of putting the tampon too far up or having it get lost.

■ While still holding the tampon in this position, use your forefinger or your other hand to gently and slowly push the plunger all the way. Pull out the applicator.

■ There are also tampons without applicators. To insert, pull the string until the end of the tampon flares out and a little recess is formed. Sitting or standing with your knees apart, put your finger in the recess of the tampon and push the tampon up into your vagina.

■ Once it's in, you should not be able to feel the tampon. If it's uncomfortable or painful, either try to push it farther up your vagina, adjust it with your finger, or remove it and try again with another tampon.

■ If you are experiencing irritation, try using a smaller size or switch to a different brand.

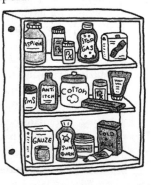

■ Though the package may say that you can flush cardboard applicators, this practice has been the cause of a number of backed-up toilets. It's usually a better idea to wrap the applicators in a bit of toilet paper and throw them in the trash. Plastic applicators and pads cannot be flushed under any circumstances.

■ All tampons come with directions complete with toll-free consumer information phone numbers, so look in the box and/or make a call if you have questions.

> *"I am a real advocate of o.b. tampons. Once you get used to them, you have a lot more control in putting them in, and they're much better for the environment because they don't use all that cardboard or plastic and come in a much smaller box. I also think that it's really important that women get to know and feel comfortable with their bodies, and because you're using your finger instead of an applicator, you can really feel how you're shaped."*
>
> —UNIVERSITY OF
> CALIFORNIA, DAVIS, '97

To remove a tampon:

■ Sit or stand in tampon-insertion position. Grasp the string and gently pull the tampon out.

■ If you're at the end of your period, or you used a tampon with more absorbency than you needed, it might take a little extra tugging, and may hurt for a few seconds. If, by mistake, you inserted the string into your vagina along with the tampon, put your finger inside and feel for the string. Once you find it, gently pull the tampon out.

■ Again, it is impossible for a tampon to get lost inside you. Sometimes women forget about a tampon and "find" it by noticing a strong, unpleasant odor; expel it when they go to the bathroom; or feel it during sex or masturbation, or when inserting another tampon.

A Few Caveats

ᘐᘐᘐ

There's no denying the convenience of tampons, but there are a few health hazards associated with tampons, and you should be aware of them before you buy your next (or first) box.

■ Using tampons can cause irritation of the vaginal walls and in some cases even tiny tears. For this reason, it is especially important to practice safer sex during and right after menstruation, because the irritation and/or tears make you more vulnerable to STDs transmission. (See "Contraception and Safer Sex," page 399.)

■ Toxic shock syndrome (TSS) is a rare but life-threatening infection caused by the *staphylococcus aureus* (or staph) bacteria that afflicts between 1 and 17 menstruating women per 100,000. Studies have shown that the higher the tampon absorbency and the longer a tampon is left inside the body, the greater the risk of developing TSS. Symptoms include a sudden high fever, vomiting, diarrhea, fainting, dizziness, or a sunburnlike rash

ECOLOGICAL AND ALTERNATIVE MENSTRUAL OPTIONS

One of the main problems with the majority of pads and tampons is that, because they are disposable and are not always packaged as sparingly as they could be, they create a lot of environmental waste. In addition, there is significant research to suggest that the bleach used in many menstrual products is itself a pollutant of the environment, not to mention of our bodies. In response to these concerns, some ecologically sound menstruation products are being made. Some of the options include:

▲ Chlorine-free disposable pads.

▲ Washable pads (made out of a type of plastic and/or absorbent cloth).

▲ Nonchlorine-bleached, all-cotton tampons. Available in some drugstores and health food stores, these tampons don't contain synthetics, optical whiteners, surfactants, fragrances, or rayon fibers.

▲ The Keeper, a brand of menstrual cap made of plastic. It looks like a cervical cap but is worn lower in the vagina and catches the menstrual blood. It can be washed out every few hours and then reinserted.

▲ The diaphragm, which can be used to catch the flow, thus serving a dual function as contraceptive and menstrual device.

If you choose to use a nondisposable method (especially those worn inside the vagina, such as the menstrual cap and diaphragm), make sure to speak with a health care practitioner about how to use it safely. Ask how it should be cleaned to avoid the growth of bacteria which can cause TSS, among other things.

"I started using the Keeper after Ms. magazine did an article about environmental menstrual products. My sister bought one, but she wasn't into using it, so I tried it and I really like it. It seems like a good way to be more environmental. I couldn't handle going back to pads and it actually saves me a lot of money on tampons."
—MACALESTER COLLEGE, '91

often most distinct on the palms and soles of the feet. If you develop these symptoms during your period, remove your tampon right away and see a doctor immediately. TSS symptoms may not appear until a few days after your period. To reduce risk, wash your hands before inserting a tampon, change your tampon every four to six hours, especially on heavy-flow days, and avoid high-absorbency tampons.

■ It appears that some scientists at the Federal Drug Administration (FDA) have discovered trace levels of dioxin (a by-product of the chlorine-bleaching process used at paper and pulp mills) in commercially manufactured tampons. Since it has yet to be established at what levels dioxin is toxic to human beings, the tampon industry has generally not responded to charges that tampons may be toxic. If you don't want to wait for the "offi-

☼ *A recent study found that men were significantly more irri-*

cial" conclusions, you might try some of the ecological and alternative options to tampons (see the box on the facing page).

■ Some tampons come fully equipped with their own deodorant. Menstrual fluid shouldn't have much of an odor until it comes into contact with the air, so deodorant tampons are unnecessary. They can be irritating to your body as well. In women who are sensitive, they can cause itching and may trigger vaginal infections.

OOH THE PAIN . . . DYSMENORRHEA AND PMS

The vast majority of ovulating women experience some sign that their hormones are a-bubble beyond simply menstruating. The signals can range from a touch of water retention and irritability to lawn-mower-in-the-lower-abdomen sort of cramps to the tell-tale pimple that announces their "little friend's" imminent arrival.

Primary dysmenorrhea, or painful periods, is a fancy name for menstrual cramps and other symptoms that appear in the first few days of the period in the absence of any physical problem. These include lower abdominal pain; pain in the leg or thigh; backache; nausea; vomiting; bloating; dizziness; and diarrhea.

The most popular explanation for dysmenorrhea is that at the end of the cycle, progesterone levels in the body drop. This allows prostaglandin levels to rise, causing the uterus to contract and expel the lining. A prostaglandin excess can increase the length of contractions and cause cramping. (This is why taking an anti-prostaglandin, such as ibuprofen, brings relief.) Dysmenorrhea symptoms are most acute in the late teens and early twenties, when women begin to menstruate more regularly.

The term "secondary dysmenorrhea" refers to menstrual pain and cramping that is related to fibroids, cysts, endometriosis, and pelvic infection. It needs to be treated by a health care practitioner.

Premenstrual Syndrome (PMS) refers to the set of over 150 physical and emotional symptoms that may occur in the luteal phase of the menstrual cycle (between ovulation and the menstruation).

Statistically, symptoms peak in a woman's mid-thirties, and are most acute in the four to five days before her period begins and during ovulation. PMS symptoms include:

▲ Bloating as a result of increased water retention.
▲ Acne outbreaks due to increased oil production.
▲ Swelling and increased sensitivity and soreness of the breasts. Women often find that their breasts become a bit lumpier as well, especially those with a family history of cysts.

▲ Heightened sensitivity, "emotionalism," exaggerated mood swings, and/or crankiness.
▲ Increased tiredness/lethargy.
▲ Constipation or diarrhea.
▲ Sugar, fat, and salt cravings (ice cream and chocolate are perennial favorites).
▲ Depression.
▲ Low self-esteem and feelings of insecurity or guilt.
▲ Insomnia.
▲ Forgetfulness, clumsiness, and spaciness.

It is only recently that PMS has been acknowledged as a bona fide physical problem, and not something that women are just imagining. The exact cause of PMS, and why different women have different symptoms, is unknown, but most researchers agree that the rising and falling levels of various hormones are at the root of the problem.

Different clinicians define PMS differently, and many women use the term "PMS" for any and all menstruation related symptoms. For this reason, it's important to describe the specific symptoms you're experiencing, rather than just tell your practitioner that you have PMS. And if you experience symptoms that are abnormal to you or are unusually extreme or long lasting, see your practitioner.

Symptom Busters

☜☜☜

The following, alone or in combination, may help prevent and relieve the myriad physical and emotional problems associated with dysmenorrhea and PMS.

■ Eat healthily. A few days before your period, cut down on salt, sugar, caffeine, and alcohol (or avoid them altogether), as they have been known to increase PMS symptoms. You may also wish to take a multivitamin and make a special effort to eat a well-balanced diet before and during your period. Diuretics (which some women take in hopes of reducing bloating) all contain caffeine and tend to aggravate, rather than relieve, symptoms.

The foods we crave can actually intensify the symptoms of PMS. For example, many women find that before menstruation their desire for sugar increases. However, after a short sugar high, blood sugar levels go down to below normal and can exacerbate PMS symptoms, such as depression, crankiness, and tiredness.

■ Take a nutritional supplement. Some women have found that a bit of safflower oil may help to temper the chemical that causes swelling and cramping. In addition, taking vitamin B_6, vitamin E, magnesium, iron, and/or zinc may reduce PMS symptoms. Excessive tiredness may also be a sign of anemia: Women with especially heavy flows are prone to anemia, and you may want to take an iron supplement and/or discuss the possibility of anemia with your doctor.

■ Exercise. Many women find that exercise—even as little as a half hour a few times a week—helps to reduce symptoms.

■ Sleep. Getting a good night's sleep for the few days before and during your period (and taking a quick afternoon catnap when the symptoms are at their worst) can aid in the prevention and relief of symptoms.

■ Relax. Have someone give you a massage (or massage yourself), take a warm bath, or use a heating pad. Many women also find that meditation and/or relaxation techniques are helpful. (See "Learning to Relax," page 250.)

■ Find a comfortable position. Many women find that relaxing in the fetal position reduces the pain of menstrual cramps. Lie on your side and curl up with your knees to your chest. Some people like to place a pillow between their knees. Others like to lie on their stomachs, with or without their knees tucked under them.

■ Engage in sexual activity. Orgasm or sexual arousal can help ease pain.

■ Take an anti-inflammatory/anti-prostaglandin drug. Taking ibuprofen a few days before you are about to ovulate (to relieve mittelschmerz) and before and during your period, can reduce the inflammation and pain of cramps. Prescription medications such as naproxen (or Naprosyn or Anaprox), an antiprostaglandin, can help to reduce pain as well as shorten the length and lessen the flow of the period.

It's especially important not to overdo it with any cramp medication. The muscles that cause the cramps are the same ones that help expel the lining, and you don't want to relax them too much or you may face other problems. If the pain is so bad that you feel like you'll need a dozen Advil to deal with it, it's time to make an appointment with your gynecologist or health practitioner.

"Yoga class has been my savior. Doing yoga is the only way that I have managed to deal with my cramps and bloating. It helps me to relax and to center myself. By working on my breathing and my body I can handle the pain. I think every woman should take yoga!"
—UNIVERSITY OF OREGON, '95

■ Consider synthetic hormones. Use of the Pill, Depo-Provera, or Norplant has helped relieve or temper severe cramps and/or mood swings.

■ Try holistic remedies. Acupuncture, herbal treatments, aromatherapy, meditation, massage, and other treatments have been shown to be quite effective in both relieving the symptoms and lessening their severity and duration.

■ Try therapy. Some women who experience mood swings and/or depression in relation to their menstrual cycle have found it helpful to join a support group or to talk with a mental health practitioner about their options. (See "More Than Just the Blues," page 247.)

MENSTRUAL PROBLEMS

If you have problems with menstruation beyond what's normal for you, such as extreme pain before and/or during menstruation, or pain that lasts longer than usual, see a gynecologist and/or other practitioner. Also, see a practitioner if any of the following occur:

■ Your period comes more often than

changes before their period, but only 10-20% suffer from bona fide PMS.

every 20 days or less often than every 35 days.

■ You have breakthrough bleeding (bleeding—excessively or just "spotting"—between periods).

■ Pain occurs between your periods, with or without spotting.

■ Your cramps or menstrual pain last longer than a few days into your period, do not relate to your period, are significantly more severe than what's normal for you, and/or are interfering with your ability to work, concentrate, and function happily.

Disorders That May Cause Menstrual Pain or Irregularity

೧ල೧

ENDOMETRIOSIS

What it is: Endometriosis is a disease that occurs when the tissue that lines the uterus (the endometrium) grows outside of the uterus, usually in other parts of the pelvic area. Because this tissue responds to the hormones that dictate the menstrual cycle (it builds up and bleeds, just as it would in the uterus), endometriosis can result in internal bleeding and the formation of cysts and scar tissue.

Symptoms: It may cause severe pelvic discomfort during menstruation, ovulation, and intercourse and can result in irregular menstrual flow, scarring, infertility, miscarriage, ruptured ovarian cysts, and other serious health problems.

Relief/treatment: Endometriosis is very difficult to diagnose. It may be diagnosed by pelvic examination, but gen-

erally laparoscopy (a surgical method of examination) is needed to make a definitive diagnosis. To relieve symptoms, hormonal treatments (such as birth control pills) are often effective in relieving pain and minimizing internal bleeding. In some cases, surgical removal of tissue is necessary. There have been recent breakthroughs in drug therapy that have proven especially successful when used in combination with surgery. Methods such as meditation, acupuncture, acupressure, and herbal therapies have also proven helpful for many women.

Other: Endometriosis is commonly misdiagnosed as pelvic inflammatory disease (PID).

UTERINE FIBROIDS

What they are: Uterine fibroids are noncancerous tumors attached to the wall of the uterus. Some fibroids are on the inside of the uterus, some are on the outside, and some are totally contained within the uterine wall itself.

Symptoms: Symptoms depend on the size, number, and/or placement of the fibroids. A large percentage of fibroids are small and unobtrusively placed, and do not have any apparent symptoms. They may be detected during a routine gynecological exam. Others may cause back pain, urinary problems, bleeding between periods, increased menstrual flow, and/or pain and may inhibit conception.

Relief/treatment: If fibroids are not causing problems, they are often not treated but are regularly monitored. If fibroids are obstructing or interfering with physiological functioning, they should be treated. They may be surgically removed or reduced by noninvasive means, including a special diet,

Overall, 25% of all women over age 30 will have uterine fi-

stress management, acupuncture, and/or other holistic remedies.

OVARIAN CYSTS

What they are: Ovarian cysts are fluid-filled sacs that appear on the surface of the ovary.

Symptoms: Ovarian cysts are quite common. Small, unobtrusive, benign ones may not cause symptoms and may only be discovered by a pelvic exam. Others may cause abdominal swelling, infrequent periods, pain, and/or painful intercourse.

Relief/treatment: The majority of cysts disappear on their own after a few menstrual cycles. Cysts that are related to endometriosis, are cancerous, impede normal ovarian and reproductive functioning, or cause pain should be surgically removed. Benign cysts are often treated with hormone therapy, stress reduction, acupuncture, and/or herbal remedies.

ACTIVIST IDEAS

■ Organize a monthly information session for women to attend before their first gynecological exam. Have a health services practitioner give a description of what will happen during the exam, a basic anatomy lesson, and information about other gynecological and reproductive health services the school offers, such as dispersal of birth control, STD and pregnancy testing, and/or administration of the morning-after pill.

■ Make posters that give detailed instructions how to give breast self-exams, laminate them so they're water-resistant, and hang them in locker room and dorm showers.

■ Have a fun and informative Menstrual Madness day. Have workshops on such topics as the historical, religious, and folkloric significance of menstruation, creating a menstrual ritual, relieving PMS symptoms, and the politics of menstrual products. Have a rap session where women can share their most horrible and funny menstruation experiences. If you really want to go all out, have all participants boogie to the Rolling Stones' "Let It Bleed" at the end of the day. Who knows, maybe a pad or tampon manufacturer would be interested in sponsoring the event and handing out free samples.

RESOURCES

General Information

AMERICAN COLLEGE OF OBSTETRICIANS AND GYNECOLOGISTS
409 12TH STREET SW
WASHINGTON, DC 20024-2188
(202) 638-5577
Maintains a resource center for the public on ob/gyn questions. Publishes numerous materials about sexual and reproductive health, available upon request.

FEDERATION OF FEMINIST WOMEN'S HEALTH CENTERS
633 EAST 11TH AVENUE
EUGENE, OR 97401
(503) 344-0966
Provides referrals to their own 11 clinics and to other progressive, women-friendly clinics nationwide. Has numerous publications, and you can order a low-cost speculum and get information about self-exams from them.

Endometriosis

ENDOMETRIOSIS ASSOCIATION
8585 NORTH 76TH PLACE
MILWAUKEE, WI 53223
(800) 992-3636 [ENDO]
(414) 355-2200
FAX: (414) 355-6065
Makes referrals to local organizations, groups, and practitioners offering support for women with endometriosis. Provides information about the current research on and treatment methods for endometriosis. Offers phone and crisis counseling. Publishes numerous materials, including a bimonthly newsletter.

Menstruation

MENSTRUAL HEALTH FOUNDATION
104 PETALUMA AVENUE
SEBASTAPOL, CA 95472
(707) 829-2744
FAX: (707) 829-1753
Provides information about menstruation. Publishes a catalog of environmentally sound menstrual products.

PMS

MADISON PHARMACY ASSOCIATES; PMS ACCESS
P.O. BOX 9326
MADISON, WI 53715
(800) 222-4767 [PMS]
(800) 558-7046
(608) 833-7046
FAX: (608) 833-7412
Primarily functions as a pharmacy and an information base recommending self-help techniques to relieve the symptoms of PMS. Provides general informa-

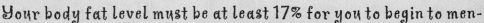

Your body fat level must be at least 17% for you to begin to men-

tion and personal consultation through its toll-free numbers. You can also order its literature, audio and video tapes, slide programs, and newsletter. Makes referrals to local health practitioners and clinics who work to address the problems of PMS.

Environmentally Sound Menstrual Products

THE KEEPER
BOX 20023 MS
CINCINNATI, OH 45220
(800) 500-0077

Sells the Keeper, a reusable menstrual product. Call to receive information and/or an order form.

MODERN WOMEN'S CHOICE
3415 JARIET ROAD
RR3 LADYSMITH, BC VOR2EO
CANADA
(604) 722-7013
FAX: (604) 722-7019

Sells numerous environmentally sound menstrual products. Catalogs are available upon request.

WOMAN KIND
900 EAST WAYZATA BOULEVARD
SUITE M310
WAYZATA, MN 55391
(800) 862-9876

Sells numerous environmentally sound menstrual products. Catalogs are available upon request.

SEVENTH GENERATION
49 HERCULES DRIVE
COLCHESTER, VT 05446-1672
(800) 456-1177

Sells numerous environmentally sound products, including reusable panty liners, maxi pads, and flannel pads. Catalogs are available upon request.

Breast Cancer

NATIONAL ALLIANCE OF BREAST CANCER ORGANIZATIONS (NABCO)
9 EAST 37TH STREET, 10TH FLOOR
NEW YORK, NY 10016
(212) 889-0606
(800) 719-9154
FAX: (212) 689-1213

A nonprofit organization that provides information on all aspects of breast cancer and promotes affordable detection and treatment. Makes referrals to local practitioners/clinics. Organizes political action/advocacy work to influence public and private health policy on issues that relate to breast cancer. Publishes numerous materials, including a newsletter, avaliable upon request.

SUSAN G. KOMEN BREAST CANCER FOUNDATION
5005 LBJ FREEWAY, SUITE 370
DALLAS, TX 75244
(800) 462-9273 [IM-AWARE]: HELPLINE
FAX: (214) 450-1710

Promotes breast cancer research. Provides information about breast self-exam and early detection, treatment options, and referrals to support groups.

Y-ME: A NATIONAL BREAST CANCER ORGANIZATION
212 WEST VAN BUREN
CHICAGO, IL 60607
(312) 986-8228
(800) 221-2141
FAX: (312) 986-0020

National hotline staffed by women in recovery, or recovered from breast cancer. Provides information, makes referrals to local organizations and practitioners.

MAMMACARE PROGRAM
P.O. BOX 15748
GAINESVILLE, FL 32604
(800) 626-2273 [MAM-CARE]

Runs classes on how to give breast self-exams. Creates early detection teaching materials, such as silicone breast models.

Breast-feeding

LA LECHE LEAGUE INTERNATIONAL (LLLI)
1400 NORTH MEACHAM ROAD
SCHAMBURG, IL 60173
(800) 525-3243
(708) 519-7730
An organization dedicated to breast-feeding. Provides information, supplies breast-feeding products, publishes materials about breast-feeding and related issues.

Breast Implants

FOOD AND DRUG ADMINISTRATION (FDA)
BREAST IMPLANT INFORMATION
OFFICE OF CONSUMER AFFAIRS
5600 FISHERS LANE
HFE-88
ROCKVILLE, MD 20857
(301) 443-3170
Has a 60-page information package about breast implants, available on request.

For more information about breast implants, contact women's health organizations listed in the "Staying Healthy" Resources, page 000.

Further Reading

ⓥⓥⓥ

It's Your Body: A Woman's Guide to Gynecology, Niels H. Lauersen and Steven Whitney (Berkley, 1992).

No Need to Be Afraid . . . First Pelvic Exam: A Handbook for Young Women and Their Mothers, Ellen Curro (Linking Education and Medicine, 1991).

Take This Book to the Gynecologist with You, Gale Malesky (Addison-Wesley, 1991).

How to Stay out of the Gynecologist's Office, The Federation of Feminist Women's Health Centers (Woman to Woman Publications, 1981).

A New View of a Woman's Body, The Federation of Feminist Women's Health Centers (Feminist Health Press, 1991).

The Medical Self-Care Book of Women's Health, Bobbie Hasselbring, et al. (Doubleday & Co., 1987).

The New Our Bodies, Ourselves: Updated and Expanded for the '90s, The Boston Women's Health Book Collective Staff (Simon & Schuster, 1992).

Menstrual Health in Women's Lives, Alice H. Dan and Linda L. Lewis, eds. (University of Illinois Press, 1992).

Menstruation, Health and Illness, Diana Taylor (Hemisphere Publishing, 1991).

The Wise Wound: Myths, Realities, and Meanings of Menstruation, Penelope Shuttle and Peter Redgrove (Bantam, 1990).

Living with Endometriosis: How to Cope with the Physical and Emotional Challenges, Kate Weinstein (Addison-Wesley, 1987).

STDs, HIV & AIDS Facing the Facts

In this day and age, it is nearly impossible not to know at least *something* about sexually transmissable diseases (STDs). Almost every first-year orientation includes at a minimum a cursory mention of HIV and the admonition "If you're going to have sex, use a condom." But even those of us who attend schools that provide a thorough, up-to-date program on STDs and HIV may not know as much as we ought to. And although the latest data on everything from HIV to herpes to genital warts to "the clap" is available at campus health services, through student groups, local organizations, national hotlines, and even on the Internet, many of us turn to far less reliable sources for information—people and places that can't or don't provide the latest accurate, unbiased information. As a result, misinformation about how STDs can be transmitted (and how they *cannot* be transmitted), how to protect yourself, and who can get them is prevalent. This misinformation accounts for the spread of STDs on college campuses, as well as for the spread of fear that can paralyze us and prejudice us.

STDs are not just personal problems, they're social problems. The stigma attached to STDs, and especially to women with STDs, makes us apt to ignore even the obvious symptoms of the diseases in ourselves and reluctant to get the treatment we need. And because of the special issues that women face with regard to the detection, transmission, symptoms, and effects of STDs, it is particularly important that we sift through all the hype and get the facts.

A note about this chapter's organization: Although in the mid-1990s other STDs are far more prevalent than HIV, by and large they can be cured or at least successfully treated, while HIV is deadly. Further, the issues around the transmission, testing, treatment, and politics of HIV are far more complex. Accordingly, we have separated HIV and AIDS out and address them

WOMEN AND STDs

Women are more susceptible to contracting STDs than are men, due to the physical shape, position, and structure of our sexual and reproductive organs. For example, in heterosexual intercourse, studies indicate that women may be from 4 to 10 times more likely to become infected with a male partner's STD than vice versa. We're also less likely to notice an STD than men are because we are more often asymptomatic (have no obvious symptoms) than men. And even if signs do appear, since the bulk of women's sexual and reproductive organs are internal, evidence of an STD may go unnoticed. This can have very serious consequences. STDs have the potential not only to impair our ability to get pregnant, but also to cause complications during pregnancy, birth, and nursing (in addition to all the effects they cause in both men and women). All too frequently, damage occurs before there is any indication of a problem. For all these reasons, it is especially important for women to get tested if there is even the slightest chance of infection.

in the latter part of the chapter. (See page 381.)

TRANSMISSION OF STDs

STDs do not exist because sex is "dirty," but because certain bugs, bacteria, and viruses are present in infected people's body fluids (blood—including menstrual blood—semen, pre-seminal fluid ("pre-cum"), feces, breast milk, vaginal secretions), and sometimes on their skin and pubic hair (in the case of pubic lice). Depending on the organism responsible for the disease, STDs may be passed by genital-genital, genital-oral, or genital-anal contact, skin contact, or blood contact between a woman and a man, a woman and a woman, or a man and a man. This contact may or may not be of a "sexual nature"—despite the name, you don't necessarily need to have sex in order to contract an STD. Depending on the STD, sharing needles, having semen or vaginal secretions enter into the body through a cut, or coming into contact with infected skin can be enough to transmit it. In addition, many of these diseases can be passed from a mother to her baby before or during birth or through nursing.

THE DISEASES

"My doctor wondered aloud how a 'nice girl' could get such a disease. I told him, 'The same way that not-so-nice girls do.'"

—GEORGETOWN UNIVERSITY, '95

Little Creatures

PUBIC LICE ("Crabs")

Cause: Small bugs called lice (*Pthirus pubis*) that attach themselves to the sides of pubic hair (and other body hair) and live on blood.

Transmission: Pubic lice (or "crabs") are most often passed by physical contact, but because they can live for approximately 24 hours outside of the body, they can be transmitted through sharing towels, clothes, and bedding as well. The lice literally jump from carrier to carrier.

Symptoms: Severe itching in hairy places (pubic area, armpits, eyebrows, scalp); the presence of tiny bugs, grayish in color (except after they've eaten, when they are rust-colored and bloated), or tiny white nits (lice eggs) in pubic or other body hair (you may need a magnifying glass to see them); small bluish marks on the skin (bites); inflamed, irritated skin from scratching. Symptoms appear three to six days after infection.

Treatment: Lice can be successfully exterminated by using a prescribed shampoo, lotion, or cream containing lindane (such as Kwell). Nonprescrip-tion drugs like RID or A-200 Pyrinate work as well for most people. These treatments should not be used near the eyes; use an ophthalmic petroleum jelly instead. Clothes, towels, and bedding should be washed twice in the hottest possible washing machine cycle and dried in a dryer, or dry-cleaned. Sexual partners should be treated simultaneously as should roommates if you've had close contact or shared clothes. If you have a pet, talk to your vet about whether you should treat it. Examine area closely for any signs of lice or nits three days after treatment.

Note: Children, pregnant women, and people with very sensitive skin should not use lindane. In these cases, some practitioners will prescribe crotamiton (Eurax), but many recommend the safer (albeit smellier) sulfur ointment for three consecutive nights.

SCABIES

Cause: Mites that burrow and lay eggs under the skin.

Transmission: Like lice, scabies are highly contagious and may be passed by direct (bodily) or indirect (towels, clothes, etc.) contact. But because they can live for a longer period away from the body, may have a dormant period, and are too small to see, they are more easily transmitted than lice.

Symptoms: Severe itching all over the body; small, reddish lines, marks, or scabs, usually on the arms, hands, and legs, in armpits and folds in the skin, and under breasts; and reddish, irritated skin from scratching. Symptoms appear several weeks after first infection. If you are reinfected, itching will begin in a matter of days.

Treatment: The most common treatment for scabies is lindane cream or lotion (such as Kwell) applied over the entire body, left on for 8 to 12 hours, and then showered off. There may be some itching after treatment. As with lice, clothes, towels, and bedding should be washed twice in the hottest possible washing machine cycle and dried in a dryer, or dry-cleaned. Sexual partners should be treated simultaneously. See the treatment for pubic lice for what to do about roommates and pets.

Note: Children, pregnant women, and people with very sensitive skin should not use lindane. See the note in pubic lice for alternatives.

Very Little Creatures

TRICHOMONAS VAGINALIS/ Trichomoniasis/"Trich"

Cause: A protozoan (a one-celled organism).

Transmission: Trichomoniasis is most often transmitted by genital-genital or genital-anal contact, though it can be passed by sharing towels, bathing suits, washcloths, or (extremely infrequently) toilet seats.

Symptoms: A frothy, yellowish or greenish vaginal discharge; itching; pain during urination and/or sexual intercourse; increased frequency of urination; foul odor; urinary tract infections. Symptoms usually appear four days to three weeks after infection. Men are often asymptomatic.

Treatment: Antibiotics.

Note: Metronidazole (brand name: Flagyl), the antibiotic most effective in the treatment of trich, can produce

WARNING SIGNS OF STDs

The following is a general list of symptoms common but not unique to a number of STDs; they can also occur with disorders that are not sexually transmitted. If you are experiencing these symptoms, you should visit a health practitioner.

▲ Sores, blisters, bumps, pimples, warts, or rashes on/in/near genitals, anus, or mouth

▲ Swelling or redness in throat not associated with a cold

▲ Swelling or tenderness in genital area or lymph nodes

▲ Unusual vaginal discharge or odor

▲ Pain in the pelvic area or deep in the vagina during intercourse

▲ Burning or itching in or around the vagina

▲ Bleeding from the vagina (other than menstruation)

very serious side effects when combined with alcohol. It may also cause complications during pregnancy or feelings of depression. And like all antibiotics, it can cause birth control pills to lose effectiveness.

Smaller Still—Bacteria

CHLAMYDIA

Cause: *Chlamydia trachomatis,* an ooligate intracellular parasite which has both bacteria- and viral-like qualities.

Transmission: Chlamydia is primarily transmitted through direct genital-genital and genital-anal contact. Less commonly, it can be spread to the mouth or eyes, and from mother to baby during vaginal birth.

Symptoms: Sixty to eighty percent of women infected with chlamydia are asymptomatic—they neither see nor feel the disease. Those who do have symptoms may experience a yellowish vaginal discharge; itching or burning sensations in the genital region; pelvic or abdominal pain; bleeding between periods or after intercourse; pain during urination and/or intercourse; or inflammation of the cervix. If symptoms do appear they generally occur anywhere from one to three weeks after infection. Health practitioners, however, can often detect the disease by analyzing a vaginal culture. Men with chlamydia experience discharge from the penis; burning or itching of the urethra; pain or swelling in the testicles; and nongonococcal urethritis (NGU), an infection of the urethra. (Though a number of STDs can cause NGU, chlamydia is the most common culprit, responsible for over 45 percent of cases.)

Treatment: Antibiotics. After completion of this treatment you should have a follow-up visit.

Note:
■ Chlamydia is currently the single most prevalent STD in the U.S. Because so many women are asymptomatic, if you are sexually active, it's a good idea to get an annual chlamydia test.

■ Left untreated, chlamydia can lead to pelvic inflammatory disease (PID) and infertility. (See page 375.)

■ The traditional test for chlamydia requires a cervical swab (similar to a Pap smear); however, a more accurate urine test has recently been developed.

■ Chlamydia can induce serious complications during pregnancy and childbirth, including ectopic pregnancy, miscarriage, premature birth, and postpartum infections. If it's transmitted to the baby, the child risks contracting pneumonia or conjunctivitis.

■ Often chlamydia and gonorrhea are transmitted together. If your practitioner wants to test for one of these, have him or her test for both.

GONORRHEA

Cause: The jelly-bean-shaped *neisseria gonorrhea* bacterium that enters the body through mucous membranes in the vagina, urethra, cervix, anus, and mouth.

Transmission: Gonorrhea is most often transmitted by genital-genital, genital-oral, and genital-anal contact.

Symptoms: Many people are asymptomatic, but indications can include a yellow-green vaginal discharge; pain during urination, bowel movements, menstruation, and/or intercourse; fever; and abdominal pain. If symptoms occur, they usually appear a few days to a few weeks after contraction of the disease. Men experience a discharge from the penis, and pain and tenderness in the testicles.

Treatment: Antibiotics. You'll need a follow-up visit and culture seven days after you finish taking them.

Note:
■ Left untreated, gonorrhea can lead to pelvic inflammatory disease (PID) and infertility. (See page 375.)

■ Because the test for gonorrhea isn't the most accurate, many practitioners

40 million people will have chlamydia by the year 2000.

recommend having two consecutive tests after possible exposure and/or after treatment.

■ Often gonorrhea and chlamydia are transmitted together. If your practitioner wants to test for one of these, have him/her test for both.

SYPHILIS

Cause: A spirochete containing the bacterium *Treponema pallidum* that enters the body through the mucous membranes or cuts in the skin.

Transmission: Syphilis is spread through contact with syphilitic sores (chancroid) or genital-genital, genital-oral, and genital-anal contact.

Symptoms: Syphilis is a disease that occurs in several stages. In the primary stage, approximately two to eight weeks after contraction of the disease, a painless, hard red-rimmed sore or lesion appears on or in the vagina, cervix, anus, or mouth (or less commonly on the breast or fingers). It disappears two to six weeks after it appears. Between six weeks and six months after this, symptoms of the second stage develop, which may include a rash all over the body or just on the palms of the hands and the bot-

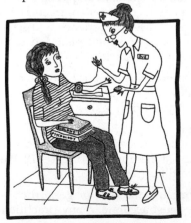

toms of the feet; flu-like symptoms, such as fever, sore throat, or nausea; inflammation of the eyes and joints; hair loss; and small, moist, flat growths that appear on the mucous membranes. This stage usually lasts one to eight weeks.

After this second stage, outward symptoms usually subside, but the bacteria continue to wreak havoc on the body. After 10 to 20 years of this latency period, the severe symptoms of the tertiary, or late, stage of syphilis appear: insanity, heart disease, brain damage, blindness, paralysis, and even death.

Treatment: Antibiotics. You must have at least two follow-up blood tests after treatment.

Note:
■ Syphilis can cause complications during pregnancy. All pregnant women should be tested. Many HIV test sites also test for syphilis.

Very, Very, Tiny—Viruses

ⓥⓥⓥ

HUMAN PAPILLOMA VIRUS (HPV)/Genital Warts/Condyloma

Cause: The human papilloma virus (HPV), a virus in the same family as the one that causes skin warts. (The symmetrical, hard warts on the hands or feet are different from, and do not cause, genital warts. However, HPV lesions may appear on the hands.)

Transmission: Genital warts are transmitted through skin-skin contact with warts (usually through genital-genital, genital-oral, and genital-anal contact). The warts themselves are highly contagious right before they appear and while they exist. It is unclear how eas-

PELVIC INFLAMMATORY DISEASE (PID)

Pelvic inflammatory disease (PID) is not an STD, but rather a condition caused by STDs (and in between 5 to 10 percent of cases, other gynecological disorders). PID is an infection of the lining of the uterus, the fallopian tubes, and/or ovaries that develops when bacteria (usually those causing gonorrhea or chlamydia) travel into these organs and are left untreated.

PID can inflict serious damage, including severe scarring that can cause infertility or ectopic pregnancy (when a fertilized egg implants in a fallopian tube rather than the uterus), and peritonitis, a life-threatening condition. PID is often misdiagnosed as endometriosis, and vice versa. (See page 366 for more information about endometriosis.)

PID is not contagious, but the diseases that cause PID are. Indications that you might be suffering from PID include abdominal pain or backache; vaginal bleeding (other than menstruation); foul-smelling discharge; persistent fever, chills, nausea, and vomiting; pain during vaginal intercourse; increased menstrual cramps and flow;

frequent urination; general fatigue; and swollen abdomen.

PID is sometimes difficult to diagnose, and may require a number of different tests and procedures such as a culture, a blood test, a laparoscopy, and/or a biopsy. If it's diagnosed early enough, PID can be treated with antibiotics, but in its later stages it may require surgery. When being tested for PID, it is important to test for the STDs that may have caused PID, and have your partner(s) tested and treated as well.

Because PID often goes unnoticed in its early stages, it is good practice, if you are sexually active, to be tested for the STDs that can cause PID at your annual gynecological checkup. Because the IUD greatly increases your susceptibility to PID (by lowering resistance to infection, irritating the uterine lining so infection can set in more easily, and giving bacteria easy access to the upper reproductive system via the string), it is especially important to use a condom or other latex barrier if you have an IUD. (See page 417 for more information on the IUD.)

ily HPV is passed between partners when warts are not present. But because it is very hard to predict when an outbreak has occurred—they may be present on your vaginal walls or your cervix, or in your partner's urethra, but not on the skin you see and touch—always practice safer sex if you or the person you are with has HPV. (See "Safer Sex," page 421.)

Symptoms: Warts that resemble skin warts when located on the exterior genitalia, and appear soft and fleshy when on the internal genitalia. They may be round, oval, or asymmetrical, and be grayish, pinkish, brownish, or whitish in color. The warts can occur singly or in clusters on the anus, labia, vagina, and cervix in women (and on the anus, testicles, penis, and urethra

LIVING WITH HPV (GENITAL WARTS) AND HERPES

Millions of people are infected with herpes (HSV) and genital warts (HPV), and their lives are affected only minimally. Having genital warts or herpes does not mean you can't have a fulfilling, safe sex life. Though HSV and HPV are chronic conditions (they can be treated but not cured), they shouldn't preclude sex or adversely affect your future relationships. The main thing to remember is to practice safer sex (see page 421) and not to engage in sexual activity during an outbreak—even with a condom, dental dam, or other latex barrier. Not only can sweat that has come in contact with the virus seep outside the latex area, but it is difficult to keep sores or warts that are not on the penis or inside the vagina fully covered by latex. In addition, even if both you and your partner have the virus you should still avoid sex during an outbreak because the virus can be introduced to new sites or a different strain can be transmitted. (For more information on viruses in general, see "HIV Explained," page 382.)

"I was really scared when my yearly checkup Pap smear came back 'abnormal.' I had no problems or symptoms of anything. It turned out to be HPV."

—UNIVERSITY OF MAINE
AT ORONO ,'95

in men), and are usually (but not always) painless. There may be burning, itching, pain, or bleeding in the genital area. Warts appear one to six months after contraction of HPV.

Treatment: There is no known cure for HPV. While there are a number of methods used to remove the warts and diminish any unpleasant symptoms, they rarely completely clear the body of the virus. Treatment with trichloriacetic acid podofilox (Condylox) or other chemicals, freezing (cryosurgery), surgery, and electrocautery are the most popular removal methods. To alleviate symptoms, some use interferon or other antiviral drugs, but many believe that removal using the above-mentioned methods offers equal results for less money and without the risk of side effects.

Note:
■ Because the virus remains in the body even after warts are removed, recurrences are common. The severity and frequency vary among individuals and generally decrease with age.

■ Hormonal changes during pregnancy can trigger outbreaks.

■ Even though HPV rarely complicates pregnancy, it is still important to tell your doctor if you are pregnant and have a history of HPV.

■ Do not use over-the-counter wart removal products to self-treat HPV.

■ Though Pap smears don't test directly for HPV, the virus often causes abnormal Pap results. There is, however, a link between HPV and cervical dys-

> *"I kept getting little pimples in my bikini area. I would freak out and get really depressed because I was convinced I must have herpes or something. It turned out that I had a gynecologist appointment just when one appeared, and I asked her about it. It turned out to just be an ingrown hair."*
>
> —COLLEGE OF THE HOLY CROSS, '97

plasia, a precancerous condition, so if you are infected, be sure to have a Pap smear every three to six months.

HERPES

Cause: A virus that exists in two forms: herpes simplex 1, or oral herpes (cold sores on the lips or mouth), and herpes simplex 2, or genital herpes.

Transmission: Direct contact with herpes sores transmits the virus. Herpes is extremely contagious just before and during an outbreak. Lip sores can cause genital lesions if oral sex occurs when the virus is "shedding." It is unclear how easily the virus is transmitted when no sores are present, but because it is not always possible to know when an outbreak will recur or when sores are present but not visible, in theory, there is no totally safe time.

Symptoms include:

Oral herpes: Fever blister, canker, or cold sore on lips, gums, tongue, or face.

Genital herpes: Painful blisterlike sores or lesions on the outer/inner labia, clitoris, anus, vagina, and/or cervix in women, and the penis, anus, or urethra in men. Sores first appear as red bumps resembling pimples, then come to a head and turn into watery, crusty blisters covered by a yellowish secretion. Sometimes blood will also appear. The sores will open and ooze, then scab over and heal. Often accompanying these sores are flu-like symptoms, enlarged lymph nodes in the groin area, and pain during urination and intercourse. The length of outbreaks vary (usually between 7 to 15 days), and they occur at different rates for different people; some experience only a couple of recurrences, while for others they are quite frequent.

Generally, the first outbreak is the most severe and lasts the longest. It is often accompanied by flu-like symptoms (fever, chills, aches, fatigue, and swollen glands and lymph nodes) and/or may begin with an itching/tingling/burning sensation, pain, or feelings of pressure. The first outbreak usually occurs three days to four weeks after contraction of the disease.

Treatment: Though there is no known cure for herpes (once you contract it, you carry the virus and have the potential for outbreaks for life), there are ways to minimize the pain, discomfort, and duration of the sores, and to increase the time between outbreaks.

Oral herpes: Over-the-counter canker sore medications can help alleviate the discomfort and shorten the life of outbreaks. For sores on the face, if bacterial infection occurs, some doctors recommend a prescribed or over-the-counter antibiotic cream or ointment.

Genital herpes: Acyclovir (Zovirax) is an antiviral medication that may be applied to sores to help speed the healing process, but is most often taken orally or injected to reduce the number and severity of recurrent outbreaks. Other medications, such as idoxuridine and lysine (an amino acid) are used with less success.

In 1994, between 48 and 50 million Americans carried the virus.

To minimize outbreaks: Aside from the onset, outbreaks are related to how well the immune system is able to keep the virus at bay. Illness (including HIV), stress, and/or diet may all play a role in outbreaks. Use relaxation techniques, exercise, and get sufficient sleep, especially if you feel a recurrence coming on, and maintain a healthy diet (and take a multivitamin and extra vitamin C). Some believe that foods containing arginine (such as nuts, cola, seeds, and chocolate) and caffeine may trigger outbreaks.

During a genital herpes outbreak: Wear cotton underwear and loose-fitting clothes; sit in a warm bath with Epsom salts and baking soda; treat sores with drying agents like corn-starch, aloe vera gel (which also soothes), or even a hair dryer on a low setting. Taking high-potency B complex, vitamins C and E, zinc, and lysine may help speed recovery.

Note:

■ The majority of Americans carry HSV-1—that's the virus that causes a cold sore or a canker sore. Though it's rare that HSV-2 causes outbreaks on the lips, mouth, and face, an estimated 10 percent of outbreaks on the genitals are HSV-1, most often contracted through oral sex.

■ Most doctors will perform cesarean births if herpes sores are present during labor.

■ Do not donate blood during herpes outbreaks.

■ Washing well with soap and hot water can kill the virus before it enters your body; doing so after sex can help prevent transmission of the virus.

■ If you have a cold sore on your mouth or face (HSV-1), do not engage in oral sex or use saliva as lubrication in any sex play (masturbation or with others)—or to wet contact lenses.

HEPATITIS B

Cause: One of the five strains of the hepatitis virus (hepatitis A–hepatitis E).

Transmission: Genital-genital, genital-oral, and genital-anal contact and blood contact (such as through sharing needles).

Symptoms: More than 50 percent of those infected show no symptoms. Those who are symptomatic may experience extreme fatigue, jaundice, nausea, poor appetite, fever, joint and stomach pain, rash, diarrhea, and/or dark urine.

Treatment: There is no treatment for hepatitis. Those infected usually have no choice but to rest, drink a lot of fluids, take vitamins, and avoid alcohol and unprescribed drugs. In most cases, recovery is complete in one to four months, but a small percentage may develop chronic hepatitis or liver cancer. Some doctors use antiviral medications, such as alpha-interferon, to help alleviate chronic symptoms.

Note: A hepatitis vaccine is effective in preventing infection in most people. The American College Health Association and public health experts recommend the vaccine for all college students, particularly those who are sexually active. A blood test can detect the virus even when symptoms are not present.

❈ Herpes comes from the Greek "to creep." ❈ 20-30 million Americans

IF YOU THINK YOU'VE GOT AN STD

———————

I f you suspect you have an STD, make an appointment to see a gynecologist or another health practitioner as soon as possible. (Many health care clinics offer free or inexpensive STD screenings.) The sooner you treat an STD, the easier it is to cure or treat; the less chance it will cause other health problems; the less time you will have to stress, worry, and wonder about it; and the less likely you will be to infect someone else. (And some STDs, like herpes, must be detected within the first few days of the outbreak, or they are nearly impossible to diagnose conclusively.) In the time between making and having the appointment, avoid touching the area, both sexually and nonsexually. As difficult as it may be, resist the temptation to inspect, pick, squeeze, or scratch. Do not douche or use any medication, ointments, or creams unless specifically recommended by your doctor, because these can cause "false-negative" test results—negative test results that would have, but for the use of creams, ointments, and so forth, read positive.

IF YOU'RE DIAGNOSED WITH AN STD

———————

■ Treat the problem exactly as prescribed. Avoid touching the area (or having the area touched by others) during treatment—it can aggravate the problem, slow healing, and cause the disease to spread, scar, hurt, or itch more. And finish the medicine, even if you're feeling better—symptoms often subside before the STD is gone.

■ Get post-treatment checkups.

WHAT GETTING AN STD MEANS (AND DOESN'T MEAN)

Contracting an STD doesn't mean you're bad, dirty, sleazy, fast, or being punished. STDs are medical, not moral, issues (and in these times, they are also mortal issues). You should never feel embarrassed or apprehensive about asking your practitioner to examine or test you for STDs. In fact, it's not a bad idea to get screened for STDs if you've been involved in *any* potentially risky behavior—even if you've been practicing safer sex. (Most doctors do not routinely test for STDs, so you'll probably have to ask.)

Getting an STD doesn't mean you are doing something you shouldn't, but it may mean you aren't doing something you *should* be doing—namely protecting yourself from contracting a disease that can lead to a maddening itch, infertility, or sometimes even death. And even more important than knowing the symptoms and treatment methods of STDs is knowing how to avoid them. (See "Safer Sex," page 421, for more on the prevention of STDs.)

have herpes; as many as 5OO,OOO people are infected each year.

■ Notify those people with whom you have engaged in sexual and other activities that may have put them at risk of contracting the disease.

■ Wait to resume sexual and/or other risky activities until your partner(s) are tested (and treated, if necessary).

■ Remember: Being treated for and cured of an STD does not protect you from getting it again.

■ Do not share STD medication with your partner. Though you may feel fine, and it may seem to cure your symptoms, neither one of you will end up getting enough medicine to get rid of the disease completely, and only the strongest, most resistant germs will remain, making it even more difficult to get rid of the disease (though symptoms may disappear).

> **"When I got an STD I was really upset, not just because of having to deal with it, but because I got it from my boyfriend, who was supposed to be monogamous."**
> —UNIVERSITY OF VIRGINIA, '93

TELLING A PARTNER YOU HAVE AN STD

There are no two ways about it—as soon as you've been diagnosed with an STD, you have to get in touch with anyone you might have passed it to. There are many ways to disclose the information; you can do so personally or anonymously. Some clinics that offer STD treatment will do it

for you (and will not use your name). If you want to tell a partner—anyone you are, or have been in a sexual relationship with, be it for an hour or five years—yourself, but can't face it alone, make an appointment with your health practitioner and take your partner with you. This way the practitioner will be right on hand to clarify any information and answer any questions s/he may have.

Telling a partner that you have an STD is not easy. In all likelihood, the encounter will be emotional. Your partner may feel angry, hurt, or just plain shocked. You might be devastated because you could have gotten it from no one else but your partner, and the two of you were supposed to be monogamous. But for your and your partner's health and stress level, it's important to deal with it as quickly, rationally, and calmly as possible.

If you choose to tell the person (or people) yourself:

■ Find an appropriate place and time to talk. If at all possible, bring it up face to face rather than on the phone. Choose a time when you can be alone, free from interruptions, and unhurried. You may want to meet in a neutral space that is less emotionally "loaded" than your bedroom, like a library or a coffeehouse.

■ Though it may be difficult, for the moment try to separate the health issue ("what I've/we've got") from the fidelity issue ("How did I/we/you get this?"). This is especially true when the STD was acquired months (or years) before your present relationship, as can be the case with herpes or HPV, or when symptoms weren't obvious.

■ Get the facts in advance. Learn about the disease—its symptoms, how it's

"I have HPV, as do a lot of women I know, and I always tell guys I'm with before anything happens— it's my responsibility....After I told my ex-boyfriend, he was afraid to touch me, even when I assured him that if we used a condom he would be at a very, very, very small risk of getting it. I know that most of the problem was that he had no idea what warts were and how HPV is transmitted, but it made me feel terrible when he acted as if I was dirty or tainted." —UCLA, '94

spread, and how it's treated. Give your partner(s) a short but thorough description, discuss questions, and clear up misconceptions. It might help to have this book, a pamphlet, or an STD information hotline number on hand for more information.

■ Use this time to talk about safer sex in general.

■ Give your partner(s) the name and number of a clinic or doctor where information, testing, and treatment are available.

HIV AND AIDS

Though we all "know about" HIV (human immunodeficiency virus) and AIDS (acquired immune deficiency syndrome), we may not know exactly what they are, how HIV is transmitted, what the testing procedures (and politics) are, or what the special issues for women are. New information and misinformation about HIV and AIDS appear so rapidly that it can be difficult to keep track. Indeed, it is quite possible that some of the information in this chapter may be out of date within the next few years. Hopefully, the section about the lack of a cure will be. (For the latest information, contact one of the organizations listed in the Resources at the end of this chapter.) But remember, just knowing the facts about HIV and AIDS is not enough. In order to protect yourself, you also need to understand how you can get HIV and AIDS and take the appropriate steps to prevent transmission. (Practicing safer sex— using a latex barrier when engaging in oral, anal, or vaginal sex—and using clean needles are essential in the prevention of HIV. See "Safer Sex," page 421, and "Cleaning Needles," page 304, for full discussions.)

WHAT IS HIV/AIDS?

AIDS is the final stage in the progression of HIV infection. The definition includes a large number of conditions and illnesses that afflict people whose immune systems are compromised due to HIV infection to the point that their bodies are no longer able to defend themselves against illness. In fact, most of the diseases associated with AIDS are not even particularly dangerous to people who have healthy immune systems. It is only because the body has been so weakened by HIV that these illnesses, which are normally not lethal, can become life-threatening.

they rose by 18% in women, 75% of whom were women of color.

HIV, AIDS, AND STDs

Just as you can't get stomach flu from an ear infection, you can't get AIDS from another STD. The only way you can get AIDS is from the virus that causes AIDS: HIV. But when you have another STD (or any other illness), haven't eaten or slept well, or are very stressed, your immune system isn't as capable of fighting disease, and you might be more likely to become infected with HIV if exposed to it. Also, STDs that cause sores or skin irritation increase susceptibility to infection, because a partner's body fluids can enter into your body through skin damaged by cuts, scratching, and rashes. For these reasons untreated STDs can increase the likelihood of becoming infected with HIV upon exposure.

Individuals can test positive for HIV without actually showing or feeling any of the symptoms associated with HIV infection or AIDS. In fact, they may not even begin to show signs for 5 or 10 years (and sometimes even longer). Internally, however, the HIV *is* taking its toll. And a person who is HIV-positive is capable of infecting others regardless of whether or not s/he manifests any symptoms.

This means that you can become infected as a result of having unprotected anal, oral, or genital sex, sharing needles, or taking part in any other behaviors that may involve the exchange of blood (including menstrual blood), semen, vaginal secre-

tions, or breast milk with someone who is infected but has no outward signs of having the virus. Engaging in any of the above is considered risky behavior.

HIV Explained

A little bit of knowledge about the nature of viruses (particularly HIV) gives you the tools to determine "what's not safe," as well as the equally important "what *is* safe." It allows you to accurately assess the risk involved in your behavior, makes you more aware of how to protect yourself, and alleviates some of the fear that comes from misinformation.

Viruses (including HIV) are not capable of living or causing illness on their own. They need to enter a host cell, where they replicate by taking over the cell's reproductive "machinery," and then eventually spread to other cells. However, viruses don't simply invade cells at random—for every virus there is only one (or, in some cases, a few) specific cell type that can act as a suitable host. For HIV the infectable cells are those with CD4 receptors, such as the white blood cell called the T-cell. These cells are an essential part of the human immune system and are found in the fluids in which HIV is transmitted—semen, blood, breast milk, and vaginal secretions. (They are also present in other body fluids, but not in concentrations high enough to transmit the virus.) T-cells are often cited in discussions about HIV because they are easily measured and thus are commonly used to gauge the extent of infection.

Normally, a virus as fragile as HIV (it can't sustain itself for more than a few moments outside the body) wouldn't pose much of a threat to us, but because it attacks the very cells that would destroy it, it is able to survive and do damage. When a virus or bacterium (or any other disease-causing invader) enters the body, the CD4 cells and the rest of the immune system work to obliterate the virus before it can wreak havoc. Most often, these defenses are successful. However, HIV weakens the immune system's ability to fight infection. After HIV infects a CD4 immune cell, the cell's functions become impaired (after a possible lag time), and then the virus reproduces. Eventually, a new generation of viral particles are released from the host cell into the lymph glands and bloodstream, where they infect other healthy cells. The host cell then dies. In effect, the cell that is designed to destroy viruses now creates them.

As HIV multiplies, more CD4 immune cells are destroyed, and the body becomes less able to ward off disease. This leaves the body vulnerable to contracting illnesses that are very rare or nonthreatening in people with healthy immune systems, such as cytomegalovirus (CMV), Kaposi's sarcoma (KS), and pneumocystis carinii pneumonia (PCP). When a person is said to have AIDS, or "full-blown" AIDS, it means s/he has one of the diseases that the Centers for Disease Control and Prevention recognizes as defining AIDS.

FACTS ABOUT HIV

HIV is not an exclusive virus—it can infect anyone with CD4 cells, which are common to all humans: a white male intravenous drug user, a black female heterosexual honors student, a Latina lesbian, an Asian gay male. It doesn't matter where you're from, what you do, or what you don't do—if the virus gets into your body you may become infected.

You can be HIV-positive and not feel at all sick or show any signs of illness.

It is not yet proven that everyone with HIV will develop "full-blown" AIDS.

TRANSMISSION

In order for transmission to occur, body fluids containing the virus must be able to enter the bloodstream, then pass directly into a cell with the CD4 receptor (such as the T-cell). Transmission occurs most often via mucous membranes (wet surfaces where the inside of the body meets the outside, such as the mouth, eyes, anus, and vagina); through sharing needles; or from mother to baby in utero, during birth, and through breast-feeding. In addition, health care workers have contracted the virus by inadvertently sticking themselves with HIV-contaminated syringes. There also have been cases of transmission by blood transfu-

ing the virus to women; only 2% occurs from women to men.

WHAT DO ALL THE ACRONYMS MEAN?

AIDS: Acquired Immune Deficiency Syndrome

Acquired: You get it from someone; it doesn't spontaneously occur.

Immune: The body's immune system protects and defends against illness.

Deficiency: Lacking in some way. In the case of AIDS, *immune deficiency* means that the body's immune system is compromised.

Syndrome: A collection of problems or symptoms that are somehow related. A large number of health problems and symptoms are associated with HIV infection, as a response to the virus itself and as a result of immune system breakdown.

HIV: Human Immunodeficiency Virus

Human: The virus exists in people.

Immunodeficiency: Impaired immunity.

Virus: One of the many causes of disease. Viruses are responsible for causing illnesses like hepatitis, mononucleosis, the flu, and the common cold. Unlike bacteria, they do not respond to antibiotics and cannot be cured by medicine. Many viruses—such as cold viruses and influenza—are short-lived, but others—such as the herpes virus, HPV (the genital warts virus), and HIV—are lifelong.

AZT and ddI: These are two of the most common antiviral prophylactic treatments (a fancy name for preventative treatments) used to combat HIV and slow its progression in those infected. AZT is the acronym for azidothymadine and ddI is short for didanosine.

CDC: The Centers for Disease Control and Prevention, located in Atlanta, Georgia, is the agency responsible for estimating the number of Americans with HIV, classifying the ways that people contract HIV, labeling the type of behavior that puts one at risk for HIV, and determining what symptoms, disorders, and diseases are included in the definition of AIDS. The CDC also serves as a locus for research and a clearinghouse of information about health issues.

sion. However, since 1985, all donated blood has been tested for the virus and the number of new cases of HIV infection from blood transfusions is greatly reduced.

The only body fluids that are known to have a high enough concentration of HIV to transmit the virus are the above mentioned blood (including menstrual blood), preseminal fluid ("pre-cum"), semen, vaginal fluid, and breast milk. Other body fluids, such as saliva, sweat, urine, and tears, don't appear to have a high enough concentration to transmit the virus. Though just one exposure can transmit HIV, it is possible to have repeated exposures without becoming infected.

HIV cannot live without the three W's: warmth, wetness, and white

 Since 1992, heterosexual transmission has been the most

blood cells. Being rather fragile, it is quickly inactivated by exposure to the air and to household bleach, as well as to very hot and cold temperatures. Unlike the flu, you cannot catch HIV if someone with the virus coughs or sneezes near you. It can't be breathed or swallowed in, nor can it pass through healthy, unbroken skin.

Taking Precautions

"You always hear about how people our age feel like they won't get AIDS, and even though I know I can get it on a rational level, I still don't do everything I should to protect myself."

—MIDDLEBURY COLLEGE, '92

Having unsafe sex (sex that involves the potential exchange of body fluids) and sharing unclean needles (when injecting drugs, including steroids) can spread the virus. Regardless of your or your partner's sexual preference or current HIV status (unless you've undergone serial testing), heed the following:

■ If you have vaginal, anal, or oral sex, or engage in any activities that might draw blood, it is imperative that you practice safer sex. Using latex condoms and dental dams during vaginal, oral, and anal intercourse reduces but does not eliminate the possibility of transmission. (For more on protecting yourself and your partners from HIV and other sexually transmissable diseases, see "Safer Sex," page 421.)

■ If you shoot drugs, do not share works unless they are sterilized before each and every use. (See "Cleaning Needles," page 304.)

■ It's not a good idea to share razors or toothbrushes.

■ Even if *both* you and your partner are HIV-positive, it is still important to practice safer sex and use clean needles, to avoid co-infection (i.e., infection with different strains of the virus).

SYMPTOMS—HOW DO I KNOW IF I HAVE HIV?

Almost all the symptoms of early HIV infection are also symptoms of illnesses that are common among college students. Many students, upon reading the list, start questioning whether their cold, flu, mono, stress- or diet-related headaches, stomach problems, or sleeplessness may be HIV. The chief distinction is the severity and duration of the conditions. For example, a week or two of feeling tired, having swollen glands, fever, cough, and diarrhea is most probably just the regular ol' (albeit rather unlovable) flu. However, if the symptoms are prolonged, recurrent, and/or are especially acute, they may be a sign that you have a more serious illness, possibly related to HIV.

Symptoms may include some of the following:

▲ Unexplained fever that lasts more than a week
▲ Swollen glands
▲ Unusually heavy night sweats
▲ Recurring severe yeast infections or thrush (oral candidiasis)
▲ Abnormal menstrual bleeding

SAFE ACTIVITIES

❀

As important as knowing how you can get HIV is knowing how you can't get HIV. You *cannot* get HIV from:

▲ Donating blood
▲ Sitting next to or sharing food with an HIV-positive person
▲ Drinking out of the same glass as an HIV-positive person
▲ Swimming in a public pool
▲ Riding public transportation
▲ Using a phone
▲ Rocking an HIV-positive baby
▲ Drinking from a water fountain
▲ Touching a doorknob
▲ Being stung or bitten by an insect
▲ Having someone sneeze on you
▲ Sitting on a toilet seat

In addition, you cannot get HIV from close casual contact with someone who is HIV-positive, including hugging, massaging, holding hands, and light kissing. French kissing is also fine, as long as you don't have cuts or sores in your mouth.

Roommates and caretakers of people with HIV/AIDS (who are not otherwise considered to be at high risk, insofar as they don't practice unsafe sex or share needles without cleaning them first) have a rate of HIV infection equal to that of the general population.

Again, the *only* way that a person can become infected with HIV is if there is a direct exchange of infected body fluids.

▲ Sudden, unexplained weight loss
▲ Rashes, bumps, blisters on the skin
▲ Diarrhea that lasts for more than a few days
▲ Severe genital herpes
▲ Acute tiredness
▲ Chronic pelvic inflammatory disease

TESTING FOR HIV

The most common test for HIV is called the enzyme-linked immunoabsorbent assay, or ELISA, test. The ELISA test does not test for HIV itself, but rather for the presence of antibodies that the body creates when the virus is present. It can take two to six months (and in some cases it may take as long as nine months) for the virus to proliferate to the extent that enough antibodies are formed to be detected. (The time between infection and detection is called the "window period.") In other words, a negative test does not mean that a person is definitely HIV-negative, only that s/he does not have enough antibodies to test positive. Thus, a person can test negative when in fact s/he has HIV. The only way to be sure that you are HIV-negative is through "serial testing": testing negative, not engaging in any risky behavior for at least six months, and then being retested.

If the ELISA test is positive, clinicians usually perform a more specific test called the Western blot test. This is

❀ In a 1993 survey of college athletes, 11% thought HIV could be

an antigen test (a test for the virus itself). Because it's quite expensive and complex, it is generally only used to confirm a positive ELISA test. At the present time, viral cultures, in which clinicians try to grow the virus from possibly infected cells, are almost never used in HIV testing—they're time-consuming, expensive, and unreliable (in the case of HIV). New tests, such as lymph and p24 antigen studies, are also being developed to detect HIV infection.

In rare cases, people test positive when they do not have the virus (false-positive) or test negative when there are enough antibodies present to test positive (false-negative). Sometimes test results are inconclusive, often due to medication in the blood, another illness such as hepatitis, improper handling of the blood, or technical errors (all of which can cause the same sample to read positive and then retest negative). Ask about the frequency of inaccurate test results in your pre- and post-test counseling sessions. (*Note:* It is not considered false-negative when a person with HIV tests negative because the body has not had the time to manufacture a sufficient amount of antibodies to render a positive test result.)

Should I Get Tested?

ⓐⓐⓐ

Before getting tested, take the time to understand the pros and cons of knowing you are HIV-positive, and to think about where and from whom you might get the information and emotional support you would need to deal with a positive test result. Most health care experts advocate testing,

"The actual HIV test is very easy. You just go in there and talk to a counselor and get your blood taken and leave. It's all the issues around the test that make it hard."
—DUKE UNIVERSITY, '95

especially for people (and their partners) who have engaged in potentially risky behavior. Unlike other medical tests, which aren't indicated in the absence of symptoms, it is not necessary or advisable to wait until you have the symptoms of HIV before you get tested, if you believe that you might be at risk. Although discovering that you are HIV-positive is a painful, frightening thing, the sooner you know, the sooner you can begin to take the necessary steps to care for your emotional and physical health. (See "Testing Positive," page 390.) However, if you feel that you cannot bear the emotional burden of finding out you are HIV-positive at this time, or feel that a positive result will neither affect your high-risk behaviors nor prompt you to seek medical or psychological help, you might choose not to take the test.

Even though you won't find out the results of your test right away, the experience often provokes a number of different issues, feelings, and memories, and can be extremely difficult. You might want to bring a friend with you when you get tested as well as when you go in for your results. If you will not have the opportunity to meet with a counselor at the testing site before the test, or you need information or just someone to talk to while going through the testing process (or at any other time), there are numerous hotlines, support groups, and organi-

transmitted by mosquitoes and 35% by donating blood. (Wrong!) ✸

zations available. (See the Resources at the end of this chapter.)

As of this writing, it is your decision whether or not to have an HIV test, except in the following cases, when you'll automatically be tested:

■ If you enlist in the military, foreign service, and the job corps.

■ If you apply for a green card (at the U.S. Department of Immigration).

■ In order to obtain coverage by certain insurance companies.

> **"Even though I was sure I wasn't positive—I mean, there was really very little chance—I was still terrified about the whole thing. During the two weeks between taking the test and going in for my results, I obsessed over it, was completely uninterested in sex, and couldn't concentrate, and when I found out I was negative I was so happy and relieved."**
>
> **—UNIVERSITY OF MICHIGAN, '94**

■ When you donate blood, breast milk, organs, and body tissue. Your "donation" will be screened for HIV, although you may not find out if it tested positive because, in most cases, hospitals and blood banks do not keep a record of your name and often do "batch testing."

These are the only cases in which you are required to have an HIV test. It is illegal for your school, employer, or doctor to require you to take a test or to test your blood without your per-mission. (However, they can, and often will, put a lot of pressure on you to give your permission.)

Anonymous vs. Confidential Testing

Testing is either confidential or anonymous. In an anonymous test-ing situation, the testing site does not keep any record of your name. When you make an appointment, you are given a number to use for identifica-tion. The benefit of anonymous testing is that it enables you to control exactly who knows what about you, and gives you the power to determine who, when, and under what conditions you will share information about your health. With anonymous testing, you don't have to worry that people with whom you'd rather not share your HIV status (or any other intimate details of your life) will be privy to the information.

When you get an HIV test through your doctor or a clinic that provides confidential testing, the fact that you took the test will appear in your med-ical records. Though your medical records are confidential by law, the information will almost always be available to health insurance pro-viders, as well as to prospective employers (if they provide health insurance to their employees). Further-more, in some areas, if your confi-dential test comes up positive, the information will definitely not remain private—one quarter of states require physicians to report all names of those who test HIV-positive to state, county, or local health departments. (Other states require reporting of only demographic information such as age, race, and gender, and some have no reporting requirements at all.) The fact is, although it is illegal to discriminate against people with HIV or AIDS, people *have* lost their jobs, been denied health insurance, and even been refused treatment by doctors, dentists, and other health care providers. It's unfair, depressing, and infuriating, but at this time, being HIV-positive can damage more than your immune system. If it is possible, protect yourself from "unsolicited discrimination" by getting an anonymous test.

Unfortunately, anonymous testing is not available in all states. If this is the case, you can always make a confidential test anonymous by going to a place you've never been to before, using a fake name, and paying in cash (though many testing services are free).

What Happens When I Get Tested?

ᦥᦥᦥ

When you arrive for your scheduled appointment, you will meet with a trained counselor (if the testing site has counseling services) to determine your risk and discuss questions you have about the test, HIV, and what constitutes safe and unsafe behavior. After your consultation, you will have the opportunity to decide whether or not you want to be tested. If so, a technician will draw your blood. Before you leave, you will make an appointment to come back for the test result. (For the most part, clinics do not give HIV results over the phone.) When you return, you will meet with a counselor who will tell you the result and

talk with you about what it means. You will again have the opportunity to get information about HIV and gather names of local resources.

How to Get Tested

ᦥᦥᦥ

Many clinics, health centers, private doctors, city and state health departments, and other public and private organizations offer HIV testing. Some of the questions that you should ask of the places that you are considering are:

Cost and Payment Issues

▲ How much will it cost?
▲ What forms of payment do you accept (cash, check, credit card, insurance)?
▲ Are there reduced rates for students?
▲ When do I have to pay? (In person before or after the test, by mail after the test?)

Confidentiality Issues

▲ Is the test anonymous or confidential?
▲ What are the benefits and drawbacks of this type of testing?

- ▲ If I am under 18 or 21, do I need to get permission from an adult, or does an adult have to come with me?
- ▲ To whom and under what conditions will you disclose information about the fact that I was tested and my results? (Parent or guardian, insurance provider, school, boss, future employers, doctor, sexual partners, husband?)
- ▲ Will my bill state that I took the test?

Getting Information and Emotional Support

Many states require that clinics provide counseling before the test and at the time the results are given.

- ▲ Will there be someone to explain exactly what will happen—what getting tested means, and the pros and cons of getting tested?
- ▲ What are the objectives of counseling before and after the test?
- ▲ May I come in to talk about the test but not necessarily take it?
- ▲ Will I be given information about HIV and AIDS?
- ▲ May I come back to talk about the test and my feelings about it?

The Test Itself

- ▲ Do you test for anything other than HIV? (Many places also test for syphilis, hepatitis, and other diseases.)

The Logistics

- ▲ When can I get an appointment?
- ▲ How long will it take?
- ▲ How long before I get my results?
- ▲ How will I be told the results?
- ▲ May I come in and get tested with my boyfriend or girlfriend?

Testing Positive

ഗൗഗ

An essential part of coping with the fact that you have tested positive for HIV is taking the necessary steps to care for your emotional and physical health. You should seek medical care in order to monitor your health, begin treatment, and adopt a lifestyle that will allow you to live a healthier and longer life. You can take steps to avoid many of the common opportunistic infections, join support groups that can help with the difficult emotional issues surrounding testing positive, and do all that is necessary to protect present sexual partner(s) and yourself. You should also contact people with whom you have engaged in "risky" behavior, such as sexual intercourse or sharing needles, to alert them that they may be infected (you can either do this yourself or have a clinic do it for you anonymously).

"When the counselor told me that I was positive, I felt like I couldn't breathe. I felt so alone. I just wanted to run out of there, but he wouldn't let me, and now I thank him for it. . . . He told me that testing positive was a very good thing, because I had HIV whether or not I had a test to confirm it. Not getting tested wouldn't make it go away, and now that I knew, I could take steps to make my life better, and live longer."

—BROOKLYN COLLEGE,
"ONE CLASS AT A TIME"

Under the Americans With Disabilities Act, it is illegal for a doctor

Testing positive for HIV is extremely traumatic even if you have suspected you are HIV-positive for a while. You do not have to face this by yourself. There are numerous places and people you can contact for support, guidance, and information. Local and national HIV/AIDS organizations will be able to provide you with names of doctors; tips on dealing with insurance providers and employers; information about national, state, and local programs that provide assistance and offer benefits to those living with HIV; and the latest word on treatment options. Many organizations sponsor (or will refer you to) support groups, social/recreational activities, workshops, and counseling services for those with HIV and their families, lovers, and friends.

If you are positive and live in a state that requires that your name be reported before you receive medical and other benefits from the state and/or federal government, you will be required to retake the test when you talk with your doctor.

Discrimination

The 1992 revisions to the Americans with Disabilities Act protect people with HIV and AIDS from discrimination based on their illness. Even those with HIV who do not consider themselves disabled, or who do not yet manifest any symptoms, are covered by this act. The importance of this inclusion is that it reaffirms that being fired from a job, evicted from an apartment, or denied acceptance into an academic program (or the like) because you have HIV is illegal discrimination based on a medical condi-

tion, and you are entitled to take legal action against it. (For more about the Americans with Disabilities Act, see page 486 of "Breaking Down Bias.")

TREATMENTS/CURE

Although there is no cure for HIV or AIDS at this time, AZT and other prophylactic treatments are often given to delay the onset of the disease. In addition, a number of experimental medications and holistic therapies, including dietary changes and vitamin and herbal supplements, are believed to beef up the immune system and to help slow HIV's damage to the body. There are also treatments to help prevent and/or reverse some of the opportunistic illnesses that can take hold as a result of lowered immune response, as well as to alleviate some of the psychological and physical effects of HIV. (For the latest information on established and emerging treatments, the state of development of an HIV vaccine, and help with coping with the physical and emotional effects of the virus on you or

to refuse to treat someone solely because of her or his HIV status.

people you care about, see the Resources at the end of this chapter.)

THE POLITICS OF HIV/AIDS

The AIDS epidemic involves much more than just the identification, transmission, and treatment of those infected with HIV. For one thing, it reveals how much discrimination based on ignorance and fear of illness and difference exists in our society.

In addition, the AIDS epidemic has forced us to examine the politics of health care in this country. For example, it calls into question how we choose to define diseases—which groups of people and what symptoms are studied. This is important because these definitions ultimately determine who is acknowledged as needing help, and who gets it.

The Politics of Naming

In 1993 the CDC revised its definition of AIDS and HIV to more accurately reflect the advances in knowledge about the condition since it was first named in 1981. The definition was expanded to include both the problems caused directly by the virus as well as those that appear as a result of the damage it does to the immune system. The definition is also inclusive of symptoms that are not associated with white, urban, gay men. This change reflects the significant increase in the number of cases occurring in nonwhite people living in nonurban areas,

"Without question, AIDS is a woman's issue, and it is imperative that women take it upon themselves to practice proactive health care. We have been raised to believe that it is our responsibility to take care of others, but it's equally (if not more) important to take care of ourselves! See a doctor regularly, and ask questions. If something seems wrong with you, don't ignore it. Take good care of yourself! This is true whether or not you have HIV."

—BARNARD COLLEGE, '92

including lesbians and heterosexual men and women.

The revision of the AIDS definition allows those with HIV who were previously denied medical, psychological, financial, and legal assistance because their symptoms were not included in the AIDS definition to get the help they need. Beyond the benefits to individuals, a more accurate definition of who has AIDS considerably enlarges the AIDS population. This increase allows for more federal and state money to be allocated to research, prevention, education, treatment, legal protection, social programs, community outreach groups, and housing, medical, and public assistance, and other social benefits for people with HIV. It also makes the statistics about infection more demographically accurate, thereby allowing for a more equitable and proportional distribution of funding. In short, the more accurate definition allows researchers, educators, public officials,

🔅 A quarter of babies born to HIV-positive women will be infected in utero,

statisticians, and communities to gather information and offer more efficient and effective services.

WOMEN AND HIV/AIDS

As is true of most illnesses that are not female-specific, there has been relatively little research into issues of transmission, symptoms, and treatment methods of HIV in heterosexual, bisexual, and lesbian women. Because HIV was initially considered to be a "gay male disease," symptoms and experiences specific to women were completely absent from the CDC's clinical definition of AIDS until the 1993 revision. The failure to include such gynecological problems as cervical cancer and recurring severe yeast infections (as well as other disorders specific to women) meant that doctors would often not recognize or diagnose infected women as having HIV-related problems. Consequently, women with HIV died twice as quickly as their male counterparts, and a large number of women died of complications due to HIV diseases without ever having been diagnosed as HIV-positive.

Today, more attention and resources are being focused on the study and prevention of HIV in women. This is not just because of political pressure, but out of necessity—the number of HIV cases in women (particularly women of color, poor women, and/or women of child-bearing age) is increasing at a greater rate than that of any other group. Because HIV-positive mothers can pass the virus to their babies before, during, and after birth (through breast-feeding), and because women are most often the caregivers of children, it is impossible to address HIV/AIDS in women without also considering the medical, economic, social, and emotional issues surrounding the care of HIV-positive babies and children who lose their mothers to HIV/AIDS.

ACTIVIST IDEAS

- A key element in the prevention of STDs (including HIV) is to make access to information, testing, and treatment as easy and nonthreatening as possible. You can help. With the help of health services make up fact sheets about the various diseases (and don't forget to include places to go for treatment and numbers to call for more information). Get the school health center to provide free or low-cost testing and treatment of STDs, and the school health practitioners to routinely offer patients STD testing so that those who are hesitant or don't know to ask will still get the care they need. And take a stand against any practitioner who makes anyone feel ashamed or dirty because she has an STD. Talk with the director of health services, confront the practitioner directly, write a letter to the school newspaper, or suggest sensitivity training for the health center staff.

but new pre- and post-natal treatments may lower this number to 8%.

■ Form a group for people on campus living with herpes or other chronic STDs. The group can arrange a panel with medical professionals dealing with STDs, disseminate information, and lobby for more research. Members can find support, give and get advice, and investigate new treatment ideas.

■ Hold workshops on how to tell someone you have an STD. Include information on negotiating safer sex.

■ Volunteer at organizations that sponsor HIV prevention or needle exchange workshops, or organizations that offer services to people with HIV/AIDS. You can deliver meals to homebound people with AIDS, join a march or demonstration to raise money for HIV/AIDS patients or research, or give some TLC to an HIV-positive baby. Find out about such programs at your local hospital and/or HIV/AIDS organizations.

■ Plan a campus event and donate all the proceeds to an AIDS organization in your community. Or get a block of tickets to an existing AIDS benefit concert, dance, or show and promote the benefit on campus. Use it as an opportunity to disseminate information about HIV/AIDS to people on campus.

■ In order to prevent HIV/AIDS, it is essential that accurate information about safer sex is readily available and accessible. Put brochures and pamphlets about safer sex in strategic locations (like in bathrooms, lounges, library checkout desks, and near condom machines, if your school has them). Get the information out, even if neither you nor anyone you know is having oral, anal, and/or vaginal sex and/or shooting drugs (including steroids). (See "Safer Sex," page 421.)

■ Make a three-by-six-foot quilt panel in memory of a friend, lover, or family member who died of HIV/AIDS as part of the Names Project AIDS Memorial Quilt. (See the Resources for more information).

RESOURCES

Sexually Transmissable Diseases

ᘖᘖᘖ

NATIONAL STD HOTLINE
(800) 227-8922
Affiliated with the U.S. Centers for Disease Control and Prevention. Provides information about STDs. Makes referrals to local clinics, doctors, and support groups. Publishes numerous materials; confidential information available upon request.

AMERICAN SOCIAL HEALTH ASSOCIATION
P.O. BOX 13827
RESEARCH TRIANGLE PARK, NC 27709
(919) 361-8400
FAX: (919) 361-8425
Provides information about all aspects of STDs, including treatment, long-term effects, and prevention. Makes referrals to local clinics, practitioners, and support groups. Offers phone counseling and crisis intervention. Publishes numerous materials; confidential information available upon request. Organizes political action

and advocacy work involving public policy and funding related to STDs.

NATIONAL HERPES HOTLINE
(919) 361-8488
A division of the American Social Health Association. Offers phone counseling. Provides information about herpes. Publishes numerous materials, including a newsletter, *The Helper*.

HEPATITIS B INFORMATION HOTLINE
(800) 437-2873
Offers phone counseling and answers questions about Hepatitis B. Makes referrals to local organizations.

NATIONAL INSTITUTE OF ALLERGIES AND INFECTIOUS DISEASES (NIAID)
NIH BUILDING 31, ROOM 7A50
9000 ROCKVILLE PIKE
BETHESDA, MD 20892
(301) 496-5717
Provides information about and conducts research on allergies and infections diseases. Publishes numerous materials on specific allergies and diseases, available upon request.

The department of public health of almost every state has an STD division that provides information and makes local referrals to clinics and organizations dealing with the specific STD.

Check in your local phone book under "State Government Agencies: Department of Public Health."

HIV/AIDS

Information, Education, Referrals, and Political Action

State Hotlines
Almost every state has an AIDS information and referral hotline, as do some cities. You can contact the National HIV/AIDS Hotline (listed below) to get a referral to the hotline in your state, or you can call information or look in the phone book in the blue pages under "AIDS."

NATIONAL HIV/AIDS HOTLINE
(800) 342-2437 [AIDS] (24 HOURS)
SPANISH: (800) 344-7432 [SIDA]
TTY/TTD: (800) 243-7889 [AIDS-TTY]
A division of the American Social Health Association. Provides information about HIV/AIDS and prevention. Makes local and national referrals for counseling, support, testing, treatment, housing, and legal assistance. Publishes numerous materials. Sends information confidentially upon request.

CDC NATIONAL AIDS INFORMATION CLEARINGHOUSE
P.O. BOX 6003
ROCKVILLE, MD 20850
(800) 458-5231(ENGLISH, SPANISH, PORTUGUESE, FRENCH, AND CHINESE)
TTY/TDD: (800) 243-7012
A division of the Centers for Disease Control and Prevention. Provides information about all aspects of HIV/AIDS. Offers phone counseling and advice. Makes national and local referrals for counseling, treatment, housing, legal assistance, and

testing. Publishes numerous materials. Sends information confidentially upon request.

NATIONAL AIDS INFORMATION AND EDUCATION PROGRAM CENTER FOR DISEASE CONTROL AND PREVENTION
1600 CLIFTON ROAD MAIL STOP E-25
ATLANTA, GA 30333
(404) 639-0956
FAX: (404) 639-0943
Provides the latest information and educational materials about HIV/AIDS and its prevention. Sends information confidentially upon request.

PROJECT INFORM NATIONAL HOTLINE
1965 MARKET STREET, #220
SAN FRANCISCO, CA 94103
(800) 822-7422
Provides information about the symptoms and treatment of HIV/AIDS and opportunistic infections. Publishes numerous materials about HIV/AIDS, including fact sheets on such topics as women and AIDS. Sends information confidentially upon request.

GAY MEN'S HEALTH CRISIS, INC.
129 WEST 20TH STREET
NEW YORK , NY 10011
(212) 807-6655: AIDS HOTLINE
Although GMHC primarily serves the New York City area, it is an excellent organization from which to get information and

referrals. It was one of the first organizations to work on HIV/AIDS issues. (Don't let the name deceive you; it is concerned with more issues than the health of gay men.) Offers phone counseling. Makes referrals to local organizations dealing with HIV/AIDS and re-

lated issues. Organizes political action/advocacy work. Provides information on all issues related to HIV/AIDS, safer sex, gay/lesbian issues, and other related issues. Publishes numerous materials. Sends information upon request. Houses and runs the Lesbian AIDS Project, (212) 337-3532, which offers counseling, referrals, and advocacy support.

SAN FRANCISCO AIDS FOUNDATION
25 VAN NESS AVENUE, SUITE 660
SAN FRANCISCO, CA 94102
(415) 864-5855
HOTLINE (OUTSIDE NORTHERN CALIFORNIA):
    (415) 367-2437
HOTLINE (NORTHERN CALIFORNIA ONLY):
    (800) 367-2937
Offers phone counseling. Makes referrals to local and national HIV/AIDS organizations/service providers dealing with testing, medical services, counseling, housing, and food. Organizes political action/advocacy work on public policy and legislation related to HIV/AIDS. Provides information, educational materials and advice on all issues related to HIV/AIDS. Publishes numerous materials. Sends information confidentially upon request.

Houses and run the Women's AIDS Network, (415) 621-4160, ext. 2030, which makes referrals to local and national organizations that deal with women and HIV/AIDS; organizes political action/advocacy work related to women and HIV/AIDS; and provides information, educational materials, and support for women infected with HIV/AIDS.

NATIONAL ASSOCIATION OF PEOPLE WITH AIDS (NAPWA)
1413 K STREET NW, 7TH FLOOR
WASHINGTON, DC 20006
(202) 898-0414
Organizes political action/advocacy work to support people with AIDS or AIDS-related conditions. Publishes monthly

newsletters (available upon request). Provides educational materials and information. Runs speakers bureau on HIV/AIDS issues. (They are a good place to contact for suggestions of people to bring to campus to speak/educate on AIDS). Offers referral service and information service. Runs NAPWA-Link, (703) 998-3144, a computer bulletin board service that provides information and articles on a wide array of topics relating to HIV/AIDS. Also runs NAPWA-fax, which allows you to request information and articles by fax: (202) 789-2222.

PEOPLE WITH AIDS COALITION NEW YORK
50 WEST 17TH STREET, 8TH FLOOR
NEW YORK, NY 10011
(800) 828-3280: HOTLINE OUTSIDE NY
(800) 448-2775: HOTLINE IN NY
(212) 647-1415

A self-help and self-empowerment organization comprised of, and for people living with HIV/AIDS. Makes referrals to local HIV/AIDS organizations. Provides educational materials in English and Spanish. Also provides information on newly approved and experimental drugs and treatments, and the results of clinical trials. Will send information upon request.

NATIONAL CENTER FOR WOMEN AND POLICY STUDIES
NATIONAL RESOURCE CENTER ON WOMEN AND AIDS
2000 P STREET NW, SUITE 508
WASHINGTON, DC 20036
(202) 872-1770

Provides information and referrals to organizations dealing with women and AIDS and issues affecting women with HIV/AIDS.

NATIONAL NATIVE AMERICAN AIDS PREVENTION CENTER
2100 LAKE SHORE AVENUE, SUITE A
OAKLAND, CA 94606
(510) 444-2051

Runs a computer bulletin board, conferences. Houses and runs the National Native American AIDS Hotline, (800) 283-2437, a service to provide printed material about AIDS and AIDS prevention to the Native American community.

ACT UP (AIDS COALITION TO UNLEASH POWER)
135 WEST 29TH STREET, 10TH FLOOR
NEW YORK, NY 10001
(212) 564-2437
FAX: (212) 594-5141

This organization has been one of the most visible AIDS organizations in the country. It carries out direct political action and has local activist and advocacy groups throughout the country. In order to receive information it is best to write, specifying what you want, to the above address. You can also check to see if there are any ACT UP chapters in your area by looking in your local phone book. ACT UP publishes numerous materials, reports, and handbooks on HIV/AIDS legislation, statistics, prevention, and research, and on political organizing around the issue.

NATIONAL MINORITY AIDS COUNCIL
300 I STREET NE, SUITE 400
WASHINGTON, DC 20002
(202) 544-1076

Organizes political action/advocacy work to address the specific issues of different minority groups dealing with AIDS. Provides resources and educational and informational materials.

(then known as VDs), 75,000 people canceled their subscriptions.

AIDS Quilt

THE NAMES PROJECT
2362 MARKET STREET
SAN FRANCISCO, CA 94114
(415) 863-5511

This organization coordinates the making and exhibition of the AIDS Memorial Quilt (a quilt made up of three-by-six-foot panels in memory of people who have died of AIDS). Quilt panels can be made by friends, family, and lovers. The AIDS Memorial Quilt tours in pieces (it is now too large to ever be shown in its entirety) across the United States. If you are interested in making a panel, bringing part of the quilt to your campus, or supporting the project in other ways, you can contact them directly.

Discrimination

NATIONAL LEADERSHIP COALITION ON
   AIDS
1730 M STREET NW, SUITE 905
WASHINGTON DC, 20036
(202) 429-0930

Organizes political action/advocacy work to promote fair HIV/AIDS policies in the workplace, and in both public and private institutions. Provides referrals to individuals facing discrimination. Also houses the Workplace Resource Center and has information for both employees and employers about HIV/AIDS in the workplace and related issues.

Further Reading

ೋೋೋ

Risky Times: How to Be AIDS-Smart and Stay Healthy, Jeanne Blake (Workman, 1990).

A Shallow Pool of Time, Fran Peavey (New Society Publishers, 1990).

The Invisible Epidemic: The Story of Women and AIDS, Gena Corea (HarperCollins, 1992).

HIV/AIDS Periodicals

BODY POSITIVE
2095 BROADWAY, SUITE 306
NEW YORK, NY 10023
HOTLINE: (212) 721-1346
ADMINISTRATION: (212) 721-1618

THE POSITIVE WOMAN: A NEWSLETTER BY,
   FOR, AND ABOUT THE HIV+ WOMAN
P.O. BOX 34372
WASHINGTON, DC 20043-4372
(202) 898-0372

POZ MAGAZINE
OLD CHELSEA STATION
P.O. BOX 1279
NEW YORK, NY 10113-1279
(212) 242-2163

 In one study, 70% of teen women said they wanted to discuss

Contraception & Safer Sex

Playing It Smart in Risky Times

These days, "the facts of life" encompass far more than just the birds and the bees. In order to be a well-informed and sexually savvy human being, you've got to know the score on all the ways you can protect yourself against sexually transmissable diseases (STDs) and pregnancy.

Safer sex means doing what is physically and emotionally comfortable while preventing contact between your and your partner's mucous membranes and potentially infected body fluids or skin. Contraception means taking the steps required to avoid pregnancy (assuming that you don't want to get pregnant . . .). They're both about taking care of your body, being responsible for your decisions, and making choices.

Figuring out which method of contraception is right for you can be a little confusing and insisting on a condom while entwined in the throes of passion with a guy who really doesn't want to wear one (not to mention broaching the subject of sexual histories) may be difficult. But an unwanted pregnancy or an STD is certainly much more troublesome. If you've decided to engage in risky behavior—that which can transmit disease or cause pregnancy or both—you must play it safe: If you have vaginal intercourse and you don't want to get pregnant, you need to use contraception. If you engage in activities that could involve the exchange of body fluids (e.g., oral, anal, or genital sex with a man or woman) or contact with skin lesions, you need to use a latex barrier. That's simply the way it is. If you are mature enough to have sex, you've got to be mature enough to understand the facts and to protect yourself.

CONTRACEPTION

Unless you're trying to get pregnant, if you're having vaginal intercourse, you're going to need to use some form of contraception. There's a whole array of styles and methods to choose from, each with its own pros and cons, effectiveness and side effects, costs and comforts, and instructions for use. Obviously, choosing a contraceptive to fit your lifestyle requires a little thought. You may have to settle for a contraceptive that's less than perfect: Maybe the "best choice" isn't the least obtrusive or easiest to use. It's likely that whatever you pick is going to take a little getting used to. Sex in general can be a sticky business, and foams that drip and condoms that slip don't improve matters much. So take things into your own hands: If you hate condoms because they interrupt the mood, keep a bunch of them within reach, and make putting on a condom a sexy thing you and your lover do together. If you hate having to tote your diaphragm around, consider getting a second one to keep at your partner's place. Finally, don't forget that what's sexy about contraception is the peace of mind that comes with knowing you made a safe, effective choice.

Get your contraception at clinics or school health services, where appointments, pills, diaphragms, caps, and condoms are inexpensive (or free). Spermicides and condoms can also be purchased at drugstores. Talk to your partner about sharing in the contraceptive costs, too.

SO WHAT IS CONTRACEPTION, ANYWAY?

For pregnancy to occur, a sperm must travel up the vagina, through the uterus, and up into the fallopian tubes, where it must meet up with the egg, which was released that month when the woman ovulated. Then the

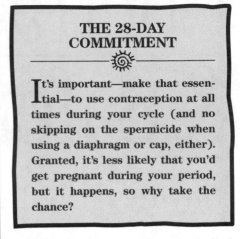

THE 28-DAY COMMITMENT

It's important—make that essential—to use contraception at all times during your cycle (and no skipping on the spermicide when using a diaphragm or cap, either). Granted, it's less likely that you'd get pregnant during your period, but it happens, so why take the chance?

sperm and the egg must join (called fertilization) and implant in the lining of the uterus. Contraception works to prevent this from occurring in a number of different ways and at different points in the process, as described below.

Abstinence means avoiding vaginal intercourse altogether. It's the most foolproof method of birth control that exists.

Physical barriers prevent sperm from entering the uterus and fallopian tubes so the egg and sperm never meet. Methods include the male condom and the female condom/pouch.

Spermicides immobilize and kill sperm on contact so they are unable to travel up into the uterus. These creams, jellies or foams are most effective when used with physical barriers.

Barrier and spermicide methods involve using a barrier to block the passage of sperm through the cervix into the upper genital tract and a spermicide to kill any sperm that happen to make it past the barrier. Methods include a condom with spermicide, the diaphragm, the cervical cap, and the sponge. Successful use of the latter three methods requires a certain level of familiarity and comfort with your body, because they need to be inserted and removed from inside your vagina. You also must know where your cervix is to ensure correct placement.

Hormonal methods prevent ovulation (so no egg is present to be fertilized), cause cervical mucus to thicken and form a barrier, and/or affect the lining of the uterus so implantation will not occur. Methods include oral contraceptives (the Pill), Norplant, and Depo-Provera.

Uterine implants affect the lining of the uterus so implantation cannot occur. The IUD, or intrauterine device, falls into this category.

Using Contraception Responsibly

Using contraception the right way involves more than just taking a pill at the same time every day or inserting a diaphragm properly. It means having protection with you when you need it. (A diaphragm won't do you much good when it's hidden in the bottom of your underwear drawer and things are getting hot and heavy in a dorm room across campus.) It means keeping tabs on your supplies (e.g., picking pills up from the pharmacy and making sure you have refills available, checking the expiration date on condoms and spermicide, having lubricant on hand). It means making and keeping all the recommended checkup and refitting appointments, and finding out the answers to your questions and concerns, no matter how insignificant or embarrassing they may seem.

METHODS OF BIRTH CONTROL

Condoms

Description: Condoms are thin sheaths of latex rubber or animal membrane that fit over an erect penis. They are available in a variety of styles, including flavored, colored, textured (e.g., ribbed), reservoir tipped (to collect semen), and/or lubricated (gel type, "dry," or spermicidal).

CONDOM COMPENDIUM

BENEFITS: Inexpensive; available over the counter; protects against STDs; few if any side effects; "one size fits all"; can be used to enhance sex play; no mess.

DRAWBACKS: Possible allergy to latex; must interrupt sex play to put on; must use a new condom before each act of intercourse; may decrease sensation for the man; may rip or tear; women must rely on their partners to use them; often need additional lubricant; must withdraw immediately after ejaculation; not reusable; when the fun is over you have a used condom on your hands.

King Charles II, who wanted to limit his number of illegitimate children.

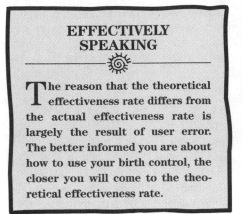

EFFECTIVELY SPEAKING

The reason that the theoretical effectiveness rate differs from the actual effectiveness rate is largely the result of user error. The better informed you are about how to use your birth control, the closer you will come to the theoretical effectiveness rate.

How it works: The condom prevents preseminal fluid ("pre-cum") and semen from entering the vagina and traveling to the uterus and fallopian tubes, thereby preventing pregnancy.

Effectiveness: When used alone, a condom has a theoretical effectiveness rate of 95 percent, and an actual effectiveness rate of 90 percent. When used with a spermicidal jelly or foam, the condom's theoretical effectiveness rate climbs to 99 percent and it provides additional protection against STDs. It's actual effectiveness is 95 percent.

STD protection: Latex condoms offer protection from STDs by blocking the exchange of potentially disease-carrying fluids (semen, vaginal secretions, feces, blood—including menstrual blood) and blocking skin-to-skin contact between the penis and vagina, anus, or mouth. Latex condoms lubricated with the spermicide nonoxynol-9 offer additional protection against pregnancy and STDs. Animal membrane condoms protect against pregnancy, but they *do not* protect against HIV/AIDS and other STDs. (For more on condoms and disease prevention, see page 423.)

Where to get them: Drugstore; erotica or condom shop; by mail order; vending machine (double check the expiration date); family planning clinic; student or women's health center.

Not recommended if: You or your partner is allergic to latex (try the newer styrene/polymer condoms); if you can't find these and he's allergic, have him use an animal membrane condom under a latex one. If you've got the allergy, reverse it. Make sure there's no lubrication on the outside of the condom worn underneath.

Reasons for failure: The condom was put on after contact occurred between the penis and the vagina; it broke because it was too old, was kept in too warm or cold a place, was used more than once, or was used with an oil-based lubricant, such as Vaseline or baby oil; it slipped as a result of too much lubricant; the penis was not withdrawn immediately after ejaculation; the condom was not handled properly during withdrawal.

Other:
- Besides sterilization, condoms are the only currently available method of contraception for men.

- Allergies to condoms are often caused by the lubricant, spermicide, or

"We all know all the benefits of using condoms—they're cheap, prevent AIDS, prevent pregnancy, and all that—but the benefit that no one talks about is that they— how should I say this—help men out in the premature ejaculation department."

—OBERLIN COLLEGE, '93

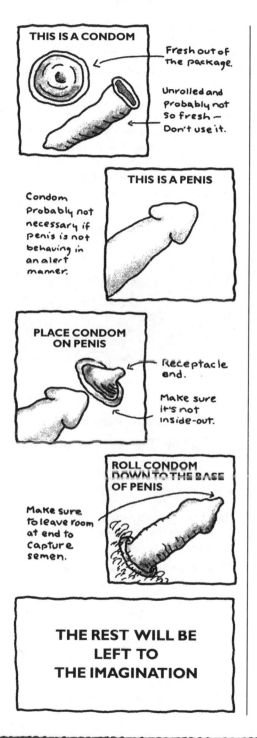

THIS IS A CONDOM

Fresh out of the package.

Unrolled and probably not so fresh — Don't use it.

THIS IS A PENIS

Condom probably not necessary if penis is not behaving in an alert manner.

PLACE CONDOM ON PENIS

Receptacle end.

Make sure it's not inside-out.

ROLL CONDOM DOWN TO THE BASE OF PENIS

Make sure to leave room at end to capture semen.

THE REST WILL BE LEFT TO THE IMAGINATION

preservatives, not the latex. Try using another brand of condom or a condom with a "dry" or silicone lubricant.

■ Reservoir tips and lubricants help prevent breakage. Lubrication can also increase sensation and comfort: Squeeze a small bit of lubricant (preferably one with spermicide) in the tip of the condom before putting it on to increase his pleasure (and, if you have no allergies, a little lube on the outside can increase *your* pleasure).

Instructions:

Note: Put the condom on before any contact occurs between the penis and vagina, anus, or mouth. The clear fluid that comes out of the penis before ejaculation contains both sperm and the organisms that carry STDs.

1. Open the package with care. (More than a few panting couples have had the unfortunate experience of recklessly tearing open the condom package and finding that they've torn the condom as well.) And be careful of fingernails, teeth, jewelry, or anything else that could rip the condom.

2. With one hand, pinch the tip of the condom and hold it to the tip of the penis. (This is to avoid trapping air in the condom.) If you are not using a reservoir-tipped condom, pinch a bit more latex to leave a small amount of space at the tip of the condom to catch the ejaculated semen. With the other hand, unroll the condom onto the erect penis as far as it will go.

■ If your partner is uncircumcised, make sure his foreskin is pulled back before putting on the condom.

■ Use a lubricant to help prevent condom breakage. Make sure that the lubricant is water-based—K-Y Jelly, Astroglide, Wet, or spermicidal jelly will work—and *not* oil-based (e.g.,

CONDOM FAILURE

If the condom slips off his penis or breaks: Have your partner withdraw his penis immediately. Insert some spermicidal jelly or foam right away to take care of any "sperm spills." Do not douche! Though it may seem as if you'd be washing the semen out, you actually can push the sperm (and potentially any germs that cause STDs) up farther, increasing the possibility of fertilization.

In either case, use a new condom before resuming sexual activity. If he has already ejaculated and you think you are ovulating or will be soon, you might consider using the morning-after pill. (See page 420.)

of the condom. Otherwise the condom might slip off, causing semen to spill. To prevent semen from leaking out after the condom is off, make a knot in the open end before you throw it out.

4. Do not flush condoms—they can cause major plumbing problems or get stuck somewhere just out of sight, only to reappear when you least expect them. If discretion is a concern, wrap the used condom in tissue before you throw it away.

Female Condom/Vaginal Pouch

Description: The Reality Female Condom is a thin, seven-inch-long tube of prelubricated, loose-fitting polyurethane with a rubber ring at each end—one that fits over the cervix like a diaphragm, and another that hangs outside the vagina to keep the condom in place.

How it works: The condom/pouch prevents preseminal fluid and semen from entering the cervix, thereby preventing pregnancy.

Effectiveness: The theoretical effectiveness rate is 90–95 percent, and the actual effectiveness rate is 85 percent. The condom/pouch is more effective when used in conjunction with spermicide.

Vaseline or baby oil). Oil-based lubricants (as well as many of the creams used to cure yeast infections) corrode latex and will cause the condom to break or tear. On the same note, wash your hands of lotions, oils, or creams before handling the condom.

■ For the best protection against pregnancy, as well as against STDs, use a spermicidal jelly or foam with the condom for extra protection during vaginal or anal intercourse.

■ After the condom is on, squeeze out any air that may be trapped inside by smoothing it down from tip to base.

3. After intercourse, make sure your partner withdraws his penis immediately (before his erection subsides) while holding on to the opening

STD protection: The female condom/pouch offers protection from STDs by preventing the exchange of potentially disease-carrying fluids and skin-to-skin contact between the penis and vagina. Male condoms provide a bit more protection from STDs spread by body fluids, since they fully contain the semen; with the female condom, there is a possibility that semen can drip out onto unprotected areas. (For more on the pouch and disease prevention, see page 425.)

Where to get it: Drugstore, family planning clinic, or student/women's health center.

Not recommended if: You are allergic to polyurethane or latex.

Reasons for failure: The condom twisted or broke; semen dripped out.

Other:
■ Because it's looser and thinner than a male condom, it may allow for more sensation.

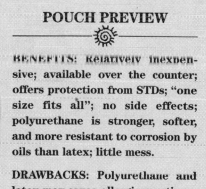

POUCH PREVIEW

BENEFITS: Relatively inexpensive; available over the counter; offers protection from STDs; "one size fits all"; no side effects; polyurethane is stronger, softer, and more resistant to corrosion by oils than latex; little mess.

DRAWBACKS: Polyurethane and latex may cause allergic reactions; putting pouch in may interrupt sex play; must use new pouch before each act of intercourse; may decrease sensation; can rip or break; may be difficult to insert and remove.

■ It's the only form of women's contraceptive that's effective in preventing both pregnancy and STD transmission.

Instructions:
1. Squeeze the inner ring and insert into vagina past the pubic bone.
2. Check that the inner ring covers the cervix and that the pouch is not twisted.
3. For extra protection from pregnancy and HIV, insert some spermicide inside the pouch. (The pouch has also been known to squeak, and lubricant can help prevent this.)
4. Right after intercourse, clasp the bottom closed, then twist the end to prevent semen from dripping out, remove it, roll it up in tissue, and throw it away.

Spermicidal Jelly, Foam, and Vaginal Contraceptive Film

Description: Spermicidal jelly, foam, suppositories, film, and tablets contain chemicals that immobilize and kill sperm on contact. They can be used alone, in conjunction with a diaphragm or cervical cap, or as a lubricant with a condom.

How they work: Spermicides prevent pregnancy in two ways—they block the opening of the cervix and prevent sperm from entering the uterus, and they kill the sperm as well.

Effectiveness: Used alone, the theoretical effectiveness rate of spermicidal jellies and foams is 95–97 percent, and the actual effectiveness rate is 82 percent. When used with a condom, the theoretical effectiveness rate is 99 percent, and the actual effectiveness rate is 95 percent. (Because coverage of the cervix is key to the effectiveness of spermicides, foams are considered the most effective, suppositories and tablets the least.)

STD protection: Spermicides containing the chemical nonoxynol-9 not only kill sperm, but can reduce the risk of infection from the viruses, parasites, and bacteria that cause AIDS, gonorrhea, syphilis, chlamydia, trichomoniasis, and herpes. (However, if the spermicide irritates your vagina or cervix, it may provide an easy entry for STDs and do more harm than good.) Next to abstinence, using a spermicide with a condom provides the best protection against STDs.

Where to get them: Drugstore, some supermarkets, family planning clinic, campus health services.

Not recommended if: You or your partner is allergic to spermicide; you have chronic urinary tract infections.

Reasons for failure: Not inserted before each act of intercourse; not inserted deeply enough to fully cover cervix; too little used; inserted too early; suppositories not given ample time to foam; douched away less than eight hours after last act of intercourse; spermicide too old (check the expiration date) or stored improperly.

Other:

■ Allergies to nonoxynol-9 are relatively rare, occurring in less than 5 percent of the population, and therefore reactions are usually to preservatives or other ingredients in the spermicide. If you have a problem with one brand, try another.

■ If you are allergic to spermicide, you can still benefit from the protection spermicides provide against pregnancy and STDs if your partner squeezes a bit of spermicidal jelly into the tip of his condom before he puts it on (an added benefit: This will also increase his sensation).

■ If you are allergic to spermicide, check to make sure that the condoms you use aren't lubricated with it.

■ Because spermicide reduces the number of "friendly" bacteria in your vagina but not the E-coli bacteria, the use of spermicide—especially in con-

---

SPERMICIDE SUMMARY

BENEFITS: Inexpensive; available over the counter; provides excellent protection from STDs when used with a condom and *some* protection from STDs when used alone; jelly can act as a lubricant.

DRAWBACKS: Not very effective as a form of birth control or as STD protection when used alone; possible allergic reaction; may aggravate urinary tract or vaginal infections; may interrupt sex play; must be used before each act of intercourse; tastes terrible.

"Many people don't use birth control because it's messy, it can be expensive, it cuts down on pleasure, it breaks the flow of things, and 'cause they're lazy. It also requires that people really think about what they're doing—what sex means to them and all—and people just don't want to deal with it. . . . And people think, 'Nothing can happen to me—I can't get a disease or get pregnant.'"

—BRYN MAWR COLLEGE, '95

junction with a diaphragm, which puts pressure on the bladder—can aggravate urinary tract infections. (For more on urinary tract infections, see page 220.)

Instructions:

1. You must insert the spermicidal jelly, suppositories, film, or foam immediately before intercourse. (If using suppositories or tablets, you must wait 10 to 15 minutes to let them foam.)

2. You must insert an additional application immediately before each act of intercourse, even if you are using the spermicide with a condom or diaphragm.

3. In order for it to be effective, you must keep the spermicide in place for eight hours after intercourse before washing or douching it away.

Diaphragm

Description: The diaphragm is a shallow dome of soft latex rubber supported by a flexible rim that fits between the top of the back vaginal wall and the pubic bone, fully covering the cervix. Diaphragms must always be used in conjunction with a spermicide.

How it works: The diaphragm works in two ways: The latex dome creates a physical barrier that prevents sperm from traveling into the upper genital tract, and the spermicide kills any sperm that try to get around the rim.

Effectiveness: The theoretical effectiveness rate of the diaphragm is 97 percent, and the actual effectiveness rate is 85–90 percent.

STD protection: Although the diaphragm protects the cervix with sper-

---

DIAPHRAGM DIGEST

BENEFITS: Relatively inexpensive; provides *some* protection from STDs; can be inserted two hours in advance if spermicide is reapplied directly before intercourse; lasts for a year (or longer); reusable (though new spermicide is needed before each act of intercourse).

DRAWBACKS: Must be fitted by a health care practitioner; must be used with a condom for adequate STD protection; possible allergy to latex or spermicide; may aggravate urinary tract infections; can interrupt sex play if not inserted ahead of time; requires manual dexterity (and perhaps a bit of practice) to insert and remove; must insert spermicide before each act of intercourse; slight risk of toxic shock syndrome (less than one in two million).

---

into the vagina. Elephant dung mixed with honey was a later favorite.

micide and latex, it does not protect the vagina. Use a condom with a diaphragm to safeguard yourself against STDs.

Where to get it: You must be fitted for a diaphragm by a health practitioner (usually a gynecologist, nurse-practitioner, or nurse-midwife); you can fill your prescription at any pharmacy. Spermicidal jelly is available in drugstores.

Not recommended if: You have a severely displaced uterus; you don't feel comfortable touching yourself; you are allergic to latex or spermicide; you are susceptible to urinary tract infections.

Reasons for failure: Not enough (or any) spermicide used; improper fit; inserted incorrectly; diaphragm has holes, tears, or cracks; removed sooner than six hours after intercourse; diaphragm was jarred loose during intercourse.

Other:

■ As is the case with many contraceptives, diaphragms have a high first-year failure rate, which is most often due to a user's unfamiliarity with it. Your health practitioner should show you how to use it and make sure you have your insertion and removal techniques down pat before you leave the office. You might want to make an appointment with your practitioner for a week after you get the diaphragm, and come to the appointment with it already in so s/he can check to see if you've inserted it correctly.

■ Take good care of your diaphragm. Wash it with plain, mild soap and water after use; store it in its case away from heat; examine it regularly for cracks, brittleness, and holes; do not let it come into contact with oil-based

creams—wash your hands before insertion and removal if you have used moisturizer or suntan lotion.

■ Get refitted once a year and/or if you gain or lose more than 10 pounds or have a baby.

■ If you use it during your period, it will catch blood and prevent menstrual messes—but don't keep it in for more than six hours.

Instructions:

Note: The diaphragm may be inserted up to two hours before intercourse. If it has been in place longer, insert additional spermicidal jelly or foam into the vagina with an applicator before intercourse.

1. Hold the diaphragm dome side down, like a bowl. Squeeze between a teaspoon and a tablespoon of spermicidal jelly inside the bowl of the diaphragm. Using your fingertip, spread a thin layer of jelly around the rim to increase effectiveness.

2. Relax and get into a position that allows you to comfortably insert the diaphragm. Different positions work for different women; some insert the diaphragm while lying down, others sit, stand, or squat.

---

3. To insert the diaphragm, hold it in one hand, dome side down, and press the opposite sides of the rim together so that the rim of the diaphragm folds into an elongated oval shape. With your other hand, spread your labia apart, and insert the diaphragm into your vaginal canal. With the dome portion angled toward your back, push it along the back wall of your vagina as far as it will go. Make sure that the near rim (the last portion of the diaphragm to enter your body) is tucked up behind your pubic bone, which feels like a small ledge.

4. Run your finger around the rim of the diaphragm to make sure it's securely in place, and feel through the dome for your cervix to make sure that it has been completely covered. Once the diaphragm is in correctly, you shouldn't be able to feel it.

5. Insert additional spermicidal jelly or foam before each subsequent act of intercourse. Do not remove your diaphragm to do this. Leave the diaphragm in place for six hours after your last act of intercourse, but do not wear it for more than 24 consecutive hours.

> *"Even though I practiced putting in my diaphragm over and over, it wasn't exactly smooth sailing the first time I put it to the test. I wanted to be extra-safe, so I squeezed in about three times more spermicide than I needed, making the little bugger so slippery that when I tried to put it in, it shot out of my hand, across the room, and right into his face."*
>
> —BOWDOIN COLLEGE, '90

A CERVICAL CAP CAPSULE

BENEFITS: Relatively inexpensive; can be inserted in advance (no interruption of sex play); once inserted, protects for 48 hours; lasts for one year (or longer); reusable (with reapplication of spermicide before each act of intercourse).

DRAWBACKS: Must be fitted by a practitioner; must be used with a condom for adequate STD protection; latex or spermicide may cause an allergic reaction; can interrupt sex play if not inserted ahead of time; requires manual dexterity (and perhaps a bit of practice) to insert and remove; cannot be used during menstruation.

Cervical Cap

Description: The cervical cap is made of soft latex rubber that is slightly thicker than the latex of the diaphragm. It is smaller than the diaphragm and is shaped like a large thimble. The cervical cap fits specifically over the cervix, and is used with spermicidal jelly or cream.

How it works: The cervical cap fits snugly over the cervix, and is held in place by a suction seal created between its rim and the cervix, where it acts as a barrier to sperm. The spermicide you use will immobilize and kill any sperm it comes in contact with.

Effectiveness: The theoretical effectiveness rate of the cervical cap is 97 percent, and the actual effectiveness rate is 85–90 percent.

STD protection: Because the cap does not protect the vagina, you must use a condom to safeguard yourself against STDs.

Where to get it: You must be fitted for a cervical cap by a health practitioner at a doctor's office, family planning clinic, or campus health services. Spermicidal jelly is available in drugstores.

Not recommended if: You are allergic to latex or spermicidal jelly or cream; you have cervical tears or lacerations; you have genital warts; you have or have had dysplasia or cervical cancer; you don't feel comfortable touching yourself.

Reasons for failure: Not enough (or any) spermicide used; improper fit; inserted incorrectly; the cap has holes, tears, or cracks; you removed it sooner than six hours after intercourse; use

during your period breaks the suction seal that holds the cap to the cervix; cap was jarred loose during sex.

Other:

■ Make sure you have your insertion and removal techniques down before leaving your practitioner's office.

■ Despite the fact that the cap has been available in the U.S. for more than five years (and has been used in other countries for a far longer time), sizes and styles are still limited. Therefore, not everyone can be fitted for a cervical cap.

■ The cap should not be used during menstruation. Your menstrual flow will break the suction on the cap; also, because of the cervix's altered shape at this point in your cycle, the cap might not fit as well.

■ Get refitted after you have a baby.

Instructions:
Note: You may insert the cervical cap up to several hours before intercourse.

1. Fill the cervical cap approximately one third full with spermicidal jelly or cream. Do not spread spermicide on the rim.

2. Relax and get into a position that allows you to insert the cap easily and comfortably. Different positions work for different women. Try lying down, standing, squatting, or sitting.

3. To insert the cervical cap, hold it in one hand, dome side down, and press the sides of the rim together. With your other hand, spread your labia, and insert the cap into your vagina. Push the cap up to your cervix. Release the cap, allowing it to fit directly over your cervix. Turn the cap around your cervix once to ensure that a seal has been created.

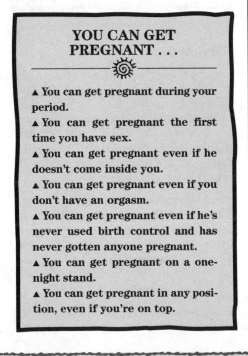

YOU CAN GET PREGNANT . . .

▲ You can get pregnant during your period.

▲ You can get pregnant the first time you have sex.

▲ You can get pregnant even if he doesn't come inside you.

▲ You can get pregnant even if you don't have an orgasm.

▲ You can get pregnant even if he's never used birth control and has never gotten anyone pregnant.

▲ You can get pregnant on a one-night stand.

▲ You can get pregnant in any position, even if you're on top.

4. Run your finger around the cap to make sure that it completely covers your cervix. Feel the rim to make sure that a suction seal has been created and the cap is sealed against your cervix.

5. You do not need to reinsert spermicidal jelly or foam each time you have repeated acts of intercourse. Leave the cervical cap in place for at least six hours after the last act of intercourse.

6. Do not wear the cap for more than 48 hours.

Contraceptive Sponge

Note: At the time of this writing, the sponge is no longer being produced. However, we have chosen to include it, as another company may begin manufacturing and distributing it again.

Description: The contraceptive sponge is made of soft polyurethane foam and is shaped somewhat like a cervical cap. It has a small cloth loop attached to it for removal and is disposable. The sponge covers the cervix and is infused with a spermicide that is activated when the sponge is dampened (before use).

How it works: The sponge covers the cervix and thus blocks the passage of sperm into the uterus. It also contains a spermicide (released by adding a bit of water to the sponge and squeezing a few times) that kills sperm on contact.

Effectiveness: The theoretical effectiveness rate of the sponge is 90–95 percent, and the actual effectiveness rate is 70–80 percent. There is a high user failure rate with the contraceptive sponge, since it is available over the counter and many users do not know how to insert it properly.

SPONGE SYNOPSIS

BENEFITS: Can be inserted in advance (no interruption of sex play); once inserted protects for 24 hours; "one size fits all."

DRAWBACKS: No longer available (see note); must use with a condom for STD protection; polyurethane or spermicide may cause allergic reaction; may aggravate urinary tract or vaginal infections; can interrupt sex play if not inserted ahead of time; requires manual dexterity (and perhaps a bit of practice) to insert and remove; cannot be used during menstruation; may cause itching and discomfort; not reusable; slight risk (less than one in two million) of toxic shock syndrome; spermicide tastes terrible.

STD protection: Though the sponge protects the cervix with spermicide, it does not protect the vagina, so you must use a condom with the sponge to safeguard yourself against STDs.

Where to get it: Drugstore, campus health services, family planning clinic.

Not recommended if: You are allergic to polyurethane or spermicide; you are susceptible to urinary tract infections or yeast infections; you don't feel comfortable touching yourself.

Reasons for failure: Not inserted properly; not moistened and squeezed before inserting; removed sooner than six hours after intercourse; sponge shifted during intercourse.

Other:

■ Women who aren't usually irritated by spermicides may have discomfort or itching due to the unique way in which the spermicide in the sponge is released.

■ Because of the risk of toxic shock syndrome, the sponge should not be used during menstruation.

Instructions:

1. Carefully read the instructions that come with the sponge.

2. Remove the sponge from its plastic covering. Wet the sponge with approximately two tablespoons of water, then squeeze (don't wring!) the sponge between your fingers and make sure that it foams (this indicates that the spermicide is activated).

3. To insert the sponge, hold it in one hand, dome side down, and press the opposite edges together. Spread your labia with your other hand, and insert the sponge into your vagina, dome side facing back, pushing it to the top of your vaginal canal in front of your cervix.

4. Run your finger around the sponge to make sure that it completely covers your cervix.

5. The spermicide in the sponge is effective for the duration of its use; you do not have to insert any spermicidal jelly or foam if you have repeated acts of intercourse. You must leave the sponge in place for six hours after the last act of intercourse.

6. It can be used for a maximum of 24 consecutive hours. It will not provide effective birth control for longer than this and should be removed and discarded. Never reuse a sponge.

Birth Control Pills

Description: Combination birth control pills, containing the synthetic hormones estrogen and progestin, are the most commonly prescribed. They mimic the effects of the naturally occurring estrogen and progesterone, which regulate the menstrual cycle. Two types are available: monophasic (all the pills provide the same hormone dosage) and triphasic (the pills' dosage varies to more closely resemble the menstrual cycle). Mini-pills containing progestin are rarely prescribed in the U.S. because they aren't as effective, since they don't suppress ovulation.

Pills come in packages of 21 or 28. In the 28-day pack, the last 7 pills (which you take just before, during, and right after your period) are placebos, included just so you don't get out of the habit of taking the pill.

How they work: Birth control pills prevent pregnancy by interrupting

---

PILL POINTS

※

BENEFITS: No interruption of sex play; nothing to prepare; can reduce risk of ovarian cysts, ovarian and endometrial cancer, pelvic inflammatory disease (PID), and benign breast tumors; causes lighter periods; can help alleviate menstrual cramps and endometriosis symptoms; no mess.

DRAWBACKS: Relatively expensive; prescription required; no protection from STDs; must take pill every day; may cause annoying side effects; may increase risk of blood clots, strokes, and heart attacks (especially in women who smoke or are over 35).

※ Women who both take the Pill and smoke are 39 times at

RISKS OF HORMONAL CONTRACEPTIVE METHODS

For nonsmoking women under age 35 with no major health problems, hormonal contraception is quite safe and extremely effective. However, there are health risks associated with using it. Women who use the Pill, Norplant, or Depo-Provera have an increased likelihood of developing blood clots, which can cause stroke, cardiac arrest, and other problems. Further, in the rare case that a woman using a non-estrogen hormonal contraception gets pregnant, she is at increased risk of having an ectopic pregnancy (the fertilized egg will develop in the fallopian tube, not the uterus). Be sure to discuss these and other risks with your prescribing practitioner.

If you use hormone-based contraception, contact your practitioner immediately if you experience:

▲ Sharp chest pain

▲ Sudden shortness of breath

▲ Sudden severe headache or vomiting, dizziness, fainting, vision or speech problems, weakness, numbness in arm or leg

▲ Severe pain and/or swelling in the calf or thigh

▲ Unusually heavy vaginal bleeding

▲ Severe pain or tenderness in lower abdomen

▲ Coughing up blood

and changing the normal menstrual cycle. The main function of the combination pill is to suppress ovulation by creating higher levels of estrogen in the body than normal. Without ovulation, the fertilization of an egg by sperm (and resulting pregnancy) cannot occur. The progestin in combination birth control pills inhibits the growth of the uterine lining so that even if fertilization does occur, the egg will not be able to implant itself in the wall of the uterus. In addition, the progestin causes the cervical mucus to become thick and dry so that sperm have a difficult time traveling through it.

Effectiveness: The Pill is a highly effective form of birth control if used correctly. The combination pill has a theoretical effectiveness rate of 99.6 percent, and an actual effectiveness rate of 97 percent. The mini-pill is slightly less effective.

STD protection: None.

Where to get them: You must get a prescription from a health practitioner at a doctor's office, family planning clinic, or campus health services. If the clinic or health center doesn't provide them, you've got to pick them up at a pharmacy.

Not recommended if: You smoke (especially if you're over 35); you are very overweight; you have diabetes, high blood pressure, or high cholesterol, or a family or personal history of blood clots or stroke, liver disease, cancer (especially breast or uterine cancer), migraine headaches, sickle-cell anemia, or depression; you are not responsible about taking the pills

greater risk of heart attack than those who do neither.

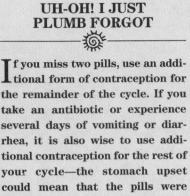

UH-OH! I JUST PLUMB FORGOT

If you miss two pills, use an additional form of contraception for the remainder of the cycle. If you take an antibiotic or experience several days of vomiting or diarrhea, it is also wise to use additional contraception for the rest of your cycle—the stomach upset could mean that the pills were improperly or incompletely absorbed by your gastrointestinal tract.

every day at the same time or about protecting yourself from STDs; your mother took diethylstilbestrol (DES, a synthetic estrogen used to prevent miscarriage) before you were born.

Reasons for failure: You failed to use a backup method if you missed two pills or you experienced several days of vomiting or diarrhea; you failed to use a backup contraceptive during the first month you started the Pill; you took other medications that rendered the Pill less effective (see below); you failed to take a pill every day.

Other: Significant side effects may include blotchy skin, varicose veins, nausea, breakthrough bleeding (spotting), vision problems, weight gain, acne, depression, and/or breast tenderness. Many of the side effects, such as nausea and spotting (which are very common in the first month of use), should go away after three months. If they don't, see your health practitioner about switching to another brand or form of pill.

■ The Pill continues to protect against pregnancy when you have your period and are either not taking any pill or are taking placebos. But during this time, like always, the Pill does not protect from STDs.

■ Taking the Pill with your evening meal often eliminates the problem of Pill-related nausea.

■ The Pill inhibits absorption of some vitamins (such as B and E), so you may want to invest in a good supplement.

■ Women on the Pill are twice as likely to develop blood clots after surgery than women who aren't.

■ Certain antibiotics, anti-fungals, anti-inflammatories, barbituates, anti-convulsants, antidepressants, and anticoagulants reduce the Pill's effectiveness and vice versa.

■ If you experience spotting or "breakthrough bleeding" (especially if you've been on the Pill for more than three months), use an additional form of birth control and call your health care practitioner.

■ The Pill can affect tests for thyroid functions, blood sugar level, and cholesterol level.

Instructions:
1. Take one pill at about the same time every day. If you forget to take a

pill, you should take one as soon as you remember. If you forget to take two pills in a row, take two as soon as you remember and two more the next day, and use a backup method of birth control for the rest of your cycle. (Obviously this does not apply if you forget to take a placebo.)

2. If you think you might be pregnant, see your health practitioner immediately.

3. If you want to stop taking the Pill, call your practitioner to discuss it. If you can't reach him or her, finish your package before you quit—doing so will make it easier for your body to reregulate your menstrual cycle.

Norplant

Description: Norplant is a highly effective contraceptive that provides continuous protection against pregnancy for up to five years. It consists of six slender, matchstick-sized silicone capsules containing the synthetic hormone levonorgestrel (a progestin), which are inserted under the skin of the upper arm in a fan-shaped configuration. Norplant can be removed before the end of the five-year period, at which point fertility should be restored to normal. Because it contains no estrogen, the potential risks (and benefits) associated with estrogen will not exist.

How it works: The capsules slowly release small amounts of progestin over the five-year period. This prevents pregnancy by inhibiting the full development of the uterine lining, and by keeping the cervical mucus thick and dry so that sperm have a difficult time traveling through.

Effectiveness: The theoretical effectiveness rate of Norplant is 99.7 per-

cent, and its actual effectiveness rate is 98.9–99.6 percent.

STD protection: None.

Where to get it: A minor surgical procedure is required to insert and remove the capsules. The procedure can be performed in a doctor's office, family planning clinic, or student/women's health center.

Not recommended if: You have liver problems, unexplained vaginal bleeding, or a history of heart attacks, stroke, blood clots, cysts, or chest pain; you have a family or personal history of breast cancer; you are not responsi-

NORPLANT NOTES

BENEFITS: Protects from pregnancy for five years; you don't have to keep buying birth control; no interruption of sex play; can reduce risk of ovarian and uterine cancer, and pelvic inflammatory disease (PID); can cause lighter periods; can help alleviate menstrual cramps and endometriosis symptoms; convenient; no mess.

DRAWBACKS: Initial cost outlay is high; requires sometimes painful minor surgery to implant and remove; no protection from STDs; can cause heavy or irregular periods or stop them altogether; may cause annoying side effects; may cause abnormal follicular (egg-sac) growth in ovary; removal may be difficult; return to fertility after removal may be delayed for up to two years.

cancer by 50%, ovarian cancer by 40%, and benign breast cysts by 90%.

ble about protecting yourself from STDs; you're looking for short-term birth control.

Reasons for failure: Inserted incorrectly; sudden weight gain; used longer than five years.

Other:

■ May cause unpleasant side effects, such as irregular periods, headaches, blotchy skin, nausea (especially in the first three months of use), vision problems, weight gain, acne, depression, and breast tenderness. After two years of consecutive use, contraceptive effectiveness goes down (very) slightly in some women.

■ Norplant implants manufactured now are made from a less dense tubing than the original product, making it more effective and suitable for more women.

Depo-Provera

Description: Depo-Provera, available since 1971 as a treatment for endometrial cancer, has recently been approved for contraceptive use in the U.S., though it has been in use for decades in other countries around the world. It is injected in the arm or buttock and provides three months of protection. Depo-Provera contains depot-

---

DEPO-PROVERA DETAILS

❀

BENEFITS: Protects from pregnancy for three months; no interruption of sex play; can reduce risk of ovarian and uterine cancer, and pelvic inflammatory disease (PID); may cause lighter periods; can help alleviate menstrual cramps and endometriosis symptoms; no mess.

DRAWBACKS: Expensive; prescription required; no protection from STDs; may cause annoying side effects; may cause heavy or irregular periods (or stop them altogether); you have to have a shot every three months; may increase the risk of osteoporosis (brittle bones); it takes 6–18 months after last shot to completely regain fertility.

---

medroxyprogesterone (DMPA), a synthetic progesterone. Like Norplant, it contains no estrogen.

How it works: The progestin injection prevents pregnancy by inhibiting the full development of the uterine lining, and by keeping the cervical mucus thick and dry so that sperm have a difficult time traveling through.

Effectiveness: The theoretical effectiveness rate of Depo-Provera is 99 percent, and its actual effectiveness rate is 98.9–99.6 percent.

STD protection: None.

Where to get it: A health practitioner must give you the injection at a doctor's office, family planning clinic, or campus health services.

Not recommended if: You have liver disease, unexplained vaginal bleeding, or a history of bone problems, heart attacks, stroke, blood clots, or chest pain; you have a family or personal history of breast cancer; you are not responsible about going for a shot every three months; you are not responsible about protecting yourself from STDs; you want short-term birth control.

Reasons for failure: Did not get an injection within three months of your last one.

Other:
■ You must have an injection every three months. It may cause unpleasant side effects such as irregular periods, headaches, blotchy skin, nausea, weight gain, acne, depression, and breast tenderness.

**IUD
IN A NUTSHELL**
❋

BENEFITS: Initial cost is high but costs even out in the long run, as you don't have to keep buying birth control; no interruption of sex play; nothing to prepare; no mess.

DRAWBACKS: Must be inserted and removed by a practitioner; no protection from STDs (actually, increases susceptibility to STDs); increases risk of pelvic infection; risk of sterility or harm to uterus; may cause painful periods, cramping, and/or spotting.

■ If need be, you can get your shot up to four weeks early.

Intrauterine Device

Description: Intrauterine devices (IUDs) are small objects inserted into the uterus that prevent pregnancy. IUDs must be inserted and removed by a health practitioner.

How it works: Exactly how an IUD prevents pregnancy is not fully understood. It is speculated that an IUD causes a low-grade irritation in the uterus that inhibits fertilization by preventing the normal buildup of the uterine lining and thus the implantation of the fertilized egg.

Effectiveness: The IUD's theoretical effectiveness rate is 98–99.2 percent, and its actual effectiveness rate is 95–97 percent.

STD protection: None. In fact, IUDs increase susceptibility to STDs, as unwelcome invaders can use the string as a handy pathway into the uterus. Also, the low-grade irritation the IUD causes in the uterus can make it easier for STDs to take hold.

Where to get it: You must have the IUD inserted and removed by a health practitioner at a doctor's office, family planning clinic, or student/women's health center.

Not recommended if: You haven't been pregnant and you want to have children someday; you have a history of gynecological problems; you are not responsible about protecting yourself from STDs; you are uncomfortable about reaching into your vagina once a month to feel for the string (to make sure the IUD has not become dislodged).

❋ The Copper T-380 IUD can be left in place safely for 10 years. ❋

Reasons for failure: Inserted and/or positioned incorrectly.

Other:

■ The incidence of serious gynecological disorders related to IUD use prompted a mass recall of some brands and caused most others to be removed from the market. If you have or are considering getting an IUD, discuss the risks with your practitioner.

■ You may wish to seek the opinion of more than one practitioner.

■ IUDs should be removed before beginning treatment for STDs.

■ If you can't feel the string on your IUD, call your doctor immediately.

FERTILITY AWARENESS AT A GLANCE

BENEFITS: Inexpensive; no side effects.

DRAWBACKS: Not a very effective form of contraception; requires willpower; can be difficult and time-consuming; offers no protection against STDs.

Note: This method should *not* be confused with the much less reliable "rhythm" method.

Fertility Awareness ("Natural Birth Control")

Description: Fertility awareness is the method of avoiding pregnancy by knowing when you are ovulating and abstaining from vaginal intercourse during that time. Some women, mainly for religious reasons, use this as their only form of contraception.

Other women use it as a means of augmenting another form of birth control.

How it works: Determining the time when you are fertile can be accomplished through several methods, including monitoring basal body temperature (BBT), cervical mucus changes, and menstrual calendars. Fertility awareness also takes into account the fact that sperm can live for as long as five days in a woman's fallopian tubes, therefore lengthening the time when it is unsafe to have unprotected intercourse. Learning how to accurately predict when you are fertile requires extensive instruction from a health care practitioner.

Effectiveness: Fertility awareness can range in effectiveness from 60 to 90 percent. In order for it to be effective, it must be practiced precisely, correctly, and consistently. One of the problems with this method is the fact that it may require a great deal of self-control from both partners to abstain from having intercourse during the fertile periods, which can be 10 or more days every month.

STD protection: None.

Where to get it: If you are interested in using fertility awareness as a form of contraception, it is essential that you receive proper instruction. Talk to your health care provider or to a women's health organization for a referral.

Not recommended if: You don't have the willpower to abstain from sex during the times when pregnancy is possible, or you're not willing or able to take the time and effort necessary to monitor your body.

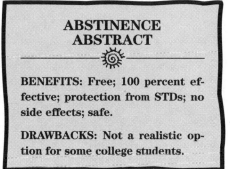

Other: Fertility awareness is more often used by women who want to get pregnant, to determine when they're ovulating.

Abstinence

Description: Abstaining from intercourse.

How it works: If no vaginal intercourse occurs (and no semen comes into contact with the vagina) pregnancy cannot occur.

Effectiveness: 100 percent.

STD protection: The term abstinence is commonly defined as "abstaining from any behavior that puts one at risk of contracting STDs." By this definition, abstinence is as safe as it gets. But, if you do everything except have vaginal intercourse you may still be at risk of contracting STDs.

Where to get it: The point is, you *don't* get it.

Not recommended if: You don't have the willpower to abstain from sexual intercourse.

Other: There are an infinite number of wonderful, romantic, erotic, sensual things you can do with a partner that don't involve sexual intercourse.

ABSTINENCE ABSTRACT

BENEFITS: Free; 100 percent effective; protection from STDs; no side effects; safe.

DRAWBACKS: Not a realistic option for some college students.

BIRTH CONTROL METHODS THAT DO *NOT* WORK

Withdrawal

Withdrawal, also called coitus interruptus, means having unprotected vaginal intercourse up until the point when your partner is ready to ejaculate, at which time he withdraws his penis and ejaculates away from the vagina. Unfortunately, this method doesn't account for preseminal fluid, which contains up to half a million sperm (and all you need is one . . .). Withdrawal does not protect against STDs, either.

Douching

Douching with water or another solution immediately after intercourse in an effort to wash semen out of the vagina is not an effective method of birth control. Sperm swim very quickly and are likely to enter the cervix before they can be washed away. Also, douching can force semen into the uterus, increasing the likelihood of pregnancy.

THE MORNING-AFTER PILL

If you have unprotected intercourse during or close to ovulation, you may want to consider taking the "morning-after" pill, a medication with the hormonal equivalent of about four birth control pills. Women who have been advised against using birth control pills should not use the morning-after pill.

The morning-after pill does not prevent the fertilization of an egg by a sperm, but rather affects the lining of the uterus so that a fertilized egg can't implant itself. It basically brings on your period. Taking the pills within three days of having unprotected intercourse or experiencing a birth control mishap (though preferably within 24 hours), then again 12 hours later, is 99 percent effective in preventing pregnancy. Morning-after pills are available from a gynecologist, women's clinics, and/or campus health centers.

Vaginal bleeding, cramps, breast tenderness, nausea, and headache usually occur within a week after taking the pills but are not sure signs of effectiveness. Normal menstruation should return within four to six weeks; if not, get a pregnancy test.

Before you take the morning-after pill, it is important to evaluate what you would do if a pregnancy did occur even after taking the pills, since the hormones in the treatment can cause problems in the pregnancy.

The long-range health effects of the morning-after pill have not been conclusively studied. It is possible that frequent use could have harmful effects. It should only be used as an emergency backup option for preventing a likely pregnancy.

The morning-after pill is not the same as RU 486. It is not considered an abortifacient. (For more on RU 486, see page 450.)

Rhythm Method

The rhythm method estimates when a woman is capable of getting pregnant by assuming that women ovulate 14 days after the first day of their period. It requires a completely regular, 28-day menstrual cycle, which is not common among college women, as our own lifestyles can include many of the factors that can cause menstrual irregularity, such as high stress, eating and sleeping at odd hours (especially around midterms and finals), and living with other menstruating women (whose cycles affect one another's).

Other factors, such as exercise, heredity, and how long a woman has menstruated, also affect a woman's cycle. The rhythm method offers no protection against STDs.

"If you can't handle being up front and assertive about the guy wearing a condom, you aren't ready to have sex."

—BRYN MAWR COLLEGE, '95

SAFER SEX

If you choose to have oral, genital, and/or anal sex, you need to take precautions against sexually transmissable diseases (STDs). Sex is serious business, and either abstaining from risky behavior or practicing safer sex is a necessity, not a choice. It is vital that we protect ourselves and others from diseases that can cause discomfort, pain, infertility, and even death.

Learn the facts. That way, you can make educated choices about what risks, if any, you choose to take. If you take the time to teach yourself what's

"I do peer education at after-school high school programs. When we talk about generic stuff, like condoms, everyone knows what to say and can depersonalize it. But when I brought in a speaker, a 21-year-old with HIV (who got the virus when she was their age), it made it really hard for them (and me) to think that it couldn't happen to them."

—STATE UNIVERSITY OF NEW YORK
(SUNY) AT BUFFALO, '97

risky, what's not, and why, you won't worry or wonder if you're being safe.

The point of safer sex is to:

■ Prevent transmission of body fluids (no semen in mouth, anus, or vagina; no blood in mouth, anus, or vagina).

■ Prevent skin contact with warts or sores.

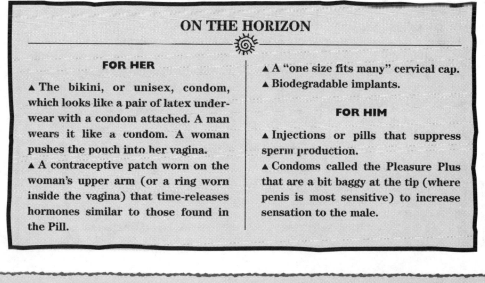

ON THE HORIZON

FOR HER

▲ The bikini, or unisex, condom, which looks like a pair of latex underwear with a condom attached. A man wears it like a condom. A woman pushes the pouch into her vagina.

▲ A contraceptive patch worn on the woman's upper arm (or a ring worn inside the vagina) that time-releases hormones similar to those found in the Pill.

▲ A "one size fits many" cervical cap.
▲ Biodegradable implants.

FOR HIM

▲ Injections or pills that suppress sperm production.
▲ Condoms called the Pleasure Plus that are a bit baggy at the tip (where penis is most sensitive) to increase sensation to the male.

■ Prevent pregnancy.

■ Have consensual sex.

■ Feel both physically and emotionally comfortable.

What's required:

■ Using latex condoms during oral, vaginal, and anal sex.

■ Using dental dams, plastic wrap, or a cut condom during oral-vaginal and oral-anal sex.

■ Using latex gloves when putting finger or hands in a partner's vagina or anus, especially if you have a cut on your hand.

■ Communicating with your partner(s) about staying safe.

■ Being assertive and open about your needs (on a health, sexual, and emotional level).

■ Respecting the choices of people you have sex with, and having them respect yours. (You can't separate what is "emotionally" safer sex from what is "physically" safer sex.)

■ Paying attention to your and your partner's bodies. Or more specifically, · learning what "healthy" and "normal" looks, smells, and/or feels like, and being on the lookout for any unusual bumps, rashes, discharge, or odors. This said, many STDs, including HIV, can be symptomless, so a healthy appearance should not be an excuse to not practice safer sex.

Activities in which there is no possibility of fluid exchange and no contact with infected skin are safe. These include dry kissing, touching healthy unbroken skin or touching while wearing latex gloves, massage, masturbation, phone sex, cybersex,

---

TALKING IT OVER

Practicing safer sex reduces your risks significantly, but it doesn't eliminate them. As of now, there is no 100 percent foolproof method of making potentially "unsafe" activities safe. Though HIV cannot travel through latex, there is always the possibility that there may be a tear in the condom or dam. Or a tiny cut or abrasion in uncovered skin can allow HIV a point of entry. Or body fluids may accidentally find their way into contact with mucous membranes. And because HPV (human papilloma virus, which causes genital warts) and herpes can be transmitted before obvi-

ous signs of infection are present, what appears to be safe behavior may not be. Don't just rely on latex and a quick visual examination to protect yourself. Discuss sexual history with potential partners before getting hot and heavy. It's good practice to put off "risky" activities until you feel you are both being honest about your pasts, and are comfortable enough with each other to do everything necessary to minimize your risk of passing along or getting a disease. If you choose to be sexually intimate with someone you don't know well, you need to be especially careful.

---

talking dirty, hugging, rolling around, playing with toys (unshared), and watching your partner turn her/himself on. French kissing is safe, too, as long as you don't have cuts or sores in your mouth.

Many STDs are spread by bacteria or viruses that travel in blood (including menstrual blood), vaginal secretions, semen, pre-cum, urine, feces, and breast milk. The germs can enter into the body through mucous membranes (such as the mouth, vagina, urethra, and anus) during any kind of intercourse or oral sex and also through cuts in the skin. For diseases like genital warts and herpes, transmission can occur via contact with the affected area right before and during an outbreak, and possibly between outbreaks. (For a full discussion of STDs and their transmission, see "STDs, HIV, and AIDS," page 369.)

SAFER-SEX SHOPPING LIST

Keep all the necessary safer-sex implements nearby when you are having sex—if they're right there you won't be tempted to forgo the condom, and won't have to break the mood to get up and search the room for that tube of spermicide.

Condoms

Note: For more info on condoms, see pages 401–404.

Condoms will provide STD protection during vaginal, anal, and oral sex. In addition to using a new one after he ejaculates, you should also use a new condom when switching from anal sex to vaginal or oral sex, even if he doesn't come, because fecal bacteria can cause a multitude of problems. Make sure you use latex condoms that specifically say they protect against STDs. Animal membrane condoms do not protect against STDs and many novelty condoms may not provide adequate protection.

"At the big drugstore in town they have all of these so-called novelty condoms on display with the real, latex ones. They can be fun, but they may not be as effective. You have to read the box pretty carefully to make sure you're getting what you need."

—UNIVERSITY OF ROCHESTER, '92

Put the condom on before any contact occurs between the penis and vagina, anus, or mouth. The clear pre-seminal fluid that comes out of the penis before ejaculation contains both sperm and the organisms that carry STDs. You should also put condoms on sex toys (dildos, vibrators) that are going to be shared (put a clean condom on for each person, each time the toy "changes hands").

SAFER SEX AT A GLANCE

WHAT TO AVOID	HOW IT CAN HAPPEN	MAKING IT SAFER
Semen coming in contact with (mucous membranes in) mouth	Fellatio, blow job (oral sex on a man)	Use a latex condom
Vaginal secretions coming in contact with (mucous membranes in) mouth	Cunnilingus (oral sex on a woman)	Use a latex/plastic wrap dam
Semen coming in contact with (mucous membranes in) vagina	Vaginal intercourse	Use a latex condom
Semen coming in contact with (mucous membranes in) rectum	Anal intercourse	Use a latex condom
Vaginal secretions coming in contact with (mucous membranes in) vagina	Sharing dildos or other sex toys, or vulva-vulva or vulva-hand-vulva contact	Use a latex condom on the dildo; wash the dildo and change the condom for each partner
Vaginal secretions coming in contact with (cuts in) hands	Touching, fisting	Wear latex gloves
Contact with STD-caused blisters and lesions	Sex play with someone who is having a herpes, HPV, or syphilis outbreak (or right before)	Avoid contact during the outbreak, even with latex. At other times, use latex and spermicide, and wash after contact with the area
Blood coming in contact with (mucous membranes in) mouth, (cuts in) hands	Touching or cunnilingus on a woman during menstruation	Use a very large piece of plastic wrap/latex dam; latex gloves

 The earliest vaginal pouches were hollowed out okra pods or goat

DO UNTO YOUR CONDOMS

Germs that cause STDs (including HIV) can't pass through latex, and thus latex condoms have been rightfully lauded as an essential part of the safer-sex experience. However, latex is far from perfect—if it's not treated correctly, it has a tendency to rip and leave you unprotected.

Cold, heat, light, and especially oils cause latex to disintegrate. Even if a condom you've found in your glove compartment seems fine and doesn't break, it can still be corroded enough to allow STD transmission to occur. The following will help you make sure your condoms are ready to roll.

Give it the condom freshness test:

▲ Check the expiration date (especially on vending machine condoms).
▲ Before opening the wrapper, squeeze it and feel for air trapped inside the condom package to be sure the condom is still factory-sealed.
▲ The condom itself should be soft and pliable. If it won't stay unrolled, feels brittle or dry, or sticks to itself, throw it away and use a new one.

In addition:

▲ Do not inflate, stretch, or poke condoms before use.
▲ Do not reuse condoms. Use a new condom for each act of intercourse, oral sex, or anal sex.
▲ Once a condom comes off, never put it back on—even if ejaculation did not occur.
▲ Once ejaculation occurs, take the condom off and dispose of it.
▲ Be aware of fingernails, rings, and teeth; they can snag and damage a condom.
▲ Store condoms in a cool, dry place.

Dental Dams

Dental dams are six-inch-square pieces of latex that can be spread across the vagina or anus and held in place during oral sex to prevent contact between the vagina or anus and one's partner's mouth. You can buy dams at women's erotica shops, pharmacies, and dental supply houses. You can also make your own by unrolling an unlubricated condom and cutting from bottom to tip, or by cutting the fingers off of a latex glove. (Be sure to wash off the powder that coats the inside of most latex gloves before use.)

Plastic wrap is also a good alternative—you can cut it into whatever size or shape you want, and it comes in a rainbow of translucent colors. To increase sensation and safety, cut off a large piece, squeeze some lubricant containing nonoxynol-9 on it, and fold it over to make a plastic-wrap-and-lube sandwich.

Note: Do not use "microwavable" plastic wrap, which contains tiny holes large enough for viruses to pass through.

Female Condom/Vaginal Pouch

The vaginal pouch offers effective (although not 100 percent) protection against STDs, and could play a key role in fighting the rising incidence of HIV in women. You and your partner may want to trade off wearing your

bladders. The more modern version was FDA-approved in 1993.

respective condoms. (The vaginal pouch is also a useful alternative if your partner has trouble maintaining an erection when he puts on a male condom.) The polyurethane lining in the vaginal pouch is stronger than the latex used in male condoms, and on the whole, it's softer, thinner, and more resistant to oils. (See page 404 for more on the female condom.)

NOT-QUITE-PERFECT PROTECTION

Condoms (both female and male) will not offer full protection from STDs that are spread by skin-to-skin contact (such as herpes or HPV) unless the condom fully covers all sores or warts. Similarly, because condoms do not cover pubic hair, they cannot protect against pubic lice or crabs. (But because the portion of the female condom that hangs out of the vagina covers a portion of the labia, it offers better protection against these STDs than does the male condom.)

Water-Based Lubricants/Spermicides

Using a lubricant on the outside of a condom (or a prelubricated condom) can make intercourse not only more pleasurable but safer as well—the lubricant helps reduce friction, making the condom less likely to rip or tear. (This is especially true with "thinner" condoms, which tend to dry out very quickly.)

Make sure that your lubricant is water-based, such as K-Y Jelly, Astro-glide, Wet, or spermicidal jelly, and not oil-based, as is Vaseline. Oil-based lubricants (as well as many of the creams used to cure yeast infections) corrode latex and can cause the condom to break or tear. (On the same note, wash your hands of lotions, oils, or creams before handling the condom.)

Some lubricants contain spermicide. The spermicide nonoxynol-9 has been shown to kill HIV and other viruses and bacteria that cause STDs, and is therefore a good secondary source of protection to use with condoms. However, in the case that you have a sensitivity to nonoxynol-9 or other components of the jelly, cream, film, foam or suppository in which it's contained, the spermicide may be doing you more harm than good in preventing the transmission of STDs. If your sensitivity causes any open sores, blisters, or rashes, especially on the mucous membranes, these could be the perfect conduit for STD transmission. If you are sensitive, you can still get some of the increased protection (contraceptive or anti-STD) that a spermicide offers by squeezing a bit of it into the tip of your partner's condom before he puts it on.

Latex Gloves

Disposable latex gloves (the kind health care practitioners use) help prevent the transmission of diseases through cuts, scrapes, or blisters on your hands when you come into contact with body fluids during activities such as touching, fingering, or fisting. The gloves come in small, medium, and large sizes, and are available at pharmacies. You can also get them in big economy-size boxes from medical supply houses.

The new Pleasure Plus condom, which enhances sensitivity

Finger Cots

Finger cots look like mini-condoms and are meant to act as a one-finger latex glove. They're good if you have a cut, blister, scratch, or a hangnail, but latex gloves are safer, as fluids can get in over the top of a finger cot pretty easily. They may be hard to find, but ask at a pharmacy or medical supply house.

Bleach

Even when you're using a condom on a dildo, vibrator, or any other sex toy, it's still important to wash your playthings properly. After you're done, clean and disinfect them in a solution of soapy water and 10 percent bleach. (Be sure to rinse them very well with clear water after washing.)

MAKING SAFER SEX FUN: LOVE YOUR LATEX

Many people consider safer sex to be less erotic and spontaneous than unsafe sex. Though it does take some organization and discipline, these efforts have valuable rewards. Practice, planning, creativity, caring for yourself and your partner(s), and a sense of humor are all key to making safer sex fun and enjoyable. Below are some tips on making the use of latex barriers more pleasurable:

To increase stimulation during vaginal or anal intercourse with condoms:

■ Use a water-based lubricant on the outside of the condom or on the vulva and around the vagina or anus to reduce dryness.

■ Put a drop of the lubricant in the inner tip of the condom before it's put on. (Use one with nonoxynol-9 for increased protection.)

■ See if everything they say about ribbed and studded condoms is true. Just make sure they're latex and provide adequate STD protection.

General tips on making oral sex through latex more appealing and pleasurable:

■ Try a flavored condom or dam, one of the flavored water-based lubricants, or something you find in your fridge— as long as it does *not* contain any fats or oil. (This means no chocolate syrup, no whipped cream, no icing, no peanut butter, etc.)

■ Wash off the powder or cornstarch from condoms, dams, and gloves before you begin.

Making fellatio (blow jobs) through latex more appealing and pleasurable:

■ Use an unlubricated condom. Lubricated condoms suffice, but the lubricant tastes so bad (especially if it's nonoxynol-9) that you may lose not only "that loving feeling," but your lunch as well.

■ Use a condom without a receptacle end. They are perfectly positioned to induce a gag reflex.

via a bulbous tip, was preferred by over 70% of both sexes. ☼

EXCUSE ME, I HAVE TO POWDER MY NOSE

Though getting up and running to the bathroom right after sex isn't the most romantic thing you can do, paying a quick visit to the toilet, shower, or sink may help you prevent STD transmission. Urinating after vaginal intercourse helps flush out some of the germs that cause STDs as well as those that cause urinary tract infections. Gently washing with soap and water after sex may help prevent transmission of herpes, HPV, and HIV. But watch how you wash: Scrubbing your genitals, especially with something rough like a washcloth or sponge, can irritate the area or give you tiny abrasions. These create an opening for HIV and other disease-causing germs to enter the body. It's important to treat your mucous membranes with the gentleness and consideration they deserve. As an alternative to full-fledged washing, you might want to try premoistened towelettes, such as those made for babies' bottoms. Not only are they gentle to the skin, but they can help kill germs. And they're small enough to keep tucked into your purse, jacket, or backpack.

While gentle washing may reduce the risk of transmission, douching after vaginal sex can *increase* the risk. Douching pushes the critters that cause STDs into the upper reproductive tract, and washes away the body's natural defenses against germs—the vaginal secretions that work to fight infection and the mucus lining the vaginal walls that acts as a protective physical barrier.

And on the subject of bathroom antics . . . don't brush or floss your teeth right before performing oral sex. (You can give yourself little cuts large enough to let the HIV in.)

■ Use an unribbed condom—sucking or rubbing your lips against a ribbed condom for too long will make your mouth/lips/tongue numb.

■ You can also buy condoms specifically designed for oral sex that are thinner and sometimes scented or flavored. (However, do not use these special condoms for intercourse or cut them up for use as dental dams—they are too thin and will break.)

Making cunnilingus through latex more appealing and pleasurable:

■ Don't use too much lubricant, or you won't be able to get a good grip on the latex.

■ For better (and easier) coverage, have your partner hold the two upper corners of the dam while you hold the lower. Or try one of the "hands-free" harnesses like the Dammit (adjustable leather thigh straps that hold the dam in place) or underwear that has a replaceable latex crotch.

■ Use flavored or colored dental dams or condoms.

■ Put a flavored, edible lubricant on the side of the dam/condom facing your mouth.

In 1995, 9 out of 10 Americans said sex-ed classes should teach about

■ Use a transparent condom or plastic wrap.

To increase sensation when using latex gloves:

■ Use tight-fitting gloves.

■ Squeeze some lubricant in the fingers of gloves before you put them on (however, do not use lubrication inside a finger cot—it can slip off).

■ Use a lubricant on the outside of the glove.

LAYING IT ON THE LINE

■ The sad fact is that many doctors and clinicians believe that we can never be completely sure that we are free from STDs. In rare cases, tests can be inaccurate, and because we may never have any identifiable symptoms of STDs, we might not even think to get tested in the first place. However, it is possible to be *almost* positive that you are free from STDs. If you and your partner are healthy, you've never participated in any "risky" behavior, and you both have serial-tested (see page 386) negative for all types of STDs, and you've committed to monogamy, you might be able to stop using latex barriers for disease prevention without risk.

■ Having sex with many partners does not cause STDs. A person who has 30 partners, none of whom have STDs, will have less of a chance of catching one than a person who is mutually monogamous with a person who has an STD. But in reality, the more partners you have, the greater the chance that one of them will have an STD.

CONDOM COMEBACKS

"I promise, you won't get anything from me."
"And without a rubber, you won't get anything from me."

"I've never used a condom."
"All the more reason I want you to wear one with me."

"I don't have a condom."
"I do."

"I'm too big for a condom."
"Then you're certainly too big for me."

"OK, we need to have the mandatory condom discussion. You're going to wear one. End of discussion. Let's move onto more exciting things."

"Real men don't wear condoms."
"I guess I don't have sex with real men."

"Condoms are a real turn-off."
"And sexually transmitted diseases are a turn-on?"

"But you're on the Pill."
"This isn't just about pregnancy."

It doesn't feel as good with a condom.

You won't feel anything without one.

And it's hard enough to find out about just one person's sexual history . . .

■ There is a significantly greater risk of a man infecting a woman during heterosexual intercourse than vice versa. Semen has an especially high content of white blood cells, meaning that if HIV (or another disease carried by white blood cells) is present, it will be present in a high concentration. Further, it remains in the vagina after intercourse, and the mucous membrane lining of the vagina is more susceptible to small tears than the skin of the penis is. Anal sex is even riskier, because the lining of the rectum is even more susceptible to tears than the vagina is. The bottom line: If there is any question, it's time to bring out the latex.

■ If you are continuing to have sex with someone with whom you *did not* have safer sex in the past, you should begin to have safer sex with him or her now. Do not assume that you both must have "caught all of each other's diseases by now," because STD transmission doesn't work that way. You may catch an STD the very first time you're exposed to it, or you may not catch it until the 50th exposure. It's never too late to start having safer sex.

■ Even if both you and your partner have a presently incurable STD (such as herpes, HPV, or HIV), you should still practice safer sex. There are different strains and complexes of the same viruses, so partners can complicate each other's cases by introducing new strains of the disease. Practicing safer sex is especially important if you and your partner are HIV-positive, so the two of you will be protected against other STDs and other random invaders that may weaken your immune system or be a serious health threat if your immune system is already compromised.

■ If you are pregnant, you have even more reason to practice safe sex, as the germs that cause STDs can severely complicate pregnancy, labor, and delivery, and can cause birth defects.

■ Whether it's with the same person or multiple partners, never reuse condoms, dams, gloves, finger cots, or plastic wrap—throw them away and start fresh each time.

ACTIVIST IDEAS

■ Start a letter-writing campaign that encourages pharmaceutical companies to do more research and to develop better and safer contraceptive methods—for women *and* men.

■ Encourage your campus health services to provide contraception at low or no cost to students and to work with pharmaceutical companies that make contraceptives to get free samples and/or bulk discounts on contraception for students.

■ Lobby government officials to make sure that contraception remains untaxed and accessible to all who need or desire it. Advocate lowering the cost of condoms and spermicides because they prevent the spread of STDs.

■ Set up a table displaying samples of all the different types of contraception and safer sex items so that people can learn how to use them and where to obtain them. Get health services to participate (perhaps a gynecologist or nurse could join you at the table). Make sure you have the latest, accurate information. Don't forget to mention how effective each method is at preventing STDs.

■ Find an expert who could lead a safer-sex workshop and invite him or her to come to your school. The workshop could include some or all of the following activities:

▲ Hand out information, answer questions, dispel myths, and discuss issues about safer sex.

▲ Have people anonymously write their questions on scraps of paper and pass them to the front of the room, then answer and discuss them. Plant a few important questions in the pile, in case your group doesn't prove to be very candid.

▲ Pass out a variety of condoms. You might also like to have some water-soluble lubricants (plain, with spermicide, and/or flavored) available, too. Give everyone a chance to see

what latex can (and can't) handle— how far it stretches, how easily it breaks, and what happens when it's exposed to Vaseline or baby oil. Hand out scissors so people can practice making dental dams. Bring some bananas, carrots, zucchinis, or dildos to practice putting them on. Amaze the group by rolling a condom on a small cantaloupe or softball.

■ Forgo the flowers, candy, and little love poems. This Valentine's Day, have campus sweeties send each other safer-sex baskets. Raise money for your club, sorority, dorm, or a charity of your choice by selling little packages containing a lovely array of condoms, dams, water-soluble lubricant, and information about making safer sex fun.

NO GLOVE, NO LOVE!

RESOURCES

PLANNED PARENTHOOD FEDERATION OF
AMERICA
810 SEVENTH AVENUE
NEW YORK, NY 10019
(800) 829-7732 [PPFA]
(212) 541-7800
FAX: (212) 245-1845
Organizes political action/advocacy work on behalf of reproductive rights and women's health. Makes referrals to local Planned Parenthood clinics that provide the services you need. Most offer low-cost basic gynecological care, contraception, and counseling. Many offer abortion services. To find a clinic near you call (800) 230-7526. You will automatically be con-

without using any form of contraception will become pregnant. ☼

nected to the closest clinic. Local clinics are also listed in the white pages of your phone book. *Note:* individual Planned Parenthood services vary.

ADVOCATES FOR YOUTH
1025 VERMONT AVENUE NW
WASHINGTON, DC 20005
(202) 347-5700
Provides information and education about birth control, STDs, and safer sex. Organizes political action/advocacy work to influence public policy and legislation. Publishes numerous materials on contraception in English, Spanish, and French, available upon request.

FAMILIES OF THE AMERICAS FOUNDATION (FAF)
P.O. BOX 1170
DUNKIRK, MD 20754
(800) 443-3395
(301) 627-3346
Trains instructors to teach natural family planning and sex education. Provides sex education and information. Maintains a library of resources on family planning and contraception. Makes referrals to local organizations and clinics. Publishes numerous materials in English, Spanish, French, Portuguese, Chinese, and Arabic.

ALAN GUTTMACHER INSTITUTE
120 WALL STREET
NEW YORK, NY 10009
(212) 248-1111
AND
1120 CONNECTICUT AVENUE NW
WASHINGTON, DC 20034
(202) 296-5756

Conducts research and policy analysis, and furthers public education. Promotes programs and policies regarding contraception and other women's reproductive health issues. Publishes numerous materials, available on request.

Further Reading

⊌ඛ⊌

The Fertility and Contraception Book, Julia Mosse and Josephine Heation (Faber and Faber, 1991).

From Abortion to Reproductive Freedom: Transforming a Movement, M. G. Fried, ed. (South End Press, 1990).

How Not to Get Pregnant, Sherman J. Silber (Warner, 1990).

Contraception: A Guide to Birth Control Methods, Bonnie Bullough and Vern L. Bullough (Prometheus, 1990).

Birth Control and You, Elizabeth K. White (Budlong, 1990).

If You Get Pregnant

Assessing Your Options

In this age of sexually transmitted diseases that can kill you, information about pregnancy almost always plays second fiddle to information about disease prevention, and contraception, if mentioned at all, rarely gets more than a footnote's worth of attention in safer-sex workshops. It's almost as if pregnancy is considered an inconvenient but curable problem—one that can be over and done with in nine months or less. The reality is, an unplanned pregnancy doesn't feel like an easily solvable, uncomplicated problem when you're going through it.

Regardless of the circumstances surrounding the pregnancy, when a woman becomes pregnant unintentionally, there are certain steps she must take. She needs to become informed about her options and evaluate them in the context of her life. She will most probably want to talk to the father, and perhaps discuss it with a friend, family member, clergyperson, therapist, or hotline volunteer at a reproductive rights organization. She then needs to make a decision and act on it.

Note: What follows barely scratches the surface of all the physiological, health, and emotional issues surrounding a full-term pregnancy, birthing, and postpartum care. These topics are too important and complex to be addressed adequately in a chapter in this book. If you choose to carry to term, seek advice from your health care provider, as well as from the numerous pregnancy guides available. See the Resources at the end of this chapter.

THE PREGNANCY BASICS

The dramatis personae in conception are the egg cell and the sperm cell; the setting is one of the fallopian tubes, inside the female body. (See page 349 for a diagram of the internal female reproductive organs.)

When a man and a woman are

having intercourse and the man has an orgasm and ejaculates, semen (a whitish fluid that ranges in consistency from runny to viscous) spurts from the tip of his penis into the vagina. The semen contains between 300 and 500 million spermatozoa, or sperm cells, as well as other secretions that help them survive in what is (to a sperm cell) the rather hostile environment of the internal female reproductive system. The sperm swim up through the vagina and cervix into the uterus, and finally into the fallopian tubes. (Actually, a man doesn't have to ejaculate directly into the vagina in order for conception to take place. Preejaculatory fluid is loaded with sperm, so even if the man withdraws before coming, pregnancy can occur. And in some cases, all it takes is for the man to ejaculate near enough the vaginal opening for the sperm to find their way in.)

The egg is the largest human cell—approximately the size of the period at the end of this sentence. At ovulation, the ovary releases a mature egg into the fallopian tube, and the cilia, or small hairs, within help it make its way through the tube to the uterus. If it encounters and unites with a sperm cell during the journey, and everything goes well, the newly formed zygote (fertilized egg) will travel to the uterus, implant itself in the uterine lining, and grow. (If the egg is not fertilized, it will dissolve, the uterus will shed its lining and menstruation will occur. See "The Menstrual Cycle," page 355.) Very infrequently, the zygote gets stuck along the way and begins to grow in the fallopian tube. This is called an ectopic pregnancy, and can be life-threatening without proper medical attention.

The egg is viable, or able to be fertilized, anytime within 24 hours after ovulation. Sperm can live in the vagina, uterus, and fallopian tubes from 3 to 5 days on average, and in some cases, even longer. A sperm can fertilize an egg anytime during its life, so even if ovulation occurs several days after intercourse, pregnancy is still possible.

Ovulation occurs about 14 days before menstruation begins, and thus it occurs at different times for different women, and it can vary from month to month in individual women. (If you have a 25-day cycle, you will ovulate on day 11; if the next month your cycle is 28 days, you will ovulate on day 14, etc.) For this reason, there is no predictably safe time to have unprotected vaginal intercourse if you don't want to get pregnant. You can only know when you ovulate in retrospect, and you never know how long your partner's sperm will live. Despite what you may hear to the contrary, it *is* possible to get pregnant if you have unprotected vaginal intercourse during your period (because sperm can live for a while in the fallopian tubes). Further, it is especially important to practice safer sex during this time, not only because blood has a higher concentration of HIV than any other body fluid of those infected with the virus, so if you are HIV

I WAS UP ALL NIGHT STUDYING FOR MY PREGNANCY TEST . . .

The most common reasons why home pregnancy tests give inaccurate results:

▲ The test was done too soon after conception and there was not a high enough concentration of hormones in the urine.

▲ The directions were not followed precisely.

▲ The expiration date on the test had passed.

▲ You took a drug that interfered with the results. Most medications do not affect the test, but there are some, including fertility drugs, that may. Check the package insert or call the toll-free consumer info line.

▲ The urine was too weak. (It's best if the urine has been in your bladder for at least an hour. To be extra sure, use your first morning urine.)

▲ The test was damaged or has a factory defect. (Though the companies that make pregnancy tests do serious quality control and package them to prevent damage from occurring, it may still happen. If you suspect a test might be damaged or defective, call the company's toll-free number to get a refund.)

▲ You have an ectopic pregnancy (the fertilized egg is implanted in the fallopian tube, not the uterus).

positive your partner would be at especially high risk, but also because the cervix opens slightly during menstruation, giving the germs that cause all types of STDs easy access to the upper reproductive system where they can cause irreparable damage. See "Safer Sex," page 421, and "STDs, HIV, and AIDS," page 369, for more information.

AM I PREGNANT?

There are no definitive early physical signs of pregnancy. A late period could be due to stress, travel, diet, illness, or extremely strenuous exercise. And ironically enough, nausea, changes in appetite, cramps, and moodiness might just be an indication that your period is coming. However, if your period is late, you have PMS-like symptoms you don't ordinarily have, and had unprotected intercourse (or a contraceptive mishap), you should consider having a pregnancy test.

"The later my period was, the more sick to my stomach, edgy, and tired (and nervous) I got. Finally, my best friend couldn't take it anymore and bought a home pregnancy test.... About a half hour after the test read negative, I got my period."

—UNIVERSITY OF CINCINNATI, '98

Early Signs of Pregnancy

ᘒᘒᘒ

Typical physical reactions begin about the time of the first missed period.

- ▲ Breast tenderness, swelling, or tingling
- ▲ Fatigue
- ▲ Nausea or "morning sickness" (which can occur anytime during the day, not just in the morning)
- ▲ Frequent urination
- ▲ Water retention/bloating
- ▲ Cramps
- ▲ Moodiness
- ▲ Indigestion and constipation
- ▲ Increased or decreased appetite

If you think that you may be pregnant, it is important to find out for sure as soon as possible. If it turns out you're not, you can save yourself an enormous amount of worry. If you are pregnant, and you decide to carry the pregnancy to term, the sooner you start prenatal care, the better; if you decide to end the pregnancy, the earlier the procedure, the safer (and cheaper) it will be.

PREGNANCY TESTS

Pregnancy tests work by detecting the presence of hormones that women produce after conception.

Home pregnancy tests: Home pregnancy tests are available over-the-counter at drugstores, and offer convenience, privacy, and reliable answers if performed correctly. (In general, the simpler the home pregnancy test, the less chance of user error.) Some tests can detect pregnancy in as early as six days after conception, though in general, most recommend that you wait until at least a day after you have missed your period before taking the test. If a home test reads positive (which is almost always an accurate indication of pregnancy), or it reads negative but your period doesn't come within a few days, you should make an appointment for a clinical pregnancy test.

> *"Having a pregnancy scare knocked some sense into me. I realized that I needed to get a little more serious about birth control, and a little more serious about not getting AIDS or something."*
> —TEXAS A&M UNIVERSITY, '93

Clinical pregnancy tests: When you go for a clinical test (available at campus health services, labs, other health clinics, or doctors' offices), a health practitioner will perform a blood or urine test (most clinics offer both, but urine tests are less expensive and equally accurate), give you a pelvic exam (to see if your uterus is tender or enlarged) and a breast exam (glands around the areola change during pregnancy), and ask you questions about symptoms. You should know the date of your last period, the average length of your cycle, as well as any medications you are taking or have taken in the last month or so.

■ Many clinics, both on and off campus, offer free or sliding-scale pregnancy tests. Depending on your health insurance carrier and the state where you have the test, your insurance may cover the cost. Be aware that some places that offer pregnancy tests may have an ulterior motive. (See "Roadblocks," page 452.)

■ Even if the clinic is "walk-in" (no appointment needed), call before you go so you'll know what to bring, when and where to go, which payment methods they accept, and any other pertinent information. You might also want to ask if there are some hours that are better than others in terms of time spent waiting.

■ For the most accurate results (especially early on in the pregnancy), tests should be done on the first morning urine. Ask the clinic if you'll need to bring yours with you. (If so, be sure to use a very clean glass jar.)

■ Unless stated otherwise, pregnancy tests, like all medical tests, are confidential, meaning that the clinic cannot tell *anyone* about the results.

■ You might want to ask a supportive friend or your partner to come along.

"Part of being responsible about sex is knowing that no contraception is 100 percent effective and discussing what you'd do if you got pregnant."
—SWARTHMORE COLLEGE, '93

Getting the Results

An unexpected pregnancy can be confusing and frightening. It can fill you with many conflicting emotions: happiness, fear, anger, shock, anxiety, guilt, excitement, power, and serenity. It can be thrilling to realize that you are capable of pregnancy—even if the pregnancy is not something that you planned or wanted.

PREGNANCY OPTIONS

Once you have determined that you are pregnant there are three main options open to you. You may continue the pregnancy and keep the baby, you may continue the pregnancy and place the baby for adoption, or you may terminate the pregnancy by means of abortion. Unfortunately, an unplanned pregnancy won't go away by itself. It can't be prayed, wished, ignored, denied, stressed, drunk, drugged, or cried away (though all have certainly been tried). Not dealing with your pregnancy as quickly as possible limits your options and can increase the likelihood of complications. There are many resources that can provide you with information and support during and after the decision-making process.

In your search for information,

A DECISION OF ONE'S OWN

Depending on where you are in your life, it might not be immediately obvious what to do when you learn that you're pregnant. You may want to seek the counsel of others just as you would with any other serious dilemma. Though the opinions and wishes of people you trust and respect will often influence your thinking, the final decision is still *yours*. It is your right, privilege, and responsibility to make your own choice about what to do with your body. After all, you will be living with the decision for the rest of your life.

Even if you choose to follow the advice of others, do so because you feel that you are making the best choice for you, based on your own priorities, needs, resources, opinions, experience, and desires. You do not have to justify your decision or apologize for it to anyone. Nor do you have to explain it, analyze it, or talk it over with others—unless, of course, you want to.

make sure you go to an individual or organization that can provide you with an evenhanded discussion of all your choices. (See the Resources at the end of this chapter.) Once you are familiar with all the options and what they entail (depending on the laws of your state and the quality and philosophies of different facilities, agencies, and services available to you), you will need to make a decision.

Deciding What to Do

෧෧෧

The first step in making your decision is to take a good look at yourself and your life. Assess your financial, emotional, and personal realities. Think about your present and future plans, where you live, what you do, how you support yourself, your religious and ethical beliefs, and the relationships you value in your life. Consider how each of the options would affect your

"I had an abortion, not because it was exactly what I wanted, but because at this point in my life, I couldn't handle a pregnancy, and definitely not a baby. . . . Sometimes you have to decide by process of elimination."

—UNIVERSITY OF NEVADA–
LAS VEGAS, '96

life. What changes would need to be made? Are those changes possible and/or desirable?

Choosing what to do may be easy, or it may be extremely confusing and stressful. It may bring up painful issues and memories, both directly and indirectly connected. Unless you've been trying to get pregnant, very rarely will one option seem completely perfect—and often no choice will seem even halfway decent. It's natural to have many different, often conflicting feelings. You may want to talk with the father, a parent or other

"Almost all the talk about having the right to choose is in relation to the right to choose to have an abortion. People always forget about the right to have a baby if you want to. As a woman with a disability, I am especially sensitive to this. When women with disabilities or other 'undesirables' get pregnant, many doctors really push abortion, and even in some cases, sterilization."

—UNIVERSITY OF CHICAGO, '97

family member, a friend, a therapist, a doctor or other health practitioner, a clergyperson, or a dorm counselor to help sort out the issues and weigh the choices.

Telling Him You're Pregnant

ⓥⓥⓥ

Though deciding what to do is ultimately your choice, in most cases you'll probably still want to discuss the options with "the guy." There are many good reasons to involve men in the decision-making process. After all, even though you are the one who is pregnant, you didn't get that way yourself. If it is possible, having the father's emotional (and financial) support usually makes everything easier to handle. And if we fail to hold men as accountable as we hold ourselves for the consequences of our actions, then we perpetuate the idea that men have no responsibility in sexual relationships. However, it may be that you

do not want to tell the father; trust your instincts and do whatever is necessary to protect yourself emotionally and physically.

If the pregnancy wasn't planned, you will inevitably feel uncomfortable and nervous telling the father, and you should be prepared to feel some ambivalence in response to his reaction. Even if you have previously discussed the issue, it may still be difficult to make the decision. For many, the choice seems totally obvious when speaking hypothetically, but when the situation becomes reality, everything gets a little murky. For example, even if you both had already decided that you would terminate the pregnancy in the event that your contraception failed, you may feel a sting when he first mentions the word abortion. Or perhaps you felt sure that you wanted to marry him and raise a family with him, but now suddenly the thought of spending the rest of your life together makes you uneasy. The tension and emotion of the situation can make you react strongly and impulsively to things that wouldn't ordinarily bother

you. Expecting that you may be pleasantly and/or unpleasantly surprised by your (and his) feelings and behavior, and keeping the following tips in mind, may make it all a bit easier.

■ Before you talk, think about what *you* want and write it down. Of course, you don't have to have your mind clearly made up, but it's important to consider what you want and need without any outside influence, persuasion, or pressure.

■ Choose a time to talk when you will have the time and privacy to deal with the issues and emotions the conversation may raise.

> *"Even though my boyfriend and I discussed the issue many times—even right before the test—and totally agreed that I would have an abortion, I couldn't help but think about what it would be like to be a mother ... imagining myself with a stroller and everything. All of a sudden the decision wasn't so cut and dried as I thought."*
>
> **—UNIVERSITY OF MICHIGAN, '94**

■ Remember whom you're dealing with. If he has a tendency to get quiet and withdrawn when faced with important or stressful issues, don't interpret his silence as not caring. Likewise, if his way of dealing with a problem is through humor, don't get offended if at first he seems to be making light of the subject. And if he's someone you don't know all that well, don't expect him to know you well, either.

■ Even if you have already made up your mind, at least show him the courtesy of listening to what he has to say. Let him get his feelings out, and remember that he may have a different way of reacting than do you.

■ Both of you will probably feel a lot of different emotions. Try not to make any rash decisions because of the intensity of the conversation and experience.

■ Be up front and direct. Ask for what you need. Don't tell him that you don't care what he thinks if you really do. Openly express how you feel about being pregnant as well as what you want to do and why. Give him a chance to do the same.

■ Remember how you felt when you first found out and keep in mind that he is hearing something new. You might have already had a chance to think about and work through your feelings for some time. Cut him a bit of slack as he absorbs the news.

■ Don't demand that he express all his feelings and know exactly what he wants to do right away. You should give him a chance to think about the issues, especially if his opinion is important to you.

■ Part of the decision-making process is figuring out what responsibilities each of you will have in carrying out the decision. Identifying the specifics may actually help you make your choice: If you opt to terminate your pregnancy, is he going to come with you when you go for the abortion? Will he pay for part or all of the expenses, whether for an abortion, prenatal/medical expenses, or child

"If men want to be part of the decision, they should do it before sex by asking the woman what she would do if she got pregnant. If he disagrees, then he shouldn't have sex with her. I believe once a guy has sex, he acknowledges that he doesn't have the final say if pregnancy happens. It'd be great if partners could discuss and agree on what to do when the woman finds out she's pregnant, but in cases where that can't happen, women have the final say."

—BRYN MAWR COLLEGE, '94

support? Will he have no part in the decision? If you have a baby, who will have the financial and parental responsibilities? Will you marry and keep the baby? Will you carry the baby to term and then put it up for adoption together or will you do it alone?

CARRYING TO TERM

If you intend to continue your pregnancy, whether or not you plan to keep the baby, it is important that you seek prenatal care as soon as possible from an obstetrician-gynecologist or nurse-midwife that you trust. (For an in-depth discussion of finding and dealing with practitioners, see page 234.) Good prenatal care involves regularly seeing a health practitioner who will teach you about the hows and whys of pregnancy and delivery and give you direction about monitoring and modifying certain aspects of your life, such as diet, exercise, smoking, and drug/alcohol consumption. If you are unable to afford prenatal care, there are a number of clinics that will provide it free. (See the Resources at the end of this chapter for places to get more information about prenatal care.)

"Just because a pregnancy is unplanned doesn't mean it's a problem. My husband and I had been going out for three years and planned on getting married after graduation, so we just got married sooner, and I took some time away from school. . . . I'm going to be graduating this May, and my beautiful daughter, Celia, will be in the audience watching me."

—PENN STATE UNIVERSITY, '94

College health services vary in terms of what services they offer pregnant students. Few school health services offer comprehensive prenatal care, though they might be good places to connect with other students who are pregnant and get referrals to practitioners, delivery options, Lamaze and other prepared-childbirth classes, and exercise classes for pregnant women. Women's centers, the office for returning students, local hospitals and clinics, city departments of health, and other public and private agencies are also good places to get information, referrals, and support.

Pregnancy is emotionally and physically demanding. Keep in mind, though, that while pregnancy can be taxing on the mind and body, in almost all cases it doesn't require that you put your life on hold for nine months. Many women remain at school or their job right up until their first contraction. Though it may not be easy, being prepared for potential problems related to the emotional, physical, economic, medical, cultural, and social issues surrounding pregnancy will certainly make everything run a bit smoother:

■ Some of the common side effects of pregnancy—e.g., tiredness, morning sickness, indigestion, mood swings, and aches and pains—can make a college student's stressful life even more so. You may want to talk with your professors, campus health services, the counseling center, and/or your health care provider for advice about balancing it all. You may need to budget your time more efficiently, perhaps drop a class or two or take an incomplete, turn in assignments early, or write a paper in lieu of doing an in-class presentation. Although pregnancy is not considered a disability, the office of disability services at your school may be a good source of support. The staff should be familiar with antidiscrimination legislation, be able to offer good advice and resources to help you successfully comanage your schoolwork, job, and the strains of pregnancy, talk with your professors on your behalf, and help you arrange a leave of absence if the need arises. If they are not willing or able to help, they can surely recommend a place that can.

■ If you receive financial aid, find out if it will be affected if you need to cut your course load or take time off. If you are unable to complete the designated number of credits, maintain the minimum GPA, complete your independent-study project, play starting center on the women's ice hockey team, or work with radioactive isotopes in your work-study job as a lab technician, there is a chance that you may be required to pay back the aid and/or be denied aid for the following term (or the term when you return). Most schools handle these issues on a case-by-case basis. If you have a feeling that the school won't be understanding, you should consider speaking with a lawyer and/or a reproductive rights organization (such as one of those listed in the Resources at the end of this chapter) before you broach the subject. (For more information, see "The Financial Aid Maze," page 75, and "Leaves of Absence," page 41.)

■ In addition to academic issues, you'll be facing a set of social issues. If you are unmarried—or even more so, unpartnered—you will have to contend with the stigma of being an unwed mother. When the hormones are flowing through your body like white water, stares, pointing, and whispering can be especially hard to handle, even if you know full well that what others think and say doesn't

"On the one hand, it was really good that [my boyfriend] agreed that an abortion would be best and all, but I couldn't help wondering if it was that he didn't want to have a baby, or he didn't want to have a baby with me. It's like I didn't have trouble with choosing what to do.... I had trouble dealing with everything the choice meant (both rationally and irrationally)."

—UNIVERSITY OF NORTHERN
IOWA, '94

matter. Colleges are notorious rumor mills, and it's not a bad idea to talk with other women who've been through it before to come up with a few coping strategies. And because it's much easier to deal with everything when you've got a trusty pal by your side, plan to meet friends for meals, after class for the walk across campus, to go to sporting events, etc.

■ You may find yourself feeling a bit isolated. Sometimes even those who urged you to continue the pregnancy convey scorn that you got yourself into this "jam" and not give you the support you expected. Your friends may act a bit weird around you, not know what to say, and consciously or unconsciously exclude you. Or you may exclude yourself if your gang is going on a 10-mile hike, or out to a smoke-filled café or a party or bar where you'd feel uncomfortable being the only one drinking soda. Your friends may need and want a few pointers about how to support you. For the most part, you will probably

find that they'll support your decision (even if they wouldn't choose the same one) and will offer to be your Lamaze partner, make you nutritious meals, lend you the notes if you couldn't make your 9:00 class because of morning sickness, and drive you to the hospital when the time comes. You may also want to get involved with (or start) an on- or off-campus group with other pregnant women for additional help, answers, companionship, and support. Adoption agencies, women's health organizations, hospitals, and even campus health services may have groups.

"There are a lot of amazing reasons to have a baby, but the biggest mistake that anyone can make is thinking that a baby will save their relationship. I'll tell you, if you are not getting along, or feel unhappy or whatever, three A.M. feedings, changing diapers, and doctor's appointments, not to mention the stress of pregnancy, will only make things worse."—UNIVERSITY OF CALIFORNIA,
SANTA CRUZ, '97

■ Even if health services doesn't offer prenatal care, pay one of its practitioners a visit. Because clinicians who work at health services are especially in tune with the issues and needs of students, they may be able to offer you advice or a perspective that an off-campus clinician would not.

■ It is against the law, according to the Pregnancy Discrimination Act of 1964,

of medical care for a premature baby for 1 day is about $2,500.

for you to be discriminated against on the basis of your pregnancy, status as a mother, or related conditions. (See "Breaking Down Bias," page 463.)

ADOPTION

The subject of adoption often brings up conflicting images and feelings. For women who do not feel that abortion is an option for them but do not have the time, desire, maturity, and/or resources to raise a child, adoption may seem the logical choice, but it's not necessarily a simple one to make. You may feel guilty thinking that you'll be "abandoning" the baby. You may wonder how a future lover or husband might react when he finds out that you've had a baby. You may be worried that the child won't be raised with love and kindness. Or you may be concerned that the adoptive family will have a different religion and/or value system from yours. You may fear that the decision will come back to haunt you, as it does for nearly every soap opera character who gives up a baby for adoption. You may fear that in the delivery room you'll realize that you want to keep the baby, but you'll feel you won't be able to. (You can always change your mind at this point—a birth mother cannot relinquish rights to her baby until after delivery.)

If you decide you want to carry to term and place the baby up for adoption, you'll have to make decisions based not only on your needs and wishes now, but also on what you think your needs and wishes might be later in life. Very tricky stuff. Because adoption and "father's rights" laws vary from state to state, as do the orga-

"After the baby was born, I thought everything would snap back to normal ... but it wasn't that easy. I was proud of myself for bringing a new life into the world but I also had mood swings and panic attacks for four months after delivery ... and my parents, who never wanted me to go through with it in the first place, were very impatient with me. I don't want to make people scared to go through with their pregnancy, but I want to tell them what was hard about it for me in the hopes that it will be easier for them."
—MARQUETTE UNIVERSITY, '98

nizations that serve as sources of support, it is impossible to go into specific regulations and options here. See the Resources at the end of this chapter for ways to get more information.

An uncanny thing you'll notice, especially in the rather friendly and easygoing college atmosphere, is that the moment you begin to show, total strangers will ask you questions about your pregnancy, flash you a nice smile, or feel obliged to share their special recipe for mashed peas that no baby can refuse. Though these gestures are almost always performed with the kindest of intentions, if you aren't planning to keep the baby, they can make you feel upset, uncomfortable, and resentful. The pregnancy and birth experience is quite different for women who choose to be involved only for the first nine months than for those who are starting a family. There are no baby showers, no excited relatives, and it's hard to know what to tell people. Many women find that friends and family don't want to discuss the pregnancy, hoping that by not acknowledging it, it will be over quickly and they can pretend it never happened.

But whether or not you're going to keep the baby doesn't make any difference in terms of the physical and emotional strains of pregnancy. You'll still need to go for check-ups, still experience indigestion, mood swings, weight gain, and labor pains. For this reason, women who plan to give the baby up for adoption need to be especially vigilant about seeking out emotional, financial, and medical support from friends, family, therapy groups, health centers, and perhaps even the people who will adopt. Reputable adoption agencies will provide counseling and support for the birth mother. You may choose to participate in a group living arrangement sponsored by an adoption agency. These organizations offer room and board in exchange for sharing in the cooking, housework, and other chores. Many of these places are religiously affiliated, and you may be required to attend services, follow dietary rules, and adhere to strict dress and behavior codes. Such programs may be helpful in that they provide women with a support network of other women who understand what they're going through.

Another issue to consider is how involved you want to be in the adoption process. You can arrange a "sealed" adoption, in which all records are kept confidential. This means that the adoptive parents and child will not have access to information about the birth parents (you and the father of the child), nor will you have access to information about the adoptive family.

This type of adoption almost always occurs with the assistance of an agency that screens potential adoptive parents. Ask about what kind of emotional, financial, and/or medical assistance they can provide you during and directly after the pregnancy, and how they screen prospective adoptive families. You should also find out what happens if you decide you want to keep the baby. You can also choose an "open" adoption, in which there is more of a direct connection between the adoptive and birth parents and you may have more control in choosing the adoptive parents. Through ads in adoption organization newsletters and school newspapers, health practitioners, and word of mouth, you will find a number of families seeking to adopt. The arrangements and the level of interaction between the adoptive and birth parents varies significantly —sometimes the relationship is no more than an interview and exchange of money to cover your living and medical expenses during pregnancy; sometimes a long-lasting friendship develops. Because procedures, laws, and the rights of birth and adoptive

parents vary from state to state, and because of the enormous amount of paperwork involved, if you are not working with a reputable agency (and sometimes if you are), it is imperative that you work with a lawyer specializing in adoption to protect yourself, to clarify the agreement, and to avoid problems later on.

ABORTION

Abortion is legal in the United States through the second trimester of pregnancy. Restrictions, regulations, and accessibility vary depending on your age, state, and location. Abortion procedures, costs, and the risks involved all depend on how early in the pregnancy the abortion is performed. First trimester abortions (which are performed between 6 and 12 weeks after the first day of your last menstrual period) are the safest and cheapest, and 9 out of 10 abortions are performed during this period. Clinics tend to be less expensive than private doctors, and only those with special training (most often licensed MDs) provide services. (See "Finding a Clinic," page 451.) Wherever you go, you should receive counseling before

CAMPUS HIGHLIGHT

In 1987, women at Hampshire College in Amherst, MA, organized "The Fight for Abortion Rights and Reproductive Freedom," a conference that has since become an annual event. Participants from across the country spend two days in workshops, lectures, and discussions, sharing information and activist tactics and networking. Though the conference focuses on women's reproductive rights, there are also sessions on such topics as organizing in of-color communities in the U.S., lesbian and bisexual rights, and violence against women. The conference is free, and sponsors provide housing, meals and childcare as well.

and after the procedure, and you must return for a postabortion checkup two weeks after the procedure.

The Abortion Procedure

Though there are a number of different procedures available from clinic abortion providers, most abortions in the first trimester and early to mid-second trimester are done by vacuum aspiration dilation and evacuation (D&E), a scary-sounding name for a relatively simple procedure. Early abortions provided by competent physicians pose very little health risk.

They are almost always done on an outpatient basis (with minor differences in the methods of dilation of the cervical opening and evacuation of the uterus in the early to mid-second trimester). The D&E procedure can still be used between the 16th and 24th weeks, though it is more complex then than when it is done earlier because the fetal tissue is larger and the uterus is more delicate. Second trimester D&Es are usually performed under general anesthesia. Still, this method is preferred by women's health advocates and practitioners over the considerably higher-risk and more expensive alternatives. (See the Resources at the end of this chapter for places where you can get detailed descriptions of other procedures.)

At the time of the abortion, you will have a pregnancy test to make sure that you are pregnant, and you will have a limited physical exam to check your breasts, lungs, heart, and blood pressure. You should also have a blood test to check if you have Rh-negative blood, in which case you should get a shot of Rhogam within 96 hours of the abortion. This will eliminate the possibility of complications stemming from Rh incompatibility in future pregnancies. You may also have a pelvic sonogram. The doctor will then perform a pelvic exam to feel the size and shape of the uterus. The cervix will be numbed by an anesthetic.

Three types of anesthesia are usually available for abortion procedures: local (which only numbs the necessary areas), augmental intravenous (an injection of a painkiller such as Demerol and a tranquilizer such as Valium), and general (which puts you "out cold"). Different clinics and doctors may, however, restrict your choices. When choosing an anesthetic, it is important to consider both your personal needs and the health risks. Local is considered the least risky form of anesthesia, and general is the most. One such potential risk of general anesthesia, for example, is that a relaxed uterus bleeds more than one that is not relaxed. Also, it has been shown that the rate of injury to the uterus and/or cervix fallopian tubes is greater when women are under general anesthesia. Local anesthesia involves numbing the cervix and uterus with injections of an anesthetic, similar to numbing the gums before a tooth is pulled. Augmental anesthesia relaxes the patient, but not to the point of unconsciousness. It may cause grogginess and nausea.

"I felt like I didn't have a choice, so I had an abortion. But now I believe that if I had really thought about it I could have found a way to have my baby. If you get pregnant, really think about everything. Don't let yourself freak out and go on automatic pilot. You might realize that you could have the baby and stay in school and do what you want with your life also." —North Florida State University, '90

Next, the cervical opening is dilated. Dilation occurs naturally during childbirth, and even slightly during menstruation to allow the release of the menstrual fluid. In the abortion procedure, dilation is induced by the use of dilator rods. A series of blunt-tipped, narrow rods that successively increase in diameter are inserted into the cervical opening to gently stretch the muscle. Then a narrow plastic tube, connected to a machine called a vacuum aspirator, is inserted through the dilated cervix into the uterus. The suction action of the machine empties out the contents of the uterus. The aspirator is generally used for a minute to a minute and a half. Then, if tissues still remain, a procedure called curettage may be performed, depending on the doctor, how far along the pregnancy is, and the patient's anatomy. Using a smooth plastic or metal instrument called a curette, the doctor gently feels along the uterine wall to dislodge any remaining tissue. Then the aspirator is used again briefly to remove anything remaining in the uterus. The second aspiration usually lasts between four and seven minutes. This is the entire procedure.

"When someone on TV has an abortion, they always freak out afterward. I didn't feel sad or regretful after my abortion. I felt relieved, happy, and free."

—EMORY UNIVERSITY, '98

While the procedure is not pleasant, it should not be more painful than menstrual cramps. If it is, tell your doctor what you are feeling. When the procedure is over you will spend a half hour to an hour in a recovery room. You should receive a pill to help your uterus contract to its previous size, and a painkiller to ease any discomfort and cramping this may cause.

Vaginal bleeding occurs after the procedure. For some women it is very light, while for others it is heavier than a period. This bleeding is normal and may last for several days. Typically, you will be given a prescription for five days' worth of antibiotics to help reduce the risk of infection.

Aftercare
ᎨᎨᎨ

It is important to take care of yourself properly after an abortion. Take the medicine as prescribed, and watch for any warning signs of infection. Because it takes time for your cervix to close completely after dilation (the time varies from woman to woman), your uterus is particularly susceptible to infection. Do not take a bath (showers are OK) or insert anything into your vagina for two weeks following the procedure—no tampons, penises, fingers, tongues, or douches. For one week following the abortion, do not exercise strenuously, and avoid taking large doses of aspirin or vitamin C, which may cause increased bleeding. And by no means blow off your postabortion checkup.

In addition to the vaginal bleeding, many women experience drowsiness, nausea, breast discharge and tenderness, and cramping in the days following the abortion. Contact your doctor or clinic if:

▲ You develop a temperature of over 100.4°F (you should take your temperature at least once a day for the first five days after the abortion).
▲ You have either no vaginal bleeding or bleed excessively (soaking through more than one pad per hour).
▲ You bleed for more than 14 days.
▲ You do not menstruate within eight weeks.

▲ You continue to have symptoms of pregnancy after a week following the abortion.

▲ You experience severe cramping.

Equally important, give yourself some time to deal with the emotional after-effects. You may experience mood swings as a result of the hormonal changes that accompany pregnancy and its termination. You may have a number of feelings stemming from issues around the abortion itself, getting pregnant, the relief that it's over, and/or your relationship with the man involved. The majority of clinics require you to meet with a counselor, alone or with a group, before and/or after the procedure, to help you address fears, feelings, and questions that you may have.

You can get pregnant in the time between the abortion and your first period, so be sure to use birth control. Clinics almost always include information about birth control options during the counseling session after the abortion.

Risks

ଓଡ଼ିଆ

There are risks involved with all medical procedures, including abortion. The method of abortion and the length of pregnancy determine the degree of risk. Though a D&E abortion during the first trimester is statistically one of the safest surgical procedures around—considerably less dangerous than carrying a pregnancy to term and giving birth—complications, both minor and serious, may occur.

■ **An incomplete abortion** occurs if any pregnancy tissue remains in the uterus after the abortion procedure.

The risk of incomplete abortion is greatest when the procedure is performed before six weeks after your last menstrual period, because the pregnancy tissue is so small. Symptoms include lack of postabortion bleeding and severe cramping.

■ **Infection** can be caused by the retention of tissue in the uterus. Symptoms include fever and severe abdominal pain.

■ **Hemorrhaging** (excessive bleeding) after an abortion can be caused by injury to the uterus during the procedure, or by a failure of the uterus to contract. Soaking through more than one large sanitary pad per hour indicates excessive bleeding.

■ **Perforation or injury to the uterus or cervix** occurs if an instrument used during the procedure punctures or otherwise injures the uterus or cervix. Injuries to the uterus usually heal by themselves, although there is the risk of injuring other organs in the abdominal cavity when perforation occurs.

■ **Future fertility** may be affected if there are complications as a result of the abortion, such as injury to the cervix or fallopian tubes. However, one or even several abortions without complication will have no effect on a woman's fertility.

ALTERNATE MEANS OF ABORTION

RU 486

RU 486 (mifepristone) is an abortion-inducing pill that provides women with a noninvasive, safer, simpler, and less expensive alternative to early surgical (D&E) abortion. The drug has been in use in France since 1988, and is used in China as well. Though RU 486 has not yet been approved in the United States, it is undergoing trial testing. It remains to be seen if and when it gains Food and Drug Administration approval.

Invented in 1980 by the French doctor Étienne-Émile Baulieu and manufactured by Roussel-Uclaf (hence the "RU"), the drug works by blocking the action of progesterone, the hormone chiefly responsible for keeping the uterine lining intact during pregnancy. When progesterone is inhibited, the lining sheds, taking any fertilized eggs with it.

RU 486 must be prescribed by a doctor. A woman is given a pill, then goes back to the doctor two days later for a dose of prostaglandin (which causes uterine contractions), which is administered either by injection or vaginal suppository. After a week, she returns for an examination to ensure that the abortion has gone smoothly. (If the uterine lining hasn't been totally expelled, the doctor will perform a surgical abortion. This occurs in fewer than 5 percent of RU 486 abortions.) At this time, RU 486 is not recommended for women who smoke, are over age 35, have had a recent cesarean section, or have health prob-lems relating to circulation or blood pressure.

In addition to its use as an abortifacient, studies have indicated that the drug shows great promise in the treatment of endometriosis, fibroid tumors, and breast, prostate, and brain cancers. Its possible uses as an estrogen-free contraceptive are also being researched.

MENSTRUAL EXTRACTION

Menstrual extraction was developed by a group of women in a women's health collective in the early 1970s as an alternative method of abortion. The initial thinking behind menstrual extraction was that because abortions are not generally complicated procedures, there is no reason for women's reproductive lives to remain in the hands of doctors and courts when we can take care of ourselves.

Menstrual extraction is a suction procedure through which the contents of the uterus are emptied. If a fertilized egg is in the uterus, it will also be removed. In addition to its use as an abortion procedure, menstrual extraction can be used to shorten and/or lessen a heavy period, by removing all the menstrual fluid at one time.

Menstrual extractions are done by highly trained women in advanced health self-help groups. They are not done at hospitals or other medical facilities. Never ever attempt any type of home abortion on yourself.

RU 486 is 96% effective in terminating pregnancy in the first 9 weeks.

Finding a Clinic

೦೦೦

Private doctors, hospitals, clinics, and some organizations (such as Planned Parenthood) perform abortions. Clinics are often the best place to go—for the most part, their practitioners have the most experience, and they are often the easiest places to get an appointment.

The best way to find a clinic is through a recommendation from someone you trust. Pro-choice groups, both on and off campus, as well as women's collectives and some health organizations, are good resources, too. At many schools, campus health services will be able to provide you with information.

Be aware that, especially in areas where verbal and physical harassment of clinic workers is common, the person on the other end of the line might not sound as friendly and helpful as you'd like, and may not go into detail about the procedure over the phone.

Questions to Ask When You Call to Make the Appointment

■ How much does the procedure cost? Does the cost include follow-up appointments and any necessary prescriptions?

■ What forms of payment do you take? (Cash, check, credit card, insurance, Medicare?)

■ Are there any legal requirements I

have to meet before getting an abortion? (See "Roadblocks," on the next page.)

■ Do I have to come in for a separate appointment or for counseling before the procedure? Will there be a follow-up appointment?

■ What abortion procedure do you normally use for women at my stage of pregnancy? How long will it take?

■ What are the available forms of anesthesia?

■ Are there any foods or medications I should not eat or take for a period of time before the appointment? What about alcohol?

■ Should I bring a urine sample? (Clinics and doctors will give you a pregnancy test before the procedure. Because first morning urine is best for this, some places will ask you to bring some in a clean glass jar.)

■ Are there protesters outside the clinic? If so, do you or a local women's group provide escorts? (See page 454 for more information.)

If it is an issue for you, make it clear that it is important that your confidentiality be maintained, and ask for tips about ways to insure this as much as possible. As with any other medical procedure, having an abortion should become part of your medical records. Though these records are supposed to be completely confidential, your insurance provider may have access to the information. In addition, in some states, abortion providers are required to inform (or obtain consent from) your husband if you're married. If you're under 18, you may be required to get your parents' consent.

If you have any special health issues or concerns (such as allergies to

Studies show that it may also be effective in treating ovarian cancer. ❀

specific anesthetics, antibiotics, or other medications, a chronic illness, a physical disability that would require the use of an examining table that provides additional support, or the like) or take prescription medication(s), be sure to mention it when you are scheduling the appointment.

If you were not already planning to bring someone with you, find out if you should and/or if the clinic will have someone there who can support you and take you home, if necessary.

Roadblocks

〰〰〰

By law, abortion is legal for women in the United States who are in their first or second trimester of pregnancy. But restrictive local, state, and federal legislation, misinformation, the shortage of medical practitioners who perform abortions, the expense, personal and public opinion, and fear of harassment and potential violence can create enormous roadblocks for women who want to exercise their right to choose abortion, or who simply want accurate information about it.

Because restrictions on abortions are designed to make obtaining an abortion as difficult as possible, once you've decided to have one, you should start the usually complicated

and time-consuming process immediately, to ensure that when you do get your abortion, it is a safe one.

The obstacles to an abortion vary from state to state. Check the Resources at the end of this chapter to learn how to find an organization that can provide information specific to your state.

Women Under 18

Parental consent/notification: In some states, in order to obtain an abortion, women under 18 years of age must have a written note of permission from one or both parents, tell (or have the clinic tell) one or both parents, or obtain a "judicial bypass" by going to court and having a judge determine that they are capable of making "mature, rational decisions." Of course, if and when a bypass is granted, a woman could be in her second trimester—too far along for a safe, relatively low-risk abortion.

Accompanied by an adult: Some states don't require you to tell your parents, but do require that, if you're under the age of 16 or 17, you must be accompanied to the clinic by someone over 18.

Married Women

Husband consent/notification: In some states, a married woman must have a written note of permission from her husband, tell (or have the clinic tell) her husband, or, as with a woman under 18, obtain a "judicial bypass" by going to court and having a judge determine that the woman is capable of making "mature, rational decisions" before she can get an abortion.

All Women

Fake clinics: Antiabortion groups have been known to set up clinics that appear legitimate, but when women come in seeking pregnancy tests and information about options, they are given inaccurate (and often frightening and dissuasive) information about abortion (often including lectures, threats, or biased films). There have even been numerous cases in which women who were pregnant were told that they weren't if the "clinic" workers suspected the women might have an abortion if they knew the truth. Fake clinics advertise in the same places that clinics that provide abortion services do. If you are seeking an abortion or unbiased information about all your options, talk with a local pro-choice or feminist group to verify a clinic's authenticity before calling. And before you make an appointment at a clinic, ask straight out if they perform abortions.

It is illegal for places that do not perform abortions to say that they do, but keep in mind that they may try to avoid the issue. You are under no obligation to give your name and number or any other personal information, and in fact should not do so until they state specifically and explicitly that they are licensed to provide abortions.

Informed consent/waiting period: In some states, women must meet with a counselor or read information approved by the state, then wait for a period of time (often a day) before they can get an abortion.

Local gag rule: When a gag rule is in effect, it is illegal for clinic workers, counselors, doctors, nurses, and other health professionals and practitioners in publicly funded facilities to talk, give advice, or provide information about abortion or give referrals to clinics. If there is a gag rule in effect in your area, and you want more information on abortion, you can call a private gynecologist or a state hotline, or see the Resources at the end of this chapter.

Insurance/Medicaid: In many states, neither private health insurance nor Medicaid will cover the cost of an abortion.

> "You have to be really careful. I went to this place that gave free pregnancy tests that I saw listed in the yellow pages. They took my urine and said that it would be an hour and a half, which I thought was kind of strange, because the test I did at home took only a few minutes. When I asked if I could leave and come back, they said I should wait, then sat me in a room where there were three other girls, and turned on the most horrifying, disgusting movie filled with antiabortion propaganda."
>
> —WASHINGTON UNIVERSITY, '93

Out of the Courtroom—
Into the Street

୭୭୭

It is not uncommon to see members of "pro-life" (or anti-choice) groups demonstrating at clinics, hospitals, doctors' offices, and other facilities that provide abortion services across the country. Different groups operate in different ways, from silent vigils

"There was no question in my mind that I wanted to have the abortion, but the protesters really freaked me out and I actually had to cancel my appointment and come back another day because I was so upset by their harassment."

—NEW YORK UNIVERSITY, '95

and prayer services to harassing patients and staff people to acts of violence. In the wake of increased violence, and consequent pressure from legal, medical, legislative, and political groups, there's been a call for more rigorous enforcement of laws protecting patients, doctors, and clinic workers from verbal and physical harassment. The first amendment rights to freedom of speech and freedom of peaceful assembly do not extend to harassment, trespassing, disturbing the peace, and the physical blocking a woman from exercising her legal right to a safe abortion.

In response, pro-choice groups, women's health advocates, law enforcement agencies, and the clinics themselves often provide escorts to give women emotional and physical support by walking with them past the protesters into the clinic. Although occasional altercations between escorts and protesters may make some feel even more uncomfortable than if the escorts weren't there at all, for the most part, escorts are very helpful and reassuring.

Having a run-in with protesters can be very upsetting, especially for a woman who feels vulnerable facing an emotionally difficult procedure. You can (and should) talk about your feelings with the counselors and other people you meet with in the clinic. (That's what they're there for.) Here are a few tips that may make you feel less intimidated if faced with anti-abortion protesters:

■ When you call the clinic or doctor to make an appointment, ask about protesters and for any suggestions on dealing with them.

■ Bring a caring friend for moral support through the whole procedure.

■ Ignore the protesters. Do not talk, respond, or try to explain yourself to them. Stare straight ahead and walk with confidence.

"All the laws and restrictions don't stop women from having abortions—they just make it harder to have the safest, easiest, least expensive abortions. Abortion is a legal medical procedure—but we're supposed to feel bad, guilty and dirty, ashamed and evil, if we have one. So they make it really expensive so it'll take us a while to gather money together, and they won't allow people to talk about it, and they put these laws together that make it so we have to travel four hours three times, and they won't import the abortion pill because God forbid we should have a less painful, private, cheap, much safer method!"

—OBERLIN COLLEGE, '92

✸ 100,000 women a year died from illegal abortions before 1973.

■ Remember, it is illegal for protesters to block, touch, or threaten you. If they do, say, "Excuse me," and keep on walking. If they don't move, inform them that you know your legal rights and that you will call the police to file a formal complaint.

"I am pro-choice. This does not mean I think abortion is necessarily right (or wrong for that matter). I am simply saying that I believe women should have the choice to do what they feel is right."

—WICHITA STATE COLLEGE, '94

ACTIVIST IDEAS

■ Support pregnant women on campus. Set up a group that can hook women up with a Lamaze partner, a ride to doctor's appointments, or other women who have been pregnant (especially those who also had an "on-campus pregnancy") to talk with.

■ Organize a pregnant student exercise group. To find a good program, check out the books and audio- or videotapes on the subject; call a women's health organization, ob-gyn, or family planning clinic; and/or talk to an exercise therapist. Studies show that exercising during pregnancy can make for an easier delivery, a healthier baby, and a healthier mom. (All participants should seek their doctor's consent before enrolling in the class.)

■ Create a pamphlet of information about resources, legislation, and services with regard to pregnancy, adoption and abortion. Include what services are offered on campus and in the community, the college/university policy on pregnancy discrimination, the state laws on abortion, access to prenatal care, and adoption (in both legalese and "plain English"), as well as the names and numbers of local agencies that arrange (or give information about) adoption and places that provide pregnancy testing, prenatal care, and/ or abortions.

■ Organize a program on the medical, social, political, financial, and legislative issues around unplanned pregnancy. Have workshops on topics such as "deciding what to do" with students who've been through it and experts who can discuss the options; the history of reproductive rights in the United States; the facts and controversy around RU 486; the midwifery movement; new reproductive technologies; the biology of reproduction; and the politics of adoption.

RESOURCES

Pregnancy

AMERICAN COLLEGE OF OBSTETRICIANS AND
GYNECOLOGISTS (SEE PAGE 366)

PREGNANCY HELPLINE
(800) 228-0332
Offers phone counseling and advice to pregnant women. Makes referrals to local organizations that provide adoption, abortion, and prenatal care services.

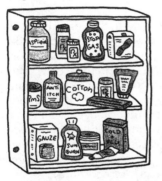

NATIONAL MATERNAL AND CHILD HEALTH
CLEARINGHOUSE
8201 GREENSBORO DRIVE, SUITE 600
MCLEAN, VA 22102
(703) 821-8955 EXT. 254
Provides information about pregnancy, labor, breast-feeding, and infant care. Publishes series of materials on maternity and child health, available for free upon request.

HEALTHY MOTHERS, HEALTHY BABIES
NATIONAL COALITION (HMHB)
409 12TH STREET SW
WASHINGTON, DC 20024
(202) 863-2458
Provides information and answers questions about childbirth. Publishes numerous materials including informative advice on prenatal care, nutrition, and infant mortal-

ity, as well as directories of over 70 local member associations that can provide educational materials about prenatal care.

CHILDBIRTH EDUCATION FOUNDATION (CEF)
P.O. BOX 5
RICHBORO, PA 18954
(215) 357-2792
Promotes the reform of childbirth methods and works to advance certified nurse-midwives, birthing centers, and alternative birthing methods. Trains childbirth educators in Lamaze and breast-feeding. Publishes information about childbirth. Makes referrals to local centers and practitioners offering natural childbirth alternatives.

Adoption

There are public, private, religious, and nonsectarian agencies and organizations that provide a range of services, such as housing and medical care through birth and adoption, and legal help. You can find them, as well as information about your rights and the adoption laws in your state, through social service agencies, religious groups, medical practitioners, and local adoption groups and agencies, as well as through the national organizations listed below.

NATIONAL ADOPTION INFORMATION
CLEARINGHOUSE (NAIC)
11426 ROCKVILLE PIKE, SUITE 410
ROCKVILLE, MD 20852
(301) 231-6512
FAX: (301) 984-8527
Provides information on adoption, including international, federal, and state laws on adoption, crisis pregnancy centers, adoption agencies, and research projects. Makes

referrals to local agencies and organizations. Publishes numerous materials on adoption, including *The National Adoption Directory*.

ADOPTIVE FAMILIES OF AMERICA (AFA)
3333 HIGHWAY 100
NORTH MINNEAPOLIS, MN 55422
(612) 535-4829

Provides assistance to persons on all sides of the adoption process and supports individuals through the adoption process (putting up children for adoption, and adopting). Provides information and answers questions about adoption. Makes referrals to local adoption agencies and adoptive parents support groups, among other organizations dealing with adoption. Publishes numerous materials, including the magazines *Ours* and *Adoptive Families.*

NORTH AMERICAN COUNCIL ON ADOPTABLE CHILDREN (NACAC)
970 RAYMOND AVENUE
ST. PAUL, MN 55114
(612) 644-3036
FAX: (612) 644-9848

Provides information about the adoption process. Makes referrals to agencies and organizations for those wanting to put their children up for adoption and for those wanting to adopt. Works with a network of adoptive parents support groups in the U.S. and Canada and coordinates the largest adoption-related conference in North America annually. Publishes numerous materials, including *Adoptalk.*

AMERICAN ADOPTION CONGRESS (AAC)
1000 CONNECTICUT AVENUE NW, SUITE 9
WASHINGTON, DC 20036
(202) 483-3399

Conducts research and educational conferences on adoption. Provides information about adoption procedures. Makes referrals to organizations dealing with adoption. Publishes numerous materials on adoption, including a newsletter called *Decree.*

NATIONAL COUNCIL FOR ADOPTION (NCFA)
1930 17TH STREET NW
WASHINGTON, DC 20009
(202) 328-8072

Maintains a library on all subjects related to adoption. Publishes numerous materials, including *Adoption Factbook.*

Abortion

You can find out about local abortion providers or check up on those you found by consulting with your school health services or local pro-choice advocacy organizations.

THE NATIONAL ABORTION FEDERATION
1436 U STREET NW, SUITE 103
WASHINGTON DC 20009
(202) 667-5881
(800) 772-9100: NATIONAL ABORTION FEDERATION HOTLINE

A national professional association for abortion service providers. Provides information on the variety and quality of abortion services offered, answers questions and provides advice on such topics as abortion procedure, judicial bypass, and legislation restricting abortions. Makes referrals to local abortion providers who are members of their organization. In addition, makes referrals to places that offer assistance with funding abortions. Publishes

materials on abortion, including several books, information packets, and a variety of fact sheets.

PLANNED PARENTHOOD FEDERATION OF AMERICA

810 SEVENTH AVENUE
NEW YORK, NY 10019
(212) 541-7800
FAX: (212) 245-1845
NATIONAL OFFICE: (800) 829-7732
(800) 230-7526 [PLAN]: FOR A REFERRAL TO THE PLANNED PARENTHOOD CLINIC NEAREST YOU. THEY ALSO PUBLISH A CLINIC DIRECTORY.

A federation of organizations working to make sure contraception, abortion, sterilization, and infertility services are available to all as a central element of reproductive health. It supports family planning efforts throughout the globe. They are affiliated with numerous state and local Planned Parenthoods that provide free and/or low-cost medical services. Many clinics will: provide abortion services and/or refer you to clinics that do; provide information about gynecological care, women's health care, contraception, and other family planning; make referrals to organizations that can help facilitate judicial bypass.

NATIONAL ABORTION RIGHTS ACTION LEAGUE (NARAL)

1156 15TH STREET NW, SUITE 700
WASHINGTON, DC 20005
(202) 973-3000

Organizes advocacy and political action work to keep abortion safe and legal. Coordinates the Campus Organizing Project and other grassroots political action projects. Supports pro-choice candidates, research on abortion and birth control methods, leadership training, and public education programs. Provides information on all areas of abortion legislation and can make referrals to those needing assistance with judicial bypass or other abortion restrictions.

NARAL has local affiliates in each state. If you cannot find a local NARAL affiliate in the phone book, you can get information by contacting the national office.

THE RELIGIOUS COALITION FOR REPRODUCTIVE CHOICE

1025 VERMONT AVENUE NW, SUITE 1130
WASHINGTON, DC 20005
(202) 628-7700

Organizes political action/advocacy work through a coalition of 36 religious organizations and denominations that work to safeguard the legal option of abortion, as well as promoting research and legislation on areas of reproductive rights and other health issues. Maintains and runs the Women of Color Partnership Program, which addresses reproductive health issues and the role of the church as well as male responsibility from the perspective of women of color.

CATHOLICS FOR A FREE CHOICE

1436 U STREET NW, SUITE 301
WASHINGTON, DC 20009
(202) 986-6093

Does educational and political action and advocacy work that supports the right to legal reproductive health care, especially family planning and abortion. Publishes numerous materials, including *Conscience: A Newsjournal of ProChoice Catholic Opinion.*

THE ABORTION ACCESS PROJECT

P.O. BOX 686
JAMAICA PLAIN, MA 02130
(617) 738-9497
FAX: (617) 576-0923

A grassroots coalition of reproductive rights activists and health care providers dedicated to making abortion truly accessible. Provides information and referrals.

ACLU Reproductive Freedom Project
122 Maryland Avenue
Washington, DC 20002
(202) 675-2337
Through litigation, advocacy, and public education seeks to uphold the rights of individuals to decide whether or not to bear a child. Strives to ensure that all have access to sexuality education, contraception, abortion, prenatal care, and childbearing assistance.

The ProChoice Resource Center
174 East Boston Post Road
Mamaroneck, NY 10543
(800) 733-1973
Fax: (914) 946-1481
A national nonpartisan nonprofit organization that trains and advises pro-choice grassroots groups and coalitions in how to identify, educate, and activate pro-choice supporters. Provides guidance and technical assistance to pro-choice groups throughout the country.

Further Reading

ॐॐॐ

Pregnancy

The Complete Book of Pregnancy and Childbirth, Sheila Kitzinger (Alfred A. Knopf, 1989).
A Good Birth, a Safe Birth: Choosing and Having the Childbirth Experience That You Want, third revised edition, D. Korte and R. Scaer (Harvard Common Press, 1992).
The New Our Bodies Ourselves, Boston Women's Health Book Collective (Simon and Schuster, 1992).

What to Expect When You're Expecting, revised and expanded second edition. Arlene Eisenberg, Hedi E. Murkoff, and Sandee E. Hathaway, B.S.N. (Workman, 1991).
Mother to Be: A Guide to Pregnancy and Birth for Women with Disabilities, Judith Rogers and Molleen Matsumura (Demos Publications, 1992).
The Whole Birth Catalog, Janet Isaacs Ashford, ed. (The Crossing Press, 1983).

Adoption

The Adoption Resource Book, third edition. Lois Gilman (HarperCollins, 1992).
The Adoption Triangle: The Sealed or Opened Records—How They Affect Adoptees, Birthparents, and Adoptive Parents, second edition. A. Sorosky, A. Baran, and R. Pannor (Corona Publications, 1989).
Helping Women Cope with Grief, P. Silverman (Sage Publications, 1981).

Abortion

A Woman's Book of Choices: Abortion, Menstrual Extraction, and RU-486, Rebecca Chalker and Carol Downer (Four Walls, Eight Windows, 1992).
Abortion Without Apology: A Radical History for the 1990's, Nina Baehr (South End Press, 1990).
Woman's Body, Woman's Right: Birth Control in America, revised edition. Linda Gordon (Penguin, 1990).
RU 486: The Pill That Could End the Abortion Wars and Why American Women Don't Have It, Lawrence Lader (Addison-Wesley, 1991).
Abortion and Woman's Choice: The State, Sexuality, and Reproductive Freedom, revised edition. Rosalind Pollack Petchesky (Northeastern University Press, 1990).

Part Five

Fighting Back

Breaking Down Bias

Prejudice, Harassment & Discrimination

Bias is present on even the most integrated and enlightened college campus. For many of us who grew up in relatively sheltered, homogeneous environments, college can be the first time we witness, experience, and even perpetrate bias. (Though, as women, most of us have probably had at least a brush with sexism.) Bias comes in many different forms. In addition to sexism, we may encounter racism, anti-Semitism or heterosexism, to name just a few of the "isms" present on campus. The consequences can be as benign as having someone assume

you came from a big family because you're Catholic, as hurtful as having them believe that you got into school only because of affirmative action, or as serious as being rejected from grad school or being denied a promotion because of your gender or race.

Now is the time to take a look at what prejudices you might have arrived with, and to figure out how to deal with prejudices you might run into. Ideally, college trains you to live and work in the "real world." Part of that training is defining your own identity; learning to be open to other opinions, approaches, beliefs, and

By age 2, children can distinguish race and gender.

THE VOCABULARY OF BIAS

BIAS is a predisposition toward or against a person, group, thing, or approach. It is generally based on assumptions or beliefs rather than evaluation or merit. *Note:* A measure of bias on anyone's part is to be expected and not necessarily criticized. At a certain level, we can't separate our thoughts, actions, and reactions from who we are and what we're used to. Without some sense of bias, we wouldn't have constructive arguments, editorial pages, or even distinct personalities. The point is to try to be aware of and responsible for our biases, knowing when they add an element of flavor or challenge—and when they diminish or exclude.

A STEREOTYPE is a generalization about a group of people that characterizes them as a whole, disregarding their individual differences. Even when a stereotype itself is not negative, its impact is: Any stereotype can cause or encourage us to relate to people based on preconceived notions rather than on what they have to say for themselves.

PREJUDICE means, literally, prejudgment: an attitude or opinion, often based on a stereotype, formed before finding out what someone or something is really like. Prejudice is usually negative or hostile; even when it takes a "positive" form, that by nature means it's favoring one group, person, or thing at the expense, exclusion, or rejection of another. Prejudice tends to run deep—often in a family or community—and is not easily dismantled simply by presenting someone with facts contrary to his or her opinion.

DISCRIMINATION is prejudice in action. When prejudice on the part of an individual or an institution is systematic and/or serves to deny people or groups of people their civil rights, education, or employment, then prejudice becomes discrimination.

SCAPEGOATING is the act of placing false blame on an individual or group. Scapegoating is caused by—and serves to reinforce—prejudiced attitudes.

RACISM is prejudice or discrimination based on assumptions or stereotypes about people with a particular skin color or features. A racist attitude assumes that someone's race is the primary determinant of his or her personality and/or ability. Racism exists among individuals, but it is often "institutionalized"—sanctioned and perpetuated, explicitly or implicitly, by the practices or attitudes of an existing power structure.

SEXISM is prejudice or discrimination based on negative assumptions or stereotypes regarding gender. Like racism—and all its "ism" cousins—sexism can be individual or institutional, and it can lead to violence.

ANTI-SEMITISM is prejudice or discrimination against Jews, either directly or simply by invoking stereotypes about them. Anti-Semitism is sometimes considered to be a form of racism, since Nazis and other anti-Semites, past and present, refer to the Jewish people as the "Jewish race."

HETEROSEXISM is the assumption that heterosexuality is the "normal" way of life. A related term is "homophobia," which connotes a negative attitude toward or fear of gay, lesbian and bisexual people.

CLASSISM is prejudice or discrimination based on negative assumptions and sterotypes of people based on their socioeconomic class. Class includes real or assumed wealth, educational level, and/or social status.

ABLEISM is prejudice or discrimination based on real or perceived ability, directly or through the assumption that everybody has certain abilities.

LOOKSISM is prejudice or discrimination based on physical appearance.

AGEISM is prejudice or discrimination based on real or perceived age.

backgrounds; and recognizing and handling those situations where someone else is not respectful of your identity or ideas.

THE SPECTRUM OF BIAS

"There is nothing more destructive than the racism in America. Every newspaper, except for the black papers, is written from a white perspective, every TV show depicts my people looking stupid, every bit of history in this country has been made with the blood of my people, and so I am angry about the discrimination in this society, and I am angry not only for myself but for the entire black race."

—DUKE UNIVERSITY, '96

Bias, like violence against women (see ""Ending the Silence," page 491), happens along a continuum. It can range from assumptions and opinions to comments, demands, threats, and acts of violence; it can take the form of a joke, an insult, or a pattern of sexual harassment.

No one is completely without bias. But instead of ignoring it or pretending it doesn't exist, it's important to be aware of the ways in which it operates in your own life. The following questions have no right or wrong answers. But they will help you identify and understand your own biases and those of your community.

"I didn't realize until recently how much racism I had experienced. Being at Princeton and being Latina, I might as well wear a sign that says, 'No, I am smart, I don't speak English poorly, and as far as I know, I didn't get in because of affirmative action—it was because of my accomplishments—but if it was, I don't care.'"

—PRINCETON UNIVERSITY, '95

■ Do you form opinions about people based on what they look like, where they're from, where they hang out?

■ In class, do you make assumptions about people's intelligence and the validity of their contributions based on what they look like, their accent, or their background?

■ Are you more apt to listen to, take notes on, comment on, and agree with questions and comments on subjects unrelated to identity from students of your same background?

■ Do you feel that bias against certain groups is more "permissible" than bias against others?

■ How do you react when you're teased, excluded, ignored, or talked about in a negative way?

■ Are there terms and assumptions about members of groups to which you belong (or don't belong) that are more damaging, dangerous, and offensive than others?

■ How and in what situations (both general and specific) does being part of a majority group have an advantage? When is not being part of a majority a disadvantage?

■ Were you a member of a minority or majority while growing up? Were most people of the same race, socio-economic class, religion, ethnicity as you? Are you in the minority or majority on campus? How does that make you feel?

■ How would you react if someone accused you of being racist? Sexist? Homophobic? Ableist? Would you react more strongly to some than others?

■ Do you tell jokes that stereotype or judge others? Is it OK as long as you are a member of the group that the joke makes fun of?

■ How do you feel about interracial or interfaith dating? How would you feel if after a few months of phone, letter, and/or on-line communication with a person you completely "clicked" with,

"I was annoyed when my roommate told me that she had never met a Jewish person and wanted to learn all about Jewish people from me. I felt like, Why do I have to represent all Jews? . . . On the other hand, it showed she was open and not wanting to make assumptions based on prejudice. It was also a bit of a warning: 'If I say or do something that offends you, know that I am ignorant about Jews and want to learn not to be.' She told it like it was—and we could work from there."

—HOBART AND WILLIAM SMITH COLLEGES, '90

WORDS CAN HURT: BIASED REMARKS

✺

"Certain people are destroying the curve in this class."

"You don't look Jewish."

"Did you hear the one about the blonde and the . . . ?"

"You're just filling the quota."

"Are you a member of a gang?"

"If you wore makeup and dressed nicely, guys would like you and you wouldn't have to be a lesbian."

Guaranteed you have heard a remark like one of those above. Was it directed to you, or did you overhear it? Who said it—a stranger, a classmate, a professor, or a boss? Did you object, approve, laugh, say nothing? Have you said similar things yourself? Are they really that bad?

Although threats and acts of violence are the most blatant instances of bias, the use of biased language— however subtle—can be every bit as harmful. Linguists acknowledge that language does more than reflect or express thought; our thoughts are shaped by the words that we use to form them. Language can create, reinforce, and perpetuate bias and prejudice. So be careful of what you say, even if you're joking among friends. And if you're wounded by a remark, even if it's one that you simply overheard, don't think you're being oversensitive. If you're up to it, confront the speaker about the comment.

"When I was having a hard time in calculus, someone actually turned around and said to me: 'That's impossible; you're Asian, and you chinks are all good at that stuff.' "
—UNIVERSITY OF CALIFORNIA, SAN DIEGO, '92

you found out your correspondent was of a different race or religion, had a disability, or was very rich or poor?

■ Do you tend to make friends only or mainly with people from a similar background to yours?

■ How would the world be different if people didn't make assumptions about ability and value based on attributes like gender, class, race, or sexual orientation?

■ How do you feel when people ask you to respond to questions as a "spokesperson" for an entire group? ("What do women/Asians/Jews think about . . . ?")

"Every black woman experiences racism and sexism. You can pretend you don't see it, but every one of us knows what it feels like to be excluded, to be oppressed, and to be hurt. It affects us very deeply. It makes us believe that we aren't able to do things that we can, it makes us feel like we aren't of use. . . . Sisters, you gotta raise your consciousness and get with the program—start helping yourself and helping our people."
—SPELMAN COLLEGE, '96

"I struggle with being an open-minded person while still being a practical person. Theoretically, I really have a problem with stereotypes and assumptions, but because of the nature of this society, in which people wear their beliefs on their sleeves and birds of a feather do flock together, there may actually be some accuracy in the stereotypes."

—UNIVERSITY OF CALIFORNIA,
BERKELEY, '92

Remember, the point of being inclusive, open-minded, and tuned in to bias—your own and others'—is not just to Do the Right Thing or to Be a Good Person. It's about accepting individuals for what they are—individuals. It's about allowing yourself to be challenged, and open to new and unfamiliar experiences. And on the flip side, it's about making sure that you get the respect and opportunities that you deserve.

IDENTIFYING DISCRIMINATION IN THE CLASSROOM

Discrimination is not always easy to identify. It can take subtle forms: hints, maneuvers, innuendos. You might be sure about the effect—say, a lower grade—but only have "a feeling" about the cause—e.g., racism on the part of the TA. Maybe your professor is prejudiced or maybe s/he's just a jerk who makes life miserable for everyone.

There is no single, surefire way to tell when discrimination in the classroom is taking place, but certain signs can point in that direction. Some are open to misinterpretation, and some are more alienating and harmful than others; they can all occur in matters of degrees. But they're good starting points for observation—and possibly for recording evidence.

■ Does the professor disproportionately call on one group, race, or gender?

■ Does the professor disproportionately interrupt or correct one certain group, race, or gender?

■ Does the professor ridicule or humilate any group, race, or gender when its members are speaking?

■ Does the professor make remarks that generalize about one group, race, or gender's ability to handle the course material?

■ Does the professor make sexist, racist, homophobic, etc., wisecracks or

assignments
1. Work too hard.
2. No excuses.
3. Limit partying.
4. Make me proud that I am a professor.
5. Don't sleep in class.

use stereotypes in examples presented to the class?

And on a more subtle level . . .

■ Does the professor tend to ask men factual questions and women for their subjective opinion?

■ Does the professor always use men as the protagonists in examples of case studies or word problems? (And/or when women are used, are they portrayed as clumsy or silly, or in traditional gender roles?)

■ Does the professor call the male students "men," and the female students "girls" or "ladies"?

■ Does the professor ask just students of a certain race or gender to answer interesting, complex questions and reserve the objective, yes/no, short-answer ones for others?

■ Does the professor seem to grade more harshly or leniently, depending on a student's race or gender? Every school maintains certain criteria upon which a student's performance should be evaluated. If you think these criteria were not followed, or that the criteria are themselves unfair, talk to the faculty or dean's office that handles academic affairs. If you feel you are being discriminated against, you may also wish to contact organizations dealing with students' legal rights, educational equity, and/or sexual discrimination.

It's also important to be aware of the ways in which the subjects you're studying can be subtly or overtly biased. When we study the history of civilizations, cultures, and nations, it is often the study of the history of the men—and often privileged, nonminority men—in those cultures. When we study advances that have been

"I was the first woman to arrive at my Spanish conversation class. There were a few male students, obviously friends, who were joking around with the professor. When I walked in they all stopped talking and looked me over. Then one of the guys asked the prof how to say 'tits' in Spanish and they all started talking about my 'big tits.' When other women came in, [the male students] would comment on the size of their 'tits,' too. The professor was laughing hysterically and totally egging them on! I dropped that class and have not taken a Spanish class since."
—COLUMBIA UNIVERSITY, '92

made in science, we are often studying the contributions made by white men and their effect on men. When we learn about medical studies that purport to teach us about the human body, we are usually dealing with studies that have been conducted about men. When we interpret literature, we often discuss the struggle of the individual male protagonist against the world, without considering what the text has to tell us about women or people of other races. While there's nothing inherently wrong with studying kings and popes, F. Scott Fitzgerald and Copernicus, testosterone production and Hamlet's angst, the problems arise when our courses, professors, and departments—either actively or passively—determine the value of texts and ideas, based on gender or race.

Again, these determinations may be tough to detect. The questions below may have subtle or complicated answers, but you can use them as starting points to help you figure out if your classes have a sexist bias.

■ Are all the books on the syllabus written by white men? If there's just one book written by or about a woman/women or member of another race does it feel like a token? Is it discussed in as much depth as the rest of the curriculum?

■ Are the experiences of women or relevant racial/ethnic groups brought into historical or literary discussions?

■ Are the experiences of white men treated as the experience of all "people," and the experiences of women or members of minority groups, if discussed at all, treated as "female people" or "minority people"?

■ When people in the class raise such questions, are they listened to or simply dismissed as "narrow," "single-issue," or "PC"?

If you're uncertain about whether or not your professor and/or course material is biased, you might want to ask someone else's opinion. You can gain useful insight by running it by

> "There's a game being played on my campus. It's called Guess L.'s Race. People come up to me and say, 'Hmmm, you are Chinese, right, no, wait—Japanese, but you kind of look Korean, too. What the hell ARE you?'"
>
> —SYRACUSE UNIVERSITY, '96

both someone familiar with the situation and someone totally removed. Describe the comment(s), incident(s), or syllabus and see what they think. Bear in mind, though, that women who describe or report classroom discrimination are often told that they are overreacting and are advised to "stick it out." Sometimes that's good advice, but sometimes it's an automatic response to squelch a potential stink. Make sure to talk to someone you trust, and get a second opinion if you want one. And above all, trust yourself.

SEXUAL HARASSMENT

The Equal Opportunity Employment Commission (EEOC) classifies sexual harassment as a form of sexual discrimination under Title VII of the 1964 Civil Rights Act. According to the EEOC, sexual harassment encompasses "unwelcome sexual advances, requests for sexual favors, and other verbal or physical conduct of a sexual nature."

Though the definition itself is fairly clear, confusion can still arise in trying to determine what behaviors fit the definition. The nature of alleged harassment can shift depending not only on specific facts, words, and actions, but also on the relationship between the two parties, the context of the situation, its effect on the "harassee," and, more often than not, on conflicting opinions between the two parties about what constitutes harassment in the first place. What might be flirting to one person might be annoying—or worse—to another.

Like rape, sexual harassment is not about sex; it's about power. It's about invading someone's space, making someone uncomfortable, intimidating someone, establishing or asserting dominance, and/or using sexual language or coercion as a tool. For this reason, sexual harassment is of particular concern in the workplace and in the classroom. It can interfere with one's rights to equal education, employment, and opportunity.

According to the EEOC, sexual harassment can be said to have occurred when (1) submission to such conduct is either explicitly or implicitly made a term or condition of an individual's employment; (2) submission to or rejection of such conduct by an individual is used as the basis for employment decisions; or (3) such conduct has the purpose or effect of unreasonably interfering with an individual's work performance or creating an intimidating, hostile, or offensive working environment. "Quid pro quo" (literally, "this for that") and "hostile environment" are two general categories of sexual harassment. Quid pro quo occurs when opportunities or benefits are somehow linked to a demand for sexual conduct; many cases include the stated or implied threat that a job or promotion depends on accepting sexual advances. A hos-

"Especially at a northern, very PC college like Sarah Lawrence, telling someone they're racist is the quickest way to turn them off to anything you might want to say—they get so busy defending themselves, trying to 'prove' they're not. I had one woman start listing all the rap and hip-hop shows she'd seen. What I'd like is people to be thankful when someone confronts them on their unintentional racism, and understand that it takes work to undo the effects of living in a racist society."
—SARAH LAWRENCE COLLEGE, '95

tile environment involves "unwanted, personally offensive sexual attention"—grabbing, aggressive or explicit remarks, lewd jokes—that is not directly associated with threats or repercussions.

It's clear how this pertains to school if you substitute "classroom" for "workplace" and "grade" for "employment." Even student-to-student harassment can be a means of quid pro quo (in the context of leadership positions, for example) or simply create an environment hostile enough to interfere with someone's ability to fully participate and perform well in school.

But of course, hearing someone say, "If you don't sleep with me, you'll fail," or "Nice hooters!" is much less ambiguous than "I think it would be beneficial to discuss your paper over a cup of coffee" or "You know, you look really great in that dress." Once again,

AM I BEING HARASSED OR DISCRIMINATED AGAINST?

"When I was in college I heard the African-American writer Ntozake Shange read from her work and answer questions. Someone asked her about how to deal with racism at Yale, and after asking what year the woman was in, Shange said, 'You want to look carefully and see whether you're uncomfortable mainly because Yale is racist and sexist, or mainly because you're a freshman in college.' Shange knows that racism and sexism are daily realities. But especially in an unfamiliar environment, the 'isms' aren't the cause of every insecurity, frustration, or obstacle. To automatically blame them for all of the problems that are part of college is to miss the opportunity to work on these problems ourselves."
—*YALE UNIIVERSITY, '90*

In order for something to be considered harassment or discrimination, in legal terms, you will need to prove the following:

▲ The harassment or discrimination occurred.

▲ It was unsolicited. (Wearing sexy clothing or asking for a performance review is *not* considered solicitation of sexist or racist comments.)

▲ A reasonable person of your same gender/race/religion would find the harasser's/discriminator's behavior similarly offensive.

▲ The behavior is related to your race/gender/religion (e.g., you were fired because of who you are—not because you did a lousy job).

WHAT MIGHT **NOT** BE HARASSMENT OR DISCRIMINATION

▲ When someone asks you for a date after you've turned him down before—irritating, maybe, but not necessarily harassing.

▲ A supervisor's shifting around job duties or positions. She may make bad choices and carry them out in obnoxious ways, but it's part of her job.

▲ Being assigned books or having class discussions about topics that are potentially painful or offensive, if it's relevant to the class (e.g., it's legitimate to include material that contains anti-Semitic remarks in a course on Nazi Germany).

▲ Nonmalicious practical jokes.

▲ Well-intentioned compliments on clothing or appearance.

▲ Ignorance (e.g., someone uses terms, makes jokes, or holds assumptions that s/he doesn't recognize as offensive and derogatory).

▲ A negative performance evaluation, either at work or in class—as long as it's reasonable, constructive, and impersonal.

▲ Sexual or intimate relationships between supervisor and supervisee, teacher (or TA) and student, RA and student. Such relationships may present a conflict of interest or violate other regulations, but they are not automatically exploitative or coercive.

Women are 9 times more likely than men to quit their jobs and 5 times

if you're not sure how to evaluate what's happened or happening, seek out other opinions. Your school should have an explicit policy, echoing the EEOC's, on sexual harassment. If it's not in the catalog, your RA, dean, ombudsperson, or the office of affirmative action should have access to a copy. Feminist groups on campus can also be a great source of support and information. Talk to someone you trust about the incident(s). If you feel physically threatened, talk to someone right away.

Why should you talk to someone even if you aren't sure it's harassment or you aren't interested in dealing with the issue? Not only does harassment violate your rights, but it can also interfere with your emotional, social, and physical sense of well-being. Experts note that women who've been harassed report feelings and responses similar to those of rape survivors, including lack of confidence and self-esteem, inability to concentrate, self-blame, anger, frustration, depression, anxiety, and fatigue. Even if you don't pursue disciplinary action, make sure to take care of yourself, not only so that you're best able to get fair grades and fair employment, but also so that your future in school—and your future, in general—is not permanently affected.

That said, when you seek support from college employees, such as dorm counselors, campus police, faculty advisors, graduate residents, professors, deans, departmental heads, coworkers, and supervisors, realize that they may not understand sexual harassment and may react to your story with disbelief. Their loyalties may lie elsewhere (the dean, for example, may be more concerned with keeping a widely published harassing professor at your school than in keeping you. Realize the limits of those you are talking with, and if you don't like their responses or ideas for resolution, seek others who may be more helpful.

Remember, too, that even if the behavior may not be considered harassment in a court of law, that does not mean it isn't inappropriate, damaging, painful, and important to stop. It is perfectly acceptable to protest anything that you feel is offensive. If a guy puts up a poster of a scantily clad, super-busty woman on his door and it offends you, you have every right to ask him to take it down.

DECIDING WHAT TO DO

A fraternity holds a wet T-shirt contest to raise money for the United Way. The fella next door loudly and constantly refers to women as "bitches." Someone in your French seminar asks you if you "played your race card" when applying to schools. Your professor gives a lecture on how Japanese women are subservient to "their men," then asks you, a fourth generation Chinese-American woman, to comment.

ONLINE
Does anybody out there want to talk for a while? I don't feel like working...

SOFTWARE
SHORT STORIES
GAMES
COMPUTER BASICS
DICTIONARY

FINAL DRAFT

more likely to transfer in-company because of sexual harassment.

In cases like these, there may be no question that you feel offended and upset but you might not be quite sure what to do. Confronting bias is rarely as easy as some of the diversity awareness materials would lead us to believe. There are all sorts of reasons why you might feel apprehensive about taking action. You could risk being labeled oversensitive or histrionic. The time, energy, and/or risks involved in confronting the entire fraternity system, your prof, or the guy who will be living on your hall for the next seven and a half months may be far more difficult to endure than the offhand comments and piggery. And you may worry that no one will believe you, they'll think you're overreacting, or you'll get a reputation as a troublemaker.

But by addressing the problem you may put an end to it, gain respect and thanks from others, bring an important issue to the surface where it can be addressed, revise outdated policy, and perhaps change the minds of an ignorant few. Furthermore, the self-confidence boost that comes from speaking up or taking a stand is always a plus.

Each time you confront bias, you'll have to judge for yourself whether what you'll gain by taking action outweighs what you may lose. Trust your instincts.

BEFORE TAKING ACTION

Before you take action, either formally or informally, take the time to do the following:

■ Assess the situation. Is it bias? Talk-

ing to others (especially witnesses) can help you sort out the issues, and they can stand behind you when you're confronting the bigot on your hall or testify in your behalf, as well as provide emotional support. (See "Who Can Help," page 476, for more places and people to help you with this.)

■ To get a clear picture (as well as have evidence in case you want to file a formal complaint), keep, collect, and create records. Even if you think that your case is not very serious or that you will not pursue formal action, keep records so that you'll have all the information you need should you decide to write a letter to the perpetrator or report the incident later. Write down detailed accounts of every instance of bias, including date, time, place, and witnesses. Record what was said and done and how it made you feel. Save any notes, pictures, or messages from the offender. Don't throw anything away in anger. If you have to defend your allegations, this evidence will be crucial. Offenders usually operate when nobody is around. If it's your word against his or hers, any corroboration of your testimony will help. If you do have witnesses, ask them to write down what they saw. Ask for copies and keep them in a safe place.

As you take action to stop the situation, keep equally detailed records of all communications (letters, phone calls, meetings, etc.) with officials on campus or supervisors at work from whom you seek help. It is probably a good idea to follow up any verbal agreements with letters to the relevant offices. These can help later if you have problems with the manner in which your complaint was handled.

■ Set goals about what you want to accomplish. Obviously, a minimum is to have the behavior stop. You may want to see some sanctions taken against the offender. You may want him or her to make a formal apology or to attend a class or workshop on the subject of bias. You may want him or her to be relocated, fired, or expelled. Write down what your ideal outcome would be and then write down what the minimum requirements for a resolution would be. You will be weighing these possible outcomes against the effort that it will take for you to see them realized.

■ Understand the consequences of all the options. Though you have the law on your side and you're doing an important thing, it won't necessarily be easy. Get a feel for what you're up against, possible pitfalls and roadblocks, and the time, energy, and (possibly) money that may be involved, so you can plan accordingly.

DEALING WITH HARASSMENT OR BIAS INFORMALLY

If the offensive behavior is not severe, and you just want it to stop, it may be sufficient to tell the person who is harassing you to desist. Don't worry about hurting the person's feelings, and don't feel you have to be polite. For example, if a woman on your hall always makes an obnoxious comment about your ethnicity when you pass, you can simply tell her to cut it out in no uncertain terms. To feel safer or more confident, you may want to have a friend and/or someone in an official capacity with you. You might also consider writing a letter (see page 478). If

the behavior is more threatening, however, this may not be your best option.

The benefit of handling the problem informally is that it's the least time- and energy-consuming, most confidential way possible to get the problem solved. In addition, if you do end up filing a formal complaint, your case will be stronger if you can show that you tried to deal with the problem yourself. (Of course this doesn't apply if you feel that talking to the offender could be dangerous or would exacerbate the situation, rather than resolve it.)

Speaking Up

ଊଊଊ

It's not easy to figure out a response—or whether to respond at all—to prejudiced or sexist remarks. Sometimes it's difficult to tell if the person who makes them is biased, mean-spirited, or just plain ignorant. If something is offensive to you, it can be hard to explain precisely why. If you don't say anything, you might feel incriminated, a party to the offense; but if you do, you may fear being labeled oversensitive, humorless, defensive. And if you find yourself in the position of needing to confront a TA, professor, boss, or other superior, the stakes are even higher.

Still, as difficult and complicated as it may be, many diversity experts and school administrators do recommend speaking out against offensive speech, whether directed at you or overheard. Some feel it is a responsibility to the slighted group and to the community at large.

Theoretical issues aside, what should you actually say? Don't feel that you have to prepare an elaborate

WHO CAN HELP

There is no uniform policy that all colleges follow when dealing with harassment or discrimination. The best ways to find out about your options for getting support or filing a complaint on campus are by asking the dean of student life (or another of the people mentioned below) about what is offered at your school as well as by referring to your school's catalog. (Your school may also have a hand-book or other publication on these issues.) You do not have to divulge anything about your case; just ask about the proper procedures and places to go and then choose your course of action.

Although each campus is different, they all have some sort of hierarchy. In most cases it is a good idea to start at the bottom of the hierarchy and work your way up.

YOUR ADVISOR OR DEPARTMENT HEAD is usually a good place to start if you're having problems with a profes-sor or TA.

RESIDENT ADVISORS will generally provide information and referrals, help develop options, and accompany you in a formal process.

COUNSELING/MENTAL HEALTH SER-VICES will provide support and coun-seling, will help develop options, and will provide referrals. The campus psy-chiatry service must by law report cer-tain kinds of abuse.

DEANS' OFFICES: The dean has the power to initiate change. You may start with an assistant dean, depending on the situation. Confidentiality is not guaranteed when you speak to most deans; the dean is part of a larger administrative network and may not be completely unbiased with regard to your situation.

THE OFFICE OF AFFIRMATIVE AC-TION: Campuses that receive federal funding were required to establish offices of affirmative action after the passage of Title IX. These offices are intended to serve all students, staff, and faculty. Serving as an on-campus complaint office, the purpose of these offices is to avoid lawsuits for the school. They are supposed to address any problems with campus safety and discrimination on the basis of race, sex, religion, national origin, ethnic-ity, etc. However, because they are not independent of the school, they may be more or less helpful, depending on the situation. Some schools have offices that are better equipped than others.

THE OMBUDSPERSON: The role of the ombudsperson is to be a designated neutral source of impartial, confiden-tial information about available options, and/or to provide assistance in resolving conflicts informally. The office is independent of the other offices of the university, and theoreti-cally the ombudsperson has access to all files. The ombudsperson will direct you further if s/he can't handle your problem.

In one study, 78% of Cornell women students had encountered sex-

CAMPUS GRIEVANCE COMMITTEES: Depending on your school, different offices (such as the office of student life or dean's office) will have established grievance committees that try to help resolve problems. Generally these committees will maintain confidentiality and work independently of the office of affirmative action.

STUDENT GROUPS (such as an Asian, African-American, Latina, lesbian, or women's groups) are often great sources of support and information (and sometimes even inside information). And if the college is being less than accommodating in addressing your problem, having the support of many people who are threatening negative publicity can work miracles.

STUDENTS WHO HAVE BEEN THROUGH THE PROCESS: Individuals at your school or on other campuses who have dealt with issues similar to yours may be extremely helpful in developing tactics to overcome roadblocks.

ACADEMIC DEPARTMENTS: While professors in the African-American, Hispanic, Asian, or women's studies departments (or others that are personally or academically involved with political action and the rights of oppressed groups) may not be able to assist you in an official capacity, they are often good sources of information about campus policies and politics, your rights, what constitutes discrimination, and people who will be the most helpful to you. Tenured faculty members—especially those who have the university wrapped around their little finger—are always good to have on your side.

LAWYERS: If you're at a university with a law school, get in touch with professors and student groups that work on antidiscrimination issues. Organizations may also offer legal assistance.

OFF-CAMPUS ORGANIZATIONS: Local, state, and national groups that work against discrimination can provide information and support as well. (See the Resources at the end of this chapter.)

If you're concerned about confidentiality, bring it up before you get into the details of your case. Depending on the incident, some of the above people or groups may be required to try to stop the offending behavior when they're notified of abuse and thus may not be able to keep confidentiality.

speech that offers a full, airtight, sociolinguistic explanation for your position. You may want to ask the person to please repeat himself. You may also want to challenge him to back up his opinion by asking, "What makes you think so?"

Or else it may be enough to start out with, "You know, I think you're making a lot of assumptions about . . ." If you're not sure what to say, say so. You don't need to get fancy, and you don't necessarily need to get angry—just say what's on your mind. The person probably won't be thrilled to hear your opinion, and may or may not stick around for you to fully articulate your feelings, but at least you won't have let the moment pass while worrying about your word choice. You may also find out that you misunderstood the person's intent, and she may see how what she said could have been misconstrued. (But if you feel threatened by the person's response, get yourself out of the situation and report the incident to a dorm official or another administrator.)

Some bias-driven comments are far less subtle than the kind discussed above. They may include the use of racial, gender, or other types of slurs; overt spoken or written (on paper or on-line) threats against a group or individual; and obscene phone calls. Some of these incidents are isolated; some may be repeated. Many venture into the realm of hate speech/crimes and harassment. (Federal laws on bias crimes are continually changing. Currently, only those behaviors that include a threat or act of violence are legally recognized as bias crimes.) In some such cases, telling the perpetrator you're offended won't be effective and could be dangerous. For ways of addressing these overt forms of bias,

"Anti-Semitism happens on a lot of levels; it is everything from calling a Jewish woman a JAP (Jewish American Princess), which reinforces a stereotype about us, to defacing synagogues, to what happened at my friend's school where the mezuzot (boxes that Jews put on their doorposts containing a prayer) were stolen off of the doors of over 50 students. People like to talk about how anti-Semitism doesn't happen anymore, but you try being one of a few Jews in North Dakota, or even one of a lot of Jews in New York, and I guarantee you will find virulent anti-Semitic stereotypes everywhere."

—New York University, '93

see below. (For more about the issue of violence against women, see "Ending the Silence," page 491.)

Write a Letter

ᔆᔆᔆ

If you don't feel up to orally confronting someone whose behavior you find offensive or if previous attempts to resolve the situation have failed, you can write him or her a letter. Letter-writing is an effective means of getting your point across and resolving a conflict for a number of reasons. The process of composing the letter allows you to clarify the situation to both yourself and the addressee; having all the facts, feelings, and suggestions for recourse down in ink leaves less room for miscommunication or misunderstanding. In addition, taking the time to write sends a strong message that you see this as an important matter. The harasser will not think you were joking or flirting, or that you were just casually irked. Another advantage of a letter rather than a face-to-face confrontation is that you won't run out of time or be interrupted, ignored, "tuned out," intimidated, or misinterpreted. And in allowing the offender to read (and reread) the letter at his or her leisure with time to think it over, you won't have to face an irrational, angry, or defensive initial reaction. Lastly, the addressee knows that you have a copy of the letter and that you could make copies for others. The threat of a stink alone is often enough to provide the offender with the impetus to resolve

the issue quickly and completely. (For this reason, you may want to indicate in the letter that you've spoken about the issue with someone else, especially if prior attempts to resolve the situation have failed.)

The letter should be clear, honest, and to the point. The first section should describe what happened, without analysis. ("Your comment that girls hate dissection and get woozy when they use a scalpel," is preferable to "your sexist comments about women and science.") Give details about dates, places, and behaviors using specific examples. In the second section, describe how the incident(s) made/makes you feel (angry, unable to trust, depressed, manipulated, etc.), as well as how the harassment has affected your life (dropping a class, failing to finish a job task, moving out, etc.). The third section should convey what you would like to see happen

---

SPEAKING OUT AGAINST HATE SPEECH

Speech and writing can be symbols of hatred and acts of bias. In recent years the politics of interpreting and responding to hate speech have been the focus of increased debate on campuses around the country. When people make racist, sexist, anti-Semitic, homophobic, and/or other statements you find offensive and hateful, you don't have the right, in most cases, to censor their speech. But you do have the right to speak out against what they say, to celebrate what they denigrate, and to correct their misinformation. What guarantees others the right to voice their

opinions guarantees you the right to respond.

It's easy to talk about the theoretical fine line between one group's right to free speech and another group's civil rights, but it's harder to identify it. When you encounter hate speech, find an organization on campus that identifies with the group being attacked or one that deals with civil rights to get support and help you figure out what to do. Different schools have different policies about what is permissible on campus; look into your school's policy before determining your course of action.

---

nation based on race; 23,919 on gender; and 19,884 on age.

TRUST YOURSELF

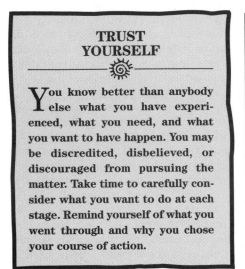

You know better than anybody else what you have experienced, what you need, and what you want to have happen. You may be discredited, disbelieved, or discouraged from pursuing the matter. Take time to carefully consider what you want to do at each stage. Remind yourself of what you went through and why you chose your course of action.

next (you want an apology, you want the behavior to stop, etc.). Do not make threats or promises you won't carry out or keep, hurl insults or obscenities, or blame yourself for the person's actions.

Before you send it (preferably via certified mail or by hand, so you can verify that it was received), have someone you trust look over the letter. (Your school's ombudsperson, trained in just this sort of thing, could be a good person to ask.) Be sure to keep a copy of the letter and a record of all subsequent interactions with the offender. This will be important should you decide to press formal charges later or in the event of an investigation into your case or other cases of harassment.

Get an Agent

You can also ask another person to talk to the offender for you. An RA can help with problems in your dorm. Your boss may be able to talk to a

coworker, and a TA may be able to talk to your prof. But choose your agent carefully. It's probably best not to hand the job to someone occupying a rung in the higher reaches of the campus hierarchy without first trying to address the problem on your own, especially if you won't be present to straighten out the facts and answer the questions that will inevitably arise.

Try Mediation

Some schools (and workplaces) have official mediators to help work out solutions. They hear both sides of the story and help the parties come to some sort of agreement. If you decide to proceed with mediation, make sure that the mediator is trained, and that the agreement you reach is put in writing. If you are not satisfied with the process or the outcome (for instance, if the offender doesn't abide by the agreement), you have the right to complain again and/or change your course of action. One major problem with mediation is that it doesn't take into

account the power differences between the people involved, so in conflicts between students and faculty, or employees and employers, the cards may be stacked against the less powerful. If you do opt to mediate a dispute between you and, say, a professor, see if you can get an advocate to attend the sessions with you.

Anonymous Reporting

୭୭୭

If you don't want to have any type of investigation and don't feel comfortable addressing the problem yourself, you can file an anonymous report with the head of the department, the office of affirmative action, campus security, or the office that compiles statistics about instances of bias on campus. Though no formal action can be taken from an unsigned report, reporting does allow the campus to get a more accurate picture of the bias that students face, and may be a factor in the creation of new policies. (Campus security should also have forms for the anonymous reporting of rape and sexual assault. See "Ending the Silence," page 491, for more infomation about reporting these crimes.)

TAKING FORMAL ACTION

Taking action against harassment and discrimination is not always easy, swift, or safe. Fortunately, though, more and more schools are putting together explicit guidelines for students who are reporting and pursuing complaints of bias and sexual

harassment, and guidelines for the administrations to use when following up and responding. In other words, as far as campuses are concerned, these problems are starting to be recognized and legitimized.

The steps for taking formal action are different on every campus. But most follow a silmilar scheme. First, you'll probably need to file your complaint with the office of affirmative action or of student life or with a campus grievance committee, which will then decide if the complaint merits a hearing. Or, you may need to make your case before a panel in a preliminary hearing so that the school may do an investigation and decide whether the case is worthy of formal arbitration. If the school decides to grant you a hearing, you may need to write up another complaint that meets the specifications of the body that will hear your case.

Keep in mind that even if policies at different colleges are worded very similarly, they may be carried out differently. Each campus will have some administrators who are supremely helpful and supportive, some who will tell you what you want to hear but won't do anything, and some who will be rude and unhelpful. The personalities, power, and positions of those involved will determine the best way to proceed. Investigate the history of student grievances on campus, try and dig up some insider information on who's helpful and who's not, and seek the support and advice of people you can trust when considering filing a formal complaint. (See "Who Can Help," page 476, for places and people that may assist you.) Learn about issues like deadlines, statutes of limitations (the laws governing the amount of time after which a crime was perpetrated that it can be prosecuted), and the rules around countercharges (when the accused files charges of harassment and slander against the complainant). Also find out about the school's policy on protecting the complainant from retaliation—further harassment or punishment, such as failing the student or making verbal or physical threats "to get her back" for filing the case.

Formal Complaints or Charges at School or Work

ଓଡ଼ଓ

Filing a formal complaint, either at school or at work, usually requires that you name the person who has harassed or otherwise offended you, and that s/he be informed of your complaint. (Some schools will keep your name confidential to provide for your safety and help prevent retaliation, but the perpetrator will eventually need to know your name so s/he can formulate an appropriate defense.) Filing a formal complaint is the only method of getting the offender punished officially, outside of filing civil or criminal charges. Often a formal investigation and hearing are part of this process.

Several things should be considered before making a decision to file formal charges. Find out if past complaints at your school or workplace have brought satisfactory results. Schools legitimately claim that they cannot take actions against an accused harasser unless a formal hearing leads to a finding of guilt; but in fact, some administrations haven't taken action against even those who are found to be

guilty. The people you encounter may be very vague about the policies and procedures on certain issues, such as confidentiality. When campuses/workplaces have no written procedures, they may create new ones for each case to suit their needs. In addition, many schools have no policies to deal with retaliation and do not guarantee the complainant any protection against the abuser.

Despite all of these potential problems, some people have been successful. Many women find that pressing charges helps in the healing process, and it can feel good when someone is held accountable for his or her actions.

Anatomy of a Formal Complaint

ଓଡ଼ଓ

You may have several different avenues for officially reporting and/or taking formal action against discrimination or harassment. Find out at which office you should file the complaint or send a letter expressing your desire to press formal charges (check the catalog or talk to someone listed in "Who Can Help," page 476). It should contain the following:

■ The date of your letter.

■ The name of the person you are charging.

■ A description of the incident(s) of harassment: a rough chronology of events (include place, time, and date); all relevant facts; the effects of the incident(s) on you; names of anyone else affected; reference to the existence of any relevant evidence; in the case of sexual harassment, confirmation that you made clear that the advances were unwanted; information about whether the behavior was repeated, how you felt, and how the behavior affected your ability to study or carry on normal activities (optional).

■ A statement of your desired outcome from this complaint (for example, removal of the accused abuser from on-campus housing, funding from your school for a period of time to allow you to make up academic credits lost due to the harassment, expulsion of the accused abuser, or termination of his/her employment).

■ A summary of all previous actions you took toward resolving the abusive situation.

■ Preferred times for the formal hearing (the sooner the better!).

■ A request that you be informed prior to any and all communications with the accused (optional).

■ A request that restrictions be placed on the accused with regards to his having any contact with you (optional).

If possible, hand-deliver the letter and have someone in the office sign a statement that the letter was received that day. Otherwise, have it sent by certified mail. Keep copies of all written transactions between you and the office.

The office should respond with a letter requesting further information (if needed), stating the date and time of the hearing, details about the format of the hearing (how many witnesses, if you can have an advocate, etc.), and (sometimes) a copy of a written response from the accused. If you don't hear from them within a week after your first letter, give them a call.

At the Hearing . . .

☉☉☉

There is no uniform procedure for hearings on campus. Some hearings are closed to all not directly involved in the case, whereas others may recommend or require that you have an advocate (or even a lawyer) with you. In most cases, the charges will be clarified, and both you and the defendant will have a chance to present your story and answer questions posed by members of the hearing committee. You may be asked to bring witnesses to testify on your behalf.

If your school allows it, bring a trusted friend or advisor to support you. Go to the hearing and take careful notes if it's not too distracting—if it is, have someone else take notes for you. Ask if you can record the hearing. The proceedings can get heated, so try to make sure you aren't interrupted and that you have the chance to make all your points.

After everything has been presented, the office presiding over the case will probably tell you when they will make a decision and when they will notify you. Call them if they do not respond within the specified time. Keep notes on any delays and other details concerning the handling (or mishandling) of your case. If you are unsatisfied with the resolution or the handling of your case, you have the options of either going outside of your school or appealing your case to the provost or president. If you go off campus, you may continue a charge against the accused, or you may file charges against your school for violating its responsibilities to prevent and eliminate bias.

Policies may vary, but one thing is uniform across the board: You are entitled to a fair hearing by law. If you suspect at any point during the procedure that the process is unfair, you may wish to call an organization specializing in students' rights or in the legal rights of victims of harassment or discrimination for advice about your options.

REPORTING BIAS TO AUTHORITIES OFF CAMPUS

If the discrimination or harassment was perpetrated by someone who was not affiliated with your school and you want to take action, you should still talk to school officials, women's groups, or the office of affirmative action about what to do. If you want to press charges, they may be able to help you find a lawyer, work with the police or related governmental or community agencies that address such issues. (See the Resources at the end of this chapter to find organizations that can provide you with information and referrals.)

There are a number of different ways to report bias crimes or incidents of harassment, and depending on the situation, some will be more appropriate than others. In any case, you have to determine what you feel comfortable with. Most of the same guidelines listed earlier for reporting abuse on campus or at work apply when you are reporting a crime to the police or another outside agency.

If you decide to report the incident, you are not required to pursue the prosecution of the case. To obtain assistance from the police and/or to report the crime, you can call the police precinct in which the crime occurred.

Even if you don't want to take any official action, consider reporting the incident to the appropriate office and/or campus security. This option is useful for several reasons. It provides your school with information about the number and type of harassment and bias incidents, giving administrators a clearer picture of what's going on in the community. Reporting the incident to the authorities may also help to vent your anger and get validation from others, but without formal charges it will probably be difficult to actually punish the offender.

If you feel that your case has been mishandled by your school, or you want to file additional complaints, you can contact the office of civil rights at the Department of Education, your state's commission against discrimination, or the Equal Employment Opportunity Commission. It can evaluate whether your school mishandled your case and/or whether the school policy and procedures are in compliance with local, state, and federal laws. Documents and details are very important, and you must submit the claim within a certain number of months from the last date of alleged discrimination.

■ **Civil Lawsuits:** You can file a lawsuit against an individual offender and/or against your school or workplace in a civil court. The charges could be breach of an employment contract, intentional infliction of mental duress suffered from harassment, or injury due to an assault, to name a few. Filing deadlines and statutes of limitations vary from state to state and even among districts, so if you think there's even a chance you'll want to take this route, get legal counsel early

YOUR RIGHTS ON THE JOB

Employers have historically had the right to fire employees at will (unless there is a written contract between employer and employee that specifies potential causes for termination, or the employee is a member of a union that defines grounds for dismissal). This broad right is limited by federal laws that prohibit discrimination against individuals on the basis of age, race, or gender. In addition, although federal law does not do so now, many districts prohibit discrimination on the grounds of marital status and/or sexual orientation. In addition, if someone is fired for not agreeing to date or get physically involved with an employer, it is illegal.

on. This route has the advantage of allowing you to be in control of the legal process—you may decide when to take legal action and when to stop if you are or are not satisfied with the results. You are not subject to the whim of governmental agencies, police officers, or district attorneys. Since this takes place in a civil court, you are awarded monetary settlement for damages if your suit is successful. The drawbacks to this option are that it costs money, it can take years to settle, you may have to continue to attend school or work with the offender, and s/he will not be convicted of criminal charges.

■ **Criminal charges:** This may be the best route to take for faster action in extreme cases and in cases of physical abuse. You can take the perpetrator to court and ask for a restraining order. In order to file criminal charges, you must contact the police department, and you should secure some kind of legal counsel. You can get advice about what steps to take from organizations dealing with issues of individual's rights, discrimination, violence against women, bias crimes, and/or student rights.

CURRENT LAWS AFFECTING HARASSMENT AND DISCRIMINATION

Title IX of the Education Amendments of 1972, prohibits discrimination on the basis of gender in educational programs and extracurricular activities (including employment, admission, campus housing, facilities, access to course offerings, counseling, funding, athletic programs, clubs and organizations, and other college run programs.) According to this law, facilities by sex may differ, but they must be equal. For example, housing and sports may be segregated, but all must have access to them. Both students and employees of federally funded schools are covered by this legislation. Three types of institutions are exempt: religious institutions (in cases where the antidiscrimination provision is contrary to specific religious tenets); military institutions (in certain instances); and both private and public single-sex undergraduate institutions (in admissions). Title IX also requires schools to set up an office of affirmative action to hear complaints and enforce antidiscrimination regulations on campus.

CAMPUS HIGHLIGHT

Students at Brown University in Providence, RI, started the group Allies for Change in 1992. Its mission is to explore the ways in which students, as a diverse community, can work to understand and eliminate discrimination and prejudice. Through workshops, seminars, research projects, and conferences, Allies looks at how we learn bias against others and internalize negative messages about ourselves; how gender, race, class, religion, culture, and sexual identity function in our lives; how we all have experience as being both oppressed and oppressing others; and how both "insiders" and "outsiders" (members and nonmembers of identity groups) can work to make social change.

In a nutshell, Title IX is the catch-all that prevents discrimination on the grounds of gender under any circumstances. "No person shall, on the basis of sex, be excluded from the participation in, be denied the benefits of, or be subjected to discrimination in any education program or activity receiving federal financial assistance in the form of grants, loans, and/or contracts."

Title VII of the Civil Rights Act of 1964 and the subsequent amendments prohibits discrimination on the basis of race, color, national origin, sex, and religion. It does not cover religious institutions and schools or companies with fewer than 16 employees.

In 1980, the Equal Employment Opportunity Commission (EEOC), the body that enforces Title VII, ruled that protection for sexual harassment is covered by the statute. "Unwelcome sexual advances, requests for sexual favors, and other verbal or physical conduct of a sexual nature constitute sexual harassment when submission to such conduct is made either explicitly or implicitly a term or condition of an individual's employment; when submission to or rejection of such conduct by an individual is used as a basis for employment decisions affecting such individual; or such conduct has the purpose or effect of unreasonably interfering with an individual's work performance or creating an intimidating, hostile, or offensive working environment."

Other guidelines require institutions to implement programs to educate and prevent discrimination and punish those individuals who violate the established guidelines.

The 1992 Americans with Disabilities Act (ADA) requires that public places, whether publicly or privately owned or funded, be accessible to all people regardless of disability. The ADA gives a grace period to already existing schools, organizations, and companies to give them time to restructure, raise funds, and complete the changes required to increase accessibility and lessen discrimination. Excluded from regulation are religiously affiliated organizations and places of worship, and private clubs.

The act also reaffirms the illegality of discrimination based on disability. It prohibits the creation or enforcement of such rules as requiring a driver's license for ID, prohibiting animals who aid the disabled from

 By some estimates, 30% of female college students will come

entering buildings, allowing only one person in a dressing room, or charging a fee for items or services such as interpreters, TDD machines, or elevator use.

The Education Family Rights and Privacy Act of 1974 (more commonly known as the Buckley Amendment) guarantees that students above the age of 18 have the right to see their student record upon request. Students have the sole right to determine who can see their records (although school faculty who have an educational interest in the student may also see it). These records cannot be released to anyone without student permission. If a student is a minor (under the age of 18) and a dependent (as defined by the Internal Revenue Service), his/her parents have the right to access these records. When you waive your rights to see part of your academic record (such as a recommendation), your parents also waive this right. An addendum to the amendment prohibits "hiding" criminal records within academic records.

"After I became disabled I got a new perspective on the world. I realized how much discrimination there is against people with disabilities, and I'm not just talking about people's attitudes. It's illegal, as well it should be, for places like restaurants to not serve someone because they're black, or for clubs to not allow women to join. But until the new ADA, places could openly discriminate against people in wheelchairs—for example, if there is no ramp or the door's too small to allow a wheelchair to fit through."
—*TUFTS UNIVERSITY, '97*

ACTIVIST IDEAS

■ One of the biggest stumbling blocks in bias awareness groups is that we are so afraid to admit our biases, we tend to become defensive rather than enlightened. Organize a bias awareness campaign that operates on the premise that we all have prejudices, and that it's far more useful to acknowledge, understand, and dismantle them, than it is to deny them.

■ Rally in support of laws that protect women, people of color, gays and lesbians, ethnic and religious minorities, and recent immigrants from bias crimes. Educate students on campus about the legal, political, financial, educational, and social implication of overturning legislation that works to ensure equal opportunity for all.

■ Have students submit signed or anonymous accounts of bias they have experienced in their lives and publish them in a magazine that also includes suggestions for combating bias. Have individuals and/or campus groups write up answers to questions such as "What does being Muslim mean to me?" "What would I like people of other races to know about how I and people of my race experience discrimination?" "Why do I mostly hang around with people with whom I share a common heritage?" It might work particularly well if done after the occurrence of a particularly jolting incident on campus or in combination with a bias awareness week or celebrations in conjunction with Black History Month (February), Women's History Month (March), and Asian-Pacific-Islanders Awareness Month, often held in April.

■ Work to get a better understanding of the bias experienced by members of other groups. For example, if you consider yourself to be heterosexual, pin a gay/lesbian rights button on a conspicuous place on your knapsack, walk around campus or the local area, and take note of how you're treated and how vulnerable you feel. If you're used to being in the majority, hang out where your race, religion, or ethnicity is in the minority. Or borrow a pair of crutches from health services and take a day to go to class, ride public transportation, go shopping, and hit the stacks in the library to gather books for a research paper. Though these activities will not make someone who is part of the majority, straight, and/or fully able bodied truly understand all the roadblocks and prejudices out there, they will inevitably make you aware of bias in ways that being told about it couldn't.

RESOURCES

DEPARTMENT OF JUSTICE
CIVIL RIGHTS DIVISION
10TH STREET CONSTITUTION AVENUE NW
WASHINGTON, DC 20530
TO FILE A COMPLAINT: (202) 514-4718
SWITCHBOARD: (202) 514-2000
Enforces all federal civil rights legislation. Accepts and investigates complaints in areas of discrimination, such as hate crimes, employment, housing, Americans with Disabilities Act, and addresses issues of discrimination on the basis of gender, race, disabilities, etc. Provides information about your rights and makes referrals to other appropriate organizations.

COMMISSION ON CIVIL RIGHTS
1121 VERMONT AVENUE NW, SUITE 800
WASHINGTON, DC 20425
(800) 552-6843
Addresses discrimination and civil rights complaints. Provides information about civil rights laws and what course of action can be taken if they are violated. Makes referrals to local Commissions on Civil Rights.

To find your state and local Commissions on Civil Rights, look in your telephone book under: "U.S. Government, Civil Rights Commission," con-

☀ Studies have found that professors often ignore nonwhite students.

tact your local Federal Information Center (see "Managing Your Money" Resources, page 128), or call the number above.

9 TO 5: NATIONAL ASSOCIATION OF WORKING WOMEN

238 WEST WISCONSIN AVENUE, SUITE 700
MILWAUKEE, WI 53203-2308
(414) 274-0925
(800) 522-0925:
FAX: 414-272-2870

Provides crisis counseling and detailed advice for dealing with sexual harassment and other forms of discrimination in the workplace. Although the organization primarily deals with the workplace they make referrals to local organizations and offer assistance to women dealing with all forms of sexual harassment. Also operates the Job Survival/Rights Hotline which automatically routes you to the 9 to 5 office nearest to you. For more information about 9 to 5 see the Resources in "Working Women," page 184.

EQUAL EMPLOYMENT OPPORTUNITY COMMISSION (EEOC)

1801 L STREET NW
WASHINGTON, DC 20507
(800) 669-4000
(202) 663-4264
TDD: (800) 800-3302

Makes referrals to local EEOC offices. Provides information and answers questions about all areas of employees' rights, including information about policies on hiring, firing, unemployment, discrimination, and sexual harassment. Enforces numerous acts against discrimination, including Title VII of the Civil Rights Act of 1964, which prohibits discrimination on the basis of race, color, religion, sex, and national origin; the Pregnancy Discrimination Act; the Age Discrimination Act; the Equal Pay Act; and the Americans with Disabilities Act. They accept and investigate discrimination complaints. Conduct research and provide information about your rights. Publishes numerous materials on all areas of discrimination and how to file complaints, available for free upon request. Accepts and processes complaints against employers. Local EEOCs exist in every state and can provide you with more specific information and assistance.

AMERICAN CIVIL LIBERTIES UNION

132 WEST 43RD STREET
NEW YORK, NY 10036
(212) 944-9800

Provides legal and other assistance to individuals experiencing civil rights and/or economic discrimination. Conducts research to monitor civil rights legislation and violations. Publishes numerous materials about individual rights. As one of the oldest and largest civil rights organizations in the country, they can assist you in finding local branches and/or other organizations that can help.

Organizations for Specific Groups

The following organizations assist individuals and communities in responding to specific forms of discrimination. In addition, they organize on behalf of particular groups to raise awareness about and to reduce discrimination. In addition to the organizations listed below, numerous community organizations assist individuals experiencing discrimination, as well as working against discrimination. You may wish to contact national and/or local activist, political action organizations, community centers for referrals and/or assistance dealing with discrimination. Although, not directly in their scope, the following organizations should also be able to provide you with referrals to organizations that can address your specific needs.

spend less time responding to their questions, and offer them less praise.

AMERICAN-ARAB ANTI-DEFAMATION COMMITTEE
4201 CONNECTICUT AVENUE NW, SUITE 500
WASHINGTON, DC 20008
(202) 244-2990
Assists individuals and communities in responding to anti-Arab hate speech and discrimination. Publishes numerous materials and organizes political action/advocacy to raise awareness.

ANTI-DEFAMATION LEAGUE OF B'NAI B'RITH
823 UNITED NATIONS PLAZA
NEW YORK, NY 10017
(212) 490-2525
Assists individuals and communities in responding to anti-Semitic hate speech and discrimination. Publishes numerous materials and organizes political action to raise awareness about anti-Semitism. Organizes diversity training and awareness programs to reduce all forms of discrimination. Local offices exist throughout the country. In addition, provides referrals to other local organizations that can provide assistance.

HUMAN RIGHTS WATCH
WOMEN'S RIGHTS PROJECT
1522 K STREET NW, SUITE 910
WASHINGTON, DC 20005
(202) 371-6592
Assists individuals dealing with discrimination and documents discrimination and violence against women.

NATIONAL GAY LESBIAN TASK FORCE
1734 14TH STREET NW
WASHINGTON, DC 20009
(202) 323-6483
Organizes political action/advocacy to promote gay and lesbian rights, and works to raise awareness about discrimination against gays and lesbians. Provides assistance to individuals dealing with discrimination on the basis of sexual orientation, and makes referrals to local organizations that can provide additional help.

NOW LEGAL DEFENSE AND EDUCATION FUND
99 HUDSON STREET, 12TH FLOOR
NEW YORK, NY 10013
(212) 925-6635
Provides assistance to women dealing with sexual harassment and other forms of discrimination. Provides legal assistance, advice, and information about your rights. Publishes numerous materials about discrimination.

See the Resources at the end of "Community and Identity," page 553, for more organizations that deal with the issues and concerns of people of color.

Further Reading

ೲ

Get Smart: What You Should Know (But Won't Learn in Class) About Sexual Harassment and Discrimination, Montana Katz and Veronica Vieland (Feminist Press, 1993).

Back Off! How to Confront and Stop Sexual Harassment and Harassers, Martha J. Langelan (Fireside, 1993).

The Lecherous Professor: Sexual Harassment on Campus, Billie Wright Dziech and Linda Weiner (University of Illinois Press, 1990).

Ivory Power: Sexual Harassment on Campus, Michele A. Palindi (State University of New York, 1990).

The Rights of Students the Basic ACLU Guide to a Student's Rights, 3rd ed. Janet R. Price, Alan H. Levine, and Eve Cary (Southern Illinois University Press, 1988).

The Rights of Women: The Basic ACLU Guide to Women's Rights, Susan Deller Ross and Ann Barcher (Southern Illinois University Press, 1993).

In a '92 poll, ⅓ of women said they'd been harassed on the job.

Ending the Silence

WOMEN'S RESOURCE CENTER
BOWDOIN COLLEGE
24 COLLEGE STREET
BRUNSWICK, ME 04011

Violence Against Women

Only very recently has "violence against women" become a phrase we recognize and understand. Our culture and legal system are gradually beginning to acknowledge the phenomenon for what it almost always is: acts of violence committed against women because they are women. Crimes such as stranger rape, date rape, domestic violence, sexual assault, and stalking have at their core not only an individual's anger or a personal grudge, but also a basic presumption that a woman's life and body lack value. Acts such as these lie at one extreme end of a continuum that includes sexist remarks, sidewalk harassment, and workplace or classroom discrimination. (For more about these topics, see "Breaking Down Bias," page 463). This continuum has little to do with sexual desire or being frustrated, seduced, or horny; it's about attitudes toward women and abuse of power. Violence against women can affect you, even if it doesn't "happen" to you: It's what makes you not go the the gym because there's no one to walk with; it's what makes you leave a party after getting groped on your way to the keg; it's what makes you stop going to a class because your TA won't stop asking you out.

Certain power relationships and circumstances particular to college campuses may exacerbate and complicate incidents of violence against women. They can affect how, where, and why violence happens, and how, where, and whether or not it is reported and addressed. First, there's the social scene: drinking, partying, and the pressure to make friends, fit in, and go along. Then there's the academic scene: the professor you need a good grade from, the boss at the job you need to meet tuition costs. There's also the campus itself: late-night treks from the library, unlocked doors in laid-back dorms. And finally, there are the college disciplinary systems, formal and informal: the administration's interest in protecting its reputation, the varsity team's or the fraternity's interest in protecting its own.

Fortunately, however, universities have not escaped the recent tide of increased awareness about violence against women. Most college administrations and campus police have developed specific response policies; students have established peer hotlines and support groups. And most fundamentally, terms such as "date rape" and "stalking" are now widely used and accepted, allowing women to define their experiences both personally and legally.

WHAT FORMS CAN VIOLENCE AGAINST WOMEN TAKE?

Words and attitudes can be violent. People can cause hurt not only by raising their hand against someone else, but also by simply raising their voice continually or making negative comments. Such words and attitudes can damage a woman's self-esteem and emotional well-being as well as limit her physical freedom and her personal opportunities. (For a discussion of nonphysical harassment and discrimination, see "Breaking Down Bias," page 463.)

This chapter will define and discuss the acts as well as the threats of physical violence that affect women simply because they are women. "Physical assault" is a broad term that refers to such unsolicited physical contact as hitting, kicking, slapping, or punching. Physical assault can occur in all types of settings and among all types of people. But when women are the victims, physical assault often occurs within the context of sexual or sexualized violence, violence that's bred from the notions that men derive their power from their physical prowess and that women derive their value—or lack thereof—from their sexuality.

Abusive Relationships

Abuse can happen in any relationship—gay or straight, new or committed, romantic or platonic—and refers to one person's exertion of power to dominate, coerce, or control the other. The abuse is often physical, but may also be psychological, verbal, or economic (e.g., restricting a partner's access to work or money). It can take the form of jealousy and possessiveness, insults and threats, violence and rape.

A single incident of assault absolutely counts as abuse, but abuse in relationships tends to develop and perpetuate itself over time. Abusive relationships often cycle through periods of calm and reconciliation and periods of tension and violence. During the "good" times, it can be easy for the victim of violence to believe what she may very well want to believe: that her partner is truly sorry, that it wasn't as bad as all that, that he had just had a bad day, that he only did it because he loves her so much, that it won't happen again. Abusers may also say manipulative or hurtful things, such as "You're the only person I can talk to" or "I'll kill myself if you ever leave me," which may cause the victim to believe that the abuse is somehow her fault.

Causing a victim to believe abuse is her fault is part of the abuse itself. Abuse is never the victim's fault. But this characteristic of abusive relationships sheds light on one of the most

In the days following the murder of Nicole Brown Simpson,

complicated aspects of the situation: why women stay in such relationships. It's easy to ask: "Why doesn't she just leave?" Why can't she quit the job, drop the class, file formal charges, leave her boyfriend/girlfriend? But these questions don't have simple answers. A woman may be made to feel deserving of the abuse. She may have a family history that has led her to believe that abuse is normal. She may feel that since she's made a commitment, submitted to violence, or "let it happen" before, she no longer has the right to pick up and go. Her feelings of love and allegiance may get mixed up with her concerns about her family, grades, research project, or public image. Her abuser may control all her money; her abuser may watch her every move.

Seeking help can be particularly difficult for lesbians in abusive relationships. Not only are there fewer resources that address their specific needs, but they may be fearful about encountering homophobia if they go to the police or school officials. They may also be apprehensive that speaking out would serve to further stigmatize lesbians.

"*I was in a sexually abusive relationship as a freshman in college. I felt so alone that I stayed with the guy, thinking that if I made the relationship work, the rapes wouldn't be so terrible. He was an alcoholic and a heavy drug user—only after I got out of it did I realize I never had any control in the relationship.*"

—*GETTYSBURG COLLEGE, '94*

These justifications for staying are complex and human, but they are also misguided and dangerous. No matter how long a woman has been in such a relationship, no matter how sincerely an abuser insists on his or her love and commitment to change, no matter how deeply a victim believes that it's up to *her* to fix things, she can and should do whatever it takes to get out. There are people and organizations who will be there to help her right away and over time (see "Sources of Support," page 503). And specifically, if she is afraid that leaving will make her abuser violent—or more violent—she should consider taking out a restraining order (see the next page).

Getting Out of an Abusive Relationship

Many women feel stuck in abusive relationships because their abuser controls their money, because they don't know how they'll escape with the children, because his or her home is the only home they know. Though college women are perhaps less likely to find themselves in these particular circumstances, that doesn't mean it's easy for them to leave unhealthy relationships. In addition to the often universal feelings of self-blame or dependence, college women may have their own set of obstacles: "Can I leave him without leaving school?" "Domestic violence hotlines sound like they're for married women—do I qualify?" "If I hit him in self-defense, am I still entitled to help?"

In short, the process of convincing yourself to leave can be as difficult and scary as the act of leaving. The cycles of denial, dependence, and justification are profound and complicated, but ultimately, all you need to ask yourself is: Has s/he hit or threatened to hit me in the past? Has s/he been verbally abusive, controlling or domineering? The answer should probably be either yes or no; "Yes, but . . ." should send up a red flag. Don't make any excuses for your abuser or for yourself. If these questions give you pause but you don't feel capable of leaving, talk to someone who cares about you and trusts you. You do not have to "qualify" for a domestic violence hotline—or at least for a serious conversation with a friend, parent, counselor, RA, dean, or other faculty member. But if anyone tries to dismiss, downplay, or trivialize what you have to say, talk to someone else.

These guidelines should make the act of leaving safer and as definitive as possible:

Your safety comes first. If s/he hits you or threatens to hit you, try to get out immediately, even if—in fact, *especially* if—s/he threatens you or pleads with you. Get to a friend's room or a public place, or at least to a phone where you can call for help. Don't be afraid or embarrassed to call the campus or local police —or even to scream—just because s/he's not a stranger. You can ask the police to make an arrest, or just to protect you so that you

can leave. If you don't call the police, make sure that you have a safe place to stay where s/he can't find you, until you figure out what to do next. Don't stay anywhere alone.

The police are there to help you: If you do call the police, you are entitled to ask the police to arrest the abuser; if they refuse, you can make a "civilian arrest," in which case the police must help you take the person to the police station and fill out arrest forms. If the police try to dismiss an incident of violence as some sort of young lovers' spat, let them see you write down their names and badge numbers and let them know you'll be reporting them to a commanding officer, civilian review board, legislator, or district attorney. You can also go to the police to file a complaint or request an arrest at any time.

Save evidence. If you are visibly injured at any time, try to get someone to take color pictures. Save any torn or bloody clothing, broken objects, or threatening notes. You may need such evidence to get a restraining order or if you press charges.

Consider taking out a restraining order or order of protection. Requirements and procedures vary from state to state, but your state's family or criminal court should be able to issue an order requiring your abuser to stay away from you (and your children, if any). You may need to provide evidence (such as bruises or photographs of injuries) or witnesses. Call the court or a domestic violence hotline for details. It may also be possible to do the same through campus channels: Ask a dean or other faculty member for guidance. These orders do not mean that you are automatically safe, just that you can call the police or campus security to have an abuser arrested if s/he violates such an order.

Trust yourself. Our courts, our colleges, and our culture are only very gradually beginning to understand and accommodate issues of violence against women. Many people might still believe that young women, single women, lesbian women, successful and bright college women, "can't" be in abusive relationships. But abuse can happen to anyone, and misunderstanding can be its greatest perpetuator. If you feel threatened, uncomfortable, or are hurt, speak up and get out. Support will be there for you.

CHILD SEXUAL ABUSE, INCEST, AND OTHER FAMILY VIOLENCE

"I was sexually abused as a child (around 5–10 years old) by my sitter's son and came to this realization last year. Since then I have been trying to get myself refocused with the help of my friends and my journal. It was molestation, but not as 'bad' as some other stories that I have encountered. Since [my realization] only happened last year, thoughts, ideas, and feelings are still fresh in my mind.... I am very proud of my survival and am successfully finding ways in which what happened has caused my life to change for the better."

—COLUMBIA UNIVERSITY, '96

Child sexual abuse is any sexual behavior, with or without actual physical contact, imposed on a child. Children may be abused by parents, stepparents, uncles, aunts, siblings, grandparents, neighbors, family friends, baby-sitters, doctors, clergy, therapists, teachers, and strangers. "Incest" is sexual abuse by a family member or a trusted individual who is considered "part of the family." All forms of child sexual abuse can result in emotional and/or physical trauma.

One of the most difficult aspects of child sexual abuse and incest is that although these experiences may have happened in childhood, they may still affect the lives of women and men, consciously and subconsciously, years after the abuse. Survivors of childhood abuse may remember everything or nothing that happened, or they may begin to remember what happened only gradually and sporadically. If you know or believe you were sexually abused as a child—especially if you haven't already gotten support—the pressures of adjusting to and getting through college can be acute; painful memories can be triggered in unexpected ways.

If you have experienced childhood abuse, incest, or other family abuse but have not fully resolved the issue for yourself, it is important to find support and people to talk with. If the abuse is ongoing, you should take the same steps as dealing with any other type of sexual assault. (See "Sources of Support," page 503.)

SEXUAL ASSAULT

"Sexual assault" includes rape, child sexual abuse, incest, and other sexual acts that are physical and nonconsensual, forced, manipulated, and/or coerced. Specific acts of sexual assault can take such forms as unwanted touching of one's intimate parts, such as a sexual organ, buttocks, or breasts; forced kissing; or bodily penetration. Strictly speaking, such actions are illegal. However, one of the most complicated aspects of sexual violence is understanding how the same acts (such as making out, intercourse, oral sex, or anal sex) that we may consent to and enjoy in one context become violating and offensive in another—and where and when that line gets crossed. (See "What Is Consent?" on the facing page.)

RAPE

Legal definitions of rape vary from state to state. In general though, rape is defined as nonconsensual forced penile penetration of the vagina. Some definitions include penetration by fingers or other foreign objects. Other definitions include anal or oral penetration or they may be called sexual abuse or sodomy. An act is "nonconsensual" when a person does not consent to it or is unable to consent (because she is drunk, unconscious, or otherwise incapacitated). Types of force may include verbal coercion, physical violence and/or intimidation, and threats (verbal and/or physical).

Acquaintance Rape

Statistics indicate that "stranger rape"—rape by an unknown assailant (our most familiar image of a rapist)—constitutes only 15 percent of all reported rapes. On the other hand, "acquaintance" or "date" rape, in which the victim knows her rapist, constitutes 85 percent of reported rapes.

Campus statistics are even more dramatic: About 90 percent of college rape victims know their attackers, and 57 percent of them are attacked by dates. Four out of five campus sexual assaults are committed by students.

Though acquaintance rape is much more common than stranger rape, it can also be much more difficult to identify, resolve, and prosecute, especially on campus. Many acquaintance rapes occur on dates or between people who are in a relationship, whether new or established. This type of rape, then, violates not only a woman's body, but also her trust—of her date and of her own judgment: "He's a nice guy—how could he be a rapist?" "I should have known better than to get so trashed at a fraternity party." Her perspective on what happened may be obscured: "I consented up to a point—when did it become rape?" "I said no this time, but I'd said yes before—is that rape?" (see "What Is Consent?" on the facing page). Her knowing that he is around campus may make it tough to speak up: "Our groups of friends overlap—how will they react?" "If I say something is he going to bad mouth me to the whole squash team, his frat, and everyone else he knows?" "What if I run into him in the student center?"

The above questions are hard to

☼ *Nearly ⅓ of female homicide victims are killed by their husbands or boy-*

RACIAL AND ETHNIC STEREOTYPES AND SEXUAL ASSAULT

Racist and sexist rape myths stereotype women of color and Jewish women in ways that can, directly or indirectly, justify sexual assault of them. African-American women may be seen as "easy" and wild, Latin women as passionate and flirtatious, Asian women as mysterious and submissive, Jewish women as frigid and domineering. This stereotyping by race and/or ethnicity can compound the obstacles to reporting and coping with rape. It can make some women more vulnerable to rape and less "credible" as victims and it can increase the trauma of those who are assaulted. Women of color may avoid reporting an attack for fear that the police, the courts, the media, the administration, or even family members won't believe them. A woman may have absorbed or "internalized" the stereotypes to the point where she is not even sure what happened was rape. Rape survivors of color should make sure to consult someone with a particular sensitivity to racial identity and sexual assault.

answer for both individuals and institutions. Just as the issue of acquaintance rape itself is still murky, so in many cases are official campus policies for addressing it. On many campuses the same judicial boards originally established to adjudicate cases of plagiarism and honor code violations now step in to settle allegations of rape—with little understanding of the crime and great interest in keeping such cases out of the hands of public authorities. (For more on campus judicial procedures, see "Reporting and Prosecuting," page 505.)

Colleges are, however, offering more and more support services for all kinds of rape and sexual assault; anyone who is raped or otherwise assaulted, even if she opts not to press formal charges, should to talk to someone trained in or sympathetic to the issue and its resonance on campus. (See "Sources of Support," page 503.)

WHAT IS CONSENT?

The precise legal definition of "consent" (to a sexual act) is central to the understanding, prevention, and prosecution of rape and sexual assault. But the legal definition is not consistent from state to state—and neither is the way we and others define consent from situation to situation.

Many states classify rape as any situation in which a victim does not give consent or is incapable of consent because she is unconscious or asleep; unable to communicate; inebriated; or physically helpless. When stranger rapes are investigated or prosecuted—and/or when a victim is visibly injured—the issue of consent is not usually called into question. Lawyers defending alleged acquaintance rapists, on the other hand, often distort the issue by invoking myths about women and their sexual behavior: They may assert that a defendant assumed that the sur-

friends. ✺ In 1990-91, the number of reported rapes rose by 59%. ✺

WHY DO FRATERNITIES GET SUCH A BAD RAP?

We all know that not every fraternity is Animal House and not every Greek brother is a date rapist who plies his date with spiked punch. But by and large, the statistics about fraternities and sexual assault support some of these stereotypes. Studies have shown that a disproportionate number of campus sexual assaults are committed at fraternity houses and by fraternity members. A 1989 study by the University of Illinois at Urbana-Champaign, for example, found that fraternity members were responsible for 63 percent of the sexual assaults on that campus. The problem is especially pronounced on campuses where most or all of the drinking takes place at the Greek houses, and/or where the houses are off campus.

What is it about fraternities that gives us these skewed numbers? Despite the fact that plenty of Greek brothers are good guys and plenty of fraternities are assets to their communities, traditional fraternity culture tends to demean women. Notions of brotherhood, masculinity, and loyalty are sometimes twisted into principles of male superiority that exclude and degrade women. At its worst, this spawns "rituals" such as "rude-hoggering" (hooking up with the "ugliest" woman at the party), "bagging" (cornering and flashing a woman), and systematic, calculated rape and gang rape (proving each member is as "man" as the next).

All too often, women who are sexually assaulted by frat members don't report it. They may feel they should have known better; they may not remember the details because they were drunk; they may not be able to face the conflict with the perpetrator and *all* his brothers; they may doubt that the college would ever discipline its prized athletic recruits.

Fortunately, many fraternities have begun to make changes: Some frats have banned alcohol; some have outlawed "hazing"; some local and national chapters have gone coed; some require rape awareness training in their initiation; some have trained peer counselors to keep an eye out for trouble at parties.

Unfortunately, women still need to keep an eye out, too. If you're new on the party scene, find out the word on the frats: Which are the notorious houses; who are the notorious scammers, etc. If you feel like you're being hit on hastily and insistently, get your antennae up. You and a friend might even want to consider developing some sort of system of checking in with one another.

It's a real pain to feel as if we have to take special precautions or need special protection. But like it or not, common street smarts can be crucial. When your personal safety may be up against institutionalized abuse of women—followed, perhaps, by institutionalized slaps on the wrist—the stakes are really pretty high.

☼ Male attackers are viewed as less responsible for a rape if they were

vivor's miniskirt, dirty dancing, writing sexual fantasies in a journal, drinking, going to the rapist's room, kissing—or even saying no—meant yes.

While the question of consent can be intentionally misrepresented, it can also be legitimately misunderstood. What sexual activities we want and don't want vary among different settings and different people. How we convey our own consent or read our partner's can be complicated, subtle, and ambiguous. One way to ensure mutual understanding is to "check in" with your partner as you go, listening carefully for either agreement or discomfort and asking him or her to do

> "People need to know that though states define consent, it is up to a jury to determine if consent was indeed given. In some cases, if someone doesn't kick and scream, it is considered consent. In other cases, like at Antioch College [which has a very explicit consent policy that its students are required to follow] partners must clearly agree on what's going to happen and what's not. In a well-publicized court case it was determined that if a woman convinces a rapist to wear a condom it does not mean that she consented. But in too many cases, if a woman wasn't bruised and bloody, or if she wore sexy clothing, then consent was implicitly given."
>
> —TEMPLE UNIVERSITY, '96

the same. Of course, signals may be missed or misinterpreted, and some people might feel uncomfortable about communicating directly and asserting what they want. There are no easy answers: The best you can do is trust yourself and your instincts.

You may also want to find out about campus rape and consent policies: Call your dean's office, the campus rape crisis center, and/or women's center for more information.

WHAT TO DO IF YOU'VE BEEN ASSAULTED

An experience of assault can be not only frightening, but also complicated and confusing. You will certainly have some decisions to make—about seeking support, about pressing charges, about making sense of what happened. But don't let the emotional and legal questions stand in the way of the first order of business: making sure you are physically safe. Only when you're safe should you even begin to consider what's next.

Immediate Steps

If you have just been raped or otherwise assaulted:

■ **Get to a safe place.** If you can at least get to a phone, call 911, a friend, campus security, the campus health services, campus sexual assault hotline, the police, or an area rape crisis center (if you dial "411," the operator should be able to put you in touch with the last). *Note:* Calling the police for help initially does not commit you to make a signed statement.

■ **Get support.** Even if you are already safe, call a friend, a family member, or a rape crisis center volunteer who can talk or be with you through your next steps. (For more about seeking support, see page 503.)

■ **Resist the urge to shower or change clothes.** Even if you haven't decided whether or not to go to the police, you should take steps to preserve evidence in case you do need it. Do not shower or change clothes; in a case of forced oral sex, do not eat, drink, or rinse your mouth out. If you do change clothes, put what you were wearing in a paper bag (because plastic doesn't "breathe" it can spoil the evidence).

■ **Consider getting medical attention.** Many sexual assault survivors feel that going to the hospital—being poked and prodded, reliving the event—is the last thing they'd want to do. Date rape survivors may believe that what happened is not "real" rape and therefore that they don't deserve "real" medical treatment. But you should think very seriously about going to a nearby emergency room: There, hospital staff can check for injuries that you may be unaware of, counsel you about and test you for possible sexually transmitted diseases, and discuss pregnancy prevention options. They can also collect evidence that may be crucial if you do file charges. Hospitals will not automatically alert the police about the rape. If you talk to a rape crisis center, ask if there's a hospital they

recommend, if they can call ahead for you, and if they can send an "advocate" to be with you if you're alone (hospitals may also provide this service). Keep in mind that you may also ask to be examined by a female doctor.

■ **Do not deny yourself treatment because you think you can't pay.** Your health insurance policy may or may not cover an emergency room visit, but you cannot be denied care, even if you can't pay. Also, if your state has a victims' compensation law, you may be entitled to reimbursement for medical

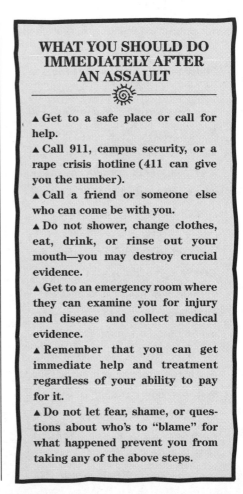

WHAT YOU SHOULD DO IMMEDIATELY AFTER AN ASSAULT

▲ **Get to a safe place or call for help.**

▲ **Call 911, campus security, or a rape crisis hotline (411 can give you the number).**

▲ **Call a friend or someone else who can come be with you.**

▲ **Do not shower, change clothes, eat, drink, or rinse out your mouth—you may destroy crucial evidence.**

▲ **Get to an emergency room where they can examine you for injury and disease and collect medical evidence.**

▲ **Remember that you can get immediate help and treatment regardless of your ability to pay for it.**

▲ **Do not let fear, shame, or questions about who's to "blame" for what happened prevent you from taking any of the above steps.**

 By some estimates, 1 in 4 women will be attacked by a rapist

and/or counseling costs. A rape crisis or state victim services hotline would know the details; in New York, for example, you can apply for compensation from the state Crime Victims' Board only if you have reported the assault to the police. By the same token, coverage of your medical costs by school insurance may require that you contact health services immediately or soon after the attack.

What Will Happen in the Emergency Room—and Why It's Important to Go

❧❧❧

You may look and feel physically fine, and you may want more than anything to just go home, shower, and go to bed. But going to the hospital will ensure not only that you are physically OK, but also that the police will have the evidence they'll need to pursue an investigation. (Even if you think you won't prosecute, it's advisable to have the evidence collected while you can.)

Any hospital can take care of a sexual assault victim, but some hospitals are specially equipped with evidence collection kits, private examining rooms, and/or personnel specifically trained to handle the medical and psychological needs of survivors of sexual assault. If you have the time and the presence of mind, check with a rape crisis center before you go to see which hospital they might recommend. In general:

■ A hospital that provides sexual assault survivor advocates should have one there for you soon after you register (or possibly earlier, if someone called ahead). The advocate should guide you through the process in the emergency room. If there's no one to be with you, call a friend or a rape crisis center who should have trained advocates available to you.

■ You will need to fill out various forms. You will probably be asked about medical insurance, but in any case, you cannot be denied care. Your school health plan, if you're on it, should cover your exam.

■ Medical personnel will ask you about the assault before doing a physical exam. It's very important that you explain exactly what happened. They are not there to judge you, but to treat and help you, and they need all the information they request. What you say will be kept confidential.

■ The medical examination is both external and internal. Following a general exam, the doctor will perform a pelvic exam almost identical to the routine exam you would have at the gynecologist's. If it's your first pelvic exam, be sure to tell the doctor.

■ Many hospitals have rape evidence collection kits that take doctors through a process of collecting evidence such as semen, hair, and material from under a victim's fingernails. In any case, make sure—or have your advocate or friend make sure—that such evidence is being looked for and noted, even if you don't yet know if you'll make a signed statement.

■ Emergency rooms can be confusing and chaotic places. Not even the most well-meaning, sensitive practitioner can know what you need to feel comfortable. If something hurts or bothers you, say something.

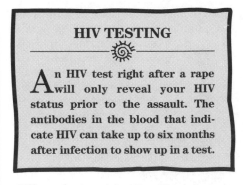

HIV TESTING

An HIV test right after a rape will only reveal your HIV status prior to the assault. The antibodies in the blood that indicate HIV can take up to six months after infection to show up in a test.

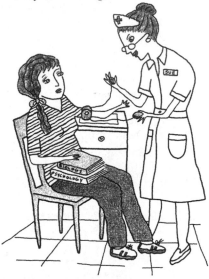

EMOTIONAL AND PSYCHOLOGICAL REACTIONS

Healing is an intensely personal process. It is spiritual, emotional, intellectual, and physical. In the short and long terms, healing can involve working through issues of fear, betrayal, trust, anger, guilt, shame, loneliness, isolation, body image, sexuality, suicide, depression, and strength. It doesn't necessarily follow a direct or logical route; there is no "right" or "normal" way to respond to a rape or assault. Everyone responds differently to crisis situations; no one can predict what her own reactions might be. You might talk constantly or sit silently, feel frightened or feel angry, want to be with someone or want to be left alone—or all of the above in quick succession. The important thing is to allow yourself your reactions without criticizing or second-guessing them. They are all normal. But if you're scared, lonely, or desperate, call a friend or hotline.

One very typical reaction is to blame oneself for what happened: "I should have known better than to walk there." "Maybe everyone but me knew that going to someone's formal means you have sex with him afterward." "Did my dress send the wrong message?" But no dark alley, romantic date, or tight dress is an excuse for rape. It was not your fault. You may not really believe that right away, but don't let feelings of self-blame cause you to feel undeserving of medical care or personal support. Figure out what you need *now* and get it—there will be time later to sort out the rest.

Over time, many sexual assault survivors find themselves unable to concentrate, paralyzed by fear, constantly anxious, getting bad grades, wanting or deciding to leave school. All of these responses are normal. The effects can be lessened by getting professional help and being around supportive people.

Many women find it difficult to feel comfortable in even the safest, most comfortable and loving intimate relationships for a long time after an experience of sexual assault. (See the box below.)

Sources of Support

༄༄༄

Because the issue of sexual assault is so fraught with misunderstanding, confiding in someone else about it is not a straightforward, simple prospect. How you perceive yourself or others after an experience of assault may depend on your communities, background, and beliefs. You may

wonder: "What if they think I'm over-reacting?" "What if they tell me I was stupid to be in that situation in the first place?" "How can I burden someone with this during midterms?" "He told me he'd make my life hell if I told anyone—what am I supposed to do?"

If you feel you can't tell a friend or family member, there are plenty of other sources of support to fall back on. It's important to talk to someone so that you can maintain perspective and avoid feeling isolated. Here are some possible resources:

■ **A resident advisor or dorm counselor.** RAs should be trained in offering personal support as well as advice on avenues of disciplinary action.

■ **A campus or local rape crisis hotline.** The number should be listed in

---

BEING SEXUAL AFTER AN EXPERIENCE OF SEXUAL ASSAULT

An abusive sexual experience can have a profound effect on your sexuality. It can effect your ability to trust, making it difficult to feel safe and comfortable with a partner. You may not want to be touched in ways that remind you of the assault. There may be times when you feel separated from your body during sex, or you might experience flashbacks. And because sexual abuse carries a negative stigma, it can be hard to talk about it. You may be embarrassed or blame yourself, and be afraid of how others would perceive you if they knew that you'd been abused.

Talking with your partner can

help. It also may be useful to find a therapist who can help you work through your pain and fears. For information on how to find someone to talk to, see "Finding a Therapist or Group," page 261.

"I have a male lover who was sexually abused as a child. We have talked about it and I know he's not always comfortable being sexual. I try to be aware of what he wants because I know he is used to being forced as a child and I don't want him to do anything he doesn't want with me."
—*WAYNE STATE COLLEGE, '95*

---

mit rape if they were certain they wouldn't get caught.

HOW TO RESPOND WHEN A FRIEND TELLS YOU SHE'S BEEN ASSAULTED

When a friend confides in you about an experience of sexual assault, it's hard to know what to do. Use these guidelines as suggestions, but don't worry about "getting it right" to the point where you're not even listening. The most important thing is to let her know you're there and you care. You can always refer her to someone who's professionally trained to tackle legal questions and psychological issues. However, if you truly feel that for some reason of your own you are unable to support her, you should at least help her find someone else to talk to. Otherwise:

▲ LISTEN, LISTEN, LISTEN. Let her tell you what happened in her own words and at her own pace. Try not to interrupt and interject your own stories or comments. Also, don't start trying to figure out "what to do" right away. Just listen.

▲ DON'T QUESTION THE STORY'S VALIDITY. Even if the story sounds strange or hard to believe, just let it go and keep listening. Things like "I can't imagine him doing something like that; he's usually such a nice guy" can be frustrating to hear and make it hard for your friend to keep her grasp on what happened.

▲ DON'T BLAME HER. Don't assert or even imply that your friend was somehow responsible for what happened. If she seems to be blaming herself, hear her out and listen to how she feels, but let her know that the victim of an attack is never responsible for it. Give her time and don't browbeat her; she may not be willing to believe this right away.

▲ DON'T TELL HER NOT TO BE UPSET. It's pointless, and may sound to her like you're trivializing her feelings and what happened to her.

▲ ASK HER WHAT SHE NEEDS. Does she want you just to listen? Or does she want advice or some other kind of help from you? Don't make assumptions or try to read her signals, no matter how well you know her.

▲ SUPPORT HER in getting the medical and psychological attention she needs. You can't force her to go to a doctor or counselor if she doesn't want to, but you could at least let her know what the advantages might be so that she is able to decide for herself.

▲ MAKE SURE SHE'S SAFE. Talk to campus security or the police if you have reason to believe that her attacker still poses a threat. Otherwise, just make sure she's physically secure.

If your friend's experience of sexual assault was in her past, and you aren't able to give the support she needs, there are plenty of places to go and people she can speak with. See the Resources at the end of this chapter, and the information in "A Friend in Need," page 327, and "Finding a Therapist or Group," page 261.

☼ About a quarter of boys aged 13-15 think it's OK for a

the phone book or with information. You can call anonymously, with specific questions, or just to talk about how you're feeling.

■ **A medical doctor.** Physical problems can arise as a direct or indirect result of assault. Stress and anxiety can cause physical symptoms, and a doctor may be helpful. A rape crisis hotline may be able to recommend a doctor sympathetic to the problems particular to sexual assault.

■ **A support group.** A hotline or women's center may be able to recommend a support group for survivors of sexual assault. Such groups may not provide formal therapy; what they usually offer is a safe space to talk and be with people who are going through the same things.

■ **A therapist.** You may feel that your healing process demands professional attention. In this case, you might want to ask a rape crisis center to refer you to a therapist who has experience working with women who've been assaulted or abused. You may have several options: a one-time meeting versus ongoing care, individual or group therapy. Depending on the circumstances and state laws, you may be eligible for reimbursement of counseling costs—check with a rape crisis or victims' services hotline.

REPORTING AND PROSECUTING

For some women, taking legal action against an identified rapist or attacker is a given, part of a need for personal and/or public justice. However, only 5 percent of college women rape survivors even report the crime to the police, and only 1 percent of male students who rape are prosecuted. Some women don't report the crime because they're not sure they were "really" raped; some let it go because they prefer to leave the incident behind them.

Still other survivors may want to take some sort of action but are afraid to. They've heard stories about accusers being dismissed, harassed, or threatened; about victims forced to expose and defend their sex lives on the witness stand; about codes of silence that impede investigations and protect perpetrators. This final concern is often a reality on campuses. Despite the growing number of peer counseling services, Take Back the Night marches, and sexual harassment awareness campaigns, when it comes to decisive discipline, colleges often remain unwilling to take action.

A university's first course of action is often to meet with the survivor to explain the advantages of settling the case through the university's own disciplinary system. Taking this

> "'Rape' is a strong word that did not apply to my case. When I was looking for help I was insecure because I felt I had to be raped in order for the system to help me. I didn't feel like I could call the rape crisis hotlines or rape crisis centers because I was 'only' assaulted. (I was wrong.)"
>
> —UNIVERSITY OF ROCHESTER, '90

man to rape his date "if he spent a lot of money on her." 🌀

"Schools like mine don't release all of the correct statistics. For example, my school stated in the campus guide to safety that from August 1991 to December 1992 there were no sexual assaults reported to campus security. The guide stated that zero 'forcible and non-forcible' rapes were reported, even though I spoke with a woman who logged a report herself."

—GUILFORD COLLEGE, '97

route can amount to a university board—often made up of faculty, staff, and students originally convened to handle plagiarism and the like—trying and sentencing an alleged felony; legal experts say that this maneuver may constitute a violation of a victim's right to due process. On many campuses, "convicted" rapists are suspended or put on probation rather than kicked out or prosecuted (which means that survivors might run into their attackers on campus). They are eventually awarded their diplomas, while their victims may have left school to put their lives back together.

Even those women who are brave enough to try to press charges with local authorities may not get very far, despite the fact that the Campus Sexual Assault Victims' Bill of Rights grants survivors the right to ask off-campus authorities to investigate on-campus sexual assaults. Some legal experts, citing examples of plea bargaining that resulted only in misdemeanor charges and probation—and still spotless records—suggest that connections between campus officials

CAMPUS HIGHLIGHT

In 1991, students at Columbia University in New York City, frustrated by the lack of a formal policy about sexual assault and inadequate services for survivors of sexual assault and other kinds of violence, petitioned the University Senate for the creation of a student-run, on-campus rape crisis center. In February of 1992, "the RCC" opened to provide assistance to male and female survivors of sexual, physical, and emotional violence and those who care about them. The 20 to 30 active volunteers offer in-person and phone crisis counseling and referrals to places that provide therapy, legal, advocacy, and medical services, and to activist groups that do work around issues of violence against women.

and local DAs' offices make prosecutors unwilling to take on such cases.

If you feel intimidated by all this, that's exactly the point. These impasses, wrist-slaps, plea bargains, and spotless records have the effect—if not the intention—of scaring women away from rocking the boat. If you're up to it, this system would be quite an important one to take on. If you're not up to it, at least not yet, that's fine, too. Your job is to respond to and recover from rape in the way that you think is best for you. So there's no "right" plan of action, but there are some things you should keep in mind as you think about what to do.

Submitting a signed statement. Calling the police does not require you to submit a signed statement officially reporting the incident. However, in order for the police to do their job—pursue a formal investigation (which could lead to the state pressing charges against the rapist)—they will need a signed statement from you. And so they understandably will urge you to give one. Before you do, find out what it will mean with regard to your obligation to testify later. An advocate should be a good source of information about the pros and cons of submitting a statement. (There is also the option of the unsigned statement. Although the police don't like it, it allows a record to be kept on file in case the person is ever accused of a crime again.)

Some local and campus police departments now have "sensitive" crime units with officers specially

IMPORTANT LEGISLATION

THE STUDENT RIGHT TO KNOW AND CAMPUS SECURITY ACT of 1990 and the subsequent Higher Education Amendments of 1992 put into effect new requirements for preventing, reporting, and prosecuting sex crimes on campus. The act requires all colleges and universities that receive federal funding to compile and make available statistics on rape and other crimes on campus. In addition, policies, disciplinary consequences, and resources about sexual harassment and assault, and information about school security measures and awareness programs to prevent it must also be readily available. The act also requires that survivors be given assistance in changing living arrangements and academic requirements to protect them from having to live near or go to class with the accused.

This law prohibits universities from downplaying or hiding occurrences of violence and crime on campus. However, officials have many ways to circumvent reporting acts of crime on campus in order to preserve their school's reputation. For example, some schools have been known to count only those rapes reported to have occurred in dormitories. Check with your school's office of public information to make sure that data is being collected—if it's not, or if the numbers seem iffy, talk with the campus women's center or another group about challenging them.

THE VIOLENCE AGAINST WOMEN ACT, passed in May 1993, authorized $65 million for courses in public junior high schools on the prevention of rape. Additional money was granted for college classes. The act also provides monetary restitution for survivors of sex crimes; new federal penalties for spouse abusers who cross state lines; a national task force to combat violence against women; doubling sentences for perpetrators of rape; and grants to states to improve safety for women in streets, parks, and public transit.

"dressing provocatively" cannot be used as defense for sexual assault.

trained to deal with the particular physical and emotional circumstances of sexual assault cases and survivors. You may also be able to fill out your report with a female responding officer if you wish. Finally, going through the police is also a way of making sure the crime is officially registered and recognized.

Find out what your options are. If you were assaulted on campus or by a member of the college community, ask a trusted RA, dean, or other faculty member about school disciplinary procedures—and how effective they've been in the past. Have they ever handled a case of sexual assault? What was the result? (See page 481 for information about filing a formal complaint on campus.)

Campus grievance committees cannot convict someone of a crime—only the courts can do that. If you want to prosecute the case in civil or criminal court (off campus)—usually your only option for legal recourse if the perpetrator wasn't a student, faculty or staff member, or otherwise affiliated with the school—get in touch with local groups that work on issues of violence against women. They can give you information about policies and procedures specific to your state, tips and tricks for navigating the legal system, help finding a lawyer, and support during the trial. See the Resources at the end of this chapter and at the end of "Breaking Down Bias," page 488. Also see page 484 for more information about taking legal action outside the college.

You can change your mind. Find out about your state's statute of limitations for prosecuting sex crimes (for example, it's five years in New York).

If you think you might ever decide to prosecute, make sure the evidence is/was in order at the hospital (see page 501).

If you don't take formal action, make sure you have some other means of dealing with what happened. For some rape survivors, prosecuting their attacker is a matter not only of public safety but also of personal healing. But again, if you decide not to pursue an investigation or prosecution, consider engaging in another activity—counseling, a support group, volunteer work—that will help you feel like you're back in charge. Often after the initial impact of a violent experience has subsided, more subtle and unconscious effects arise.

Try to make sure that the crime is counted. Even if you are not planning to submit a statement, you should file an anonymous report with local and/or campus police so that they include your attack in their statistics on crime. Call them or a sexual assault survivor's advocacy group to find out how to do this.

You can also write a letter (anonymously if you wish) to the local or campus paper to make sure people know what happened and, where appropriate, suggesting courses of action: Does a sidewalk need to be better lit? Are students leaving dorm doors open carelessly? Should women consider buddying up at parties? If you're moved to even more direct action, talk to the campus women's center (or a group of supportive friends) about putting together a mini- (or maxi-) awareness campaign: posting signs where the attack occurred, organizing a speak-out, lobbying the university for new streetlights.

☼ 98% of rape survivors never see the arrest or prosecu-

If the sexual assault was perpetratrated by another student or by a college employee and you want to bring disciplinary action against the person, you can file a complaint and request a hearing. See "Taking Formal Action," page 481.

ACTIVIST IDEAS

■ Raise awareness about the prevalence of violence against women at college and in the community and empower women to stand up against violence by organizing an annual Take Back the Night event. It can be as simple as holding a march, with placards and flyers containing statistics about rape and assault, names and numbers of resources for victims of violent crime, and slogans of the "Women Unite, Take Back the Night" and "We Demand Safe Streets and Freedom from Violence" ilk or it can include rallies and speak-outs, where survivors of assault can share their stories. There should be trained counselors present to help survivors deal with the strong feelings and painful memories that inevitably arise.

■ Create a pamphlet that lists basic facts about sexual assault, campus policies, and names and numbers of local resources that can provide emotional, medical, educational, and legal services. Post them in campus buildings, laminate them and put them up near outdoor public phones, and distribute them by leaving piles in baskets in heavy traffic areas, sending them through campus mail, including them in first year orientation packets, and asking RAs to hand them out to residents.

■ Help survivors of rape and sexual assault get the support and assistance they need. Volunteer in a local rape crisis center or battered women's shelter. Staff a sexual assault hotline. Support women on campus filing charges against their assailants. Donate food, toiletries, clothing, toys, and cooking utensils to a battered women's shelter.

■ Join or start an "advocate program" where volunteers accompany rape survivors to the hospital right after assault. Local rape crisis centers, emer gency rooms, the police, and/or cam pus security will receive a list of volunteers who are "on-call" for the evening to be notified if assistance is needed. Arrange for people involved with rape awareness and advocacy, crisis counseling, health care, and law enforcement officers to provide training to volunteers.

■ Bring the clothesline to your campus. Contact the National Network Office of the Clothesline Project (P.O. Box 822, Brewster, MA 02631, (508) 385-7004) about starting a "survivor clothesline" on campus. Women bring in shirts for themselves or other survivors of sexual or domestic violence and they are displayed on a clothesline. The display serves as a symbol of strength and solidarity of survivors and provides a tangible demonstration of the number of women whose lives are impacted by sexual violence.

tion of their attackers; only 2% of rapes ever go to trial.

RESOURCES

Most of the organizations/hotlines that use the terms "rape," and/or "domestic violence" also serve women dealing with all forms of sexual and physical assault and are generally good places to find referrals.

To find your local rape crisis/domestic violence hotlines: Dial 911, 411, or your operator and they should be able to connect you. Most centers/crisis lines are listed in the phone book under "Rape Crisis," "Domestic Violence," "Suicide Intervention," or "Crisis Counseling."

In addition, local women's centers and/or your local hospital are often good places to find assistance or referrals to organizations that can help. And many schools have their own or affiliated rape crisis centers and should be able to provide you with help.

Hotlines

All of the following hotlines will maintain confidentiality and if, for any reason, they need to call you back, they will be discreet.

RAPE, ABUSE, AND INCEST NATIONAL
    NETWORK (RAIN)
252 10TH STREET NE
WASHINGTON, DC 20002
(202) 544-1034
FAX: (202) 595-1401
HOTLINE: (800) 656-4673 [HOPE]
This 24-hour hotline automatically connects you to the rape/sexual assault/domestic violence hotline nearest to you. In some cases you will speak first with an answering service, which will take your first name only and contact a counselor

who will respond to your call immediately.

The counselors can make local referrals to address such issues as legal assistance, support groups, or immediate medical/counseling needs.

CHILD HELP, USA
6463 INDEPENDENCE AVENUE
WOODLAND HILLS, CA 91367
(800) 422-4453/(800) 4 [A-CHILD]
This 24-hour hotline provides crisis intervention and counseling. Can advise you about your legal rights. Makes local referrals to organizations that deal with child and/or sexual abuse, and other forms of assault. Publishes numerous materials on sexual and physical abuse, including national statistics, information about individual's rights, and abuse prevention available upon request.

SEXUAL ASSAULT VICTIMS HOTLINE
1520 EIGHTH AVENUE
MERIDAN, MISSISSIPPI 39302
(800) 643-6250
This 24-hour hotline provides counseling and referrals to local rape crisis centers and organizations that provide assistance to individuals dealing with sexual assault.

NATIONAL ORGANIZATION FOR VICTIMS
    ASSISTANCE (NOVA)
1757 PARK ROAD NW
WASHINGTON, DC 20010
(800) 879-6682 [TRY-NOVA]
(202) 232-6682
FAX: (202) 462-2255
24-hour hotline provides crisis counseling, information about your options and rights, and referrals to organizations that address issues such as domestic violence, child abuse, and sexual assault. Makes referrals to local organizations. Publishes materials

on prevention and response to violent crime. Maintains a speakers bureau, library, and clearinghouse on federal and state legislation.

NATIONAL VICTIM CENTER
2111 WILSON BOULEVARD, SUITE 300
ARLINGTON, VA 22201
(800) 394-2255 [FYI-CALL] (REFERRALS 9–5)
(703) 276-2880 (MAIN OFFICE)
Provides information to crime victims. Makes referrals to local organizations. Publishes materials on such issues as rape, gang violence, and domestic violence.

Political Action Groups

NATIONAL COALITION AGAINST DOMESTIC VIOLENCE (NCADV)
P.O. BOX 34103
WASHINGTON, DC 20043-4103
(202) 638-6388
OR
P.O. BOX 18749
DENVER, CO 80218
(303) 839-1852
A national organization with affiliates in every state. Makes referrals to local and state coalitions against domestic violence, as well as to local counseling and advocacy organizations. Organizes political action to prevent and end violence and to improve federal legislation. Provides information, statistics about violence against women. Runs projects on related forms of violence and discrimination such as racism and homophobia.

NATIONAL COALITION AGAINST SEXUAL ASSAULT
912 NORTH SECOND STREET
HARRISBURG, PA 12102
(717) 232-7460
Has local rape crisis center affiliates throughout the country. Organizes political action and awareness education to prevent and end sexual violence, and makes refer-

rals to organizations that provide services to survivors. Publishes numerous materials on topics such as child sexual abuse, acquaintance rape, and sexual harassment.

Further Reading
ꙮꙮꙮ

The Courage to Heal: A Guide for Women Survivors of Sexual Abuse, Ellen Bass and Laura Davis (Harper & Row, 1988).

Quest for Respect: A Healing Guide for Survivors of Rape, Linda Braswell (Pathfinder, 1992).

If You Are Raped, Kathryn M. Johnson (Learning Publications, 1992).

Everything You Need to Know About Date Rape, rev. edition, Frances Shuker-Haines (Rosen, 1992).

Acquaintance Rape: The Hidden Crime, Andrea Parrot and Laurie Bechhofer, eds. (Wiley, 1991).

Surviving Sexual Violence, Liz Kelly (University of Minnesota Press, 1989).

Sexual Assault: How to Defend Yourself, Dan Lena and Marie Howard (Lifetime, 1990).

Violent Betrayal: Partner Abuse in Lesbian Relationships, Claire M. Renzetti (Sage, 1992).

Do Tell Someone! Inner Turmoils Surrounding Sexual Abuse Victims, Yvonnia M. Houston (Shane, 1992).

Safety First

At Home & on the Go

The world isn't as harsh and cruel as big-screen bloodbaths might lead you to believe, but it's not like Dorothy's Kansas, either. So no matter what else is on your mind—your history final, spring break, auditioning for the orchestra or finishing that term paper—save a little corner of it to look out for your personal safety.

Even the most Edenic of college campuses can be the backdrop of petty and more serious crimes. And by knowing a few basics, you can reduce the likelihood of becoming a victim and empower yourself at the same time. This doesn't mean you should go to every class with a bevy of escorts, wear a bulletproof vest to your winter formal, or obsess over any and all of the things that could possibly happen to you. (The point is to take care of yourself, not freak yourself out.) What it does mean is that you should learn to think preventively.

The first commandment of safety is not to take it for granted. Start to look at it as an integral part of your life—an elemental part of your total health program. Like regular exercise, a good night's sleep, frequent flossing, and a nutritious diet, carrying yourself as if you're the world's bantamweight champion and taking basic precautions should become a natural part of your everyday life. Since we were wee toddlers, we've been told how to think preventively about danger: "Don't talk to strangers," "Don't get in the car of someone you don't know." "Don't walk alone at night." Now that just seems like common sense. With a little practice, the following advice on personal safety at home, in transit, and away from home will all become second nature as well.

HOME, SWEET HOME

One benefit to living on campus or in college housing is that the school is responsible for taking care of your security. Different schools take this responsibility more or less seriously. Some do not let visitors, such as delivery people or prospective students, past a security desk without an escort who lives in the building. Some have security officers make rounds, checking up on campus buildings a few times a day. Some require residents to sign in and out. Others don't even have locks on dorm front doors. Obviously, the strictness of security policies depends a lot on the location of the school and the needs of the students. But often, a school's estimate of what's required for student safety isn't enough to make students feel safe. And it may take a violent incident on campus before a school will upgrade the level of security.

If you feel that the security policy in your dorm is too lax or is not being well enforced, and you feel unsafe and nervous, bring it up at the next dorm meeting or student government open forum. Alternatively, write a letter or get a petition together, listing specific problems and possible solutions and signed by your fellow dormmates, and send it to campus security, the dean of student life, and any other administrators that might have a say in the matter. If the school can't provide additional security, band together with your cohabitants and take charge of the problems yourselves. Sign up for shifts to staff a security desk at the building entrance. Make it a policy that students meet delivery people at the dorm entrance rather than allow-ing them to wander the hallways. Set up a mirror in the elevator, so people can see if someone's lurking in a corner before they enter. Require that all visitors sign in and out. If you see a stranger or suspicious-looking person roaming the halls, contact campus security if you feel uncomfortable approaching him or her yourself. Have emergency numbers placed near all the hall phones, and instructions about what to do in case of fire or earthquake posted on the walls.

In addition to making your communal environs safe, take steps toward making your personal space safe and secure. Whether you are living on or off campus, in an apartment or in a dorm, take the following precautions:

■ If your dwelling has an elevator, never get on if someone suspicious is either already on or about to enter with you. Trust your instincts. Once on, always stand near the control panels (specifically, the alarm button). If you feel threatened, press the alarm button and as many other buttons as you can, so the elevator will open on the next floor. Be similarly wary of isolated places, such as the basement, laundry room, infrequently used stairwells, and tunnels or passageways, especially late at night.

■ It's a good idea to keep your room locked both when you are and are not there. If you live in a building where

PROTECTING YOUR VALUABLES

You're more valuable than your valuables are, but a little safety can go a long way toward keeping your stuff where it belongs—with you. Remember the following, whether you're on the road in your own car or a big ol' Greyhound; going shopping for groceries at the corner market or at a bazaar in Morocco; at the library or the campus canteen.

▲ Be discreet with your valuables. Don't flash your jewelry in inappropriate places, or leave a wad of cash in full view in the backpack at your feet in a library carrel. Don't leave your wallet or other valuables out on your dresser. Turn rings with stones around so only the band shows, and tuck chains into your shirt when riding on big-city public transportation.

▲ Don't leave your bag unattended. Don't hang it on a chair in the library or dining hall. When on the go keep your bag shut and next to your body and your money in your front pocket or closed compartment of your purse.

▲ Keep all doors—car, dorm, apartment, and so forth—locked at all times, even if you're just stepping out for a second to run a quick errand.

▲ Avoid carrying your keys in the same place you carry any ID bearing your address.

▲ Insuring your stuff can be affordable, so look into traveler's and renter's insurance. Campus security may be a good source of information.

▲ Keep an inventory of your valuables, with descriptions and serial numbers, in a place where it's not likely to be stolen along with your stuff, to use in the event of a burglary.

▲ When you're loading and unloading your precious belongings as you move from one dorm room to another, don't leave your car or truck unattended. It only takes a few minutes for someone to run off with your entire CD collection.

▲ It's best not to keep anything of value in an unattended car (or at a minimum, not in clear view).

▲ Consider purchasing a Chapman lock or a "Club" that attaches to your steering wheel. They are likely to get you a reduction in your car insurance, as well as to deter thieves.

▲ A car with out-of-state plates is more likely to be vandalized, because travelers are more likely to have stuff stowed in the trunk, and are less likely to stick around to find the crooks than residents would be. Display something that would identify you as from the area (e.g., a school parking permit or school sticker in the window, or something else "student-esque").

"I never used to lock my door when I was in my room. Then one afternoon when I was napping, two kids came in soliciting money for their basketball team. I woke up in a fog and didn't have my glasses on, but I gave them a couple of bucks from my pocket. Later on, I discovered they'd swiped my wallet. After that I locked the door when I was asleep or in the shower."

—HARVARD UNIVERSITY, '93

everyone keeps his or her door open at all times, at least lock up when you go to sleep.

■ Just as you wouldn't want to remove the locks from your doors, resist the urge to remove safety gates and/or window jams. Indeed, they may obstruct your view, prevent you from airing out your room in a jiffy, and look a bit unfriendly, but they do enhance your safety, protecting both you and your valuables. Also, there is every possibility that your school/ landlord will slap huge fines on you if you remove them.

■ Don't lend your keys out or tell people the combination to the front door or to your room.

■ Don't let in anyone you don't know, including representatives of local utility companies, campus security, or pest control, without first seeing some form of ID. If you aren't expecting a repairperson, say, call the company to verify that the service person is indeed legit.

■ If your room becomes uninhabitable or unsafe due to an emergency, such as a flood, a power failure, or a broken window, door, or lock, call the campus housing maintenance office if you are in campus housing (there should be a 24-hour number) or your landlord if you're off campus. If you feel uncomfortable there, stay with a friend until the problem can be fixed.

■ Because in an emergency you can forget the simplest things and you don't have time to go leafing through a phone book, post all the important numbers by every phone: campus security, campus EMS, police, fire, ambulance, poison control, doctors' numbers, parents' numbers, and numbers of places you spend a lot of time (work, boyfriend's, sorority, astrophysics lab, computer center, etc.).

Telephone and On-line Safety

The telephone can come to your aid in finding help when you need it, but it can compromise your safety and security if you inadvertently use it to give privileged information about yourself. For example, do not have an answering machine or voice-mail message that might make you appear an easy target—for instance, one that says that you're away for an extended period of time or that you are a woman living alone. (Many people like to use "we" instead of "I.") If your first name reveals your gender, protect yourself by only using your first initial and last name in the phone book (and on door nameplates, or apartment directories).

Don't give away personal information about yourself, including name, address, credit card number(s), and bank account number(s), to an unsolicited caller. Check out who's calling, why they need the information, and exactly how it will be used before revealing anything. Ask if they can send or fax information or to give you their phone number, so you can call them back and verify what they're telling you.

■ If you get a crank or obscene call, hang up quietly as soon as you recognize it's a crank. Don't try to figure out who's on the line. If you're upset, don't let the caller know—it's probably his or her primary objective.

■ If you receive repeated crank calls or any kind of phone harassment, and you're on a campus network, call the campus operator and security to report it. If you're off campus, call the operator. He may connect you to an annoyance call bureau, which can give you suggestions on what to do. The police and phone company can trace the calls. Some states offer Caller ID, a service that displays the number of the caller when the phone rings and while you're talking. There is a monthly fee for the service and you have to buy the Caller ID box.

■ If you consistently receive hang-ups or wrong number calls someone may be trying to find out about your schedule. Call campus security or the police for suggestions on what to do. And even if you're alone, you might say, "No, it's not for you—it's another wrong number" out loud as you hang up.

■ If you receive harassing E-mail, many computer networks have sysops (system operators) who monitor postings/public listings and to whom you can report harassment—they may have the power to suspend users who abuse their computer accounts. On the

Internet, you may have less chance for recourse, but you can still ask the seasoned net surfers at the school computing center, or even the local police for advice.

EMERGENCIES

E mergencies of the hard-drive-crash-while-spell-checking-an-unsaved-and-overdue-term-paper ilk are more common at college than fires, earthquakes, and floods. But it's always best to be prepared for them nonetheless.

Fires

If your dorm is like most, it's been standing, unchanged and unrenovated, since the early '60s (that's 1860s in some places). And if you're off campus, it's likely that your place isn't brand spanking new, either. In some of these buildings, one unattended iron could burn down the house. Recognizing the hazard, most dorms don't allow appliances like toasters, microwaves, hot pots, or popcorn poppers. Though these rules are rarely strictly enforced, always attend to all electric gadgets, and be cautious when reading, relaxing, worshipping, or seducing by candlelight or with incense.

To be prepared for a fire, locate the fire alarm and fire extinguisher closest to your room and the bathroom you use most frequently, and in places you hang out. Keep a fire extinguisher in the kitchen as well. Make sure there is a working smoke detector in every room you occupy and check the batteries occasionally (it's recommended that you change them when you reset your clock for daylight time). Plan an escape route in case of emergency. If you have impaired mobility, discuss with your RA and/or roommate how you will evacuate if you need to.

If a Fire Breaks Out

■ If an electric appliance bursts into flames, unplug it and douse it with the fire extinguisher (or pour a lot of salt or baking soda on it). If hot oil on the stove ignites, turn off the burner and do the same. Never pour water on electrical or oil fires. Other small fires can be stamped out or extinguished by throwing a blanket over them, but a fire extinguisher is always a good bet, even if it seems like overkill. In a building that's packed with people and full of combustible materials like paper, overreacting is always preferable to underreacting.

■ If you detect a fire but don't know where it is, or it is not instantly extinguishable, and you can safely get to an alarm, activate it immediately. If you hear a fire alarm, evacuate immediately. Never assume that a fire alarm is a test, not only for your safety but also for your sanity: If everyone takes their good ol' sweet time evacuating the premises during a fire drill, the powers

DIALING 911

✸

If you find yourself in a situation in which you have to report some kind of crime, you will need to give out as much useful information as clearly and quickly as possible. Take a deep breath and tell the 911 operator:

WHO: A good description of the assailant(s) and the victim(s)

WHAT: What happened, who's hurt, and how seriously they're hurt

WHERE IT OCCURRED: Street address or dorm address, along with a landmark, if applicable ("the corner of Main and Eighth, right across the street from the bowling alley").

WHAT'S HAPPENING NOW: What direction the assailant went—in what color car, with whom, etc.

You do not have to give the operator your name.

that be will inevitably insist on staging yet another 3:00 A.M. test.

■ If you are in your room when the fire alarm sounds, awaken any sleeping roommates. Grab only the room or house key, if you can quickly locate it. Feel the doorknob and the door. If they are hot, do not open the door; if they aren't, open it slowly. If smoke rushes in, close the door and remain inside. Use a bed sheet or blanket to fill the cracks under the door(s). If possible, open the window two thirds at the top to allow hot air and gases to escape, and one third at the bottom to allow you to breathe, and wave a towel or bright-colored garment to alert people to your presence. (The fire department will be looking for this sign.) If you can leave the room, follow the predetermined exit route. Use the stairways— never the elevator. When exiting in smoky conditions, cover your nose and mouth with a wet towel and crawl to the nearest exit. Your head should be approximately seven inches off the ground. Try to stay calm. (It may not be easy, but try your darndest.)

Earthquake

ᗯᗋᗯ

Going to school on the West Coast certainly has its advantages—some of the most beautiful places in this country lie west of the Rockies. But what's an idyllic landscape on the surface isn't so friendly a few miles down, and students have to know what to do if the land starts to rock. Schools that lie on or near the San Andreas fault will probably have emergency instructions posted in the dorms or hand out flyers at orientation. For information about safety and evacuation procedures specific to your school, talk to an RA or campus security. Here are a few general tips to follow in case an earthquake strikes.

Once you feel an earthquake, head straight for the nearest door frame and stand or sit under it (they are constructed to withstand pressure), or dive under a sturdy table. Lie with your hands over your head. Stay clear of windows and anything else made of

glass. Once the building has stopped moving, evacuate immediately by stairs, not by elevator. If you are driving when the tremors begin, move away from overpasses, underpasses, and bridges, pull over to the side of the road, and get out of your car. Get clear of power lines, trees, or other objects that could fall on you. After the quake is over tune in to television or radio news to find out the extent of the damage and any special instructions (for example, it may not be safe to drink the water).

ᗯᗋᗯ

(For information on dealing with medical emergencies, see page 236. For information on dealing with drug- or alcohol-related emergencies, see page 313. For dealing with rape or other forms of sexual assault, see "Ending the Silence," page 491).

OUT AND ABOUT: SAFETY IN YOUR NEIGHBORHOOD

When outside the comfort of your home sweet home—walking around campus, going to and from your off-campus job, hitting the local thrift store for some good cheap pickin's, or exploring the city—keep alert and aware of what's going on around you. So much of being safe involves relying on your sharpened instincts. Every campus poses its own dangers. You'll know best—by word of mouth, what your advisors say, handouts from campus security, and so on—which routes you should avoid, which buildings don't have guards after midnight, and generally how to

SAFER DATING

"Depending on where I'm going, I sometimes stuff a $10 bill in my bra, enough to get me home safe, just in case I lose my bag or it gets stolen."
—*SAN DIEGO STATE UNIVERSITY, '96*

Before you go out with someone you don't know too well:

▲ Write down your date's name, address, and phone number, where you're going, and when you plan to be back, and leave them with a friend. At the very least, tell someone (a roommate or a friend) these things. If you change your plans, make a call.

▲ Don't go on blind dates unless they are arranged by someone you know and trust.

▲ Even if you don't expect to pay, don't go anywhere without some cash—a little change in case you need to make a phone call, enough money to get you home from wherever you're going (with a bit to spare). If nothing else, bring a bank card and a few quarters.

▲ Take it easy on the alcohol if you're with someone you don't know well. Drugs and alcohol can seriously impair judgment and make it more difficult for you to control what happens. Do not get intimately involved with someone that you don't know well if either you or s/he is very drunk or high. If you choose to use drugs or alcohol, especially in social settings, be responsible and do it only with friends who will watch out for your safety.

---

avoid dangerous situations. Don't let the initial safety orientation and the advice that follows freak you out. There's a big difference between being cautious and walking around in a suit of armor—replete with a can of mace and five whistles that blow in five different tones.

■ Get to know the area—the locations of phones (including emergency phones), the campus security station, the police station, and the hospital, as well as more than one route between school and your assorted off-campus destinations. You should also get acquainted with the people in your neighborhood. Say hello to the shopkeepers, the folks who are always sitting out on their porch, and the beat police officers you pass every day. They'll look out for you and be more willing to help you if you're familiar to them.

■ Carry yourself with confidence. You don't have to possess a black belt in karate to confidently walk down the

campus. Often, both victim and victimizer have been drinking.

street, but it doesn't hurt to act as if you do. Most attackers are looking for a vulnerable person, someone who looks unsure of herself, or doesn't know where she's going, not someone who looks like she owns the sidewalk. So walk with authority, even if it's only an act. Look like you know exactly where you're going. Remember, you have a right to take up space.

■ Pay attention to who's walking behind, in front of, and across the way from you. If someone looks menacing, cross the street and walk in the opposite direction from him or her. As quickly as possible get yourself into the nearest group of people or store. If a car approaches you and someone inside threatens you, scream and run in the opposite direction from the way the car is headed.

■ Carry as few bags and books as possible. You're not designed like a pack horse, so it's not surprising that you can't run as quickly when you're saddled down as you can when you're carrying only the bare essentials. If you need to lug three notebooks, a laptop, and a 40-pound Shakespeare anthology to and from the library,

invest in a backpack, which is less movement-inhibiting than a shoulder bag (and better for your pack, to boot).

■ Vary your route. If you go to the library from 6:00 to 10:00 every evening, try alternating between a few well-lit routes home.

NIGHT CRAWLERS

Students are always on the move in the middle of the night, and, as common sense dictates, you have to take special precautions when it's dark. Areas that may be bustling by day become deserted, it's hard to see, and people have a tendency to do things that make them less alert than in the daytime. For example, the later it is, the better the chances are that you're tired, your thoughts are consumed by the exam you're up cramming for, you're exhausted after a night of painting the town red, or a tad inebriated from the punch at the African Heritage house fund-raiser. The problem is, these are the times we need to be especially careful. Don't ruin your fun or your concentration by

"I am a vocal feminist and I'm physically strong, but even so I always ask someone to walk me home after dark. It is very disempowering to feel that I can't walk across campus alone, but I would rather be disempowered than be a crime statistic." —YALE UNIVERSITY, '96

worrying about all the dangers lurking around every corner. But do take steps that can minimize your chances of getting hurt.

■ Avoid walking alone at night, even if it means you have to ask your lab partner to take a detour to drop you off at your dorm or apartment. If your school operates a campus shuttle, find out where it leaves from and when, and take it, even if it means waiting 10 minutes for it. If the school does not operate a shuttle, investigate the possibility of getting such a service. Other good night-walking tips: Keep alert. Keep an eye on your surroundings. Don't walk next to bushes or dark doorways, or in deserted places. Don't wear headphones.

■ If you bike, run or walk at night, try to team up with others and stick to well traveled routes. If you're on a road, be aware that drivers may have difficulty seeing you and may be less alert than during the day.

■ Anytime you choose to drink or use other drugs, know that your reflexes and judgment will probably be affected, and act accordingly. Ditch your pride or the need to prove that you can hold your liquor. You know full well when you should ask a trusted friend to help you home. Follow that instinct, even if it requires that you ask said friend to leave the party for 15 minutes. Walking home alone when you're less than capable of watching out for yourself is not a good move. Someone who's obviously inebriated—who isn't coordinated enough to fight off an attack and will probably not remember what happened too clearly—is an assailant's favorite target. (For tips on responsible drinking and drug use, see page 310.)

WOMAN-POWERED VEHICLES

A bike can be your best friend. It can get you where you want to go fast, it's not as troublesome or expensive to maintain as a car, and while you're mounting rough hills, you're getting a workout and building strength and endurance. The same goes for Rollerblading—another fun, quick, and potentially aerobic way to get around. However, some of the best things about biking and blading can get you into trouble. For example, if you overestimate your stamina you can find yourself stranded five miles from home, too exhausted to put foot to pedal or wheel to ground. Here, some cruising tips.

■ Adjust your workout to the weather. On 95°F cloudless days, bring along a bottle of water to prevent dehydration. If you need to ride in the rain, snow, or ice, go easy when you brake to avoid skidding or hydroplaning. (The same goes for driving a car.)

■ Be meticulous about safety gear. Always wear a helmet. Yes, they are among the dorkiest-looking of creations, but they're also practical. For safety's sake, forgo coolness. With in-line skates wear knee pads and wrist guards as well.

■ Be especially careful when you start to "feel the burn." Riding or blading when you're tired can make you more prone to injury, because your form won't be as good, and to accidents because you'll have slower reflexes and less strength to stop short.

■ You also have to make sure that others can see you. The bike should have

but it's especially good in fog and hard rain and at twilight. ☀

SAFER SELF-DEFENSE

The best weapon against being mugged or attacked is avoiding it all together. Being aware and alert and thinking preventively will hopefully keep you from ever being in a situation in which you'd need to avert an attack. But if you feel threatened, your voice, your body, a loud whistle, or a can of pepper spray or mace may ward off an attack if used properly, and may be very dangerous for you if used improperly. You can provoke an already nervous assailant by screaming or blowing a whistle instead of just quickly handing over your things. "Protective" devices like guns, mace, and clubs often cause injury to the bearer or are grabbed by the assailant and used against you.

In fact, the smartest course is often to not use a weapon at all. Sometimes just giving the attacker what he wants is the safest course of all. For example, if you are mugged, hand over what you've got as quickly and smoothly as possible. The mugger is probably as scared as you are—don't push him. The goal is to get him away from you and the episode over and done with as soon as possible. The point is, if you choose to wield one of the weapons below, it is important to know when to use it; but it's just as important to know when *not* to use it.

▲ VOICE: People are much less responsive to helping someone who screams "Rape!" or "Help!" than they are to an emergency that may potentially affect them, too. Scream "Fire!" instead.

▲ BODY: Karate, tae kwon do, and many other martial arts or self-defense classes teach you how to kick butt, build your confidence level, and help you feel more secure. You can also get a good workout, network with a group of people who share your safety concerns, and, on many campuses, fulfill your physical education requirement. Hopefully, you'll never have to try out your moves outside class, perhaps partly because the strength and confidence you'll exude just may deter would-be attackers. If you are interested in finding a class and your school doesn't offer any, check with a campus women's group, campus security, a community organization like a Y, or the yellow pages under self-defense or karate and martial arts. And take a look at the resources at the end of this chapter.

▲ WHISTLE: A good, loud police or referee's whistle can attract attention and possibly scare away a potential attacker when used where people are within hearing range. Wear the whistle on a cord around your wrist like a bracelet—never around your neck, as the attacker could seriously injure you (intentionally or not) to keep you from using it.

▲ MACE AND PEPPER SPRAY (where legal): When used incorrectly, these can prove extremely dangerous. You need to be close enough to the attacker to get a good amount of the spray on his face. If you are too far away or the spray doesn't work, you

‌‌‌
⚙ 80% of deaths from bicycle-related accidents are from head injuries, most

may enrage him more than disable him. Further, if you're standing in a strong wind, the spray may blow into your face. Read the instructions that come with the product. It's also not a bad idea to call the local police station for handy tips on proper use.

▲ GUNS: According to a *Mother Jones* magazine report, keeping a gun in your home makes it three times as likely that someone will be killed there, and guns purchased for self-defense far more often hurt or kill someone unintentionally than hurt or kill an attacker. These are the facts. For the sake of your own and others' well-being, if you do choose to own a gun, it is your responsibility to register it according to the laws of your state, learn how to use it properly from a qualified (preferably certified) instructor, practice, and be obsessively meticulous about safe use and storage.

If you are attacked, realize that you are not to blame. Even the most cautious person will not be guaranteed a life free from violence and robbery. This is because we can't control what others do. You can take steps toward avoiding potentially violent and/or dangerous situations, prepare for emergencies, and learn what to do (and not to do) if an emergency arises, but you just can't always prevent something from happening. It is not your fault if you are in the wrong place at the wrong time or you misjudge someone's character or intentions. Nothing you say, wear, or do justifies violence.

reflectors and lights, and if you plan to ride or blade at night and/or in poorly lit areas, consider investing in reflectors to wear on your person. There are reflector stickers to put on your helmet and reflector vests like crossing guards wear. If you don't want to glow, at least wear a light-colored shirt or jacket. Many students who bike in busy places or in traffic like to wear a police whistle and use it like a horn.

■ Just as when you're walking, you need to be alert when you're riding or rolling. Ditch the headphones when you're traveling in traffic or densely populated areas, or after dark, when you'll need your hearing to make up for what you'll lose in sight.

■ Always make sure your equipment is in tip-top shape. For example, if you're biking, check your tires and/or your brakes before every trip. It's also wise to carry a portable pump and mini-repair kit when you're making anything but the shortest trips and to get to know a bit about the mechanics of your mode of transportation. Learn how to do emergency repair—what to do if the bike chain or a skate wheel falls off in a remote place, for example. Places that sell or rent bikes and blades, the phys-ed department, professional biking or in-line skating organizations, or an outing club may give classes or have information on upkeep, repair, and safety.

■ Bikes and blades are often expensive pieces of machinery, so much so that others may want them enough to threaten you with violence for them. When going out through turf you're not familiar with (as far as terrain and population) ask a buddy to come along with you.

of which could have been prevented if the rider had been wearing a helmet. ☼

AUTO-NOMOUS WOMAN

A car is more complex than a bike, and safety, security, and maintenance are more complex as well. Most of the following is common sense, but in your rush to catch the 6:15 P.M. movie or turn in your take-home final, you may forget the basics. Don't. As a reminder:

Keep your car properly maintained. A poorly tuned car is more likely to break down, often at an unfortunate time. Keep tabs on your tires, your oil, and your gas. Don't drive on a near-empty tank, worn tires, or brakes that sound funny. As logic dictates, be especially diligent about checking the car before and during a trip cross-country (or cross-state). If you don't feel equipped to examine and evaluate the health of your auto, bring it to a full-service gas station for a quick checkup. If you suspect the car might need a more serious inspection, ask around for the name of a reputable mechanic/service station. If your school offers a course in auto repair, students or faculty in the program would be a good place to get a recommendation. You can also ask professors, shopkeepers, the office that handles parking permits on campus, or campus security.

Know the basics of emergency repair. Just as it's important to keep your vehicle in good shape, you should learn how to fix simple problems, in the event that, despite your careful maintenance, something goes awry. You don't need to know how to take an engine apart and put it back together again while blindfolded (though that would certainly be impressive)—you just need to learn the basics, such as how to change a tire, change the oil, put coolant in an overheated radiator, and jump-start a battery. If you don't want to (or don't trust yourself to) keep it all in your head, stash a how-to auto maintenance manual in your glove compartment (available at bookstores). Every modern woman should know that "dipstick" and "lug nut" aren't just good pet names for ex-boyfriends.

Travel with emergency equipment. It's a good idea to have on hand a blanket (to put out a fire or keep you warm), jumper cables, a white cloth to tie to your car to signal that you need help or a purchased or homemade CALL FOR HELP sign, a flashlight, maps, a first-aid kit, a spare tire, a bottle of water (especially if you're going to be driving in a hot, dry, sparsely populated area), and a bit of high-energy food that doesn't spoil (trail mix is a perennial favorite). In addition, you should always travel with a jack and lug wrench to change a tire and flares or flashers.

Whenever possible, travel on well-lit and more populated streets. Keep doors locked at all times and windows rolled up at night and in questionable neighborhoods. Actually, it's a good idea to keep your car locked both when you're in it and when you're not. When parking in the late afternoon or evening, find a spot that will be well lit when you return to your car. Always approach the car with your keys in hand and check the backseat of your car before you get in.

Dealing With Car Problems

಄಄಄

■ **Locking the keys in:** Police used to be able to help if you locked your keys in your car, but because of liability problems, most no longer will. You might need the help of a gas station or a towing service. If you have a car that has manual door locks, you may want to try the wire hanger trick: Untwist a wire hanger, bend the end into a nickel-sized loop, stick it between the window and the rubber around it, and try to catch and lift the lock. Unfortunately for people who lock their keys in the car (and fortunately for people who leave their valuables in plain view), this doesn't always work—but it's certainly worth a try.

■ **Breaking down on the highway:** Resist the urge to leave the car and walk along the side of the road to find help. Similarly, do not hitchhike, especially if you are alone. (And do not pick up hitchhikers.) If your car breaks down on the highway, put a white "flag" on the door handle or a sign in the window that faces traffic, and wait for a uniformed highway patrol officer to assist you. If someone other than a patrol officer approaches first, roll down the window only enough to pass them some change for a phone call and a note with a description of

the car. Do not open your door for a total stranger.

■ **Being followed:** If you think you're being followed, drive to a well trafficked area. Slow down a bit and see if the car passes you. If the car keeps following you, drive somewhere for help, like a gas or police station, or a crowded place where you can phone for help. Do not stop in a deserted area.

■ **If you are not able to drive:** If you get sick and need medical attention while driving in an unfamiliar place, try to get to a restaurant or gas station and ask for help. If you can't do this get to a phone and call 911. If you are unable to drive, pull over to the side of the road and put up a white flag or sign (see above) to signal that you need help. If you can wait for a while for help, keep your car locked and do not open the door for a stranger. Ask anyone who stops to send help. If you're feeling really terrible, you may have to trust strangers and let them take you to the hospital.

If you have been drinking alcohol to the point of legal intoxication, do not even attempt to drive home yourself. To avoid temptation, give a sober friend your keys. (See page 312 of "Use and Abuse" for ways to avoid driving intoxicated or with someone who is intoxicated.)

■ **Sirens behind:** If you are pulled over by the police, do not get out of your car. Not only is it safest for you to stay inside with the windows rolled up until you're sure whoever stopped you is a police officer, but the police prefer you to do so. They regard someone who's gotten out of the car as a potential threat. Have your license and registration ready to hand over.

■ **Accident:** If you get into an accident at night in a remote place and there has been no serious damage done to person or car, do not get out of the car. Either wait inside until a police officer arrives, or drive to a police or gas station (or other well-lit, populated area) and report the accident to the police.

If you see an accident and emergency vehicles have not yet arrived, take note of the location, the colors and makes of the cars involved, and get to a phone to call the police. Unless you are trained to provide assistance, it's best for everyone if you call the professionals. As you're driving away from an accident, signal oncoming cars that there's a problem ahead by putting on your low lights if it's daytime, and flashing your brights if it's night.

LONG-DISTANCE SAFETY

Hittin' the road anytime soon? Maybe you have to drive back to school after the winter break. Or

maybe you're planning a trip to somewhere you've always wanted to go—Graceland or Thailand, for example—over the summer or for a semester abroad. Nothing can be more fun or enlightening than setting out in search of your "inner self," old ruins, or mastery of a foreign language. Still, even the best-planned trip can fall short of perfection if you don't think preemptively about safety. But if you prepare, the world really is your oyster, and it's your decision when and how to navigate through the briny deep.

On the Road

■ Plan to follow a specific route, and make an itinerary. Don't travel without an up-to-date map. Without being too inflexible, don't stray too far from your predesignated route.

■ Have immediate access to a stash of emergency money via a bank card or a credit card with a decent credit limit (See "Money Matters," page 104, for more information.) Be prepared for unexpected costs: a car breakdown, a medical emergency, a typhoon that might land you in a hotel instead of your tent.

■ Keep in consistent contact with at least one person on the home front. Check in at prearranged times. Make sure you have a calling card number, which you can get through your phone company. (You may even want to rent a cellular phone for long trips—often a less expensive proposition than you'd imagine.)

■ Rest when you are tired. It is not a good idea to drive or find yourself in a foreign train station when you are exhausted and therefore more vulnerable to accidents and attacks.

■ If possible, get phone numbers and addresses of people in the places where you plan to travel (consult with friends and family). That way, if you get into a bind, you'll have the number of a local who can help you out.

■ Consider getting property protection in case your valuables are stolen.

■ Travel with others as often as possible. Not only will this reduce the number of cars on the road, but it can help in an emergency, since two heads are better than one.

■ Think about becoming a member of the Automobile Association of America (AAA) if you're on the road a lot. See the Resources at the end of this chapter for information.

Once You Get There

🌀🌀🌀

■ Whenever possible, confirm your sleeping arrangements in advance. If you need reservations, make them. If you're staying with a friend (or a friend of a friend), call before you arrive and remind them when you plan to turn up. Get explicit directions on how to get there from the train or bus station, the airport, or the main road. The last thing you want to do is arrive in a strange city or town in the middle of the night with no idea of where you are going.

■ If your hotel room or residence is far from the center of town and you want to go in for dinner or entertainment, inquire about the safest way back. Ask

"There are a lot of places that don't look too kindly on young women traveling alone at night. I see girls who didn't grow up in the South come to Arkansas and drive around playing really loud rock music and smoking cigarettes out the window. If they don't get hassled by the cops, they'll sure get it from the guys."

—UNIVERSITY OF ARKANSAS, '94

about public transportation: At what time do buses or subways stop running? Do taxis run all night? Can you walk through a well-lit and adequately populated section of town to reach your abode?

■ If you're abroad, educate yourself about local customs. Without specifically trying, you may send an inappropriate signal simply because you don't know what's acceptable behavior. For example, wearing shorts inside a mosque, church, or synagogue is not only disrespectful but may also make you prone to attack. If it's 110°F and you choose to wear shorts anyway, that's your prerogative. But be informed. Pay a visit to the American consulate in the area, or better yet, talk to a frequent traveler or to a resident of the area to become acquainted with the local customs and codes of behavior. Travel books also may be a good source for this information as well.

■ Learn at least a few key words of local language (including the address where you're staying). In addition to "please," "thank you," "where is?" and "how much?" learn polite forms of address and "doctor" and "police."

ACTIVIST IDEAS

■ Make up key chains to sell or give away with the campus security emergency number on them and a few of your favorite, school-specific safety tips. (Security may even cover the cost.)

■ See if a campus security representative can come to a dorm meeting for a safety orientation.

■ Take classes in basic first aid and CPR, so you can be prepared to help in an emergency.

RESOURCES

Prevention and Personal Safety

CAMPUS VIOLENCE PREVENTION CENTER
THE ADMINISTRATION BUILDING, ROOM 107
TOWSON STATE UNIVERSITY
TOWSON, MD 21286
(410) 830-2178
Provides information and answers questions about crime and safety on campus—both how to take preventive actions and how to respond when things do happen. Publishes materials for students about methods for prevention.

SECURITY ON CAMPUS
215 WEST CHURCH ROAD, SUITE 200
KING OF PRUSSIA, PA 19406-3207
(610) 768-9330
Publishes numerous materials on campus safety, including such topics as guidelines for self-defense, your rights as a student, and safety procedures. Provides information, answers questions, and offers advice about campus safety and security, as well as prevention.

AUTOMOBILE ASSOCIATION OF AMERICA
   (AAA)
1000 AAA DRIVE
HEATHROW, FL 32746-5063
(407) 444-7000

This is the national headquarters of the AAA, a federation of 122 clubs throughout the U.S. and Canada. It can refer you to the club nearest you. All clubs provide emergency road service, travel and route advice, and safety information, among their many services.

To Find Self-Defense Classes

Many schools offer self-defense classes through their physical education departments. If not, local community centers, rape crisis centers, YM/YWCAs, martial arts schools, and dance studios often offer self-defense courses, or should be able to refer you to a place that does. In addition, you can contact one of the organizations listed below for more information:

THE AMERICAN WOMEN'S SELF-DEFENSE
   ASSOCIATION
713 NORTH WELLWOOD AVENUE
LINDENHURST, NY 11757
(516) 225-6262
Publishes materials on women's self-defense techniques. Works to raise awareness and increase the involvement of women in self-defense courses. Makes

In a national poll, 56% of women say worrying about crime

referrals to local self-defense organizations and classes for women.

CHIMERA
SELF-DEFENSE FOR WOMEN
59 EAST VAN BUREN, # 714
CHICAGO, IL 60605
(312) 759-1707

Sponsors personal safety and self-defense classes and makes referrals to regional and local organizations and classes. Publishes materials and provides information about women and self-defense.

IMPACT PERSONAL SAFETY
1930 VENTURA BOULEVARD, SUITE 200
TARZANA, CA 91356
(800) 345-5425

Sponsors personal safety classes that teach applied self-defense with padded mock assailants and makes referrals to regional and local self-defense organizations and classes for women. Publishes materials and provides information about women and self-defense.

RESOURCES FOR PERSONAL EMPOWERMENT MODEL MUGGING PROGRAM
P.O. BOX 20316
NEW YORK, NY 10021
(800) 443-5425

Sponsors personal safety classes that teach applied self-defense with padded mock assailants and makes referrals to regional and local self-defense organizations and classes for women. Publishes materials and provides information about women and self-defense.

FEMINIST KARATE UNION
1426 SOUTH JACKSON STREET
SEATTLE, WA 98107
(206) 325-3878

Offers self-defense, self-protection, and karate training to women. Makes referrals to local groups offering classes. Publishes numerous materials about women and self-defense, including *Fear into Anger: A Manual of Self-Defense for Women, Peace of Mind,* and *Acquaintance Rape.*

THE LOS ANGELES COMMISSION ON ASSAULTS AGAINST WOMEN
6043 HOLLYWOOD BOULEVARD, SUITE 200
LOS ANGELES, CA 90028
(213) 462-1356

Publishes numerous materials about women's self-defense including: *Self-Defense Women Teaching Women* (a video and manual package) and *Women's Self-Defense: A Complete Guide to Assault Prevention.*

Part Six
Defining Yourself

Community & Identity

Finding Your Place

College is an opportunity to explore and celebrate where we came from, who we are, and who we ultimately want to be. It's a time to hone our individuality among those who are both different from and similar to us. From those who are different, we learn to value our uniqueness and appreciate the rich tapestry of our college campus. From those who are similar, we learn about the importance of community and the strength and security to be found there.

Although college may not be the first time we have faced issues of identity and community, for many of us it may be the first time we've thought seriously about what they mean. Maybe you were raised in a fairly insular Mexican-American neighborhood but find yourself on a predominantly white campus. Before you may have taken your Chicana identity for granted, but now recognizing and cel-ebrating your heritage has become important to you. Or, as the daughter of a Japanese-American woman and an African-American man, you find that the tensions between the two communities make you feel alienated. Or perhaps you grew up in an observant Baptist community and, away from it, are questioning some of its tenets and looking for other members who are going through the same thing. (Or, on the flip side, maybe your religion meant little to you before and now you'd like to explore it.) Perhaps you are coming up against blatant sexism for the first time and hate how powerless it makes you feel. In each of these scenarios, you are faced with exploring your personal identity as it relates to your identity within a community. This can be exciting and terrifying at the same time. But trying to make connections between what we learn and who we are is part of what the college experience is all about.

WHY NOW?

There are myriad reasons why, on a college campus, issues of community and identity are suddenly front and center:

■ Pressure on you to figure out not just what you're going to be when you grow up, but who.

■ The new environment. Chances are that your college has a much more diverse student body than did your high school, prompting you to examine exactly where you fit in. Or your campus could be more homogeneous than you're accustomed to, which would also raise identity issues.

■ Exposure to new ideas. College is a time when you're exposed to as many ideas as there are students, professors, reading lists, and rallies. So if your consciousness wasn't raised before, guaranteed it'll get a good boost before first year is over.

■ Unspoken permission to "go wild": In college you suddenly have the license, if not the mandate, to be yourself, whatever that may mean on any given day.

■ You realize that whether you like it or not, you are making assumptions

MULTICULTURALISM IN THE CLASSROOM

Over the past 30 years, the standard college curriculum has undergone a transformation. From being almost exclusively focused on the Western canon, it has evolved to include the study of other cultures and civilizations and the work of people who have traditionally been ignored, or at best put on the back burner (including women, and indigenous and colonized people, and/or people of color). This does not mean that what historically has been considered important, like the classics, has to be discarded. Rather, the concept of what is fundamental is expanding to include more perspectives.

So why has multiculturalism become such a heated subject on college campuses? One of the main reasons is that communities have started to actively assert their identities. When any one group affirms its stature, the value of all that has previously believed to be important is implicitly challenged. For example, until relatively recently, women's experiences, writing, art, etc. were not considered to be relevant or worthy of study by the vast majority of academicians. It wasn't until women started to organize as a group that women's studies was taken seriously.

The same has been true for the development of African-American studies, Asian studies, Latino studies, and the like. And such efforts have affected not only academia but society in general. The old never gives way to the new without a fight, and some of the tension that has arisen around multiculturalism stems from this basic aspect of life.

based on gender, race, religion, sexual preference, hairstyle—you name it—and you get a better feel for how deeply rooted the negative messages are, and see the importance of working to change them.

■ You're meeting new people who don't know a thing about your reputation as the science whiz, your work to improve racial harmony, or your name that's hard for a native English speaker to get on the first try. On the one hand, this enables you to focus on whichever aspects of yourself that you want; on the other hand, because people know nothing about you, they'll make assumptions about you based on outward appearances and first impressions.

■ The end of innocence. You're no longer protected by youth, ignorance, or your parents from the facts of oppression and prejudice. Issues like discrimination in lending, admissions, hiring, and housing are now very real, threatening, and pertinent to your life.

EXPLORING YOUR IDENTITY

When someone asks you to define yourself, you may have a litany of things that you can say: "I'm a student," "I'm from Missouri," or "I'm a gymnast." Anytime you say these things, you assert your individuality while affirming your common bond and/or experience with others who share those parts of your identity. Your identity is constantly evolving. When you move to a new place, become involved in a new activity, or explore a part of your past, you may

"There was a song I used to sing at camp, 'Different people are fun to know/It's the difference that makes it so . . .' Now I realize it was a premonition that I would go to Oberlin. After growing up in a very homogeneous suburb, it was wonderful to be immersed in a campus awash with people of all races, religions, sexualities, and cultures. Through interaction with so many different people, I probably learned more about myself in my 4 years at Oberlin than I had in my 18 years before."

—OBERLIN COLLEGE, '92

begin to identify yourself differently or emphasize new aspects of who you are and what groups or ideas you are connected to. You may identify yourself by race, religious or political affiliation, nationality, sexual preference, socioeconomic class, physical characteristics, major, and/or where you hang out. And depending on both

internal and external forces, such as whom you're with, what you're talking about, and how you're feeling, you may choose to reveal different aspects of yourself, flaunting, hiding, loving, despising, and ignoring different parts of your identity at different times.

Visible and Invisible Identities

Some of the ways in which we identify ourselves may be more visible than others. While some identities, such as gender and race, are generally visible, others, such as sexual preference, religious or political affiliations, and family background, are less visible or even invisible unless deliberately revealed. All of us possess a rich combination of visible and invisible identities, and we make choices about when and where to make them known, depending on whom we are with and how comfortable we feel.

Choosing to be open about different parts of yourself always has risks. For example, you may feel that people will have a negative reaction to finding out where you grew up, what your mother does for a living, that your "boyfriend" is a girlfriend, or what your religious beliefs are. You may fear

that people will judge you unfairly, and thus prefer to discuss certain topics or aspects of yourself only with people whom you trust and who understand what you are talking about.

However, hiding aspects of yourself can cause you to feel alone and hollow, as if a part of you is something to be ashamed of. Being open about who you are and what is important to you can give you a sense of pride and strength and can be empowering not only for yourself but for others as well. The more that women of various backgrounds are honest about who they are and proud to share their experiences, opinions, and beliefs, the better role models we'll have and the more society will be forced to address our varied needs and recognize our many contributions. However, there may be times when it could be inappropriate and/or dangerous to be open about yourself. Only you can weigh the pros and cons of revealing your identity.

Broadening Our Horizons

Despite our being complex and multifaceted women, we are often labeled and pigeonholed by others before we have a chance to define ourselves. Perhaps you have had the experience in one of its many incarnations: You're assumed to be the "expert" on disabled women simply because you are visually impaired, or asked to speak for all Native American women because you are of Comanche heritage. Whatever shape your experience of being stereotyped has taken, chances are it's been uncomfortable and maddening. Although it may leave you vulnerable to misunder-

FINDING LIKE-MINDED FOLK

"One of the main reasons that I went to UCLA is that I knew there was a big Latino community. But when I got to school, I found that the kinds of things that they were involved in weren't what I cared about, and I felt like I had two choices, either to transfer to a school that had the type of community I wanted, or to make it into something I wanted, because there was no way that I was not going to be involved in something so important to me."

—UCLA, '96

Colleges often have countless communities, but if you're new at school, you may have to seek them out. One of the best ways to do this is through campus organizations. There are probably groups organized along racial, religious, political, and gender lines that can serve to introduce you to people who share your interests, culture, and background. For information on finding the right group, see "Scouting Out On-Campus Groups," page 594.

Remember, though, that one group can rarely address all of your ideas, issues, and identities, and you may need to try more than one before you find exactly what you are looking for. Some women really enjoy organized campus groups and others find that they're just not their cup of tea; their community becomes the people they consider friends, the people with whom they study, eat, and hang out. It is also not unusual to belong to several "groups" simultaneously or serially during college.

In addition, just having interests in common doesn't mean you will necessarily like the people who share your passions. If you find your interests within a certain group diverge from the norm, there are probably others who feel the same way. Try calling a meeting about the issue(s) you feel strongly about and see if there is any response.

If you find that no existing campus group really meets your needs or interests, you can create your own. (See "Starting Your Own Organization," page 596).

standing, asserting your identity is actually often a way of nipping these often limiting and sometimes damaging assumptions in the bud. It is only through learning about others and letting them learn about us that we can combat stereotypes.

Fortunately, most campus environments give us access to diverse cultural, political, and social resources.

Between the student body, libraries, extracurricular activities, special events, and course offerings, there are many creative ways to explore cultures, ideas, and histories that we might not otherwise have access to. By trying out and learning about a broad range of things, we can figure out what is important to us, what types of communities we'd like to be a part of,

COMMUNITIES TO WATCH OUT FOR

Groups that use any of the tactics listed below to recruit prospective members or to keep members involved are often called cults. By definition alone, it's not always so easy to distinguish a cult from a religion or branch of a religion—or even from a sorority, for that matter. Cults are often linked to religious traditions but not necessarily accepted or recognized by the mainstream organizations within a religion. It's important to be aware that such groups often recruit on campuses, knowing that many of us are vulnerable because we are looking for community, going through big changes in our lives, and willing to try new things. Some of the things you should watch out for are:

▲ People you don't know who ask you to do things with them, such as come to dinner or go away on a retreat, or who are offering you gifts with "no strings attached."

▲ People who won't leave you alone, who make you feel guilty, pressured, or uncomfortable, even when you have clearly said "No thanks" to their overtures.

▲ Involvement in a group that is making you feel powerless to do what you want or need to do for yourself.

▲ Feeling scared or unable to leave a community.

▲ People who make financial demands, asking you to give them money and/or making you feel financially dependent on them for your survival.

▲ Feeling coerced into believing the group's philosophy, or doing certain things such as initiation rites that you otherwise might not choose to do, and may even feel uncomfortable doing.

▲ Becoming isolated from your friends and/or family members as a result of group involvement.

▲ People who promise to solve your problems and provide you with friends and/or community.

and what activities we enjoy. Knowledge gives us choices, and choices allow us to lead fuller and richer lives. To take advantage of the resources on campus, you might want to try:

■ Taking classes in departments or subjects that you might not normally consider.

■ Reading books about your own or other cultures, or reading novels by "minority" writers.

■ Writing papers or doing research for classes on topics outside of your major, or on topics not necessarily covered in the syllabus.

■ Joining cultural and/or ethnic organizations or going to their events.

■ Attending community celebrations, cultural gatherings, food fairs, political events, and lectures.

■ Making friends with people who have backgrounds that are different from your own.

☼ 76% of Americans attended religious services in 1993. ☼ 46%

- Engaging in activities that involve a diverse group of people you might not otherwise meet.

- Exploring the different communities and neighborhoods near you.

FINDING A COMMUNITY

One of the main ways in which we express our identities in college is by being involved in formal or informal groups on campus. We all feel as if there are some people who just understand us better than others. Chances are, these are the kind of people that we are going to want to hang out with and confide in because they are going through the same things we are. We feel that we can talk to them without having to explain everything. Whether they're part of an organization or just our friends from our first-year dorm, these people make up our communities and are a fundamental part of the shaping and understanding of our identities.

A community is a group of people with common causes, strengths, or histories who get together to share ideas, pray, organize, raise awareness, counsel, and/or shoot the breeze. These groups are formed in different ways and around different issues. People may come together around race/color, sexual preference, religious affiliation, and/or political, social, or artistic interests. And in many cases, communities share more than one of these, such as an organization of black women painters or Catholic lesbians.

If you have an identity that is not part of the campus "mainstream"—perhaps you are a feminist at an over-whelmingly conservative university, or a Buddhist in the Bible Belt—it may feel all the more crucial for you to find a community that affirms your minority identity. You may find that a community can offer positive perspectives on aspects of your identity that are commonly distorted in a mainstream university and in society at large. A community can also offer positive role models and be an important political tool, helping to effect change in institutions that discriminate. By joining a community you can take action and mobilize with others, celebrate who you are and what you share, and educate others about the things that interest, concern, or involve your group.

You may find that participation in a group gives you an entirely new direction in life, or that it was just a passing interest. Whatever the case, when you affiliate with a community, chances are you'll learn something new, clarify and personalize what you're studying in a class, gain a deeper understanding of yourself and your family, contextualize your community in history, help to preserve traditions and rituals, work against oppression and discrimination, meet like-minded people, and/or just share some good food—or bad food, as the case may be.

It's important to remember, however, that just because we share certain traits doesn't mean that we are inherently compatible, unified birds of a feather. There are differences not only between communities but also within them, which is one of the reasons most large communities are made up of many smaller ones. However, there is no getting around the fact that our identities and communities are commonly shaped around distinctions of gender, race, religion, sexual orientation, ethnicity, and/or ability. For example, although people who are black come from a huge variety of backgrounds, our society happens to place a lot of importance on racial categorization, so chances are that as a black woman you'll have a lot of shared experiences—namely racism and its ramifications—with other women who are black. For this reason, skin color may become the common ground on which you'll want to organize.

COMMON THEMES OF IDENTITY ON CAMPUS

It would be impossible to delineate all the ways in which themes of gender, race, religion, sexual orientation, ethnicity, and/or ability affect us in a global sense, and it wouldn't be any easier to cover the many ways they affect our college experience. What fol-

lows, then, are simply some ideas about the impact these "categories" may have in shaping who we are and how we define ourselves in college.

Gender

ⓥⓥⓥ

If you are like a lot of women, college may be the first time you become attuned to issues of gender. Maybe you're sensing that the men in the class get called on to answer the really interesting questions. Or maybe living with a group of women and watching some of them starve themselves makes you acutely aware of the emphasis placed on looks and the price we pay for it. Or maybe you realize that the things you once thought of as your own limiting personality traits—shyness, lack of confidence, a seeming inability to get your questions answered, your ideas heard, your needs met—were at least in some part societally imposed and reinforced because of your gender.

Issues you understood before on a theoretical level may suddenly come to life when you or a close friend is raped on a date, sexually harassed by a professor, or treated like a child by health services. You may have heard the phrase "The personal is political," but when you are offered a lower starting salary than a male peer or aren't getting the recognition you deserve from your biology professor simply because you're a woman, it suddenly applies to you. All of these things serve to make you realize that, in many ways, you may have more in common with a woman who grew up in an environment completely different from yours and less with a guy from your hometown than

☀ In one survey, 63% of those women who felt there was a need for a

you previously thought. No matter who you are or where you come from, being a woman informs your experience of the world, and certainly of college.

What Does Feminism Mean?

On its most basic level, feminism is a movement and ideology that acknowledges and addresses the inequality of men and women in our society and recognizes the achievements, intelligence, strength, and power that women possess in their many different roles. Feminism is a celebration of women's ideas, accomplishments, contributions, abilities, and sexuality. Being a feminist is exercising and seizing your right as a woman to define yourself, to make your own choices, and to create a society where women's lives and work are valued. It also encompasses working against such social problems as sexism and its ramifications including discrimination and verbal, emotional, physical, and/or sexual violence against women. Though all feminists agree that there is inequality between the sexes, many differ about what is at the root of this inequality, what perpetuates it, what changes in society are necessary to resolve it, and what are the best tactics to achieve equality.

To many women these days, feminism has a negative connotation. Even women who believe in the basic feminist principles of equal rights, equal pay, equal representation, and freedom of choice (in all aspects of their lives) are sometimes reluctant to describe themselves as feminists because it brings to mind negative stereotypes, "radical" beliefs and tactics, or association with groups or ideas that have excluded women who

SEPARATISM
☀

"I think it's ridiculous when whites feel like there's something wrong with my hanging with only brothers and sisters. I fail to believe that they really want to join our group. . . . They're just threatened when they see a group of black students together."
—UNIVERSITY OF CONNECTICUT, '95

Some communities are more diverse than others. For example, as undergrads and as women we are all members of a broad community of female students. But as African-Americans or Russians or lesbians and/or Jews we may belong to a tighter community as well. We turn to this community for support and to be with people who understand us. But to others our hanging out together may seem separatist.

It is important to recognize why people of similar backgrounds or interests find it necessary to spend time together, particularly if on their campus they're in a minority. In their classes and dorm they may feel isolated or like a "token." Getting together with people who understand where they're coming from can be a relief. It can also allow them to explore their heritage, network, and/or focus on their own art, music, growth, politics, and scholarship in an environment that does not have their issues as its primary concern.

strong women's movement did not consider themselves feminists. ☀

are not white, middle class, and heterosexual. As more women challenge these connotations and work to form groups that respect and celebrate the similarities *and* the differences among women, this negative connotation will dissipate.

On campus there are many ways to learn about and express feminist beliefs, ranging from being attuned to gender issues and forming groups and coalitions with women from a diversity of backgrounds to volunteering at a rape crisis center, signing up for women's studies classes, and/or taking part in rallies and marches for women's rights.

Race and Ethnicity

◔◕◔

"I'm at Howard, and for the first time in my life being black puts me in the majority. When I go to classes, lectures, discussions, and political events, they are geared toward me and who I am. . . . I know that when I leave here and be in the minority again, but it feels great to have the tables turned, and I know these years are making me stronger to be able to deal with the fact that as a black woman in America, I have a lot of battles left to fight."

—HOWARD UNIVERSITY, '98

Racial and ethnic diversity, empowerment, and discrimination are certainly some of the hottest topics on college campuses. And correspondingly, personal issues of racial identity become particularly salient in college, whether you are in the minority or the majority. While you may be learning about your heritage and taking pride in it, chances are you are also becoming more aware than ever of the ramifications of your skin color and the privilege or penalty attached to it. If you're white, this may be the first time that you've actively thought about what that means in this society, instead of just taking it for granted. And if you're a student of color, you may not only be tapping into what's important about being, say, African-American, but also coming face to face with the consequences of being black in a white society. Suddenly you are in a place where you feel a strong sense of what not being white means politically, socially, theoretically, and practically *and* have the opportunity to explore it and work to change it. The fact that all of this is happening at a time in your life when the stakes have never been higher only intensifies matters: In preparation for forging your destiny in a racially stratified world, your campus communities can offer the social support, the political clout, and the personal empowerment to help ensure that you get the same education as everyone else, the same opportunities upon graduation, and the tools to help you win the inevitable battles you'll face along the way.

There are a number of reasons why college may be the first time you've felt it important to define yourself in terms of your race. Maybe others are already taking the liberty of doing it for you, and you're tired of their assumptions, prejudices, and stereotypes and want to head them off

Of the 249 million people counted in the 1990 U.S. Census,

at the pass by asserting your racial identity. Or maybe in embracing your race you are gaining a sense of strength and belonging, and feel as if you've found your voice for the first time. Or maybe you've *always* defined yourself in terms of race and now find that by being in the majority on campus or by joining a black sorority, you finally feel that you have both the needed support and the forum in which to express your convictions.

Women of Color

Instead of emphasizing national origin or specific ethnicity, many women have chosen to bond with other non-white women to address shared experiences of growing up and living in a society dominated by racial distinctions. The term "women of color" is relatively new, and distinguishing yourself as such means celebrating heritages, cultures, religions, lan-

"I have seen people do the funniest things when describing how black people look—this one guy spent all this time describing how this other guy looked and when I finally asked him, 'Is he black?' he said all sheepishly, as if it was a sin to say it, 'Yeah, he's black!' People are sometimes so concerned with how they should refer to black people that they try to be color blind, but that's not the point of it. He's black—what are you going to do, pretend he isn't? I don't want people to act as if I'm not black, I want them to see it and to realize that it is not only OK but great!"
— BOSTON COLLEGE, '95

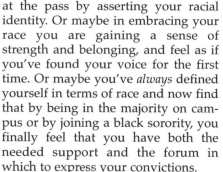
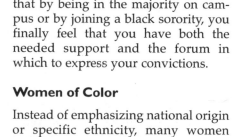

assignments
1. Work too hard.
2. No excuses.
3. Limit partying.
4. Make me proud that I am a professor.
5. Don't sleep in class.

guages, and skin colors that have historically been denied, denigrated, and distorted. The inclusion of gender in the term demonstrates that a woman's race cannot be separated from the fact that she is a woman, and that as a woman she will experience her culture and religion from a distinct and valuable point of view.

In some instances, however, it may not serve all women of color to be seen as a homogeneous group, as women of color have many different ethnicities and concerns. An African-American women's group may want separate space in which to grow strong and identify its own concerns and priorities. A Korean-American group may want the same. But they each may find it effective and useful to come together to discuss issues common to both groups, such as creating a stronger curriculum in non-Western studies or the hiring of more minority professors. As a woman of color on campus, you may want to join a group that focuses on racial and ethnic pride, on creating change in campus policy, and/or on socializing with people with whom you share a common heritage and culture.

"My mom's white and my dad's black, and all the kids in my family except for me have skin the color of dark caramel—I'm very light-skinned. My parents got divorced when I was pretty young, and my dad got custody of all of us. . . . People would assume that I was adopted, and someone told me that people had, more than once, wondered if my dad had kid-napped me—why else would a white girl be with a black man and a bunch of dark-skinned kids? . . . Until I got to college I didn't really have a context in which to talk about or think about how all this affected me. I gained enough sup-port and confidence to proudly assert my identity, and rather than be ashamed or embarrassed about myself, I've started to teach people that what you see isn't always what's inside."

—*University of Texas at Austin, '96*

Religion
〰〰〰

When everything is unfamiliar and changing all the time, as it often is in college, you may find that your religious beliefs soothe and stabilize you, helping you to deal with the weird twists and monkey wrenches campus life inevitably hurls your way. But college can also be a time when your religion faces some hard scrutiny. First, the university setting can be a very secular place, due to the prevailing notion that religious faith and rational thinking are mutually exclusive. What you've always thought of as universal truths are suddenly called into question when your philosophy prof argues that there is no truth and no objectivity. And second, chances are that this is the first time you've actu-ally had the opportunity to choose whether or not to practice your reli-gion. You may find that away from home the practical ramifications of your religious beliefs—dietary restric-tions, classes or social events missed because of holy days, etc.—may sud-denly seem burdensome, or at the very least isolating. Or the ritual and rou-tine may be the only thing that keeps you sane while at the same time pro-viding you with an instant sense of community.

You may also find that in college you become attuned to issues speci-fic to religious women. Women have always been active in their religions, but their role in maintaining and per-petuating their traditions has not always been acknowledged. In addi-tion, in many religions women have not had equal access to positions of power and felt alienated by certain tenets. Consequently, a lot of women have tried to figure out which aspects of their tradition they want to keep and which ones they want to work to change. The relatively progressive setting of a college campus is often the ideal place to examine these questions. Most campuses have numerous religious organizations in which to explore and express your religious identity. If you find it frightening or guilt-inducing to be doubting or questioning your tradition, just remember that religion has stood up to centuries of scrutiny. And it may be that your inquiry will only serve to solidify your beliefs.

Sexual Orientation

ⓥⓔⓥ

Plain and simple: Some people—heterosexuals—are attracted exclusively (or primarily) to members of the opposite sex; some—homosexuals (lesbians and gay men)—are attracted exclusively (or primarily) to members of their own sex; and some—bisexuals—fall somewhere in between. But the personal and social meanings of our attraction to others are considerably more complex than these clear cut definitions.

"I am attracted to both sexes. It depends on who I meet, if that specific person is sexy, intelligent, and communicative. I am attracted on a person-by-person basis and I feel that for me, this is my sexuality."

—ALBERT EINSTEIN SCHOOL OF
MEDICINE, '97

It's a girl-date-boy world out there, and your basic college campus is no exception. Unless you tell people otherwise, you are generally presumed to be hetero. Still, college has traditionally been one of the safer places to explore your sexuality if you are questioning your orientation, and to "come out" if you are a lesbian or bisexual. You are almost certain to find people who will accept, understand, and affirm your sexual identity. Because of this, college can be the ideal place to gather strength and courage to face the challenges of loving women in a straight world.

On any college campus, you'll find that lesbians have opinions, desires, and realities that are as varied as those of heterosexual women. Lesbians are of all classes, races, religions, and cultures. For some women on campus, the term "lesbianism" will carry the political significance of being independent from men—that is, not depending on men financially, emotionally, or sexually. Some lesbians view coming out as an act of resistance to popular culture and morality. And some prefer to be called "gay" or "women-oriented," claiming that the term "lesbian" is linked to a white, Western, nonradical women's movement.

TIPS ON COMING OUT

In the same way that you hope that others will be sensitive to what you are experiencing and recognize how difficult it is for you to divulge what may seem like your biggest secret, you must also try to be sensitive to their situation. Doing so may help coming out be the positive, affirming event it can be.

▲ Consider who you're dealing with. Before coming out to someone, ask yourself: Is she understanding? Nonjudgmental? Has she stuck by you in the past? You can test the waters by asking her general questions about the topic of homosexuality. Usually, this will give you some insight into the person's ability to respect your sexual orientation. But prepare yourself to be surprised as well.

▲ Pick a time when you can actually talk; don't just "drop a bomb" and leave. If you choose to come out in a letter, make it clear that you're available to talk about it as well.

▲ Realize that even friends who are accepting of your identity may be surprised if you suddenly reveal parts of yourself that they didn't know about before—especially if they feel close to you. They may feel as if you have been lying to them, or be hurt that you didn't previously trust them with something so important to you.

▲ If you feel comfortable doing so, try to ask if they have any questions about what you've told them. You may even want to provide them with some articles, suggestions of books that they can read, or people they can talk with to get more information.

▲ Try not to be defensive; expect that they might get angry and upset.

▲ Be prepared for paradoxical reactions. For example, your roommate may simultaneously feel worried that you might make a move on her and insulted when you tell her that she has absolutely nothing to worry about.

▲ Remember that even the most loving, accepting, and open-minded folks may be thrown for a loop when you come out to them. Your parents' fantasies about your wedding and your friends' fantasies about setting you up with their boyfriends' roommates may die hard.

▲ Be prepared to deal with questions that you may find offensive. Give good, solid, clear, and nondefensive answers to such statements as "Can't you find a man?"; "It's only a phase"; "Are you doing this to hurt us?"; "You

Coming Out

"Coming out" is a term used to acknowledge one's lesbianism/gayness/bisexuality to oneself or to others. It comes from the expression "coming out of the closet," the closet being a metaphor for a hiding place. Declaring your attraction to women can bring up a torrent of conflicting feelings: It can be simultaneously terrifying and thrilling, with attendant feelings of anger and relief. All your life you have probably been socialized

just need a little therapy"; and "I should have never allowed you to go to such a liberal college." See the Resources at the end of this chapter and check your local bookstore, library (particularly those in the women's and/or gay/lesbian studies departments), or mail-order catalogs for books that can help with these tricky issues.

▲ Remember that you may have been thinking about and dealing with your attraction to women and the attendant ramifications for a while and have moved beyond the confusion, anger, fear, and questions that accompanied your early coming-out process. Allow your friends and family to go through the same process of coming to terms with your sexual identity, ungraceful as it may be.

▲ Find support. Coming out can be a scary, lonely process. A loving community of gay and/or straight friends can make all the difference. Even if you don't immediately identify with the people active in the gay/lesbian alliance on campus, they can nonetheless be good sources of advice and can possibly introduce you to people you find more your style. On many campuses, the gay/lesbian alliance is pretty male-centered, but you can find women lurking on the periphery or in affiliated groups.

to think heterosexual is "right" and homosexual is "wrong", so it's no wonder it's a big deal.

Some women see coming out as an important political statement and a way to eradicate lesbian invisibility and oppression. If a woman tells the

world that she is a lesbian, the world can no longer deny that lesbians exist. When lesbian doctors, actresses, mothers, professors, politicians, and navy lieutenants come out, they create role models for other lesbians, people to look up to and to respect. Other women see coming out as an entirely personal decision, one each woman must make for herself. Either way, the majority of women who come out as lesbian or bisexual find it liberating to reveal this important aspect of themselves.

At the same time, however, coming out can mean "disappointing" family, being rejected by friends, and setting yourself up for physical and verbal harassment and discrimination in health care, jobs, insurance, custody, and housing. (Many schools, however, have anti-discrimination policies that protect students from institutional bias based on sexual orientation.) And if you are part of other campus communities that are central to your identity (e.g., ethnic/religious/sports groups, or a sorority), you may face

the very real risk of being rejected or ostracized by members.

A lesbian or bisexual woman constantly makes choices about when, where, and whether or not to come out. If you are having difficulty coming out or need someone to talk about it with, you might want to seek out women involved with the lesbian community on campus, on the net, or in off-campus organizations, or a therapist experienced in issues of sexual identity (you may even be able to find a gay or lesbian therapist with whom to speak).

"I can remember sitting in my room when I was 13 and first considering my desire for women. I would write poems about how messed up what I wanted was. I did not know anyone else in my family or school that felt the same way. I was angry that I might have to give up my nice, safe, heterosexual ideas about a husband, a career, and 2.5 kids. I was terrified, really. And yet, the idea of making love to girls seemed so sexy and so natural. When I fooled around with a girl for the first time at 16, at first I felt afraid, but then I just knew it was right. I could tell. Making love to another girl was like reaching the moon, like coming home, like loving myself for the first time. I was relieved and psyched. I was coming out, coming into myself."

—COLUMBIA UNIVERSITY, '92

Disabilities and Abilities

Because the majority of college students can see and hear well, move around easily and without pain, and read at an average speed, their abilities are often taken for granted and accommodations for and understanding of those who can't are not integrated into college life. For this reason, having a disability on a college campus can have a profound effect on your experience, your attitudes about the world and yourself, and others' attitudes about you.

What we deem "disability" is linked to our expectations about what people can and can't do. Our society values physical strength and agility, and the ability to get things done quickly and to take care of one's needs. It values visual and verbal communication and intelligence as measured by tests of reading, writing, abstract reasoning, "rational and logical" thinking, and clear expression. It's important to note, too, that women with disabilities are subject to the double oppression of sexism and ableism, and many have to deal with the burden of other forms of discrimination, such as racism, homophobia, and anti-Semitism, as well.

What Is a Disability?

Disabilities come in many forms. Some, such as mobility impairments, are outwardly apparent. "Hidden" disabilities, such as some chronic illnesses, and most learning and emotional disabilities, are less obvious. The Americans with Disabilities Act (ADA) includes the following in its definition of disability: cancer, heart

"The civil rights movement and women's movement have been really good at identifying how this society is structured to benefit white rich men, at everyone else's expense. . . . But then they hold meetings in places that you can't get to in a wheelchair. It's like they're saying, 'Well, some kinds of exclusion are OK. . . .'"

—OHIO STATE UNIVERSITY, '95

disease, diabetes, mental retardation, emotional/mental illness, specific learning disabilities, HIV disease (symptoms or no symptoms), TB, drug addiction, and alcoholism, as well as other permanent or temporary physical or mental conditions that hinder a "major life activity," such as walking, breathing, seeing, learning, working, hearing, taking care of oneself, and performing manual tasks.

What Is a Learning Disability?

A learning disability (LD) has nothing to do with intelligence. It's a disorder that affects the manner in which some-one processes, retains, and/or expresses information. LDs can affect reading comprehension, spelling, written expression, math computation, organizational skills, time management, and problem solving. Sometimes they can also cause difficulty with social skills. They are often very frustrating and can be inconsistent, manifesting themselves in only a few subject areas or contexts, or erratically in several subject areas. Vision or hearing impairment and speech disorders, as well as feeling uncomfortable, nervous, insecure, ill, or bored, can all affect a person's ability to learn, but these are not considered to be LDs.

On the one hand, the college environment is becoming more and more accommodating to and accepting of students with learning disabilities: Colleges offer emotional and educational support and are some of the best places to find the latest information about LDs. On the other hand, as college is a learning environment, it is one of the hardest places to have an LD. Therefore, it is important to know

"I wasn't really challenged that much in my high school classes, but college was different. All of a sudden I was having so much trouble studying, concentrating, finishing tests, and getting papers in on time. It made me really upset and I started seeing a therapist, who ended up sending me to an LD specialist. It turns out that I had an LD, and once I got the appropriate support and help, I could get back on track." —YORK COLLEGE, '97

both what learning disabilities are as well as how to get a diagnosis and assistance in dealing with one while at school.

> *"I've had teachers who think that they're really helping me by making me take tests in the same amount of time as other students or not being lenient about deadlines. They think it'll make me feel good about myself, that I won't have to be reminded that I'm different or 'less capable.' But it's like, I've gotten over being ashamed of my LD, it's a fact of life. Giving me extra time on a test is something I need. They would never ask a person with a broken leg to run the 50-yard dash because everyone else in her gym class is doing it or because she'll be reminded of her accident if she doesn't."*
>
> —KENYON COLLEGE, '92

Diagnosing Disabilities

Temporary or permanent disabilities can develop as a result of illness, accident, depression, trauma, or anxiety, or they may come to light in a new environment. If you feel that you might have an undiagnosed disability and would like to learn about places and people who do testing and evaluation, get more information about general or specific aspects of disabilities, or access entitlement and services, check with:

▲ The office or department responsible for services for disabled students at your school. (This is always a good place to begin.)
▲ Your state's board of disability services.
▲ Local chapters of disability rights organizations.
▲ Social service agencies that provide programs and resources for and about people with disabilities.
▲ Disabilities professionals and/or doctors or therapists who work with disabilities issues.

> *"My professors have a hard time understanding that I have a learning disability because I can articulate myself really clearly, grasp difficult ideas, and get high grades on oral reports. It just takes me a while to write a paper and a test. They're not used to someone like me—they assume that someone is a 'good' student or a 'bad' student, and disabled students are, by virtue of the fact that we're disabled, 'bad' students."*
>
> —LOUISIANA STATE UNIVERSITY, '96

REVEALING YOUR HIDDEN DISABILITY

"My disability isn't apparent if you pass me on the street, but that doesn't mean that it's 'less serious' or it doesn't affect me. People I know who have apparent disabilities talk about how people assume that they're unable to do a lot of things that they can, and they have to explain this over and over. I have the opposite problem. People assume that I can do things I can't, and I have to explain this over and over."

—RICE UNIVERSITY, '90

Depending on the circumstances, students with "invisible" or "hidden" disabilities may choose to reveal their condition to those around them, including friends, professors, doctors, employers, admissions officers, and school administrators.

For example, if you have a "hidden" disability, such as a learning disability, the most persuasive benefit of letting others know is that it opens access to the growing services, protection from discrimination, and resources available to people with disabilities. But identification may affect insurance rates and can also carry a stigma, which might outweigh the benefits. If a disability is intermittent and usually manageable, or you are able to get all the help you need through other channels, you may prefer not to tell others. It is important to weigh the pros and cons carefully, and it may be helpful to talk, anonymously if you wish, to the office of disability services at your school to find out your options. Remember, talking to them doesn't mean that you have committed yourself to anything.

"For the same reasons it's important for me to come out as a lesbian, I think it's important to come out as disabled. If people were more open about their disabilities, then everyone would realize how many people have disabilities and those of us with disabilities would feel a sense of community and know we're not alone."

—UNIVERSITY OF CALIFORNIA, —SANTA CRUZ, '98

Culture

As important as the above themes are in determining our identity, they are all informed by our culture: our set of customs, behaviors, attitudes, and beliefs. We see everything through the veil of culture. Differences in standards and values, the way we respond to a crisis, choose to celebrate, talk about ourselves or our families, and/or are politically active may stem from cultural or ethnic backgrounds. Culture determines how we understand the world and what we see as right and wrong, normal and not normal. In college your culture may be made apparent to you, either by how you fit in or how you stand out, and stepping back and taking a look at the beliefs that shaped you can be a very powerful part of learning about who you are. You can celebrate your culture while understanding the blind spots you might have because of it.

Many of us come from "mixed origins"—households or communities that take from more than one cultural background. Especially when the values of one clash with the values of another, we can simultaneously feel like an insider and an outsider. Negotiating our multiple identities and finding a place in communities that respect us as the multifaceted women that we are is a key element of college and beyond.

In many circumstances and in many cultures past and present, the voices and ideas of women have not been valued. It is crucial then that we, as women, have communities and friends that support and listen to us, think we are special and important, and share our ideas about life and identity. We deserve to have communities in which we can create, grow, gather, and strengthen our identities.

ACTIVIST IDEAS

■ Choose a weekend day to hold a campus-wide teach-in celebration, where different groups and communities would have a chance to set up a table, run programs, bring speakers, and give presentations about their concerns and beliefs. It should be a day where all are invited to ask the questions they always wanted to ask, participate in or observe real or mock ceremonies, taste ethnic foods, do folk dances, listen to music from rap to salsa to Klezmer to Gaelic, share personal experiences, learn about individual and community pride in the face of discrimination and prejudice, and understand some of the important issues on-campus, locally, nationally, and worldwide. Involve as many different groups on campus in the planning—i.e., fraternities and sororities, the administration, academic departments, clubs and campus organizations, sports teams, etc., in order to bring out a big crowd.

■ So, who are you? Take a good look at yourself. Think about how, where, when, and with whom you grew up, your race, your gender, your religious beliefs, and your culture and how it has all shaped your past (and present) experiences, your view of the world, whom you choose as friends, your "values," and your desires.

※ In a 1994 national survey, 71% of respondents said they had a

RESOURCES

Disabilities

EDUCATIONAL EQUITY CONCEPTS
NATIONAL CLEARINGHOUSE FOR WOMEN
 AND GIRLS WITH DISABILITIES
114 EAST 32ND STREET, SUITE 701
NEW YORK, NY 10016
(212) 725-1803
FAX: (212) 725-0947
Makes referrals to local organizations, support groups, and practitioners that can provide assistance to disabled women. Provides information about financial aid, health, and reproductive issues. Publishes materials about disabilities services for women. Organizes political action/advocacy work to promote programs for girls and women with disabilities.

HEATH RESOURCE CENTER: THE NATIONAL
 CLEARINGHOUSE ON POSTSECONDARY
 EDUCATION FOR PERSONS WITH
 DISABILITIES
1 DUPONT CIRCLE, SUITE 800
WASHINGTON, DC 20036
(202) 939-9320
Publishes materials, including a newsletter about college disabilities services. Conducts research about and monitors disabilities services provided to students. Provides information on topics such as financial aid, legislation, testing, and other disability services. Organizes political action/advocacy work on behalf of disabled students.

African-Americans

NATIONAL COUNCIL OF NEGRO WOMEN
1001 G STREET NW, SUITE 800
WASHINGTON, DC 20001
(202) 628-0015
FAX: (202) 628-0233

An umbrella organization serving to promote the leadership of black women. Serves as a clearinghouse of information for the activities of black women. Sponsors self-help projects on both the national and local levels. Makes referrals to local black women's organizations and other, more general organizations working for racial and gender equality. Organizes political action/advocacy on issues of equality and women's leadership. Publishes materials, available upon request. Maintains local chapters and affiliates throughout the country.

NAACP (NATIONAL ASSOCIATION FOR THE
 ADVANCEMENT OF COLORED PERSONS)
4805 MOUNT HOPE DRIVE
BALTIMORE, MD 21215-3297
(410) 358-8900
Organizes political action/advocacy work to promote the advancement of African-Americans and reduce racism in the United States. Publishes materials on all issues of concern to African-Americans. Maintains a youth and college division, which runs national programs to promote the leadership of black students and facilitates student organizing. In addition, the education

division of the NAACP provides information and resources on a wide variety of topics, including reducing racism, civil rights, promoting and celebrating African-American culture, and organizing around African-American issues. Makes referrals to both local and national organizations dealing with all issues of concern to African-Americans. Maintains local chapters and affiliates throughout the country.

Women of Color

WOMEN OF COLOR RESOURCE CENTER
2288 Fulton Street, Suite 103
Berkeley, CA 94704
(510) 848-9272
A clearinghouse of information for and about women of color. Publishes a national directory, updated continually, of organizational resources for women of color. Makes referrals to both local and national women of color organizations working on everything from political action to social issues.

Lesbians, Bisexuals, and Gays

NATIONAL GAY AND LESBIAN TASK FORCE
2320 17TH STREET NW
WASHINGTON, DC 20009
(202) 332-6483
FAX: (202) 332-0207
TTY/TDD: (202) 332-6219
Organizes political action/advocacy to improve public policy and legislation with regard to gay and lesbian rights. Acts as a clearinghouse of information for gay and lesbian issues and organizations. Makes referrals to local organizations and has affiliates throughout the country. Maintains a database of campus gay/lesbian/bisexual groups. Administers a campus project that produces a newsletter with information on violence and defamation against gay and lesbian students, among other issues.

PARENTS, FAMILIES, AND FRIENDS OF LESBIANS AND GAYS (PFLAG)
1101 14TH STREET NW, SUITE 1030
WASHINGTON, DC 20005
(202) 638-4200
Provides information and services to parents, families, and friends of lesbians and gays. Maintains a network of, and makes referrals to, local support groups throughout the country to promote the well-being of both lesbians and gays and those who care about them. Publishes materials to assist in communication and education, including *Coming Out to Your Parents*. Organizes political action/advocacy work to influence public policy and legislation.

BISEXUAL RESOURCE CENTER
95 BERKELEY STREET, SUITE 613
BOSTON, MA 02116
(617) 338–9595
Publishes an international directory of bisexual organizations and groups. Organizes political action/advocacy to promote gay, bisexual, and lesbian rights. Offers social, political, and educational programs for bisexuals.

LESBIAN AVENGERS
208 WEST 13TH STREET
NEW YORK, NY 10011
(212) 967-7711 EXT. 3204
Grassroots group that organizes direct action to promote lesbian rights and visibility. Has local chapters in communities and on campuses throughout the country. Contact the national office to find out more information about starting a group, or to get a referral to groups in your area.

Asians

ORGANIZATION OF CHINESE AMERICANS
1001 CONNECTICUT AVENUE NW, SUITE 707
WASHINGTON, DC 20036
(202) 223-5500
FAX: (202) 296-0540

Works to promote the advancement and empowerment of Chinese-Americans, in specific, and all Asian-Americans, in general. Engages in political action/advocacy work on behalf of Asian-American civil and political rights. Organizes numerous cultural, political, educational, health, and professional programs on both the national and local levels. Runs a college outreach program, which assists Asian student groups (not only Chinese groups) to facilitate programming and communication. Makes referrals to local and national Asian groups.

The following Asian students organizations rotate their main headquarters but can be found by contacting the student activities office on your campus, at a school near you, a local Asian organizations, or the Organization of Chinese-Americans: Asian-Pacific-American Medical Students Association; Asian-Pacific-American Law Students Association; East Coast Asian-American Student Union; Midwest Asian Student Union; Atlantic Coast Asian-American Student Union; Asian-Pacific Coast Students Union; and the Asian-American Graduate

Students Association. These groups organize regional and national conferences and activities and facilitate the formation and development of Asian student groups at campuses throughout the country.

Latina/os

NATIONAL COUNCIL OF LA RAZA
1111 19TH STREET NW, SUITE 1000
WASHINGTON, DC 20036
(202) 785-1670
FAX: (202) 785-0851
Works to promote the empowerment and advancement of Latinos in the United States. Provides assistance to organizations working with Latinos. Conducts research on issues such as education, employment, health, immigration, and civil rights. Organizes political action/advocacy work to promote legislation and public policy that advance the cause of Latinos. Makes referrals to local organizations. Runs the College Leadership Forum which works to establish a national computerized network of organizations and individuals serving Latino students. Provides training, technical assistance, and other resources to student groups and organizations serving students.

NATIONAL CONFERENCE OF PUERTO RICAN WOMEN
5 THOMAS CIRCLE
WASHINGTON, DC 20005
(202) 387-4716
Promotes the full participation of Puerto Rican women and other Latinas in their economic, social, professional, and political life. Offers workshops, training seminars, and conferences on various topics. Organizes political action/advocacy work to improve public policy and civil rights legislation for all Latina/os. Makes referrals to local and national Latina/o groups. Offers scholarships and provides assistance to

Latina students wishing to organize. Publishes materials available upon request.

MANA: A NATIONAL LATINA ORGANIZATION

1725 K STREET NW, SUITE 501
WASHINGTON, DC 20036
(202) 833-0060

National organization working to promote the advancement of Latinas. Maintains local chapters throughout the country and makes referrals to national and local Latina/o organizations. Runs mentoring programs to foster the leadership, educational and professional development of Latinas. Organizes political action/advocacy around issues of human and civil rights, and health and reproductive rights. Assists campus groups in organizing. Offers scholarships for Latina students. Publishes materials on areas of concern for Latinas, available upon request.

Jews

NATIONAL HILLEL/THE FOUNDATION FOR JEWISH CAMPUS LIFE

1640 RHODE ISLAND AVENUE NW
WASHINGTON, DC 20036
(202) 857-6560

National Jewish campus organization with local Hillel organizations on campuses throughout the country. Organizes and facilitates cultural, political, social, and religious programming on local and national levels for Jewish students of all backgrounds and affiliations. Makes referrals to local and national groups, organizes events, and provides assistance to Jewish students throughout the country and abroad. Publishes an annual directory of Jewish campus organizations, and Jewish student newsletters.

MA'YAN: THE JEWISH WOMEN'S PROJECT

180 WEST 80TH STREET
NEW YORK, NY 10024
(212) 580-0099

FAX: (212) 799-0254

Promotes the leadership and advancement of Jewish women in all areas of life: religious, professional, communal, philanthropic, artistic, and political. Organizes feminist programs for Jewish women and assists in the formation and networking of Jewish women's groups throughout the country.

Christians

UNITED MINISTRIES IN HIGHER EDUCATION RESOURCE OFFICE

7407 STEELE CREEK ROAD
CHARLOTTE, NC 28217
(704) 588-2182

Organizes ecumenical Christian student groups of all denominations on campuses throughout the country. Publishes a national directory of ecumenical ministries in higher education. Makes referrals to campus and other local Christian groups.

CATHOLIC CAMPUS MINISTRIES ASSOCIATION

300 COLLEGE PARK AVENUE
DAYTON, OH 45469-2515
(513) 229-4648

Organizes and oversees Catholic students groups on campuses throughout the country. Makes referrals to campus and other local Catholic groups. Publishes materials to help Catholic students organize on campus. Holds national and regional conferences for Catholic students.

Other Religions

Many campuses also have groups for students of religious/cultural traditions not covered by the organizations listed above, such as organizations of Hindu, Buddhist, Sikh, and Muslim students. In addition, many schools and/or communities have women's spirituality/religious organizations. In order to find them contact your student activities office or local religious community center.

Cults

CULT AWARENESS NETWORK
2421 WEST PRATT BOULEVARD, SUITE 1173
CHICAGO, IL 60645
(312) 267-7777
Provides information and publishes materials about cults in general, and about specific groups. Makes referrals to organizations that can provide additional assistance to individuals seeking information about cults and/or recovery services.

AMERICAN FAMILY FOUNDATION
INTERNATIONAL CULT EDUCATION PROGRAM
P.O. BOX 1232, GRACIE STATION
NEW YORK, NY 10028
(212) 533-5420
Provides education, maintains a speakers bureau, and offers educational materials to schools and individuals. Conducts research about specific cults. Publishes materials about cults, including information about specific cults on college campuses, cult awareness, and preventive education, as well as updated listings of educational and audio-visual resources, mental health professionals, legal experts, and experts in cult ritual abuse. Offers and makes referrals to local recovery services.

Further Reading

The list of excellent books dealing with issues of community and identity and the specific histories of women from all backgrounds is abundant and always increasing. The books that follow are by no means comprehensive, but they are intended to help you find some idea of where to start reading about the topics covered in the chapter. You may also just want to try browsing in your local bookstore or library for books that catch your eye. New things are being published on these topics every day.

Making Waves: An Anthology of Writings By and About Asian-American Women, Asian Women United of California, ed. (Beacon Press, 1989).

Aiiee! An Anthology of Asian-American Writers, Chin Frank, et.al., eds. (Mentor, 1991).

Truth Tales: Contemporary Stories by Women Writers of India, Kali for Women, eds. (The Feminist Press at the City University of New York, 1990).

Native American Women: A Contextual Bibliography, Rayna Green (Indiana University Press, 1983).

That's What She Said: Contemporary Poetry and Fiction by Native American Women, Rayna Green, ed. (Indiana University Press, 1984).

Blacks in College: A Comparative Study of Students' Success in Black and White Institutions, Jacqueline Fleming (Jossey-Bass, 1984).

Home Girls: A Black Feminist Anthology, Barbara Smith, ed. (Kitchen Table/Women of Color Press, 1983).

This Bridge Called My Back: Writings by Radical Women of Color, 2nd edition, Gloria Anzaldua and Cherrie Moraga, eds. (Kitchen Table/Women of Color Press, 1983).

All the Women Are White, All the Blacks Are Men, but Some of Us Are Brave: Black Women's Studies, Gloria T. Hull, Patricia B. Scott, and Barbara Smith, eds. (Feminist Press, 1983).

The Tribe of Dina: A Jewish Women's Anthology, Irena Klepfiez and Melanie Kaye-Kantrowitz (Sinister Wisdom Books, 1986).

Coming Out to Parents: A Two-Way Survival Guide for Lesbians and Gay Men and Their Parents, Mary V. Borhek (Pilgrim Press, 1983).

Bisexuality: A Reader and Sourcebook, Thomas Geller, ed. (Times Changes Press, 1990).

Beyond Tolerance: Gays, Lesbians, and Bisexuals on Campus, Nancy J. Evans and Vernon A. Wall, eds. (American College Personnel Association, 1991).

Is It a Choice? Three Hundred of the Most Asked Questions about Gays and Lesbians, Eric Marcus (HarperSanFrancisco, 1991).

With Wings: An Anthology of Literature By and About Women with Disabilities, Marsha Saxton and Florence Howe, eds. (Feminist Press, 1987).

Living with a Learning Disability, Revised edition, Barbara Cordoni (Southern Illinois Press, 1990).

Yes You Can: A Helpbook for the Physically Disabled, Helynn Hoffa and Gary Morgan (Pharos, 1991).

In 1993, the Episcopal church elected its first American woman bishop.

Negotiating Relationships

Family, Friends & Lovers

For many of us, our relationships give us the opportunity to expand our emotional and intellectual horizons. They provide us with sounding boards for our ideas and feelings and outlets for our fears and frustrations, and they add depth, meaning, and texture to our lives. Our relationships allow us to fulfill our need for intimacy and at the same time help us explore and reaffirm our own identities.

College is a veritable hothouse for growing relationships of every genus and variety. Living and working arrangements that put you in close—make that very close—proximity to other students provide the opportunity to meet a slew of new people (many of whom may be quite different from those you grew up with). You'll find yourself sharing your hopes, ambitions, and even innermost fantasies with people you never would have dreamed of sitting next to in your high school cafeteria. These new relationships can help you gain insight into your values, talents, and personality quirks; challenge—or confirm—your most deeply held convictions; or awaken you to a subject, activity, or belief you never considered.

ADJUSTING TO THE FIRST FEW MONTHS OF COLLEGE

Your first months on campus can be a heady mix of old and new. One night you're having 40 different conversations in 10 different dorm rooms, the next you're burning up the phone lines to your mother, your brother, and half your high school class. In the space of a month, you might meet a potential lifelong friend, a handful of classmates you'd like to

"I was miserable for the first month or so of school. I thought that was a little abnormal. I mean, college is supposed to be the best time of your life. You meet tons of new people and do fun things—but all I wanted to do was be alone. I missed my mom."

—PITZER COLLEGE, '94

date, and/or a neighbor who shares your guilty pleasure of lip-synching ABBA songs behind closed doors.

There'll probably be times when you experience a little loneliness, even if you were itching to get to school. Finding yourself in a place where you barely know a soul can leave you feeling unsure of yourself and aching for the familiar. Luckily, there are plenty of ways to relieve the symptoms of homesickness. Writing a letter, making a call, or regaling your new friends with tales of your old gang's exploits can make the separation process a little more manageable. Getting involved on campus and settling into a niche (even if you'll just occupy it for the first few weeks) is also a good way to distract you from thoughts of how much more comfortable you feel at home—or at least to get you out of your room and away from all the snapshots you've plastered on your wall. You may want to talk to your RA—she is trained to help you adjust to your new surroundings, and can be a good sounding board, source of advice, or surrogate parent during the rough periods. And remember: Your homesickness will ease up, though it might take a few weeks or months to disapppear entirely.

INDEPENDENCE ISSUES

Leaving home means taking a big—and sometimes bittersweet—leap into independence. For many people, going away to college marks the beginning of adulthood. But the transition rarely happens overnight. It's entirely normal to simultaneously rely upon your parents as a source of support and resent them for it, and to shift between being upset that your mom doesn't offer advice and being irritated when she tries to tell you what to do.

Adjusting to your new responsibilities and independence may be startlingly easy, a complete nightmare, or most likely, a bit of both. There's an expectation that now that you're in college you should be able to field any new troubles that roll your way, but it can be extremely helpful to get a few adult perspectives on the adult-sized decisions you're facing. A parent may be able to provide wise and objective counsel on a change in major, your tentative career plans, or the roommate you just can't seem to communicate with. Accepting advice from a parent or another adult doesn't necessarily mean you're not thinking for your-

"I can remember resenting my parents for encouraging me to go away to school. I called into question the value of leaving home. I knew it was the right decision—after all, they weren't forcing me, it was my decision—but it didn't feel right to just leave my family."

—BROWN UNIVERSITY, '95

☀ In 1991, a mere 6% of U.S. households fit the stereotype of

self or you aren't capable of making your own decisions; it just means that you're drawing on a trusted source of wisdom. And who better to seek advice from than someone who both knows you and wants what's right for you?

When Worlds Collide

இஇஇ

It's a given that your family won't understand every factor that's influencing the choices you make at college. To a degree, most parents expect this, and accept that you're making decisions for yourself. But what happens when the directions you've chosen aren't ones they would have chosen for themselves or for you? The daughter of two accountants may find it a tough row to hoe when she announces her choice of an English major (the emphasis in Elizabethan poetry should *really* flip them out). Or a Woodstock veteran might wonder where she went wrong when her daughter joins the Young Republicans group on campus.

Growing up inevitably means growing apart from your family in some ways, and you may start noticing that your values and opinions don't always match theirs. College exposes you to a lot of new ideas, and your parents may not be quite as

WHEN THERE'S TROUBLE AT HOME

Your feelings about being away from home may be especially confusing or hard to handle if you're leaving a troubled situation behind. You may feel relieved, guilty about feeling relieved, or worried about not being there for your siblings, parents, grandparents, or high school friends. If you have a history of fighting with a particular parent or sibling, or if your family has been affected by divorce, death, or alcohol/drug abuse, a little distance and time might make it easier to deal with painful issues. For one thing, not having to deal with someone on a day-to-day basis can make the tensions in your relationship a little more manageable. Second, you may be able to gain perspective on the situation when you're not immersed in it. And third, people's strengths, as well as their faults, tend to stand out when viewed from afar.

If you're comfortable with the idea of talking about problems over the phone, then by all means do it. Or it may be easier to address issues in a letter (and remember, not every letter has to be mailed—it often helps just to put your thoughts and feelings on paper). Talking with someone at a campus counseling center can also be a big help in sorting out unresolved issues, especially if you're worrying about things at home to the point that it's difficult to concentrate on your studies or social life. (See "Finding a Therapist or Group," page 261, for information on finding someone to talk to.)

employed father, stay-at-home mother, and 2.5 children.

STAYING IN TOUCH WITH SIBLINGS

"Before I went away to school, my little brother and I were really close. Now he doesn't even like to talk on the phone. And when I come home over break, it takes awhile for him to warm up to me."
—SARAH LAWRENCE COLLEGE, '95

It's important to let siblings (especially younger siblings) know that you are thinking of them even though you can't always be there. (If they're really young, they might not even understand why you've gone in the first place.) Calling home to speak with them, bringing them up for a football game or concert, or sending a silly postcard, a "voice letter" on tape, a sweatshirt with your school's logo on it, or pictures of your dorm room, your new pals, and the most scenic campus views can make a world of difference to them and to your relationship. (All of the above activities work well for other family members, too.)

"You start to realize in college that some of the advice your parents give you actually is valuable."
—UNIVERSITY OF ILLINOIS, CHAMPAIGN-URBANA, '92

another's right to a different world-view. Below are some tips to help bridge the chasm:

■ If your phone conversations are beginning to resemble a particularly heated episode of *Crossfire* or your folks don't quite get what the Society for Creative Anachronism is all about, don't give up—just give it some time. Send them a copy of your favorite organization's newsletter, or balance a political discussion with topics like your shared passion for the Chicago Cubs. Better yet, bring them up for a weekend. Welcome them with open arms, take them to a class, introduce them to your new friends, go on a campus tour, make them take you out to dinner. . . . After 48 hours of on-campus family bonding, they'll see how impressively you've got everything under control, and will be more likely to see you as the savvy, independent undergrad you are.

■ It can be especially difficult to find a common ground with your family when they have very specific ideas about what your college years should lead up to. If your grandfather has his heart set on you becoming the first doctor in the family but the sight of blood sends you into a tizzy, the time will come when you'll have to explain to him—gently but firmly— that you appreciate his interest and concern, but you just don't think you are cut out for the career he has in mind.

accepting of them as you are. Sometimes new interests, social and political beliefs, or involvement in certain activities can cause a serious communication gap to open up. You may love and respect your folks, but you don't have to embrace their entire set of values, just as they don't have to embrace all of yours. What's important is that you acknowledge and respect one

※ 84% of women will call a woman "just to talk;" only 40% of men ever do.

■ It also helps to take a step back and view things from your family's perspective. Remember, while you're busy spreading your wings, they've got to deal with an empty nest, and it's not always easy for even the most free-thinking parents to face the fact that their daughter is becoming a mature, responsible adult like themselves. After all, they probably have been trying to keep a pretty close watch on you for 18-odd years—be patient if they're finding the habit hard to break.

Phoning Home

ꙮꙮꙮ

Unless you are commuting to school or your campus is close enough for you to head home on weekends, most interaction with your family will probably take place over the phone. This can be a highly effective means of communication for both you and your family, but problems do occur, typically when the quality and quantity of the conversations don't meet both parties' expectations.

For example, if you're feeling a tad neglected—as if you're out of sight, out of mind—let your family know that it's important to you to hear from them every once in a while. You may find that they were deliberately trying to let you have your space, and would love to talk more often.

Perhaps more common are parents who want to be up on every nuance of your life, and resent that you don't call more frequently. Recognize that it may be hard for them to not have you in their day-to-day life, and that they may not realize how busy you are. After you've cleared the air, establish a fairly regular phone schedule with the folks back home. If

you want, choose a set time and day each week to call. Should more garrulous p's find it tough to stick with your agreed-upon plan, remind them gently but firmly that you love talking to them every 20 minutes or so, but that your homework is keeping you so busy that it might be a good idea to talk just once or twice a week. Or ask them to write you a letter or even E-mail you, if that's an option. Chances are, no matter what your original situation was, once they realize that you're sticking to whatever calling schedule you've agreed upon, they'll see that they're still occupying a significant space in your life and back off a bit.

> *"I really missed my family the first few weeks of school. They never called. I thought it was because they didn't think of me. So I called them and my mom said she was afraid to call because she didn't want to embarrass me. I told her how I'd been feeling, and now we talk at least once a week."*
>
> —SANTA CLARA UNIVERSITY, '94

Commuting From Home

ᘒᘒᘒ

If you live close enough to campus, you may opt to commute from home. Naturally, though, you won't want to repeat your high school existence just because you're hanging with the fam for a bit longer. Laying down some ground rules can help you and your family make your transition from high school senior to first-year college student a smooth one. Living at home may be even more complicated if you were living on your own for a while before returning to the homestead. In this case, it may be especially important to have an explicit conversation on how you plan to conduct your life. You might want to consider the following issues when you're working out your new arrangements:

Your transportation. If public transportation is not an option and you don't have your own car, you may have to work out a transportation plan that meets everybody's needs. Or maybe your family can help you finance some wheels of your own. (A bicycle is an environmentally correct, heart-healthy alternative if you live close enough to campus.)

Your household duties. If you have previously been expected to help out with such chores as grocery shopping, cooking, or cleaning, it's safe to assume you still will be—but you might want to work out a schedule for your chores that meshes with your class, study, and work schedule. Special situations like exam week or a 20-page paper that was due first thing yesterday should be taken on a case-by-case basis; letting everyone know in advance that you're going to be tied up is an effective and considerate way of getting yourself off KP duty, if absolutely necessary.

Your independence. Sometimes progressing to a more mature level of existence when you're still under your family's roof can be tricky. Offering to pay your folks a little something in the way of rent—even if it's just a token amount—is a big step toward showing you're ready for adult responsibilities and privileges. And if friends are nervy enough to ask you what you're still doing under your family's roof, your best response—besides giving them the hairy eyeball—is to let them know that staying home for the short term will enable you to do what you want further on down the road.

You'll probably want to negotiate a new curfew (if you had one to begin with), although it's probably a good idea to let everyone know if you're going to be coming home on the late side. Look at cluing your family in as a simple common courtesy rather than a constraint on your freedom.

Your campus connection. Living at home means you'll have to work a little harder to keep up with what's happening at school. Putting yourself on mailing lists, subscribing to the school newspaper, and making it a point to stick around for lectures, readings, or club meetings can help you stay posted. It may also require extra effort to develop and maintain friendships. If late-night rendezvous at the library aren't an option, try scheduling coffee or lunch dates between classes, and/or coming in on weekends.

(See other hints for commuting from home on page 135 in "A Room of Your Own.")

Homeward Bound

☙☙☙

You've just pulled in the driveway, and you haven't been hugged this much since . . . well, since you *left* for school. Your aunt's teary-eyed, your father's beaming, and assorted siblings and family pets are grouped adoringly round your ankles. At long last you're home, and suddenly, you know just how Dorothy felt.

A week later, your mother is nagging you to do the five loads of laundry you lugged back with you, your grandma has asked for perhaps the hundredth time what you're doing on Saturday night, and to top it off, someone's spilled an entire Diet Coke on the psych paper you've been trying (unsuccessfully) to complete.

When the expectations for your homecoming are running high on both sides, it can be tough for the actual event to live up to its billing. You envisioned a warm and fuzzy snuggle in the bosom of your family, but things are turning out to be just a little pricklier. Your family is a bit confused by the minor but definitely perceptible shifts in your relationship. They may not understand why you get a little snippy after being asked a million and one questions about every little detail of your college existence, or why you would want to hang out with your col-

lege friends when "you can see them all the time." To top it off, no one knows exactly where you fit into the scheme of things: You're somewhere between a regular family member and a guest, and the lines of what you're expected to participate in are seeming a little blurry.

Even if you've been really looking forward to going home, it can take a few days to adjust once you're there. Reports of family feuds breaking out not 20 minutes after you walk in the door are not uncommon; things can get tense pretty quickly when you're used to doing things one way and your parents another. You might find yourself seriously missing all the quirky little freedoms that college has to offer (e.g., coming and going as you please, eating a half a box of Cap'n Crunch washed down with Mango Madness Snapple for dinner, taking a two-hour nap without anyone trying to feel your forehead).

> "Coming home after my first term at school was really hard. It was weird to be with my parents again. Anytime I wanted to go anywhere, I had to ask for their permission. It was hard living under their rules again."
>
> —STANFORD UNIVERSITY, '95

But not every homecoming has to be sprinkled with tension-filled moments, as long as you and your family are willing to adjust to the fact that you are all are on a slightly different footing. Though there's no avoiding every altercation, the following tips may help make the transition a little smoother:

■ Try not to be impatient with your family's need to ask numerous questions about your social or academic life at school. It can be fun to have such an attentive audience for your stories, and you might even find yourself appreciating the fact that they take such an interest in all your doings.

■ Nip potential scheduling conflicts in the bud. Let them know what your plans are going to be ahead of time so no one is tempted to cook a menu composed entirely of your favorite foods on the same night you're planning to dine out with friends.

> *"I was really worried about coming home that first time. My sister's relationship with our parents changed when she went away to school—they grew apart. But when I came home for Thanksgiving, it felt great to be around my family again. Sure it wasn't exactly as it had been, but I wouldn't have wanted it to be."*
> —OREGON STATE UNIVERSITY, '94

■ If your parents are the type who need to know where you're going and when you'll be back, it's probably easier just to fill them in than to fight about it.

■ Asking your family if there's anything you can do to help with the evening meal or offering to wash their whites with yours is always greatly appreciated. And working side by side on even the dullest task gives you a great chance to catch up on what's new in one another's lives.

MAINTAINING OLD FRIENDSHIPS

> *"My best friend from high school and I had a really tough time saying good-bye to each other. We've been friends for 11 years. I mean, you just don't say, 'See you later!' to someone you've known for that long."*
> —WILLAMETTE UNIVERSITY, '95

Seeing your old friends on that first break home can be a little surreal. Often the dynamic of the friendship was based on seeing each other just about every day. Now that you're in different places it can feel hard to connect. You may bump into the "you had to be there" syndrome: Certain experiences, jokes, and situations just won't come across if the two of you aren't in the same place, and it's easy for the day-to-day nuances of your separate existences to get lost in the translation. Usually all it takes is a few hours to get back on track—and the recognition that your friendship will change. Ask a lot of questions about what she is doing and don't get hyped about it if it takes a little time to feel totally comfortable together again.

Still, as time wears on, you might notice that you and a friend are on

STAYING IN TOUCH WITH FRIENDS FROM HOME

Even though your new friendships are progressing nicely, there are times when you'd chuck 'em all for one spin through the DQ drive-thru with a carload of your best high school buddies. Fortunately, out of sight doesn't have to mean out of mind. Try these tried and true ways to keep in touch:

▲ With family obligations, dental appointments, and shopping trips tugging at your vacation time, it might be harder than you think to squeeze in quality time with your friends, so it's not a bad idea to schedule the days or evenings you'll spend together before you even leave campus. If you want to bond to the fullest, arrange to spend a spring break together away from the family homestead.

▲ Get all your friends to go on-line. Many campuses offer free E-mail in their computer labs.

▲ As E. B. White said in *Charlotte's Web*, "It is not often that someone comes along who is a true friend and a good writer." If, like Wilbur, you've encountered someone who's both, letter writing can be a wonderful way to keep in touch—not to mention one of the cheapest.

▲ Take turns phoning each other so one person doesn't bear the brunt of the long-distance bills. If it's cheaper for one of you to call, the other can send a check for half of the damage.

▲ Send each other care packages during finals week.

▲ If it's doable, take turns road-tripping to see each other throughout the year.

markedly different trajectories. (Of course, this can happen with the friends you've made *on* campus, too.) For example, you might be headed to Osaka to immerse yourself in Japanese culture, whereas your friend is heading back to the 'burbs to plan her wedding to a high school sweetheart. It's tempting to focus on the differences that have sprung up between the two of you, and to weigh your friend's choices against your own. But dwelling on your dissimilarities isn't going to close the gap in your interests, nor will comparing your choices with the ones she's made. Obviously, you are separate people with different passions and talents, and it's going to take correspondingly different ways of life to make you happy.

That doesn't mean you shouldn't take an active interest in your friend's new pursuits and passions. First off, it'll act as the glue that holds you together. Second, who knows—you might learn something new. Third, seeing the new things your friend is into can help you recognize what directions you're moving in and why. And don't be afraid to discuss it all with your friend: Comparing and contrasting who you were with who you're becoming can draw the two of you even closer together.

more friends or relatives who were 100 or more miles away.

FORGING NEW FRIENDSHIPS

It's not uncommon to feel a little bit at a loss when it comes to the task of making new friends in college (or anyplace else, for that matter). During your last couple of years in high school you were probably a part of a comfortable, close-knit gang. You may not even remember how you hooked up with your high school friends in the first place. But fear not: If you did it once, you can do it again. And years later, when looking fondly back upon your college chums, you won't remember how you met up with any of them, either.

Where Do You Go to Find Friends?

First and foremost, remember that you and your fellow first-years are all passengers on the same boat. Nobody else knows anybody either, so don't feel as though you're starting off at a disadvantage. And not to worry: It's darned near impossible not to get

to know the folk coexisting on the floor of your dorm—you'll be constantly running into your neighbors in the elevator, in the cafeteria, and in the lovely communal bathrooms.

Get involved in the activities that pique your interests and you'll meet people who share them. You could join a campus political organization, write for the school paper, sign up for an intramural sport, join a film lovers' club, or do volunteer work or any other extracurricular activity that puts you into the social swim. Try hanging out at your student union; particularly at the beginning of the year, it'll be loaded with flyers, tables, and bulletin boards advertising every imaginable campus activity, and it's a prime gathering place for students of every stripe. Classes can yield up lots of potential pals, too. Don't hesitate to approach the woman whose contributions to your Religion and Society class discussion seem to mark her as a kindred spirit.

If you're feeling a little timid, it may seem easier to stay home and

> "One evening early on freshman year, several members of our floor took it upon themselves to conduct a room-by-room poll of who had lost their virginity, and where and when they'd done it. By midnight of that very same evening, the results were in and the most outrageous revelations had been gossiped over. . . . I swear at least four or five new friendships began that night."
>
> —UNIVERSITY OF IOWA, '92

72% of women and 42% of men say they would not give up

alphabetize your CDs. But resisting the urge to hole up in your room means you'll probably have a better time, and you'll definitely have a better chance of meeting people.

> "My circle of friends in high school were of great support to me. Once I got to college, I was lonely, and a little scared. I thought I would never meet anyone."
> —UNIVERSITY OF WASHINGTON, '94

Making Time for Studies

〰〰〰

After you've been at school for a few semesters, the issue will likely be less one of making friends than figuring out how to fit in your studies and other activities around them. There are few places in the world as social as a college campus. And for many of us, college is the first time we're living with friends. The temptation can be to spend most of your time hanging out, engaging in all manner of discussion, be it philosophical or frivolous. This isn't a problem in and of itself (as said before, some of the best learning takes place outside the classroom). But if you find yourself cutting class to take part in an ultimate Frisbee tournament or pulling all-nighters to play poker, you may have to reevaluate your priorities. It's true, friends are lifelong, but so are the analytical skills you learn in class. The key is to strike a balance between the two. This is usually simpler than it sounds. It just involves stopping talking about all the work you have and going off to do it.

WOMAN'S BEST FRIEND

A roommate who doesn't want to borrow money or clothes and is always happy to see you may sound tempting. But before you're seduced by a Free Puppies sign, remind yourself that owning a pet isn't just sloppy kisses and endless games of fetch.

Although an animal's companionship can be as rewarding as a person's (and in some cases infinitely more), a pet may be too much to take on in your college years. Think about it: Does your schedule permit frequent walks? Can you afford food and veterinary care? How will you replace your roommate's cashmere sweater after Spot uses it as a chew toy? Who will care for Fluffy when you spend the semester in France—or march on Washington over the weekend?

What's more, most on- and off-campus landlords frown on animals. Of course, you could smuggle your live cargo into your room, but all that secretiveness would get tiresome soon. And how long will a Great Dane fit in your jacket?

Even if you can't take on a pet full time, you can still make animal friends. Walk dogs for local senior citizens. Care for an out-of-town prof's cat. Volunteer at the humane society. Or lunch with the leeches in the biology building.

Keeping in Touch

Even though you're surrounded by pals in college (and even if you spend an extravagant amount of time with them), maintaining friendships can take work. A lot of friendships flourish because students are thrown together, whether it's in a dorm or classroom, or through involvement in an activity. With schedules changing every semester, dorm assignments every year, and involvement in activities ebbing and flowing, students can be torn apart as quickly as they're thrown together. So if you want to stay close to your costar in *A Raisin in the Sun* or last semester's lab partner, you may have to put in a little extra effort. Although scheduling lunch or coffee can seem overly formal and like another demand on your already limited time, it may mean the difference between cementing a friendship and drifting apart.

WHAT TO DO WHEN YOU HATE HER HONEY

What's the best course of action when you think your best friend's paramour is slimy, skanky, or just plain unworthy of her?

Simple: You keep it to yourself. This is one of the few situations when honesty is not the best policy. Telling your friend exactly what you think of her main squeeze is not a good idea, unless it means so much to you to spill the beans that you're willing to risk your relationship with her. If she demands that you tell her honestly what you think of the one who makes her heart pound and your skin crawl, do it as tactfully as possible so it's not painfully uncomfortable every time the three of you are together. It never hurts to add that you're happy that the object of her affections is keeping her so happy. And most likely, you'll mean it.

The diplomatic method should be likewise employed if your friend asks you for advice on how to handle a problem in her relationship. It's not wise to criticize her honey or to shriek, "Thank heavens you've seen the light!" when she confesses that her lover isn't as close to ideal-mate status as she'd originally thought. Instead, try to get her to focus on the real issues at hand: Is the problem she's complaining about easily cured with double doses of communication and compromise? You might also try posing the million-dollar question: When all is said and done, does the relationship make her happy?

And keep in mind that if you do wind up doling out specific advice, don't expect your friend to act immediately on everything you say—assuming she agrees with you—as few relationships change overnight. In the meantime, the two best things you can do for your friend are to be supportive of whatever decisions she makes, and to hear her out when she needs it.

 60% of conversations between women are about "personal"

Who's More Important, Anyway?

ⓥⓥⓥ

Everyone knows what it's like to have a friend drop off the face of the earth after she takes a hit from Cupid's arrow: You wind up spending equal time missing her and wanting to blow her off. A better solution, though, would be to let your friend know exactly how you feel when she puts you on the back burner to make room for a significant other. She may have been too blinded by her grand passion to even notice the toll it's been taking on your friendship. Recognize, though, that your friend will want to make time for her honey, and that you probably won't be able to hang with her 12 hours out of 24. But if she's not willing to invest some time in the friendship, she may not be the soulmate you thought she was.

It works both ways. If you're the one making the love connection, be sure you're giving your friends more than the busy signal. Splitting your attention equally between platonic and romantic relationships can be a

> "Starting sophomore year, my friend became more interested in guys and a boyfriend than in keeping our friendship strong. It got so bad that the only time we would do anything together was when she was between relationships, which wasn't all that often. I finally confronted her—she'd been oblivious to my discontent. We're getting along better now."
>
> —SCRIPPS COLLEGE, '94

difficult but worthwhile task. Take a hard look at your upcoming social calendar. Are you making enough time to meet up with the women or men who are your best buddies? And don't forget to cultivate the occasional new friendship as well.

ROOMMATES

It stands to reason that the first person you're going to bond with when you hit campus is your roommate. Sometimes you don't know what you'd do without her—for instance, after she coaxes you out of a finals-induced nervous breakdown. Other times her little quirks drive you up a wall—does anyone really need to play 45 minutes' worth of alarm tag before they're fully awake?

Let common sense call the shots when it comes to interactions with your roommates. Open lines of communication, a strong hands-off-without-asking-first policy when it comes to clothes and other goodies, and a healthy tolerance for one another's pet peeves and idiosyncrasies will go a long way toward ensuring peace and harmony between you and your cohabitants. A roommate may not even be aware that she's driving you crazy with one of her habits. Just letting her know that you're finding something she does particularly irksome can sometimes clear up the problem once and for all.

Take mental notes on what makes your roommate happy or upset, overjoyed or completely furious, and refer to them occasionally. Being in tune with each other's moods, quirks, and foibles ensures that you'll stay in bet-

TAKING THE BEAST BY THE HORNS

"I never knew how to argue before I went to college. Even though I grew up in a progressive household, I internalized the idea that women are supposed to be agreeable and accommodating, and I took any criticism as a complete attack on and rejection of my whole self. . . . Learning conflict resolution and assertiveness training have made my relationships so much more fulfilling, and have improved my self-esteem a thousandfold."
—WELLESLEY COLLEGE, '94

Whether you're talking about a relationship with a friend, lover, or family member, unless you're diligent about steeling yourself against every little misunderstanding and lapse of courtesy, you're going to have the occasional . . . er, disagreement. Knowing that probably won't make it any easier to have it out, but an argument doesn't have to cause a total communication breakdown. In fact, a "good" argument—one blessed with diplomacy and the desire to hear the other person's side—can do the opposite, clearing the air and preventing small conflicts from turning into irreconcilable differences. Following are ways to help ensure that a bad situation has a good outcome:

▲ Try to ignore your first instinct to attack, defend, or lose your temper as an argument heats up. Staying calm, cool, and reasonably collected can spell victory for both sides.
▲ Fault the behavior, not the person.

Say that you find your friend's habit of always being late annoying—not that you find *her* annoying.
▲ Make an effort to see things from the other person's point of view. You may learn a few new things about the situation at hand—and your role in it.
▲ Admit it when you're wrong. You've got to love a person who's willing to shoulder some—or all—of the blame (when appropriate). And if your friend/partner/relative sees that you're willing to admit to fault, she will be less likely to go on the defensive, and more likely to hear what you have to say.
▲ Listen. Do your best not to interrupt, defend, debate, thwart, resist, or tune out the other person while she's making her point.
▲ If the two of you just can't seem to get anywhere in resolving your conflict, call a time-out. After you both have had a chance to reconsider your positions, you may find that they've shifted enough to allow a compromise or that you care more about the relationship than about being right.
▲ Once you've come up with a solution, it's not a bad idea for you to do a quick recap of all the points you've resolved. That way, there's less chance the argument will recur.

"I've always followed the 'fighting fair' method. Before I get angry, I ask myself: 'Am I fighting because I want to fight or because I want to resolve something?'"
—PITZER COLLEGE, '93

ter harmony, and you'll be able to resolve differences more quickly if and when they do arise. (You also may want to keep track of when her exams, papers, and other projects are due, so you can be extra nice or at least non-confrontational during these periods.) Knowing each other's background and upbringing can also bring about a certain understanding, if not tolerance, of the behavioral tics that make you bug-eyed. Maybe your roommate comes from a big family whose ruling motto is "share and share alike," in which case she may be more likely to borrow clothes or other possessions without asking. Or if you learn that your roommate never had to help out with cleaning and tidying up at home, it shouldn't surprise you that her side of the room resembles Pigpen's abode. Communication styles can be handed down through the generations as well. One roommate might be descended from a long line of highly confrontational types who view heated argument as the best way to "get everything out in the open," one might be of the "say that nothing's wrong but snap at anything that moves" ilk, while you prefer to work out problems in a low-key, matter-of-fact way. Being aware of conflicting personal styles will help you read each other better and not take things personally shouldn't be.

THE ROAD TO ROMANCE

At no other time in your life will you be presented with so many options for dating than when you are in college. Sampling from the dating smorgasbord that's spread out before you provides a great opportunity to get acquainted with your own tastes and compatibilities. And a college campus offers limitless possibilities for an afternoon or evening out. A night at the theater, a sporting event, a poetry reading, or just a stroll through your campus can be fertile ground for a romance to take root.

As for the cons of college dating, studies, classes, and extracurricular activities can all make claims on the time that's needed to get a relationship rolling. In fact, the loose, informal nature of college romance can postpone a shift into a steady dating mode in which the two of you are seeing each other on a one-on-one basis. All in all, whether you're seeking out a serious romance, or just a fun compadre to hang out with occasionally, most colleges supply a hard-to-equal range of romantic possibility.

Intimate Relationships 101

There's nothing quite like finding yourself in an intimate relationship that's in full swing. Hooking up with someone romantically can cast a rosy glow on nearly all aspects of your life. It's like an emotional springtime: Your world takes on brighter shades, and even the mundane details of a daily existence are infused with a new vitality. You feel footloose and fancy-free, shedding emotional restraints like so many layers of winter clothing.

By their very nature, however, romantic relationships also involve a fair share of stormy weather. No matter how hard the two of you try, the moment you step over the platonic line (and what a moment it is), the intensity factor in your relationship is going to change. You're going to be much more aware of each other on a physical level—just brushing past that special someone can trigger pulse-quickening, knee-weakening tremors. You'll also be more sensitive to the emotional details of your relationship. Things that might not have bothered you a whit when you were just friends can take on major importance when you're lovers.

That's why intimate relationships require so much energy and upkeep once you're beyond the getting-to-know-you stage. Learning to trust someone physically and emotionally requires time, patience, caring, and mutual respect, but it's a process that's key to the growth and health of any relationship. Granted, letting down your guard for another person isn't always easy. But that's exactly what relationships are for: revealing the facets of your identity that can get lost in the day-to-day shuffle and in doing so rediscovering the inestimable freedom of just being yourself.

You Say Tomayto, I Say Tomahto

ೞ

All relationships require a little maintenance in the form of—what else? —good communication. But when you sense that things between you and the person you're dating are going off-track, it's not always easy to bring it up, especially if it's hard to pinpoint exactly what's going wrong. Still, bringing it up is exactly what you have to do.

Before you have the big discussion, determine exactly what's bothering you. If it's not easy to put your finger on the problem, ask yourself, are his actions contributing to the problem? His attitude? What he does or doesn't say? Could it just be that your expectations for the relationship are out of sync? Also consider that the problem may lie in a simple misunderstanding. For example, your boyfriend may think he's doing you a favor by planning your entire weekend together, while you think he's being overbearing.

No matter what the problem is, the quicker you can let each other know what's on your collective minds, the better. Letting a problem fester isn't going to do either of you any good. Tell your boyfriend what your needs are as well as what behaviors aren't acceptable to you and why and ask him to do the same. Such conversations are never easy. But if you go into them with a low-key, nonconfrontational approach, a willingness to compromise, and a sense of humor you'll likely find that the negotiation process isn't as awkward or acrimonious as you imagined it would be.

Sometimes you'll find that you just need to cut each other some slack. No one is going to meet all your hopes and expectations all the time. So choose your battles wisely. If your darling is doing something only mildly irritating, let it go, and work instead on the habits or behaviors that you really don't think you can live with.

If your relationship continually

FALLING FOR A FRIEND

He's the one who taught you to play pool. You've spent hours studying together, you helped him throw his roommate's surprise party, and you've turned to each other as a source of romantic advice. The problem is, you seem to be noticing more and more lately what a great smile he has, and you're starting to have some pretty heady *When Harry Met Sally*-style fantasies. . . .

If you find yourself in this situation—and college's vast potential for spawning both requited and unrequited relationships makes it a real possibility—you have several options. If you're the strong, silent type, you might be tempted to just stick it out and not say a word, hoping that he'll get the clue and make the first move. You might try to up the romance factor in your activities: Ask him to go to a concert, make him dinner, or, if you're especially brave, invite him out with you and an already established couple. But be prepared: He may not get the hint for some time—or he may just be ignoring it if he'd rather keep things the way they are.

Choosing to reveal your feelings is obviously the more direct and speedy route, but it can be awkward, especially when you're worried about how it will affect your friendship. So before you disclose your feelings, be sure you're ready for the relationship to change (including in a nonromantic direction).

If he leaps at the chance to become your boyfriend as well as your buddy, congratulations. (But keep in mind that you both may need some time to get used to the boost in the intensity of your relationship. The expectations you place on someone you're smooching are higher, too. If he forgot to call you back when you were friends, it was no big deal, but let him try it when he's your boyfriend. . . .)

The eminently less desirable and trickier outcome is that he's more comfortable with the two of you being just friends. Now the challenge is to maintain the friendship despite your revelation. If you truly think you can manage it, assure him that you understand and you'll do your best to keep *your* feelings from interfering with your friendship. It may take some time before you're comfortable with him in all the ways you were before you spilled the beans, but stick it out.

makes you unhappy or your fights are especially heated or frequent but you want to stay together, consider seeking the help of a counselor. A relationship that has crossed the line into physical violence (or threatens to) is one you need to get out of as quickly and by any means possible. Remember, no one has the right to hurt you, no matter what has been said or done. Telling a friend, calling a hotline, and heading for your campus health service are all good first steps to take. (For more information about getting out of an abusive relationship, see "Ending the Silence," page 491.)

Breaking Up

ᦉᧁᧁ

If your relationship seems to have more bad days than good, and all your efforts to improve matters just don't seem to be working, it may be time for the two of you to break up.

Should you decide to call it quits (or if you're on the receiving end of the decision), give yourself some time to feel miserable. A reasonable mourning period—say, a few days to a few weeks, depending in part on how long you went out—is a natural part of the bounce-back process. (If you're hurting really badly, or the pain just isn't going away, you may want to seek a little counseling.) Recovering from a bad breakup is like recovering from a virus: You may still feel hot, weak, or shaky, your symptoms return when your resistance is low, and there's nothing to do but wait it out. But before you give up all hope of recovery, note the following tips to help get you back in on your feet:

- We've all heard this before, but get out there and get busy. Resist the urge to hole up in your room. Fill your new free time by hanging out with friends, catching up on your studies, or doing a little volunteer work. Before you know it, Mr.-or-Ms.-Not-Quite-Right will be invading your thoughts less and less.

- Let yourself be sad for a while. Don't wallow indefinitely, but give yourself some time to let it all hang out emotionally, rather than trying to bottle up your unhappiness.

- Don't forget to exercise. There's nothing like a good workout to lift your mood, energize you, and make you feel powerful and in control.

HOW MUCH IS TOO MUCH?

A common sticking point in relationships is determining how much time you should be spending together. It's likely that one of you will require more personal space than the other does. If you've spent every night together for the past eight days, it's only natural that someone is going to want to come up for air. If it's your partner who's pulling back, it doesn't mean that s/he doesn't care for you or want to be around you—it might just mean s/he needs to spend the afternoon shooting hoops with some friends. Likewise, there are going to be times when the last thing you want to see is the sight of him or her taking up space on your sofa while you're trying to finish putting your art portfolio together. Honoring one another's wish for some time apart can only have positive results for both of you—not to mention for the friends who are half-expecting to see your picture on a milk carton.

38% of women and 28% of men say they can find someone at-

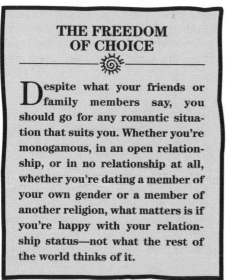

THE FREEDOM OF CHOICE

Despite what your friends or family members say, you should go for any romantic situation that suits you. Whether you're monogamous, in an open relationship, or in no relationship at all, whether you're dating a member of your own gender or a member of another religion, what matters is if you're happy with your relationship status—not what the rest of the world thinks of it.

■ Unless you are absolutely certain it won't be torture for either one of you, resist the temptation to call or hang out with your ex. You need a little time alone to get over him or her.

■ Again, talk to a professional if you're really having a hard time getting over the relationship.

EXPLORING YOUR SEXUALITY

Whether you're in a relationship or not, a healthy sense of your own sexuality depends on getting to know one person intimately: yourself. Discovering your sexuality is a lifelong process that involves learning who you are and what gives you the most pleasure. It's understanding your needs and desires, and how they can be fulfilled. It's feeling comfortable in your own skin and getting to know and accept your body for what it is. It's becoming familiar with the range of responses that you have when you're touched. And it's knowing how your body reacts when it's next to another. Sexuality is an essential part of your emotional and psychological makeup, so you should never feel that you don't deserve to explore it to the fullest. No explanations, labels, or rationalizations are necessary to justify what you like, what you do, what you'd like to do, what you don't want to do, or who you do it (or not do it) with. Your relationship with your sexual self should be a source of pleasure and excitement that enriches every aspect of your life, not something that makes you feel ashamed, embarrassed, or guilty.

But understanding and accepting yourself isn't always that easy—your own emotions, beliefs, or inhibitions can be obstacles to getting to know yourself as a sexual being. There may be inherent contradictions in what you want and don't want, fears about what is "acceptable," and the conflicting

"I despise pornography in a political sense, but it turns me on anyway. For years I would feel guilty about it and think that I was a bad person because of it. Now I just accept it. There is nothing wrong with me if something that is supposed to turn people on turns me on, too.... I actually find it somewhat exciting that I can derive some sort of pleasure or arousal from an image and that my sexuality is complex and multifaceted."
—UNIVERSITY OF VIRGINIA, '93

tractive only if s/he has similar religious beliefs to their own.

pressures to "be sexual and enjoy it" on the one hand and to "pet your dog, not your date" (or yourself) on the other hand.

Social mores and expectations can have a dramatic influence on how you relate to both your own sexuality and other people's. Gender roles, the media, religion, our communities, past relationships, and your friends, lovers, and family can influence your perceptions of "good" sex and "bad" sex, and what's sexy and what's not. On one level, it can be useful and interesting to decode the messages that are affecting your attitude toward what turns you on. You may then choose to challenge those ideas and see what happens when you decide that you're not going to censor your desires. (See "Sex, Lies, and Stereotypes," below.)

But on another level, it doesn't really matter why you get pleasure from one thing and not another. There is no "right" or "wrong" way to feel. The goal is to feel comfortable enough to explore what is satisfying to you and to accept what you discover without evaluating it or judging it. Delving deep down and checking out some of the most intense and personal aspects of who you are is pretty powerful

> "One of the most liberating parts of sex for me was realizing that someone else thought my curves and fat were soft and exciting. The fact that someone else thought my body was beautiful helped me to see it that way. I wish that I could have realized it alone, but now I will always know it for myself."
>
> —GRINNELL COLLEGE, '91

stuff. And it can be especially wonderful when you do it with another person in a context where you feel safe enough to let your guard down and enjoy it.

Sex, Lies, and Stereotypes

꩜꩜꩜

Sexual stereotypes—misguided or negative assumptions about sexual behavior that are race-, class-, or gender-based—are some of society's less positive contributions to our perceptions about sexuality. Stereotypes based on gender roles (which dictate that we should look or act in ways that match narrowly defined expectations about what a woman is supposed to do, think, and feel) are hard to miss. The old double standard that men who sleep around a lot or love sex are "studs" but women who do the same are "sluts" has remained, with few exceptions, an accepted perception. Women are assigned a variety of not very flattering adjectives—like "frigid," "passive," "loose," "submissive," "delicate," or "easy"—when it comes to describing female sex roles and behaviors. Such labels are sometimes used in conjunction with racial stereotyping: e.g., "Latin women are hot" or "Asian women are submissive." Although stereotypes and their consequences are in the process of being challenged and dispelled, there are still plenty of them to go around.

Another way that society can influence our perceptions of ourselves and our sexuality is by holding up images of what a sex god or goddess is supposed to look like. Having a body like a Hollywood starlet's is not a prerequisite for a good sex life, but accepting the way you look can be. Granted, it might be hard to feel sexy when all you can think about is the five pounds you put on last month. But dwelling on or distorting the reality of how you look is self-defeating. In order to reap the full rewards of your own sexuality you've got to love your body for what it is. Besides, your partner might delight in what you consider a physical drawback.

The Anatomy of Arousal

ⓥⓥⓥ

Sex is more than just a series of hormone-triggered reactions. Your feelings about yourself, your partner, and even the environment you're in are intrinsically linked to your sexual responses; arousal is as much an emotional as a physical state. Sometimes as little as a brief touch, a song lyric, a whiff of a familiar cologne, or even watching a C-SPAN debate on health care reform (hey, whatever blows your skirt up) can stimulate your desire. Other times, a romantic dinner for two, complete with champagne, can-

dles, and strolling musicians, isn't enough to get you in the mood.

Physically speaking, when you get aroused, your pelvic region, clitoris, and vagina become swollen and engorged with blood. The whole area feels full and warm, and your vagina produces a fluid that makes it and your labia wet and slippery. Your clitoris becomes erect and sensitive to touch. Your pelvic muscles contract, your nipples harden, your skin flushes, and your breathing gets heavier.

CHALLENGING SEXUAL STEREOTYPES
❋

The first step in safeguarding ourselves and others against stereotypes is to assess how they operate in our own lives. Do you take it for granted that a man has to make the first move? Do you make assumptions about a partner's sexual experience, behavior, and desires based on his/her background? Do you allow fears about homosexuality to make you feel uncomfortable about forming close friendships with other women or exploring your curiosities or fantasies?

On a positive note, thinking about sexual stereotypes gives us a context in which to examine our own beliefs and experiences. And the effect of revealing stereotypes for what they are extends beyond bedroom doors to bring freedom and acceptance into our relationships with our friends, family, coworkers, and ourselves.

THE FIRST TIME

"When I got to college there was such a focus on intercourse, I was convinced that I was the only person my age who was still a virgin. (I was totally wrong.) I would preface remarks with 'Even though I'm still technically a virgin, I've done everything else.' Why did I have to justify myself? Why did I feel so embarrassed when I told people I was going out with?"

—UNIVERSITY OF NEBRASKA, '87

The first time you have sex with another person might be scary, awkward, painful, intense, disappointing, or exhilarating or a combination of the above. Chances are you'll be nervous because you're doing something new and because it's probably been built up into a big, big deal. Just as you probably weren't able to ride a bicycle perfectly the first time out, you probably won't be an expert the first time you try intercourse or giving a "blow job." It takes time to learn about your body and desires, to say nothing of your lover's body and desires.

Below are a few things to consider when you are thinking about having sex for the first time:

▲ As hard as it may be, do not allow yourself to feel pressured to have sex. Only you will know when you're ready, meaning that you're emotionally comfortable with the idea, and that you are responsible enough to assert your needs and limits and to take the appropriate measures to protect against unwanted pregnancy and sexually transmissable diseases. (See "Contraception and Safer Sex," page 399.)

▲ If you have an intact hymen, your first experience with vaginal penetration may cause bleeding and/or some pain. (For more about the hymen, see page 348.)

▲ Before penetration, for the sake of pleasure, comfort, and ease, you should be aroused so your vaginal muscles are relaxed and your vagina is well lubricated. You may also want to use a water soluble lubricant, especially if you're using a condom. (And, given the risk of possible STD transmission or a pregnancy, it would be in both your best interests to use a condom and spermicidal jelly.)

▲ There's no predicting how you'll feel after the first time. You may be so overwhelmed with emotion that you start to cry, so nervous that you're a bit distracted, or have a "that's it?!?" feeling.

▲ If your experience doesn't rival a big screen sex scene, remember it takes time to learn what makes you and your lover feel good. Frankly, if we all used our first sexual experience as the basis for our sexuality, many of us would have never given sex another chance. Work with yourself and your lover to learn what you each like.

The average length of an erect penis? In one survey, men's average

As arousal heightens and the tension in your pelvic region builds, the clitoris retracts under its hood. As the inner labia are stimulated directly or indirectly, the clitoral hood moves back and forth over the glans, the highly sensitive nodule of tissue and nerve endings that's underneath. An orgasm occurs when the tension is released in a series of involuntary and intense muscular contractions of the uterus, anus, and vagina that release the blood from the pelvic area. Some women compare this release of tension to a sneeze, others to a slow, spreading warmth. The sensations are often felt through the entire pelvic region, and to some degree, even throughout your body.

In recent years, there's been much talk about the G-spot, an acorn-size region behind the front wall of the vagina (between the cervix and the back of the pubic bone) that for some women may be highly sensitive. When this spot is stimulated in these women, it causes an intense orgasm that is often accompanied by a gush of fluid (that is not urine) through the urethra. If you are interested in locating the G-spot and all its possibilities, there are a number of books available to show you exactly where it is, and there are special curved vibrators that can make the hunt that much easier.

So What Happens to Men?

ᖇᖇᖇ

When a man becomes aroused, his blood pressure, breathing rate, and heart rate rise, and his pelvic region becomes increasingly sensitive. His penis fills with blood, becomes larger and erect, and his testicles move in closer to his body. His nipples become hard and the glans of the penis and the testicles become flushed and increased in size. Clear preseminal fluid, which contains a high concentration of sperm, may ooze from the tip of the penis.

Orgasm begins with emission—when secretions from the prostate and other internal glands in the pelvic region and sperm from the testicles flow to the base of the urethra. Soon after emission occurs, contractions of the penis and urethra force this mixture, called semen, through the tip of the penis in spurts, and the man ejaculates. These highly pleasurable contractions are felt throughout the pelvic and rectal areas. After orgasm, blood leaves the genitals and pelvic region, and the genitals return to their previous size, shape, and color.

The Big O

ᖇᖇᖇ

It's pretty safe to say that no two orgasms are exactly alike. When you have an orgasm, or come, it can resemble a mild shiver, a ripple, or a series of intense rolling or pulsing waves. It can feel like a chain reaction of small orgasms or one big explosive one. It may remain centralized in the vaginal or pelvic region or it may move upward and outward through your whole body. Many women reach orgasm after clitoral stimulation but there are other ways to reach it, including, for a few, nipple stimulation alone. Some of us may need to take a breather following an orgasm, while others may want to get right back to business (provided their partner is ready and willing).

answer: 10 inches; women's: 4 inches. The Kinsey Institute says 5-7. ✵

> *"Being able to have an orgasm was an important thing for overcoming my lack of value for my body. It's such a creative thing that my body can create such incredible, vibrant pleasure. . . . Having an orgasm is like sheer sweetness."*
> —Tufts University, '89

But no matter how amazing orgasms can be—and for the most part, they do live up to the hype—they aren't the be-all and end-all of every sexual experience. The time you spend working up to an orgasm or basking in its glow can be just as fulfilling as the orgasm itself. Plus, nothing kills a sexy mood faster than trying to keep track of who's climaxing and how often.

Also remember that just because you don't climax every time or have multiple orgasms doesn't mean you're "frigid." Many women find it tough to have an orgasm via penetration alone—they may need a little manual stimulation as well. However, if you're not having orgasms and you'd like to, you can teach yourself how. Sex therapists and counselors recommend practicing solo. Then, once you've become familiar with your sexual response and feel comfortable having an orgasm, you'll know what it takes to have one with others.

Getting Into the Act

ೲೲೲ

The benefits of finding out your own patterns of sexual arousal and orgasm are many and varied. Putting a finger (so to speak) on exactly what turns you on is almost a surefire means of finding sexual satisfaction. Two of the easiest ways to explore what works for you sexually are masturbation and fantasy.

Masturbation is a means of exploring the particulars of your sexual response: what kind of pressure feels good, where it feels good, and how fast or slow you like to be touched. On top of being able to give yourself instant gratification, if you know precisely what gives you pleasure, you'll be able to communicate your needs to a lover more effectively. Masturbation can also help keep you in touch—literally—with your body's needs and rhythms, help relieve stress and help you relax and fall asleep.

Sexual fantasies—mental images or scenarios that trigger arousal—can

> *"I think the most important thing for women to know is how to masturbate: Lie down, get comfortable, and close your eyes. Get into how it feels when you touch your face, your breasts, your arms. Go into the bath and let a warm stream of water fall on your vagina. . . . Think about your whole body . . . or someone you are attracted to. Look at pictures that turn you on. Read erotic prose or poetry. Play sexy music. Fantasize or talk "dirty" to yourself. Suck on something. Use feathers, ice, lubrication, a pillow, or a vibrator to spice up an evening with yourself. I'm telling you, it is good!"*
> —The New School, '90

be another way to shed some light on what makes you tick sexually. Whether it's a quick MTV-style flash of an image or something resembling a fully scripted feature film, a fantasy can have a surprisingly powerful aphrodisiac effect. (And it doesn't necessarily have to resemble a porn movie in any way.)

When it comes to fantasy, your imagination's the limit. Your fantasies may not necessarily affect what you do or want in reality, though they may give you ideas about areas to explore. Because they are only fantasies, feel free to imagine scenarios you probably wouldn't actually find yourself in, for example, being entwined with someone you don't know or don't want to know or wouldn't be entwined with if you did know. And because they are only fantasies, they shouldn't make you feel scared, dirty, or bad.

COMMUNICATION ISSUES

Sex is one of the most powerful experiences that two people can share. Through physical intimacy you can express love, friendship, lust, desire, caring, need, and excitement, and learn about each other, each other's bodies, and your different pleasures.

There is no right way to have sex—no one way to be sexual with another person. That's part of the fun. You can spend hours entangled in each others' limbs, kissing and cuddling. You can explore your lover's body with your fingers or your tongue, or touch your own body. You can be rough or gentle. You can make up nicknames for each other that may

> *"Being sexual with another person is the most intense way to speak to another human being. I am always amazed by our bodies, how one touch can calm someone down and another touch can make them scream with, well, you know."*
>
> —CALIFORNIA STATE UNIVERSITY AT NORTHRIDGE, YEAR WITHHELD

or may not be appropriate to repeat in polite company. You can tease and tickle each other with words, fingers, or feathers or swap fantasies and feelings in person or by phone, E-mail, or letter. You can read to one another from erotic literature or rent an erotic movie. You can play strip poker, strip Scrabble, or naked Twister or dress up in sexy clothes or lingerie. You can try flavored condoms, dental dams, and lubricants. You can blindfold your partner or tie him up with scarves. (*Note:* If you are going to be playing games where "no" doesn't mean no, make sure you designate an alternate "stop" word. Choose a nonsexual term together, such as "purple" or "pumpkin pie" to let the other know when you've had enough.) If you are excited and happy, you can hoot and holler (but heed the schedule of your roommates). And who says sex has to be serious? A good laugh (not at your partner's expense, of course) can erase an awkward moment or create a sense of camaraderie that fosters emotional—as well as physical—bonding.

Different strokes for different folks is all too true, especially when it comes to sex. What makes some people go gaga with delight makes others uncomfortable or causes them pain, and the only way you're going to know is via clear communication. Don't assume your partner will like what you like—an especially easy trap to fall into if you're having sex with another woman—or will always like the same thing every time. Similarly, you may need to teach your partner what you like. You can be direct and ask what your partner likes and say what you like. Or you can show what you enjoy by what you say, by how you sigh, or by how you move your body.

> "Sometimes it's really nice when you're not an automatic sexual match. It means you've got to explore together and find out what the other wants. Asking for what I wanted made me really think about how to make someone else feel good. It even opened up other parts of our relationship."
>
> —University of California at Riverside, '96

THE LINGUISTICS OF SEX

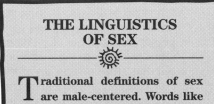

Traditional definitions of sex are male-centered. Words like "foreplay," "afterplay," and "intercourse" partition the sexual experience and turn the focus of sexual activity to vaginal penetration and male orgasm. In addition to excluding lesbian sex, this vocabulary makes other components of the sexual experience, such as touching, kissing, hugging, and massaging "less important" or a means to an end.

Similarly, many women feel that the traditional, intercourse-based definition of virginity doesn't describe their attitudes or experiences, particularly in its emphasis on something that is lost. In fact, many women feel that by losing their virginity they are in fact gaining something, i.e., a new way to express intimacy and a new appreciation of the pleasure their bodies can bring them.

Many women feel uncomfortable communicating during sex and may be quiet and undemanding in bed because they're afraid it will break the mood. And some have been implicitly taught that their partner's pleasure is more important than their own. Granted, getting pleasure from giving pleasure is an important part of sex. You may engage in certain activities because your partner enjoys them and you enjoy pleasing your partner (and s/he may do the same for you). Or because of time constraints and mood there may be times when you both don't "get your turn." But if you find you are compromising too often, it could be a problem. If your partner's

SEXUAL HEALING

For many of us, talking about sex with a partner is not easy, especially when things aren't going well. If you're trying to convey what gives you pleasure or learn what your partner likes during sex, you may feel like you're the protagonist of a dime-store novel. And if you have to bring up a problem, you may feel as if you are conducting a sex therapy seminar. We all want to get pleasure and to please the person we're with, but it can still be surprisingly difficult to say, "A little to the left, please," or even "*Passez le vibrateur, s'il vous plait.*" But introducing a little conversation into the proceedings can work wonders:

▲ Use positive reinforcement when you like something: "This feels so good." "I love it when you. . . ." "Do that again!" Or if you're more the nonverbal type, when your partner's on to something good, breathe heavily into his or her ear, move around, stroke whatever you can reach, or stop moving or stroking.

▲ Make sure that any negative feedback you must give is well-padded with positives.

▲ Don't say that it's really wonderful and that you're seeing "that which is most holy" if you're not.

▲ Teach him or her by example. Touch your partner in the manner or at the pace that you'd prefer—it's likely s/he'll get the hint.

▲ Along the same lines, ask your partner, "Does this feel good? How about when I do that?" or to describe in detail what it feels like when you touch different parts of his or her body in different ways.

▲ Use whatever vocabulary you feel comfortable with discussing intimate matters. Language that works in the bedroom doesn't have to be suitable for the classroom. Nor does it have to be racy or raunchy.

▲ Keep it light. Sex does not have to be serious.

▲ Be specific. Say how fast, how slow, how hard, how gentle (you get the idea).

▲ Take matters into your own hands. If your partner is having problems figuring out where it is you like to be touched, take his or her hand in yours and place it exactly where it needs to go. And don't stop there; gently demonstrate what kind of pressure and rhythm you'd like applied. The idea of introducing a game of "show and tell" into your bedroom may take a little getting used to for both of you, but it's certainly an effective and pleasurable teaching method.

needs are always being fulfilled and yours aren't, or if you feel "used" or as if your desires are not considered important in the relationship, discuss this with your partner.

Safer Sex—Not Just Latex

Safer sex involves more than using latex barriers to protect against dis-

sex; 42% sometimes do; and 44% do so as often as their male partners.

ease (see "Safer Sex," page 421). It involves knowing and respecting your partner's boundaries, asking if you're not sure if you're overstepping them, and making sure your own boundaries are known and respected.

When you have sex, you communicate using more than just words. However, this can leave you open to a great deal of ambiguity. You can misinterpret each other. A sigh of pain can sound like a sigh of pleasure. A gesture might mean your partner's knee is twisted and you need to change your position, that s/he doesn't want to go any further, or that s/he's having an orgasm. It's preferable to have a conversation before things get hot and heavy, but even if you do, it's imperative to check that you're reading your partner accurately while you're atangle. You've got to be especially explicit in your communication when you're with someone new or trying something new. Saying something like, "If anything makes you uncomfortable you'll tell me, right?" or even a simple, periodic "You OK?" is a good habit to get into. And speaking up if you feel uneasy, no matter why or when, is your responsibility to yourself and to your partner.

ACTIVIST IDEAS

■ Everyone—and especially first-year students—experiences some degree of homesickness and has awkward times when trying to renegotiate relationships with folks back home. But in general, students are reluctant to talk about or admit to their homesickness or difficulty adjusting (or at least not until after the fact), and attendance at an optional forum on these issues is quite likely to be pretty weak. So address these issues straight on in mandatory dorm meetings. Have people share their homesickness remedies, laugh and learn from older students' experiences working out the first visit home, and brainstorm ways to avert and/or resolve some of the inevitable conflicts and miscommunications that will arise between students and parents, siblings, and old friends. Pair up participants and pass out role-playing assignments or discussion topics such as, "Your mom wants you to major in something 'practical.' You've found that if don't spend the rest of your life studying postmodern Latin American women writers, your life will have no meaning"; or "You want to introduce your not necessarily prejudiced but certainly ignorant father to your new beau who's of a different race than you are," or "You come home from break and each family member has independently arranged to spend every moment with just you." Make it fun and interactive—it may not be a bad idea to invite a peer counselor or a counselor from health services to join in, but don't let it become a "relationships are hard" lecture. And because students who are living at home need to work out the relationship issues in person, on a daily basis, first-year students who aren't living in dorms should also be invited to join the groups.

■ Organize a series of informal discussion groups on such topics as how sex changes relationships; how you know if you're ready to have sex; the various often conflicting messages we get about sex; what is virginity; social pressures to have sex and not to; the connection between love and sex; women's erotica and how it differs from traditional pornography; and feelings about sex in the age of AIDS (include the basics of safer sex as well). Though some of the most potent social messages do revolve around heterosexual intercourse, the straight crowd certainly has no monopoly on these issues. Try to form groups with people representing all points on the sexual spectrum.

RESOURCES

STEPFAMILY FOUNDATION
333 WEST END AVENUE
NEW YORK, NY 10023
(212) 877-3244
Offers support to people dealing with the issues of step family relationships. Makes referrals to local support groups and professionals who can provide counseling. Publishes materials about step families and provides information about related issues.

SEX INFORMATION AND EDUCATION COUNCIL OF THE UNITED STATES (SIECUS)
130 WEST 42ND STREET, SUITE 350
NEW YORK, NY 10036-7802
(212) 819-9770
Promotes sex education and health care. Provides information on human sexuality. Publishes reports, books, bibliographies, and other information on sexuality.

DOWN THERE PRESS
938 HOWARD STREET, #101
SAN FRANCISCO, CA 94103
(800) 289-8423
Publishes numerous women-friendly, sex-positive books about sexuality and how to have fun with it. Write or call to request a free catalog of publications.

EVE'S GARDEN INTERNATIONAL, LTD.
119 WEST 57TH STREET
NEW YORK, NY 10019
(800) 848-3837

AND

GOOD VIBRATIONS
1210 VALENCIA STREET
SAN FRANCISCO, CA 94110
(415) 550-7399
Two warm, friendly, sensitive sex-positive stores dedicated to helping people enjoy and express their sexuality. (Eve's Garden is specifically for women.) They both sell sex toys, books, and other erotica. Call or write to request a free mail-order catalog.

SEXUAL ADDICTION ACCESS HELPLINE
(800) 362-2644
Provides counseling to people dealing with sex addiction and makes referrals to local support groups and practitioners.

and women "living together." Another 1½ million were same-sex partnerships.

Further Reading

〰〰〰

The Family Interpreted, Deborah Anna Leupnitz (Basic Books, 1988).

Women in Families, Marsha McGoldrick, Carol Anderson, and Fromma Welsh, eds. (W. W. Norton & Co., 1991).

Just Friends: The Role of Friendships in Our Lives, Lillian B. Rubin (Harper & Row, 1985).

You Just Don't Understand: Women and Men in Conversation, Deborah Tannen (Ballantine Books, 1990).

Uncoupling: Turning Points in Intimate Relationships, Diane Vaughan (Oxford University Press, 1986).

The Dance of Anger: A Woman's Guide to Changing the Patterns of Intimate Relationships, Harriet G. Lerner (Harper & Row, 1985).

The Kinsey Institute New Report on Sex: What You Must Know to Be Sexually Literate, June M. Reinisch and Ruth Beasley (St. Martin's Press, 1991).

The New Joy of Sex: A Gourmet Guide to Lovemaking revised edition, Alex Comfort (Pocket Books , 1992).

The Joy of Selfloving, Betty Dodson (Crown Books, 1987).

Enabling Romance: A Guide to Love, Sex, and Relationships for the Disabled (and the People Who Care About Them), Erica Klein and Ken Kroll (Crown Publishing, 1992).

The Lesbian Sex Book: A Guide for Women Who Love Women, Wendy Caster (Alyson Publications, 1993).

Susie Sexpert's Lesbian Sex World, Susie Bright (Cleis Press, 1991).

The Playbook for Women about Sex, Joani Blank (Down There Press, 1982).

The Good Vibrations Guide to Sex, Anne Semans and Cathy Winks (Cleis Press, 1994).

Also check out books written or edited by Lonnie Barbach:

For Yourself: The Fulfillment of Female Sexuality (Signet, 1975).

Erotic Interludes: Women Write Erotica (HarperPerennial, 1986).

Pleasures: Women Write Erotica (HarperPerennial, 1984).

Books by Nancy Friday:

My Secret Garden (Pocket Books, 1973).

Forbidden Flowers (Pocket Books, 1975).

Women on Top (Pocket Books, 1991).

Getting Involved

Lending a Hand, Taking a Stand

You could probably make it through your college career just going to class, studying, and attending to a few other essential matters. For the sake of a lively, exciting, and diverse campus, thank goodness most of us don't do this. The fact is, the listings in the course catalog represent only a small portion of the riches your campus offers. If it's like most schools, there are opportunities to get involved in music, theater, politics, service, and journalism, and many other areas that may have no connection to your official curriculum but nonetheless provide the chance to do a whole lot of learning (not to mention have a whole lot of fun). Getting involved with one or more of the organizations on campus or in the community will allow you to hone your skills, act on your beliefs, and become a more worldly person. And chances are, long after you've forgotten all the time lines, formulas, and verb conjugations you crammed into your head the night before that last final, you'll still have the friendships, leadership skills, and feelings of accomplishment you developed during your involvement.

GETTING STARTED

Campuses are filled to the gills with activities and opportunities. There are theater groups, school publications, intramural and varsity sports, sororities and fraternities, issue-oriented organizations, orchestras and choral groups, community service projects, religious programs, and academic and preprofessional clubs, to name just a few. Often, the hard thing to do is figure out which group or activity you want to join. Here are a few things to bear in mind while you're assessing your choices:

■ There's plenty of time to get involved. Don't feel like you need to join everything your first week or that you can't try something new in your second semester senior year. You have time to check out all the organizations that interest you.

■ Use the opportunity to challenge yourself, and get involved with groups of people who don't look just like you or think like you.

■ Don't bite off more than you can chew. Even if you feel you *have* to play on the ice hockey team, volunteer at a youth center, edit the poetry journal, *and* organize a food drive for a local shelter, think twice. If you have no time to think, eat, or sleep because you are running from meeting to meeting, chances are you won't be able to put enough into any of the activities and you won't enjoy them much, either.

■ Don't feel like you can't get involved because you don't have the knowledge and training necessary to offer what's needed. Many groups provide formal training (or can recommend places to get it) or buddy-up new recruits with veterans to learn the ropes. And chances are you'll find that the skills you already have, your enthusiasm, your desire to learn, and a week or two of experience will be all you need to get in the swim of things.

■ The participants may be as important as the goals of the group. A great group of people can breathe life into an uninteresting project, and a boring group can suck all the life from a challenging, exciting one.

> *"When I got to school I couldn't believe how many groups there were that addressed all the issues that were important to me, and at freshman orientation I signed up for a good 20 of them. I enjoyed getting all the attention at first, but by the end of the second month at school I was heavily involved in four organizations while running a campus-wide activity for a fifth. When I failed two midterms, I realized (at the insistence of my parents) that I needed to reassess my priorities."*
> —WASHINGTON UNIVERSITY, '97

■ Beware the pressure. Active members are the lifeblood of campus organizations, and they are usually not shy about asking a lot from you. Remember that just because you attend a couple of meetings and want to help out doesn't mean you are married to an organization. You can always say no to demands on your time.

■ Recognize that as your needs and interests change (as well as your living situation, class and work schedules, lovers, and academic focus), so will your level of involvement in different groups. Don't feel guilty if even though you spent every spare hour production managing the campus paper one semester, you're too busy (or even simply not inclined) to do it the next. Help find and train a replacement and move on.

FEAR OF COMMITMENT

"Getting involved" can seem like a scary prospect. You may be afraid that when you're looking just to spend a bit of time doing something you enjoy and care about, you'll be expected to make a commitment that will leave little time or energy for anything else. But just because you don't have the time or energy to tutor a spunky junior high school student, assist a homebound person with AIDS, or do advocacy work at the local courthouse, that doesn't mean you can't do something for the causes you think are important. The fact is, there are many ways to "do good," have fun, make change, and get involved, even if you only have a few hours to spare.

▲ Support people and groups who are doing work you think is admirable. Donating time and/or money is one way, but letting them know you appreciate their work is another. Telling someone who's involved in a big-sister program that you've noticed how happy her "little sister" looks when they're together or sending a note to a safer-sex educator thanking her for her presentation can have a real impact.

▲ Write a paper about a current campus, community, or world issue for a class, and upload it on-line.

▲ Send a note (or E-mail) to school, community, state, or national officials expressing your views. Or write a letter to the campus paper, go on-line and post in a newsgroup, or bring up the topic when hanging out with a group of friends.

▲ Recycle your term paper rough drafts and soda cans, buy a can or two of beans for the food drive, donate a shirt you never wear to a clothing drive, and sign a petition.

▲ Attend a rally, read student magazines, and go to student concerts. Campus groups need participants as much as they need organizers. Even if you don't have the time to participate in the planning, by all means, enjoy it.

▲ Give when and where you can. You don't have to volunteer every day (or even every week) in order to make a difference.

▲ Put up a sign; display a bumper sticker; wear a button.

▲ Vote.

▲ Make the world a better place by example. Say thank you, treat other students with respect, don't forget to tell your friends how great they are, write a letter to your grandma every so often, stick up for people who are being treated unfairly, make it a point to meet and explore relationships with people who are different than you are. What may seem like a little thing—saying, "I think you made a great point today in class," being friendly to the person checking IDs at the library, holding the door for someone—can make you and others feel appreciated and important. And isn't that one of the ultimate goals of service?

1991 and '93, women's average contribution rose 2.3%, men's dropped 5.7%.

SORORITIES—SISTERHOOD IS POWERFUL

"People always mention initiation period when they talk about the problems with sororities. Pledging can be difficult, but it's your decision whether or not you want to do it. . . . For me, choosing to push myself and see how much I could do was really worthwhile—it made me a stronger and more confident person."

—UNIVERSITY OF VIRGINIA, '96

One of the most popular ways that women get involved on campus is by joining sororities. At schools big and small, sororities may offer a sense of belonging to a time-honored tradition (which may be shared with mothers, aunts, sisters, and grandmothers), a locus for school and community service, an opportunity to hone leadership skills, a support group, a network for life, and a great gang of friends all wrapped up into one. Plus, in some cases, you get a beautiful house to live in as well.

On the downside, by their very nature sororities are exclusive. You can't join even the most lenient of houses without an invitation. And if it is your first college experience, being rejected from the sorority of your choice isn't exactly getting off on the right foot. In addition, sororities have a way of dominating members' social life, can take up a lot of time (by requiring you to attend meetings and parties), and cost quite a bit, too.

THE CHANGING FACE OF GREEK LIFE

On many campuses, the Greeks have been getting some heat in recent years, which can be mostly attributed to the high incidence of fraternity-related sexual assault, underage drinking, and hazing and initiation rituals that cause members harm. But the fraternity and sorority systems have been making some changes. There's been an effort to address problems through seminars on sexual assault and date rape, workshops on eating disorders and body image, programs dealing with (or initiating bans on) the use of alcohol and other drugs, and diversity awareness training. Rules about rush and initiation period, drinking, and hazing are being more strictly enforced. There is increased emphasis on community service. (And fraternities and sororities formed for the sole purpose of doing community service, such as Alpha Phi Omega, are becoming very popular.)

"The pervasive image of sororities is Scarlett O'Hara types sipping mint juleps on the porch of their stately mansion. Black sororities are totally different. We are a close-knit group and very committed to our community, including other women of color on campus and around the world. It's an affirming place, a loving place, a place that makes me proud to be a black woman."

—BARNARD COLLEGE, '97

Coed frats are also popping up on campuses across the country.

GETTING TO KNOW YOU: RUSH

"Rush week is like a job interview from hell. You have to kiss butt, send in references, wear uncomfortable clothing, and be nice to everyone. But instead of them paying you once you're accepted, you have to pay them."

—*VANDERBILT UNIVERSITY, '96*

Though there are many schools that have informal rush, rush is usually a structured, meticulously planned event. You and your fellow rushees may be separated into groups and assigned a rush leader who will accompany you on all the week's visits, offering advice, moral support, and quick beauty fixes whenever needed. Rush week consists of a series of parties given by every sorority on campus. (Some of them have catchy themes like "Fly the Friendly Skies with Theta Pi," in which all the "actives"—charter members of the sorority are dressed up as flight

attendants.) The parties give you opportunities to mix and mingle with each and every member of the various houses. (So brush up on possible small-talk topics, as you'll want to keep the conversational ball rolling as you circulate among the actives.) The events start out pizza-party informal and end with many a ceremonial flourish on "bids night."—the all-important evening when you pick your house and your house picks you.

TAKING THE PLEDGE

Most houses have a clandestine initiation process that involves learning house secrets, getting to know the other women, and doing fun and silly activities. It also may involve mild to intense humiliation at the hands of your sisters-to-be. It's tough to say no in situations like initiation, when the reigning philosophy is that suffering together will make you closer and that what doesn't kill you will make you stronger. However, if you don't feel up to the pressure and proceedings, remember that you do not have to continue. If you decide you don't want to be a part of the sorority, dropping out will not prevent you from having a flourishing social life during your college years. If you want to quit, have a one-on-one with your "big sister" or "pledge mom" or another active you think may be understanding. Chances are, if you explain your reasons for dropping out in a diplomatic, nonaccusatory manner, everyone will understand. And if they don't, as your mom would say, what kind of friends are they, anyway?

SCOUTING OUT ON-CAMPUS GROUPS

College catalogs, orientation materials, and the back-to-school edition of the paper usually list the names, numbers, and meeting places of campus organizations. Not that you'd need such a list when these materials appear, as the groups are usually quite active and visible at the beginning of fall semester. However, in February, when you're hankering for a new project or an emotional support group, darned if they (and the lists) don't all seem to have disappeared into the tundra that is your campus.

How do you find what's happening where? Checking out the following sources should lead to clues.

■ The student activities office or student government office should know about the existence, philosophies, reputation, and activities of every campus group.

■ Academic departments will know of conferences, academic societies, pre-

---

FACILITIES, FACILITIES, FACILITIES

Take advantage of everything that comes free (or cheap) with the price of tuition. Depending on where you go to school, you might play squash or tennis; go skating, swimming, and skiing; take weight training, yoga, dance, and aerobics classes; and have access to all the equipment you'd need for a pick-up softball game or pillow polo match for next to nothing (and even, possibly, get gym credit to boot). You can try your skills at disk jockeying or producing a film or a local-access TV show, or reserve a soundproof room in which to rehearse with your not-ready-for-the-studio band, Taste the Cow. There may be a language lab in which to dabble in a bit of conversational Portuguese in your spare time or a screening room where you can have a public viewing of the video of your grandparents' 50th wedding anniversary party. There are many student- and/or university-run art collectives that allow you access to a darkroom and photo-processing chemicals, a pottery kiln, and woodworking and metal shop studios.

In addition, libraries are often taken for granted, and not recognized as places to catch up on all the latest newspapers and magazines, listen to CDs, watch videos, borrow sheet music, and play with CD-ROMs. (And rummaging through rare book rooms and special collections is one of the most underrated activities around. Even those who burn their books at the end of the semester can't help but feel a thrill when looking at letters, writings, and pictures of the famous and infamous.) Plus, the campus computing center can be more than just a place to print out papers. It can be where you learn to surf the net, become acquainted with machines and programs that will make you an A-1 job applicant, and release yourself from the shackles of technophobia.

---

professional organizations, special lectures, and presentations.

■ Bulletin boards in dorms, dining halls, libraries, academic and recreational buildings, and the student center often have the newest and most current listings. (And if you pull off a few staples, you're sure to uncover some less current listings as well.)

■ The campus newspaper and radio station usually provide up-to-date info.

■ Pay a visit to the appropriate facilities (the theater to find out about acting groups, a soup kitchen to find out about helping the needy, the athletics office to find out about sports, etc.).

■ Asking your friends and classmates is a time-honored way of learning about groups and activities.

"I used to hate it when people would join the paper or do community service because they wanted it on their résumé or their parents pushed them to do it. But it doesn't really matter why people start to participate in campus groups; they always end up being so thankful they did, and they always get much more out of it than they thought."

—WEST CHESTER UNIVERSITY, '95

CAMPUS HIGHLIGHT

In 1982 a group of students, staff, and faculty at New York City's Hunter College School of Social Work who were interested in promoting community activism started the Education Center for Community Organizing (ECCO), a teaching and networking group for local activists. It organizes events ranging from large-scale conferences to informal coffeehouses, is home to a library of materials and a job file for organizers, and provides training for people working for peace, equality, and social and economic justice.

LENDING A HAND: COMMUNITY SERVICE

Thousands of students do some type of public service during their college years. They get involved in such projects as helping to renovate or build housing for the homeless, teaching English to recent immigrants, cleaning up neglected city parks, or volunteering in an after-school program for kids. Most students start volunteering to help others, but find that they end up getting as much out of it as they give, if not more. Doing community service provides the opportunity to learn from people you might not otherwise encounter, and the brush with their lives can enrich yours. The blind woman that you read to has an incredible collection of jazz albums and great stories to share; the kids you play baseball with offer spontaneous affection; even the irascible old man at the soup kitchen has quite a few things to teach you about assertiveness.

> *"It's easy for people to feel overwhelmed with all the problems they see. They want to help everybody, and work on everything, but can't figure out where to start, so they end up not doing anything. . . . People should just start somewhere, choose something."*
>
> —*COLLEGE OF THE HOLY CROSS, '94*

It can be hard to make the first move toward volunteering. The problems you want to address can seem so insurmountable that you think that your time won't make a difference. Or you may feel scared or uncomfortable about working with disadvantaged, ill, or elderly people. These feelings are legitimate, but usually there's a way around them. Even if your efforts only help one person for a short time, you've still made a valuable contribution. And most service organizations provide training.

Many schools have a community service office that can hook you up with a variety of service opportunities. If yours doesn't, try researching them yourself by contacting the student activities office, career services, or the student government office, by looking under "Social and Human Services" in the yellow pages. Also see the Resources at the end of this chapter.

STARTING YOUR OWN ORGANIZATION

If you've grilled the staff, faculty, and students and pored over every campus publication and posting area, and you still haven't found anyone who's doing what you want to do, get together with a few like-minded folks and start a group of your own. It can be as informal as a discussion group in your dorm room or as organized as starting a new sorority chapter or establishing a multicultural center. At most schools, in order to get funding, access to facilities, permission to post notices in prime locations, and approval to cosponsor events with other groups, you'll need to get official recognition from the student government, dean of students, and/or another organization. This may require writing a statement of purpose, creating a budget, presenting a list proving you have the required number of members, and/or appearing in front of a committee. You can get additional details on the process from the course catalog, RAs, deans, or ac-

BE A CULTURE VULTURE

Campuses are saturated with culture. Take advantage of it. You probably won't have access to the same offerings at the same low cost in the "real world." Check out:

EXHIBITS: Many schools have an art gallery or even a museum that sponsors lectures and offers mini-courses or tours. Pay a visit every so often to catch the visiting exhibits. Even if your school doesn't have a formal space devoted to the visual arts, departments often sponsor student/faculty art shows, and the library may sponsor exhibits of or about writers, letters, and/or literary history.

LECTURES: It's likely that some of the most inspiring minds around, spanning the political, literary, and academic spectrum, will visit your campus and share their ideas, opinions, and latest work with you. Their lectures may be sponsored by departments, campus groups, community organizations, alumni, the dean's office, or health services. They may be in a formal setting with podium or in a casual setting around a table. Grabbing a group of friends and going to hear a student, faculty member, or visitor wax eloquent (or occasionally not so eloquent) about a subject, and discussing it over coffee or beer afterward, is a quintessential college experience.

DEMONSTRATIONS: Attend a rally to support a cause, learn about the issues, or keep tabs on "the opposition." There are few things as exciting and empowering as standing up for what you believe in.

WORKSHOPS AND DISCUSSION GROUPS: As evidenced by the proliferation of online discussion groups (ranging from alt. Ernie and Bert to alt. quantum theory), discussing topics from the arcane to the personal to the just plain silly is the bread and butter of human existence. Workshops, discussions, and conferences are easy to find on campuses.

THE ARTS: Confirm or refute your feelings about classical/reggae/new age/alternative/rap/jazz/blues/salsa/opera/religious music; modern/Impressionist/performance art; Shakespeare/Harlem Renaissance/musical/epic/modern theater; Hollywood/experimental/foreign film; and country/square/modern/ballroom/hip-hop/disco/ballet/slam dancing.

COMMUNITY EVENTS: Explore traditions, cultures, and ideas to which you've never been exposed. Challenge yourself to attend lectures by people with whom you disagree, or programs on topics you never thought about or don't fully understand. Attend a Passover seder, a women's discussion group, a Kwanzaa celebration, a Chinese New Year party, a salsa dancing class, High Mass, or a gay/lesbian pride march on National Coming Out Day. (And extend this learning into your academic experience by taking an African-American, Asian, Middle Eastern, Arctic, and/or lesbian studies class.)

tributed money and 68% contributed time to charitable organizations.

tive members in established campus groups. But the most important thing you need to do is hone your leadership skills and get organized.

LEADERSHIP AND COOPERATION: ORGANIZING

Getting involved with campus activities provides invaluable opportunities to develop leadership and organizational skills. Usually groups are small enough that if you want to take on a lot of responsibility you can. But being a key player in an organization can take a lot of hard work. Below are some tips on running a smooth ship.

■ Anticipate and deal with problems that could alienate people and divide the group. Even a group of "haters of hierarchy," devoted to collective decision making, will have its share of power struggles and egos. In most cases, they are not the result of members trying to take over the group, but rather of the fact that people (legitimately enough) like having their voices heard and getting credit for their work and expertise. "Human nature" issues inevitably arise when a bunch of people get together; acknowledging and dealing with them constructively is what working in groups is all about.

■ Let people speak. The stupid can spawn the brilliant, so if you're brainstorming, don't inhibit the process by squelching others' ideas.

■ Strike a balance between sticking to an agenda and keeping things or-

"The most important thing I learned at college is that it's important to find out the issues and needs of others and be sensitive to them. The second most important thing I learned is that it's not always possible to address everyone's issues and take care of everyone's needs at once, and that's OK.... Rather than trying to plan an activity that everyone will love, do a lot of different things that a variety of people will like."
—EARLHAM COLLEGE, '96

derly, and fostering a spontaneous and fun atmosphere in which new members feel comfortable contributing.

■ Delegate. The more people who feel they've made a contribution the better. On most campuses, there's more than enough enthusiasm and desire to help out. Unfortunately, groups that desperately need help often lose people, as members leave feeling that there was nothing for them to do or that they weren't valued. If you've got 20 students clamoring to help, focus your time on organizing the tasks so that they can. And don't delegate just menial tasks. In general, the more responsibility people have, the more they will give.

■ Make a timetable and stick to deadlines. Finished is better than perfect.

■ Ask for feedback. The goal is to plan a good event, help others, and to learn and/or enjoy yourselves. Learn from your mistakes and successes, and thank people when they give construc-

☀ People are almost 4 times more likely to do volunteer work

tive criticism. Though it can sting when you hear it, heeding it will make future events better.

■ Be a mentor. Involve younger students in the decision-making process. Many a wonderful campus group has fizzled into nonexistence once the gregarious leader graduated, because she did not share her knowledge, responsibility, and contacts.

■ Take risks. Try out creative ideas that may or may not work. So your "hands-on" shadow puppet workshop wasn't exactly a smashing success, and using purple and orange food coloring to make the food at your sorority homecoming banquet match your school colors wasn't exactly appetizing— when else in your life will you be able to have such glorious failures?

■ Be flexible and clear, especially when you're working in coalition with other organizations. Compromise and clarity as to each group's responsibilities are key.

"In order to put a theoretic framework into action you'll have to make certain compromises. This isn't selling out. This is getting things done."

—BROWN UNIVERSITY, '94

SPONSORING EVENTS ON CAMPUS

Whether you want to sponsor a food and clothing drive for a local shelter, hold a demonstration against a campus policy, throw a kickin' Oktoberfest party, or give a chamber music concert, the planning and execution of the event is basically the same. You'll need to establish:

What (and why): Establish your goals and parameters. Do you want to stage a rally to increase the group's visibility on campus? Throw a fund-raising party that will be talked about for generations to come? Organize a film festival to introduce your schoolmates to the beauty of silent film? Plan an outing to clean up a local beach, park, or playground? Write down your goals and how your event will meet them.

When: Check around before you inscribe your event on the calendar in permanent marker. For the sake of maximum attendance and good relations with other groups and communities on campus, do everything in your power to avoid scheduling your event for the same time (or right around the time) as those of like-minded groups holding programs slated to attract the same folks you hope to attract. Also heed religious or cultural holidays, big campus parties, and possibly, major sporting events. But bear in mind that even planning six months ahead and keeping a constant watch on the school schedule doesn't guarantee that your event won't conflict with something—even if it's just your cochair's mother's birthday or the season finale of the hottest TV show of the moment. However, conflicts may occasionally work to your advantage. Scheduling a non-sports-related function during the Super Bowl or a nonalcoholic alternative to the annual all-campus Dionysius worship weekend can translate into insta-success.

Where: When choosing a place, consider the number of people you expect

FUNDING YOUR GROUP, EVENT, OR CAUSE

The first place to seek funding for a group and/or event is the school student government and activity association. Most schools have a certain amount of money that they give to these groups to distribute to campus programs and organizations. If you come up short after you go through the regular channels, try the dean's office or academic departments. They may have discretionary funds set aside to sponsor events they are particularly interested in. For example, if you are planning an event dealing with intergroup relations, you might approach the dean's office with a budget and project proposal or summary and ask if it is interested in supporting the event. Similarly, other campus or community groups may be interested in cosponsoring certain types of events.

BUDGET CHECKLIST

EXPENSES:

Xeroxing	$
Advertising	$
Food/drink	$
Phone calls	$
Miscellaneous supplies	$
Room rental fee	$
Honorarium	$
AV equipment	$
Other expenses	$
TOTAL:	$

INCOME:

Grants:

From student government	$
From campus organizations	$
From outside sources	$
Donations	$

Other sources:

Entrance fees (estimate number of attendants)	$
Food booth	$
T-shirt booth	$
TOTAL:	$

COOL, a national college community service organization, started in

to attend, the available facilities on campus, the mood of the event, and the cost. Depending on the event—the size, sponsorship, activity—you may be required, in accordance with the Americans with Disabilities Act, to hold the event in a wheelchair-accessible location. If you are unsure about how to accommodate the needs of students with disabilities, talk to the office of disability services, the dean's office, the scheduling office, or campus or community groups that provide services to or work for rights of people with disabilities.

How: Depending on the event, the organizing process can be as simple as posting a few leaflets, making a few calls, and buying a box of Fig Newtons, or it can be as complex as making plane and hotel reservations for speakers, securing funds, finding volunteers to work at the event, hiring a sign language interpreter, arranging to have a building kept open late, borrowing a VCR and mike, obtaining a sound permit, filling out special forms if you will

serve alcohol or collect money, and getting OKs from the administration, security, food services, other group members, and cosponsoring organizations. Even if it seems like it's not necessary, make up a list including the names, phone numbers, and specific duties of the people involved and general information about the event and hand out a copy to all the pertinent parties. Don't forget to arrange for people to come early and set up, manage everything during the event, clean up afterward, and write thank-you notes later.

Publicity

வ௸

Get the word out! The most potentially fabulous event will flop if no one knows about it. With any publicity, make sure to include the event's time, date, location (directions or a little map may be a good idea), cost (if any), and sponsors, a number to call for more info, and whether the event is wheelchair-accessible. Also note if food will be served. (A given: Advertising free goodies is one of the best ways to boost attendance.)

Methods of Publicity

■ Posters/flyers: Make them direct, legible, and graphically attractive. It's a good idea to follow your school's posting rules. Posters you've tacked up in illegal spots will probably be removed and may get the group in trouble.

■ Mailings: Sending notes or flyers to people who have expressed interest and/or signed a mailing list may be to your benefit, but think hard before doing a full-campus mailing. The expense, the people-power required, the waste of paper, and the fact that the majority of all-campus mailbox stuffings end up scattered on the floor unread may not make it worth your while.

■ Direct phone calls/voice mail.

■ Announcements in classes and the dining hall; at other organizational or dorm meetings and sports events; and on campus TV or radio stations.

■ Ads in newspapers/newsletters.

■ Tabling (setting up a table in a strategic location and handing out information about the event): You can get petitions signed, disseminate information, and, if allowable, sell stuff while you're out there.

■ Media attention: Getting media attention during and after the event is important, too. When doing symbolic actions—protests, letter-writing campaigns, effigy burnings—or edu-

cational campaigns, a little media coverage will go a long way. If the point is to show the world your support or dissent or to disseminate information, then it pays to make sure that those who report news on campus (and off campus, if appropriate) are told of the event, treated well when they are there, and thanked if they write an article or give a mention.

A couple of other tips:

■ See if other campus and community groups will help you publicize your event (you can give their members free or discounted admission in return).

■ For information on the proper format of press releases, the names and addresses of local media contacts, and general PR and publicity tips, pay a visit to the office of alumni relations, career services, large active organizations on campus (the student government may be a good place to start), or the library.

ACTIVIST IDEAS

■ Get together with representatives from other campus organizations and create a guide to planning events on campus. It should include:

▲ Rooms on campus that are available to reserve or rent
▲ Rules and guidelines about "acceptable" activities
▲ Where to go for inexpensive copies and supplies
▲ Names and numbers of people in the scheduling office
▲ A step-by-step guide to organizing an event on campus

▲ What the planners' responsibilities in terms of alerting security and the administration are
▲ Contact names and numbers of campus groups
▲ Sample press releases
▲ Ideas on where to send press releases
▲ How to get an organization approved
▲ How to petition for money
▲ Regulations and tips on accommodating the needs of students with disabilities and/or dietary restrictions

▲ Special issues for organizing in a diverse community, including the dates of important holidays

■ Disseminate resources and information for and about women on your campus. It can be a pamphlet, an electronic resource, a special edition of a campus paper or magazine, or a collectively organized and written handbook. Include such topics as:

▲ People, places, services, and organizations that address the needs of women. (Many of them will address men's needs, too.) Include contact names and numbers at campus organizations, health services, counseling services, support groups, and academic services, as well as the office of career services, office of affirmative action, and community groups. Also include the names of faculty, staff, and administrators who do a good part of their work with, for, and about women.

▲ A description of who in the administration does what (and where).

▲ Tips on personal safety, and step-by-step instructions on dealing with emergencies.

▲ Information on scholarships and grants offered to women.

▲ Policies, including the text of the sexual harassment and discrimination policies and the procedure for filing a complaint.

▲ A history of women at the school and a discussion of some notable alumnae.

■ Confront prejudice and ignorance by supporting and celebrating the diversity on campus—attend programs sponsored by gay/lesbian/bisexual groups, the Asian, black, Latin, and Native American student associations, the Buddhist, Catholic, Christian, Jewish, Muslim, and other religious groups (whether you "are" or you "aren't").

RESOURCES

Student Organizations

UNITED STATES STUDENT ASSOCIATION (USSA)
1012 14TH STREET NW, SUITE 207
WASHINGTON, DC 20005
(202) 347-8772
FAX: (202) 393-5886
Coalition of student governments and organizations throughout the United States. Organizes political action/advocacy to promote public and educational policy on behalf of students in postsecondary education. Promotes student activism, leadership, and organizing around a wide variety of issues. Provides technical and organizing assistance to student groups. Maintains a database of student organiza-

sports ranked 1, volunteer work, 2, and sororities/fraternities, 3. ☼

tions throughout the country and makes referrals to national and local groups working on a diversity of topics. Maintains caucuses/affiliates for students who are women, of color, disabled, gay, lesbian, or bisexual, among others. Publishes numerous materials on student activism, including organizing manuals and voter registration guides. Runs national conferences for student activists.

CAMPUS OUTREACH OPPORTUNITY LEAGUE (COOL)
1511 K STREET NW, SUITE 307
WASHINGTON, DC 20005
(202) 637-7004
FAX: (202) 637-7021

National organization that helps college students/groups establish and run all types of community action/service programs. Holds national conferences to bring together campus leaders and has numerous affiliated organizations throughout the country. Maintains a national database of student/campus groups engaged in communal and political action and advocacy. Makes referrals to local and national groups engaged in all areas of community service. Publishes numerous materials to assist in student organizing.

STUDENT ENVIRONMENT ACTION COALITION (SEAC)
P.O. BOX 1168
CHAPEL HILL, NC 27514
(800) 700-7322 [SEAC]
(919) 967-4600
FAX: (919) 967-4648

Coalition of autonomous student and community groups working on environmental and social action issues across the country. Acts as a clearinghouse to support student organizing and leadership. Holds both national and regional conferences. Maintains a database of student organizations and makes referrals to local and community organizing groups. Publishes

numerous materials, including a national newsletter. Provides information on a variety of topics such as how to start groups, fundraise, and conduct environmental campus audits.

THE YOUNG WOMEN'S PROJECT
923 F STREET NW
WASHINGTON, DC 20004
(202) 393-0461
FAX: (202) 393-0065

Works to promote the leadership and advancement of young women. Conducts national conferences. Organizes mentoring and leadership training programs. Provides peer technical assistance to help in the formation and maintenance of young women's groups and initiatives on campuses throughout the country. Publishes numerous materials, including the 730-page organizing bible, *The Young Women's Handbook*. Runs national conferences and has numerous local affiliates.

STUDENTS ORGANIZING STUDENTS FOR YOUNG WOMEN'S HEALTH
1600 BROADWAY, SUITE 404
NEW YORK, NY 10019
(212) 977-6710

Promotes leadership development of young women throughout the country through national programs and local com-

munity and campus affiliates. Works in coalition with students and women's groups to organize political action and educational forums on issues of concern to young women, especially those relating to women's health, such as sexuality, teenage pregnancy, and reproductive rights. Runs mentoring programs and the Field Organizer Program in which college women design a women's health education/action project or event.

General Women's Activist Organizations

Listed here are some of the more established women's activist organizations. There are many, many other national, regional, and local groups that you can hook up with as well. The organizations listed below should be able to refer you to other women's groups that do the kind of work that interests you. You can also try looking on your campus and at local community and women's centers to find local activist groups. (Also see the Resources at the end of every chapter to find listings of organizations working on specific issues.)

NATIONAL ORGANIZATION FOR WOMEN (NOW)
1000 16TH STREET NW, SUITE 700
WASHINGTON, DC 20036
(202) 331-0066
FAX: (202) 785-8576
One of the largest and oldest feminist political activist groups in the United States. As a multi-issue women's organization they organize political action/advocacy work on public policy and legislation to promote women's rights, advancement, and leadership. Works on issues related to all areas of equal rights, pay equity, legal rights, such as welfare reform, reproductive rights, and lesbian rights. Maintains

local chapters throughout the country and on college campuses and assist students in political organizing around women's issues. Conducts research on women's issues. Publishes numerous materials on all areas of concern to women's rights. Maintains a listing of and makes referrals to numerous women's and other political action organizations throughout the country. Organizes national conferences, coalitions, rallies, and campaigns on behalf of women's rights.

FUND FOR THE FEMINIST MAJORITY
1600 WILSON BOULEVARD, #704
ARLINGTON, VA 22209
(703) 522-2214
Does lobbying, education, and political action around rights to domestic violence. Maintains local chapters throughout the country. Runs the largest abortion clinic defense project in the nation. Publishes numerous materials, including a newsletter.

NATIONAL HOOK-UP OF BLACK WOMEN
5117 SOUTH UNIVERSITY
CHICAGO, IL 60615
(312) 643-5866
Maintains a national database of and makes referrals to organizations serving black women in all areas of life. Maintains local chapters throughout the country, which can provide more comprehensive local referrals. Conducts research and publishes numerous materials on the status of black women in America.

WOMEN'S LEGAL DEFENSE FUND
1875 CONNECTICUT AVENUE NW, SUITE 710
WASHINGTON, DC 20009
(202) 986-2600
Does political action work to promote equal rights and opportunities. Publishes numerous materials on policy relating to women's issues. Works in coalitions with groups to influence public policy and pro-

mote education about women's rights, in specific, and human rights in general.

NATIONAL WOMEN'S POLITICAL CAUCUS
1275 K STREET NW, SUITE 750
WASHINGTON, DC 20005
(202) 898-1100
Supports women political candidates in national, state, and local government.

CONGRESSIONAL CAUCUS FOR WOMEN'S ISSUES
2471 RAYBURN BUILDING
WASHINGTON, DC 20515
(202) 225-6740
Organization of congresspeople who work on women's issues, promote women in politics, and conduct research on women's issues. Monitors legislation and public policy that impacts on women's lives.

Organizations Researching Women and Politics

CENTER FOR THE AMERICAN WOMAN AND POLITICS
EAGLETON INSTITUTE OF POLITICS
RUTGERS UNIVERSITY
NEW BRUNSWICK, NJ 08901
(908) 828-2210
FAX: (908) 932-6778
Conducts research and provides information and statistics on women and politics. Publishes numerous materials, including newsletters and fact sheets. Organizes non-partisan voter education forums.

INSTITUTE FOR WOMEN POLICY RESEARCH
1400 20TH STREET NW, SUITE 104
WASHINGTON, DC 20036
(202) 785-5100
FAX: (202) 833-4362
Conducts non-partisan public policy research on issues relating to women, health care, labor law reform, and/or welfare. Publishes materials on public policy affecting women and makes refer-

rals to women's organizations involved in activist and community work.

There are numerous political action committees that fundraise for candidates in certain parties and/or with certain political agendas and beliefs. Three prominent PACs supporting women candidates are: Women's Campaign Fund, EMILY's (Early Money Is Like Yeast—It Rises) List for democratic women, and WISH List (Women in the Senate and House) for republican women.

Making Your Voice Heard in Washington

To register to vote or find out about any voting issues, contact your "County Registrar of Voters," which should be listed in the blue pages of your phone book, under "Government Agencies" or under the name of your county.

LEAGUE OF WOMEN VOTERS
1730 M STREET NW
WASHINGTON, DC 20036
(202) 429-1965
Keeps tabs on the big issues in Congress and provides information about how to get involved in the political process. Publishes numerous materials, including local and federal voting guides and *Go Tell It to Washington: A Guide for Citizen Action*, which includes a Congressional directory. Chapters across the country can provide information about topics, including voting rights, registration, and current legislative issues. Facilitates citizen political action and provides information about how to contact and influence city, state, and federal governments.

OFFICE OF RECORDS AND REGISTRATION
1036 LONGWORTH HOUSE OFFICE BUILDING
WASHINGTON, DC 20515
(202) 225-1300

SPEAK YOUR MIND

Our government can't be "of the people and for the people" if "we the people" don't tell the people who represent us what's on our minds. Here's how to reach them via traditional mail or on-line:

WHITE HOUSE COMMENTS LINE
(202) 456-1111
Leave a message here to have your comments, opinions, and suggestions tallied. This is a great number to hand out at political rallies—you can plan a "call the White House day" and bombard the comments line with calls about a specific issue.

THE PRESIDENT
The White House
Washington, DC 20500
Internet address:
president@whitehouse.gov

THE VICE PRESIDENT
The White House
Washington, DC 20500
Internet address:
vice-president@whitehouse.gov

SENATORS
The Honorable *(first and last name of Senator)*
United States State Senate
Washington, DC 20510
For your senator's Internet address, call the Capitol switchboard at (202) 224-3121.

REPRESENTATIVES
The Honorable *(first and last name of Representative)*
United States House of Representatives
Washington, DC 20515
For your representative's Internet address, send E-mail to:
congress@hr.house.gov

MEMBERS OF THE CABINET
The Honorable *(first and last name of cabinet member)*
(Position on the Cabinet, i.e., "The Secretary of Labor")
Washington, DC 20210

(Check the blue pages in the telephone book for the addresses and phone numbers of local and state officials.)

Maintains directories of Senate and House members' addresses and phone numbers, as well as information on governmental agencies. Makes referrals to the government officials or agencies that can best serve your needs.

FEDERAL GOVERNMENT SWITCHBOARD OPERATORS
(202) 606-2424
Maintains directories of all government agencies and departments. Will connect you with the office that can most appropriately meet your needs.

LEGISLATIVE STATUS OFFICE
(202) 225-1772
Provides information on the status of all federal legislation and the dates of committee hearings.

SUPERINTENDENT OF DOCUMENTS
U.S. GOVERNMENT PRINTING OFFICE
WASHINGTON, DC 20402
(202) 783-3238

---

litical beliefs, the White House would be buried under 1050 tons of mail.

Publishes materials on all things political. The U.S. government, policies, laws, etc. Call for free government publications or a catalog of publications.

HOUSE DOCUMENT ROOM
B-18 ANNEX 2
WASHINGTON, DC 20515
(202) 255-3956
To get a copy of a bill in the House of Representatives, if you know its number.

SENATE DOCUMENT ROOM
SH-BO4
WASHINGTON, DC 20510
(202) 224-7860
To get a copy of a bill in the Senate, if you know its number.

Note: You can also acquire copies of legislation by contacting your congressional representative's office.

Sororities

NATIONAL PANHELLENIC CONFERENCE
3901 WEST 86TH STREET, SUITE 380
INDIANAPOLIS, IN 46268
(317) 872-3185
National umbrella confederation of women's sororities. Provides information about sororities throughout the country. Makes referrals to local chapters of sororities. Publishes numerous materials. Assists campus groups in facilitating programs, addressing problems, and organizing locally, regionally, and nationally.

NATIONAL PAN-HELLENIC COUNCIL
INDIANA MEMORIAL UNION, SUITE 30
BLOOMINGTON, IN 47405
(812) 855-8820
National umbrella confederation of African-American fraternities and sororities. Provides information about African-American sororities/fraternities throughout the country. Makes referrals to local chapters. Publishes numerous materials. Assists groups in facilitating programs, addressing problems, and organizing locally, regionally, and nationally.

Further Reading

෨ඉ෨

How to Make the World a Better Place for Women in Five Minutes a Day, Donna Jackson (Hyperion, 1992).

Women Activists Challenging the Abuse of Power, Anne Witte Garland (Feminist Press, 1988).

Organizing for Social Change, Steve Max, Jackie Kendall, and Kim Bobo (Seven Locks Press, 1991).

(See the Resources at the end of "Community and Identity," page 553, for groups organizing around identity politics/issues.)

🌀 From '90 to '94, the number of women congressional candidates rose by 64%.

Part Seven

Odds & Ends

FEEDBACK, PLEASE

We see this book as an ongoing process and hope to include in future editions whatever you (and we) think we left out in this one. Please let us know what you feel is missing, how the treatment of what's here could be improved, what you liked, and what you didn't. We have included the following list of questions to inspire you to write or E-mail your thoughts, ideas, opinions, and deeply held beliefs about our book and/or college life in general. In short, we'd love to hear from you because, as we see it, this book is every bit as much yours as it is ours.

Personal Information

Please include:
▲ Name
▲ Current address
▲ Phone
▲ Permanent address
▲ Phone
▲ Electronic address
▲ School name
▲ Date of matriculation
▲ Expected date of graduation
▲ Area(s) of study

The Dirt on This Book

■ Are there topics that should be included or removed from the book, or given more or less attention? Do you have personal experiences, tips, warnings against potential pitfalls, or unanswered questions about any of these topics?

■ What about the resources? Are there any we should add, revise, or remove? What were your experiences with the organizations listed?

■ What kind of things should we keep in mind while revising the book? Do you feel as if the book speaks to you?

The Scoop on Women in College

■ What issues do you think are important to college women today?

■ What information or resources were or would have been helpful when you started college (and grad school, if applicable)? What advice or info would you give an incoming first-year woman?

■ What type of support/groups/services are or would have been helpful during your undergraduate education?

■ Are there issues, events, or ideas on your campus that you think it would be useful for others to know about?

Please return to:
Rachel 5133@aol.com (E-mail), or Rachel Dobkin and Shana Sippy, The College Woman's Handbook, 1 Astor Place, Box PHL, New York, NY 10003.

Thank you very much.

STAT SOURCES

Following are the sources for the statistics, facts, and bits of trivia that run along the bottom of each page.

ALL THINGS ACADEMIC
The Class System: Page 1: *U.S. News and World Report*; p. 2-3: U.S. Department of Education; p. 4: *Failing at Fairness: How America's Schools Cheat Girls*, Myra and David Sadkir; p. 6: *What Are the Chances?* Bernard Siskin and Jerome Staller with David Rorvik; p. 8: *How to Make the World a Better Place for Women in Five Minutes a Day*, Donna Jackson; p. 9: *U.S. News*; p. 10: *How to Make the World a Better Place for Women*, p. 12: National Women's Studies Association; p. 14: National Science Board; p. 16: *365 Days of Women Calendar*, Workman Publishing; p. 18: *Barron's Profiles of American Colleges* p. 19: *New York Teacher*.

Burning the Midnight Oil: Page 20: R.H. Bruskin Associates; p. 21: Faber-Castell; p. 22: Ebbinghaus Retention Curve; p. 24: *Time*; p. 25: *365 Days of Women Calendar*; p. 26: *The New York Times*; p. 27: Accountemps/*On an Average Day. . .*, Tom Heymann; p. 28: Library of Congress/America Online; p. 30: *The Unofficial U.S. Census*, Tom Heymann; p. 31: *The Nonsexist Communicator*, Bobbye D. Sorrels; p. 32: *The Great Divide*, Daniel Evan Weiss/Gallup Poll; p. 33: National Academy of Sciences.

Off the Beaten Track: Page 34: Educational Testing Service (ETS); p. 36: *365 Days of Women Calendar*; p. 38: Institute of International Education; p. 39: *Choices? A Student Survival Guide for the 90s*, Bryna J. Fireside; p. 40: *The 1995 Information Please, Women's Sourcebook: Resources and Information to Use Every Day*, Lisa DiMona and Constance Herndon; p. 41: *Money*; p. 42: *Educational Record*; p. 43: *U.S. News*.

Making the Leap: Page 44: *U.S. News*; p. 45: 1990 U.S. Census; p. 46: American Council on Education, Office of Women in Higher Education; p. 48: American Council on Education; p. 50: *U.S. News*; p. 52: Women's College Coalition; p. 54: *Newsweek*; p. 56: *Why It's Great to Be a Girl*, Jacqueline Shannon; p. 57: *U.S. News*; p. 58: ETS/*U.S. News*; p. 60: *U.S. News*; p. 62: U.S. Census; p. 64: *U.S. News*; p. 65: *Money*; p. 66: *Barron's Profiles of American Colleges*; p. 68: *Barron's Profiles*; p. 70: *Barron's Profiles* .

MONEY AND HOME
The Financial Aid Maze: Page 75: National Commission on Student Financial Assistance; p. 76: *Money*; p. 78: ETS; p. 80: *U.S. News*; p. 81: *U.S. News*; p. 82-3: *Directory of Special Programs*; p. 84: *Directory of Special Programs*; p. 86: *U.S. News*; p. 88: *How the Military Will Help You Pay for College*, Don M. Betterton; p. 90: Association of Fundraising Counsel; p. 92: National Network on Women as Philanthropists; p. 94: *Money*; p. 96: Hewitt Associates; p. 98: *U.S. News*; p. 100: National Network on Women as Philanthropists; p. 102: *The International Scholarship Directory*, Daniel J. Cassidy.

Money Matters: Page 104-5: *365 Days of Women Calendar*; p. 106: *Unofficial U.S. Census*; p. 107: Rutgers University; p. 108: International Council of Shopping Centers; p. 109: *What Are the Chances?*; p. 110: *Rules of Thumb*, Tom Parker; p. 112: *Facts! That Matter*, Les Krantz; p. 114: *In an Average Lifetime...*, Tom Heymann; p. 116: *Resourceful Women*, Shawn Brennant and Julie Winkelplek; p. 118-9: *The Consumer Bible*, Mark Green; p. 120: *What Are the Chances?*; p. 122: R.H. Bruskin Associates; p. 124: Consolidated Information Bureau of New York; p. 125: *The Consumer Bible*; p. 126: Dick Israel, Congressperson Sam Gibbons' Office; p. 127: *Facts! That Matter*; p. 128: *Facts! That Matter*; p. 130: *What Counts: The Complete Harper's Index*.

A Room of Your Own: Page 131: *The Great*

Divide; p. 132: *U.S. News;* p. 134-5: *Facts! That Matter;* p. 136: *The Consumer Bible;* p. 137: *In View;* p. 138: *Money;* p. 140-1: American Movers Conference; p. 142: *On an Average Day...,* Tom Heymann; p. 144: *Facts! That Matter;* p. 146: NYNEX; p. 148: American Movers Conference; p. 150: *The Great Divide;* p. 151: *On an Average Day...;* p. 152: *The Great Divide;* p. 153: *The Consumer Bible;* p. 154: *What Are the Chances?;* p. 155: Internal Revenue Service; p. 156: *The Consumer Bible.*

Working Women Page 158: *Why It's Great to Be a Girl;* p. 159: *How to Make the World a Better Place for Women;* p. 160: *The Internship Explosion in America,* Tom Callahan; p. 162: *Women's Sourcebook;* p. 164: *Women's Sourcebook;* p. 166: *U.S. News;* p. 168: *Glamour;* p. 170: U.S. Department of Labor; p. 172: 9 to 5; p. 174: *The American Woman 1990-1991,* Sara Rix; p. 176: *Money;* p. 178: National Association of Temporary Services; p. 179 *Cosmopolitan;* p. 180: *Facts! That Matter;* p. 182: *Time;* p. 184: The Glass Ceiling Commission, U.S. Department of Labor.

OF SOUND BODY AND MIND
The Big Three: Page 189: Gallup Poll; p. 190: Domino Pizza/*Glamour;* p. 191: *Time;* p. 192: *The PDR Family Guide to Women's Health and Prescription Drugs;* p. 194: *Our Bodies, Ourselves,* Boston Women's Health Collective; p. 196: *Technology Review;* p. 198: Anorexia Nervosa and Related Eating Disorders, Inc.; p. 200: American Dietetic Association; p. 202: Archives of Pediatrics and Adolescent Medicine; p. 204: Bob Hope International Heart Research Institute; p. 206-7: Better Sleep Council; p. 208: *The New York Times;* p. 210: Lieberman Research.

Staying Healthy: Page 212: *Sassy;* p. 214: *The Complete Home Healer,* Angela Smyth; p. 216: *The PDR Family Guide to Women's Health;* p. 218-9: The *PDR Family Guide to Women's Health;* p. 220: *The Good Housekeeping Illustrated Guide to Women's*

Health, Kathryn A. Cox; p. 222: *The PDR Family Guide to Women's Health;* p. 223: *Mademoiselle;* p. 224: The Berkeley Wellness Center; p. 226: Task Force for Compliance; p. 228: *Newsweek;* p. 230: *Facts! That Matter;* p. 232: *Journal of the American Medical Association;* p. 234: University of California, Santa Cruz; p. 235: American College of Obstetricians and Gynecologists; p. 236: *The Good Housekeeping Illustrated Guide to Women's Health;* p. 238: *The Western Journal of Medicine*/Center for Substance Abuse Treatment; p. 240: *Women's Sourcebook;* p. 242: *Journal of the American Women's Medical Association;* p. 244: *Women's Sourcebook;* p. 246: *Time*/CNN.

More Than Just the Blues: Page 247: Pennsylvania State University/*Harper's;* p. 248: *U.S. News;* p. 250: The Olfactory Research Fund; p. 251: *Facts! That Matter;* p. 252: *Women's Sourcebook;* p. 253: *All About Eve: The Complete Guide to Women's Health and Well-Being,* Tracy Chutorian Semler; p. 254: Charter Hospital of Thousand Oaks; p. 256: University of Chicago; p. 258: National Institute of Mental Health/U.S. Department of Health and Human Services; p. 259: National Institute of Mental Health/*All About Eve;* p. 260: *All About Eve;* p. 261: *Mirabella;* p. 262: National Institute of Mental Health; p. 263: *Psychotherapy Finances/New York;* p. 264: American Psychiatric Association; p. 265: p. 266: *All About Eve;* p. 268: *New York;* p. 270: *The PDR Family Guide to Women's Health;* p. 271: American Academy of Family Physicians; p. 272: *Facts! That Matter.*

Real vs. Ideal: Page 274: *Sassy;* p. 275: *The Beauty Myth,* Naomi Wolf; p. 276-7: *Time;* p. 278: *Never Too Thin,* Eva Szekely; p. 280: The National Institute of Compulsive Eating; p. 281: U.S. Department of Health and Human Services; p. 282-3: Anorexia Nervosa and Related Eating Disorders, Inc.; p. 284-5: *Women's Sourcebook;* p. 286: Mattel/*Harper's*/*Women's Sourcebook;* p. 288: *The Beauty Myth;* p. 290: Jean Kilbourne; p. 292: *The Boston Globe.*

Use and Abuse: Page 293: *Time*; p. 294: *Sassy*; p. 296: Columbia University's Center on Addiction and Substance Abuse; p. 298: *The PDR Family Guide to Women's Health*; p. 300: *Harper's*; p. 301: Harvard School of Public Health/*Journal of the American Medical Association*; p. 302: National Household Survey on Drug Abuse; p. 303: *Alcohol and Drugs are Women's Issues*, P. Roth; p. 304: Associated Press; p. 305: *All About Eve*; p. 306: *Ms.*; p. 307: *Time*; p. 308: University of Michigan; p. 310: National Council on Alcoholism and Drug Dependence; p. 311: American Psychiatric Association; p. 312: *Facts! That Matter*; p. 313: *Sassy*; p. 314: *Mademoiselle*; p. 316: *Women's Sourcebook*; p. 318: *Scientific American*; p. 320: Alcoholics Anonymous; p. 321: *The Good Housekeeping Illustrated Guide to Women's Health*; p. 322: *All About Eve*; p. 324: *The Recovery Book*, Al J. Mooney, M.D., Arlene Eisenberg, Howard Eisenberg.

A Friend in Need: Page 326: Harvard School of Public Health/*Journal of the American Medical Association*; p. 328: *The Great Divide*; p. 330: *The New Hite Report*, Shere Hite; p. 332: Harvard School of Public Health/*Journal of the American Medical Association*; p. 334: *The Good Housekeeping Illustrated Guide to Women's Health*; p. 336: U.S. Census/*USA Today*/*The Great Divide*; p. 338: American College Health Association.

SEXUAL AND REPRODUCTIVE MATTERS

Know Your Body: Page 343: *New England Journal of Medicine*; p. 344: *Image: Journal of Nursing and Scholarship*; p. 346: American Cancer Society; p. 348: Maidenform; p. 349: *The PDR Family Guide to Women's Health*; p. 350: National Cancer Institute; p. 351: *The Advocate*; p. 352-3: *The PDR Family Guide to Women's Health*; p. 354: *The PDR Family Guide to Women's Health*; p. 356: *Why It's Great to Be a Girl*/ *Anatomy of Love*, Helen E. Fisher; p. 358: *The Question of Rest for Women During Menstruation*, Dr. Mary Jacobi; p. 360: *Women's Sourcebook*; p. 362:

The PDR Family Guide to Women's Health; p. 364: *The PDR Family Guide to Women's Health*; p. 366: *The PDR Family Guide to Women's Health*; p. 368: *The PDR Family Guide to Women's Health*.

STDs, HIV, and AIDS: Page 369: *Women's Sourcebook*; p. 370-1: *The American Woman 1994-1995*, Sara Rix; p. 370-1: National Institute of Allergy and Infectious Diseases; p. 372-3: Centers for Disease Control and Prevention; p. 374-5: Centers for Disease Control and Prevention; p. 375: *The PDR Family Guide to Women's Health*; p. 376 American Social Health Association; p. 378: *The PDR Family Guide to Women's Health*; p. 379: U.S. Department of Health and Human Services; p. 380: Centers for Disease Control and Prevention; p. 382: *Women's Sourcebook*; p. 384: Centers for Disease Control and Prevention; p. 386: Michigan State University/BACCHUS; p. 388: Centers for Disease Control and Prevention; p. 390: The ACLU AIDS Project; p. 392: National Institutes of Health; p. 394: World Health Organization; p. 396: *365 Days of Women Calendar*; p. 398: Ortho Pharmaceutical Company.

Contraception and Safer Sex: Page 400: *The Good Housekeeping Illustrated Guide to Women's Health*; p. 402: K. Carr; p. 404-5: *Women's Sourcebook*; p. 406: *The PDR Family Guide to Women's Health*; p. 408: Ortho Pharmaceutical Company; p. 409: *The PDR Family Guide to Women's Health*; p. 410-1: Ortho Pharmaceutical Company; p. 412: *The Good Housekeeping Illustrated Guide to Women's Health*; p. 414: *The Good Housekeeping Illustrated Guide to Women's Health*; p. 416: Ortho Pharmaceutical Company; p. 417: *All About Eve*; p. 418: *Women's Sourcebook*; p. 420: *Medical Tribune*; p. 422: *Glamour*; p. 424: *The PDR Family Guide to Women's Health*; p. 426: Emory University; p. 428: ABC News; p. 430: *Contraceptive Technology*; p. 432: *FDA Consumer*.

If You Get Pregnant: Page 433: Planned Parenthood; p. 434: *Our Bodies Ourselves*; p. 436: Alan Guttmacher Institute; p. 438: *U.S. News/Sassy*; p. 440: *American Family Physician*/

National Center for Health Statistics; p. 441: Joycelyn Elders/*Women's Sourcebook*; p. 442: *Scientific American*; p. 444: *How to Make the World a Better Place for Women*; p. 445: National Council for Adoption; p. 446: Guttmacher Institute; p. 448: *All About Eve*; p. 449: Guttmacher Institute; p. 450: University of Medicine and Dentistry of New Jersey/*Time*; p. 452: Guttmacher Institute; p. 454 National Abortion Rights Action League; p. 456: Guttmacher Institute; p. 458: Population Action International; p. 460: The Center for Population Options.

FIGHTING BACK

Breaking Down Bias: Page 462: *"Prejudice Puzzle" Teacher's Guide*, National Public Radio/*Making a Difference*, Lynn Duvall; p. 464: *U.S. News*; p. 466: National Institute Against Prejudice and Violence; p. 468: UCLA; p. 470: *Did You Know: Fascinating Facts and Fallacies about Businesses*, D. Keith Denton and Charles Boyd; p. 472: The National Council for Research on Women; p. 474-5: *Women's Sourcebook*; p. 476: Cornell University; p. 478 *Don't Believe the Hype*, Farai Chideya; p. 480: *New York Times/Glamour*; p. 482: *Working Woman*; p. 484: *Working Woman*; p. 486 *Money*/Michele A. Paludi; p. 488: *In View/Blacks in College*, Jacqueline Fleming, PhD; p. 490: *Working Woman*.

Ending the Silence: Page 491: U.S. Student Association; p. 492: National Domestic Violence Coalition on Public Policy/*Time*; p. 494 U.S. Student Association; p. 496: *Ms.*; p. 497: The American Woman 1994-1995; p. 498: *Journal of American College Health*; p. 500: U.S. Student Association/*Young Women's Handbook*; p. 502: Association of American Colleges, Project on the Status and Education of Women; p. 504: *What Are the Chances?*; p. 506: ACLU; p. 508: *Women's Sourcebook*; p. 510: American Medical Association/*Time*.

Safety First: Page 512: *U.S. News*; p. 514: *The Great Divide*; p. 515: *Money*; p. 516:

p. 517: *Money*; p. 518: Harvard School of Public Health; p. 520: *Facts! That Matter*; p. 522: *Sassy*; p. 524-5: Roper Reports; p. 526: *The American Woman 1994-1995*; p. 528: ABC News.

DEFINING YOURSELF

Community and Identity: Page 533: U.S. Census; p. 534: *Making a Difference*; p. 536-7: *Making a Difference*; p. 538: *Independent Sector*; p. 539: *The Great Divide*/Gallup Poll; p. 540: *Women's Sourcebook*; p. 542: U.S. Census; p. 544: *Los Angeles Times/The Great Divide*; p. 546: *The New York Times*; p. 548: *The Janus Report*; p. 549: The Hedrick-Martin Institute; p. 550: President's Committee on Employment of People With Disabilities; p. 552: Times Mirror Center for the People and the Press; p. 554: *The Advocate*; p. 556: *The College Finder: 475 Ways to Choose the Right School for You*, Steven Antonoff; p. 558: *The American Woman, 1994-1995*.

Negotiating Relationships: Page 559: *The New Hite Report*; p. 560: U.S. Census; p. 562-3: *The Great Divide*; p. 564: Hallmark; p. 566: *The Great Divide*; p. 568: *Women's Sourcebook*; p. 570: *The Great Divide*; p. 572: *Women's Sourcebook*; p. 574: *U.S. News*; p. 576: *Parents*/Kane, Parsons and Associates; p. 578: *Ladies' Home Journal*; p. 579: *Mademoiselle*; p. 580: *One Medicine: A Tribute to Kurt Benirschke*, O.A. Ryder and M.L. Byrd; p. 581: *The Kinsey Institute New Report on Sex*, June Reinisch; p. 582 Center for Marital and Sexual Studies; p. 583: *The New Hite Report*; p. 584: *The Kinsey Report*; p. 586: U.S. Census; p. 588: *Facts! That Matter*.

Getting Involved: Page 589: *Independent Sector*; p. 590-1: *Independent Sector*; p. 592: National PanHellenic Conference; p. 593: Alpha Phi Alpha; p. 594: *Independent Sector*; p. 596: *Independent Sector*; p. 598: *Independent Sector*; p. 600: Campus Outreach Opportunity League; p. 602: *The College Finder*; p. 604: *Women's Sourcebook*; p. 606: *How to Make the World a Better Place for Women*; p. 608: Fund for the Feminist Majority.

Index

A

H

I

J, K

L

M

N

O,P

T

U, V

W, Y, Z

Date Due

BRODART, INC.   Cat. No. 23 233   Printed in U.S.A.

RACH   **IPPY**

achel Dob ... feminist ac ... computer ... year at Bowdoi ... Maine, she re ... York City to ... Pro-Choice mar ... NOW-NYC. ... Barnard Colleg ... degree in wome ... ogy in 1992. Wl ... art direction, la ... The Barnard/Co ... book, as well as ... work for Sister, ... paper, and Lil ... women's maga ... extensive acade ... cational work ... gender, and sex ... currently worki ... sultant and hop ... site where college women can network, exchange ideas, share knowledge, or just chat.

rn and raised in ... ia, but since ... College in 1989 ... st Coast transes ... pes isn't perma- ... pent most of her ... promoting inter- ... nd organizing ... ical forums on ... man rights. She ... le major in his- ... 1993. Being the ... ndian father and ... ther, it's no sur- ... rently studying ... a Masters pro- ... ersity. She plans ... rite and teach at